standard catalog of

OLDSMOBILE

1897-1997

John Chevedden and Ron Kowalke

Published by

700 E. State Street • Iola, WI 54990-0001
Telephone: 715/445-2214

Please call or write for our free catalog of automotive publications.
Our toll-free number to place an order or obtain a free catalog is 800-258-0929
or please use our regular business telephone 715-445-2214
for editorial comment and further information.

ISBN: 0-87341-484-5
Printed in the United States of America

CONTENTS

STANDARD CATALOG SERIES

The concept behind Krause Publications' "standard catalogs" is to compile massive amounts of information about motor vehicles and present it in a standard format that the hobbyist, collector, or professional dealer can use to answer some commonly asked questions.

Those questions include: What year, make, and model is the vehicle? What did it sell for new? How rare is it? What is special about it? In our general automotive catalogs, some answers are provided by photos and others by the fact-filled text. In one-marque catalogs such as this one, additional information such as trucks, pace cars, prototype/concept identification, motorsports milestones and interesting Oldsmobile facts is included in the back of the book.

Chester L. Krause of Krause Publications is responsible for the basic concept of creating the standard catalogs covering American cars. David V. Brownell, of *Special-Interest Autos*, undertook preliminary work on the concept while editing *Old Cars Weekly* in the 1970s. John A. Gunnell continued the standard catalog project after 1978. *The Standard Catalog of American Cars 1946-1975* was first published in 1982. Meanwhile, Beverly Rae-Kimes and the late Henry Austin Clark, Jr., continued writing and researching *The Standard Catalog of American Cars 1805-1942*, which was published in 1985. In 1987, *The Standard Catalog of Light-Duty American Trucks 1900-1986*, was compiled by John Gunnell and a second edition of the 1946-1975 volume was printed. In 1988, the 1805-1942 volume by Kimes and Clark appeared in its second edition. Also in 1988, James M. Flammang authored *Standard Catalog of American Cars 1976-1986*, which went into its second edition in 1990. More recently, the 1946-1975 book was re-edited during 1992 and a third edition of the 1805-1942 book was released in 1996.

While the four-volume set of standard catalogs enjoyed high popularity as all-inclusive guides for car and light-duty truck collectors, there seemed to be many auto enthusiasts who focused their energies on only one make of car or multiple makes made by closely related manufacturers. This led to creation of standard catalogs about Chrysler Corp., FoMoCo, GM makes, and American Motors. This, the *Standard Catalog of Oldsmobile 1897-1997*, is a continuation of our examination of the offerings of General Motors, following our successful standard catalogs detailing the histories of Chevrolet, Buick, Cadillac and Pontiac.

The Standard Catalog of Oldsmobile was compiled by an experienced editorial team consisting of the automotive staff of Krause Publications and numerous experts within specific areas of Oldsmobile history. A major benefit of this "teamwork" has been the gathering of more significant facts about each model than a single author might find.

No claims are made that these catalogs are infallible history texts or encyclopedias. Nor are they repair manuals or "bibles" for motor vehicle enthusiasts. They are meant as a contribution to the pursuit of greater knowledge about many wonderful vehicles. They are also much larger in size, broader in scope, and more deluxe in format than most other collector guides, buyer guides, or price guides.

The long-range goal of Krause Publications is to make all of the catalogs as nearly perfect as possible. At the same time, we expect they will always raise new questions and bring forth new facts that were not previously unearthed. All our contributors maintain an ongoing file of new research, corrections, and additional photos that are used, regularly, to refine and expand future editions.

Should you have knowledge you wish to see in future editions, please don't hesitate to contact the editors at *Standard Catalog of Oldsmobile*, editorial department, 700 East State Street, Iola, WI 54990.

ACKNOWLEDGMENTS

While there are two authors' names listed on the cover of this book, the *Standard Catalog of Oldsmobile* was made possible through the work of many dedicated, generous, knowledgeable people who are enthusiasts of both Oldsmobile and the collector car hobby in general. In alphabetical order, these individuals are:

Ken Buttolph, the late Dennis Casteele, the late Henry Austin Clark Jr., Helen J. Earley, James M. Flammang, John Gunnell, Gary Hoonsbeen, Beverly Rae Kimes, James T. Lenzke and Roy Nagel.

It would not have been possible to complete this book without your guidance and contributions. Thank you all!

ABBREVIATIONS

ABS - anti-lock braking system
bhp - brake horsepower
Brgm - Brougham
BSW - black sidewall tires
bus cpe - business coupe
cabr - cabriolet
cid - cubic inch displacement
Cl Cpl - Close Coupled
conv - convertible
conv cpe - convertible coupe
conv sed - convertible sedan
cpe - coupe
cu. in. - cubic inch
Cus Conv - Custom Convertible
Cus Sed - Custom Sedan
cyl - cylinder
Del Conv - Deluxe Convertible
Del Cpe - Deluxe Coupe
Del Lan Sed - Deluxe Landau Sedan
Del Sta Wag - Deluxe Station Wagon
dr - door(s)
EFI - electronic fuel injection
Eight - eight-cylinder model
ft. - foot/feet
gal - gallon(s)
GM - General Motors Corp.
hatch - hatchback
HEI - high energy ignition
hp - horsepower
HO - high output
HT - hardtop
in. - inch(es)
lan cpe - landau coupe

lan sed - Landau Sedan
lb.-ft. - pound-feet
limo - limousine
MFI/MPFI - multi-port fuel injection
mm - millimeters
mpg - miles per gallon
mph - miles per hour
OHC - overhead cam
OHV - overhead valve
phae - phaeton
rds - roadster
rds cpe - roadster coupe
rpm - revolutions per minute
RPO - regular production option
SAE - Society of Automotive Engineers
sed - sedan
SFI/SPFI - sequential fuel injection
Six - six-cylinder model
SOHC - single overhead cam
Spl Sed - Special Sedan
Spl Sta Wag - Special Station Wagon
Spt Cabr - Sport Cabriolet
Spt Cpe - Sport Coupe
Spt Phae - Sport Phaeton
Spt Rds - Sport Roadster
Spt Sed - Sport Sedan
sq. in. - square inch(es)
sta wag - station wagon
TBI - throttle body fuel injection
tr sed - touring sedan
VIN - Vehicle Identification Number
w/ - with
w/o - without

CATALOG STAFF

Manager of Books Division: Pat Klug
Old Cars Division Publisher: Greg Smith
Old Cars Editorial Director: John Gunnell
Old Cars Books Editor: Ron Kowalke
Old Cars Weekly News & Marketplace Editors: Chad Elmore, James T. Lenzke
Pricing: Ken Buttolph

Book Production Team: Bonnie Tetzlaff, Ethel Thulien, Cheryl Mueller, Patsy Morrison, Tom Nelsen, Tom Payette
Photo Graphics: Ross Hubbard, Kara Gunderson
Camera Room: Julie Mattson, Gerald Smith
OCR Scanning: Carol Klopstein
Cover Design: Paul Tofte

PHOTO CREDITS

AA - Applegate & Applegate
CX - Car Exchange
DC - Dennis Casteele
HAC - Henry Austin Clark, Jr.
HJE - Helen J. Earley
IMS - Indianapolis Motor Speedway

JAC - John A. Conde
JAG - John A. Gunnell
JG - Jesse Gunnell
O - Oldsmobile Division
OCW - Old Cars Weekly
TVB - Terry V. Boyce

HOW TO USE THIS CATALOG

APPEARANCE AND EQUIPMENT: Word descriptions help identify trucks down to details such as styling features, trim and interior appointments. Standard equipment lists usually begin with low-priced base models. Then, subsequent data blocks cover higher-priced lines of the same year.

VEHICLE I.D. NUMBERS: This edition features expanded data explaining the basic serial numbering system used by each postwar vehicle manufacturer. This data reveals where, when and in what order your vehicle was built. There is much more information on assembly plant, body style and original engine codes.

SPECIFICATIONS CHART: The first chart column gives series or model numbers for trucks. The second column gives body type. The third column tells factory price. The fourth column gives GVW. The fifth column gives the vehicle's original shipping weight. The sixth column provides model year production totals (if available) or makes reference to additional notes found below the specifications chart. When the same vehicle came with different engines or trim levels at different prices and weights, slashes (/) are used to separate the low price or weight from the high one. In some cases, model numbers are also presented this way. In rare cases where data is non-applicable or not available the abbreviation "N.A." appears.

BASE ENGINE DATA: According to make of vehicle, engine data will be found either below the data block for each series or immediately following the specifications chart for the last vehicle-line. Displacement, bore and stroke and horsepower ratings are listed, plus a lot more data where available. This edition has more complete engine listings for many models. In other cases, extra-cost engines are listed in the "options" section.

VEHICLE DIMENSIONS: The main data compiled here consists of wheelbase, overall length and tire size. Front and rear tread widths are given for most trucks through the early 1960s and some later models. Overall width and height appears in some cases, too.

OPTIONAL EQUIPMENT LISTS: This section includes data blocks listing all types of options and accessories. A great deal of attention has been focused on cataloging both the availability and the original factory retail prices of optional equipment. Because of size and space limitations, a degree of selectivity has been applied by concentrating on those optional features of greatest interest to collectors. Important option packages have been covered and detailed as accurately as possible in the given amount of space. When available, options prices are listed.

HISTORICAL FOOTNOTES: Trucks are already recognized as an important part of America's automotive heritage. Revealing statistics; important dates and places; personality profiles; performance milestones; and other historical facts are highlighted in this "automotive trivia" section.

SEE PRICING SECTION IN BACK OF BOOK.

OLDSMOBILE — SERIES F — SIX: Oldsmobile continued its two series format in 1938 with the F, or six-cylinder, continuing to be the division sales leader. This would mark the final year for the two series format. New front end treatments were found on both series and the F-models offered a slightly cleaner front end package. Mechanically things stayed almost exactly the same, the six powerplant developed 95 horsepower.

I.D. DATA: Serial numbers were located on frame left side rail under hood. Starting: [Series F] California built-CF-504001; Linden, N.J. built-LF-545001; Lansing, MI built-F-600001. Starting: [Series L] California built: CL187001; Linden, N.J. built-LL-197001; Lansing, MI built-L-212001. Ending: [Series F] California built-CF-510598; Linden, N.J. built-LF-551236; Lansing, MI built-F-662212. Ending: [Series L] California built-CL-188760; Linden, N.J. built-LL-198759 and Lansing, MI built-L-228126. Engine numbers were on upper left corner of cylinder block. Starting: F-series: 828001; L-series: 296001. Ending: F-series: 905000; L-series: 298859. On engine codes any engine with C-prefix first letter was California built. F, L or G letter prefix indicates Lansing production. LF, LG or LL numbers indicate Linden, New Jersey, built engine.

Model No.	Body Type & Seating	Price	Weight	Prod. Total
Series F, 6-cyl.				
383667	2-dr. Conv.-3P	1046	3360	1184
383627B	2-dr. Bs. Cpe.-3P	873	3205	8538
383627	2-dr. Clb. Cpe.-3P	929	3215	5632
383601	2-dr. Sed.-5P	919	3275	3975
383611	2-dr. Tr. Sed.-5P	944	3285	22,390
383609	4-dr. Sed.-5P	970	3290	1477
383619	4-dr. Tr. Sed.-5P	995	3305	36,484

ENGINE: [Series F] Inline, L-head. Six. Cast iron block. B & S: 3-7/16 x 4-1/8 in. Disp.: 230 cu. in. C.R.: 6.1:1. Brake H.P.: 95 @ 3400 R.P.M. Main bearings: four. Valve lifters: mushroom. Carb.: single downdraft, automatic choke. [Series L] Inline, L-head. Eight. Cast iron block. B & S: 3-1/4 x 3-7/8 in. Disp.: 257 cu. in. C.R.: 6.2:1. Brake H.P.: 110 @ 3600 R.P.M. Main bearings: five. Valve lifters: mushroom. Carb.: duplex downdraft with automatic choke.

CHASSIS: [Series F] W.B.: 117 in. O.L.: 190-7/16 in. Frt/Rear Tread: 58/59 in. Tires: 16 x 6.50. [Series L] W.B.: 124 in. O.L.: 197-7/8 in. Frt/Rear Tread: 58/59 in. Tires: 16 x 7.00.

TECHNICAL: Sliding gear synchromesh transmission. Speeds: 3F/1R. Floor mounted center gearshift, column mounted on optional semi-automatic. Single plate clutch. Shaft drive. Spiral bevel, semi-floating rear axle. Overall ratio: standard: 4.375:1; semi-automatic: 3.55:1. Cast iron drum, hydraulic brakes on four wheels. Pressed steel wheels. Wheel size: 16 x 4.50. Drivetrain options: Safety automatic transmission ($100.00).

OPTIONS: Dual sidemount ($65.00). Bumper guards (2.00 each). Radio (standard radio 53.00; deluxe radio 66.50). Heater (standard hot water heater 14.45; deluxe hot water heater 19.95). Clock (header board clock 12.25, electric clock 15.00). Cigar lighter (1.75). Radio antenna (turret top antenna 7.00). Seat covers (standard 12.95; deluxe 16.95). Dual windshield defroster (8.25). Defroster fan (4.40). Gearshift ball (50 cents). Wheel chrome mouldings (10.75). Exhaust deflector (1.00). License plate frames (2.75). Luggage compartment mat (1.75). Luggage compartment light (1.25). Fender markers (3.25). Fog lamps (6.25). Winter grille covers (1.00). Locking gas cap (1.50).

HISTORICAL: An air-cooled battery introduced this model year, Safety Automatic Transmission (shared with Buick) continued this model year. Calendar year sales and production: 93,706. Model year sales and production: 99,951. C.L. McCuen was the general manager for Oldsmobile.

BODY STYLES

Body style designations describe the shape and character of an automobile. In the early days, automakers exhibited great imagination in coining words to name their products. This led to descriptions that were not totally accurate. Many of the car words were taken from other fields: mythology, carriage building, architecture, railroading, and so on. Therefore, they have no "correct" automotive meanings; only those brought about through actual use. Some seeming inconsistencies have persisted to recent years, while other imaginative terms of past eras have faded away. One manufacturer's sedan might resemble another's coupe. Some automakers have persisted in describing a model by a word different from common usage, such as Ford calling the Mustang a sedan. Following the demise of the pillarless hardtop in the mid-1970s, various manufacturers continued using the term hardtop to describe their sedans. Some used the descriptions pillared hardtop or thin-pillared hardtop to label what most call a sedan. Descriptions in this catalog generally follow the manufacturers' terms, unless they conflict strongly with accepted usage.

TWO-DOOR (CLUB) COUPE: The Club Coupe designation seems to come from club car, describing the lounge or parlor car in a railroad train. The early postwar Club Coupe combined a shorter-than-sedan body structure with the convenience of a full back seat, unlike the single-seat business coupe. Club Coupe has been used less frequently after World War II, as most two-door models have been referred to as coupes. The distinction between two-door coupes and two-door sedans has grown fuzzy, too. Hudson used the term Club Coupe until 1954, the year the company merged with Nash to form AMC.

TWO-DOOR SEDAN: The term sedan originally described a conveyance seen only in movies today: a wheel-less vehicle for one person, borne on poles by two men...one ahead and one behind. Automakers pirated the word and applied it to cars with a permanent top that seated four to seven people (including driver) in a single compartment. The two-door sedan of recent times has sometimes been called a pillared coupe or just plain coupe, depending on the manufacturer's whims. On the other hand, some cars commonly referred to as coupes carry the sedan designation on factory literature. One of AMC's most unusual two-door sedans was the Pacer.

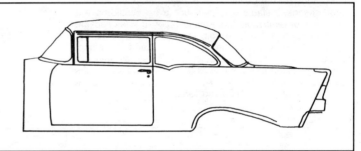

TWO-DOOR (THREE-DOOR) LIFTBACK COUPE: Originally a small opening in the deck of a sailing ship, the term hatch was later applied to airplane doors and to passenger cars with rear liftgates. Most automakers called these cars hatchbacks, but AMC used the term liftback. Various models appeared in the early 1950s, but weather tightness was a problem. The concept emerged again in the early 1970s, when fuel economy factors began to signal the trend toward compact cars. Technology had remedied the sealing difficulties. By the 1980s, most manufacturers produced one or more hatchback models, though the question of whether to call them two-doors or three-doors never was resolved. Their main common feature was the lack of a separate trunk. Liftback coupes may have had a different rear end shape, but the two terms often described essentially the same vehicle. The Gremlin was an interesting hatchback coupe that AMC created.

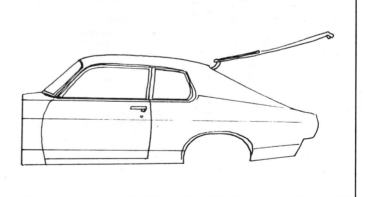

TWO-DOOR FASTBACK: By definition, a fastback is any automobile with a long, moderately curving, downward slope to the rear of the roof. This body style relates to an interest in streamlining and aerodynamics and has gone in and out of fashion at various times. Some fastbacks (Mustangs for one) have grown quite popular. Others have tended to turn customers off. Certain fastbacks are really two-door sedans or pillared coupes. Four-door fastbacks have also been produced. Many of these (such as Buick's late 1970s four-door Century sedan) lacked sales appeal. Fastbacks may or may not have a rear-opening hatch. The Hudson Hornet's fastback styling helped it in stock car racing and the AMX's aerodynamic lines helped its dragstrip and road racing performance.

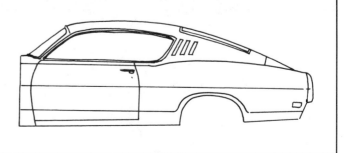

TWO-DOOR HARDTOP: The term hardtop, as used for postwar cars up to the mid-1970s, describes an automobile styled to resemble a convertible, but with a rigid metal or fiberglass top. In a production sense, this body style evolved after World War II. It was first called hardtop convertible. Other generic names have included sports coupe, hardtop coupe or pillarless coupe. In the face of proposed federal government rollover standards, nearly all automakers turned away from pillarless cars by 1976 or 1977. **FORMAL HARD-TOP:** The hardtop roofline was a long-lasting fashion hit of the postwar era. The word formal can be applied to things that are stiffly conservative and follow the established rule. The limousine, being the popular choice of conservative buyers who belonged to the establishment, was looked upon as a formal motor car. When designers combined the lines of these two body styles, the result was the Formal Hardtop. This style has been marketed with two- or four-doors, canopy or vinyl roofs (full or partial) and conventional or opera-type windows, under various trade names. The distinction between a formal hardtop and plain pillared-hardtop coupe (see above) hasn't always followed strict rules. AMC did not offer this body style.

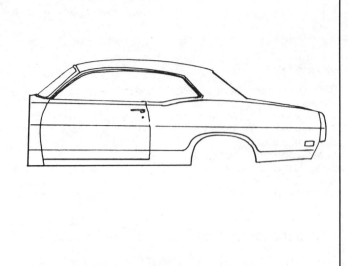

CONVERTIBLE: To depression-era buyers, a convertible was a car with a fixed-position windshield and folding. When raised, the top displayed the lines of a coupe. Buyers in the postwar period expected a convertible to have roll-up windows, too. Yet the definition of the word includes no such qualifications. It states only that such a car should have a lowerable or removable top. American convertibles became almost extinct by 1976, except for Cadillac's Eldorado. In 1982, though, Chrysler brought out a LeBaron ragtop; Dodge a 400; and several other companies followed it a year or two later. Today, many other cars are available in the convertible format. The last AMC ragtop was the Alliance convertible, offered in 1985 and 1986.

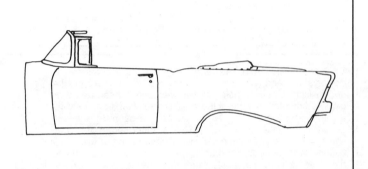

ROADSTER: This term derives from equestrian vocabulary, where it was applied to a horse used for riding on the roads. Old dictionaries define the roadster as an open-type car designed for use on ordinary roads, with a single seat for two persons and, often, a rumbleseat as well. Hobbyists associate folding windshields and side curtains (rather than roll-up windows) with roadsters, although such qualifications stem from usage, not definition of term. Most recent roadsters are either sports cars, small alternative-type vehicles or replicas of early models. Hudson built its last roadster in 1931. Nash ended production of true roadsters in 1930, although a "convertible-roadster" (with roll-up windows) was cataloged through 1932.

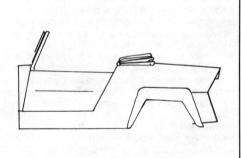

RUNABOUT: By definition, a runabout is the equivalent of a roadster. The term was used by carriage makers and has been applied in the past to light, open cars on which a top is unavailable or totally an add-on option. None of this explains its use by Ford on certain Pintos. Other than this usage, recent runabouts are found mainly in the alternative vehicle field, including certain electric-powered models. The most famous runabout in the AMC family of cars is the first Rambler.

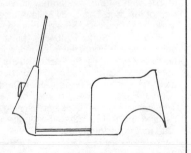

FOUR-DOOR SEDAN: If you took the wheels off a car, mounted it on poles and hired two weight lifters (one in front and one in back) to carry you around in it, you'd have a true sedan. Since this idea isn't very practical, it's better to use the term for an automobile with a permanent top (affixed by solid pillars) that seats four or more persons, including the driver, on two full-width seats.

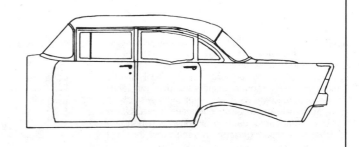

FOUR-DOOR HARDTOP: This is a four-door car styled to resemble a convertible, but having a rigid top of metal or fiberglass. Buick introduced a totally pillarless design in 1955. A year later most automakers offered equivalent bodies. Four-door hardtops have also been labeled sports sedans and hardtop sedans. By 1976, proposed federal roll-over standards and waning popularity had taken their toll of four-door hardtop output. Only a few makes still produced a four-door hardtop. They disappeared soon thereafter. AMC's 1957 Rambler Rebel is probably the company's most famous four-door hardtop.

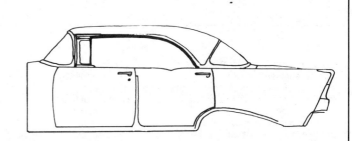

FOUR-DOOR PILLARED HARDTOP: Once the true four-door hardtop began to fade away, manufacturers needed another name for their luxury four-doors. Many were styled to look almost like the former pillarless models, with thin or unobtrusive pillars between the doors. Some, in fact, were called "thin-pillar hardtops." The distinction between certain pillared hardtops and ordinary (presumably humdrum) sedans occasionally grew hazy.

FOUR-DOOR (FIVE-DOOR) LIFTBACK: Essentially unknown among domestic models in the mid-1970s, the four-door liftback or hatchback became a popular model as cars grew smaller and front-wheel drive caught on. Styling was similar to the original two-door hatchback, except for the extra doors. Luggage was carried in the back of the car. It was loaded through the hatch opening, not in a separate trunk. AMC's first hatchback sedan, a five-door model, appeared in the 1984 Encore line.

LIMOUSINE: This word's literal meaning is 'a cloak.' In France, limousine means any passenger vehicle. An early dictionary defined limousine as an auto with a permanently enclosed compartment for 3-5, with a roof projecting over a front driver's seat. However, modern dictionaries drop the separate compartment idea and refer to limousines as large luxury autos, often chauffeur-driven. Some have a movable division window between the driver and passenger compartments, but that isn't a requirement.

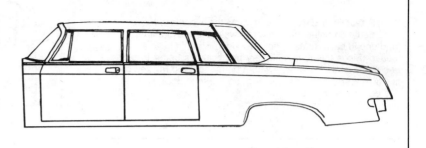

TWO-DOOR STATION WAGON: Originally defined as a car with an enclosed wooden body of paneled design (with several rows of folding or removable seats behind the driver), the station wagon became a different and much more popular type of vehicle in the postwar years. A recent dictionary states that such models have a larger interior than sedans of the line and seats that can be readily lifted out, or folded down, to facilitate light trucking. In addition, there's usually a tailgate, but no separate luggage compartment. The two-door wagon often has sliding or flip-out rear side windows.

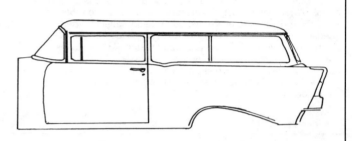

FOUR-DOOR STATION WAGON: Since functionality and adaptability are advantages of station wagons, four-door versions have traditionally been sales leaders. At least they were until cars began to grow smaller. This style usually has lowerable windows in all four doors and fixed rear side glass. The term "suburban" was almost synonymous with station wagon at one time, but is now more commonly applied to light trucks with similar styling. Station wagons have had many trade names, such as Country Squire (Ford) and Sport Suburban (Plymouth). Quite a few have retained simulated wood paneling, keeping alive the wagon's origin as a wood-bodied vehicle. AMC was famous for introducing the four-door hardtop (pillarless) station wagon in the mid-1950s.

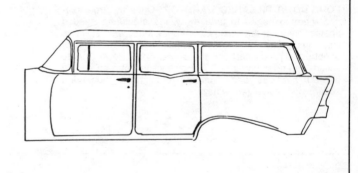

LIFTBACK STATION WAGON: Small cars came in station wagon form too. The idea was the same as bigger versions, but the conventional tailgate was replaced by a single lift-up hatch. For obvious reasons, compact and subcompact wagons had only two seats, instead of the three that had been available in many full-sized models. The Hornet Sportabout station wagon should become a collectible example of this body style, along with early American Eagle station wagons.

DIMENSIONS

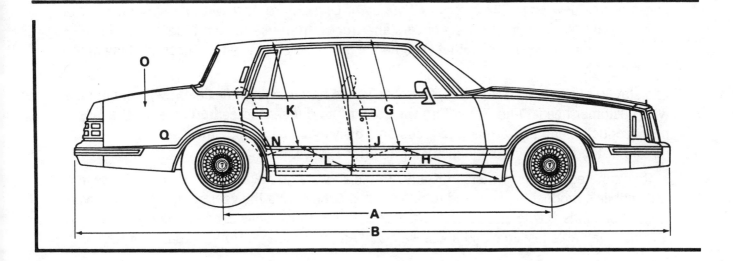

DIMENSIONS
Exterior:
A Wheelbase
B Overall length
C Width
D Overall height
E Tread, front
F Tread, rear
Interior—front:
G Headroom
H Legroom
I Shoulder room
J Hip room
Interior—rear:
K Headroom
L Legroom
M Shoulder room
N Hip room
O Trunk capacity (liters/cu. ft.)
P Cargo index volume (liters/cu. ft.)
Q Fuel tank capacity (liters/gallons)

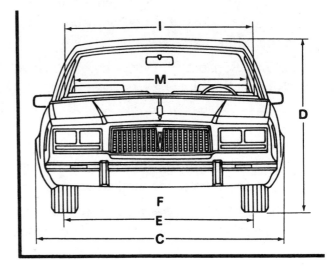

FOREWORD

On August 21, 1997, Oldsmobile celebrates its first 100 years in the automobile business, making it the first American car company to reach the centennial milestone. Not only has Oldsmobile outlived more than 2,500 other vehicle companies that have taken a stab at the horseless carriage, but it has made its mark in the industry as a leader. As you thumb through the pages of this new book, the *Standard Catalog of Oldsmobile*, you will find we've manufactured and marketed a great variety of cars and trucks; from high-priced to low, from large to small. In addition, you'll notice that Oldsmobile has been an innovator, accomplishing many industry firsts.

To stay in business for 100 years, Oldsmobile has had to remain flexible ... staying in tune with customer needs. And as we turn the corner into our second century, we sport a whole new product lineup and a renewed focus on satisfying customers ... the right ingredients to remain at the forefront of the industry for another 100 years.

I thank the editors and writers of Krause Publications who have taken the time to research Oldsmobile's product heritage and to publish this book during the year of our 100th anniversary. Thousands of auto enthusiasts and especially our Oldsmobile car club members will find it to be a valuable resource and a keepsake of "America's longest running car marque."

Oldsmobile's first 100 years

Before you begin your search in this book for information on a specific Oldsmobile model, let me take a minute to tell you about where Oldsmobile has been and where we are headed in the future.

It was Ransom Eli Olds who established the Olds Motor Vehicle Company way back in 1897. At that time he was given the charge to "build one carriage in as nearly perfect a manner as possible." While vehicle production was limited at first, only four cars over the next two years, the company experienced rapid success in 1900 with the development of the famous gasoline runabout called the Curved Dash Oldsmobile. The runabout would become the best selling vehicle in the United States during these early years of the auto industry, garnering nearly one-third of the market.

The Curved Dash was a success because Olds had three necessary elements of any successful business ... a good product, a capable and dedicated workforce and a marketing plan. Olds' marketing plan was pitched as being better than the competition at the time -- the horse.

Olds became a part of General Motors in 1908 and through the efforts of its talented people, took credit for many firsts in the industry over the years. Here's just a few of the things Oldsmobile is famous for:

* First to pioneer automobile mass production

* First to establish a distribution system ... both foreign and domestic

* First to develop an automotive supplier system

* Won the first transcontinental race to Portland, Oregon, in 1905

* Developed chrome plating on auto parts in 1925
* Offered a semi-automatic transmission in 1937 and a fully automatic transmission in 1940, known as the Hydra-Matic transmission.
* Developed the first modern high-compression V-8 engine in 1949, called the Rocket V-8
* Offered the first fluid-injected turbocharged engine in 1962, called the Jetfire
* Brought to market the first modern front-wheel drive car in 1966, the Toronado
* With the Cutlass, achieved the rank of best-selling car in the United States in 1976
* The Oldsmobile Aerotech set the world's records of 257 and 267 mph for the closed course and the flying mile in 1987
* Oldsmobile offered the first in-vehicle Navigation Information System for sale in the United States in 1994

Oldsmobile moves into its second century

As the market changed during the late-1980s and early-1990s, Oldsmobile faced many new challenges. The company needed to re-establish itself as an industry leader and it needed a plan that would lead to continued success as the company moved into its second century.

Today, Oldsmobile is aggressively following its "Centennial Plan." Starting with the Aurora, introduced in 1995, Oldsmobile is now developing vehicles that are intended for import-minded customers who are generally younger and a little more upscale than those customers who were targeted in the past. Once the company's new products are in place, Oldsmobile will be the logical choice for buyers looking for a domestic vehicle with an international flavor.

It is a pleasure to be a part of this fine company as it celebrates its centennial. During this anniversary year, we will not only introduce several new products that will surely change the look and feel of Oldsmobile for years to come, but we will also begin our drive into the future with enthusiasm as we leverage our great heritage to begin a successful second century.

Many thanks to Krause Publications for highlighting Oldsmobile's first 100 years. May you enjoy success in the future and we look forward to working with you again when we celebrate 200 years in 2097.

Darwin E. Clark
Oldsmobile General Manager
Vice-President, General Motors Corp.

OLDSMOBILE HISTORY

The history of Oldsmobile begins before its official 100th anniversary on August 21, 1997. Ransom Eli Olds built his first car in 1891, a steamer, and a second car in 1892. In 1895 he turned his attention to the internal combustion engine. In the summer of 1896, he completed his first gasoline-powered car. The engine produced five horsepower with a top speed of 18 mph. Technically, it wasn't an "Oldsmobile" as that name wasn't registered until 1900.

The car was successful enough to prompt Edward Sparrow and Samuel Smith to give Oldsmobile additional money to start production. Accordingly, a new firm called The Olds Motor Vehicle Company was incorporated on August 21, 1897. This is today recognized as the founding of Oldsmobile and the 100th anniversary of Oldsmobile will be celebrated on August 21, 1997.

Oldsmobile built and sold four cars in three months, but was interrupted by a strike. Sparrow lost faith in Olds and pulled out. However, Smith did not and put up most of the money for incorporation of a new venture on May 18, 1899, called Olds Motor Works. The new automaker's first car was a 7 hp, two-cylinder model for $1,250, but it attracted few orders.

Meanwhile, Oldsmobile seemed more interested in developing electric cars than improving the gasoline model. However, there was a fateful fire that destroyed the Olds factory on March 9, 1901, along with Ransom Oldsmobile's prototype electric and a few other experimental cars. Only one car was saved, a lightweight one-cylinder runabout with a curved dash.

Olds was on vacation at the time in California. He took the first eastbound express train and then made the momentous decision to concentrate on a single model, the surviving curved dash design. Olds produced a credible 425 cars in 1901.

The Lansing Chamber of Commerce offered its former 52-acre fairground site for the new Oldsmobile factory absolutely free. Oldsmobile built his new factory in Lansing, Michigan.

By 1903 production was up to 4,000 cars. However, Olds was criticized for not doing enough to develop new cars since the curved dash wouldn't sell forever. Sam Smith's son, Fred, pushed for a two-cylinder companion model.

In January 1904, a dispute over new products broke out at a board meeting. Ransom Olds replied with a short speech and then announced he would resign. A month later he sold his stock.

Curved dash sales climbed to 5,508 units in 1904. The first of Smith's new models in 1905 was a curved dash derivative, still with a one-cylinder engine, but priced $100 higher. Other models shared a new two-cylinder engine and a $1,250 price.

Meanwhile, Ransom Olds was approached by Lansing entrepreneurs who offered to back him in a new automobile company. This became the Reo Motor Car Company representing Ransom E. Olds' initials. Ironically, Olds adopted the same new product policy for Reo that he had previously opposed at Oldsmobile.

In 1906 Oldsmobile developed the Model S with a front-mounted four-cylinder engine selling for $2,250. It weighed 2,200 pounds and was capable of 40-45 mph.

In 1908 Oldsmobile introduced its first six-cylinder engine on the Model Z and KR. These carried the same $4,200 price, which made them direct competitors for the Packard 30, Locomobile Series E and Peerless Model 18. Displacement was a massive 453 cubic inches with 45 hp. The Z and KR did not do well because they were in a small, select market, overcrowded with cars with more prestigious names than Oldsmobile.

By the middle of 1908 Oldsmobile was more than a $1 million in debt and Oldsmobile seemed doomed. At this time, William C. Durant who was buying car companies to build General Motors into a complete car line automaker, bought Oldsmobile. He paid $17,279 cash, with the remainder of the price paid in General Motors stock, $1.8 million in preferred shares, and $1.2 million in common shares.

In 1909 Durant sent a Buick Model 10 over to the Oldsmobile Lansing, Michigan, plant. In the Oldsmobile workshop, before startled Olds brass, Durant had the Buick chassis sawed off across the middle and split down the center. Metal was then added to make a new chassis with a longer wheelbase and a wider track to accommodate a roomier, more expensive body. Existing springs, axles, driveline and engine were retained. The concept was to price the new Oldsmobile $250 more than the Buick 10, but less than the rest of the Olds line.

However, the Model 20 was soon discontinued in 1910, leaving Olds without a low price entry. But the real mistake was the new Limited, a larger six-cylinder car. It was built on a 130 inch wheelbase and weighed over two tons. It was powered by a giant 700 cubic inch engine producing 60 hp with an impressive top speed of 75 mph. The Olds catalog described the Limited as creating, "A new standard of luxury in motoring, a combination of the smooth-running six-cylinder Oldsmobile engine, improved spring suspension, and large 42 inch tires produces the easiest-riding car every built." But at $4,600, it was far above any Cadillac and was not an easy car to sell. In 1911 the Limited price increased to $5,000.

The four-cylinder Autocrat was introduced in 1911 with 40 hp. Prices ranged from $3,500 to $5,000. In 1912 the four-cylinder Model 40 Defender was introduced with 35 hp, priced from $3,000 to $3,600.

Cost cutting was given high priority and in 1913 the Model 40 Defender prices were slashed by $500 to $2,500, and the four-cylinder Autocrat was discontinued. The Model 53 replaced the Limited and sold for a full $1,800 less at $3,200. It had a new L-head six-cylinder with 50 hp. In 1913 C.W. Nash was named general manager at Olds. Under Nash, Olds immediately began experimenting with quality light cars.

Oldsmobile thus began moving away from uppercrust products toward a more lucrative market for quality light cars. In 1914 the Model 42, known as the "Baby Olds," was introduced on a 110 inch wheelbase for $1,285. It had a 192 cubic inch four-cylinder with 30 hp. In 1915 the Model 42 Baby Olds was upgraded with a two inch longer wheelbase and the price was reduced to $1,285. Only 400 of these were built in 1914, but the Baby Olds generated a considerably higher volume in 1915.

Late in the year, Oldsmobile introduced its first popularly-priced V-8 car, the Model 44 with 246 cubic inches and 40 hp. In 1915 tops and windshields were made standard on all Oldsmobiles.

In 1916 Oldsmobile began producing closed cars in significant volume. Six-cylinders were discontinued while the four-cylinder Model 43 and V-8 Model 44 remained.

In 1917 Oldsmobile introduced a light-6, the Model 37. Its weight averaged 2,400 pounds and it had 40 hp from its valve in-head engine. Two closed models were available in the 1917 Model 37 line, a coupe and a sedan.

In 1918 Oldsmobile produced kitchen trailers for World War I, while maintaining car output at 1917 levels. Oldsmobile made 11,037 six-cylinders, now designated Model 37A and 8,132 of the V-8 Model 45A. The war restricted changes. In 1918 two closed models, called All Season cars, continued to sell well despite a price $700 higher than open models.

Oldsmobile production more than doubled in 1919 to 39,042 cars. The major new product was the Oldsmobile economy truck, powered by the new 224 cubic inch Northway 4 with 40 hp and priced from $1,250. The Oldsmobile economy truck sales in 1919 were 5,617. Passenger cars, meanwhile, received only minor changes. The Model 45A V-8s were joined by Model 45B, which was basically an up-market version on a longer 122 inch wheelbase.

In 1921 the unchanged top-of-the-line Model 46 was joined by the new and slightly smaller Model 47 with a long-stroke 233 cubic inch V-8. It was an L-head design with only two main bearings. The price range on this new "light-8" was $1,695 to $2,295.

In 1923 the Oldsmobile line was largely unchanged except that production started on the new Model 30-A in July. Significant Model 30-A production wasn't achieved until October when the 1924 models debuted. Early Model 30-As, however, were designated 1923 models.

The 30-A was a low-priced six-cylinder, little changed from the 1920-21 six-cylinder engine. Its chassis was similar to the four-cylinder model 43-A, except for a five inch shorter wheelbase. The key selling point was the price, which ranged from $795 to $1,095, making this one of the industry's least expensive six-cylinder cars and no more expensive than the last of the four-cylinder cars. Oldsmobile four-cylinders and V-8s were discontinued in 1923. Thus Oldsmobile had only six-cylinders from 1924 to 1931.

The 1924 models carried the designation 30-B and were identical to the late 1923 Model 30-A. The 1923-24 six-cylinder engine had 169 cubic inches and continued through 1926. For 1925 it became model 30-C and in June 1925 it became the Model 30-D. Mechanical changes were minimal but radiator and hood were revised, cowl lights were standardized, chrome plating replaced nickel on radiator shells and a new center mount instrument panel was introduced. Prices increased a little and production remained steady with 34,334 units for the year.

In 1926 the Model 30 became the 30-D and in 1927, the 30-E. The six-cylinder engine increased to 185 cubic inches for 1927.

The 30-D continued in 1927 and minor modifications were made to suspension and wheel size that resulted in lower bodies. There were more closed bodies in deluxe versions of the coupe, coach and sedan. Volume hit a new peak with 57,878 units for the calendar year.

The 1927 Oldsmobile was officially titled 30-E and first appeared in mid-1926. Oldsmobile introduced four-wheel brakes with no price increase in January 1927. Olds had another sales record reaching 79,282 units.

In 1928 the Model 30 was superseded by the similarly priced F-28. It introduced a new 197 cubic inch side-valve six-cylinder that was appreciably smoother than the more primitive 1923-vintage Model 30 engine. The new six-cylinder continued in production through 1933 without basic alteration. In 1928 the fuel pump replaced the vacuum tank.

In 1929 the F-28 was re-badged as the F-29. Division head, I.J. Reuter, was determined to hold it at the original price to assure the maximum sales, so alterations were minor.

The all-new 1929 Oldsmobile Viking was not a "junior" Oldsmobile such as the LaSalle was to Cadillac or the Marquette was to Buick. The Viking was an upscale Oldsmobile built on a 125 inch wheelbase and powered by a 90 degree V-8 with 259 cubic inches. Weight averaged two tons. Although the Viking was introduced in April 1929, the decision to introduce it was made in 1925 and design work started in 1926. It had horizontally set valves, which gave a unique triangular-section combustion chamber. Oldsmobile sold 5,259 Vikings in 1929 and only 2,738 Vikings in 1930. Production was suspended in the summer of 1930, never to be resumed.

In 1930 the F-30, a redesigned Oldsmobile was introduced with new styling by General Motors' Art and Color Studio. It had a lower chassis and smaller diameter wheels. In 1931 it became the F-31 and wheel diameter was reduced again for a lower look. Starting prices were reduced to $845 for the standard business coupe and two-door sedan.

In 1932 Oldsmobile introduced a new L-head straight 8-engine for the new L-32 series. Its 240 cubic inch displacement continued through 1936 and produced 82 hp. Except for the engine, the L-32 was a twin to the six-cylinder line now designed as an F-32. Oldsmobile's 1932 styling changes followed those at other GM divisions with smoother body contours, more flowing fenders, hood ventilator doors, slightly slanted windshields and outside windshield visors deleted. In 1932 the six-cylinder F-32 displacement was 213 cubic inches.

In 1933 the streamlining trend gained momentum in the all-new Oldsmobile bodies. The re-bodied straight-8 models also received a four inch longer wheelbase (119 inches) than the six-cylinder models. For 1933 only, the six-cylinder displacement increased slightly to 221 cubic inches. The 1933 Oldsmobiles featured "no-draft ventilation" with pivoting wind-wings developed by Fisher Body. The wind-wings were on both the front door and aft of the rear door.

The 1934 Oldsmobile had a highly swept grille, which was scaled back for 1935. The chassis received "knee-action" front suspension and Oldsmobile adopted Bendix four-wheel hydraulic brakes ahead of its sister divisions, except LaSalle. Remarkably, Oldsmobile sales doubled during this Depression year.

Oldsmobile introduced the all-new "Turret-Top" bodies in 1935. Oldsmobile smashed its all-time 1929 sales records and delivered 183,152 cars for the calendar year. Oldsmobile front doors were suicide doors, hinged at the back.

Oldsmobile quickly returned to front hinge doors in 1936. Otherwise the 1936 bodies were little changed. Both the six- and eight-cylinder engines introduced light aluminum pistons to replace cast-iron pistons. Sales continued upward reaching 187,638 for the calendar year.

The 1937 Oldsmobile switched to a lighter X-member chassis, which allowed the passenger floor to be lowered 3-1/2 inches. The 1937 Oldsmobile also received a new straight-8 of 257 cubic inches for 110 hp. There was also a new six-cylinder with 229 cubic inches and 95 hp. This displacement would be retained through 1940. Both engines were machined on the same lines and had high parts commonality to minimize production costs. In 1938 Oldsmobile introduced coil springs for its rear suspension.

Oldsmobile again introduced new bodies in 1939. The F-39 Series 60 was the entry-level series and was powered by a de-bored 216 cubic inch version of the familiar six-cylinder now producing 90 hp. It sold as low as $770 in business coupe form, undercutting the low-end Pontiac and also encroaching on Chevrolet territory. In 1939 the smaller 60 Series Oldsmobile had a 215 cubic inch six-cylinder and the 70 Series, a 229 cubic inch six-cylinder.

Oldsmobile's Hydra-Matic transmission, the industry's first automatic transmission, was the big news for 1940. It was subsidized at the low price of $57.

In 1941 Oldsmobile offered six- and eight-cylinder engines in all series. The top-of-the-line 90 Series could have a six-cylinder and conversely the entry 60 Series could have an eight-cylinder. In 1941 the Special 60 Series introduced the four-window town sedan, a step toward the notchback sedans of the late 1940s. In 1941 the new six-cylinder displacement was 238 cubic inches. The 1941 engines were unchanged through 1947. In 1942 all Oldsmobile series had front fenders that extended to the front doors plus a complex grille with a two-tier bumper.

The 1946 Oldsmobile introduced a completely revised grille, while most 1946 cars had only minor front end revisions. The new grille is significant because it set an evolutionary trend in Oldsmobile grille design for the next decade.

Although the initial postwar engines were carryovers from 1942, the revolutionary Kettering overhead-valve "Rocket V-8" engine was soon introduced in 1949. The Rocket V-8 started a design trend that dominated the industry's horsepower race of the 1950s. The Rocket V-8 was the industry trendsetter. Although Hudson had a powerful six-cylinder that out-raced Oldsmobile for a short period, the Hudson 6 set no industry direction. The Hudson six-cylinder was a significant anomaly on the road to higher performance, but did not predict future technology for the industry.

In 1948 the Oldsmobile 98 was completely re-styled and introduced an exclusive new body. The redesigned 1948 Oldsmobile 98 was an upscale move, using the same body as the Cadillac 61 and 62 Series. The 98 set the "Futuramic" styling theme for the re-styled 1949 Oldsmobile 76s and 88s, waiting another year for their first postwar redesign. The 98 "Futuramic" styling was applied to the new and smaller 76/88 body, shared with the all-new 1949 Chevrolet and Pontiac.

In the late 1940s Oldsmobile and General Motors took a more evolutionary approach toward the elimination of stand-out fenders. The 1948 Oldsmobile 98 front fender completely faded away, while the rear fender continued to stand out. By contrast, the 1949 Ford and Mercury front and rear fenders completely disappeared in their initial postwar redesign.

In 1949 Oldsmobile decided at the last minute to introduce the 98's powerful overhead-valve V-8 in the 88 series. The principle advantage of the V-8 for the 88 was its lighter body. It gave the 88 higher performance than the 98 with the identical engine. It showed the potential of the new OHV V-8 in a lighter car. The V-8 was so successful that the six-cylinder Oldsmobile was phased out at the end of 1950. The 1949 Oldsmobiles with the new V-8 were the hottest performing cars in dealer showrooms in the late-1940s.

Oldsmobile again led the industry when it introduced two-door hardtops in 1949. It wasn't until 1951 that Packard and Hudson introduced two-door hardtops, followed by Mercury in 1952.

Another important postwar trend, where Oldsmobile played a leading role, was the development and widespread use of major convenience options, starting with the automatic transmission in 1940. In the late-1940s and early-1950s, the percentage of Oldsmobiles built with Hydra-Matic increased dramatically. Power steering and brakes, and air conditioning followed in the early 1950s.

The 1950s also marked the era of longer, lower and wider bodies for American cars. For instance, the Oldsmobile 88's length went from 202 inches in 1950 to 218 inches by 1959. Meanwhile, the width increased from 75-3/16 to 80.8 inches and the height was reduced from 64-1/16 to 56 inches.

The Oldsmobile 98 promptly received its second postwar redesign in 1950. The two-door hardtop introduced a full wraparound rear window. The 1950 Oldsmobile 98 four-door sedan also introduced a sedan wraparound rear window. The 98s were also the first Oldsmobile to have a fade-away rear fender.

At the start of the 1951 model year, only the 88 and 98 models appeared. The redesigned Super 88 model was not ready until the end of March. It was heavier than the base 88, now essentially a carryover 1950 Series 88 model with less trim. Although the base 88 was at the bottom of the line, the potent V-8 was standard.

In 1952 the Super 88 and 98s gained 25 hp through a new "Quadra-Jet" down-draft four-barrel carburetor. The 1954 Oldsmobile co-introduced the wraparound windshield to the complete line. In 1954 only the Oldsmobile, Buick and Cadillac lines had this feature. By 1955 virtually all cars had wraparound windshields.

The 1957 Oldsmobile introduced a new V-8 displacement of 371 cubic inches, which continued through 1960. The 1957 Oldsmobiles had a re-worked suspension with retrograde rear leaf springs replacing coils. The 1958 Oldsmobile introduced New-Matic ride. It used four air springs and an automatic self-leveling feature with an extra large high pressure tank.

The 1959s represented a drastic re-style for Oldsmobile. It contrasted to the 1957 and 1958 Oldsmobiles that had a heavy look that lagged behind Chrysler's trendsetting 1957 "Forward Look." The 1959 Oldsmobile was targeted to surpass the Chrysler styling theme and resulted in new extremes of long, low and wide cars with fins.

The drastic 1959 re-style introduced a greater difference between the hardtops and sedans. Both two- and four-door hardtops were two inches lower than the respective sedans.

The 1959 Oldsmobile offered a 371 cubic inch engine for the 88s and 394 cubic inch engine for the Super 88 and 98. Rare options in 1959 included air suspension with 0.5 percent installation rate, limited slip differential with 5.2 percent installation rate, while air conditioning was gaining popularity with a 15.2 percent installation rate.

The 1960 Oldsmobile used entirely new sheet metal with fins deleted, a retreat from the 1959's styling excesses. The 1961 Oldsmobile was entirely redesigned, again following more conservative lines. Reversing the industry trend, bodies were slightly higher in 1961.

The other major news in 1961 was the introduction of the F-85, Oldsmobile's first compact car. The midyear 1961 Oldsmobile F-85 coupe was the first production Oldsmobile named Cutlass, a name that will continue into Oldsmobile's second 100 years.

In 1961 Oldsmobile returned to the conventional windshield, eclipsing the wraparound windshield fad. The 1961s also evolved away from the wraparound rear window. The four-door hardtop models had a wide C-pillar with a slight wraparound rear window. In 1962, this feature was expanded to the four-door sedans. The 1962 two-door hardtop roof line was radically redesigned to resemble the silhouette of a convertible with a wide C-pillar and small rear window.

The 1961 and 1962 Oldsmobile 88s and 98s were called the "extruded look," with full-length parallel body sculpting. This design trait was also shared with the Buick and Pontiac. The 1962 full-size Oldsmobile had front and rear re-styling but door sheet metal remained the same. In 1963 the 1961-64 platform was freshened with entirely new sheet metal. In 1964, again only the front and rear were modified.

Although the F-85 was introduced as a compact car in 1961, it was completely redesigned and enlarged to intermediate dimensions in 1964. Ironically, the price change was minimal. A key factor was the replacement of the expensive aluminum 215 cubic inch V-8 engine with a larger and less expensive cast-iron 330 cubic inch V-8. The 1964 Jetstar 88 entry-level full-sized Oldsmobile borrowed the new 330 cubic inch Jetfire Rocket V-8 from the all-new F-85/Cutlass.

The 1964-1/2 Oldsmobile F-85 4-4-2 option (code B-09) evolved from the police pursuit package. The initial 1964-1/2 4-4-2 package denoted four-speed floor shift manual transmission, four-barrel carburetor and dual exhaust.

The F-85 and the Cutlass, which was the top-of-the-line F-85 series, continued their 1964 bodies through 1965. They were completely re-skinned in 1966, introducing a tunnel-back recessed rear window.

In 1965 the 4-4-2 designation denoted a 400 cubic inch V-8, four-barrel carburetor and dual exhaust. The 4-4-2 package also included heavy-duty suspension, wider wheels and tires, special rear axle and driveshaft, heavy-duty engine mounts/steering gear/frame, front and rear stabilizer bars, 11 inch clutch, 70 amp battery and special nameplates.

The 1965 re-styling introduced an entirely new body for the full-size 88 and 98 Series plus a larger 425 cubic inch Super Rocket V-8.

The most important news for Oldsmobile in 1966 was the front-drive Toronado, the first front-drive American car since the 1937 Cord 810. The Toronado had concealed headlights and prominent wheel arches inspired by the Cord. Other Toronado styling aspects were soon adopted by other Oldsmobile series.

In 1966 the Oldsmobile Cutlass introduced the Cutlass Supreme four-door hardtop. This was the first intermediate four-door hardtop. Oldsmobile was four years ahead of Ford and Mercury in introducing four-door hardtop intermediates.

In 1968, the F-85/Cutlass was entirely new. The two-door models used a short 112 inch wheelbase while the four-door models had a 116 inch wheelbase. This departed from the usual practice of using identical wheelbases for two-door and four-door models. Added to this wheelbase proliferation was the Vista Cruiser, which in 1964 had a five inch stretch from the four-door sedan to a 121 inch wheelbase.

The first Hurst/Olds was introduced in 1968 as a limited production hardtop or coupe based on the 4-4-2. It featured a special 455-cid/390-hp V-8 with Turbo Hydra-Matic transmission, Hurst dual-gate shifter, H/O emblems plus a special black and silver paint combination. Limited production totaled 515.

The F-85 and Cutlass retained the 1968 body through 1969. They were re-skinned in 1970 and were scheduled to be completely redesigned in 1972. However, a major General Motors strike postponed the new generation until 1973.

Oldsmobile introduced its all-time largest V-8 with 455 cubic inches for 1968. The 1971 Oldsmobiles were entirely re-styled and remained basically unchanged through 1976. The principal changes during this six-year run were stronger bumpers (to meet federal requirements) and the transition of the two-door models into coupes. The 88 was re-styled to coupe format in 1974 and the 98 hardtop was converted to a coupe in 1975 with a large opera window.

The principal change in the 1971 through 1978 generation Toronado was the introduction of an opera window in 1974. This transformed the Toronado hardtop into a coupe. The sales of the successfully downsized 1979 Oldsmobile Toronado doubled to just over 50,000.

The redesigned 1973 Cutlass was heavy for an intermediate, weighing nearly 4,000 pounds. Oldsmobile retained this body until its dramatic downsizing in 1978. The weight of these cars was highlighted by the fact that the downsized full-size 1977 Oldsmobile 88 models weighed less than pre-downsized 1977 Cutlass series.

The 1971 Oldsmobile Custom Cruiser was the largest conventional station wagon ever built. It featured a novel clamshell rear tailgate with the bottom-half of the tailgate sliding under the floor of the cargo area and the top-half of the tailgate retracting into the roof.

In 1973-1/2 Oldsmobile introduced the compact Oldsmobile Omega which was a lightly modified Chevrolet Nova, based on the 1968-74 Nova body. It introduced Oldsmobile's first hatchback.

The Oldsmobile Omega body was redesigned for 1975. Although the 1975 Omega was introduced a year after the late-1973 Arab oil embargo, it was too far in development to be lightened for better fuel efficiency. This body would remain until the arrival of the downsized front-drive X-platform in April 1979, as early 1980 models.

In response to the energy crisis, Oldsmobile first reduced engine sizes, then it downsized bodies. For example, in 1975 Oldsmobile introduced a small-block 260 cubic inch V-8 in the compact Omega when it was re-styled, but not downsized.

Oldsmobile produced 891,000 cars for 1976, a quarter million more than 1975, retaining third place in the industry. Oldsmobile's great strength was the intermediate Cutlass.

1976 was the last year for the 455 cubic inch V-8 in the 98 and front-drive Toronado. The Chevrolet inline six for the Omega

and Cutlass disappeared after 1976, replaced by Buick's superior V-6. Buick had just repurchased its V-6 tooling from American Motors, which stopped using it for Jeeps.

Oldsmobile's revolutionary downsizing started in 1977 with the full-size 88 and 98 models. Next came the intermediate Cutlass in 1978, followed by the Toronado in 1979 and the Omega in 1980. The Omega was the most radical early downsizing because, in addition to a substantial weight reduction, it made the transition to transverse front-drive format. The Omega had rack and pinion steering, all coil-spring suspension and a transverse Pontiac Iron Duke four-cylinder engine or new Chevrolet 2.8 liter V-6. The downsized 88/98 and intermediate Cutlass retained rear-drive.

In 1977 the Oldsmobile had its first million car year with 1,135,803 sales. The Cutlass Supreme sold 632,812 units, a considerable achievement considering this was the final year for the 1973-77 body. In 1977 the Toronado XSR model (production models were called XS) introduced a radically changed roof line with an extreme wraparound rear window with creased corners, coupled with a T-top (never made available on a production model). At the other end, the sub-compact Starfire got a four-cylinder in 1977.

One year after their dramatic downsizing, the 88s and 98s introduced a second radical advancement for fuel efficiency, the 350 cubic inch diesel V-8. The diesel was derived from Oldsmobile's conventional gasoline V-8. Its internal components and seals were strengthened, but not adequately. Oldsmobile diesels initially sold well, especially during the 1979 Iranian oil crisis, and were used by all other GM divisions. The new diesel V-8 had a 21 mpg city EPA mileage rating and a 30 mpg highway rating -- impressive for a full-size car. Oldsmobile diesels were advertised as the first diesel V-8 passenger cars.

In introducing the new downsized 1978 Oldsmobile Cutlass styling, there was concern about maintaining its best-selling status. The notchback coupes sold well. However, the "aeroback" two- and four-door sedan models did not. This necessitated a crash program to develop notchbacks from the aeroback four-door platform. Notchbacks were introduced in 1980 and four-door sales increased over 100 percent. In 1978 and 1979 the Oldsmobile 4-4-2 package was available only on the unpopular "aeroback" two-door body style and consequently, sales suffered.

In 1979 Oldsmobile introduced a 260 cubic inch diesel V-8, followed by a V-6 diesel in 1982. At one point nearly one in five Oldsmobiles was diesel powered. Eventually there were many complaints about mechanical problems, which led to lawsuits and bad ink. Diesels hung on until 1985 but their sales diminished steadily.

In 1980 the full-sized 88 and 98 models got extensively revised sheet metal. Weight was reduced by 150 pounds without downsizing. Aerodynamics were also improved. The 1980 Oldsmobile Delta 88 V-8 diesel was rated 22 mpg city and 34 mpg highway with an impressive highway range of 918 miles.

In 1980 the 307 cubic inch V-8 was made standard in the 98 and Toronado, replacing the 350 cubic inch V-8. The 350 cubic inch diesel engine was a $960 option on the 1980 Cutlass. In 1981 a new four-speed automatic overdrive transmission was introduced.

In 1982 the Oldsmobile Cutlass Ciera debuted on the new front-drive A-body platform. This was an extended and modified Omega X-body platform. Fortunately, it did not suffer from the recall reputation of the X-body and remained in the Oldsmobile line through the end of 1996, an all-time record for the longest production run for any Oldsmobile platform.

The 1982 Oldsmobile Cutlass Ciera accompanied rather than replaced the rear drive Cutlass. It introduced an 85 hp 4.3-liter V6 diesel, which was also available on the rear drive Cutlass. In 1982 Oldsmobile introduced the Firenza, its version of the new GM J-body. It was front-drive with a transverse mounted inline four-cylinder.

1983 was a good year for Oldsmobile in selling 916,583 cars. This was down from the over a million units a year sold in the 1977 through 1979 period, but was still a sound performance.

Oldsmobile again topped a million sales each year from 1984 to 1986. In 1984, the front-drive Oldsmobile Cutlass Ciera was GM's best selling front-drive intermediate and introduced a new five-door wagon. Oldsmobile achieved second place in 1985 with 1,165,649 sales, surpassing Ford by 16,222 units.

In 1985 Oldsmobile introduced its all-new 98 Series version of the General Motors C-body, now offered only with a V-6. It also made the transition to front-drive and was also 500-600 pounds lighter than its predecessor. This was a radical change for a genuine full-sized car.

In 1985 Oldsmobile also introduced its Cutlass Calais version of General Motors N-body, an upscale version of the J-body introduced in 1982. It debuted in coupe, followed by a four-door sedan in 1986. Again, this was a front-drive configuration.

In 1988 the new Oldsmobile Cutlass Supreme was introduced on the GM10 platform with front drive. Four-door versions were introduced a year later.

Oldsmobile and C&C, Inc. produced 55 replicas of the 1988 Cutlass Supreme Indy pace car, based on the GM10 coupe platform. It featured a turbocharged version of the new twin-cam Quad 4 engine and aircraft-type heads-up display (HUD). It led to introduction of a Cutlass Supreme convertible late in the 1990 model year. However, the Oldsmobile Cutlass Supreme convertible had a "structural top bar" and a V-6 replaced the turbo Quad 4.

The new 1990 Oldsmobile Silhouette, built on the same platform as the Pontiac Transport and the Chevrolet Lumina minivans, had composite skin panels similar to Pontiac's Fiero and the Saturn. The 1990 Oldsmobile Toronado was stretched to eclipse the stubby rear-deck styling introduced in 1986. In 1990 the Oldsmobile Cutlass Supremes were available as four-door sedans for the first time.

In 1992 the Oldsmobile 1988 Royale was redesigned in only four-door sedan form with coupes deleted. The 1992 Oldsmobile Cutlass Supreme convertible offered the "twin dual cam" 3.4 liter V-6 as a new option in Oldsmobile's 95th anniversary year.

The all-new 1992 Oldsmobile 88 Royale had anti-lock brakes standard on the upper-level LS model.

The 1995 Oldsmobile Aurora four-door replaced the Oldsmobile Toronado two-door. It had a 4.0 liter 250-hp V-8, a downsized Cadillac Northstar.

Ransom E. Olds

Oldsmobile General Managers

R.E. Olds	1897-1904
*F.L. Smith	1904-1908
W.J. Mead	1908-1912
O.C. Hutchinson	1912-1913
C.W. Nash	1913-1916
Edward VerLinden	1916-1921
A.B.C. Hardy	1921-1925
Irving J. Reuter	1925-1930
**D.S. Eddins	1930-1932
Irving J. Reuter	1932-1933
C.L. McCuen	1933-1940
S.E. Skinner	1940-1950
Jack F. Wolfram	1951-1964
Harold N. Metzel	1964-1969
John B. Beltz	1969-1972
Howard H. Kehrl	1972-1973
John D. Baker	Nov./Dec. 1973
Robert J. Cook	1974-1983
Joseph J. Sanchez	1983-1985
William W. Lane	1985-1989
J. Michael Losh	1989-1992
John D. Rock	1992-1997
Darwin E. Clark	1997-

* Henry Russel, president

** Acting general manager

OLDSMOBILE 1897-1942

1897 Oldsmobile, gasoline experimental, JAC

OLDSMOBILE — Detroit & Lansing, Michigan — (1897-1942 et seq.) — The Olds Motor Vehicle Company was organized in Lansing, Michigan, on August 21, 1897, and Oldsmobile remains today America's oldest manufacturer of automobiles. The selection of 1897 as the official Olds beginning in the automotive field is somewhat arbitrary, because Ransom Eli Olds had already been experimenting for a decade by that time. Indeed, he tested his first car in 1887, a cumbersome three-wheeled steamer that ran but not very well; in 1891 he followed with another steamer that ran better and even made the pages of *Scientific American*. His first gasoline car arrived in 1896, a dos-a-dos four-seater perched high on its chassis, and powered by a single-cylinder 5 hp engine. Several others resulted, which in turn resulted in Ransom Olds organizing the Olds Motor Vehicle Company that August in 1897 because the family business of P.F. Olds & Son (renamed Olds Gasoline Engine Works in November) was too busy being one of the biggest manufacturers of gasoline engines in central Michigan to get into the automobile business. By the middle of 1898, Olds had managed to produce only a half-dozen cars at best. This lamentable situation was resolved on May 8, 1899, when Olds Motor Works was organized with a capital stock of a half-million dollars, acquiring the previous Olds businesses, and finally getting things moving. Ransom Old's personal investment was $400; $199,600 was provided by lumber millionaire Samuel L. Smith, whose sons Frederick and Angus had just graduated from college and needed gainful employment. With so much money now on hand, Ransom Olds returned to experimentation. From 1899 to 1900 about 11 different automobiles were built (some of them electrics) in the new Olds factory in Detroit, and plans were made to put a number of them on the market in 1901. But it didn't happen that way. Although there is no evidence that anyone at Olds Motor Works started it, the fire at the plant on March 9, 1901, was later referred to by Fred Smith as "the best move ever made by the management." Rescued from the blaze was a single gasoline runabout upon which all company hopes now were focused. It was the curved dash Oldsmobile, as delectable a little car as ever was built. Powered by a single-cylinder four-stroke engine developing 7 hp at 500 rpm and good for "one chug per telegraph pole," the Olds featured an all-spur geared

two-speed transmission, center chain drive, two longitudinal springs running fore and aft that served as side frame members, a total weight of 700 pounds and an asking price of $650. Many people asked for it. From 425 cars in 1901, Olds production rose to 2,500 in 1902, 4,000 in 1903 and 5,508 in 1904. The curved dash Oldsmobile was America's first quantity-produced car. No doubt its success encouraged others of mechanical mind to enter the automotive field, and persuaded those with the money to invest that the automobile was not a passing fad but a potentially viable business. This is not to discredit the pioneering of Alexander Winton, with whom Ransom Olds diced, incidentally, at Ormond-Daytona in 1902, pitting his single-cylinder racing Olds Pirate against Winton's four-cylinder Bullet I. (Neither claimed victory, both said they put up 57 mph.) But Winton, the first in America to set up orderly production of a gasoline automobile, was building relatively expensive cars in relatively small numbers in Cleveland. In Detroit (and from 1904 back home in Lansing), Ransom Olds was building cars that more people could afford — and he was building many more of them. Certainly, too, Olds Motor Works proved to be probably the best apprentice training school in America. Many subsequent key figures in the industry got their start putting together the curved dash Oldsmobile. The factors contributing to the car's success included an all-out promotion campaign (extensive advertising, and performances at fairs throughout the Midwest), young Roy Chapin's epic drive to New York City during the fall of 1901 for the automobile show, the cross-country trek of L.L. Whitman and Eugene Hammond in 1903, followed by the transcontinental of two curved dashes nicknamed Old Steady and Old Scout in 1905. Despite popular assumption, the curved dash Oldsmobile was not the only model offered by Olds Motor Works during these years, nor was it discontinued in 1905 when production reached 6,500 cars, and Gus Edwards and Vincent Bryan wrote "In My Merry Oldsmobile." The demise of the curved dash had been a foregone conclusion the year before, however, when Ransom Olds and the Smiths quarreled regarding the car's future — and Olds lost. By now the Smiths were anxious to move on to bigger and more luxurious cars, and because Olds was not, he left the company in January 1904 and soon thereafter began manufacture of the Reo. Meanwhile, the Smiths continued the curved dash in production through 1907, though relegating it further and further back in the company catalog as rather grander Oldsmobiles began to take its place, the grandest a 36 hp four on a 106-inch wheelbase (fully 60 inches longer than the curved dash) and priced at $2,750 as the "Palace Touring" and "Flying Roadster" in 1907. Whether it was that America was not yet ready to accept a big Oldsmobile, or that the Smiths couldn't manage as well without Olds, or simply that one generally cannot sell more $2,750 cars than $650 ones anyway, the result was a nosedive in the marketplace. In 1906, 1,600 Oldsmobiles were produced, in 1907 just 1,200, in 1908 down further to 1,055. But by December of 1908 William C. Durant had bought Olds Motor Works for his new General Motors company. The Smiths received $17,279 in cash and a little over $3 million in GM stock. Billy Durant received a company in financial distress. "That's a hell of a price to pay for a bunch of road signs," he commented regarding the nationwide network of Olds billboards that seemed to be one of the company's chief tangible assets. But Durant was aware as well that the Olds name and history were intangible assets worth far more. Durant made many foolish purchases for General Motors; Olds Motor Works was not one of them. By now there was a $4,500 six-cylinder Oldsmobile (introduced for 1908), which was continued with the $2,750 four for 1909, together with a new smaller $1,250 four called the Model 20

that was makeshifted from the Buick Model 10 — and which accounted for 5,325 of the 6,575 Oldsmobiles sold that year. No doubt the Olds 20, built just that one season, was produced to bring some fast cash into the company's treasury because in 1910 and for the years following, Oldsmobiles were all-out luxury cars: the four-cylinder Special followed by the Autocrat and Defender, and the Limited, with six cylinders, 707 cubic inches, a wheelbase that stretched 138 inches in 1911 over wheels a colossal 42 inches in diameter. It was the Limited that inspired the famous William Hamden Foster painting, "Setting the Pace." The Limited's pace was a wicked 70 mph. By 1913, when the Defender was reduced in price and a less formidable six replaced the Limited, the future course of Oldsmobile as a builder of quality cars of medium price was set — this policy cemented with introduction of a smaller $1,285 four (the "baby Olds") in 1914, and two years later by an attractively priced V-8 announced at $1,295 and continued in production through 1923. Production of 10,507 cars in 1916 doubled to 22,613 in 1917. By this time, having been ousted from General Motors once, Billy Durant was back at the helm again, though his GM tenure would irrevocably end in November 1920. Oldsmobile seems not to have suffered in that turmoil, though GM asked Olds president Edward Ver Linden to leave shortly thereafter (purportedly for lending himself money from the Olds treasury without GM knowledge), and A.B.C. Hardy, longtime Durant associate, took over the Olds managership. It was Hardy who made all Oldsmobiles sixes in 1924, and Cannon Ball Baker who proved their stamina by taking a new Model 30 six (which was introduced at only $750) cross-country that year in 12-1/2 days. Olds production in 1924 was 44,854 cars, double that of 1922. In 1928 — now with Irving Reuter in charge — production doubled again, to 86,593. The reason this time was the

new F-28, a 197.7-cubic inch 55 hp (up from 40) six, with the four-wheel brakes introduced on Oldsmobiles the year previous. During the year the stock market crashed, Oldsmobile topped the 100,000 mark for the first time. The Viking V-8, an Olds companion car introduced for 1929, didn't long survive, however, and for a while it appeared Oldsmobile might not either, as production dropped to 17,502 cars in 1932. Synchromesh in 1931 and a new 82 hp straight-eight for 1932 had not helped Oldsmobile fortunes during the Depression's early years, but there was an upswing in 1933 to 36,072 cars when Oldsmobiles received fresh new styling highlighted by what journalists of the day referred to as "beaver-tail rears" — and a terrific surge to 82,150 cars in 1934 when Oldsmobile offered independent front suspension. Heading Oldsmobile now was former engineer C.L. McCuen. With the economy recovering, what Oldsmobile represented — good, solid transportation in a wide line of sixes and eights at good prices — brought good fortune to the company: 183,752 cars in 1935, 187,638 in 1936, 212,767 in 1937. For the 1938 model year the company introduced its "Safety Automatic Transmission," admitting that "a certain amount of manipulation of the gear selector" was necessary for full performance. But for 1940, Hydra-Matic arrived as a fully automatic four-speed transmission available as a $57 option on all Oldsmobiles. The company called it "the most important engineering advancement since the self-starter." In 1941, Oldsmobile had its best year thus far: 230,703 cars. On January 1, 1942, the venerable name Olds Motor Works gave way to Oldsmobile Division, General Motors. The month following, Sherrod E. Skinner (who had replaced McCuen in 1940) turned all efforts to war production. Ammunition would be the Oldsmobile specialty until peace came.

1901 Oldsmobile, with Roy Chaplin at the tiller, JAC

Oldsmobile Data Compilation by Dennis Casteele

Curved Dash Olds Data Compilation by Gary Hoonsbeen

1901-1902-1903

OLDSMOBILE — MODEL R (CDO): The Model "R" was the first of three models to be known as the Curved Dash Oldsmobile and the first car produced by the Olds Motor Works to bear the name Oldsmobile.

Its design was conceived in late 1900 and a dozen or so prototypes were built before the Detroit factory was destroyed by fire in March of 1901. Production cars first reached the public in late summer of 1901 and it is generally accepted that about 425 cars were built that year.

The Model "R" CDO was a two-passenger car that could be fitted with an optional dos-a-dos (French for back to back) seat to carry one additional adult or two small children. The body was fabricated from wood and the design was distinctive with its toboggan-like front. The body was painted black with trim in a cherry color. The frame and body were decorated with a gold pin striping.

The engine crankshaft was designed to hold the flywheel, planetary transmission and high speed clutch assembly. A third outboard bearing, mounted on the frame, supported this additional weight and load. The transmission contains a reverse, brake and low speed drum. A chain drive sprocket is located between the reverse and brake drum. The outside surface of the low speed drum also serves as the high speed clutch plate. A shifting lever at the right side of the operator controls the low speed and reverse transmission bands along with the mechanism that engages the high speed clutch pads.

A brake pedal on the floor operates the transmission brake band. Next to the brake pedal is a foot throttle that connects to the carburetor via a thin iron wire.

All Curved Dash Oldsmobiles are right-hand drive and steered by a tiller. A crank handle is permanently fixed to the engine and extends out the side of the body such that the operator can start it while sitting in the seat.

The Model "R" CDO was changed during the years it was sold and major changes did not coincide with the calendar year. The earliest Model "R" cars were first modified during 1902 by adding truss rods under the front and rear axles, providing an emergency brake system in the rear differential housing, the carburetor was changed from a crude mixer requiring a fuel pump to a simple floatless design that was gravity fed from the fuel tank and relocating the water tank to allow more water capacity.

Another round of major changes was introduced in mid-1903, which included redesigning the differential housing to a more conventional bolt together style from ones that screwed together, changing the cylinder head block so a separate water jacket sleeve was no longer needed along with adding some cooling fins, replacing the #44 block chain with a #46 roller chain and improving the water cooling by replacing the smooth tubed radiator and centrifugal pump with a finned radiator and a positive flow gear pump.

The early Model "R" Oldsmobiles were equipped with tubeless 28 by 2-1/2 inch tires on wire wheels. During the life of the Model "R" as many as seven other variations of wheels were offered. These include 12- and 14-spoke wooden artillery wheels, a metal-spoked wheel and a staggered-spoked design. All these were offered for both tubeless and 28 x 3 clincher tires.

There is some evidence that the production of the Model "R" Oldsmobile continued well into 1904 with rear hub brakes added primarily for the foreign market.

Early Model "R" Oldsmobiles were supplied with a three-inch bicycle bell mounted on the tiller, which was replaced by a bulb horn in 1903. Lights were offered as an option and were supplied by "Neverout." A buggy top was also an option and supplied either in leather or rubber cloth. If the top was ordered a special bag was installed under the inside of the curved dash to hold the side curtains.

I.D. DATA: Serial numbers were found on compression release pedal, patent plate and cylinder head casting. Starting: (1901) 6000. (1902) 6451. (1903) 10000. Ending: (1901) 6450 (est.). (1902) 9999. (1903) 19999. Note: It appears blocks within these serial number ranges were not used.

Model No.	Body Type & Seating	Price	Weight	Prod. Total
R	Two-Passenger	650	650	—

1901 Oldsmobile, curved dash, runabout, OCW

1902 Oldsmobile, curved dash runabout, OCW

ENGINE: Horizontal, one-cylinder. Cast iron block. B & S: 4-1/2 x 6 in. Brake H.P.: 4-1/2 @ 600 R.P.M. Main bearings: two. Valve lifters: mechanical. Carb.: mixer.

CHASSIS: [Series R] W.B.: 66 in. Frt/Rear Tread: 5 in. Tires: 28 x 3.

1903 Oldsmobile, curved dash runabout, OCW

TECHNICAL: Planetary transmission. Speeds: 2F/1R. Controls located on right side of driver-hand control. Clutch: fingers (four). Chain drive. Semi-floating rear axle. Overall ratio: 3.1666:1. Mechanical brakes on rear differential and transmission. Tubeless/clincher-wooden artillery wheels.

OPTIONS: Top. Fenders.

HISTORICAL: Calendar year production: (1901) 425. (1902) 2,500 (est.). (1903) 3,924.

1904

OLDSMOBILE — MODEL "6C" (CDO): The Model "6C" Curved Dash Oldsmobile was first introduced to the public in April of 1904 and looked almost identical to its predecessor, the Model "R." It remained in production until the end of calendar 1904. Although the Models "R" and "6C" appeared to be the same they were in fact totally different cars. The body on the "6C" was slightly larger and contained more reinforcing, the running gear was heavier and stronger, the transmission contained only a low speed and reverse, drum and hub brakes were added to the rear wheels while retaining the brake in the rear axle differential housing.

A new Holley carburetor was used that contained a conventional cork float. The wheels remained 28 x 3 and 12-spoke artillery wheels were standard. Early Model "6C" cars used ball bearings in the front wheels but these were replaced with roller bearings after a few hundred cars. The rear wheel hub brakes were first supplied with external bands but this was later changed to internal expanding brake shoes.

The body was all wood, painted black with a bright red trim. There is some evidence that dark green cars were also offered. Controls for operating the "6C" were almost identical to those on the earlier model "R".

I.D. DATA: Serial numbers were located on patent plate and brass plug on cylinder head. Starting: 20000. Ending: 25000 (est.).

Model No.	Body Type & Seating	Price	Weight	Prod. Total
6C	Std. Rbt.-2P	650	800	2500

ENGINE: Horizontal, one-cylinder. Cast iron block. B & S: 5 x 6 in. Brake H.P.: 7 @ 600 R.P.M. Main bearings: two. Valve lifters: mechanical. Carb.: Holley Model 4.

OLDSMOBILE — TOURING RUNABOUT — ONE-CYLINDER: The Oldsmobile Touring Runabout was larger than the Model "6C" Curved Dash Oldsmobile. It was popularly known as the "French Front" model. The wheelbase was 10 inches longer than that of the Curved Dash. The Touring Runabout had a conventional hood with louvers on the side, twin bucket seats to accommodate two passengers and a sloping rear deck. The fenders were larger than those used on the Curved Dash and a steering wheel was featured. The horizontal engine was mounted under the "body," which was little more than a pedestal held in place with just four bolts. Standard equipment included pressure feed lubrication, jump spark ignition, single chain drive, angle steel frame, tires and tools. A 1904 Oldsmobile advertisement read, "For business or pleasure, in rain or sunshine, the pioneer runabout has no equal. It is always ready. It represents the latest and best in automobile construction — the product of the largest automobile plant in the world." Colors for the Touring Runabout were dark red or dark green. Oil brass side lamps were included.

I.D. DATA: Serial number information not available.

Model No.	Body Type & Seating	Price	Weight	Prod. Total
TR	Tr. Rbt.-2P	750	NA	Note 1

Note 1: Production of the Touring Runabout and Light Tonneau combined is estimated at 2,500 units.

ENGINE: Horizontal, one-cylinder. Cast iron block. B & S: 5 x 6 in. Brake H.P.: 7 @ 600 R.P.M. Main bearings: two. Valve lifters: mechanical. Carb.: Holley Model 4.

OLDSMOBILE — LIGHT TONNEAU — ONE-CYLINDER: Another new 1904 model was the Oldsmobile Light Tonneau Touring Car. It was a four-passenger model with a detachable tonneau body. With the tonneau removed, it looked like a larger version of the Touring Runabout. It was built on a chassis with an eight inch longer wheelbase than the Touring Runabout. The hood on both models did not cover an engine, but instead housed the gas and water tanks and battery. The list of standard equipment and body finish colors was the same for both models. The tonneau incorporated rear entrance provisions with a door in the center of the rear. The car could be ordered with or without a rear seat. Oil brass side lamps were included.

I.D. DATA: Serial number information not available.

Model No.	Body Type & Seating	Price	Weight	Prod. Total
LT	Lt. Tonn. w/o rear seat-2P	850	NA	Note 1
LT	Lt. Tonn. w/rear seat-4P	950	NA	Note 1

Note 1: Production of the Touring Runabout and Light Tonneau combined believed to be 2,500 units.

ENGINE: Horizontal, one-cylinder. Cast iron block. B & S: 5-1/2 x 6 in. Brake H.P.: 10 @ 600 R.P.M. Main bearings: two. Valve lifters: mechanical. Carb.: Holley.

1904 Oldsmobile, curved dash runabout, HAC

CHASSIS: [Series "6C"] W.B.: 66 in. Frt./Rear Tread: 56 in. Tires: 28 x 3. [Touring Runabout] W.B.: 76 in. Frt./Rear Tread: 56 in. Tires: 28 x 3. [Light Tonneau] W.B.: 83 in. Frt./Rear Tread: 56 in. Tires: 30 x 3-1/2.

TECHNICAL: [All models] Planetary transmission. Speeds: 2F/1R. Controls located outboard of right-hand driver's position. Disk type clutch. Semi-floating rear axle. Overall ratio: 3.44:1. Mechanical two-wheel brakes. Clincher type wood artillery wheels.

OPTIONS: Leather top. Bulb-type horn. Rear seat in Light Tonneau ($100.00).

HISTORICAL: Introduced April 1904. *The Production Figure Book For U.S. Cars* shows total production of 5,508 cars and commercial vehicles combined. Other sources say that 2,234 Curved Dash models were assembled in 1904.

Innovations: New models introduced. Steering wheels used on new models. Holley carburetor introduced. Curved Dash engine had larger bore size, larger cooling system, improved main bearing design and rear drum brakes.

R.E. Olds left Oldsmobile and formed Reo Motor Car Co. By the end of the year Olds employment rose to an all-time high of 500 workers. Two slogans used in 1904 were "You see them wherever you go. They go wherever you see them," and "All roads alike to the Oldsmobile." Oldsmobile was America's top automaker in 1904. One advertisement offered, "A captivating and beautifully illustrated automobile story *Golden Gate to Hell Gate*," which would be sent to interested parties upon receipt of a two-cent stamp. Oldsmobile also claimed "Record breaking sales" and "a host of satisfied customers."

1905

OLDSMOBILE — MODEL B (CDO): The Model "B" Curved Dash Oldsmobile was introduced in early 1905 and remained in production until late 1906. It looked very much like its predecessors the Model "R" and "6C" but was an entirely new design.

The engine was similar to the Model "6C" but contained more reinforcing. The connecting rod was changed to a marine type, with a separate cap, while the models "R" and "6C" had a hinged bearing cap. The water jacket inlets and outlets were also improved over the Model "6C" to eliminate hot spots in the cylinder head. The flywheel on the Models "R" and "6C" had spokes whereas the Model "B" flywheel was cast with a few holes between the hub and the rim.

1905 Oldsmobile, touring runabout, OCW

1905 Oldsmobile, side entrance touring, JAC

All the spring leaves on the Model "B" run from the front to rear axles. On the earlier models only the bottom spring leaf is continuous with the upper leaves terminating at the frame leaving a long gap, which is filled with a wooden block.

The front axle on the Model "B" does not contain a truss rod and there are two truss rods on the rear. The Model "B" did not use a brake drum in the rear differential housing but a brake drum was added to the transmission. Two brake pedals were used, one for the rear hub brakes and one for the transmission brake.

I.D. DATA: Serial numbers located on patent plate and brass plug on cylinder head. Starting: 50000. Ending: 52000 (est.).

Model No.	Body Type & Seating	Price	Weight	Prod. Total
B	Std. Rbt.-2P	650	NA	NA

ENGINE: Horizontal, one-cylinder. Cast iron block. B & S: 5 x 6 in. Brake H.P.: 7 @ 600 R.P.M. Main bearings: two. Valve lifters: mechanical. Carb.: float type.

OLDSMOBILE — TOURING RUNABOUT — ONE-CYLINDER:
The Touring Runabout was carried over with no major changes. The two-passenger model again had a louvered hood, with top access door, containing fuel, water and battery. The radiator was again of honeycomb design. Standard equipment included a steering wheel on a brass column, brass-plated side lamps, horizontal seven horsepower one-cylinder engine under the body, two-speed and reverse planetary transmission, pressure feed lubrication, jump spark ignition, single chain drive, angle steel frame, 76-inch wheelbase, 28 x 3-inch tires and tools. Colors were once again dark green and red.

I.D. DATA: Serial number information not available.

Model No.	Body Type & Seating	Price	Weight	Prod. Total
TR	Tr. Rbt.-2P	750	NA	NA

ENGINE: Horizontal, one-cylinder. Cast iron block. B & S: 5 x 6 in. Brake H.P.: 7 @ 600 R.P.M. Main bearings: two. Valve lifters: mechanical. Carb.: Holley.

OLDSMOBILE — LIGHT TONNEAU — ONE-CYLINDER:
The Light Tonneau or rear-entrance Tonneau Touring car was carried over unchanged. Standard equipment included a four-passenger detachable tonneau body, single-cylinder horizontal engine under body, two-speed reverse and planetary transmission, pressure feed lubrication, jump spark ignition, single chain drive, angle steel frame, 83-inch wheelbase, 3-1/2 x 30-inch tires and tools. Advertisements from 1905 did not state whether it was available without a rear seat. There was now a Light Delivery Car, actually a van, built on this chassis. It sold for $1,000, but is technically a commercial vehicle. The Light Tonneau again had brass side lamps and colors were dark green and red.

I.D. DATA: Serial number information not available.

Model No.	Body Type & Seating	Price	Weight	Prod. Total
LT	Lt. Tonn.-4P	950	NA	NA

ENGINE: Horizontal, one-cylinder. Cast iron block. B & S: 5-1/2 x 6 in. Brake H.P.: 10 @ 600 R.P.M. Main bearings: two. Valve lifters: mechanical. Carb.: Holley.

OLDSMOBILE — SIDE ENTRANCE TOURING — TWO-CYLINDER:
Cycle and Automobile Trade Journal said that the new two-cylinder Oldsmobile Touring Car was "quite a departure for this concern." It was of side entrance design and the body sections sat on two pedestals. The front section had twin bucket seats and doorless open sides for passenger access. The rear pedestal carried a wide tonneau with a solid back. Passengers entered the rear tonneau by means of hinged doors that shielded the area between the two pedestals, the tonneau and the bucket seatbacks. The body was constructed of wood and finished in dark blue. Running gear was painted yellow, making an attractive combination. Standard equipment included the two-cylinder horizontally-opposed engine mounted amidships, two-speed and reverse planetary transmission, mechanical lubrication, jump spark ignition, single chain drive, angle steel frame, 30 x 4-inch tires in rear, 30 x 3-1/2-inch tires in front, tools and brass oil lamps. The factory claimed a top speed of 40 mph. The two-cylinder car had a conventional hood and honeycomb brass radiator up front.

I.D. DATA: Serial number information not available.

Model No.	Body Type & Seating	Price	Weight	Prod. Total
TR	2-dr. Side Ent. Tonn. Tr.-5P	1400	2350	NA

ENGINE: Horizontal-opposed. Two-cylinder. Cast iron block. B & S: 5-1/4 x 6 in. Brake H.P.: 20 @ 600 R.P.M. Main bearings: four. Valve lifters: mechanical. Carb.: Holley.

CHASSIS: [Series "B"] W.B.: 66 in. Frt./Rear Tread: 56 in. Tires: 28 x 3. [Touring Runabout] W.B.: 76 in. Frt./RearTread: 56 in. Tires: 28 x 3. [Light Tonneau] W.B.: 83 in. Frt./Rear Tread: 56 in. Tires: 30 x 3-1/2. [Two-Cylinder Touring] W.B.: 90 in. Frt./Rear Tread: 55 in. Tires: (front) 30 x 3-1/2; (rear) 30 x 4.

TECHNICAL: [All models] Planetary transmission. Speeds: 2F/1R. Right-hand (outboard) mounted gearshift. Disk type clutch. Semi-floating rear axle. Overall ratio: 3.44:1. Two-wheel mechanical brakes. (Two-cylinder touring also has third brake acting on transmission). Wood-spoke artillery wheels.

OPTIONS: Bulb horn (w/c). Leather top (CDO). Brass dashboard "grab" rail.

HISTORICAL: Calendar year production: 6,500 [all models]. Innovations: New two-cylinder model. Marine-type connecting rods in CDO engine. Improved CDO engine waterjacketing. Improved springs on Curved Dash models.

This was the last year that Oldsmobile ranked as America's number one automaker. A new high of 612 employees produced 36 cars per day. Percy Megargel and Dwight Huss made a cross-country trip in a Curved Dash Oldsmobile, nicknamed "Old Scout," which is still owned by the company. Oldsmobile was a member of the Association of Licensed Automobile Manufacturers. One ad slogan used in 1905 read, "The Best Line of Light Cars ever placed on the market."

1906 Oldsmobile, straight-dash runabout, OCW

OLDSMOBILE — CURVED DASH MODEL "B" — ONE-CYLIN-DER: The Model "B" Curved Dash Oldsmobile was carried over. The primary change was the addition of several accessories as standard equipment to perk-up sagging popularity of this model. A top and storm front with celluloid windows was now included at regular price by the time of the New York Automobile Show at the old Madison Square Garden. Oldsmobile was not showing the Curved Dash in much of its 1906 advertising.

I.D. DATA: Serial number information not available.

Model No.	Body Type & Seating	Price	Weight	Prod. Total
B	Std. Rbt.-2P	650	NA	Note 1

Note 1: Oldsmobile built 100 one-cylinder cars in 1906. Only some of these had Curved Dash styling. The others were Straight Dash types.

ENGINE: Horizontal, one-cylinder. Cast iron block. B & S: 5 x 6 in. Brake H.P.: 7 @ 600 R.P.M. Main bearings: two. Valve lifters: mechanical. Carb.: Holley Model 4.

1906 Oldsmobile (Howard Coffin at wheel), touring runabout, JAC

OLDSMOBILE — STRAIGHT DASH MODEL "B" — ONE-CYL-INDER: In 1906, Oldsmobile offered a "straight" or "piano box" front for the Model "B," in addition to the Curved Dash. The running gear was essentially the same for both models. The body was of wood, as in previous models, painted black or green with

red trim. Controls for operating the Model "B" remained the same as earlier models with the exception of an extra brake pedal (see 1905).

I.D. DATA: Serial number information not available.

Model No.	Body Type & Seating	Price	Weight	Prod. Total
B	Std. Rbt.-2P	650	NA	Note 1

Note 1: Total production of the Model "B" was 100 units including both Curved Dash and Straight Dash styles.

OLDSMOBILE — MODEL "L" — TWO-CYLINDER: The two-cycle Model "L" was a new updated and upgraded two-cylinder automobile. One advertisement described it as "the sensation of the season." It was available as a four-five passenger touring car with a rear tonneau attached. It also came as a runabout, with twin bucket seats and no tonneau attachment. The tonneau used was of side entrance design. The car also had low-cut front doors, making it what was known as a "fore-door" model. The hood and radiator were much higher than in the past and the fenders much fuller. Standard equipment included brass headlamps and side lights, a pressed steel frame, selective sliding gear transmission, bevel gear drive and a 24 hp engine that was claimed to have "only three working parts in the motor itself." Oldsmobile said that this rare machine was "the only novelty in automobiles in five years." It had no gears, valves or guides in the engine. Tools and batteries were located in a box on the right-hand runningboard. Taillights and a horn were included.

I.D. DATA: Serial number information not available.

Model No.	Body Type & Seating	Price	Weight	Prod. Total
L	2-dr. Rbt.-2P	1150	1800	Note 1
L	4-dr. Tr.-4/5P	1250	2000	Note 1

Note 1: Total production was 100 units with no breakout according to body style.

ENGINE: "Double-Action" (two-cycle). Two-cylinder. Cast iron block. B & S: 5 x 5 in. Brake H.P.: 24. Carb.: one-barrel.

OLDSMOBILE — MODEL "S" — FOUR: Oldsmobile's new Model "S" line was promoted as "the best thing on wheels." The large car was said to be of European style and came as a Gentleman's Roadster or Palace Touring Car. Both had a new four-cylinder engine under the hood and featured clamshell front fenders, runningboards, straight-back rear fenders and a high hood/radiator line. The roadster could be ordered with a mother-in-law seat on the rear deck. The front axle was well forward, under the radiator, giving an extra-long wheelbase. Standard features included a pressed steel frame (channel section) with a sub-frame supporting the motor and radiator, sliding gear transmission, bevel gear drive, two acetylene lamps, two oil lamps, a horn and a full set of tools. Runningboards and fenders were designed for easy removal. An accessory cape type folding top was available for the Palace Touring Car. Other features included mechanical valves, forged steel connecting rods, a two-section aluminum crankcase, gravity feed, 15-gallon gas tank, jump spark ignition with four unit dash coils, pump cooling, and a clutch that could be activated by either a foot pedal or the emergency brake lever.

I.D. DATA: Serial number information not available.

Model No.	Body Type & Seating	Price	Weight	Prod. Total
L	Gentleman's Rds.-2P	2250	2100	Note 1
L	Gentleman's Rds.-3P	2250	2200	Note 1
L	4-dr. Palace Tr.-5/6P	2250	2300	Note 1

Note: Total series production was 1,400 units.

ENGINE: Vertical. L-head. Cast enbloc. Four. Cast iron block. B & S: 4-1/4 x 4-3/4 in. Brake H.P.: 26-28. Valve lifters: mechanical. Carb.: Holley.

CHASSIS: [Model "B"] W.B.: 66 in. Frt./Rear Tread: 56 in. Tires: 28 x 3. [Model "L"] W.B.: 102 in. Frt./Rear Tread: 56 in. Tires: (Frt.) 30 x 3-1/2, (Rear) 30 x 4. [Model "S"] W.B.: 106 in. Frt./Rear Tread: 56 in. Tires: (Frt.) 32 x 3-1/2, (Rear) 32 x 4.

Note: Larger wheels and tires on Model "S" Gentleman's Roadster.

TECHNICAL: [Model "B"] Planetary; [Models "S" & "L"]: Selective sliding gear. Speeds: [Model "B"] 2F/1R; [Models "S" & "L"] 3F/1R. Right-hand outboard mounted gearshift. Disk type clutch. Semi-floating rear axle. Two-wheel brakes w/transmission brake. Wood spoke artillery wheels.

OPTIONS: Mother-in-law seat. Folding top. Runningboard luggage rack. Speedometer. Side curtains. Taillights. Adjustable side lamps.

HISTORICAL: Introduced: [Models "S" & "L"] December-January 1905/1906. Calendar year production: [Model "B"]: 100, [Model "S"]: 1,400, [Model "L"]: 100. Total: 1,600.

1906 Oldsmobile, Model L, touring, JAC

Innovations: New straight dash option for Model "B." Two-cycle vertical two-cylinder engine with three working parts for Model "L." Regulation outfit, sliding gear transmission, pressed steel frame, bevel gear drive on Models "L" and "S." Engines below hood on Models "L" and "S." New European-type styling.

Oldsmobile dropped to sixth among U.S. automakers. Corporate headquarters and production facilities were centralized in Lansing, Michigan. A 1906 Oldsmobile driven by Ernest Keeler and Harry Miller competed in Vanderbilt Cup Race. Oldsmobile's 1906 advertisements included coupons to order catalogs on each model, order a large art calendar designed by George Gibbs (10 cents) and request a 25 cent one-year subscription to Oldsmobile's *Motor Talk* magazine. *Motor Talk* was devoted to automobiling.

1907

OLDSMOBILE — MODEL F — ONE-CYLINDER: The one-cylinder Oldsmobile runabout was offered for the last time. Now designated the Model "F," it was available in both Curved Dash and Straight Dash Styles. Prices and specifications were the same as in the previous year. Consult the 1906 listings for details.

1907 Oldsmobile, Model H, flying roadster, HAC

OLDSMOBILE — MODEL H FLYING ROADSTER — FOUR: The Model H was a single model series. The Oldsmobile catalog for 1907 called it a "pacemaker" and "a car which is distinctive and sportsmanlike, and has plenty of reserve power and speed."

1907 Oldsmobile, Model A, touring, HJE

OLDSMOBILE — MODEL A — FOUR: The two-model Model A series was the basic Olds for 1907. Olds claimed this design resulted in part from the Olds performance in the 1906 Glidden Tour. 1907 was the final year the old Curved Dash (or straight dash) model was to be offered; Olds would go on to bigger and more expensive cars for the next few model years.

I.D. DATA: Location of serial numbers is not available. Starting: 60000. Ending: 61200. Engine number location is not available. Starting: 54500. Ending: 55999.

Model No.	Body Type & Seating	Price	Weight	Prod. Total
H	Rds.-3P	2750	2200	Note 1
A	4-dr. Tr.-5P	2750	2600	Note 1
A	2-dr. Limo.-5P	3800	2900	Note 1

Note 1: Oldsmobile model year total was 1,200.

ENGINE: (Both Model A & H used identical engines.) Straight four. Cast gray iron block. B & S: 4-1/2 x 4-3/4 in. Disp.: 302 cu. in. Brake H.P.: 35/40. Main bearings: three.

CHASSIS: [Model H] W.B.: 106-1/2 in. Frt/Rear tread: both 55 in. Tires: front 34 x 3-1/2, rear 34 x 4. [Model A] W.B.: 106 in. Frt/Rear tread: both 55 in. Tires: front 34 x 3-1/2, rear 34 x 4.

TECHNICAL: Sliding gear transmission. Speeds: 3F/1R. Right side control lever. Steel propeller shaft drive. Overall ratio: approx. 3.1:1. Pedal operated brakes on shaft, lever operated on rear hubs. Wood artillery wheels.

OPTIONS: Standard equipment on Model H roadster and Model A palace touring included: a full set of tools, two acetylene headlights, two oil taillamps, a large horn and luggage carrier. Standard equipment on Model A limousine included: speaking tube, full toilet set, perfumery bottles, ashtray and silk trim. Model H roadster colors: red or French gray. Limousine usual colors: dark green and black. Model A palace touring colors: gray, Brewster green or red.

HISTORICAL: Innovations: introduced nickel plating. Model year sales: 1,200. Model year production: 1,200. Company president of Oldsmobile was F.L. Smith (general manager).

1908

OLDSMOBILE — SERIES M/MR — FOUR: This was a continuation of the four-cylinder Oldsmobile with a slight increase in displacement over the previous year. The M designation was applied to the touring car and MR applied to the roadster.

OLDSMOBILE — SERIES Z — SIX: The all-new six-cylinder series for 1908. Olds began to develop this engine in 1905.

OLDSMOBILE — SERIES X — FOUR: The X was a second four-cylinder car and was similar to 1907 models. It had a highly swept-back front fender design.

1908 Oldsmobile, Model M, touring, HJE

I.D. DATA: [Series M, MR & X] Location of serial number is not available. Starting: 61500. Ending: 62500. Engine number location is not available. Starting: 57000. Ending: 58000. [Series Model Z] Location of serial number is not available. Starting: 65000. Ending: 65055. Engine number location is not available. Starting: 60001. Ending: 60055.

Model No.	Body Type & Seating	Price	Weight	Prod. Total
MR	Rds.-2P	2750	2200	Note 1
M	4-dr. Tr.-5P	2750	2600	Note 1
X	4-dr. Tr.-4P	1900	2100	Note 1
Z	4-dr. Tr.-5P	4200	3000	55

Note 1: Oldsmobile model year total for MR, M and X Series was 1,000.

1908 Oldsmobile, Model X, touring, JAC

ENGINE: [Series M & MR] Inline four. Cast iron block. B & S: 4-3/4 x 4-3/4 in. Disp.: 336 cu. in. Brake H.P.: 36. Main bearings: three. [Series X] Inline four. Cast iron block. B & S: 4-1/2 x 4-3/4 in. Disp.: 336 cu. in. Brake H.P.: 32. Main bearings: three. [Series Z] Inline six. Cast iron block. B & S: 4-1/2 x 4-3/4 in. Disp.: 453 cu. in. Brake H.P.: 48.

CHASSIS: [Series M] W.B.: 112 in. Frt/Rear Tread: 55 in. Tires: front 34 x 3-1/2, rear 34 x 4. [Series MR] W.B.: 106 in. Frt/Rear Tread: 55 in. Tires: front 34 x 3-1/2, rear 34 x 4. [Series X] W.B.: 106 in. Frt/Rear Tread: 55 in. Tires: front 34 x 3-1/2, rear 34 x 4. [Series Z] W.B.: 130 in. Frt/Rear Tread: 56-1/2 in. Tires: Front 36 x 4-1/2, rear 36 x 5.

TECHNICAL: Sliding gear transmission. Speeds: 3F/1R. Right side control lever. Shaft drive. Overall ratio: approx. 3.1:1. Pedal operated brakes on shaft, lever operated on rear hubs. Wood artillery wheels.

OPTIONS: Standard equipment on Model M, MR and X included: full tool set, two acetylene headlights, two oil taillamps, horn and luggage carrier. Standard equipment on Model Z: tool set, tire irons, muffler cut-out, nine-inch headlamps, Prest-O-Lite tank and oil side and taillamps.

HISTORICAL: Won the Glidden Reliability tour. Calendar year sales: 1,055. Calendar year production: 1,055. Company president of Oldsmobile was W.J. Mead (general manager).

In late 1908 Oldsmobile became a cornerstone division of General Motors. The new six-cylinder Model Z was introduced at Madison Square Garden.

1909

1909 Oldsmobile, Model DR, roadster, OCW

OLDSMOBILE — SERIES D/DR — FOUR: The D and DR models were the main line four-cylinder cars of this model year. The D model designation was applied to the larger touring cars in this series while the DR designation was used on the roadster and rare coupe models.

OLDSMOBILE — SERIES X — FOUR: The X series was a carryover from 1908 and offered a slightly smaller four-cylinder engine than the D series.

OLDSMOBILE — SERIES Z — SIX: Introduced late in 1908, production continued on this six-cylinder series in 1909. This series was the most expensive and rarest Oldsmobile built this year and was the forerunner of the fabled Limited Series offered the next three model years.

OLDSMOBILE — SERIES 20 — FOUR: The most interesting car in the 1909 lineup was the Model 20. A direct result of Oldsmobile's new position in William Durant's General Motors, little appears on this model in period factory literature. Most accounts describe it as a thinly disguised Buick.

I.D. DATA: [Model D, DR & X] Location of serial number is not available. Starting: 62500. Ending: 63600. Engine number location is not available. Starting: 58000. Ending: 59100. [Model Z] Location of serial number is not available. Starting: 65100. Ending: 65250. Engine number location is not available. Starting: 60501. Ending: 60650. [Model 20] Location of serial number, starting and ending serial numbers and engine number location are not available. Starting: 4050. Ending: 9375.

1909 Oldsmobile, Model D, touring, HJE

Model No.	Body Type & Seating	Price	Weight	Prod. Total
D	4-dr. Tr.-5P	2750	2600	Note 1
D	4 dr. Limo.-5P	3800	2900	Note 1
D	4-dr. Land.-5P	4000	2900	Note 1
DR	2-dr. Rds.-2P	2750	2400	Note 1
DR	2-dr. Cpe.-2P	3500	2600	Note 1
X	2-dr. Spec. Rds.-2P	2000	2300	Note 1
20	4-dr. Tr.-4P	1200	2100	5325
Z	4-dr. Tr.-7P	4000	3000	Note 2
Z	2-dr. Rds.-2P	4000	2800	Note 2

Note 1: Oldsmobile model year total for D and DR Series was 1,100.
Note 2: Oldsmobile model year total for Z Series was 150.

ENGINE: [Model D & DR] Inline four. Cast iron block. B & S: 4-3/4 x 4-3/4 in. Disp.: 336 cu. in. Brake H.P.: 40. Main bearings: three. Valve lifters: mechanical. [Model X] Inline four. Cast iron block. B & S: 4-1/2 x 4-3/4 in. Disp.: 302 cu. in. Brake H.P.: 32. Main bearings: three. Valve lifters: mechanical. [Model 20] Inline four. Cast iron block. B & S: 3-3/4 x 3-3/4 in. Disp.: 165 cu. in. Brake H.P.: 22. Main bearings: three. Valve lifters: mechanical. [Model Z] Inline six. Cast iron block. B & S: 4-3/4 x 4-3/4 in. Disp.: 505 cu. in. Brake H.P.: 60. Valve lifters: mechanical.

CHASSIS: [Series D & DR] W.B.: 112 in. Frt/Rear Tread: 56-1/2 in. Tires: front 34 x 3-1/2, rear 34 x 4. [Series X] W.B.: 106 in. Frt/Rear Tread: 55 in. Tires: front 32 x 3-1/2, rear 32 x 4. [Model 20] W.B.: 91 in. Frt/Rear Tread: 54 in. Tires: front 30 x 3-1/2, rear 30 x 4. [Model Z] W.B.: 130 in. Frt/Rear Tread: 56-1/2 in. Tires: front 36 x 4-1/2, rear 36 x 5.

1909 Oldsmobile, Model Z, touring, OCW

TECHNICAL: Sliding gear transmission. Speeds: 3F/1R. Side controls. Leather faced cone clutch. Shaft drive. Overall ratio: approx. 3.1:1. Foot lever external brakes on two wheels. Artillery wheels.

OPTIONS: Model D, DR & X standard equipment: eight-inch headlights, acetylene generator, oil side and taillamps, full tool set, coat rail, foot rest, trunk rack and horn. Model Z standard equipment: nine-inch headlamps, Prest-O-Lite tank, oil side and taillamps, full set of tools and toolbox, coat rail, foot rest, horn, tire iron and muffler cut-out.

HISTORICAL: Calendar year sales: 6,575. Calendar year production: 6,575. Company president of Oldsmobile was W.J. Mead (general manager). Highest production ouput to date by Oldsmobile. General Motors influence gradually takes over. Closed car production increased.

1910

OLDSMOBILE — SPECIAL — SERIES 22-25 — FOUR: The Special series was a continuation of several years of four-cylinder Oldsmobile production. The engine was modified slightly and was linked to a four-speed transmission. It had a longer wheelbase, larger tires and an improved suspension system and the new Special nameplate was first used.

OLDSMOBILE — LIMITED — SERIES 23-24 — SIX: The factory catalog from 1910 reads: "The Oldsmobile Limited has created a new standard of luxury in motoring." This model drew heavily from Z series cars of the past two years, but the Limited series was the largest and most powerful Olds to date. The Limited name came from the catalog statement: "While the output (for 1910) has been increased, such a car cannot be produced rapidly, therefore a limited quantity can be built."

1910 Oldsmobile, Limited touring, OCW

I.D. DATA: [Special] Location of serial numbers is not available. Starting: 67000. Ending: 68525. Engine number location is not available. Starting: 62000. Ending: 63350. [Limited] Location of serial number is not available. Starting: 65500. Ending: 65825. Engine number location is not available. Starting: 60650. Ending: 60950.

Model No.	Body Type & Seating	Price	Weight	Prod. Total
Special Series				
22	4-dr. Tr.-5P	3000	NA	Note 1
25	2-dr. Rds.-2P	3000	NA	Note 1
NA	4-dr. Limo.-5P	4200	NA	Note 1
Limited Series				
23	4-dr. Tr.-7P	4600	NA	Note 2
24	2-dr. Rds.-2P	4600	NA	Note 2
NA	4-dr. C.C. Tr.-5P	4600	NA	Note 2
NA	4-dr. Limo.-5P	5800	NA	Note 2

Note 1: Oldsmobile model year total for Special Series was 1,525.
Note 2: Oldsmobile model year total for Limited Series was 325.

1910 Oldsmobile, Special, roadster, JAC

ENGINE: [Special Series] Inline, cast in pairs. Four. Cast iron block. B & S: 4-3/4 x 4-3/4 in. Disp.: 336 cu. in. Brake H.P.: 40. Main bearings: three. Valve lifters: mechanical. Carb.: Oldsmobile. [Limited Series] Inline, cast in pairs. Six. Cast iron block. Disp.: 505 cu. in. Brake H.P.: 60. Valve lifters: mechanical. Carb.: Oldsmobile.

1910 Oldsmobile, Special, touring, HJE

CHASSIS: [Special Series] W.B.: 118 in. O.L.: 174 in. Frt/Rear Tread: 56/56 in. Tires: 36 x 4. [Limited Series] W.B.: 130 in. O.L.: 186 in. Frt/Rear Tread: 56/56 in. Tires: 42 x 4-1/2.

TECHNICAL: Sliding gear, selective transmission. Speeds: 4F/1R. Side lever controls. Leather faced cone clutch. Full-floating rear axle. Shaft drive. Overall ratio: approx. 3.1:1. Internal and external brakes on two wheels. Artillery wheels.

1910 Oldsmobile, Limited roadster, OCW

OPTIONS: Mohair top ($125.00). Pantasote top (100.00). Glass front. Speedometer. Clock. Extra tires. Special signaling apparatus. Colors other than standard (green, blue, black, red) (50.00 extra).

HISTORICAL: Calendar year sales: 1,850. Calendar year production 1,850. Model year sales and production: 1,850. Company president of Oldsmobile was W.J. Mead (general manager).

Oldsmobile continued to offer some of the most powerful and expensive models built by General Motors. Employment dropped to 850. In the introduction year for the "Limited" the famous William Hamden Foster painting "Setting the Pace" was created. Prints would be used several times as Olds advertising pieces.

1911

OLDSMOBILE — SPECIAL — SERIES 26 — FOUR: The Special series was a carryover. This was the least expensive Olds series and this was the last season for the Special series. With its low volume production Olds had little need for two four-cylinder series and the Autocrat would continue into the next model year.

OLDSMOBILE — AUTOCRAT — SERIES 28 — FOUR: New for 1911, the Autocrat offered the most powerful four-cylinder engine yet seen in an Oldsmobile. Larger than the Special, the

Autocrat would be carried over to the next model year. The Autocrat shared many mechanical features with the larger Limited series Oldsmobiles.

OLDSMOBILE — LIMITED — SERIES 27 — FOUR: The Limited remained one of the largest and most powerful American cars built. The 1911 catalog stated: "In the Limited we offer a car which leaves nothing to be desired in design, construction, finish, power or equipment. It stands in the front rank of high grade cars; the greatest of a line universally recognized and ranked among leaders. The motor is the companion to the Autocrat, having the same bore and stroke and incorporating the same mechanical features."

1911 Oldsmobile, Limited, limousine, OCW

I.D. DATA: [Special series & Autocrat series] Location of serial numbers is not available. Starting: 70000. Ending: 71000. Engine number location is not available. Starting: 65001. Ending: 65999. [Limited series] Location of serial numbers is not available. Starting: 75000. Ending: 75250. Engine number location is not available. Starting: 64000. Ending: 64200.

1911 Oldsmobile, Autocrat, touring, HAC

Model No.	Body Type & Seating	Price	Weight	Prod. Total
Special Series				
NA	2-dr. Rbt.-2P	3000	NA	Note 1
NA	4-dr. Tr.-7P	3000	NA	Note 1
NA	4-dr. Limo.-7P	4200	NA	Note 1
Autocrat Series				
NA	2-dr. Rbt.-2P	3500	NA	Note 1
NA	4-dr. Tr.-7P	3500	NA	Note 1
NA	4-dr. Trbt.-4P	3500	NA	Note 1
NA	4-dr. Limo.-7P	5000	NA	Note 1
Limited Series				
NA	2-dr. Rbt.-2P	5000	NA	Note 2
NA	4-dr. Tr.-7P	5000	NA	Note 2
NA	4-dr. Trbt.-4P	5000	NA	Note 2
NA	4-dr. Limo.-7P	7000	NA	Note 2

Note 1: Oldsmobile model year total for Special Series was 1,000.
Note 2: Oldsmobile model year total for Limited Series was 250.

1911 Oldsmobile, Limited touring, OCW

ENGINE: [Special Series] Inline, cast in pairs. Four. Cast iron block. B & S: 4-3/4 x 4-3/4 in. Disp.: 336 cu. in. Brake H.P.: 36. Main bearings: three. Valve lifters: mechanical. Carb.: Oldsmobile. [Autocrat Series] Inline, Thead, cast in pairs. Four. Cast iron block. B & S: 5 x 6 in. Disp.: 471 cu. in. Brake H.P.: 40. Main bearings: three. Valve lifters: mechanical. Carb.: Oldsmobile design, constant level float. [Limited Series] Inline, T-head, cast in pairs. Six. Cast iron block. B & S: 5 x 6 in. Disp.: 706 cu. in. Brake H.P.: 60. Valve lifters: mechanical. Carb.: Oldsmobile design, constant level float.

CHASSIS: [Special Series] W.B.: 118 in. O.L.: 166 in. Frt/Rear Tread: 56 in. Tires: 36 x 4. [Autocrat Series] W.B.: 124 in. O.L.: 177 in. Frt/Rear Tread: 56 in. Tires: 38 x 4-1/2, Bailey tread. [Limited Series] W.B.: 138 in. O.L.: 198 in. Frt/Rear Tread: 56 in. Tires: 42 x 4-1/2, Bailey tread.

TECHNICAL: Sliding gear transmission. Speeds: 4F/1R. Outside lever controls. Cone clutch, springs under facing. (Special and Autocrat: leather faced cone clutch). Shaft drive, enclosed in torsion tube. Full-floating rear axle. Overall ratio: approx. 3.1:1. Expanding and contracting brakes on rear wheels, service foot pedal, emergency hand lever. Artillery wheels made of second growth hickory.

OPTIONS: Standard equipment on all series: headlights, side and taillamps, Prest-O-Lite tank, tire irons, Trauffault-Hartford shock absorbers, Dragon horn, baggage rack, robe rail, floor mat, set of tools and removable seats on some models.

HISTORICAL: Innovations: first time for air-type self-starter by Oldsmobile. Calendar year sales and production: 1,250. Model year sales and production: 1,250. Company president was W.J. Mead (general manager).

1912

OLDSMOBILE — DEFENDER — SERIES 40 — FOUR: The Defender series was new to the model line. The smaller of the two four-cylinders offered this year, the Defender was a predictor of things to come. After starting out with the small nimble Curved Dash models, Olds offerings grew to the massive Limited; in the years to come the Oldsmobiles would get a bit smaller.

OLDSMOBILE — AUTOCRAT — SERIES 32 — FOUR: The Autocrat was a carryover model. It was a large four-cylinder model sharing many components with the fabled Limited series. This was the Autocrat's final year.

OLDSMOBILE — LIMITED — SERIES 33 — SIX: In its final year of a three-year run, the mighty Limited would leave an imprint on Oldsmobile history. Its huge size and awesome powerplant made it one of the most talked about cars of the era. Although production was well under 1,000 for the three year run, several fine examples of this collector car remain today including a Limited the Olds factory has owned since the 1930s.

I.D. DATA: [Defender Series] Location of serial number is not available. Starting: 80000. Ending: 80325. Engine number location is not available. Starting: 70000. Ending: 70330. [Autocrat Series] Serial number was on brass tag under left front seat. Starting: 71100. Ending: 71600. Engine number location is not available. Starting: 66000. Ending: 66560. [Limited Series] Serial number was on brass tag under left front seat. Starting: 76000. Ending: 76250. Engine number location is not available. Starting: 64500. Ending: 64750.

1912 Oldsmobile, Autocrat, speedster, HAC

Model No.	Body Type & Seating	Price	Weight	Prod. Total
Defender Series				
NA	4-dr. Trbt.-4P	3000	NA	Note 1
NA	4-dr. Tr.-5P	3000	NA	Note 1
NA	2-dr. Rds.-2P	3000	NA	Note 1
NA	2-dr. Cpe.-2P	3600	NA	Note 1
NA	2-dr. Cpe.-5P	3900	NA	Note 1
Autocrat Series				
NA	2-dr. Rds.-2P	3500	NA	Note 2
NA	4-dr. Tr.-7P	3500	NA	Note 2
NA	4-dr. Trbt.-4P	3500	NA	Note 2
NA	4-dr. Limo.-7P	4700	NA	Note 2
Limited Series				
NA	2-dr. Rds.-2P	5000	NA	Note 3
NA	4-dr. Trbt.-4P	5000	NA	Note 3
NA	4-dr. Tr.-7P	5000	NA	Note 3
NA	4-dr. Limo.-7P	6300	NA	Note 3

Note 1: Oldsmobile model year total for Defender Series was 325.
Note 2: Oldsmobile model year total for Autocrat Series was 500.
Note 3: Oldsmobile model year total for Limited Series was 250.

1912 Oldsmobile, Limited, tourabout, HJE

ENGINE: [Defender Series] Inline, T-head, cast in pairs. Four. Cast iron block. B & S: 4 x 5-15/16 in. Disp.: 267 cu. in. Brake H.P.: 35. Main bearings: three. Valve lifters: mechanical. Carb.: Rayfield Model D. [Autocrat Series] Inline, T-head, cast in pairs. Four. Cast iron block. B & S: 5 x 6 in. Disp.: 471 cu. in. Main bearings: three. Valve lifters: mechanical. Carb.: Rayfield Model D. [Limited Series] Inline, T-head, cast in pairs. Six. Cast iron block. B & S: 5 x 6 in. Disp.: 707 cu. in. Brake H.P.: 60. Valve lifters: mechanical. Carb.: Rayfield Model D.

CHASSIS: [Defender Series] W.B.: 116 in. O.L.: 149 in. Frt/RearTread: 60 in. Tires: 36 x 4. [Autocrat Series] W.B.: 126 in. O.L.: 179 in. Frt/Rear Tread: 60 in. Tires: 38 x 4-1/2. [Limited Series] W.B.: 140 in. O.L.: 200 in. Frt/Rear Tread: 60 in. Tires: 42 x 4-1/2.

TECHNICAL: Selective, sliding gear transmission. Speeds: 4F/1R. Side lever controls. (Limited - outside lever controls). Cone clutch, springs under facing. Shaft drive enclosed in torsion tube. Full-floating rear axle, pressed steel housing. Overall ratio: approx. 3.1:1. Internal expanding brakes external contracting on rear wheels; sevice by foot pedal; emergency by hand lever. Artillery wheels of second growth hickory.

OPTIONS: Nickel trim. Gas headlamps. Side lamps. Taillamps. Prest-O-Lite tank. Pantasote top. Windshield. Luggage rack. Robe rail. Shock absorbers. Dragon horn. Jones speedometer with light. Tire irons. Tool kit.

HISTORICAL: An addition was made to the main assembly plant. Calendar year sales and production: 1,075. Model year sales and production: 1,075. Company president was O.C. Hutchinson (general manager).

1913

1913 Oldsmobile, Model 53, touring, JAC

OLDSMOBILE — DEFENDER — SERIES 40 — FOUR: Essentially a carryover, the Defender series made its final appearance this year. There were some special bodied Defenders and most of the year's production came from this series.

OLDSMOBILE SIX — SERIES 53 — SIX: This was Oldsmobile's new offering for 1913. The least expensive six-cylinder offered by Olds, this series was continued for several years. While the Limited was a well known and recognized machine, its sales were less than sustaining. Olds officials hoped this new, lighter six would sell better. The Olds catalog for the Model 53 said, "Without sacrificing any of the rugged strength and dependability for which the Oldsmobile is famous, the entire chassis of the new car has been refined, standardized and lightened."

I.D. DATA: [Defender Series] Serial number on brass tag under left front seat. Starting: 80325. Ending: 80999. Engine number location not available. Starting: 70330. Ending: 70499. [Model 53] Serial number on brass tag under left front seat. Starting: 81000. Ending: 81500. Engine number location not available. Starting: 614180. Ending: 614700.

Model No.	Body Type & Seating	Price	Weight	Prod. Total
Defender				
NA	4-dr. Tr.-7P	2500	NA	1,000 total
Model 53				
NA	4-dr. Tr.-5P	3200	4625	Note 1
NA	4-dr. Tr.-7P	3350	4700	Note 1
NA	4-dr. Trbt.-4P	3200	4635	Note 1

Note 1: Oldsmobile model year total was 500.

ENGINE: [Defender] Inline, cast in pairs, T-head. Four. Cast iron block. B & S: 4 x 5-5/16. Disp.: 267 cu. in. Brake H.P.: 35. Main bearings: three. Valve lifters: mechanical. Carb.: Ray-field, Model D. [Model 53] Inline, cast in pairs. Six. Cast iron block. B & S: 4-1/8 x 4-3/4. Disp.: 380 cu. in. Brake H.P.: 50. Valve lifters: mechanical. Carb.: float feed.

CHASSIS: [Defender] W.B.: 116 in. O.L.: 149 in. Frt/Rear Tread: 60 in. Tires: 36 x 4. [Model 53] W.B.: 135 in. Tires: front 36 x 4-1/2, rear 36 x 5.

TECHNICAL: Selective, sliding gear transmission. Speeds: [Defender] 4F/1R: [Model 53] 3F/1R. Outside lever controls. [Defender] Cone clutch, springs under facing. [Model 53] Cone clutch, leather faced. Shaft drive. Floating rear axle. Overall ratio: approx. 3.1:1. Internal expanding brakes, external contracting; service by foot pedal; emergency by hand lever. Artillery wheels made of second growth hickory.

OPTIONS: [Defender] 9-1/2 inch gas headlights, oil/electric side and taillamps, Prest-O-Lite tank, Pantasote top with cover, windshield, robe rail, shock absorbers, Dragon horn, Jones speedometer with light, floor carpet, tire irons, tool kit and black enamel and white nickel trimmings. [Model 53] Delco self-starting ignition, lighting system, 10-1/4 inch electric headlamps, storage battery, power tire pump, top with boot, windshield, robe rail, foot rest, Truffault-Hartford shock absorbers, Klaxon horn, Warner speedometer, Waltham eight-day clock, tire irons, jack and complete tool kit.

HISTORICAL: Innovations: Delco light/starting system introduced. Calendar year sales and production: 1,175. Model year sales and production: 1,175. Company president was Charles Nash (general manager). Olds was on a campaign to downsize and simplify its model offerings.

1914

1914 Oldsmobile, Model 54, touring, HJE

OLDSMOBILE — BABY OLDS SERIES — MODEL 42 — FOUR: This was an attempt by Oldsmobile to move back to the lighter car market. It was a late introduction and was the smallest Oldsmobile available in the past few model years. This type of four-cylinder car would remain a staple of the Olds lineup for the next few years.

OLDSMOBILE — SIXTH SERIES — MODEL 54 — SIX: The Model 54, a modest update of last year's Model 53, was the mainstay of the 1914 Oldsmobile lineup. The Model 54 catalog read: "While standards are the outgrowth of development, there is one standard which has made Oldsmobile development possible, and that is the desire and the ability to build each year a car just a little better than anything else on wheels — not only from an engineering standard but from an artistic viewpoint as well."

I.D. DATA: Model 42. Serial numbers located on brass tag under right front seat cushion. Starting: 84001. Ending: 84399. Starting engine number: 723700. Ending: N/A. Model 54. Serial numbers located on brass tag under left front seat. Starting: 83000. Ending: 83999. Starting engine number 646653. Ending: N/A.

Model No.	Body Type & Seating	Price	Weight	Prod. Total
42	4-dr. Tr.-5P	1350	2700	400
54	4-dr. Tr.-5P	2975	4300	1000
54	4-dr. Tr.-7P	3150	4350	1000
54	4-dr. Limo.-7P	4300	4530	1000

ENGINE: [Model 42] Inline four. Cast iron block. B & S: 3-1/2 x 5 in. Disp.: 192 cu. in. Brake H.P.: 20. Main bearings: three. Valve lifters: mechanical. [Model 54] Inline six. B & S: 4-1/4 x 5-1/4 in. Disp.: 611 cu. in. Brake H.P.: 50. Valve lifters: mechanical. Carb.: float-feed.

CHASSIS: [Model 42] W.B.: 112 in. Tires: 33 x 4, non-skid in rear. [Model 54] W.B.: 132 in., except seven-passenger touring - 139 in. Tires: 36 x 5 either Fisk or Goodyear.

TECHNICAL: [Model 42] Manual transmission. Speeds: 3F/1R. Floor shift. Clutch: cone. Shaft drive, enclosed within torsion tube. Three-quarter floating rear axle. Brakes: two-wheel rear service, foot control pedal. No drivetrain options. [Model 54] Manual transmission. Speeds: 3F/1R. Controls located right side of driver. Cone clutch. Shaft drive. Floating rear axle. Foot and hand brakes for two wheels. Wooden wheels. Wire wheels.

OPTIONS: $50 extra for any color other than green, blue or gray. Trunks: ($50.00 for single trunk, 80.00 for pair of trunks). Other options included special covers and special make tires.

TECHNICAL: The Model 42 or Baby Olds marked the return of Olds to the smaller car market. Model year and calendar year sales: total 1,400. President and general manager of Oldsmobile was C.W. Nash.

1915

1915 Oldsmobile, Model 42, roadster, HAC

OLDSMOBILE — BABY OLDS SERIES — MODEL 42 — FOUR: Oldsmobile continued the Model 42 basically unchanged for its second model year. Later in the year, this smaller four would be replaced by the larger Model 43 four. This was the first car that brought Olds back into the popular marketplace.

OLDSMOBILE — FOURTH SERIES — MODEL 43 — FOUR: Gradually during 1915 Oldsmobile's bread and butter car became the slightly larger Model 43 four. This car would carry over largely unchanged to the next model year. Wheelbase was up eight inches over the Model 42. A Delco Electric system was used for starting, lighting and ignition. Power came from valve-in-head engine of less than 200 cubic inches.

OLDSMOBILE — SIXTH SERIES — MODEL 55 — SIX: Oldsmobile had been in the big car business for several years and that segment was covered with the carryover Model 55. A large six-cylinder car, the Model 55 was a limited sales success. Easily traceable back through the 1914 Model 54 to the 1913 Model 53, the most obvious change on the six-cylinder was left-hand drive.

I.D. DATA: Model 42. Serial numbers are on the nameplate under the right front seat cushion. Starting: 84500 for touring; 91500 for roadster. Ending: 91499 for touring; 92499 for roadster. Starting engine number: 725006. Ending: N/A. Model 43. Serial numbers located on brass tag under right front seat cushion. Starting: 93000. Ending: N/A. Starting engine number: 738822. Ending: N/A. Model 55. Serial numbers located on brass tag under right front seat cushion. Starting: 92500. Ending: N/A. Starting engine number: 736531. Ending: N/A.

Model No.	Body Type & Seating	Price	Weight	Prod. Total
42-T	4-dr. Tr.-5P	1285	2495	1319
42-R	2-dr. Rds.-2P	1285	2495	1319
43-T	4-dr. Tr.-5P	1095	2620	5921
43-R	2-dr. Rds.-2P	1095	2620	5921
55-T	4-dr. Tr.-7P	2975	4186	114

ENGINE: [Series 42] Inline four. Cast iron block. B & S: 3-1/2 x 5 in. Disp.: 194.2 cu. in. H.P.: 30. Main bearings: three. Valve lifters: overhead. Carb.: float feed. [Series 43] Inline four, valve in head. Cast iron block. B & S: 3-1/2 x 5 in. Disp.: 192 cu. in. H.P.: 30. Main bearings: three. Valve lifters: overhead. Carb.: float feed. [Series 55] Inline six, L-head. Cast-iron block. B & S: 4-1/4 x 5-1/4 in. Disp.: 446 cu. in. H.P.: 50. Valve lifters: mechanical. Carb.: float feed.

1915 Oldsmobile, Model 55, seven-passenger touring, HAC

CHASSIS: [Series 42] W.B.: 112 in. Tires: 33 x 4. [Series 43] W.B.: 120 in. Frt/Rear Tread: 56 in. Tires: 33 x 4. [Series 55] W.B.: 139 in. Tires: 36 x 5. Non-skid tread on rear.

TECHNICAL: [Series 42] Manual transmission. Speeds: 3F/1R. Center, floor shift. Cone clutch. Shaft drive, enclosed within torsion tube. Three-quarter floating rear axle. Service brakes on two wheels with foot pedal control. Wheels: wooden, hickory. [Series 43] Manual transmission. Speeds: 3F/1R. Center, floor shift. Leather faced cone clutch. Shaft drive with two universal joints. Three-quarter floating rear axle. Service brakes on two wheels with foot pedal control. Wheels: wooden, hickory, natural finish. [Series 55] Manual transmission. Speeds: 3F/1R. Center, floor shift. Cone clutch. Shaft drive with two universal joints. Full floating rear axle. Service brakes on two wheels, foot pedal operated. Wheels: wooden, hickory, natural finish.

OPTIONS: $50 extra for any color other than green, blue or gray. Single or dual trunks offered. Eight-day clock. Tool set.

HISTORICAL: Calendar year and model year sales and production: 7,696. President and general manager of Oldsmobile was C.W. Nash. Oldsmobile employed 2,000 people in 1915.

1916

OLDSMOBILE — FOURTH SERIES — MODEL 43 — FOUR: A carryover was the nimble four-cylinder Model 43 with its valve-in-head engine. The roadster in this series could be fitted for a rumbleseat. This was the final four-cylinder Olds offering for awhile and the Model 42s and 43s were reliable motorcars and good sellers for Oldsmobile.

OLDSMOBILE — LIGHT EIGHT SERIES — MODEL 44 — EIGHT: Actually Oldsmobile began production of this model in August of 1915. It was the biggest of the Olds line and had a wheelbase of 120 inches. The all new Olds offered closed models plus a pair of open air models. The motoring public gave the Model 44 a warm reception with almost 8,000 sold.

I.D. DATA: Series 43. Serial numbers found on brass tag under right front seat cushion. Starting: 93000. Ending: N/A. Starting engine number: 738822. Ending: N/A. Series 44. Serial numbers found on brass tag under right front seat cushion. Starting: 109500. Ending: N/A. Starting engine number: 50000. Ending: N/A.

Model No.	Body Type & Seating	Price	Weight	Prod. Total
43-T	4-dr. Tour.-5P	1095	2260	2189
43-T	2-dr. Rds.-2P	1095	2260	2189
44-T	4-dr. Tour.-5P	1195	2750	8000
44-R	2-dr. Rds.-2P	1195	2750	8000
44-S	4-dr. Sed.-5P	1850	3160	8000
44-C	2-dr. Cabr.-2P	1775	2832	8000

1916 Oldsmobile, Model 43, roadster, HAC

ENGINE: [Series 43] Valve-in-head, inline four. Cast iron block. B & S: 3-1/2 x 5 in. Disp.: 192 cu. in. H.P.: 30. Main bearings: three. Valve lifters: overhead. Carb.: float feed. [Series 44 V-type] Eight. Cast iron block. B & S: 2-7/8 x 4-3/4 in. Disp.: 246 cu. in. H.P.: 40 @ 2000 rpm. Valve lifters: mechanical. Carb.: float feed.

CHASSIS: [Series 43] W.B.: 120 in. Frt/Rear Tread: 56 in. Tires: 33 x 4, non-skid on rears. [Series 44] W.B.: 120 in. Frt/Rear Tread: 56 in. Tires: 33 x 4, non-skid on rears.

TECHNICAL: [Series 43] Manual transmission. Speeds: 3F/1R. Floor mounted, center shift. Leather faced cone clutch. Shaft drive, with two universal joints. Three-quarter floating rear axle, Service brakes on two wheels operated by foot pedal. Wheels: wooden, hickory, natural finish. [Series 44] Manual transmission. Speeds: 3F/1R. Floor mounted, center shift. Leather faced cone clutch. Shaft drive with two universal joints. Floating rear axle. Service brakes on two wheels operated by pedal. Wheels: wooden, hickory, natural finish.

HISTORICAL: Introduced August 15, 1915. Calendar year and model year sales and production: 10,507. Company president and general manager of Oldsmobile was C.W. Nash.

Miss Amada Preuss drove a Model 44 V-8 roadster from San Francisco to New York via the Lincoln Highway in 11 days, five hours and 45 minutes to establish a new woman's transcontinental driving record. Production of closed cars increased.

1917

OLDSMOBILE — SIXTH SERIES — MODEL 37 — SIX: After a year out of the market, Oldsmobile came back with an all new Model 37 six-cylinder line. This was the less popular of the two series offered this year. Olds went back to slightly smaller cars with the Model 37 and was trying to appeal to a more popular price market than a few years ago.

OLDSMOBILE — LIGHT EIGHT SERIES — MODEL 45 — EIGHT: This model year saw a few Model 44 Light V-8s built, but the majority of the eight-cylinders produced this year were the new Model 45s. The light continued to be a sales winner for Olds. These two models gave Oldsmobile its strongest lineup in years and sales doubled over 1916.

1917 Oldsmobile, Model 45, touring, HAC

I.D. DATA: Model 37. Serial numbers located on brass plate under right front seat cushion. Starting: 150000. Ending: N/A. Engine number location: same as serial number. Starting: D-101-50000. Ending: N/A. Model 45. Serial numbers located on brass plate under right front seat cushion. Starting: 119000. Ending: N/A. Engine numbers: N/A.

Model No.	Body Type & Seating	Price	Weight	Prod. Total
37-T	4-dr. Tr.-5P	1295	2390	8045
37-R	2-dr. Rds.-2P	1467	2380	8045
37-C	2-dr. Cabr.-3P	1775	2580	8045
37-S	4-dr. Sed.-5P	1850	2616	8045
Model 45				
45-T	4-dr. Tr.-5P	1185	3066	13,440
45-T	4-dr. Tr.-7P	1185	3066	13,440
45-R	2-dr. Tr.-2P	1185	2860	13,440
45-S	4-dr. Sed.-5P	1595	3150	13,440

1917 Oldsmobile, Model 45, cabriolet, HAC

ENGINE: [Model 37] Inline six. Cast iron block. B & S: 2-13/16 x 4-3/4 in. Disp.: 177 cu. in. H.P.: 44. Valve lifters: overhead. Carb.: full float. [Model 45] Vee block. Eight. Cast iron block. B & S: 2-7/8 x 4-3/4 in. Disp.: 246 cu. in. H.P.: 58. Main bearings: two. Valve lifters: mechanical. Carb.: full float.

CHASSIS: [Model 37] W.B.: 112 in. Frt/Rear Tread: 56 in. Tires: 32 x 4, non-skid on rear. [Model 45] W.B.: 120 in. Frt/Rear Tread: 56 in. Tires: 34 x 4.

TECHNICAL: [Model 37] Manual transmission. Speeds: 3F/1R. Center, floor mounted shift. Leather faced cone cluth. Shaft drive. Floating rear axle. Service brakes on two wheels, pedal operated. Wheels: wooden, hickory, natural finish. [Model 45] Manual transmission. Speeds: 3F/1R. Center, floor mounted shift. Leather faced cone clutch. Shaft drive with universal joints. Full floating rear axle. Overall ratio: 4.5:1. Service brakes on two wheels, pedal operated. Artillery wheels, 12-spoke, naturally finished wood.

HISTORICAL: Calendar year sales and production: 10,507. Model year sales and production: 9,279. Company president was Edward Ver Linden. Oldsmobile began some war production that included building kitchen trailers for Army use and building Liberty aircraft engines. Aluminum pistons were used for the first time in an Olds engine. Employment stood at 4,000 — an all-time Olds high.

1918

OLDSMOBILE — SIXTH SERIES — MODEL 37 — SIX: Oldsmobile had a carryover line from the 1917 model year. The six-cylinders continued to be slightly more popular with Olds buyers. This series continued to emphasize the closed automobile with several versions offered.

OLDSMOBILE — MODEL 45-A — EIGHT: The light eight-cylinder designation became Model 45-A. Two versions of the touring car — a five- and seven-passenger — could be ordered and closed cars were offered as well. Oldsmobile rose to eighth place in sales in part due to the sales success of the 45-A.

I.D. DATA: Model 37. Serial numbers were located on brass plate under the right-hand seat cushion. Starting: touring cars: 150000; other 190000. Engine number location: same as serial number. Starting: D101-50000. Ending: N/A. Model 45-A. Serial numbers were located on brass plate under the right-hand seat cushion. Starting: 145000. Ending: N/A. Engine number location: same as serial number. Starting: X85000. Ending: N/A.

Model No.	Body Type & Seating	Price	Weight	Prod. Total
37-R	2-dr. Rds.-2P	1195	2380	11,033
37 T	4-dr. Tr.-5P	1195	2390	11,033
37-Ca	2-dr. Cabr.-3P	1595	2527	11,033
37-Co	2-dr. Cpe.-2P	1595	2632	11,033
37-S	4-dr. Sed.-5P	1695	2682	11,033
45A-T	4-dr. Tr.-5P	1295	3065	8132
45A-T	4-dr. Tr.-7P	1295	3095	8132
45A-R	2-dr. Rds.-2P	1550	3040	8132
45A-S Sptr	4-dr. Spt.Tr.-5P	1550	3065	8132
45A-C	2-dr. Cabr.-3P	1775	3085	8132
45A-S	4-dr. Sed.-5P	1850	3190	8132

ENGINE: [Model 37] Inline, valve-in-head. Six. Cast iron block. B & S: 2-13/16 x 4-3/4 in. Disp.: 177 cu. in. H.P.: 44. Valve lifters: overhead. Carb.: automatic compensating. [Model 45-A] Vee block. Eight. Cast iron block. B & S: 2-7/8 x 4-3/4 in. Disp.: 246 cu. in. H.P.: 58. Main bearings: two. Valve lifters: mechanical. Carb.: automatic compensating, Ball & Ball.

CHASSIS: [Model 37] W.B.: 112 in. Front/Rear Tread: 56 in. Tires: 32 x 4. [Model 45-A] W.B.: 120 in. Front/Rear Tread: 56 in. Tires: 34 x 4.

1918 Oldsmobile, Model 45-A, touring, HAC

TECHNICAL: [Model 37] Sliding gear, selective transmission. Speeds: 3F/1R. Center floor mounted controls. Leather cone clutch. Shaft drive. Spiral bevel, full-floating rear axle. Service brakes on two wheels, external contracting. Wooden wheels, hickory, natural finish. [Model 45-A] Selective gear transmission. Speeds: 3F/1R. Center, floor mounted controls. Leather cone clutch. Shaft drive. Spiral bevel, full-floating rear axle. Service brakes on two wheels, external contracting. Artillery wheels, wood, natural finish.

HISTORICAL: Calendar year sales and production: 19,165. Model year sales and production: 19,165. Company president and general manager of Oldsmobile was Edward Ver Linden.

A new engine plant was completed this year. The sportster touring — the first of several special models — was introduced.

1919

OLDSMOBILE — SIXTH SERIES — MODEL 37-A — SIX: Once again the most popular Olds offering was the six-cylinder series, this year the 37-A. Wheelbase on this series continued at 112 inches and there continued to be good availability of closed models.

1919 Oldsmobile, four-door sedan, FSA

OLDSMOBILE — PACEMAKER SERIES — MODEL 45-A — EIGHT: One of two light eights offered in 1919, this was essentially a carryover from 1918. Sales were just about equally divided between the two eight-cylinder offerings, but together they did not equal six-cylinder output.

OLDSMOBILE — PACEMAKER SERIES — MODEL 45-B — EIGHT: Wheelbase and overall size was increased slightly on the Model 45-A over the 45-Bs. Mechanically the two cars were nearly identical. Closed cars were becoming more common in the Oldsmobile light eight models.

I.D. DATA: Model 37-A. Serial numbers located on brass plate under hood on the right side of dash. Starting: 37A-2780. Ending: N/A. Engine number location: same as serial number. Starting: ED-1001. Ending: N/A. Model 45-A. Serial number located on brass plate under right seat cushion. Starting: 145000. Ending: N/A. Engine number location: same as serial number. Starting: X850000. Ending: N/A. Model 45-B. Serial numbers located on brass plate under right seat cushion. Starting: 45B-599. Ending: N/A. Engine number location: same as serial number. Starting: 45B1-11444. Ending: N/A.

1919 Oldsmobile, Model 37, two-door sedan (1,000,000th Olds), OCW

Model No.	Body Type & Seating	Price	Weight	Prod. Total
37-R	2-dr. Rds.-2P	1395	2380	21,968
37-T	4-dr. Tour.-5P	1395	2390	21,968
37 S	4-dr. Sed.-5P	1895	2632	21,968
37-C	2-dr. Cpe.-3P	1895	2490	21,968
45-AR	2-dr. Rds.-2P	1700	3065	5631
45-AT	4-dr. Tour.-5P	1700	3085	5631
45-BT	4-dr. Tour.-5P	1895	3175	5826
45-BT	4-dr. Tour.-7P	1895	3185	5862

ENGINE: [Model 37-A] Inline. Six. Cast iron block. B & S: 2-13/16 x 4-3/4 in. Disp.: 177 cu. in. H.P.: 44. Main bearings: three. Valve lifters: overhead. Carb.: automatic compensating. [Model 45-A] Vee block. Eight. Cast iron block. B & S: 2-7/8 x 4-3/4 in. Disp.: 246 cu. in. H.P.: 58. Main bearings: two. Valve lifters: mechanical. Carb.: two-stage, Ball & Ball. [Model 45-B] Vee block. Eight. Cast iron block. B & S: 2-7/8 x 4-3/4 in. Disp.: 246 cu. in. H.P.: 58. Main bearings: two. Valve lifters: mechanical. Carb.: two-stage, Ball & Ball.

CHASSIS: [Model 37-A] W.B.: 112 in. Frt/Rear Tread: 56 in. Tire: 32 x 4. [Model 45-A] W.B.: 120 in. Frt/Rear Tread: 56 in. Tires: 34 x 4. [Model 45-B] W.B.: 122 in. Frt/Rear Tread: 56 in. Tires: 34 x 4-1/2, non-skid on rear.

TECHNICAL: [Model 37-A] Selective, manual transmission. Speeds: 3F/1R. Floor mounted, center controls. Leather faced cone clutch. Shaft drive. Full-floating, spiral bevel rear axle. Service brakes on two wheels, external contracting and emergency internal expanding. Hickory wheels, natural finish. [Model 45-A] Selective, manual transmission. Speeds: 3F/1R. Center, floor mounted controls. Leather cone clutch. Shaft drive. Spiral bevel; full-floating rear axle. Service brakes on two wheels, external contracting. Artillery wheels, wood, natural finish. [Model 45-B] Selective, sliding gear manual transmission. Speeds: 3F/1R. Center, floor mounted controls. Leather faced cone clutch. Shaft drive. Full-floating, spiral bevel rear axle. Foot brake external contracting; handbrake internal expanding. Artillery wood wheels.

OPTIONS: Klaxon horn ($4.80). Heater (25.00). Clock (Sessions) (7.10). Gas tank gauge (1.55).

HISTORICAL: Calendar year sales and production: 33,425, does not include truck production. Model year sales and production: same as above. Company president of Oldsmobile was Edward Ver Linden.

Oldsmobile's manufacturing fortunes were on the way up. As a result the company began an aggressive expansion plan for its facilities in Lansing, Michigan.

1920

1920 Oldsmobile, Model 37-A, touring, HAC

OLDSMOBILE — SIXTH SERIES — MODEL 37-A & B — SIX: Oldsmobile designated its open six-cylinder cars as 37-As and closed cars as 37-Bs. The cars shared mechanical and chassis components and had few changes. The six-cylinder models continued as the most popular Oldsmobiles.

OLDSMOBILE — THOROBRED SERIES — MODEL 45-B — V-8: This was the final year for the designation 45 on the Olds V-8. Largely unchanged from 1919, the engine continued as a 246 cubic inch unit. It had detachable heads and horsepower remained at 58. Both open and closed cars were available.

I.D. DATA: Models 37-A & 37-B. Serial numbers located on a brass plate under hood on the right side of dashboard. Starting: 37-28140. Ending: N/A. Engine number location: same as serial number. Starting: D101-50000. Ending: N/A. Model 45-B. Serial numbers located on brass plate underhood on the right side of dashboard. Starting: 45-599. Ending: N/A. Engine number location: same as serial number. Starting: 45B1-11444. Ending: N/A.

Model No.	Body Type & Seating	Price	Weight	Prod. Total
Series 37-A				
37-AR	2-dr. Rds.-2P	1450	2380	14,073
37-AT	4-dr. Tr.-5P	1450	2390	14,073
Series 37-B				
37-BC	2-dr. Cpe.-3P	2145	2527	3871
37-BS	4-dr. Sed.-5P	2145	2632	3871
Series 45B				
45-BP	4-dr. Tr.-4P	2100	3160	7215
45-BT	4-dr. Tr.-5P	2100	3180	7215
45 BS	4-dr. Sed.-5P	3300	3695	7215

ENGINE: [Models 37-A & B] Inline. Six. Cast iron block. B & S: 2-13/16 x 4-3/4 in. Disp.: 177 cu. in. H.P.: 44. Main bearings: three. Valve lifters: valve in head, mechanical. Carb.: automatic compensating. [Model 45-B] Vee block. Eight. Cast iron block. B & S: 2-7/8 x 4-3/4 in. Disp.: 246 cu. in. H.P.: 58. Main bearings: two. Valve lifters: mechanical. Carb.: two-stage.

CHASSIS: [Series 37-A & B] W.B.: 112 in. Frt/Rear Tread: 56 in. Tires: 32 x 4. [Series 45-B] W.B.: 122 in. Frt/Rear Tread: 56 in. Tires: 33 x 4-1/2, non-skid on rear.

TECHNICAL: [Model 37-A & B] Sliding gear transmission. Speeds: 3F/1R. Center, floor mounted controls. Leather faced cone clutch. Shaft drive. Spiral bevel, full-floating rear axle. External contracting service brakes on two wheels, internal expanding emergency brake. Selected hickory, natural finish wheels. [Model 45-B] Sliding gear transmission. Speeds: 3F/1R. Center, floor mounted controls. Leather faced cone clutch. Shaft drive. Spiral bevel, full-floating rear axle. External contracting service brakes on two wheels, internal expanding. Selected hickory, natural finish wheels.

OPTIONS: Trojan horn ($4.80). Klaxon horn (4.80). Sessions clock (7.10). Keyless clock. Sedan heater (25.65). Hand tire pump (1.50).

HISTORICAL: Calendar year sales and production: 26,291. Model year sales and production: 25,159. Company president of Oldsmobile was Edward Ver Linden.

A major plant expansion program was completed including updated facilities for building axles, sheet metal and enameling. Oldsmobile today retains a 1920 Model 37-B sedan in its divisional collection.

1921

OLDSMOBILE — MODEL 37 — SIX: The Model 37s were direct carryovers from the previous year. Power came from the familiar inline six displacing 177 cubic inches and producing 44 hp.

OLDSMOBILE — MODEL 46 — EIGHT: Another direct carryover was the Model 46 eight-cylinder series. It had a 122-inch wheelbase and was powered by a 247 cubic inch engine with 58 hp.

OLDSMOBILE — MODEL 43-A — FOUR: Returning to the four-cylinder car after a few years, the Model 43-A was a welcome addition. Oldsmobile launched this new line with an extensive ad campaign that included the *Saturday Evening Post*.

Both open and closed Model 43-As were available, with the open cars less expensive and more popular. The Model 43-As were built on a wheelbase of 115 inches. Engines developed 43 hp.

OLDSMOBILE — MODEL 47 — EIGHT: Another new offering in this transition year for Oldsmobile was the Model 47 eight-cylinder. This was a smaller and less powerful model than the Model 46. Both open and closed cars came in this series. A 234 cubic inch engine produced 53 hp.

1921 Oldsmobile, Model 43-A, touring, HAC

I.D. DATA: Model 37 serial numbers on brass plate under hood on right side of dash. Starting: 37A-2780. Ending: N/A. Engine numbers were in same location as serial numbers. Starting: D-101. Ending: N/A. Model 46 serial numbers in same location. Starting: 46T-1. Ending: N/A. Engine numbers in same location. Starting: 46-1. Ending: N/A. Model 43 serial numbers in same location. Starting: 43A-1. Ending: N/A. Engine numbers in same location. Starting: A-1. Ending: N/A. Model 47 serial numbers in same location. Starting: 46-1. Ending: N/A. Engine numbers in same location. Starting: 47-1. Ending: N/A.

1921 Oldsmobile, Model 46, seven-passenger touring, HJE

Model No.	Body Type & Seating	Price	Weight	Prod. Total
37-R	2-dr. Rds.-2P	1450	2380	Note 1
37-T	4-dr. Tr.-5P	1450	2390	Note 1
37-C	2-dr. Cpe.-3P	2145	2527	Note 1
37-S	4-dr. Sed.-5P	2145	2632	Note 1
46-P	4-dr. Tr.-4P	1735	3160	Note 2
46-T	4-dr. Tr.-5P	1735	3183	Note 2
46-S	4-dr. Sed.-5P	2635	3695	Note 2
43-R	2-dr. Rds.-2P	1325	2742	Note 3
43-T	4-dr. Tr.-5P	1345	2767	Note 3
43-C	2-dr. Cpe.-3P	1895	2917	Note 3
47-T	4-dr. Tr.-5P	1825	2854	Note 4
47-C	2-dr. Cpe.-3P	2145	3082	Note 4
47-S	4-dr. Sed.-5P	2295	3146	Note 4

Note 1: Total production for Model 37 was 948.
Note 2: Total production for Model 46 was 745.
Note 3: Total production for Model 43 was 13,867.
Note 4: Total production for Model 47 was 3,085.

ENGINE: [Model 37] Inline. Six. Cast iron block. B & S: 2-13/16 x 4-3/4 in. Disp.: 177 cu. in. H.P.: 44. Main bearings: three. Valve lifters: mechanical. Carb.: automatic compensating. [Model 46] Vee block. Eight. Cast iron block. B & S: 2-7/8 x 4-3/4 in. Disp.: 246 cu. in. H.P.: 58. Main bearings: two. Valve lifters: mechanical. Carb.: two-stage. [Model 43] Inline. Cast iron block. B & S: 3-11/16 x 5-1/4 in. Disp.: 224 cu. in. H.P.: 44. Main bearings: three. Valve lifters: mechanical. Carb.: fuel nozzle type. [Model 47] Vee type. Eight. Cast iron block. B & S: 2-7/8 x 4-1/2 in. Disp.: 233 cu. in. H.P.: 60. Main bearings: three. Valve lifters: mechanical. Carb.: special model Johnson.

CHASSIS: [Model 37] W.B.: 112 in. Frt/Rear Tread: standard. Tires: 34 x 4, non skid on rear. [Model 46] W.B.: 122 in. Frt/rear tread: standard. Tires 34 x 4-1/2, non-skid on rear. [Model 43] W.B.: 115 in. Frt/rear tread: standard. Tires: 32 x 4 cords, non-skid on rear. [Model 47] W.B. 115 in. Frt/rear tread: standard. Tires: 32 x 4 cord, non-skid on rear.

1921 Oldsmobile, Model 43-A, four-door sedan, HJE

TECHNICAL: [Model 37] Selective, center control. Selective sliding gear transmission. Speeds: 3F/1R. Center floor shift. [Model 37] Leather faced cone clutch. [Model 46] Large, leather faced cone clutch. [Model 43] Single plate, dry disk clutch. [Model 47] Borg & Beck 10 in. disc clutch. [Model 47] Torque tube, shaft drive. Spiral bevel, full-floating rear axle. [Model 47] Overall ratio: 4.66:1. External contracting brakes on two wheels. [Model 37] National finish hickory wheels. [Model 46] Wooden, natural finish, artillery wheels. [Model 43] Wooden or disc wheels. [Model 47] Hickory, artillery wheels.

OPTIONS: Tuarc disc wheels. Wire wheels. California top. Extra spare tire. Moto-meter.

HISTORICAL: Calendar and model year sales and production: 19,157. President of Oldsmobile was A.B.C. Hardy. Employment was at 2,500.

1922

1922 Oldsmobile, touring, FSA

OLDSMOBILE — MODEL 43-A — FOUR: The Model 43-As continued as one of the most successful Olds series to date. This was a quality line of four-cylinder cars featuring both open and closed models. A special factory installed California top was available and a special sport touring model offered leather side rails, Tuarc disc wheels and special red paint. Prices were reduced for 1922.

OLDSMOBILE — MODEL 47 — EIGHT: This model year saw a great deal of overlap with two eight-cylinder series. Several sporty models were offered in this series.

OLDSMOBILE — MODEL 46 — EIGHT: Carried over largely unchanged was the Model 46. Both open and closed models were offered in limited numbers from this V-8 series.

1922 Oldsmobile, Model 47, coupe, HJE

I.D. DATA: Model 43-A serial numbers on tag under hood on right-hand front side of dash. Starting: 787. Ending: N/A. Engine numbers in same location as serial numbers. Starting: A-26395. Ending: N/A. Model 46 serial numbers in same location. Starting: 218. Ending: N/A. Engine numbers in same location. Starting: 1721. Ending: N/A. Model 47 serial numbers in same location. Starting: 1. Ending: N/A. Engine numbers in same location. Starting: 2823. Ending: N/A.

Model No.	Body Type & Seating	Price	Weight	Prod. Total
43-AR	2-dr. Rds.-2P	1095	2742	Note 1
43-AT	4-dr. Tour.-5P	1095	2767	Note 1
43-AC	2-dr. Cpe.-3P	1595	2917	Note 1
43-AS	4-dr. Sed.-5P	1745	3027	Note 1
46-ST	4-dr. Tour.-4P	1735	3115	Note 2
46-T	4-dr. Tour.-4P	1735	3125	Note 2
46-T	4-dr. Tour.-7P	1735	3130	Note 2
46-S	4-dr. Sed.-5P	2635	3695	Note 2
47-R	2-dr. Rds.-3P	1495	2910	Note 3
47-R	4-dr. Tour.-5P	1495	3175	Note 3
47-ST	4-dr. Tour.-4P	1825	3190	Note 3
47-C	2-dr. Cpe.-3P	2145	3345	Note 3
47-S	4-dr. Sed.-5P	2295	3387	Note 3

Note 1: Total production for Model 43-A was 14,839.
Note 2: Total production for Model 46 was 2,733.
Note 3: Total production for Model 47 was 2,723.

ENGINE: [Model 43] Inline. Four. Cast iron block. B & S: 3-11/16 x 5-1/4 in. Disp.: 224 cu. in. H.P.: 40. Main bearings: three. Valve lifters: mechanical. Carb.: two-stage. [Model 46] Vee block. Eight. Cast iron block. B & S: 2-7/8 x 4-3/4 in. Disp.: 246 cu. in. H.P.: 58. Main bearings: two. Valve lifters: mechanical. Carb.: two-stage. [Model 47] Vee block. Eight. Cast iron block. B & S: 2-7/8 x 4-1/2 in. Disp.: 233 cu. in. H.P.: 63. Main bearings: two. Valve lifters: mechanical. Carb.: special Johnson.

CHASSIS: [Model 43-A] W.B.: 115 in. Frt/Rear Tread: standard. Tires: 32 x 4 cord, non-skid on rear. [Model 46] W.B.: 122 in. Frt/Rear Tread: standard. Tires: 33 x 4-1/2 cord, non-skids on rear. [Model 47] W.B.: 115 in. Frt/Rear Tread: standard. Tires: 32 x 4 cord, non-skid on rear.

TECHNICAL: Selective-sliding gear transmission. Speeds: 3F/

1R. Center floor shift. [Model 43-A] Single plate, dry disc clutch. [Model 46] Leather faced cone clutch. [Model 47] Borg & Beck 10 in. disc clutch. Shaft drive. Spiral bevel, floating rear axle. [Model 43-A] Overall ratio: 4.66:1. [Model 47] 5.1:1. External contracting, internal expanding brakes on two wheels. Hickory, artillery wheels.

OPTIONS: Tuarc disc wheels. Wire wheels. Moto-meter. Trojan horn. Klaxon horn. Sessions clock. Keyless clock. Sedan heater. Tire pump.

HISTORICAL: Model and calendar year sales and production 21,499. General manager of Oldsmobile was A.B.C. Hardy. A special Olds racer set a speed record of 67 mph for 15 hours.

1923

OLDSMOBILE — MODEL 30-A — SIX: Moving back into the six-cylinder market, Oldsmobile introduced its long running Model 30 series. Production and sales of this all new model began in July and rose quickly for the balance of the year. The new six-cylinder models became the lowest priced Oldsmobiles for many years with touring car prices starting as low as $850. Both open and closed cars were offered in the series and Fisher bodies were featured. The powerplant for the new series was a 42 hp six with 170 cubic inches.

1923 Oldsmobile, Model 43-A, four-door sedan, OCW

OLDSMOBILE — MODEL 43-A — FOUR: This model year marked the end for some time for four-cylinder Oldsmobiles in general and specifically the Model 43-A. Prices came down again slightly on this series and production dropped after the new six-cylinders hit the dealer showrooms. The 43-A was one of the best selling Oldsmobile series to date.

1923 Oldsmobile, Model 47, sport roadster, HJE

OLDSMOBILE — MODEL 47 — EIGHT: Also in its final year was the V-8 powered 47 series. It would be almost a decade before Olds would again offer an eight, and then it would be a straight eight (although the companion Viking was built in 1929 and 1930). Prices were lowered in this series as well and by mid-summer the Model 47 assembly line was forever silenced.

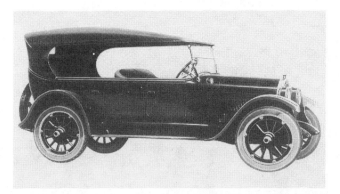

1923 Oldsmobile, Model 47, touring, OCW

I.D. DATA: [Model 30-A] Serial number was stamped on brass plate on right front door pillar. Starting: 30-1. Ending: N/A. Engine number location same as serial number. Starting: A-1. Ending: N/A. [Model 43-A] Serial number was on brass plate located under hood. Starting: 43A-1. Ending: N/A. Engine number location same as serial number. Starting: B-18501. Ending: B-27734. [Model 47] Serial number was on brass plate located under hood. Starting: 47-1. Ending: N/A. Engine number location same as serial number. Starting: 47-4601. Ending: N/A.

1923 Oldsmobile, Model 47 Super Sport, touring, OCW

Model No.	Body Type & Seating	Price	Weight	Prod. Total
Model 30-A				
30-AR	2-dr. Rds.-2P	850	2220	Note 1
30-AT	4-dr. Tr.-5P	850	2305	Note 1
30-AC	2-dr. Cpe.-3P	1250	2460	Note 1
30 AS	4-dr. Sed.-5P	1250	2570	Note 1
30-AST	4-dr. Tr.-4P	1000	2330	Note 1
Model 43-A				
43-AR	2-dr. Rds.-2P	1325	2870	Note 2
43-AT	4-dr. Tr.-5P	1345	2900	Note 2
43-AC	2-dr. Cpe.-3P	1895	3075	Note 2
43-AB	2-dr. Brgm.-4P	1795	2925	Note 2
43 AS	4-dr. Sed.-5P	1695	3140	Note 2
Model 47				
47T	4-dr. Tr.-4P	1495	3110	Note 3
47TB	4-dr. Tr.-5P	1495	3120	Note 3
47R	2-dr. Rds.-2P	1495	3085	Note 3
47S	4-dr. Sed.-5P	2295	3220	Note 3
47C	2-dr. Cpe.-3P	2145	3175	Note 3
47ST	4-dr. Tr.-4P	1825	3115	Note 3

Note 1: Oldsmobile total production for Model 30-A was 12,264.
Note 2: Oldsmobile total production for Model 43-A was 19,017.
Note 3: Oldsmobile total production for Model 47 was 2,148.

ENGINE: [Model 30-A] Inline. Six. Cast iron block. B & S: 2-3/4 x 4-3/4 in. Disp.: 169 cu. in. Brake H.P.: 42. Main bearings: three. Valve lifters: mechanical. Carb.: Zenith. [Model 43-A] Inline. Four. Cast iron block. B & S: 3-11/16 x 5-1/4 in. Disp.: 224 cu. in. Brake H.P.: 40. Main bearings: three. Valve lifters:

mechanical. Carb.: two-stage. [Model 47] Vee block. Eight. Cast iron block. B & S: 2-7/8 x 4-1/2 in. Disp.: 233 cu. in. Brake H.P.: 54. Main bearings: two. Valve lifters: mechanical. Carb.: special Johnson model.

CHASSIS: [Model 30-A] W.B.: 110 in. Frt/Rear Tread: standard. Tires: 31 x 4 cord, non-skid on rear. [Model 43-A] W.B.: 115 in. Frt/Rear Tread: standard. Tires: 32 x 4 cord, non-skid on rear. [Model 47] W.B.: 115 in. Frt/ Rear Tread: standard. Tires: 32 x 4 cord, non-skid on rear.

1923 Oldsmobile, Model 47, sport roadster, HAC

TECHNICAL: Selective, sliding gear transmission. Speeds: 3F/1R. Center floor controls. [Model 30-A] Borg & Beck, single plate clutch. [Model 43-A] Single plate dry disc clutch. [Model 47] Borg & Beck disc clutch. Shaft drive. [Model 30-A] Spiral bevel, semi-floating rear axle. [Model 43-A & 47] Spiral bevel, floating axle. [Model 43-A & 47] Overall ratio: 4.66:1. Service brakes on rear wheels. [Model 30-A] Artillery wood wheels or Tuarc steel. [Model 43-A & 47] Artillery, hickory wheels.

OPTIONS: Klaxon horn. Moto-meter. California top. Tuarc disc wheels. Wire wheels.

HISTORICAL: Calendar and model year sales and production: 34,811. Company general manager: A.B.C. Hardy.

New plant areas — including a new Fisher Body building plant — were completed this year. For the first time since the Curved Dash era, Olds tooled up for a single series powered with just one engine. "Cannonball" Baker completed a transcontinental run from New York to Los Angeles in 12-1/2 days with a Model 30-A touring car locked in high gear.

1924

1924 Oldsmobile, Model 30-B, touring, HJE

OLDSMOBILE — MODEL 30-B — SIX: Oldsmobile took a big step toward simplification with just a 30 series model — the 30-B — was offered. This would be the trend for the next few years — a single Olds series with just one engine offered. Sales improved dramatically with this single series format. Closed cars became more popular and Fisher was the body supplier.

1924 Oldsmobile, Model 30-B, four-door sedan, HAC

I.D. DATA: Serial number on plate located on right side of toe board. Starting: 30B-1. Ending: N/A. Engine location: same as serial number. Starting: B-1 . Ending: N/A.

Model No.	Body Type & Seating	Price	Weight	Prod. Total
30-BR	2-dr. Rds.-2P	880	2145	1800
30-BT	4-dr. Tr.-5P	880	2170	10,586
30-BCB	2-dr. Cpe.-2P	1175	2295	2169
30-BST	4-dr. Tr.-5P	1005	2320	8847
30-BBR	2-dr. Brgm.-4P	1365	2410	8839
30-BS	4-dr. Sed.-5P	1280	2570	3225

ENGINE: Inline. Six. Cast iron block. B & S: 2-3/4 x 4-3/4 in. Disp.: 169 cu. in. Brake H.P.: 42. Main bearings: three. Valve lifters: mechanical. Carb.: Zenith.

CHASSIS: W.B.: 110 in. Frt/Rear tread: standard. Tires: 31 x 4 cord, non-skid on rear.

TECHNICAL: Selective, sliding gear transmission. Speeds: 3F/ 1R. Center, floor mounted shift. Borg & Beck, single plate dry disc clutch. Shaft drive. Spiral bevel, semi-floating rear axle. Service brakes on rear wheels. Artillery wheels.

OPTIONS: Klaxon horn. Moto-meter. Tuarc disc wheels. Wire wheels.

HISTORICAL: Calendar and model year sales and production: 44,854. Oldsmobile general manager: A.B.C. Hardy. Oldsmobile switched to lacquer paint.

1925

OLDSMOBILE — MODEL 30-C — SIX: Olds continued to offer six-cylinder models and added both deluxe roadsters and sedans. A new and distinctive style radiator shell was featured and chrome replaced nickel plating in midyear. It had a new instrument panel and prices increased slightly. Both Model Cs and Ds were offered this year, with the 30-C being the primary model.

1925 Oldsmobile, Model 30-C, coupe, HJE

I.D. DATA: Serial number on plate on right end of front seat. Starting: 1. Ending: N/A. Engine number location: same as serial number. Starting: C-1. Ending: N/A.

Model No.	Body Type & Seating	Price	Weight	Prod. Total
30-CR	2-dr. Rds.-2P	890	2145	2090
30-CSR	2-dr. Dl. Rds.-2P	985	2270	1765
30-CC	2-dr. Cpe.-4P	1175	2460	2338
30-CS	4-dr. Sed.-5P	1285	2570	5820
30-CDS	4-dr. Dl. Sed.-5P	1375	2740	7075
30-CST	4-dr. Spt. Tr.-5P	1015	2360	4569
30-CT	4-dr. Tr.-5P	890	2200	7328
30-CD2S	2-dr. Sed.-4P	985	2440	9896

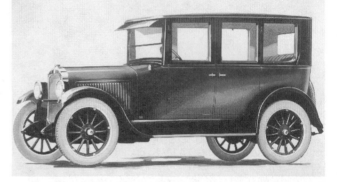

1925 Oldsmobile, Model 30-C, four-door sedan, OCW

ENGINE: Inline. Six. Cast iron block. B & S: 2-3/4 x 4-3/4 in. Disp.: 169 cu. in. Brake H.P.: 40. Main bearings: three. Valve lifters: mechanical. Carb.: Zenith.

CHASSIS: W.B.: 110-1/2 in. Frt/Rear tread: standard. Tires: 30 x 4.95 cord, non-skid on rear.

TECHNICAL: Selective sliding gear transmission. Speeds: 3F/ 1R. Borg & Beck, single plate clutch. Spiral bevel, semi-floating rear axle. Overall ratio: 5.1:1. Service brakes on two wheels. Twelve spoke, artillery wheels.

OPTIONS: Balloon tires and disc wheels ($50.00). Deluxe equipment package: Tuarc disc wheels, nickeled double bumpers, windshield wings, spotlight, aluminum step plates and enameled trunk on special platform.

1925 Oldsmobile, Model 30-C, roadster, HJE

HISTORICAL: Speed records: Floyd Clymer drove a Model 30 touring car to records climbing Lookout Mountain and Pikes Peak. Model year sales and production: 19,506. Calendar year sales and production: 43,386. Oldsmobile general manager: A.B.C. Hardy. Other highlights: a Duco finishing process was introduced. Employment rose to a record 4,250.

1926

OLDSMOBILE — MODEL 30-D — SIX: Olds remained with its single inline six engine. As with most cars of this era, closed models continued to gain in popularity. The Fisher Body nameplate had been a fixture for several years at Olds. Standard and

deluxe versions of most series cars were offered this year. A slightly different body line was offered in 1926 and two-tone paint schemes were available. Upholstery was cord material on closed cars and leather on open models.

I.D. DATA: Serial number on plate under front seat. Starting: D-1 & up. Ending: N/A. Engine number location same as serial number. Starting: D-1 & up. Ending: N/A.

1926 Oldsmobile, Model 30-D, four-door sedan, AA

Model No.	Body Type & Seating	Price	Weight	Prod. Total
30-DDR	2-dr. Rds.-2P	975	2317	1249
30-DT	4-dr. Tr.-5P	875	2225	1124
30-DDT	4-dr. Dbl. Tr.-5P	980	2380	774
30-DC	2-dr. Cpe.-2P	925	2347	1528
30-DDC	2-dr. Dbl. Cpe.-2P	990	2470	3296
30-D2S	2-dr. Sed.-4P	1025	2450	6388
30-DD2S	2-dr. Dbl. Sed.-4P	1040	2620	13,906
30-D4S	4-dr. Sed.-5P	1025	2690	3404
30-DD4S	4-dr. Dbl. Sed.-5P	1115	2700	15,302
30-DLS	4-dr. Lan. Sed.-5P	1190	2705	1205

1926 Oldsmobile, Model 30-D, deluxe coupe, OCW

ENGINE: Inline. Six. Cast iron block. B & S: 2-3/4 x 4-3/4 in. Disp.: 169 cu. in. Brake H.P.: 41. Main bearings: three. Valve lifters: mechanical. Carb.: Zenith.

1926 Oldsmobile, Model 30-D, landau sedan, AA

CHASSIS: W.B.: 110-1/2 in. Frt/Rear Tread: standard. Tires: 30 x 4.95, balloon cord.

TECHNICAL: Selective, sliding gear transmission. Speeds: 3F/1R. Center mounted, floor shift controls. Single plate, dry disc clutch. Shaft drive. Semi-floating rear axle. Overall ratio: 5.1:1. Service brakes on two wheels. Artillery, wire or steel disc wheels.

OPTIONS: Front bumper ($8.00). Rear bumper (13.45). Heater. Clock. Spotlight. K-S gas telegauge. Wire wheels. Spare tire cover. Trunk platform (15.00). Trunk (47.00). Road Commander aerlectric horn (12.50).

1926 Oldsmobile, Model 30-D, touring, HJE

HISTORICAL: Speed records: 301-mile run Chicago/Detroit less than six hours by Floyd Clymer. Calendar year sales and production: 57,878. Model year sales and production: 53,015. The general manager was I.J. Reuter. Manufacturing plant expansion was announced.

1927

OLDSMOBILE — MODEL 30-E — SIX: The 30 Series six-cylinder was again the lone Oldsmobile offering. Over the life of the series — which began in late 1923 — the E models had the most changes. The biggest change was Oldsmobile's first four-wheel brake system. Prices held steady and both open and closed models were sold in both standard and deluxe form. The deluxe package consisted of front and rear bumpers, locking moto-meter and steel disc or wooden wheels. This year was the final time the 30 designation was used.

1927 Oldsmobile, Model 30-E, sport coupe, OCW

I.D. DATA: Serial number was on tag under front seat. Starting: E-1. Ending: N/A. Engine number location same as serial number. Starting: E-1. Ending: N/A.

1927 Oldsmobile, Model 30-E, deluxe roadster, OCW

Model No.	Body Type & Seating	Price	Weight	Prod. Total
30-EDR	2-dr. Del. Rds.-2P	975	2317	2342
30-ET	4-dr. Tr.-5P	875	2335	99
30-EDT	4-dr. Del. Tr.-5P	895	2490	204
30-EC	2-dr. Cpe.-3P	875	2450	3258
30-EDC	2-dr. Del. Cpe.-3P	930	2540	5359
30-ESC	2-dr. Spt. Cpe.-3P	932	2560	3996
30-E2S	2-dr. Sed.-4P	950	2570	12,422
30-ED2S	2-dr. Del. Sed.-4P	1050	2720	11,308
Model No.	Body Type & Seating	Price	Weight	Prod. Total
30-ES	4-dr. Sed.-5P	975	2625	6945
30-EDS	4-dr. Del. Sed.-5P	1055	2780	11,298
30-EL	4-dr. Lan. Sed.-5P	1075	2785	16,792

1927 Oldsmobile, Model 30-E, two-door sedan, OCW

ENGINE: Inline. Six. Cast iron block. B & S: 2-7/8 x 4-3/4 in. Disp.: 185 cu. in. Brake H.P.: 47. Main bearings: three. Valve lifters: mechanical. Carb.: Zenith.

CHASSIS: W.B.: 110-1/2 in. Frt/Rear Tread: standard. Tires: 30 x 5.25 balloon.

1927 Oldsmobile, Model 30-E, landau sedan, OCW

TECHNICAL: Selective, sliding gear transmission. Speeds: 3F/1R. Center, floor mounted shift. Dry disc clutch. Shaft drive. Semi-floating rear axle. Overall ratio: 5.1:1. External contracting service brakes on all wheels. Disc, wooden artillery or wire wheels.

1927 Oldsmobile, Model 30-E, touring, DC

OPTIONS: Front bumper ($8.50). Rear bumper (13.45). Heater. Cigar lighter. Spotlight. Trunk (50.00). Trunk platform (15.00). Wire wheels. Spare tire cover.

HISTORICAL: Calendar year sales and production: 54,234. Model year sales and production: 82,955. Oldsmobile company president and general manager was I.J. Reuter. Plant expansion was completed. It included an enlarged engine plant, new two-story shipping dock, new engineering lab and new heat treating area. In Canada a similar "Jubilee Series" of Oldsmobiles was marketed.

1928

OLDSMOBILE — MODEL F-28 — SIX: The previous model year marked the end of the 30 series designation. For 1928 the designation F and the model year resulted in the F-28. The F designation would carry on for many years with the six-cylinders — even after eights were added. There was a new, larger and more powerful six-cylinder engine and larger chassis. Both deluxe and standard versions were offered in a variety of body styles. The deluxe package included sidemounts, trunk platform, chrome plated headlamp shells, leather boots on springs and special paint work.

1928 Oldsmobile, Model F-28, touring, HJE

I.D. DATA: Serial number on right-hand body sill under front mat. Starting: 1. Ending: N/A. Engine number location same as serial number. Starting F1. Ending: N/A.

Model No.	Body Type & Seating	Price	Weight	Prod. Total
F-28R	2-dr. Rds.-2P	995	2695	2791
F-28DR	2-dr. Del. Rds.-2P	1145	2845	200
F-28T	4-dr. Tr.-5P	995	2915	804
F-28ST	4-dr. Spt. Tr.-5P	1145	3065	2933
F-28C	2-dr. Cpe.-3P	925	2705	9164
F-28SC	2-dr. Spt. Cpe.-3P	995	2760	5079
F-28DSC	2-dr. Del. Spt. Cpe.-3P	1145	2910	1038
F-282S	2-dr. Sed.4-P	925	2790	23,572
F-28S	4-dr. Sed.-5P	1025	2890	27,849
F-28DS	4-dr. Del. Sed.-5P	1175	3040	2221
F-28L	4-dr. Lan.-5P	1085	2805	10,485
F-28DL	4-dr. Del. Lan.-5P	1235	3050	1576

ENGINE: Inline. Six. Cast iron block. B & S: 3-3/16 x 4-1/8 in. Disp.: 197 cu. in. Brake H.P.: 55 @ 3000 R.P.M. Main bearings: four. Valve lifters: mechanical. Carb.: Schebler.

CHASSIS: W.B.: 113-1/2 in. Frt/Rear Tread: standard. Tires: 28 x 5.25.

TECHNICAL: Sliding gear, selective transmission. Speeds: 3F/1R. Center, floor shift controls. Dry disc clutch. Shaft drive. Semi-floating rear axle. Overall ratio: 4.41:1. External expanding service brakes on all wheels. Wood, wire or disc wheels.

1928 Oldsmobile, Model F-28, sedan, HJE

OPTIONS: Front bumper. Rear bumper. Dual sidemount. Sidemount cover(s). Heater. Clock. Cigar lighter. Spotlight.

HISTORICAL: Introduced January 12, 1928. Calendar year sales and production: 86,593. Model year sales and production: 84,635. Oldsmobile general manager was I.J. Reuter.

In 1928 Olds reached a new employment peak of 6,234. Additional production capacity made.

1929

OLDSMOBILE — MODEL F-29 — SIX: Minor changes were made to the successful six-cylinder Olds series in 1929. Power increased slightly to 62 hp and the model line was simplified. In addition to the standard models, special and deluxe packages were available. Special equipment included: twin sidemounts, trunk rack and front and rear bumpers. Deluxe equipment included sidemounted wire wheels, trunk rack, front and rear bumpers and chrome-plated headlight shells.

1929 Oldsmobile, Model F-29, roadster, OCW

I.D. DATA: Serial number on right-hand body sill under front mat. Starting: D-1. Ending: N/A. Engine number location same as serial number. Starting: F-100001. Ending: F-196900.

Model No.	Body Type & Seating	Price	Weight	Prod. Total
F-29P	2-dr. Rds.-2P	945	2716	st.-947
F-29R	2-dr. Rds.-2P	945	2716	spl.-335
F-29R	2-dr. Rds.-2P	945	2716	del.-1013
F-29T	4-dr. Tr.-5P	945	2734	st.-18
F-29T	4-dr. Tr.-5P	945	2734	spl.-9
F-29T	4-dr. Tr.-5P	945	2734	del.-51
F-29C	2-dr. Cpe.-3P	875	2830	st.-8135
F-29C	2-dr. Cpe.-3P	875	2830	spl.-2011
F-29C	2-dr. Cpe.-3P	875	2830	del.-646
F-292S	2-dr. Sed.-4P	875	3075	st.-21,266
F-292S	2-dr. Sed.-4P	875	3075	spl.-4284

Viking: the "other" Oldsmobile

VIKING -- Lansing, Michigan -- (1929-1930) -- The Viking was one of several "in-between" cars introduced by General Motors while the Twenties still roared and the stock market hadn't crashed. It rather resembled, but was cheaper than the LaSalle, which was the less expensive companion car produced by Cadillac. It was more expensive than the Oldsmobile and was produced by the Olds Motor Works as the new upmarket companion car to the Olds F-28. It was an altogether fine car. Unlike the Olds, which was a six, the Viking was powered by an 81 bhp V-8, a 90 degree unit in which the chain-driven camshaft operated horizontal valves between the cylinder banks, rendering the valves accessible by the simple removal of a cover plate. Although announced in March of 1929 at $1,595, the price tag had risen to $1,695 by year's end. A convertible coupe, sedan and a close-coupled sedan -- all on a 125-inch wheelbase - were offered, with deluxe variations available for a few dollars more. The car's emblem was a stylized "V" -- to denote both V-8 and Viking. Doubtless had the Wall Street collapse not happened, the Viking would have survived longer. But with the onset of the Great Depression, Olds Motor Works was hard pressed to find sales enough for its Oldsmobile, which was priced at less than $1,000. Continuing to market a $1,700 car was no longer logical, and the Viking was discontinued at the end of 1930. Production had totaled 4,058 cars in 1929, 2,813 in 1930, with 353 units put together from parts already on hand in 1931.

1929 Viking, four-door sedan, OCW

1929 VIKING
Eight - 81 hp, 125" wb

	FP	5	4	3	2	1
Convertible Coupe	1595					
Sedan	1595					
Close-Coupled Sedan	1595		see pricing in back of book			

1930 Viking, convertible coupe, JAC

1930 VIKING
Eight - 81 hp, 125" wb

	FP	5	4	3	2	1
Convertible Coupe	1695					
Sedan	1695					
Close-Coupled Sedan	1695		see pricing in back of book			

Model No.	Body Type & Seating	Price	Weight	Prod. Total
F-292S	2-dr. Sed.-4P	875	3075	del.-1544
F-29S	4-dr. Sed.-5P	975	3128	st.-25,433
F-29S	4-dr. Sed.-5P	975	3128	spl.-3138
F-29S	4-dr. Sed.-5P	975	3128	del.-7197
F-29L	4-dr. Lan.-5P	1035	3140	st.-2459
F-29L	4-dr. Lan.-5P	1035	3140	spl.-601
F-29L	4-dr. Lan.-5P	1035	3140	de.-1774

ENGINE: Inline. Six. Cast iron block. B & S: 3-3/16 x 4-1/8 in. Disp.: 197 cu. in. Brake H.P.: 61 @ 2600 R.P.M. Main bearings: Four. Valve lifters: mechanical, mushroom type. Carb.: Schebler.

CHASSIS: W.B.: 113-1/2 in. Frt/Rear Tread: standard. Tires: 28 x 5.25 non-skid.

TECHNICAL: Selective, sliding gear transmission. Speeds: 3F/1R. Center, floor mounted shift controls. Single plate disc type clutch. Shaft drive. Semi-floating rear axle. Overall ratio: 4.41:1. Front Bendix three-shoe brakes, rear external contracting brakes. Wood, wire or disc wheels. Wheel size: 18 in.

1929 Oldsmobile, Model F-29, two-door sedan, OCW

OPTIONS: Front bumper. Rear bumper. Heater. Clock. Cigar lighter. Cowl lamps. Special Package — twin sidemounted spares, trunk rack and front and rear bumpers ($75.00). Deluxe Package — twin sidemounted wire wheels, trunk rack, front and rear bumpers and chrome headlight shells (130.00).

HISTORICAL: Calendar year sales and production: 97,395. Model year sales and production: 97,395. Oldsmobile general manager was I.J. Reuter.

Highest General Motors employment ever in Lansing, including Oldsmobile and Fisher body: 7,213. Three city blocks of additional land was acquired for expansion. Work started on a new administration complex.

1930

1930 Oldsmobile, Model F-30, convertible, HJE

OLDSMOBILE MODEL F-30 — SIX: Olds continued its traditional six-cylinder models in a single series. Mohair upholstery was used in most closed Oldsmobiles, with leather used in open cars. Three versions of most 1930 Oldsmobiles were available.

The standard model had basic equipment. The special models had sidemounted spare tires, front and rear bumpers and a folding trunk rack. The deluxe package included sidemounted wire wheels, both bumpers, folding trunk rack and chrome-plated headlight shells.

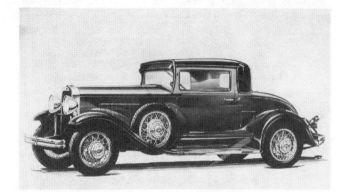

1930 Oldsmobile, Model F-30, deluxe coupe, OCW

I.D. DATA: Serial number on right-hand body sill under front mat. Starting: 1. Ending: N/A. Engine number location same as serial number. Starting: F-200001. Ending: F-252106.

Model No.	Body Type & Seating	Price	Weight	Prod. Total
30-FR	2-dr. Rds.-2P	995	2832	2979
30-FT	4-dr. Tr.-5P	965	2965	103
30-FC	2-dr. Cpe.-3P	895	2775	5008
30-FSC	2-dr. Spt. Cpe.-3P	965	2810	4870
30-F2S	2-dr.Sed.-4P	895	2840	13,165
30-FS	4-dr. Sed.-5P	995	2940	19,087
30-FPS	4-dr. Pat. Sed.-5P	1190	2950	4269

1930 Oldsmobile, Model F-30, four-door sedan, DC

ENGINE: Inline. Six. Cast iron block. B & S: 3-3/16 x 4-1/8 in. Disp.: 197 cu. in. Brake H.P.: 62 @ 3000 R.P.M. Main bearings: four. Valve lifters: mechanical, mushroom. Carb.: Model H.

CHASSIS: W.B.: 113-1/2 in. Frt/Rear Tread: standard. Tires: 28 x 5.25.

TECHNICAL: Selective, sliding gear transmission. Speeds: 3F/1R. Floor mounted, center shift controls. Dry disc clutch. Shaft drive. Semi-floating rear axle. Overall ratio: 4.54:1. Bendix three-shoe front brakes; rear external contracting brakes. Wood, wire wheels.

1930 Oldsmobile, Model F-30, touring, HJE

1930 Oldsmobile, Model F-30, convertible coupe, JAC

OPTIONS: Front bumper. Rear bumper. Heater. Clock. Cigar lighter. Spotlight. Special — sidemounts (twin), both bumpers and folding trunk rack ($35.00). Deluxe Package — sidemounts (twin wire), both bumpers, folding trunk rack and chrome-plated headlamp shells (75.00).

HISTORICAL: Calendar year sales and production: 49,994. Model year sales and production: 49,994. Oldsmobile general manager was D.S. Eddins.

Work continued on additions to the manufacturing area within Lansing.

1931

1931 Oldsmobile, Model F-31, convertible coupe, AA

OLDSMOBILE — MODEL F-31 — SIX: Olds continued to offer a single series this year, powered by the familiar six-cylinder engine. A synchromesh transmission was added. Standard and deluxe equipment packages were offered in a variety of open and closed body styles. The deluxe models came with twin sidemounts, both bumpers and a trunk platform.

I.D. DATA: Serial numbers were located on pillar of bodywork. Starting: 1. Ending: N/A. Engine number located same as serial number. Starting: F253001. Ending: F301655.

Model No.	Body Type & Seating	Price	Weight	Prod. Total
31-FCR	2-dr. Rds.-2P	995	2965	3500
31-FC	2-dr. Cpe.-3P	910	3040	3700
31-FSC	2-dr. Spt. Cpe.-3P	960	3115	4900
31-FK	2-dr. Sed.-4P	910	3155	10,555
31-FS	4-dr. Sed.-5P	960	3260	17,812
31-FP*	4-dr. Ptr. Sed.-5P	1025	3275	4415

* Deluxe models in any body style carried the letter prefix D.

ENGINE: Inline. Six. Cast iron block. B & S: 3-3/16 x 4-1/8 in. Disp.: 197 cu. in. C.R.: 5.06:1. Brake H.P.: 65 @ 3350 R.P.M. N.A.C.C. H.P. 24.4. Main bearings: four. Valve lifters: mechanical. Carb.: downdraft, Stromberg.

CHASSIS: [Series F-31] W.B.: 112-1/2 in. O.L.: 173 in. Height: 69-1/4 in. Frt/Rear Tread: standard. Tires: 28 x 5.25, non-skid balloon cord.

TECHNICAL: Synchromesh transmission. Center, floor controls. Single, dry disc clutch. Tubular, shaft drive. Semi-floating rear axle. Overall ratio: 4.56:1. Internal expanding, two-shoe self-energizing brakes. Four wooden wheels.

1931 Oldsmobile, Model F-31, Deluxe four-door sedan, JAC

OPTIONS: Both bumpers ($20.00). Rear metal tire cover (11.00). Olds/Waltham clock (15.00). Cigar lighter (1.35). Spotlight (16.50). Ornamental radiator cap (5.00). Road light (22.50). Spring covers (7.50). Seat covers (17.50). Backup light (3.50). Wheel lock (2.50). Trunk (30.00). Fender light (6.00 pair).

Accessory Groups
#1 (Bumpers, wheel lock, spare tire) ($37.50)
#2 (Items from #1 plus ornamental radiator cap, spring covers, fender lights and backup light) ($65.00)
#3 (Items from #2 plus metal tire cover, spotlight and clock) ($103.00)
#4 (Items from #3 plus radiator cap, spring covers, fender lights, backup light) ($27.50)
#5 (Items from #4 plus metal tire covers, spotlight, clock) ($77.00)
#6 (Items from #5 plus trunk) ($107.00)

1931 Oldsmobile, Model F-31, business coupe, HJE

HISTORICAL: Introduced January 1, 1931. First time Olds offered a synchromesh transmission. Calendar year sales and production: 48,777. Model year sales and production: 47,316. D.S. Eddins was Oldsmobile's general manager.

The 1931 Oldsmobile re-created the transcontinental 1905 curved dash run from New York to Portland, Oregon. Car building and shipping capacity was 800 per day in 1931.

1932

OLDSMOBILE — SERIES F — SIX: Olds retained its basic six-cylinder series again with six body styles. Despite the addition of a new eight-cylinder series this year, sales dropped dramatically from 1931 totals. A slightly more powerful six-cylinder engine was used and horsepower climbed to 74. Both series had a freewheeling system.

OLDSMOBILE — SERIES L — EIGHT: Olds came back with a two series line for 1932 adding the straight-eight powered L series. Ironically, Olds had used V-8 engines several times before — as early as 1916 — but this was the first venture with a straight-eight. Both the six- and eight-cylinder cars used the same chassis. Oldsmobile continued to offer six- and eight-cylinder engines through 1950.

I.D. DATA: Serial numbers were located on pillar of bodywork. Starting number: 1. Ending: N/A. Engine number location same as serial number. Starting: [Six] 302001, [Eight] L-1001. Ending: [Six] 316568, [Eight] L-6557.

1932 Oldsmobile, Eight, sport coupe, DC

Model No.	Body Type & Seating	Price	Weight	Prod. Total
Six-Cylinder [F Series]				
32-FCR	2-dr. Rds.-3P	1000	2870	723
32-FC	2-dr. Cpe.-3P	920	2845	1083
32-FSC	2-dr. Spt. Cpe.-3P	970	2925	1173
32-FK	2-dr. Sed.-5P	920	2960	2804
32-FS	4-dr. Sed.-5P	1000	3035	5900
32-FP	4-dr. Sed.-5P	1035	3040	2114
Eight-Cylinder [L Series]				
32-LCR	2-dr. Rds.-3P	1055	2995	394
32-LC	2-dr. Cpe.-3P	975	2970	216
32-LSC	2-dr. Spt. Cpe.-3P	1025	3045	476
32-LK	2-dr. Sed.-5P	975	3080	271
32-LS	4-dr. Sed.-5P	1055	3165	1710
32-LP	4-dr. Sed.-5P	1090	3175	2262

Note 1: Deluxe models in any body style carried the prefix letter D in model number.

1932 Oldsmobile, Eight, Deluxe convertible coupe, JAC

ENGINE: [Series F] Inline. Six. Cast iron block. B & S: 3-5/16 x 4-1/8 in. Disp.: 213 cu. in. C.R.: 5.59:1. Brake H.P.: 74 @ 3200 R.P.M. Main bearings: four. Valve lifters: mushroom type. Carb.: downdraft. [Series L] Inline. Eight. Cast iron block. B & S: 3 x 4-1/4 in. Disp.: 240 cu. in. C.R.: 5.74:1. Brake H.P.: 87 @ 3350 R.P.M. Main bearings: five. Valve lifters: mushroom type. Carb.: duplex downdraft w/automatic choke.

1932 Oldsmobile, Six, two-door sedan, HJE

CHASSIS: [Series F & L] W.B.: 116-1/2 in. O.L.: 178-3/4 in. Height: 67-7/8 in. Frt/Rear Tread: standard. Tires: 17 x 6.00, non-skid balloon cord.

TECHNICAL: Synchromesh transmission. Speeds: 3F/1R. Center, floor controls. Single, dry disc clutch. Shaft drive. Semifloating rear axle. Overall ratio: 4.56:1. Internal expanding brakes, two-shoe, duo servo. Four wooden wheels. Rear axle: 4.77:1.

OPTIONS: Both bumpers ($33.00). Sidemount covers (11.00). Electric Clock (9.85). Spotlight (18.75). Sidemount mirror (7.50 pair). Passenger sun visor (3.75). Trunk (30.00). Tire gauge (2.75). Luggage set (17.50).

HISTORICAL: Freewheeling introduced. Calendar year sales and production: 17,502. Model year sales and production: 19,239. D.S. Eddins was Oldsmobile's general manager.

1933

1933 Oldsmobile, Six, two-door sedan, JAC

OLDSMOBILE — F-SERIES — SIX: Completely restyled Oldsmobiles were introduced and once again the six-cylinder models were the most popular. The sixes now used a slightly smaller chassis. Olds called its models "style leaders."

1933 Oldsmobile, Eight, convertible coupe, JAC

OLDSMOBILE — L-SERIES — EIGHT: With a totally new styling package, the L or eight-cylinder running gear remained largely unchanged. The eight-cylinder was now larger than its six-cylinder counterpart and had a distinctive grille.

1933 Oldsmobile, Six, four-door sedan, HJE

I.D. DATA: Serial numbers were located on body pillar. Starting: Six-24001, Eight-7001. Ending: Six-50075, Eight-17600. Location of engine numbers was the same as serial number. Starting: N/A. Ending: N/A.

Model No.	Body Type & Seating	Price	Weight	Prod. Total
Six-Cylinder (F Series)				
33407	2-dr. Cpe.-3P	745	3045	1547
33428	2-dr. Spt. Cpe.-3P	780	3105	1738
33418	2-dr. Conv.-3P	825	3155	317
33401	2-dr. Sed.-5P	775	3195	3978
33431	2-dr. Tr. Sed.-5P	825	3205	5464
33409	4-dr. Sed.-5P	825	3215	7194
33419	4-dr. Tr. Sed.-5P	855	3255	5720
Eight-Cylinder (L-Series)				
33418	2-dr. Conv.-3P	925	3305	267
33407	2-dr. Cpe.-3P	845	3295	396
33428	2-dr. Spt. Cpe.-3P	880	3305	827
33401	2-dr. Sed.-5P	875	3320	203
33431	2-dr. Tr. Sed.-5P	895	3360	1901
33409	4-dr. Sed.-5P	925	3440	2639
33419	4-dr. Tr. Sed.-5P	955	3445	4357

ENGINE: [Six] Inline L-head. Cast iron block. B & S: 3-3/8 x 4-1/8 in. Disp.: 221 cu. in. C.R.: 5.3:1. Brake H.P.: 80. Main bearings: four. Valve lifters: mushroom. Carb.: downdraft, Stromberg EC-22. [Eight] Inline L-head. Cast iron block. B & S: 3 x 4-1/4 in. Disp.: 240 cu. in. C.R.: 5.5:1. Brake H.P.: 90. Main bearings: five. Valve lifters: mushroom. Carb.: downdraft, Stromberg EE-22.

CHASSIS: [F-Six] W.B.: 115 in. Height: 68-3/4 in. Frt/Rear Tread: 58-1/2/60-1/2 in. Tires: 17 x 5.50-4 ply. [L-Eight] W.B.: 119 in. Height: 68-3/4 in. Frt/Rear Tread: 58-1/2/60-1/2 in. Tires: 17 x 6.00-4 ply.

TECHNICAL: Manual/sliding gear transmission. Speeds: 3F/1R. Center, floor mounted controls. Dry-plate, single disc clutch. Shaft drive. 10-spline, semi-floating rear axle. Overall ratio: 4.56:1-standard. Bendix duo servo brakes. Four steel or wire wheels. Drivetrain options: 4.78:1 mountain gear ratio.

OPTIONS: Sidemount cover(s) ($14.00 pair). Bumper guards (3.50). Radio (Air Mate) (45.00). Heater (Deluxe) (14.95). Mirror clock (3.95). Cigar lighter (1.95). Seat covers (7.00). Spotlight (14.95). Gas tank lock (2.25). Deluxe gearshift ball (50 cents). Trunk (42.75).

HISTORICAL: Oldsmobile served as an "official car," not pace car, at Indianapolis 500. Calendar year sales and production: 36,072. Model year sales and production: 36,673. The general manager of Oldsmobile was I.J. Reuter.

1934

1934 Oldsmobile, Eight, four-door sedan, AA

OLDSMOBILE — SERIES F — SIX: Once again the basic Oldsmobile series was the six-cylinder F-series. Sales were on the rebound this year in general and Olds made a surge into sixth place in sales standings. Horsepower was upped slightly on the six and styling was mildly updated this year. GM officials seriously considered combining or doing away with either Olds, Buick or Pontiac, but by 1934 this notion had passed.

OLDSMOBILE — SERIES L — EIGHT: Despite the fact the six-cylinder models were far more popular and the engines were almost as powerful and even more dependable, Oldsmobile continued to offer the straight-eight powered L-series in 1934. The L-series continued to be a physically larger car than the F-series.

I.D. DATA: Serial numbers were on frame left side rail under hood. Starting: Six-51001; Eight-18001. Ending: Six-102103; Eight-43079. Engine numbers were on upper left corner of cylinder block. Starting: N/A. Ending: N/A.

1934 Oldsmobile, Six, four-door sedan, HJE

Model No.	Body Type & Seating	Price	Weight	Prod. Total
Series F, six-cyl.				
34457	2-dr. Bs. Cpe.-3P	650	2980	3728
* 206 additional sidemounted				
34478	2-dr. Spt. Cpe.-3P	695	3040	2135
* 236 additional sidemounted				
34451	2-dr. Sed.-5P	695	3055	4632
* 47 additional sidemounted				
34472	2-dr. Tr. Sed.-5P	725	3135	11,734
* 570 additional sidemounted				
34459	4-dr. Sed.-5P	755	3130	6492
* 522 additional sidemounted				
34469	4-dr. Tr. Sed.-5P	785	3210	19,099
* 1,682 additional sidemounted				

Model No.	Body Type & Seating	Price	Weight	Prod. Total
Series L, Eight-cyl.				
34418	2-dr. Conv.-3P	975	3350	537
* additional 378 sidemounted				
34407	2-dr. Bs. Cpe.-3P	885	3425	770
* additional 128 sidemounted				
34428	2-dr. Spt. Cpe.-3P	920	3395	1024
* additional 253 sidemounted				
34401	2-dr. Sed.-5P	895	3405	621
* additional 128 sidemounted				
34422	2-dr. Tr. Sed.-5P	925	3485	3816
* additional 475 sidemounted				
34409	4-dr. Sed.-5P	965	3490	3593
* additional 594 sidemounted				
34419	4-dr. Tr. Sed.-5P	995	3570	8857
* additional 3,445 sidemounted				

1934 Oldsmobile, Six, sport coupe, JAC

ENGINE: Inline. L-head. Six. Cast iron block. B & S: 3-5/16 x 4-1/8 in. Disp.: 213 cu. in. C.R.: 5.7:1. Brake H.P.: 84. Main bearings: four. Valve lifters: cylindrical. Carb.: downdraft single Stromberg EX22. Inline. L-head. Eight. Cast iron block. B & S: 3 x 4-1/4 in. Disp.: 240 cu. in. C.R.: 5.7:1. Brake H.P.: 90. Main bearings: five. Valve lifters: mushroom. Carb.: downdraft duplex Stromberg EE1.

CHASSIS: [Series F-Six] W.B.: 114 in. O.L.: 189-1/2 in. Height: 67-1/8 in. Frt/Rear Tread: 58 in. Tires: 5.50 x 17. [Series L-Eight] W.B.: 119 in. O.L.: 197-3/4 in. Height: 66-3/8 in. Frt/Rear Tread: 59/60-1/2 in. Tires: 16 x 7.00, four-ply.

TECHNICAL: Synchronizing/helical transmission. Speeds: 3F/1R. Floor mounted, center controls. Dry plate clutch. Shaft drive. Semi-floating rear axle, 10-spline. Overall ratio: [Series F] 4.56:1 [Series L] 4.78:1 Bendix hydraulic brakes on four wheels. Demountable steel spoke wheels.

1934 Oldsmobile, Eight, convertible coupe, HJE

OPTIONS: Bumper guards ($3.50). Radio (air mate 47.95, air chief 62.50). Heater (14.95). Clock (mirror watch 30-hour 3.95). Cigar lighter (1.50). Seat covers (standard 9.95; deluxe 11.95). Spotlight (14.95). Locking gas cap (2.25). Deluxe gearshift ball (50 cents). License plate frames (2.45). Luggage (43.75). Safety glass all windows (18.00). Group A (bumpers, spare tire covers, wheel locks and spring covers) (36.00). Group B (double windshield wiper, dual trumpet horns and automatic choke) (12.50). Group C (oversize tires, wheel trim moldings and spare tire cover) (32.00). Dealer installed Group X (right-hand inside sun visor, cigar lighter, gearshift ball, bumper guards) (7.50). Dealer installed Group Y (cigar lighter, gearshift ball, bumper guards, license plate frames, clock and wheel trim moldings) (23.95).

HISTORICAL: Calendar year sales and production: 82,150. Model year sales and production: 79,814. The general manager of Oldsmobile was C.L. McCuen. Late in 1934 Olds began a major expansion effort. A total of 2-1/2 million dollars was budgeted for equipment and major assembly line improvements. Shipping facilities also underwent renovation.

1935

1935 Oldsmobile, Six, four-door touring sedan, DC

OLDSMOBILE — SERIES F — SIX: A complete restyle came on the outside for 1935, but the mechanical nature of things stayed about the same. The F-series remained the better seller of the two models offered. A redesigned cylinder head boosted the six-cylinder output to 90 hp. Although smaller than the eight-cylinder, the main distinguishing feature of the six was its distinctive front grille.

1935 Oldsmobile, Eight, two-door sedan, DC

OLDSMOBILE — SERIES L — EIGHT: The straight-eight L-series continued to offer a full line of body styles in 1935. As in the six-cylinder model a redesigned cylinder head boosted horsepower taking the eight to the even 100 mark. Olds offered major suspension changes the previous year and the so-called "knee action" system was further fine tuned this model year.

I.D. DATA: Serial numbers were located on frame left side rail under hood. Starting: 103001-Six; 44001-Eight. Ending: 193468-Six; 73977-Eight. Engine numbers were on upper left corner of cylinder block. Starting: N/A. Ending: N/A.

Model No.	Body Type & Seating	Price	Weight	Prod. Total
Series F, 6-cyl.				
353867	2-dr. Conv.-3P	800	3155	1598
353607C	2-dr. Clb. Cpe.-3P	725	3115	200
353607	2-dr. Bus. Cpe.-3P	675	3110	8468
353657	2-dr. Spt. Cpe.-3P	725	3150	2885
353601	2-dr. Sed.-5P	755	3225	14,785
353611	2-dr. Tr. Sed.-5P	765	3235	19,821
353609	4-dr. Sed.-5P	790	3285	13,009
353619	4-dr. Tr. Sed.-5P	820	3295	34,647

* There is some indication Olds built a handful of six-cylinder station wagons this year but no production records exist on these cars.

Model No.	Body Type & Seating	Price	Weight	Prod. Total
Series L, 8-cyl.				
353867	2-dr. Conv.-3P	950	3390	910
353807C	2-dr. Clb. Cpe.-3P	870	3340	74
353807	2-dr. Bs. Cpe.-3P	860	3335	1226
353857	2-dr. Spt. Cpe.-3P	895	3380	959
353801	2-dr. Sed.-5P	895	3480	870
353811	2-dr. Tr. Sed.-5P	900	3485	4862
353809	4-dr. Sed.-5P	940	3530	2976
353819	4-dr. Tr. Sed.-5P	970	3545	18,058

ENGINE: [Series F] Inline. Six. L-head. Cast iron block. B & S: 3-5/16 x 4-1/8 in. Disp.: 213 cu. in. C.R.: 6.0:1. Brake H.P.: 90 @ 3400 R.P.M. Main bearings: four thin-wall. Valve lifters: cylindrical. Carb.: single, downdraft Stromberg EX22. Torque: 165 lb.-ft. @ 2000 R.P.M. [Series L] Inline. L-head. Eight. Cast iron block. B & S: 3 x 4-1/4 in. Disp.: 240 cu. in. C.R.: 6.2:1. Brake H.P.: 100 @ 3400 R.P.M. Main bearings: five. Valve lifters: mushroom. Carb.: duplex downdraft, Stromberg EE1. Torque: 182 lb.-ft. @ 1800 R.P.M.

CHASSIS: [Series F] W.B.: 115 in. O.L.: 188-11/32 in. Height: 67 in. Frt/Rear Tread: 58/59 in. Tires: 6.25 x 16 - four ply. [Series L] W.B.: 121 in. O.L.: 193-23/32 in. Height: 67-7/16 in. Frt/Rear Tread: 58/59 in. Tires: 7.00 x 16.

TECHNICAL: Manual, sliding gear transmission. Speeds: 3F/1R. Center, floor mounted controls. Dry plate clutch. Shaft drive. Ten-spline, semi-floating rear axle. Overall ratio: 4.44:1. Bendix-hydraulic brakes on four wheels. Demountable, steel spoke wheels.

1935 Oldsmobile, Six, station wagon, HJE

OPTIONS: Fender skirts ($11.50, lacquered and installed). Radio (standard w/antenna 51.70; deluxe w/antenna 66.25). Heater (standard 13.90; deluxe 18.65). Clock (electric 11.50). Cigar lighter (1.50). Spotlight (17.95). Right taillamp for six (5.50). Luggage compartment light (2.00). License plate frames (2.95). Defroster (3.25). Home battery charger (7.95). Fender markers (1.25). Mirror watch (4.00). Insect screen (1.50). Luggage compartment floor mat (1.75). Safety glass all windows (10.00). Group A — factory installed (bumpers, guards, spare tire and spring covers) (45.00). Group B — factory installed (dual horns, double windshield wiper and automatic choke) six-cylinder only (12.50). Group C — factory installed (oversize tires and tubes) (30.00). Group X — dealer installed (cigar lighter, gearshift ball, right-hand sun visor, mirror clock) (8.00).

1935 Oldsmobile, Eight, club coupe, OCW

HISTORICAL: Oldsmobile added its "turret top" this model year. Calendar year sales and production: 183,152. Model year sales and production: 126,768. Oldsmobile purchased the modern Durant Lansing, Michigan, plant and this became the new home of Lansing's Fisher Body operations. Olds then took over former Fisher Body floor space within the main Oldsmobile assembly plant.

1936

1936 Oldsmobile, Six, two-door sedan, AA

OLDSMOBILE — SERIES F — SIX: A mild restyle greeted Olds buyers this model year. Door handles were located from the front of the doors to the rear this year giving an easy distinguishing point from 1935 models. Headlights rose higher on the front end sheet metal this year. The six-cylinder continued as the most popular Oldsmobile. Little changed on this series mechanically.

OLDSMOBILE — SERIES L — EIGHT: The L-series remained physically larger automobiles than their six-cylinder counterparts — but styling was similar. The quickest way to distinguish the two models was in the differing grille design. Attractive fender mounted parking lamps came as standard equipment on L-series cars in 1936. Chassis-wise and mechanically, few changes were made in this group of cars over 1935 models.

1936 Oldsmobile, Six, touring sedan, OCW

I.D. DATA: Serial numbers were located on frame left side rail under hood. Starting: Six (F) — 200001; Eight (L) — 100001. Ending: Six (F) 352356; Eight (L) — 139925. Engine numbers were on upper left corner of cylinder block. Starting: Six (F) — 506001; Eight (L) — 202001. Ending: Six (F) 670000; Eight (L) — 250000.

Model No.	Body Type & Seating	Price	Weight	Prod. Total
Series F, 6-cyl.				
363667	2-dr. Conv.-3P	805	3109	2073
363607	2-dr. Bs. Cpe.-3P	665	3019	20,346
363657	2-dr. Spt. Cpe.-3P	730	3054	2831
363601	2-dr. Sed.-5P	735	3144	13,143
363611	2-dr. Tr. Sed.-5P	755	3155	46,373
363609	4-dr. Sed.-5P	795	3179	4082
363619	4-dr. Tr. Sed.-5P	820	3194	69,443
Series L, 8-cyl.				
363857	2-dr. Conv.-3P	935	3321	914
363807	2-dr. Bs. Cpe.-3P	810	3231	2181
363857	2-dr. Spt. Cpe.-3P	845	3261	959
363801	2-dr. Sed.-5P	850	3376	237
363811	2-dr. Tr. Sed.-5P	870	3385	6626
363809	4-dr. Sed.-5P	910	3401	406
363819	4-dr. Tr. Sed.-5P	935	3421	29,373

ENGINE: [Series F] Inline, L-head. Six. Cast iron block. B & S: 3-5/16 x 4-1/8 in. Disp.: 213 cu. in. C.R.: 6.0:1. Brake H.P.: 90 @ 3400 R.P.M. Main bearings: four. Valve lifters: cylindrical. Carb.: single downdraft. [Series L] Inline, L-head. Eight. Cast iron block. B & S: 3 x 4-1/4 in. Disp.: 240 cu. in. C.R.: 6.2:1. Brake H.P.: 100 @ 3400 R.P.M. Main bearings: five. Valve lifters: mushroom. Carb.: duplex, downdraft.

1936 Oldsmobile, Eight, convertible, HJE

CHASSIS: [Series F] W.B.: 115 in. O.L.: 188-13/16 in. Height: 67 in. Frt/Rear Tread: 58/59 in. Tires: 16 x 6.50. [Series L] W.B.: 121 in. O.L.: 194-3/16 in. Height: 67 in. Frt/Rear Tread: 58/59 in. Tires: 16 x 7.00.

OPTIONS: Fender skirts ($10.00 pair). Bumper guards (2.25 pair). Radio (deluxe 67.50; standard. 54.50). Heater (deluxe 16.75; standard 11.95). Clock (electric dash 11.50; mirror 4.75). Seat covers (9.80). Spotlight (15.95). Right-hand tail-lamp (for F series) (4.50). Wheel trim rings (13.55). Defrosting fan (5.25). Luggage compartment light (1.75). Luggage carrier (10.00). Visor vanity mirror (1.00). Jack (3.00). Exhaust deflector (1.00). Matching gearshift ball/cigar lighter (1.50). Grille insect shields (1.50). Home battery charger (7.95). Fender markers (2.50 pair). Luggage compartment mat (1.75). License plate frames (2.45).

HISTORICAL: Calendar year sales and production: 187,638. Model year sales and production: 200,546. C.L. McCuen was general manager of Oldsmobile.

In 1936 Olds began a vast $6 million expansion effort in Lansing.

1937

1937 Oldsmobile, Six, two-door sedan, DC

OLDSMOBILE — SERIES F — SIX: A complete restyle welcomed buyers of Oldsmobile in 1937. Once again the F-series, or six-cylinder models, were responsible for most of the sales. Less wood could be found on this new series of Fisher bodies this year. The six-cylinder had eight less inches of wheelbase. Displacement was upped slightly on the tried and true flathead six-cylinder and horsepower was increased by 5 to 95 overall.

OLDSMOBILE — SERIES L — EIGHT: A distinctive new front styling package made the Olds straight-eight series one of the most noticed cars on the road. Rolling on a wheelbase of 124 inches, cubic inches on the L series went up to 257. Horsepower went to 110.

1937 Oldsmobile, Eight, business coupe, HJE

I.D. DATA: Serial numbers were on frame left side rail under hood. Starting: [Eight] California-CL-140001; Linden, N.J.-LL-195001; Lansing, MI-L-146001. Ending: [Eight] California-CL-143240; Linden, N.J.-LL-196512; Lansing, MI-L-186544.

Starting: [Sixes] California built cars-CF-35001; Linden, N.J. built-LF-195001; Lansing, MI-F-372001. Ending: [Sixes] California-CF-364520; Linden, N.J.-LF-544720; Lansing, MI-F-503300. Engine numbers were on upper left corner of cylinder block. Starting: [Six] 670001; [Eight] 250001. Ending: [Six] 818948; [Eight] 295824.

Model No.	Body Type & Seating	Price	Weight	Prod. Total
Series F, 6-cyl.				
373667	2-dr. Conv.-3P	965	3295	1619
373627B	2-dr. Bs. Cpe.-3P	810	3220	13,908
373627	2-dr. Clb. Cpe.-3P	870	3225	7426
373601	2-dr. Sed.-5P	870	3275	9664
373611	2-dr. Tr. Sed.-5P	895	3285	38,043
373609	4-dr. Sed.-5P	920	3310	4020
373619	4-dr. Tr. Sed.-5P	945	3395	62,933
Series L, 8-cyl.				
373867	2-dr. Conv.-3P	1080	3450	728
373827	2-dr. Clb. Cpe.-3P	985	3405	2302
373827B	2-dr. Bs. Cpe.-3P	925	3395	2150
373811	2-dr. Sed.-5P	985	3480	5818
373801	2-dr. Tr. Sed.-5P	1010	3480	398
373809	4-dr. Sed.-5P	1035	3510	457
373819	4-dr. Tr. Sed.-5P	1060	3525	30,465

1937 Oldsmobile, Eight, four-door touring sedan w/trunk, DC

ENGINE: [Series F] Inline, L-head. Six. Cast iron block. B & S: 3-7/16 x 4-1/8 in. Disp.: 230 cu. in. C.R.: 6.1:1. Brake H.P.: 95 @ 3400 R.P.M. Main bearings: four. Valve lifters: mushroom. Carb.: single downdraft with automatic choke. [Series L] Inline, L-head. Eight. Cast iron block. B & S: 3-1/4 x 3-7/8 in. Disp.: 257 cu. in. C.R.: 6.2:1. Brake H.P.: 110 @ 3600 R.P.M. Main bearings: five. Valve lifters: mushroom. Carb.: duplex downdraft with automatic choke.

CHASSIS: [Series F] W.B.: 117 in. O.L.: 192-13/16 in. Frt/Rear Tread: 58/59 in. Tires: 16 x 6.50. [Series L] W.B.: 124 in. O.L.: 199-9/16 in. Frt/RearTread: 58/59 in. Tires: 16 x 7.00.

TECHNICAL: Manual, sliding gear transmission. Speeds: 3F/1R. Center, floor mounted controls. Single plate clutch. Shaft drive. Spiral bevel, semi-floating rear axle. Overall ratio: 4.375:1. Triple sealed hydraulic brakes on four wheels. Steel wheels.

1937 Oldsmobile, Six, convertible, OCW

OPTIONS: Single sidemount ($50.00). Bumper guards (3.00 pair). Radio (standard 53.00; deluxe with twin speakers 66.50). Heater (standard 13.95; deluxe 18.75). Clock (header board clock 4.25; electric clock 12.25). Cigar lighter (1.75). Seat covers (11.80). Spotlight (17.95). Dual windshield defroster (8.25). Fan defroster (6.25). Wheel trim rings (10.75).

Wheel discs (12.75). Deluxe steering wheel (12.75). Luggage compartment mat (1.75). Luggage compartment light (1.25). Fender markers (1.25). Fog lamps (6.25). Insect window screens (2.00). Winter grille cover (1.25). Winter radiator shutter controlled from instrument panel (11.35).

HISTORICAL: The safety automatic transmission was an innovation introduced late in the 1937 model year by Oldsmobile. Initially it was offered on L series cars. It was the first column shifter offered by Olds. Calendar year sales and production: 212,767. Model year sales and production: 200,546. C.L. McCuen was the general manager of Oldsmobile.

Olds began work on a new customer drive-away center at its main plant in Lansing.

1938

1938 Oldsmobile, Six, four-door sedan, AA

OLDSMOBILE — SERIES F — SIX: Oldsmobile continued its two series format in 1938 with the F, or six-cylinder, continuing to be the division sales leader. This would mark the final year for the two series format. New front end treatments were found on both series and the F-models offered a slightly cleaner front end package. Mechanically things stayed almost exactly the same, the six powerplant developed 95 horsepower.

OLDSMOBILE — SERIES L — EIGHT: The straight-eight, an Olds fixture since 1932, continued in 1938. Sales were down this year in general and Olds was in the industry's seventh sales slot. Both the six- and eight-cylinder models offered an unusual and attractive dash layout this year.

1938 Oldsmobile, Eight, four-door sedan, AA

I.D. DATA: Serial numbers were located on frame left side rail under hood. Starting: [Series F] California built-CF-504001; Linden, N.J. built-LF-545001; Lansing, MI built-F-600001. Starting: [Series L] California built: CL187001; Linden, N.J. built-LL-197001; Lansing, MI built-L-212001. Ending: [Series F] California built-CF-510598; Linden, N.J. built-LF-551236; Lansing, MI built-F-662212. Ending: [Series L] California built-CL-188760; Linden, N.J. built-LL-198759 and Lansing, MI built-L-228126. Engine numbers were on upper left corner of cylinder block. Starting: F-series: 828001; L-series: 296001. Ending: F-series: 905000; L-series: 298859. On engine codes any engine with C-prefix first letter was California built. F, L or G letter prefix indicates Lansing production. LF, LG or LL numbers indicate Linden, New Jersey, built engine.

Model No.	Body Type & Seating	Price	Weight	Prod. Total
Series F, 6-cyl.				
383667	2-dr. Conv.-3P	1046	3360	1184
383627B	2-dr. Bs. Cpe.-3P	873	3205	8538
383627	2-dr. Clb. Cpe.-3P	929	3215	5632
383601	2-dr. Sed.-5P	919	3275	3975
383611	2-dr. Tr. Sed.-5P	944	3285	22,390
383609	4-dr. Sed.-5P	970	3290	1477
383619	4-dr. Tr. Sed.-5P	995	3305	36,484
Series L, 8-cyl.				
383867	2-dr. Conv.-3P	1163	3530	475
383827B	2-dr. Bs. Cpe.-3P	989	3400	1098
383827	2-dr. Clb. Cpe.-3P	1035	3410	1136
383801	2-dr. Sed.-5P	1030	3275	143
383811	2-dr. Tr. Sed.-5P	1056	3287	1948
383809	4-dr. Sed.-5P	1081	3290	200
383819	4-dr. Tr. Sed.-5P	1107	3295	14,987

ENGINE: [Series F] Inline, L-head. Six. Cast iron block. B & S: 3-7/16 x 4-1/8 in. Disp.: 230 cu. in. C.R.: 6.1:1. Brake H.P.: 95 @ 3400 R.P.M. Main bearings: four. Valve lifters: mushroom. Carb.: single downdraft, automatic choke. [Series L] Inline, L-head. Eight. Cast iron block. B & S: 3-1/4 x 3-7/8 in. Disp.: 257 cu. in. C.R.: 6.2:1. Brake H.P.: 110 @ 3600 R.P.M. Main bearings: five. Valve lifters: mushroom. Carb.: duplex downdraft with automatic choke.

CHASSIS: [Series F] W.B.: 117 in. O.L.: 190-7/16 in. Frt/Rear Tread: 58/59 in. Tires: 16 x 6.50. [Series L] W.B.: 124 in. O.L.: 197-7/8 in. Frt/Rear Tread: 58/59 in. Tires: 16 x 7.00.

TECHNICAL: Sliding gear synchromesh transmission. Speeds: 3F/1R. Floor mounted center gearshift, column mounted on optional semi-automatic. Single plate clutch. Shaft drive. Spiral bevel, semi-floating rear axle. Overall ratio: standard: 4.375:1; semi-automatic: 3.55:1. Cast iron drum, hydraulic brakes on four wheels. Pressed steel wheels. Wheel size: 16 x 4.50. Drivetrain options: Safety automatic transmission ($100.00).

1938 Oldsmobile, Eight, convertible, OCW

OPTIONS: Dual sidemount ($65.00). Bumper guards (2.00 each). Radio (standard radio 53.00; deluxe radio 66.50). Heater (standard hot water heater 14.45; deluxe hot water heater 19.95). Clock (header board clock 12.25, electric clock 15.00). Cigar lighter (1.75). Radio antenna (turret top antenna 7.00). Seat covers (standard 12.95; deluxe 16.95). Dual windshield defroster (8.25). Defroster fan (4.40). Gearshift ball (50 cents). Wheel chrome mouldings (10.75). Exhaust deflector (1.00). License plate frames (2.75). Luggage compartment mat (1.75). Luggage compartment light (1.25). Fender markers (3.25). Fog lamps (6.25). Winter grille covers (1.00). Locking gas cap (1.50).

HISTORICAL: An air-cooled battery introduced this model year, Safety Automatic Transmission (shared with Buick) continued this model year. Calendar year sales and production: 93,706. Model year sales and production: 99,951. C.L. McCuen was the general manager for Oldsmobile.

Manufacturing efforts for cars and engines strengthened in California and New Jersey, though most Oldsmobiles continued to be built in Lansing, Michigan.

1939

1939 Oldsmobile, Six, club coupe, JAC

OLDSMOBILE — SERIES 60 — SIX: The F-series remained the bottom line Oldsmobile for the model year and as all 1939s it was completely restyled. The F-series lineup was restricted to just four body styles. A pair of coupes, a two-door and four-door were offered with no open cars in the series. The wheelbase of the F-series came down to 115 inches and a smaller displacement six-cylinder motor was fitted.

OLDSMOBILE — G-SERIES 70 — SIX: The new Oldsmobile for 1939, was actually a combination of two previous Olds offerings. Essentially the G-series cars were the larger (previously L-series) chassis fitted with the smaller (F-series) powerplant. For 1939, this automotive group was fitted with a slightly larger six-cylinder motor than F-series cars. Body styles were shared with L-series cars and a convertible could be found in both groups.

OLDSMOBILE — L-SERIES 80 — EIGHT: The top line Olds was again the straight-eight powered L-series. This was the lone year Olds would use the 80 series designation. Despite a complete external styling change, mechanics remained largely unchanged on L series cars. Interior space was increased on all 1939 models and once again the semi-automatic ("Safety Automatic") transmission was offered. A column-mounted shifter was added for standard shift cars this year.

I.D. DATA: Serial numbers were on frame left side rail under hood. Starting: [Series F (60)] California built-CF-511001; Linden, N.J. built-FL-551301. Lansing, MI built-F-663001. Starting: [Series G (70)] California built-CG-10001; Linden, N.J. built-LG-10001; Lansing, MI built-G-300001. Starting: [Series L (80)] California built-CL-189001; Linden, N.J. built-LL-199001; Lansing, MI built-L-228201. Ending: [Series F (60)] California built-CF-514115; Linden, N.J. built-LF-555385; Lansing, MI built-F-702588. Ending: [Series G (70)] California built-CG-15325; Linden, N.J. built-LG-107782; Lansing, MI built-G-354522. Ending: [Series L (80)] California built-CL-160358; Linden, N.J. built-LL-201119; Lansing, MI built-L-241850. Engine numbers were on upper left corner of cylinder block. Starting: [Series F (60)] 905001; [Series G (70)] 10001; [Series L (80)] 316001. Ending: [Series F (60)] 952701; [Series G (70)] 78471; [Series L (80)] 333127. Engines with first prefix letter C - California built. Engine with first prefix letter L - Linden, New Jersey. Engines with just single prefix letter built in Lansing, Michigan.

1939 Oldsmobile, Eight, convertible coupe, JAC

Model No.	Body Type & Seating	Price	Weight	Prod. Total
Series F (60)				
393527B	2-dr. Bs. Cpe.-3P	777	2870	5565
393527	2-dr. Clb. Cpe.-3P	833	2915	2273
393511	2-dr. Sed.-5P	838	2965	16,910
393519	4-dr. Sed.-5P	889	3000	15,948
Series G (70)				
393667	2-dr. Conv.-3P	1045	3230	1714
393627B	2-dr. Bs. Cpe.-3P	840	3040	5211
393627	2-dr. Clb. Cpe.-3P	891	3080	4795
393611	2-dr. Sed.-5P	901	3140	19,427
* additional 17 built w/sun roof				
393619	4-dr. Sed.-5P	952	3180	38,145
* additional 79 built w/sun roof				
Series L (80)				
393887	2-dr. Conv.-3P	1119	3390	472
393827B	2-dr. Bs. Cpe.-3P	920	3190	738
393827	2-dr. Clb. Cpe.-3P	971	3230	1149
393811	2-dr. Sed.-5P	992	3290	1564
* additional 2 built w/sun roof				
393819	4-dr. Sed.-5P	1043	3340	12,242
* additional 84 built w sun roof				

1939 Oldsmobile, Six, two-door sedan, AA

ENGINE: [Series F (60)] Inline, L-head. Six. Cast iron block. B & S: 3-7/16 x 3-7/8 in. Disp.: 215 cu. in. C.R.: 6.2:1. Brake H.P.: 90 @ 3400 R.P.M. Main bearings: four. Valve lifters: steel spherical mushroom. Carb.: 1-1/4 single downdraft with automatic choke. [Series F (70)] Inline, L-head. Six. Cast iron block. B & S: 3-7/16 x 4-1/8 in. Disp.: 230 cu. in. C.R.: 6.1:1. Brake H.P.: 95 @ 3400 R.P.M. Main bearings: four. Valve lifters: steel spherical mushroom. Carb.: 1-1/4 single downdraft with automatic choke. [Series L (80)] Inline, L-head. Eight. Cast iron block. B & S: 3-1/4 x 3-7/8 in. Disp.: 257 cu. in. C.R.: 6.1:1. Brake H.P.: 110 @ 3400 R.P.M. Main bearings: five. Valve lifters: mushroom. Carb.: 1-1/4 dual downdraft with automatic choke.

1939 Oldsmobile, Six, four-door sedan, OCW

CHASSIS: [Series F (60)] W.B.: 115 in. O.L.: 189 in. Height: 66 in. Frt/Rear Tread: 58/59 in. Tires: 6.00 x 16. [Series G (70)] W.B.: 120 in. O.L.: 197 in. Height: 65-3/4 in. Frt/Rear Tread: 58/59 in. Tires: 6.00 x 16. [Series L (80)] W.B.: 120 in. O.L.: 197 in. Height: 65-3/4 in. Frt/Rear Tread: 58/59 in. Tires: 6.50 x 16.

TECHNICAL: Selective, sliding gear transmission. Speeds: 3F/1R. Steering column controls. Single dry plate clutch. Shaft drive. Semi-floating rear axle. Overall ratio: 4.55:1. Hydraulic internal expanding brakes on four wheels. Steel wheels. Drivetrain options: Safety automatic transmission ($75.00).

OPTIONS: Fender skirts (streamline fender panels $15.00). Bumper guards (2.50 pair). Radio (standard 46.00; deluxe 55.00; super deluxe push button 61.00). Heater (standard hot water 13.95; deluxe hot water 18.45). Clock (glovebox 30-hour wind 4.25; electric 11.25). Cigar lighter (2.00). Radio antenna (cowl antenna 2.00). Seat covers (San Toy seat covers 11.95). Spotlight (14.50). Rear seat heater (19.95). Dual defroster (8.00). Defroster fan (4.25). Visor vanity mirror (1.00). Deluxe wheel discs (12.00). Wheel trim rings (8.50). Exhaust deflector (1.00). License plate frames (2.75). Luggage compartment light (1.25). Panel and glovebox light (1.75). Fog lamps (10.50). Winter grille cover (1.00). Locking gas cap (1.50). Backup lights (6.00). Deluxe driving lights (10.95). Fender marker lights (6.00). Windshield washer (4.75). Sunshine Turret Top (37.50). Whitewall tires (16.25). Oversize tires (20.00). Deluxe steering wheel (12.50). Oil filter (5.00).

HISTORICAL: Olds shared an innovative but rare factory sunroof with several other divisions. Runningboards were a no charge delete option for the first time this year. Calendar year sales and production: 158,560. Model year sales and production: 137,249. The general manager of Oldsmobile was C.L. McCuen.

1940

1940 Oldsmobile, 60, station wagon, JAC

OLDSMOBILE — SPECIAL — SERIES 60 — SIX: The 60 series Oldsmobile was again the bottom line in a three series lineup. Sales reached an all-time high in 1940. The 60 series grew nine inches over its counterpart in 1939. A convertible was added to the model lineup for 1940 and for the first time an official station wagon was added to factory literature of the day.

1940 Oldsmobile, 70, coupe, DC

OLDSMOBILE — DYNAMIC — SERIES 70 — SIX: This model year the 70 series did not share a wheelbase with the top of the line 90 series — but instead rolled on a 120 wheelbase of its own. This year the 95 horsepower six-cylinder engine was shared with 60 series models. Five basic body styles were to be found here: a pair of coupes, two-door and four-door sedans and a convertible.

OLDSMOBILE — CUSTOM CRUISER — SERIES 90 — EIGHT: Oldsmobile again got serious in the luxury sales race in 1940 with its 90 series models. The numerical designation was raised from the previous year's 80 tag. A buy here was the only way to obtain an eight-cylinder Oldsmobile. An exclusive 124-inch wheelbase was used. Just four 90 series models were offered. Two open cars were offered including the two-door convertible and the super rare phaeton. Also available were a club coupe and four-door sedan.

I.D. DATA: Serial numbers were on frame left side rail under hood. Starting: [Series 60] California built-CF-515001; Linden, N.J.-built-LF-556001; Lansing, MI-built-F-703001. [Series 70] California built-CG-16001; Linden: N.J. built-LG-108001; Lansing, MI-built-G-35501. [Series 90] California built-CL-190501; Linden, N.J.-built-LL-202001; Lansing, MI-L-242001. Ending: [Series 60] California built-CF-519651; Linden, N.J.-built-LF-563473; Lansing, MI-built-F-758579. [Series 70] California built-CG-21070; Linden, N.J.-built-LG-117596; Lansing, MI-built-G-417928. [Series 90] California built-CL-192700; Linden, N.J.-built-LL-205267; Lansing, MI-built-L-281191. Engine numbers were on upper left corner of cylinder block. Starting: [Series 60] 79001; [Series 70] 79001; [Series 90] 334001. Ending: [Series 60] 224652, [Series 70] 224652; [Series 90] 378661. Engine number with the first prefix letter C were California built. Engine numbers with the first prefix letter L were Linden, New Jersey, built. Engine numbers with just a single prefix letter were Lansing, Michigan, built.

1940 Oldsmobile, 90, four-door sedan, TVB

Model No.	Body Type & Seating	Price	Weight	Prod. Total
F-Series (Special) - 60				
403567	2-dr. Conv.-3P	1021	3150	1347
403527B	2-dr. Bs. Cpe.-3P	807	2950	2752
403527	2-dr. Clb. Cpe.-3P	848	2995	11,583
403511	2-dr. Sed.-5P	853	3045	29,220
403519	4-dr. Sed.-5P	899	3060	24,422
403565	4-dr. St. Wgn.-6P	1042	3542	633
G-Series (Dynamic) - 70				
403667	2-dr. Conv.-3P	1045	3290	1070
403627B	2-dr. Bs. Cpe.-3P	865	3090	4337
403627	2-dr. Clb. Cpe.-3P	901	3130	8505
403611	2-dr. Sed.-5P	912	3190	22,486
403619	4-dr. Sed.-5P	963	3230	42,467
L-Series (Custom Cruiser) - 90				
403967	2-dr. Conv.-3P	1222	3440	290
403929	2-dr. Phae.-5P	1570	3670	50
403927C	2-dr. Clb. Cpe.-3P	1069	3280	10,243
403919	4-dr. Sed.-5P	1131	3390	33,075

ENGINE: [Series 60 & 70] Inline, L-head. Six. Cast iron block. B & S: 3-7/16 x 4-1/8 in. Disp.: 230 cu. in. C.R.: 6.1:1. Brake H.P.: 95 @ 3200 R.P.M. Main bearings: four. Valve lifters: mushroom. Carb.: single downdraft with automatic choke. [Series 90] Inline, L-head. Eight. Cast iron block. B & S: 3-1/4 x 3-7/8 in. Disp.: 257 cu. in. C.R.: 6.2:1. Brake H.P.: 110 @ 3200 R.P.M. Main bearings: five. Valve lifters: mushroom. Carb.: dual downdraft with automatic choke.

CHASSIS: [Series 60-F] W.B.: 116 in. O.L.: 197-3/4 in. Height: 65 in. Frt/Rear Tread: 58/59 in. Tires: 16 x 6.00. [Series 70-G] W.B.: 120 in. O.L.: 199-3/4 in. Height: 65 in. Frt/Rear Tread: 58/59 in. Tires: 16 x 6.50. [Series 90-L] W.B.: 124 in. O.L.: 210-3/4 in. Height: 65 in. Frt/Rear Tread: 58/59 in. Tires: 15 x 7.00.

TECHNICAL: Manual, synchromesh sliding gear transmission. Speeds: 3F/1R. Column shifted. Single plate clutch. Shaft drive. Semi-floating, hypoid rear axle. Overall Ratio: [Series 60] 4.1:1; [Series 70 & 90] 4.3:1. Hydraulic brakes with cast iron drums on four wheels. Pressed steel wheels. Drivetrain options: automatic transmission: HydraMatic ($100.00).

1940 Oldsmobile, 90, convertible sedan, OCW

OPTIONS: Fender skirts ($15.00). Bumper guards (2.00 pair). Radio (standard-45.00; deluxe-56.60). Heater (dash-13.45; defroster-8.25; underseat-19.75: defroster-10.75). Clock (30-hour hand wind-5.50; electric with automatic glovebox light-12.90). Cigar lighter (2.00). Seat covers (12.85). Deluxe steering wheel (12.50). Vanity visor mirror (1.00). Wheel trim rings (8.00). Directional signals (9.85). Fog lamp (5.45 each). Back-up lights (6.00 pair). License frames (2.75 pair). Exhaust deflector (1.00). Trunk light (1.25). Winter grille cover (1.00). Locking gas cap (1.50).

1940 Oldsmobile, 90, convertible coupe, JAC

HISTORICAL: A combined effort between Olds and GM engineers produced the first HydraMatic equipped cars this model year. Although certainly not the first automatic transmission, probably the best unit to this date. Calendar year sales and production: 215,028. Model year sales and production: 192,692. The general manager of Oldsmobile was S.E. Skinner.

1941

1941 Oldsmobile, 66, station wagon, AA

OLDSMOBILE — SPECIAL — SERIES 60 — SIX OR EIGHT: Olds moved up to sixth place this model year with its three series format. The major change this year found a six-cylinder or eight-cylinder version of each series offered. The special series was a price leader that offered a pair of coupes, two- and four-door sedans, the rare station wagon and a convertible coupe. A deluxe equipment package was also offered in this long running series.

1941 Oldsmobile, 98, coupe, OCW

1941 Oldsmobile, 98, convertible, OCW

OLDSMOBILE — SERIES 90 — SIX OR EIGHT: Just a pair of fastback sedan body styles were offered in this series for 1941. A wheelbase of 125 inches was shared with the 90 series. A deluxe equipment package was offered here. The top of the line Oldsmobile in 1941 came in four body styles. Rarest of these cars was the phaeton, which was offered by Oldsmobile only in 1940 and 1941. Joining the four-door open car was a convertible coupe, club coupe and four-door sedan. This was the only year in Olds history that a Model 96 — a 90 series car with a six-cylinder engine was available. Few were sold. HydraMatic was a popular option on 90 series cars this year.

1941 Oldsmobile, 78, four-door sedan, OCW

I.D. DATA: Serial numbers were on frame left side rail under hood. Starting: [Series 60] California built-66C or 68C-1001; Linden, NJ built-66L or 68L-1001; Lansing, MI built-66 or 68-1001. [Series 70] California built-76C or 78C-1001; Linden, NJ built-76L or 78L-1001; Lansing, MI built-76 or 78-1001. [Series 90] California built-96C or 98C-1001; Linden, NJ built 96L or 98L-1001; Lansing, MI built-96 or 98-1001. Ending: [Series 60] California built-66C or 68C-8827; Linden, NJ built-66L or 68L-8622; Lansing, MI built-66 or 68-8817. [Series 70] California built-76C or 78C-6843; Linden, NJ built-76L or 78L-10426; Lansing, MI built-76 or 78-47617. [Series 90] California built-96C or 98C-3352; Linden, NJ built-96L or 98L-13195; Lansing, MI built-96 or 98-24679. Engine numbers were on upper left corner of cylinder block. Starting: [Six-cylin-

der] 225001; [Eight] 37901. Ending: [Six-cylinder] 422090; [Eight] 449095. Engines with one letter prefix (F, L or G) Lansing, Michigan. Engine with two letters prefix with first letter C built in California, with first letter L built in Linden, New Jersey.

Model No.	Body Type & Seating	Price	Weight	Prod. Total
66 Models				
413567	2-dr. Conv.-3P	1048	3355	2833
413527B	2-dr. Bs. Cpe.-5P	852	3145	6433
413527	2-dr. Clb. Cpe.-3P	893	3185	23,796
413511	2-dr. Sed.-5P	898	3190	32,475
413519	4-dr. Sed.-5P	945	3230	37,820
4135SW	4-dr. SW.-6P	1176	NA	NA
68 Models				
413567	2-dr. Conv.-3P	1089	3445	776
413527B	2-dr. Bs. Cpe.-5P	893	3260	188
413527	2-dr. Clb. Cpe.-3P	935	3330	2684
413511	2-dr. Sed.-5P	940	3335	3878
413519	4-dr. Sed. 5P	987	3390	6009
4135SW	4-dr. SW.-6P	1217	NA	NA
76 Models				
4136278	2-dr. Cpe.-3P	908	3315	353
413627	2-dr. Clb. Sed.-5P	954	3320	std. 41,938
				dlx. 6947
413609	4-dr. Sed.-5P	1010	3390	std. 31,074
				dlx. 9645
78 Models				
413627B	2-dr. Cpe.-3P	1029	3403	51
413627	2-dr. Clb. Sed.-5P	1074	3420	std. 8260
				dlx. 5338
413609	4-dr. Sed.-5P	1130	3500	std. 8046
				dlx. 7534
96 Models				
413967	2-dr. Conv.-3P	1191	3525	325
413927	2-dr. Cpe.-3P	1043	3320	2176
413919	4-dr. Sed.-5P	1099	3410	4176
98 Models				
413967	2-dr. Conv.-3P	1227	3600	1263
—	4-dr. Phae.-6P	1575	3790	119
413927	2-dr. Cpe.-3P	1059	3430	1263
413919	4-dr. Sed.-5P	1135	3500	22,081

ENGINE: Six-cylinder, same on all series. Inline, L-head. Cast iron block. B & S: 3-1/2 x 4-1/8 in. Disp.: 238 cu. in. C.R.: 6.1:1. Brake H.P.: 100 @ 3200 R.P.M. Main bearings: four. Valve lifters: mushroom. Carb.: single downdraft with automatic choke. Eight-cylinder, same on all series. Cast iron block. B & S: 3-1/2 x 4-1/8 in. Disp.: 257 cu. in. C.R.: 6.3:1. Brake H.P.: 110 @ 3400 R.P.M. Main bearings: five. Valve lifters: mushroom. Carb.: dual downdraft with automatic choke.

CHASSIS: [Series 60 (six or eight)] W.B.: 119 in. O.L.: 204 in. Frt/Rear Tread: 58/61-1/2 in. Tires: 16 x 6.00. [Series 70 (six or eight)] W.B.: 125 in. O.L.: 211 in. Frt/Rear Tread: 58/61-1/2 in. Tires: 16 x 7.50. [Series 90 (six or eight)] W.B.: 125 in. O.L.: 213 in. Frt/Rear Tread: 58/61-1/2 in. Tires: 15 x 7.00.

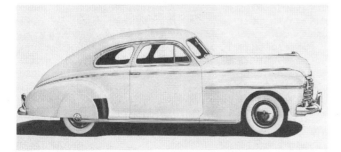

1941 Oldsmobile, 78, two-door club sedan, OCW

TECHNICAL: Sliding gear, synchromesh manual transmission. Speeds: 3F/1R. Steering column controls. Single plate dry disc clutch. Shaft drive. Semi-floating hypoid rear axle. Overall ratio: [Series 60] 4.1:1; [Series 70 & 90] 4.3:1. Sealed hydraulic, cast iron drum brakes on four wheels. Pressed steel wheels. Drivetrain options: automatic transmission ($100.00).

1941 Oldsmobile, 98, four-door sedan, OCW

1941 Oldsmobile, 98 Series, convertible sedan, TVB

OPTIONS: Fender skirts ($14.00). Bumper guards (3.75 each). Radio (deluxe 62.50; standard 52.50). Heater (condition-air heater 30.50; deluxe 22.00; underseat 19.75). Clock (30-wind 5.50; electric 12.25). Cigar lighter (2.00). Seat covers (13.75). Glovebox light (90 cents). Deluxe steering wheel (12.50). Visor mirror (1.00). Rear seat foot rests (1.85). Wheel trim rings (8.00). Turn signals (10.95). Fog lamps (10.90 pair). Backup light (4.45). License plate frames (2.75 per pair). Exhaust deflector (1.25).

1941 Oldsmobile, 76 Series, four-door sedan, HJE

HISTORICAL: Introduced September 23, 1940. Calendar year sales and production: 230,703. Model year sales and production: 270,040. The general manager of Oldsmobile was S.E. Skinner. The two-millionth Oldsmobile was built this model year. Oldsmobile focused more on war production and specialized in producing munitions.

1942

1942 Oldsmobile, 66 Series, two-door sedan, CX

OLDSMOBILE — SPECIAL — SERIES 66 OR 68 — SIX OR EIGHT: Olds stayed with its Special series as the price leader of a three series format. As with all automakers, production was halted early in the year due to the war. Both a six- or eight-cylinder engine could be ordered. Extremely rare, both a convertible and station wagon were available.

1942 Oldsmobile, 76, four-door sedan, OCW

OLDSMOBILE — DYNAMIC — SERIES 76 OR 78 — SIX OR EIGHT: The Olds "fastback" series had two body styles. It had a separate 125-inch wheelbase and the option of a six- or eight-cylinder engine.

OLDSMOBILE — CUSTOM CRUISER — SERIES 98 — EIGHT: Once again the Custom Cruiser was the Olds entrant in the luxury market. Gone was the single year offering of a six-cylinder in the 96. All cars now had the straight-eight engine. Also gone was the rare convertible sedan. An exclusive 127-inch wheelbase was used in this series.

1942 Oldsmobile, 98 Series, convertible, OCW

I.D. DATA: Serial numbers were located on upper left front face of dash. Starting: [Series 60] California built-66C or 68C-3001; Linden, N.J. built-66L or 68L-3001; Lansing, MI built-66 or 68-9001. [Series 70] California built-76C or 78C-4001; Linden, N.J. built-76L or 78L-4001; Lansing, MI built-76 or 78-26001. [Series 90] California built-98C-4001; Linden, N.J. built-98L-6001; Lansing, MI built-98-25001. Ending: N/A. Engine numbers were on upper left corner of engine block. Starting: [Six G] 424001; [Eight L] 45001. Ending: [Six G] 472869; [Eight L] 468773. Engines with single letter prefix were Lansing, Michigan, built. Engines with two letter prefix and first letter C — California built, first letter L — Linden, New Jersey, built.

1942 Oldsmobile, 98 Series, four-door sedan, AA

Model No.	Body Type & Seating	Price	Weight	Prod. Total
Series 60				
423527B	2-dr. Bs. Cpe.-3P	992	3230	1166
423527	2-dr. Clb. Cpe.-3P	1035	3205	4173
423507	2-dr. Clb. Sed.-5P	1050	3270	10,766
423511	2-dr. Sed.-5P	1040	3275	3688
423519	4-dr. Sed.-5P	1088	3320	8053
423569	4-dr. Twn. Sed.-5P	1088	3315	3888
423567	2-dr. Conv.-3P	1277	3400	848
4235SW	4-dr. SW.-6P	1376	3515	NA
Series 70				
423607	2-dr. Clb. Sed.-5P	1095	3485	14,701
423609	4-dr. Sed.-5P	1153	3510	12,566
Series 90				
423967	2-dr. Conv.-4P	1561	3740	216
423907	2-dr. Cib. Sed.-5P	1319	3620	1771
423969	4-dr. Sed.-5P	1376	3780	4672

ENGINE: [Six-cylinder] Inline, L-head. Cast iron block. B & S: 3-1/2 x 4-1/8 in. Disp.: 238 cu. in. C.R.: 6.5:1. Brake H.P.: 100 @ 3200 R.P.M. Main bearings: four. Valve lifters: mushroom. Carb.: single downdraft with automatic choke. [Eight-cylinder] Inline, L-head. Cast iron block. B & S: 3-1/4 x 3-7/8 in. Disp.: 257 cu. in. C.R.: 6.5:1. Brake H.P.: 110 @ 3400 R.P.M. Main bearings: five. Valve lifters: mushroom. Carb.: dual downdraft with automatic choke.

CHASSIS: [Series 60 Special] W.B.: 119 in. O.L.: 204 in. Frt/Rear Tread: 58/61-1/2 in. Tires: 6.00 x 16. [Series 70-Dynamic Cruiser] W.B.: 125 in. O.L.: 212 in. Frt/Rear Tread: 58/61-1/2 in. Tires: 6.50 x 15. [Series 90 Custom Cruiser] W.B.: 127 in. O.L.: 216 in. Frt/Rear Tread: 58/61-1/2 in. Tires: 7.00 x 15.

TECHNICAL: Manual, synchromesh transmission. Speeds 3F/1R. Steering column controls. Single plate dry disc clutch. Tubular driveshaft. Hypoid, semi-floating rear axle. Overall ratio: [Series 60] 4.1:1 ; [Others] 4.3:1. Sealed hydraulic, cast iron drum brakes on four wheels. Pressed steel wheels. Drivetrain options: HydraMatic automatic transmission ($95.00). Heavy-duty air cleaner (3.75). Solenoid starter (7.50). Oil filter (5.25).

OPTIONS: Fender skirts ($14.00 pair). Bumper guards (4.50). Radio (master 68.50; standard 58.00; universal 29.45). Heater (condition-air 39.95; dual-flow 23.50, underseat 22.00, universal 14.45). Clock (electric 12.95; 30-hour wind 6.00). Seat covers (satin-rayon 29.50). Spotlight (14.50). Glovebox light (1.00). Plastic steering wheel (14.00). Visor utility kit (2.95). Visor mirror (1.35). Wheel trim rings (8.00). Fog lamps (11.50). Turn signals (11.40). Backup light (4.75). Outside rear view mirror (2.50). Underhood light (1.25). Gas tank cover lock (1.25). "In-A-Car" bed (19.50).

HISTORICAL: Calendar year sales and production: 12,230. Model year sales and production: 67,999. The general manager of Oldsmobile was S.E. Skinner. Auto production stopped on February 5, 1942, for war production. Oldsmobile's main war effort was rocket and mortar shells, cannon, and aircraft propellers and engines.

OLDSMOBILE 1946-1975

1947 Oldsmobile, 98 two-door convertible, OCW

By Dennis F. Casteele

Oldsmobile has the longest historical trail of the existing domestic car builders. Over the years the Lansing, Mich.-based General Motors division has offered a genuine variety of motorcars and even a few trucks. Oldsmobiles powered by a selection of single-, twin-, six- and eight-cylinder engines with inline and V-block construction and fueled by either gasoline or diesel, have rolled the roads since 1897.

Success came to the company early and just after the turn of the century Oldsmobile was the most popular car on the road. Several editions of the nimble little Curved Dash model were marketed. Like other GM namesakes David Buick and Louis Chevrolet, Ransom Eli Olds left the firm carrying his name in the early going. Unlike Messrs. Buick and Chevrolet, Olds made a successful re-entry into the automotive field. By 1905 his new firm REO was working its way up the automotive ladder.

Joining the fledgling General Motors group in 1908, Oldsmobile slipped into the lower production, higher-quality automotive realm through the early 1920s. After a series of six-cylinder cars built to more modest price standards from the early 1920s through 1928, Olds introduced a companion car in 1929. The new line was called Viking and came upon the scene in the worst of times with a overcrowded marketplace and economic Depression. By 1930 the Viking was just a somewhat bitter memory. In 1933 things looked so bleak for GM that serious consideration was given to combining or eliminating Buick, Old-

smobile and Pontiac. Things gradually got better for Oldsmobile, however, and GM retained all of its automotive arms. Through the shortened 1942 model year Olds offered first two and then three automotive series, powered by a six or eight-cylinder inline motor. For most of this time Oldsmobile was content to hold a sales slot near the bottom rung of the industry's top 10, offering solid, if unspectacular, transportation.

The lone indication of things to come began with introduction of the Hydra-Matic transmission in 1940. For years the auto industry had flirted with the fully automatic transmission. Certainly Oldsmobile's Hydra-Matic was not the first automatic, but up until that point it probably was the best. Several years before Oldsmobile had shared with Buick the so-called Safety Automatic Transmission. It was really a semi-automatic unit and had very limited marketing success. The Hydra-Matic, backed by the research of giant GM, caught on quickly in the Oldsmobile showrooms and soon Cadillac was offering Hydra-Matic as well.

Like most of the established car building firms, Oldsmobile hit the postwar streets with warmed-over 1942 models as 1946s. The same was true in 1947 and for the junior series of 1948. It was a different story (and a strong indication of things on the immediate Oldsmobile horizon) with the 1948 Ninety-Eight models. Here an all-new appearance package called Futuramic was introduced. In 1949, Futuramic styling got the underhood boost it deserved, the new high-compression overhead valve Rocket V-8 engine. Coupled with the time-proven Hydra-Matic, the real postwar Oldsmobiles were dynamite. A big-engined/small-bodied Rocket 88 series was king of the roads and champ of the budding NASCAR stock car racing circuit in the early 1950s.

Gradually, Oldsmobile was upstaged in the performance arena by the Chrysler Hemi and the high-winding small-block Chevrolet V-8. Oldsmobile did continue to offer a variety of pleasing, well-styled, and popular cars through 1956. In 1957 Oldsmobile made another move into the high-performance arena. Divisional engineers elected to fight the competition's more exotic and more expensive fuel-injection and supercharging systems with a tri-carb based J-2 option available on most 1957 and 1958 models.

Oldsmobile, like most of the domestic car builders, moved into an automotive space age of sorts with the 1958 models. In 1961, two big developments came from the Oldsmobile camp. The personal luxury Starfire bowed as a convertible (a companion hardtop was added in 1962) and the folks from Lansing also joined the GM compact car parade with their F-85/Cutlass Series. Eventually the Cutlass nameplate would grow into the best-selling single model of the 1970s.

By the early 1960s Oldsmobile was on the move upwards on many sales and engineering fronts. An innovative chief engineer named John Beltz would move into the general manager's chair in this era. A lot of great automotive concepts were advanced by this auto enthusiast/executive. The Cutlass had once seen a brief fling with high-performance in its turbocharged Jetfire models in 1962 and 1963. Now more was on the way.

In 1964, Oldsmobile made a bold move back into the high-performance field with its 4-4-2 package. First as an F-85/Cutlass option, later as a full-fledged series, this Oldsmobile intermediate package was a real hit with the performance crowd. For those seeking a bit more zing, the potent W-cars were offered in the late 1960s. Finally, buyers who wanted to taste more luxury with their high-performance Cutlass were tempted by the limited-production Hurst/Olds.

One of the uniquely different cars of the postwar era emerged from Oldmobile, in 1966, with the introduction of the front-wheel-drive Toronado. This quickly became the Oldsmobile banner-carrier on the personal/luxury front while the Starfire was dropped. The Toronado garnered a basket full of 'buff book' and engineering awards, but never captured the market share Oldsmobile officials hoped for.

By the 1970s, the Cutlass had grown into a powerful market force beyond the high-performance arena covered by the W-cars, Hurst/Olds and 4-4-2. This position got even stronger with the introduction of the Colonnade styled Cutlass Supreme coupe in 1973. Coupled with solid sales performances from the traditional Eighty-Eight and Ninety-Eight models and a boost from the addition of the smaller Omega and new Starfire, Oldsmobile rode into third place in the industry sales race.

1947 Oldsmobile, Special Sixty four-door station wagon, 6-cyl.

1950 Oldsmobile, 88 Series Holiday two-door hardtop, V-8

1950 Oldsmobile, 88 Series two-door convertible, V-8

1956 Oldsmobile, 98 Series Holiday two-door hardtop, V-8

1961 Oldsmobile, Super 88 Holiday four-door hardtop, V-8

1964 Oldsmobile, Starfire two-door hardtop, V-8

1962 Oldsmobile, 98 Holiday four-door hardtop, V-8

1970 Oldsmobile, 4-4-2 two-door hardtop, V-8

1970 Oldsmobile, Cutlass 'S' Rallye 350 two-door hardtop, V-8

1946

1946 Oldsmobile, 60 Series four-door station wagon, 6-cyl. (DC)

SPECIAL - SIXTY SERIES - The Special or Sixty series was Oldsmobile's lowest-priced group of cars. Specials had only six-cylinder power, although an eight-cylinder was offered in other years. Interiors were tan mixture pattern cloth. Standard tire size was 6.00 x 16 inches. Leather interiors were offered on convertibles. Technical features included electro hardened aluminum pistons, full-pressure lubrication and automatic choke with fast idle mode.

OLDSMOBILE I.D. NUMBERS: Serial number (VIN) on left front door hinge pillar. Engine number on front of block above water pump and on plate on end of floorboard inside the right front door. VIN starts with a prefix having two or three symbols. First two symbols indicate series: 66=Series 66 six-cylinder; 76=Series 76 six-cylinder; 78=Series 78 eight-cylinder and 98=Series 98 eight-cylinder. Third symbol (if used) indicates assembly plant: no symbol=Lansing, Mich.; K=Kansas City; L=Linden, N.J.; C=California (Los Angeles). Beginning and ending numbers by plant and series (check prefix) were [Lansing] 66-112001 to 66-131546; 76-92001 to 76-133098; 78-33001 to 78-48769; and 98-32001 to 98-42567. [Kansas City] 66K-1001 to 66K-2431; 76K-1001 to 76K-2997; 78K-1001 to 78K-2096; and 98K-1001 to 98K-1660. [Linden] 66L-14001 to 66L-18098; 76L-13001 to 76L-18939; 78L-5001 to 78L-7588; and 98L-7001 to 98L-8956. [Los Angeles] 66C-12001 to 66C-14468; 76C-9001 to 76C-12618; 78C-5001 to 78C-6500; and 98C-5001 to 98C-6181. Engines carried mixed production serial numbers with no specific relationship to a particular assembly plant. Beginning and ending engine numbers were: (six-cylinder) 6-1001 to 6-82337; (eight-cylinder) 8-1001 to 8-36397.

SPECIAL SIXTY SERIES

Model Number	Body/Style Number	Body Type & Seating	Factory Price	Shipping Weight	Production Total
60	3527	2-dr Clb Cpe-5P	1108	3325	4,537
60	3507	4-dr Clb Sed-5P	1134	3330	11,721
60	3519	4-dr Sed-6P	1169	3355	12,747
60	3567	2-dr Conv-5P	1327	3605	1,409
60	3581	4-dr Sta Wag-6P	1795	3785	140

1946 Oldsmobile, 78 Series two-door sedanet, 8-cyl. (DC)

DYNAMIC - SEVENTY SERIES - Again the Seventy, the middle Oldsmobile series, had two fastback models. Standard equipment included front and rear bumper guards, vacuum booster pump, dual sun visors, cigarette lighter and plastic radiator ornament. Deluxe equipment included wider door trim, foam rubber seat cushion, special steering wheel, Deluxe instrument cluster, electric clock, chrome wheel trim rings and rear seat armrest. Six-cylinders were designated 76s, eight-cylinders as 78s. Cars in this series came standard with 6.50 x 16 inch tires. Technical features included: Electro-hardened aluminum pistons, I-beam connecting rods and automatic choke with fast idle feature.

DYNAMIC SEVENTY SERIES

Model Number	Body/Style Number	Body Type & Seating	Factory Price	Shipping Weight	Production Total
SIX-CYLINDER					
76	3607	2-dr Clb Sed-5P	1184	3460	32,862
76	3609	4-dr Sed-5P	1234	3655	20,604

1946 Oldsmobile, 76 Series two-door sedanet, OCW

EIGHT-CYLINDER					
78	3607	2-dr Clb Sed-5P	1264	3650	10,911
78	3609	4-dr Sed-5P	1313	3799	10,042

NOTE 1: D Style Number suffix = Deluxe; Deluxe items available on standards.

1946 Oldsmobile, 90 Series four-door sedan, 8-cyl. (DC)

CUSTOM CRUISER - NINETY SERIES - The Custom Cruiser or Ninety series Oldsmobile was the top of the line. Three models were offered and all were eight-cylinder powered. Most equipment found standard on the 60 and 70 series cars was also standard on the 90 models. Added standard equipment included: wraparound bumpers, Deluxe instrument cluster and clock, rear seat armrest and foam rubber seat cushions. Tire size was 7.00 x 15 inches. Available upholstery was either leather, broadcloth or Bedford cord.

CUSTOM CRUISER NINETY SERIES

Model Number	Body/Style Number	Body Type & Seating	Factory Price	Shipping Weight	Production Total
46-90	3969	4-dr Sed-5P	1490	3795	11,031
46-90	3907	2-dr Clb Sed-5P	1442	3715	2,459
46-90	3967	2-dr Conv-3P	1840	4075	874

1946 Oldsmobile, 90 Series two-door convertible, OCW

ENGINES

(OLDSMOBILE 60/70 SERIES SIX) Inline. Six-cylinder. L-head. Cast iron block. Displacement: 238 cid. Bore and stroke: 3-1/2 x 4-1/8 inches. Compression ratio: 6.5:1. Brake hp: 100 at 3400 rpm. Five main bearings. Solid valve lifters. Carburetor: Carter one-barrel Model WA1-504S.

(OLDSMOBILE 70/90 SERIES EIGHT) Inline. Eight-cylinder: L-head. Cast Iron block. Displacement: 257 cid. Bore and stroke: 3-1/4 x 3-7/8 inches. Compression ratio: 6.5:1. Brake hp: 110 at 4600 rpm. Six main bearings. Solid valve lifters. Carburetor: Carter two-barrel Model WDO-503S.

CHASSIS FEATURES: Wheelbase: (Special) 119 inches; (Dynamic) 125 inches; (Custom) 125 inches. Overall length: (Special) 204 inches; (Dynamic) 214 inches; (Custom) 216 inches. Front tread: (All) 58 inches. Rear tread: (All) 61-1/2 inches.

OPTIONS: Condition-air heater and ventilating system. Dual-flow heater with defroster. Deluxe radio. Standard radio. Deluxe plastic steering wheel. Electric clock. Directional signals. Safety spotlight. Auxiliary driving and fog lights. back-up light. Trunk light. Rear fender skirts. Gas tank cover lock. A three-speed manual transmission with column shifter was standard equipment on all 1946 Oldsmobiles. A fully automatic Hydra-Matic transmission -- introduced by Oldsmobile on its 1940 models -- was available as on option on any model.

HISTORICAL FOOTNOTES: Postwar production began Oct. 15, 1945, but a United Auto Workers strike on Nov. 21, 1945, halted production. Production did not resume until April 1, 1946. This held Oldsmobile's model year production to 119,388 units and kept calendar year production to 114,674 cars. Olds was the seventh largest U.S. automaker for the year. Olds woodie station wagon bodies were made by both Ionia and Hercules in 1946. The rare wagons came in a limited range of colors: black, Ambassador red, Pawnee beige and Forest green. Fender skirts were a rare option offered exclusively on Ninety Series Oldsmobiles.

1947

1947 Oldsmobile, 66 Series four-door station wagon, OCW

SPECIAL - SIXTY SERIES - More models were offered in the low-priced Special series than in the other two series. The eight-cylinder engine returned to the Special series and there were 66 and 68 versions of each body style offered. Standard equipment included: safety glass, spare wheel and tire, dual horns, vacuum booster pump and cigarette lighter. The standard interior fabric was tan mixture cloth. Standard tire size was 6.00 x 16 inches.

1947 Oldsmobile, 68 Series two-door convertible, OCW

OLDSMOBILE I.D. NUMBERS: Serial number (VIN) on left front door hinge pillar. Motor number on front of block above water pump and on plate on end of floorboard inside the right front door. VIN starts with a prefix having two or three symbols. First two symbols indicate series: 66=Series 66 six-cylinder; 76=Series 76 six-cylinder; 68=68 eight-cylinder; 78=Series 78 eight-cylinder and 98=Series 98 eight-cylinder. Third symbol (if used) indicates assembly plant: no symbol=Lansing, Mich.; A=Atlanta, Ga.; K=Kansas City; L=Linden, N.J.; C=California (Los Angeles); W=Wilmington, Del. Beginning and ending numbers by plant and series (check prefix) were [Lansing] 66-132001 to 66-163261; 76-134001 to 76-162749; 68=13001 to 68-24077; 78-50001 to 78-70213; and 98-43001 to 98-64483. [Atlanta] 66A-1001 to 66A-1045; 76A-1001 to 76A-1035; 68A-1001 to 68A-1020; 78A-1001 to 78A-1025; and 98A-1001 to 98A-1001. [Kansas City] 66K-1001 to 66K-8124; 76K-4001 to 76K-8509; 68K-1001 to 68K-2538; 78K-3001 to 78K-6132; and 98K-2001 to 98K-5269. [Linden] 66L-19001 to 66L-29555; 76L-2801 to 76L-29949; 68L-4001 to 68L-7037; 78L-8001 to 78L-14896; and 98L-10001 to 98L-18787. [Los Angeles] 66C-15001 to 66C-19520; 76C-13001 to 76C-17239; 68C4001 to 68C-5401; 78C-7001 to 78C-10011; and 98C-7001 to 98C-10515. Engines carried mixed production serial numbers with no specific relationship to a particular assembly plant. Beginning and ending engine numbers were: (six-cylinder) 6-83001 to 6-186314; (eight-cylinder) 8-37001 to 8-125584.

1947 Oldsmobile, 66 Series four-door sedan, 6-cyl. (DC)

SPECIAL SIXTY SERIES

Model Number	Body/Style Number	Body Type & Seating	Factory Price	Shipping Weight	Production Total
66/68	47-3567	2-dr Conv-4P	1627	3520	6,528
66/68	47-3527	2-dr Clb Cpe-4P	1308	3315	14,297
66/68	47-3507	4-dr Clb Sed-5P	1334	3330	28,488
66/68	47-3519	4-d Sed-5P	1369	3375	22,660
66/68	47-3581	4-dr Sta Wag-6P	2175	3715	1,460

NOTE 1: Prices and weights are for 66 model.

NOTE 2: Production figures are for 66 and 68 models.

1947 Oldsmobile, 78 Series four-door sedan, 8-cyl. (DC)

DYNAMIC - SEVENTY SERIES - The Oldsmobile middle series had two fastback body styles. Power came from either inline six- or eight-cylinder engines, hence the designations 76 or 78. There were Deluxe and standard versions of both body styles. Standard equipment included the same items that were standard on the lower series Special cars. Deluxe equipment included: a special instrument cluster, Deluxe Clock and steering wheel, foam rubber seat cushions and rear center armrests. The Deluxe package cost approximately $100, depending on model and represented a substantial savings over purchasing the same items individually. Interior fabric choices were modern-weave cloth and custom broadcloth. Tire size was 7.00 x 15 inches.

DYNAMIC SEVENTY SERIES

Model Number	Body/Style Number	Body Type & Seating	Factory Price	Shipping Weight	Production Total
76/78	47-3607	2-dr Clb Sed-5P	1392	3460	44,849
76/78	47-3609	4-dr Sed-5P	1459	3525	38,825

NOTE 1: Deluxe models had the suffix D on the style number.

NOTE 2: Prices and weights shown are for 76 six-cylinder models.

1947 Oldsmobile, 98 Series two-door convertible, 8-cyl. (DC)

CUSTOM CRUISER - NINETY-EIGHT SERIES - The top-of-the-line Oldsmobile series again had three body styles. This was the last year for the Ninety-Eight 1941 prewar body. All Ninety-Eights had the straight-eight engine. Standard Ninety-Eight equipment included the same items as the Special Series, plus a solenoid starter system. Upholstery was either custom broadcloth or leather. Standard tire size was 7.00 x 15 inches.

CUSTOM CRUISER NINETY-EIGHT SERIES

Model Number	Body/Style Number	Body Type & Seating	Factory Price	Shipping Weight	Production Total
98	47-3907	2-dr Clb Sed-5P	1642	3690	8,475
98	47-3967	2-dr Conv-5P	2040	4023	3,940
98	47-3969	4-dr Sed-5P	1690	3775	24,733

ENGINES

(68/78 SERIES SIX) Inline. Six-cylinder. Cast iron block. L-head side valve design. Displacement: 238 cid. Bore and stroke: 3-1/2 x 4-1/8 inches. Compression ratio: 6.5:1. Developed hp: 100. Electro-hardened aluminum pistons. Full pressure lubrication. Carter WA1-504S downdraft carburetor fitted with automatic choke and fast idle system.

(68/78/98 SERIES EIGHT) Eight-cylinder. L-head straight eight design. Cast iron block. Displacement: 257 cid. Compression ratio: 6.5:1. Bore and stroke: 3-1/4 x 3-7/8 inches. Electro-hardened aluminum pistons. I-beam construction connecting rods. Carter WCD-665S two-barrel downdraft carburetion. Automatic choke with fast idle system.

CHASSIS FEATURES: (Special Series) Wheelbase: 119 inches; overall length: 204 inches; front tread: 58 inches; rear tread: 62 inches. (Dynamic Series) Wheelbase: 125 inches; overall length: 213 inches; front tread: 58 inches; rear tread: 62 inches. (Custom Cruiser Series) Wheelbase: 127 inches; overall length: 216 inches; front tread: 58 inches; rear tread: 62 inches.

OPTIONS: Condition-Air heater ($52.90). Dual-flow heater/defroster ($31.80). Chrome wheel trim rings ($10.60). Plastic white sidewall discs ($12.10). Trunk light ($1.75). Chrome exhaust extension ($1.75). Left-hand outside mirror ($3.40). Visor mirror ($2.50). Underhood light ($2.10). License frame ($2.10). Electric clock ($17.40). Gas tank door lock ($1.90). Fender skirts ($17.35). Deluxe steering wheel ($17.14). Directional signals ($14.75). Fog and driving lamps ($15.55). Cadet outside visor ($30.25). Back-up light ($7.75). Rear-window wiper ($15.20). Standard 5-tube radio ($72.75) and Deluxe 6-tube radio ($82.75). All 1947 Oldsmobiles came standard with a column-shifted, three-speed manual transmission. The Hydra-Matic transmission could be ordered on any 1947 Olds for $135 extra. Special and Dynamic models came either as six-cylinder 66 or 76 models, or as eight-cylinder 68 or 78 models. Ninety-Eights (98s) were available only with an eight.

HISTORICAL FOOTNOTES: Model year production was 194,388 units and calendar year output amounted to 191,454 cars to rank seventh in the industry. On June 7, 1947, GM engineering genius Charles "Boss" Kettering put an overhead valve V-8 engine in a 1947 Oldsmobile sedan and demonstrated the car at the summer meeting of the Society of Automotive Engineers. It had a 12.5:1 compression ratio and required 94 octane gas. All 1947 Oldsmobile wood-bodied station wagons had Ionia bodies.

1948

DYNAMIC - SIXTY SERIES - This year Oldsmobile dropped the Special series designation and named both the former Special and 70 series cars Dynamics. The 60 series Dynamics were the smallest Oldsmobiles offered in 1948 and offered the greatest variety of body styles. Either six- or eight-cylinder engines were available and were designated 66 or 68 accordingly. Standard 60 series equipment included: dual horns, dual sun visors and a cigarette lighter. The Deluxe equipment package added foam rubber seat cushions, Deluxe steering wheel, Deluxe instrument cluster, clock and chrome wheel trim rings. Standard tires were 6.00 x 16 and upholstery was Bedford cord or broadcloth.

1948 Oldsmobile, 66 Series club coupe, OCW

OLDSMOBILE I.D. NUMBERS: Serial number (VIN) on left front door hinge pillar. Engine number on front of block above water pump and on plate on end of floorboard inside the right front door. VIN starts with a prefix having two or three symbols. First two symbols indicate series: 66=Series 66 six-cylinder; 76=Series 76 six-cylinder; 68=68 eight-cylinder; 78=Series 78 eight-cylinder and 98=Series 98 eight-cylinder. Third symbol (if used) indicates assembly plant: no symbol=Lansing, Mich.; A=Atlanta, Ga.; B= (Boston) Framingham, Mass.; K=Kansas City; L=Linden, N.J.; C=California (Southgate/Los Angeles); W=Wilmington, Del. Beginning and ending numbers by plant and series (check prefix) were [Lansing] 66-165001 to 66-185604; 76-164001 to 76-177725; 68=25001 to 68-33599; 78-72001 to 78-82294; and 98-65001 to 98-96882. [Atlanta] 66A-2001 to 66A-3864; 76A-2001 to 76A-3414; 68A-2001 to 68A-2817; 78A-2001 to 78A-2983; and 98A-1001 to 98A-3485. [Framingham, Mass.] 66B-9001 to 66B-2868; 76B1001 to 76B-2443; 68B-1001 to 68B-1824; 78B-no 78s made at Framingham; 98B-1001 to 98B-4559. [Kansas City] 66K-9001 to 66K-13202; 76K-9001 to 76K-12182; 68K-3001 to 68K-4851; 78K-7001 to 78K-9315; and 98K-6001 to 98K-12126. [Linden] 66L-31001 to 66L-34067; 76L-31601 to 76L-33422; 68L-8001 to 68L-9359; 78L-16001 to 78L-17830; and 98L-20001 to 98L-27179. [Los Angeles] 66C-21001 to 66C-24356; 76C-18001 to 76C-20549; 68C-6001 to 68C-7509; 78C-11001 to 78C-12951; and 98C-11001 to 98C-18076. Engines carried mixed production serial numbers with no specific relationship to a particular assembly plant. Beginning and ending engine numbers were: (six-cylinder) 6-188021 to 6-256090; (eight-cylinder) 8-127001 to 8-164285.

1948 Oldsmobile, 68 Series two-door convertible, OCW

DYNAMIC SIXTY SERIES

Model Number	Body/Style Number	Body Type & Seating	Factory Price	Shipping Weight	Production Total
66/68	48-3527	2-dr Clb Cpe-5P	1609	3240	9,326
66/68	48-3507	4-dr Clb Sed-5P	1776	3285	23,732
66/68	48-3519	4-dr Sed-5P	1677	3320	18,142
66/68	48-3567X	2-dr Conv-5P	1725	3550	3,892
66/68	48-3562	4-dr Sta Wag-6P	2614	3620	2,707

NOTE 1: Deluxes have suffix "D."

NOTE 2: Prices and weights for 66 models.

DYNAMIC - SEVENTY SERIES - Again this year, the middle Olds series had two fastback models. Standard equipment included front and rear bumper guards, vacuum booster pump, dual sun visors, cigarette lighter and plastic radiator ornament. Deluxe equipment added wider door trim, foam rubber seat cushions, special steering wheel, Deluxe instrument cluster, electric clock, chrome wheel trim rings and rear seat armrest. Upholstery was broadcloth or Bedford cord. Standard tire size was 7.60 x 15 inches.

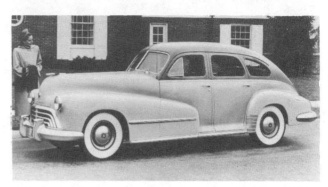

1948 Oldsmobile, Dynamic 70 Series four-door sedan, 8-cyl. (DC)

DYNAMIC SEVENTY SERIES

Model Number	Body/Style Number	Body Type & Seating	Factory Price	Shipping Weight	Production Total
76/78	48-3609	4-dr Sed-5P	1801	3525	24,646
76/78	48-3607	2-dr Clb Sed-5P	1726	3460	25,172

NOTE 1: Deluxe cars had the suffix "D" along with the body style number.

1948 Oldsmobile, 98 Series two-door sedanet, 8-cyl. (DC)

FUTURAMIC - NINETY-EIGHT SERIES - For the first time in years, Oldsmobile offered two totally different bodies during a single model year. The top-of-the-line series drew heavily on the new Futuramic styling concept that would be used by all 1949 Oldsmobiles. Standard equipment on the Ninety-Eights included a solenoid starter, fender skirts, E-Z-I rearview mirror and foam rubber seat cushions. The Ninety-Eights also included standard items from the Sixty and Seventy Dynamic models. Deluxe equipment on the Ninety-Eight added front and rear floor mats, Deluxe steering wheel, wheel trim rings, rear seat armrests and hydraulic window, seat, and top controls on convertibles. Upholstery was either broadcloth or leather. The standard tire size was 6.50 x 16.

FUTURAMIC NINETY-EIGHT SERIES

Model Number	Body/Style Number	Body Type & Seating	Factory Price	Shipping Weight	Production Total
98	48-3807	2-dr Clb Sed-5P	2708	3465	14,260
98	48-3869	4-dr Sed-5P	2151	3705	38,061
98	48-3867X	2-dr Conv-5P	2624	4035	12,914

NOTE 1: Deluxe model had "D" suffix on style number.

1948 Oldsmobile, 98 Series two-door convertible, OCW

ENGINES

(66/76 SERIES SIX) Inline. Six-cylinder. L-head. Cast iron block. Displacement: 238 cid. Bore and stroke: 3-1/2 x 4-1/8 inches. Compression ratio: 6.5:1. Developed hp: 100 at 3400 rpm. High carbon crankshaft. Four main bearings. Aluminum alloy pistons. Carter WA1-651S one-barrel downdraft carburetor with automatic choke.

(68/78 SERIES EIGHT) Inline. Eight cylinder. L-head. Cast iron block. Displacement: 257 cid. Compression ratio: 6.5:1. Bore and stroke: 3-1/4 x 3-7/8 inches. Brake hp: 110 at 3600 rpm. Aluminum pistons and I-beam connecting rods. Carter WDO-650S two-barrel downdraft carburetor with automatic choke.

1948 Oldsmobile, 98 Series four-door sedan, OCW

(98 SERIES EIGHT) Inline. Eight-cylinder. L-head. Cast iron block. Bore and stroke: 3-1/4 x 3-7/8 inches. Displacement: 257 cid. Compression ratio: 7.0:1. Brake hp: 115 hp at 3600 rpm. Carter WDO-650 SA dual downdraft carburetion with built-in automatic choke.

CHASSIS FEATURES: Wheelbase: (Sixty) 119 inches; (Seventy and Ninety-Eight) 125 inches. Overall length: (Sixty) 204 inches; (Seventy and Ninety-Eight) 213 inches. Front tread: (Sixty and Seventy) 58 inches; (Ninety-Eight) 57 inches. Rear tread: (Sixty and Seventy) 62 inches; (Ninety-Eight) 59 inches.

CONVENIENCE OPTIONS: Solenoid starter ($7). Fender skirts ($17). Dual flow heater and defroster ($32). Condition-air heater and defroster ($58). Windshield washer ($9). Standard five-tube radio ($84). Super Deluxe radio 6-tube ($94). Chrome wheel trim rings ($10). Glovebox and map lights ($2). Fog and driving lamps ($15). Safety spot light ($20). Tilting glare proof mirror ($5). Visor mirror ($2). Back-up light ($9). Turn signals ($16). Cadet sunvisor ($30). Rear window wiper ($14). All models came standard with a column-shifted manual transmission. Each 1948 Oldsmobile could be ordered with the optional Hydra-Matic Drive ($175). Engine options included the heavy-duty air cleaner ($4) and oil filter ($7).

HISTORICAL FOOTNOTES: Production was 173,661 cars for the model year and 194,755 for the calendar year. This put Oldsmobile seventh in the U.S. auto sales for the third year in-a-row. The 1948 station wagons had new combination wood and metal Fisher Body Co. bodies. The 98s featured all-new styling and engineering. They were introduced in February 1948, while the carryover "prewar" style models bowed on Jan. 15, 1948. It was the last year for the Oldsmobile 66, 68 and 78 series.

1949

1949 Oldsmobile, 76 Series four-door station wagon, 6-cyl. (DC)

SEVENTY-SIX SERIES - Oldsmobile would retain a six-cylinder engine through 1950, but 1948 was the last year for three different-sized series. The Seventy-Six was now the bottom-line Oldsmobile. The Seventy-Six and Eighty-Eight were nearly identical, except for their engines. Standard Seventy-Six equipment included: safety glass, bumper guards, dual horns, dual sun visors, cigarette lighter and solenoid starter. The Deluxe option featured foam rubber seat cushions, front and rear floor mats, special external chrome moldings, clock, Deluxe steering wheel, wheel trim rings and turn signals. Upholstery choices were Bedford cord, broadcloth and leather. Standard tire size was 7.10 x 15 inches.

1949 Oldsmobile, 76 Series two-door club sedan, OCW

OLDSMOBILE I.D. NUMBERS: Serial number located on left front door pillar on right side of cowl. Motor number on block above water pump; and on plate on floor inside right door; and on left corner of block above generator; and on front of left cylinder head at negative battery terminal. Olds 76 numbers took the form 496( )1001 to 496( )ending number. Olds 88 numbers took the form 498( )1001 to 498( )ending number. Olds 98 numbers took the form 499( )1001 to 499( )ending number. First two symbols indicate model year: 49=1949. Third symbol indicates series: 6=76; 8=88; 9=98. Fourth symbol in ( ) indicated assembly plant as follows: A=Atlanta; B=Boston (Framingham); K=Kansas City; M=Michigan (Lansing); L=Linden (New Jersey); C=California (Los Angeles/Southgate);

and W=Wilmington, Del. Remaining symbols were the unit's sequential production number. Starting number at each assembly plant was 1001. Ending numbers, by series, at each coded plant were: [76] M48479; A6595; B7168; K11687; L8703; C9069; and W8794. [88] M46245; A7203; B8544; K13460; L10496; C10512; and W13460. [98] M46908; A6327; B7508; K11676; L9576; C9508; and W8750. Motor numbers (unrelated to assembly plants) were: [Six-cylinder] 6A1001 to 6A96888; [V-8] 8A1001 to 8A193864. Engines with an "H" prefix on Hydra-Matic cars.

1949 Oldsmobile, 76 Series two-door club coupe, OCW

SEVENTY-SIX SERIES

Model Number	Body/Style Number	Body Type & Seating	Factory Price	Shipping Weight	Production Total
76	49-3527	2-dr Clb Cpe-5P	1630	3260	12,683
76	49-3507	2-dr Clb Sed-5P	1790	3290	32,019
76	49-3569	4-dr Sed-5P	1725	3335	37,505
76	49-3508	4-dr Twn Sed-5P	1715	3625	6,466
76	49-3567X	2-dr Conv-5P	2025	3845	5,338
76	49-3561	4-dr Sta Wag-6P	2735	3945	1,545

NOTE 1: Deluxe equipped models had a suffix "D" after style number.

1949 Oldsmobile, 76 Series two-door convertible, OCW

1949 Oldsmobile, 88 Series four-door sedan, OCW

1949 Oldsmobile, 76 Series four-door station wagon, OCW

EIGHTY-EIGHT SERIES - Introduced later than the other two series, the Eighty-Eight was the logical combination of the all-new Rocket V-8 engine, from the Ninety-Eight series, into the new, lightweight Futuramic Seventy-Six chassis. Standard equipment and Deluxe equipment packages were nearly identical to those listed in the Seventy-Six series section. Upholstery selection could be made from leather, cloth and leather combinations, Bedford cord or broadcloth. Standard tires were 7.60 x 15 inches. Thirteen standard colors were offered plus eight two-tone combinations.

1949 Oldsmobile, 88 Series two-door club sedan, V-8 (DC)

EIGHTY-EIGHT SERIES

Model Number	Body/Style Number	Body Type & Seating	Factory Price	Shipping Weight	Production Total
88	49-3527	2-dr Clb Cpe-5P	2025	3550	11,561
88	49-3507	2-dr Clb Sed-5P	2050	3585	28,707
88	49-3569	4-dr Sed-5P	2120	3610	46,386
88	49-3508	4-dr Twn Sed-5P	2110	3625	5,833
88	49-3567DX	2-dr Conv-5P	2420	3845	5,434
88	49-3561	4-dr Sta Wag-6P	3120	3945	1,355

NOTE 1: Suffix "D" was on all Deluxe equipped cars.

1949 Oldsmobile, 98 Series two-door convertible, V-8 (DC)

FUTURAMIC NINETY-EIGHT SERIES - This was the second year for Futuramic styling in the top-of-the-line Oldsmobile series and the first year for Rocket V-8 power. Standard equipment included all items basic to the lower two series plus foam rubber seat cushions, windshield washer and turn signals. The Deluxe 98 package had a rear center seat armrest, front and rear floor mats, special chrome body moldings, electric clock, Deluxe steering wheel, stainless steel wheel trim rings and hy-

draulic window, seat and top controls on convertibles. Upholstery choices were Bedford cord, broadcloth, leather and leather/cloth combinations. Standard tire size was 7.60 x 15 inches. Oldsmobile used this year's 98 series to introduce its popular two-door Holiday hardtop model.

1949 Oldsmobile, 98 Series two-door club sedan, OCW

NINETY-EIGHT SERIES

Model Number	Body/Style Number	Body Type & Seating	Factory Price	Shipping Weight	Production Total
98	49-3807	2-dr Clb Sed-5P	2380	3835	20,049
98	49-3869	4-dr Sed-5P	2360	3890	57,821
98	49-3867X	2-dr Conv-5P	2810	4200	12,602
98	49-3837X	2-dr Hol Cpe-5P	2973	3945	3,006

NOTE 1: Cars with "D" suffix are Deluxes.

NOTE 2: Cars with "DX" suffix have hydraulic powered accessories.

1949 Oldsmobile, 98 Series Holiday two-door hardtop, OCW

ENGINES

(SERIES 76 SIX) Inline. Six-cylinder. Cast iron block. Bore and stroke: 3-17/32 x 4-3/8 inches. Displacement: 231 cid. Compression ratio: 6.5:1. Brake hp: 105 at 3400 rpm. Solid lifters. Carter WA1-709 S single-barrel downdraft carburetor with built-in choke.

1949 Oldsmobile, 88 Series two-door convertible, OCW

(SERIES 88/98 EIGHT) Vee-block. Overhead valves. Cast iron block. Bore and stroke: 3-3/4 x 3-7/16 inches. Brake hp: 135 at 3600 rpm. Compression ratio: 7.25:1. A Carter WGD-714S dual downdraft carburetor was fitted with an automatic choke.

64

1949 Oldsmobile, 88 Series two-door club coupe, OCW

OPTIONS: Standard radio ($88). Super Deluxe radio ($96). Condition-Air heater /defroster ($67). Traffic light viewer ($5). Cadet visor ($30). Hood ornament ($5). Stainless steel wheel rings ($10). Auxiliary driving and fog lights ($19). Spotlight ($26). Turn signals ($21). Glovebox light ($2). Underhood light ($2). Trunk light ($2). Outside rearview mirror ($3). Visor mirror ($2). Exhaust extension ($2). License frame ($2). Windshield washer ($9) Back-up lights ($15). A column-shifted three-speed manual transmission was standard equipment on all Seventy-Six models. Eighty-Eight and Ninety-Eights came standard with the Hydra-Matic transmission, which was an $185 option on the Seventy-Six. A heavy-duty air cleaner cost $4.40, while an oil filter cost $9.

HISTORICAL FOOTNOTES: In 1949 Olds introduced the first all-new postwar bodies for the Seventy-Six and Eighty-Eight series. These junior Oldsmobiles shared bodies with the new 1949 General Motors B-body Chevrolet and Pontiac. Although the 1949 station wagons were entirely new, they underwent major modifications at midyear. All exterior wood was replaced with steel, trimmed to resemble the deleted real wood. Consequently, the early 1949 wagons are more valuable today in the collector car market. Oldsmobile adopted functional P-38 World War II fighter-style air scoops under the headlights. Model year output was 288,310 cars...a new Oldsmobile record! The company retained seventh slot in the U.S. industry with 282,885 cars made in the calendar year. New-car introductions took place in September 1948 and the Holiday Hardtop was added at midyear. Along with Buick and Cadillac, Olds debuted the hardtop body style. These were the industry's first true pillarless hardtops. These hardtops also introduced the first wraparound rear windows. The 1949 Olds 88 sedan could go 0-60 mph in 12.2 seconds and run the quarter-mile in 19.9 seconds, which was hot for the time. Olds 88s quickly began setting stock car racing records. Symbolizing this performance, an 88 convertible was the official pace car for the 1949 Indianapolis 500. Among its special features was a see-through plexiglas hood to show off the Rocket 88 V-8. This item was made available as a factory option, too. Red Byron won the 1949 stock car race on the sand at Daytona Beach, Fla., with a Rocket 88 coupe and Oldsmobile took five of eight NASCAR Grand Nationals held that year. Byron was named the national champion.

1950

1950 Oldsmobile, 88 Series two-door sedan, 6-cyl., (DC)

SEVENTY-SIX SERIES - This was the final year for both the Seventy-Six series and its "Big Six" engine. Olds would not offer another six-cylinder until the mid-1960s and that engine would be built by Buick. The Seventy-Six models were again nearly identical to the Eighty-Eight offerings. Standard equipment on the base models included: bumper guards, dual horns, parking lamps, dome light, rubber front floor mats, aluminum sill plates. Deluxe equipment included: foam rubber seat cushions, robe rails, stainless steel gravel shields and extra chrome moldings. Upholstery choices were striped cloth, broadcloth, nylon surrey weave and leather. Standard tire size was 7.10 x 15 inches. For 1950, a Holiday hardtop was introduced to the Seventy-Six and Eighty-Eight series and this marked the last year for an Oldsmobile station wagon until 1957.

1950 Oldsmobile, 76 Series two-door club coupe, OCW

OLDSMOBILE I.D. NUMBERS: Serial number located on left front door pillar; on right side of cowl. Engine number on block above water pump; on plate on floor inside right door; on left corner of block above generator; and on front of left cylinder head at negative battery terminal. Olds 76 numbers took the form 506( )1001 to 506( )ending number. Olds 88 numbers took the form 508( )1001 to 508( )ending number. Olds 98 numbers took the form 509( )1001 to 509( )ending number. First two symbols indicate model year: 50=1950. Third symbol indicates series: 6=76; 8=88; 9=98. Fourth symbol in ( ) indicated assembly plant as follows: A=Atlanta; B=Boston (Framingham); K=Kansas City; M=Michigan (Lansing); L=Linden (New Jersey); C=California (Los Angeles/Southgate); and W=Wilmington, Del. Remaining symbols were the unit's sequential production number. Starting number at each assembly plant was 1001. Ending numbers, by series, at each coded plant were: [76] M17502; A3149; B2879; K4931; L3501; C3715; and W3657. [88] M114848; A20617; B20092; K40988; L26001; C25800; and W26826.[98] M51635; A7949; B7412; K14934; L10157; C10157; and W10280. Motor numbers (unrelated to assembly plants) were: [Six-cylinder] 6A97001 to 6A130440; [V-8] 8A194001 to 8A568689. Engines with an "H" prefix on Hydra-Matic cars.

1950 Oldsmobile, 76 Series two-door club sedan, OCW

1950 Oldsmobile, 76 Series Holiday two-door hardtop, OCW

SEVENTY-SIX SERIES

Model Number	Body/Style Number	Body Type & Seating	Factory Price	Shipping Weight	Production Total
76	503507	2-dr Clb Sed-5P	1640	3260	5,105
76	50-3511	2-dr Sed-5P	1655	3290	6,354
76	50-3527	2-dr Clb Cpe-5P	1615	3295	3,364
76	50-3537	2-dr Hol HT-5P	1885	3335	538
76	50-3567X	2-dr Conv-5P	2010	3585	973
76	50-3569	4-dr Sed-5P	1710	3340	16,555
76	50-3562	4-dr Sta Wag-6P	2360	3610	368

NOTE 1: Style numbers for Deluxe cars carried the suffix "D".

1950 Oldsmobile, 88 Series two-door club sedan, V-8 (DC)

EIGHTY-EIGHT SERIES - In its second year the Eighty-Eight continued to be one of the hottest performers available off the showroom floor. Body and chassis were quite similar to the Seventy-Six series. A one-piece curved windshield was a midyear upgrade for the 88s. Standard and Deluxe equipment packages were identical to those listed for the Seventy-Six. Upholstery choices included broadcloth, striped cloth, nylon and a variety of colored leathers. Standard tire size was 7.60 x 15 inches.

1950 Oldsmobile, 88 Series four-door sedan, OCW

EIGHTY-EIGHT SERIES

Model Number	Body/Style Number	Body Type & Seating	Factory Price	Shipping Weight	Production Total
88	50-3707	2-dr Clb Sed-5P	1790	3460	31,093
88	50-3711	2-dr Sed-5P	1805	3490	50,561
88	50-3727	2-dr Clb Cpe-5P	1725	3485	21,456
88	50-3737	2-dr Hol HT-5P	2035	3535	12,682
88	50-3762	4-dr Sta Wag-6P	2585	3810	2,382
88	50-3767X	2-dr Conv-5P	2160	3746	9,127
88	50-3769	4-dr Sed-5P	1860	3540	141,111

NOTE 1: Style numbers for Deluxe models carried the suffix "D".

1950 Oldsmobile, 88 Series Holiday two-door hardtop, OCW

1950 Oldsmobile, 98 Series two-door convertible, V-8 (DC)

NINETY-EIGHT SERIES - The 1950 Oldsmobile 98 repeated its 1948 precedent of previewing some of next year's styling cues for the 88. The 98 was restyled after only two years. It was the first slab-sided Oldsmobile and the first sedan with wrap-around rear windows. The 98 four-door fastback curiously returned after its absence from the line in 1949. Standard equipment included all items from the Eighty-Eight plus foam rubber seat cushions, chrome interior trim, lined luggage compartment and counter-balanced trunk lid. Deluxe Ninety-Eight equipment included rear seat center armrest, Deluxe electric clock, Deluxe steering wheel and horn button, special door trim and stainless steel wheel trim rings. Upholstery choices spanned nylon fabric, striped broadcloth or leather. Standard tire size was 7.60 x 15 inches.

1950 Oldsmobile, 98 Series four-door sedan, OCW

NINETY-EIGHT SERIES

Model Number	Body/Style Number	Body Type & Seating	Factory Price	Shipping Weight	Production Total
98	50-3807	2-dr Clb Sed-5P	2095	3685	11,989
98	50-3869	4-dr Sed-5P	2165	3765	80,265
98	50-3808	4-dr Twn Sed-5P	2135	3750	1,778
98	50-3837	2-dr Hol Cpe-5P	2245	3775	8,263
98	50-3867X	2-dr Conv-5P	2615	4150	3,925

NOTE 1: Deluxe cars carried the suffix "D" in style number.

1950 Oldsmobile, 98 Series two-door club sedan, OCW

ENGINES

(SERIES 76 SIX): Inline. Six-cylinder. Cast iron block. L-head. Bore and stroke: 3.531 x 4.375 inches. Displacement: 231.5 cid. Brake hp: 105 at 3400 rpm. Compression ratio: 6.5:1. Solid lifters. Carter single-barrel downdraft carburetor model WA1-764A with automatic choke.

1950 Oldsmobile, 88 Series two-door convertible, OCW

(SERIES 88/98 ROCKET 88 V-8): Vee-block. Overhead valve. Cast iron block. Hydraulic valve lifters. Bore and stroke: 3-3/4 x 3-7/16 inches. Displacement: 303.7 cid. Brake hp: 135 at 3600 rpm. Compression ratio: 7.25:1. Five main bearings. Carter model WGD-714S dual-downdraft carburetor.

1950 Oldsmobile, 88 Series four-door station wagon, OCW

CHASSIS FEATURES: Wheelbase: (Seventy-Six and Eighty-Eight 119-1/2 inches; (Ninety-Eight) 122 inches. Overall length: (Seventy-Six and Eighty-Eight) 202 inches, all except station wagon, 205 inches; (Ninety-Eight) 209 inches. Front tread: (Seventy-Six and Eighty-Eight) 57 inches; (Ninety-Eight) 59 inches. Rear tread: (Seventy-Six and Eighty-Eight) 59 inches; (Ninety-Eight) 61-1/2 inches.

OPTIONS: Standard Condition-Air heater and defroster ($45). Deluxe condition air heater and defroster ($60). Standard radio ($85). Deluxe radio ($1 10). Futuramic electric clock ($15). Deluxe steering wheel with horn ring ($20). Stainless steel wheel trim rings ($10). Deluxe wheel covers ($17). Turn signals ($15). Safety spotlight ($23). Auxiliary driving and fog lights ($16). Back-up lights ($15). Center bumper guard ($5). Under hood light ($2). glovebox light ($2). License frames ($2). Outside rear view mirror ($3). Visor mirror ($3). Exhaust deflector

($2). Windshield washer ($7) and Cadet sun visor ($27). Traffic light view ($5). Standard transmission on all 1950s was a column-shifted manual three-speed. Hydra-Matic was available on any 1950 Olds. Heavy-duty oil bath air cleaners were available or both the "Big Six" and the Rocket V-8. A full flow oil filter was a V-8 option.

HISTORICAL FOOTNOTES: Model year output: 407,889. Calendar year output: 396,757. Rank in U.S. industry: sixth. The 1950 Oldsmobiles were introduced in December 1949. During the calendar year, the company produced 6.6 percent (13,571) of all American convertibles; 8 percent (21,482) of the hardtops; and 1.7 percent (2,650) of the domestic station wagons. With the weak showing in wagons, Olds would not build wagons again until 1957. There were 19 big NASCAR stock car races during 1950. Oldsmobiles took 10 of them, with driver Bill Rexford winning the championship. Hershell McGriff and Ray Elliott won the 1950 Mexican Road Race in their #52 Olds coupe, a 1951 model. Car owner Roy Sundstrom, of Portland, Ore., was awarded 150,000 pesos for the victory. That sounds impressive, but equated to $17,341.04 in U.S. currency. McGriff, a 32-year-old lumber truck driver, won the race by a one minute and 19 second margin. His Rocket 88 was one of 13 Oldsmobiles that competed. At the Olds factory in Lansing, Mich., S.E. Skinner occupied the general manager's desk. His designers turned out the "Palm Beach" dream car. Based on the Holiday hardtop, it featured alligator hide and basketweave wicker trim. This was the final year of the fastback body style for all three Olds series.

1951

STANDARD/DELUXE 88 SERIES - This series was also known as the 88-A series and was almost identical to the 1950 Eighty-Eight series. Near the end of the model year, 88-A production was dropped altogether and the car disappeared from later editions of the 1951 catalog. Gone for 1951 was the long running inline six-cylinder engine. Two body styles were offered. Standard features included: bumper guards, cigarette lighter, dome light, rubber floor mats, stainless steel moldings and lined trunk. Deluxe cars had foam seat cushions, rear ashtrays and stainless steel gravel shields. Upholstery choices were nylon or nylon cord. Standard tire size was 7.60 x 15 inches.

1951 Oldsmobile, 88 Series two-door sedan, OCW

OLDSMOBILE I.D. NUMBERS: Serial number located on left front door pillar on right side of cowl. Engine number on block above water pump; and on plate on floor inside right door; and on left corner of block above generator; and on front of left cylinder head at negative battery terminal. Olds 88 numbers took the form 517( )1001 to 517( )ending number. Olds Super 88 numbers took the form 518( )1001 to 508( )ending number. Olds 98 numbers took the form 519( )1001 to 519( )ending number. First two symbols indicate model year: 51=1951. Third symbol indicates series: 7=88; 8=Super 88; 9=98. Fourth symbol in ( ) indicated assembly plant as follows: A=Atlanta; B=Boston (Framingham); K=Kansas City; M=Michigan (Lansing); L=Linden (New Jersey); C=California (Los Angeles/Southgate); and W=Wilmington, Del. Remaining symbols were

the unit's sequential production number. Starting number at each assembly plant was 1001. Ending numbers, by series, at each coded plant were: [88] M19934; A2960; B2835; K4989; L3571; C3555; and W3592. [Super 88] M66062; A12364; B11103; K20775; L14291; C15413; and W15340. [98] M42674; A8556; B7590; K15277; L11584; C11027; and W10857. Motor numbers (unrelated to assembly plants) were: [V-8] 8C1001 to 8C287312. Engines with at "B" prefix on Synchromesh cars.

1951 Oldsmobile, Super 88 four-door sedan, OCW

EIGHTY-EIGHT SERIES

Model Number	Body/Style Number	Body Type & Seating	Factory Price	Shipping Weight	Production Total
88A	51-3711	2-dr Sed-5P	1815	3585	11,792
88A	51-3769	4-dr Sed-5P	1871	3610	22,848

1951 Oldsmobile, Super 88 Holiday two-door hardtop (DC)

SUPER EIGHTY-EIGHT - This middle series was restyled and completely different than the Eighty-Eight series. The tables were turned this year with the restyled 88 predicting some of the 1952 Ninety-Eight styling cues. The Rocket V-8 was the only engine available. With its five body styles the Super 88 offered buyers more selection than the other Olds series. A Deluxe package was offered on this series. It included items from both the standard and Deluxe Eighty-Eight packages, plus low pressure tires, special interior chrome door trim, exposed chromed roof bows and dual rear quarter courtesy lights. Upholstery choices were colored leathers, nylon cloth or nylon cord. Standard tire size was 7.60 x 15 inches.

SUPER EIGHTY-EIGHT SERIES

Model Number	Body/Style Number	Body Type & Seating	Factory Price	Shipping Weight	Production Total
S-88	51-3627D	2-dr Clb Cpe-5P	1928	3628	7,328
S-88	51-3611D	2-dr Sed-5P	1969	3642	34,963
S-88	51-3637D	2-dr Hol HT-5P	2231	3659	14,180
S-88	51-3667DX	2-dr Conv-5P	2333	3896	3,854
S-88	51-3669D	4-dr Sed-5P	2025	3675	90,131

NOTE 1: DX suffix indicates hydraulically-operated seat and windows.

1951 Oldsmobile, 98 Series Holiday two-door hardtop (DC)

NINETY-EIGHT SERIES - The Ninety-Eight topped the Oldsmobile line again for 1951. Three body styles were available. The four-door sedan and convertible came only with Deluxe equipment, while the Holiday hardtop was available with either Deluxe or Standard trim. Ninety-Eight standard equipment included all items from the lower series, plus illuminated ashtray, foam rubber seat cushions and extra chrome moldings. Deluxe equipment was special rear door ornament, rear center seat armrests, Deluxe electric clock, Deluxe steering wheel with horn ring and special chrome trim. Upholstery choices were nylon cord, nylon cloth and leather.

1951 Oldsmobile, 98 Series four-door sedan, OCW

NINETY-EIGHT SERIES

Model Number	Body/Style Number	Body Type & Seating	Factory Price	Shipping Weight	Production Total
98	51-3837	2-dr Hol HT-5P	2267	3762	17,929
98	51-3869D	4-dr Sed-5P	2277	3787	78,122
98	51-3867DX	2-dr Conv-5P	2644	4107	4,468

NOTE 1: Deluxe models had D suffix; suffix "X" indicated hydraulic controls.

1951 Oldsmobile, 98 Series two-door convertible, OCW

ENGINE

V-8. Cast-iron block. Overhead valves. Hydraulic lifters. Five main bearings. Bore and stroke: 3-3/4 x 3-7/16 inches. Displacement: 303 cid. Brake hp: 135 at 3600 rpm. Torque: 263 pound feet at 1800 rpm. Compression ratio: 7.5:1. Carburetor: Rochester BB two-barrel.

1951 Oldsmobile, Super 88 two-door convertible, OCW

CHASSIS FEATURES: Wheelbase (Eighty-Eight) 119-1/2 inches; (Super Eighty-Eight) 120 inches; (Ninety-Eight) 122 inches. Overall length; (Eighty-Eight) 202 inches; (Super Eighty-Eight) 204 inches; (Ninety-Eight) 208 inches. Front tread: (Eighty-Eight and Super Eighty-Eighty) 57 inches; (Ninety-Eight) 59 inches. Rear tread: (Eighty-Eight and Super Eighty-Eight) 59 inches; (Ninety-Eight) 61-1/2 inches.

OPTIONS: Radio antenna ($7). Deluxe radio ($88). Super Deluxe signal seeking radio ($113). Electric clock ($15). Deluxe wheel covers ($17). Exhaust extension ($2). Deluxe condition air heater/ defroster ($42). Back-up lights ($18). Fog and driving lights ($19). Under hood light ($2). Spotlight with rearview mirror ($25). Outside rearview mirror ($4). Visor mirror ($2). Turn signals ($21). Rear radio speaker ($18). Chrome ventshades ($14). Cadet outside sun visor ($32). Traffic light viewer ($5). Battery vitalizer ($5). Windshield washer ($10). All 1951 Oldsmobiles were fitted with identical Rocket V-8 engine. The synchromesh three-speed column-shifted manual transmission was standard equipment in all series. Hydra-Matic was a $150 option on any model, any series. An optional $6 oil filter was available on any Rocket V-8. Rear end ratios were 3.42:1, 3.64:1 or 3.90:1.

HISTORICAL FOOTNOTES: The 1951 Oldsmobiles debuted in showrooms in January 1951. Model year production was 285,615 units, while the calendar year production total included only 19 additional cars. Oldsmobile ranked seventh again. Olds built 10,500 more hardtops in 1951 than 1952. For the calendar year, the hardtops' sales amounted to 32,109 units. However, this was a lower 6.7 percent of the hardtops' industry-wide share of market. The 1.3 percent drop for Olds was due to many other automakers bringing out their own hardtops. In the calendar year, Olds also built 5.9 percent (8,322) of all U.S. convertibles, but no wagons. Hydra-Matic transmission was installed in 278,717 cars in calendar 1951. In racing, Oldsmobile captured 20 of 41 stock car racing checkered flags, but lost the annual crown to Hudson. The dropping of the Holiday hardtop, club coupe and two-door fastback in the 1951 Rocket 88 series had a negative effect on winning races. The remaining models were heavier and less aerodynamic. Curtis "Pops" Turner became a well-known Olds race driver. On the corporate front, Jack Wolfrom became the 13th general manager of Oldsmobile Division.

1951 Oldsmobile, Super 88 two-door sedan, OCW

1952

1952 Oldsmobile, 88 Series two-door sedan, OCW

DELUXE EIGHTY-EIGHT - In 1952, Oldsmobile maintained its three series format. On the bottom was a two-model series known as the Deluxe Eighty-Eight. Wheelbase, chassis features and most body features, minus a bit of extra trim, were shared with the Super Eighty-Eight. A slightly lower-powered version of the Rocket V-8 was fitted. Standard equipment included: bumper guards, gray rubber floor mats front and rear, electric clock, dual horns, aluminum door sill plates and rubber gravel shields. Upholstery was a gray basket weave corded cloth. Standard tire size was 7.60 x 15 inches.

1952 Oldsmobile, 88 Series four-door sedan, OCW

OLDSMOBILE I.D. NUMBERS: Serial number located on left front door pillar on right side of cowl. Engine number on block above water pump; and on plate on floor inside right door; and on left corner of block above generator; and on front of left cylinder head at negative battery terminal. Olds 88/Super 88 numbers took the form 528( )1001 to 528( )ending number. Olds 98 numbers took the form 529( )1001 to 529( )ending number. First two symbols indicate model year: 52=1952. Third symbol indicates series: 8=88 or Super 88; 9=98. Fourth symbol in ( ) indicated assembly plant as follows: A=Atlanta; B=Boston (Framingham); K=Kansas City; M=Michigan (Lansing); L=Linden (New Jersey); C=California (Los Angeles/Southgate); and W=Wilmington, Del. Remaining symbols were the unit's sequential production number. Starting number at each assembly plant was 1001. Ending numbers, by series, at each coded plant were: [88/Super 88] M62915; A11269; B8235; K20968; L12276; C13379; and W13681. [98] M36565; A6008; B4730; K10793; L8605; C8403; and W7733. Engine numbers (unrelated to assembly plants) were: [V-8] 8R1001 to 8R214478.

1952 Oldsmobile, Super 88 Series four-door sedan (DC)

DELUXE EIGHTY-EIGHT SERIES

Model Number	Body/Style Number	Body Type & Seating	Factory Price	Shipping Weight	Production Total
D-88	52-3611	2-dr Sed-5P	2050	3565	6,402
D-88	52-3669	4-dr Sed-5P	2110	3608	12,215

SUPER EIGHTY-EIGHT - Similar to the Deluxe Eighty-Eight, the five model Super Eighty-Eight lineup was the most popular Olds series. The Super Eighty-Eight outsold the Eighty-Eight by a six to one margin. Standard equipment included Deluxe Eighty-Eight items plus foam rubber seat cushions, stainless steel gravel shields and turn signals. Upholstery choices were broadcloth, nylon sharkskin, nylon Bedford cord or leather. Standard tire size was 7.60 x 15 inches.

1952 Oldsmobile, Super 88 two-door sedan, OCW

SUPER EIGHTY-EIGHT SERIES

Model Number	Body/Style Number	Body Type & Seating	Factory Price	Shipping Weight	Production Total
S-88	52-3627D	2-dr Clb Cpe-5P	2126	3597	2,050
S-88	52-3611D	2-dr Sed-5P	2172	3603	24,963
S-88	52-3637D	2-dr Hol HT-5P	2430	3640	15,777
S-88	52-3667TDX	2-dr Conv-5P	2595	3867	5,162
S-88	52-3669D	4-dr Sed-5P	2234	3649	70,606

1952 Oldsmobile, Super 88 two-door convertible, OCW

NINETY-EIGHT SERIES - The Ninety-Eight models remained as the top-of-the-line Oldsmobiles. The series shared the new, higher output, 160-hp Rocket V-8 with the Super Eighty-Eight. Standard-equipment on the three body styles included Super Eighty-Eight items plus carpeting front and rear, electric clock, stainless steel wheel trim rings, windshield washer and Deluxe steering wheel with horn ring. Upholstery selection was broadcloth or six colors of leather. Standard tire size was 8.00 x 15.

NINETY-EIGHT SERIES

Model Number	Body/Style Number	Body Type & Seating	Factory Price	Shipping Weight	Production Total
98	52-3037D	2-dr Hol HT-5P	2750	3874	14,150
98	52-3067DX	2-dr Conv-5P	2940	4111	3,544
98	52-3069D	4-dr Sed-5P	2532	3764	58,550

1952 Oldsmobile, 98 Series two-door convertible (DC)

ENGINES

(DELUXE 88) V-8. Cast iron. Overhead valves. Hydraulic valve lifters. Bore and stroke: 3-3/4 x 3-7/16 inches. Displacement: 303 cid. Brake hp: 145 at 3600 rpm. Torque: 280 pound feet. Compression ratio: 7.5:1. Five main bearings. Carburetor: Rochester model BB two-barrel or Carter.

(SUPER 88/98) V-8. Cast iron block. Overhead valves. Hydraulic valve lifters. Bore and stroke: 3-3/4 x 3-7/16 inches. Displacement: 303 cid. Brake hp 160 at 3600 rpm. Torque: 283 pound feet. Compression ratio: 7.5:1. Five main bearings. Carburetor either Rochester 4GC or Carter WGD four-barrel.

CHASSIS FEATURES: Wheelbase: (Deluxe and Super Eighty-Eight) 120 inches; (Ninety-Eight) 124 inches. Overall length: (Deluxe and Super Eighty-Eight) 204 inches; (Ninety-Eight) 213 inches. Front tread: 58 inches. Rear tread: 59 inches.

OPTIONS: Deluxe Condition-Air heater/defroster ($79). Deluxe 6-tube radio ($100). Deluxe radio with rear speaker ($121). Super Deluxe 8-tube radio with signal seeking ($129). Windshield washer ($10). Back-up lights ($21). Deluxe steering wheel with horn ring ($14). Cadet visor ($32). Turn signals ($24). Electric clock ($8). Self-winding steering wheel mounted car watch ($35). Compass ($8). Stainless steel wheel trim rings ($14). "Hydraulic" power steering ($185). Accessory group Z exhaust extension, visor mirror, trunk, under hood and glovebox and hand brake lights. All cars were Rocket V-8 powered with Super Eighty-Eight and Ninety-Eight models having slightly higher horsepower. An optional oil filter was available for $10; a heavy-duty air cleaner cost $11. All cars came standard with a column-shifted three-speed manual transmission. The optional Hydra-Matic could be ordered on any model, any series for $165.

HISTORICAL FOOTNOTES: Model year production: 213,419. Calendar year production: 228,452. Rank in industry: fourth (a new high for Oldsmobile). Power steering was a new option. During 1952, Oldsmobile continued to be the top-selling car in America with automatic transmission. A total of 1,737,351 Oldsmobiles were built with Hydra-Matic since the division pioneered it in 1940. (All in all, 3,837,443 American cars -- including 223,581 Olds built in calendar 1952 -- had been equipped with Hydra-Matic by the end of 1952.) During the calendar year run, Olds also made 9,500 convertibles and 33,119 hardtops, both up slightly. The Southern 500 stock car race at Darlington, S.C., on Labor Day 1952, was the biggest of three NASCAR events Oldsmobiles won in 1952.

1953

1953 Oldsmobile, 88 Series two-door sedan (DC)

DELUXE EIGHTY-EIGHT - Oldsmobile continued to offer a relatively modest entry series with just two body styles in the Deluxe Eighty-Eight series. Again a lower horsepower Rocket V-8 was exclusive to this series. Standard equipment included: bumper guards, electric clock, lined trunk, dual horns, cigarette lighter, chrome moldings and twin interior sun visors. A total of 17 colors were available with 15 two-tone combinations on the order form. Upholstery was a two-tone pattern cloth. Standard tire size was 7.60 x 15 inches.

1953 Oldsmobile, 88 Series four-door sedan, OCW

OLDSMOBILE I.D. NUMBERS: Serial number located on left front door pillar on right side of cowl. Engine number on block above water pump; and on plate on floor inside right door; and on left corner of block above generator; and on front of left cylinder head at negative battery terminal. Olds 88 numbers took the form 537( )1001 to 537( )ending number. Olds Super 88 numbers took the form 538( )1001 to 538( )ending number. Olds 98 numbers took the form 539( )1001 to 539( )ending number. First two symbols indicate model year: 53=1953. Third symbol indicates series: 7=88; 8=Super 88; 9=98. Fourth symbol in ( ) indicated assembly plant as follows: A=Atlanta; B=Boston (Framingham); K=Kansas City; M=Michigan (Lansing); L=Linden (New Jersey); C=California (Los Angeles/Southgate); and W=Wilmington, Del. Remaining symbols were the unit's sequential production number. Starting number at each assembly plant was 1001. Ending numbers, by series, at each coded plant were: [88] M19106; A3184; B3254; K4613; L3317; C3028; and W3298. [Super 88] M107336; A13333; B11410; K24976; L15787; C17946; and W16346. [98] M49567; A7826; B6610; K13956; L10234; C9887; and W9034. Engine numbers (unrelated to assembly plants) were: [V-8] R215001 to R549482.

1953 Oldsmobile, Super 88 Series Holiday two-door hardtop (DC)

DELUXE EIGHTY-EIGHT SERIES

Model Number	Body/Style Number	Body Type & Seating	Factory Price	Shipping Weight	Production Total
S-88	53-3611	2-dr Sed-5P	2065	3514	12,400
S-88	53-3669	4-dr Sed-5P	2126	3622	20,400

SUPER EIGHTY-EIGHT - Again Oldsmobile's middle series offered the most body styles and had the highest sales. The Super 88's body and chassis were similar to the Deluxe Eighty-Eight. The Super Eighty-Eight shared a higher horsepower Rocket V-8 with the Ninety-Eight. This series carried the same standard equipment as the Deluxe Eighty-Eight, plus rear seat robe rails, special rear stainless steel trim and chrome window ventipanes. Upholstery selection included nylon cloth or leather.

1953 Oldsmobile, 98 Series Fiesta two-door convertible (DC)

SUPER EIGHTY-EIGHT SERIES

Model Number	Body/Style Number	Body Type & Seating	Factory Price	Shipping Weight	Production Total
S-88	53-3611D	2-dr Sed-5P	2253	3634	36,824
S-88	53-3637D	2-dr Hol HT-5P	2448	3670	34,500
S-88	53-3667DX	2-dr Conv-5P	2615	4080	8,310
S-88	53-3669	4-dr Sed-5P	2252	3681	119,317

1953 Oldsmobile, 98 Series Holiday two-door hardtop, OCW

NINETY-EIGHT SERIES - The normally plush Ninety-Eight series got an even richer limited production model late in the year, the rare Fiesta. This model predicted 1954 styling features such as the "panoramic" wraparound windshield and also had virtually every Olds option offered, except factory air conditioning.

The regular Ninety-Eight models had all items from the lower series cars as standard equipment plus padded dash, windshield washers and Deluxe steering wheel with horn ring. Upholstery selections were broadcloth, gabardine or leather. Standard tire size was 8.00 x 15.

NINETY-EIGHT SERIES

Model Number	Body/Style Number	Body Type & Seating	Factory Price	Shipping Weight	Production Total
98	53-3037DX	2-dr Hol HT-5P	2771	3906	27,920
98	53-3067DX	2-dr Conv-5P	2963	4123	7,521
98	53-3069D	4-dr Sed-5P	2552	3798	64,431
98	53-3067SDX	2-dr Fiesta Conv-5P	5715	4459	458

1953 Oldsmobile, 98 Series four-door sedan, OCW

ENGINES

(DELUXE 88) V-8. Cast iron block. Overhead valves. Hydraulic valve lifters. Bore and stroke: 3-3/4 x 3-7/16 inches. Displacement: 303 cid. Compression ratio: 8.0:1. Brake hp: 150 at 3600 rpm. Torque: 280 pound feet at 1800 rpm. Carburetor: Carter WGD two-barrel.

(SUPER 88/98) V-8. Cast iron block. Overhead valves. Hydraulic valve lifters. Bore and stroke: 3-3/4 x 3-7/16 inches. Displacement: 303 cid. Compression ratio: 8.0.1. Brake hp: 165 at 3600 rpm. Torque: 284 pound feet at 1800 rpm. Carburetor: either Rochester 4GC or Carter WCFB four-barrels.

1953 Oldsmobile, 98 Series two-door convertible, OCW

(FIESTA) V-8. Cast iron block. Overhead valves. Hydraulic valve lifters. Bore and stroke: 3-3/4 x 3-7/16 inches. Displacement: 303 cid. Compression ratio: 8.3:1. Brake hp: 170 at 4000 rpm. Carburetor: Rochester 4GC four-barrel.

CHASSIS FEATURES: Wheelbase: (Deluxe and Super Eighty-Eights) 120 inches; (Ninety-Eight and Fiesta) 124 inches. Overall length: (Deluxe and Super Eighty-Eights) 204 inches; (Ninety-Eight and Fiesta) 215 inches. Tread: (front and rear all series) 59 inches.

OPTIONS: Deluxe Condition-Air heater/defroster ($79). Deluxe radio, six-tube push button ($100). Rear seat speaker ($20). Super Deluxe radio, eight-tube, signal seeking ($129). Back-up lights ($14). Hand brake light ($6). Windshield washer ($10). Deluxe steering wheel with horn ring ($14). Cadet visor ($33). Safety padded instrument panel ($15). Electric clock ($18). Autronic eye ($50). Tinted glass ($30). Hydraulic window and seat

controls ($131). Oldsmobile/Frigidaire air conditioning ($550). Stainless steel wheel trim rings ($12). Power steering ($165). Power brakes ($33). This year all Oldsmobiles were equipped, for the first time, with 12-volt electrical systems. All models, except the Fiesta, came standard with a three-speed manual, column-shifted transmission. Hydra-Matic, which was standard on the Fiesta, cost $132 on any other model in any series. An optional oil filter cost $10 and a heavy-duty air cleaner was $6.

HISTORICAL FOOTNOTES: The 1953 Oldsmobiles were introduced Jan. 9, 1953. By the end of the year, 334,462 cars built to 1953 model specs were made. A calendar year run of 319,414 units put Olds in seventh place. The Fiesta limited-production convertible was introduced midyear. There were big increases in calendar year production of convertibles (16,000 built) and hardtops (62,500 built). The fiberglass-bodied Starfire toured this year's auto shows. The release of heavy-duty factory parts helped make '53 Oldsmobiles more competitive in NASCAR racing. Olds captured checkered flags in nine events, including Buck Baker's win at the Southern 500. Bob Pronger set a new mark of 113.38 mph in the Flying-Mile at Daytona driving an Old 88 two-door sedan. Later, he rolled the car on the beach race course during the 160-mile Daytona stock car race, which Bill Blair won in another Olds. During this model year a fire destroyed the General Motors Hydra-Matic plant and a number of Oldsmobiles were built with the Buick Dyna-Flow automatic transmission.

1954

EIGHTY-EIGHT SERIES - A complete restyling was introduced across the board for Oldsmobile in 1954. The entry level Olds series was again the Eighty-Eight. Gone was the misleading Deluxe Eighty-Eight terminology. The bottom series was powered by slightly de-tuned Rocket V-8. A third model was added to this series -- the popular two-door Holiday hardtop. Standard Eighty-Equipment included: bumper guards, rubber simulated carpets front and rear, electric clock, lined trunk, dual horns, cigarette lighter, aluminum door sill plates and turn signals. Eighteen standard paint colors were offered in 1954 and 18 factory two-tone combinations. Upholstery was either gray, green or blue pattern cloth. Standard tire size was 7.60 x 15 inches.

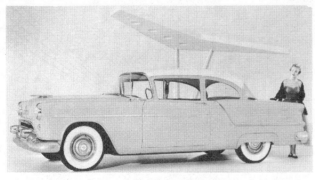

1954 Oldsmobile, 88 Series two-door sedan (DC)

OLDSMOBILE I.D. NUMBERS: Serial number located on left front door pillar on right side of cowl. Engine number on block above water pump; and on plate on floor inside right door; and on left corner of block above generator; and on front of left cylinder head at negative battery terminal. Olds 88 numbers took the form 547( )1001 to 547( )ending number. Olds Super 88 numbers took the form 548( )1001 to 548( )ending number. Oldsmobile 98 numbers took the form 549( )1001 to 549( )ending number. First two symbols indicate model year: 54=1954. Third symbol indicates series: 7=88; 8=Super 88; 9=98. Fourth symbol in ( ) indicated assembly plant as follows:

A=Atlanta; B=Boston (Framingham); K=Kansas City; M=Michigan (Lansing); L=Linden (New Jersey); C=California (Los Angeles/Southgate); T=Texas (Arlington); and W=Wilmington, Del. Remaining symbols were the unit's sequential production number. Starting number at each assembly plant was 1001. Ending numbers, by series, at each coded plant were: [88] M31457; A6390; T3992; B5394; K10213; L9056; C7066; and W7293. [Super 88] M8842; A15328; T7612; B12411; K24104; L23190; C16267; and W17294. [98] M44758; A7278; T4101; B6362; K10921; L11436; C8426; and W7779. Engine numbers (unrelated to assembly plants) were: [V-8] V1001 to V355083.

EIGHTY-EIGHT SERIES

Model Number	Body/Style Number	Body Type & Seating	Factory Price	Shipping Weight	Production Total
88	54-3611	2-dr Sed-5P	2066	3684	18,013
88	54-3637	2-dr Hol HT-5P	2230	3703	25,820
88	54-3669	4-dr Sed-5P	2126	3707	29,028

1954 Oldsmobile, Super 88 Series two-door convertible (DC)

SUPER EIGHTY-EIGHT SERIES - The Super Eighty-Eight continued to be Oldsmobile's bread-and-butter series. One of the most noticeable 1954 features was the so-called panoramic windshield previewed on the limited-production 1953 Fiesta. Standard equipment on this series included all items from the Eighty-Eight series plus chrome rocker panel moldings, deck lid ornament and foam rubber seat cushions. Upholstery selections featured a nylon and orlon cloth combination or a variety of colored leathers. Standard tire size was 7.60 x 15 inches.

SUPER EIGHTY-EIGHT SERIES

Model Number	Body/Style Number	Body Type & Seating	Factory Price	Shipping Weight	Production Total
S-88	54-3611D	2-dr Sed-5P	2189	3713	27,882
S-88	54-3637D	2-dr Hol HT-5P	2448	3758	42,155
S-88	54-3667DTX	2-dr Conv-5P	2615	3985	6,452
S-88	54-3669D	4-dr Sed-5P	2251	3755	111,326

1954 Oldsmobile, Super 88 four-door sedan, OCW

NINETY-EIGHT SERIES - A three model Ninety-Eight series was atop the Olds line. This year Olds dubbed its Ninety-Eight series convertibles 'Starfires' after the previous year's dream car. A slightly higher horsepower Rocket V-8 was shared with Super Eighty-Eight models. Standard Ninety-Eight equipment includ-

ed items from the bottom two series plus padded dash, parking brake light, courtesy light package, stainless steel wheel discs, windshield washer and Deluxe steering wheel with horn ring. Upholstery choices were nylon and leather in a variety of colors. Standard tire size was 8.00 x 15 inches.

1954 Oldsmobile, 98 Series Holiday two-door hardtop (DC)

NINETY-EIGHT SERIES

Model Number	Body/Style Number	Buy Type & Seating	Factory Price	Shipping Weight	Production Total
98	54-3037	2-dr Hol HT-5P	2570	3840	38,553
98	54-3067DX	2-dr Conv-5P	2963	4159	6,800
98	54-3069D	4-dr Sed-5P	2552	3863	47,972

1954 Oldsmobile, 98 Series Starfire two-door convertible, OCW

ENGINES

(88 SERIES) V-8. Cast iron block. Overhead valves. Hydraulic lifters. Bore and stroke: 3-7/8 x 3-7/16 inches. Displacement: 324 cid. Hp: 170 at 4000 rpm. Compression ratio: 8.5:1. Torque 300 pound feet at 1400 rpm. Carburetor Carter dual downdraft WGD.

(SUPER 88/98 SERIES) V-8. Cast iron block. Overhead valves. Hydraulic lifters. Bore and stroke: 3-7/8 x 3-7/16 inches. Displacement: 324 cid. Hp: 185: Torque 300 pound feet. Compression ratio: 8.25:1. Carburetor: Carter WCFB or Rochester 4GC, both four-barrels.

CHASSIS FEATURES: Wheelbase: (Eighty-Eight and Super Eighty-Eight) 122 inches; (Ninety-Eight) 126 inches. Overall length: (Eighty-Eight and Super Eighty-Eight) 205.26 inches; (Ninety-Eight) 214.26 inches. Front tread: 59 inches. Rear tread: 58 inches.

OPTIONS: Deluxe heater/defroster ($79). Power steering ($125). Deluxe radio ($100). Electric antenna ($20). Rear seat speaker ($14). Super Deluxe radio ($129). Back-up lights ($14). Courtesy light package ($4). Windshield washer ($10). Tinted glass ($30). Cadet sunvisor ($33). Padded dash ($17). Power brakes ($37). Air conditioning ($550). Oversize tires ($18). Whitewall tires ($30). Autronic eye ($45). Hydraulic window lifts ($165). Electric 4-way seat ($65). Stainless steel wheel trim rings ($8). Deluxe wheel discs ($30). Mimetic wire wheel discs ($60). Accessory group Z - exhaust extension, visor mirror and trunk, under hood and glove box lights ($10). Oil filter ($10). Air cleaner ($5). Hydra-Matic transmission ($165).

HISTORICAL FOOTNOTES: The 1954 Oldsmobiles were introduced on Jan. 20, 1954. Added later were Deluxe 88 and Classic 98 Deluxe Holiday hardtops and the Classic 98 Holiday convertible or Starfire convertible. The Rocket V-8 was enlarged for the first time, going from 303 cid to 324 cid through a larger bore. Olds added the Starfire "show car" name to the 1954 98 convertible. Model year production was 354,001 units. Olds took fourth place in industry output with calendar year production of 433,810 units. The '54s were the fastest Olds ever with up to 170 hp from the 324-cid block. They could do 0-60 mph in 12.4 seconds and cover the quarter-mile in 18. Calendar year production included 11,575 convertibles and 144,000 hardtops, with sales of the hardtops more than doubling from the prior year. The Cutlass F-88 dream car toured the show circuit for Oldsmobile in 1954. Oldsmobiles took 11 NASCAR victories, but then heavy-duty factory parts kits were banned.

1955

1955 Oldsmobile, 88 Series two-door sedan (DC)

EIGHTY-EIGHT - Again the entry Olds series was the Eighty-Eight with its three body styles. Exclusive to this series was a slightly de-tuned, 185-hp Rocket V-8 engine, although the 202-hp Rocket was a $35 option. Standard Eighty-Eight equipment included: turn signals, bumper guards, stainless steel moldings, dual horns, cigarette lighter, front and rear floor mats and inside rear view mirror. Oldsmobile continued to offer a number of a stylish two-tone combinations highlighted by an attractive molding package. Upholstery choices were gray, green or blue pattern cloth or moroceen and pattern cloth. Standard tire size was 7.60 x 15 inches.

1955 Oldsmobile, Super 88 Holiday four-door hardtop (DC)

OLDSMOBILE I.D. NUMBERS: Serial number located on left front door pillar on right side of cowl. Engine number on block above water pump; and on plate on floor inside right door; and on left corner of block above generator; and on front of left cylinder head at negative battery terminal. Olds 88 numbers took the form 557( )1001 to 557( )ending number. Olds Super 88 numbers took the form 558( )1001 to 558( )ending number. Oldsmobile 98 numbers took the form 559( )1001 to 559( )ending number. First two symbols indicate model year: 55=1955. Third symbol indicates series: 7=88; 8=Super 88;

9=98. Fourth symbol in ( ) indicated assembly plant as follows: A=Atlanta; B=Boston (Framingham); K=Kansas City; M=Michigan (Lansing); L=Linden (New Jersey); C=California (Los Angeles/Southgate); T=Texas (Arlington); and W=Wilmington, Del. Remaining symbols were the unit's sequential production number. Starting number at each assembly plant was 1001. Ending numbers, by series, at each coded plant were: [88] M83115; A25284; T13728; B14843; K26765; L30220; C26134; and W18188. [Super 88] M95087; A24050; T14606; B35211; K26765; L30220; C26134; and W18874. [98] M48385; A12463; T7937; B7338; K12237; L16111; C12655; and W9117. Engine numbers (unrelated to assembly plants) were: [V-8] V400001 to V983275.

EIGHTY-EIGHT SERIES

Model Number	Body/Style Number	Body Type & Seating	Factory Price	Shipping Weight	Production Total
88	55-3611	2-dr Sed-5P	2297	3690	37,507
88	55-3637	2-dr Hol HT-5P	2474	3705	85,767
88	55-3669	4-dr Sed-5P	2362	3710	57,777
88	55-3639	4-dr Hol HT-5P	2546	3695	41,310

SUPER EIGHTY-EIGHT - This year the 202-hp Ninety-Eight series engine was slipped into the Eighty-Eight body to make the Super Eighty-Eight series. An Olds buyer had more choice in this series than any other, since there were four available body styles. Standard equipment included Eighty-Eight series items plus foam rubber seat cushions, stainless steel rocker panel moldings, front seatback robe cord, spun glass hood insulation and rear window ventpanes. Upholstery choices were pattern cloth, leather and pattern cloth combinations and two colored leather combinations.

1955 Oldsmobile, Super 88 Holiday two-door hardtop, OCW

SUPER EIGHTY-EIGHT SERIES

Model Number	Body/Style Number	Body Type & Seating	Factory Price	Shipping Weight	Production Total
S-88	55-3611D	2-dr Sed-5P	2436	3755	11,950
S-88	55-3637D	2-dr Hol HT-5P	2714	3765	62,534
S-88	55-3667DTX	2-dr Conv-5P	2894	3795	9,007
S-88	55-3669D	4-dr Sed-5P	2503	3760	111,316
S-88	55-36395D	4-dr Hol HT-5P	2788	3780	47,385

1955 Oldsmobile, Super 88 four-door sedan, OCW

1955 Oldsmobile, Super 88 two-door convertible, OCW

NINETY-EIGHT SERIES - This year's Ninety-Eight again had a longer wheelbase than the Eighty-Eight. Standard equipment included items from the Eighty-Eight and Super Eighty-Eight series plus electric clock, stainless steel wheel discs, custom cushion lounge seats front and rear, hand brake light, courtesy light package, padded dash, Deluxe steering wheel with horn ring and windshield washer. Upholstery choices were covert and pattern cloth, leather and pattern cloth, leather and nylon and leather and dimple leather. Standard tire size was 7.60 x 15 inches.

1955 Oldsmobile, 98 Series Starfire two-door convertible (DC)

1955 Oldsmobile, 98 Series four-door sedan, OCW

NINETY-EIGHT SERIES

Model Number	Body/Style Number	Body Type & Seating	Factory Price	Shipping Weight	Production Total
98	55-3037	2-dr Hol HT-5P	3069	3805	38,363
98	55-3067DX	2-dr Starfire Conv-5P	3276	3890	9,149
98	55-3069D	4-dr Sed-5P	2833	3865	39,847
98	55-3039SDX	4-dr Hol HT	3140	3875	31,267

NOTE 1: Deluxe Holiday two-door hardtop carried the suffix "DX" in style number.

ENGINES

(88 SERIES) V-8. Cast iron block. Overhead valves. Hydraulic valve lifters. 3-7/8 x 3-7/16 inches. Displacement: 324 cid. Hydraulic valve lifters. Hp: 185 at 4000 rpm. Torque: 320 pound feet at 2000 rpm. Compression ratio: 8.5:1. Carburetor: Rochester 2GC dual downdraft.

1955 Oldsmobile, 98 Series Holiday four-door hardtop, OCW

(SUPER 88/98 SERIES) V-8. Cast iron block. Overhead valves. Hydraulic valve lifters. Bore and stroke: 3-7/8 x 3-7/16 inches. Displacement: 324 cid. Hydraulic valve lifters. Compression ratio: 8.5:1. Hp: 202 at 4000 rpm. Torque: 332 pound feet at 2400 rpm. Carburetor: Rochester 4GC Quadra-jet.

1955 Oldsmobile, 98 Series Holiday two-door hardtop, OCW

CHASSIS FEATURES: Wheelbase: (Eighty-Eight and Super Eighty-Eight) 122 inches; (Ninety-Eight) 126 inches. Overall length: (Eighty-Eight and Super Eighty-Eight) 203 inches. (Ninety-Eight) 212 inches. Front tread: 59 inches. Rear tread: 58 inches.

OPTIONS: Condition-air heater/defroster ($74). Power steering ($120). Deluxe radio ($94). Electric radio antenna ($21). Rear seat radio speaker ($12). Super Deluxe radio ($21). Back-up lights ($13). Hand brake light ($5). Windshield washer ($11). Deluxe steering wheel with horn ring ($15). Padded dash ($32). Spotlight ($23). Air conditioning ($550). Pedal-Ease power brakes ($58). Electric clock ($11). Autronic Eye ($45). Electric 2-way seat ($50). Electric 4-way seat ($65). Electric windows ($80). Hydra-Matic ($165). Heavy-duty air cleaner ($10). Oil filter ($6).

HISTORIC FOOTNOTES: Nov. 5, 1954, was the factory introduction date for 1955 Oldsmobiles. Dealer introductions were held exactly two weeks later in auto showrooms across America. Public announcements of the 1955 Holiday four-door hardtop were made Jan. 6, 1955, two days after Buick announced its own Riviera four-door hardtop. Sales of this totally new body style, by Oldsmobile dealers, began in March 1955. This helped make it the best-ever model year for the company with production of 583,179 units. The calendar year output was 643,549 cars, good for fifth in the industry's production sweepstakes. On a calendar year basis, the new four-door Holiday sedan outsold the Riviera sedan 174,207 to 173,527. However, the Oldsmobile lead in four-door hardtop sales lasted only the one year. Olds also increased calendar year production of convertibles to 20,218 units and Holiday two-door hardtops to 195,866. The extraction of 32 more horsepower from the 324 cid V-8 helped the 1955 Super 88 sedan trim its 0-60 mph time to 10.6 seconds and its quarter-mile time to 17.6 seconds. Tubeless tires were used in all series. Drivers Dick Rathman and Jim Pascal raced Oldsmobiles for the Wood Racing Team. This year's factory show car was the Delta, with cast aluminum wheels and

annodized aluminum bodyside trim predictive of the late 1950s plus a tachometer and console like 1960s muscle cars. The Eighty-Eight four-door hardtops had Ninety-Eight-style side trim, while the 98 four-door sedan had 88-style side trim. The Eighty-Eight had unique tear-drop cutouts in its fender skirts for this year only.

1956

1956 Oldsmobile, 88 Series two-door sedan (DC)

EIGHTY-EIGHT - Oldsmobile stayed with its three series format in 1956. The Eighty-Eight was again the entry level series. The series was expanded this year to four body styles including a new four-door Holiday hardtop. Standard equipment items were: armrests, bumper guards, lined trunk, rotary door latches, dual horns, cigarette lighter, turn signals, rubber floor mats, aluminum door sill plates and sun visors. Twenty-one factory colors were available with 26 two-tone combinations. Upholstery choices included pattern cloth in a variety of colors and trim materials. Standard tire size was 7.10 x 15 inches.

OLDSMOBILE I.D. NUMBERS: Serial number located on left front door pillar on right side of cowl. Engine number on block above water pump; and on plate on floor inside right door; and on left corner of block above generator; and on front of left cylinder head at negative battery terminal. Olds 88 numbers took the form 567( )1001 to 567( )ending number. Olds Super 88 numbers took the form 568( )1001 to 568( )ending number. Olds 98 numbers took the form 569( )1001 to 569( )ending number. First two symbols indicate model year: 56=1956. Third symbol indicates series: 7=88; 8=Super 88; 9=98. Fourth symbol in ( ) indicated assembly plant as follows: A=Atlanta; B=Boston (Framingham); K=Kansas City; M=Michigan (Lansing); L=Linden (New Jersey); C=California (Los Angeles/Southgate); T=Texas (Arlington); and W=Wilmington, Del. Remaining symbols were the unit's sequential production number. Starting number at each assembly plant was 1001. Ending numbers, by series, at each coded plant were: [88] M81004; A23776; T12624; B13634; K23009; L27865; C21622; and W20657. [Super 88] M68628; A18370; T11317; B9624; K19777; L23452; C19208; and W15808. [98] M37834; A9354; T6069; B5403; K8944; L13210; C9179; and W8063. Engine numbers (unrelated to assembly plants) were: [V-8] A001001 to A385513.

1956 Oldsmobile, 88 Series Holiday two-door hardtop, OCW

EIGHTY-EIGHT SERIES

Model Number	Body/Style Number	Body Type & Seating	Factory Price	Shipping Weight	Production Total
88	56-3611	2-dr Sed-5P	2166	3705	31,949
88	56-3637	2-dr Hol HT-5P	2330	3715	74,739
88	56-3669	4-dr Sed-5P	2226	3761	57,092
88	56-3639	4-dr Hol HT-5p	2397	3776	52,239

1956 Oldsmobile, Super 88 Series Holiday two-door hardtop (DC)

SUPER EIGHTY-EIGHT - With its five body styles the Super Eighty-Eight continued to offer the most selection and achieved the most sales. Standard equipment included Eighty-Eight series items plus front and rear carpeting, foam rubber seat cushions, courtesy lights, front fender medallions and deck lid '88' script. Upholstery choices included pattern cloth and leather in a variety of colors and combinations. Standard tire size was 7.60 x 15 inches.

1956 Oldsmobile, Super 88 two-door convertible, OCW

SUPER EIGHTY-EIGHT SERIES

Model Number	Body/Style Number	Body Type & Seating	Factory Price	Shipping Weight	Production Total
S-88	56-3611D	2-dr Sed-5P	2301	3835	5465
S-88	56-3637SD	2-dr Hol HT-5P	2520	3838	43,054
S-88	56-3669D	4-dr Sed-5P	2363	3897	59,728
S-88	56-3639SD	4-dr Hol HT-5P	2586	3905	61,192
S-88	56-3667DTX	2-dr Conv-5P	2726	3947	9,561

NINETY-EIGHT - Again in 1956, the top of the line Oldsmobile series had an exclusive wheelbase four inches longer than the two Eighty-Eight series cars. Power came from a 240-hp Rocket V-8 shared with Super Eighty-Eights. Standard equipment included all items found on the lower series plus back-up light moldings, electric clock, Jetaway Hydra-Matic Drive, padded dash, courtesy lights, power steering, windshield washers and Deluxe steering wheel. Upholstery choices were pattern cloth and leather in a variety of colors and combinations. Standard tire size was 8.00 x 15 inches either U.S. Royal, Goodrich or Firestone.

NINETY-EIGHT SERIES

Model Number	Body/Style Number	Body Type & Seating	Factory Price	Shipping Weight	Production Total
98	56-3037SDX	2-dr Hol HT-5P	3138	3978	19,433
98	56-3069D	4-dr Sed-5P	2969	4047	20,105
98	56-3039SDX	4-dr Hol HT-5P	3204	4061	42,320
98	56-3067DX	2-dr Starfire Conv-5P	3380	4107	8,581

1956 Oldsmobile, 98 Series Starfire two-door convertible (DC)

ENGINES

(88 SERIES) Cast-iron overhead valve V-8 engine. Bore and stroke: 3-7/8 x 3-7/16 inches. Displacement: 324 cid. Hydraulic valve lifters. Compression ratio: 9.25:1. Hp: 230 at 4400 rpm. Torque: 340 pound feet at 2400 rpm. Carburetor: Rochester 2GC dual downdraft. Super Eighty-Eight engine optional in this series.

(SUPER 88/98 SERIES) Cast-iron overhead valve V-8 engine. Bore and stroke: 3-7/8 x 3-7/16 inches. Displacement: 324 cid. Hydraulic valve lifters. Compression ratio: 9.25:1. Hp: 240 at 4400 rpm. Torque: 350 pound feet at 2800 rpm. Carburetor: Rochester 4GC Quadro-Jet.

CHASSIS FEATURES: Wheelbase: (Eighty-Eight and Super Eighty-Eight) 122 inches; (Ninety-Eight) 126 inches. Overall length: (Eighty-Eight and Super Eighty-Eight) 203.29 inches; (Ninety-Eight) 212.29 inches. Front tread: 59 inches. Rear tread: 58 inches.

OPTIONS: Deluxe heater and defroster ($77). Power steering ($100). Deluxe six-tube push-button radio ($96). Electric antenna ($21). Rear speaker ($14). Super Deluxe eight-tube signal seeking radio ($121). Back-up lights ($13). Parking brake light ($5) Front courtesy lights ($4). Windshield washer ($10). Deluxe steering wheel with horn ring ($13). Deluxe horn ($10). Tinted glass ($30). Cadet visor ($33). Padded dash ($18). Power brakes ($37). Electric clock ($18). Air conditioning ($400). Whitewall tires ($33). Dual exhaust ($38). Exhaust extension ($2). Autronic eye ($46). Electric 6-way seat ($86). Electric windows ($90) Deluxe wheel discs ($28). Heavy-duty air cleaner ($10). Oil filter ($6). Super Hydra-Matic Drive ($175). Jetaway Hydra-Matic ($190 on 98s only). Heavy-duty manual transmission with clutch cover and special propeller shaft (Lansing-built cars only, $15).

1956 Oldsmobile, 98 Series Holiday two-door hardtop, OCW

HISTORICAL FOOTNOTES: Factory introduction of the 1956 Oldsmobiles was Oct. 25, 1955. The dealer introductions took place on Nov. 3. Model year assemblies came to 485,459 units, equaling 7.7 percent of all U.S. output. Calendar year totals were 432,903 vehicles including 17,795 convertibles; 121,304 two-door hardtops; 128,640 four-door hardtops; and 689 early-production 1957 station wagons. Leather trim was

available in the Olds 98 Starfire convertible; the 98 Deluxe Holiday four-door hardtop; the 98 Deluxe Holiday two-door hardtop; the Super 88 convertible; and the Super 88 Holiday four-door hardtop and Holiday two-door hardtop. Even with 38 extra horses, the 1956 Olds Super 88 four-door hardtop was slower than the 1955 four-door sedan. It needed an extra .20 seconds for both 0-60 mph and the quarter-mile, due to its extra 107 pound weight. Olds took only one big NASCAR race in 1956, although Lee Petty was able to establish a new Flying-Mile record of 144 mph with an Oldsmobile at Daytona Beach, Fla. The 1956 face lift introduced a swept flank to depart from the 1954/55 boxy look.

1957

1957 Oldsmobile, 88 Series two-door sedan (DC)

GOLDEN ROCKET EIGHTY-EIGHT - To honor GM's upcoming 50th anniversary, Olds named its entry series the Golden Rockets. A complete restyling greeted Olds fans this year with a retrograde three-piece rear window treatment. Olds buyers could order a station wagon for the first time since 1950. Standard equipment included: armrests, bumper guards, turn signals, rubber floor mats and sun visors. Upholstery choices included a variety of colors and fabrics. Standard tire size was 8.50 x 14 inches.

1957 Oldsmobile, 88 Series two-door convertible, OCW

1957 Oldsmobile, 88 Series Holiday four-door hardtop, OCW

OLDSMOBILE I.D. NUMBERS: Serial number located on left front door pillar on right side of cowl; on cowl under hood; on flange on left frame, just ahead of cowl; on metal plate on top of left front end of frame; on engine number plate. Engine number on block above water pump; and on plate on floor inside right door; on left corner of block above generator; and on front of left cylinder head at negative battery terminal. Olds 88 numbers took the form 577( )1001 to 577( )ending number. Olds Super 88 numbers took the form 578( )1001 to 578( )ending number. Olds 98 numbers took the form 579( )1001 to 579( )ending number. First two symbols indicate model year: 57=1957. Third symbol indicates series: 7=88; 8=Super 88; 9=98. Fourth symbol in ( ) indicated assembly plant as follows: A=Atlanta; B=Boston (Framingham); K=Kansas City; M=Michigan (Lansing); L=Linden (New Jersey); C=California (Los Angeles/Southgate); T=Texas (Arlington); and W=Wilmington, Del. Remaining symbols were the unit's sequential production number. Starting number at each assembly plant was 1001. Ending numbers, by series, at each coded plant were: [88] M70862; A18289; T10149; B9961; K19003; L19547; C16888; and W15960. [Super 88] M52348; A13297; T9490; B6879; K14818; L16542; C14280; and W11689. [98] M33963; A8105; T5873; B4877; K8378; L10933; C7994; and W7260. Engine numbers (unrelated to assembly plants) were: [V-8] A001001 and up.

1957 Oldsmobile, 88 Series four-door sedan, OCW

1957 Oldsmobile, 88 Series Fiesta four-door station wagon, OCW

1957 Oldsmobile, Super 88 Fiesta four-door hardtop station wagon, OCW

77

1957 Oldsmobile, Super 88 two-door convertible, OCW

GOLDEN ROCKET EIGHTY-EIGHT SERIES

Model Number	Body/Style Number	Body Type & Seating	Factory Price	Shipping Weight	Production Total
88	57-3611	2-dr Sed-6P	2478	4110	18,477
88	57-3637	2-dr Hol HT-6P	2591	4119	49,187
88	57-3639	4-dr Hol HT-6P	2663	4188	33,830
88	57-3669	4-dr Sed-6P	2538	4137	53,923
88	57-3667TX	2-dr Conv Cpe-6P	2895	4392	6,423
88	57-3662F	4-dr Sta Wag-6P	2914	4433	5,052
88	57-3665F	4-dr HT Sta Wag-6P	3017	4472	5,767

NOTE 1: All 1957 Oldsmobile station wagons are called Fiestas.

1957 Oldsmobile, Super 88 Holiday two-door hardtop, OCW

SUPER EIGHTY-EIGHT - The middle Oldsmobile series was the popular Super Eighty-Eight. Wheelbase and body shells were shared with the Golden Rocket Eighty-Eights. Six body styles were offered including the newly returned station wagon. Standard equipment included all items from the Golden Rocket Eighty-Eight plus front fender chrome script, exposed chrome roof bows and side interior courtesy lights. A variety of colored cloth and leather upholstery combinations could be ordered. Standard tire size was 8.50 x 14 inches.

1957 Oldsmobile, Super 88 four-door sedan, OCW

SUPER EIGHTY-EIGHT SERIES

Model Number	Body/Style Number	Body Type & Seating	Factory Price	Shipping Weight	Production Total
S-88	57-3637SD	2-dr Hol HT-6P	2884	4171	31,155
S-88	57-3611D	2-dr Sed-6P	2687	4164	2,983
S-88	57-3639SD	4-dr Hol HT-6P	2950	4251	39,162
S-88	57-3669D	4-dr Sed-6P	2745	4186	42,696
S-88	57-3667DTX	2-dr Conv Cpe-6P	3132	4445	7,128
S-88	57-3665SDF	4-dr Sta Wag-6P	3220	4537	8,981

1957 Oldsmobile, 98 Series four-door sedan (DC)

STARFIRE NINETY-EIGHT - Again the top-of-the-line Oldsmobile series was the four model Ninety-Eight, this year officially titled "Starfire Ninety-Eight." Standard equipment included all items standard on the Super Eight-Eight plus electric windows, special emblems, power steering, power brakes and Jetaway Hydra-Matic. Upholstery choices included a variety of cloth, morocceen and leather. Standard tire size was 9.00 x 14 inches.

STARFIRE NINETY-EIGHT SERIES

Model Number	Body/Style Number	Body Type & Seating	Factory Price	Shipping Weight	Production Total
98	57-3037SDX	2-dr Hol HT-6P	3578	4458	17,791
98	57-3067DX	2-dr Conv-6P	3838	4747	8,278
98	57-3069D	4-dr Sed-6P	3396	4450	21,525
98	57-3939SDX	4-dr Hol HT-6P	3649	4525	32,099

1957 Oldsmobile, 98 Series Starfire Holiday two-door hardtop, OCW

ENGINES

(88/SUPER 88/98 SERIES) Cast-iron overhead valve V-8 engine. Bore and stroke: 4 x 3-11/16 inches. Displacement: 371 cid. Hydraulic valve lifters. Compression ratio: 9.5:1. Torque: 400 pound feet at 2800 rpm. Brake hp: 277 at 4400 rpm. Carburetor: Quadra-Jet four-barrel.

CHASSIS FEATURES - Wheelbase: (Golden Rocket Eighty-Eight and Super EightyEight) 122 inches; (Starfire Ninety-Eight) 126 inches. Overall length: (Golden Rocket Eighty Eight and Super Eighty-Eight) 208.2 inches; (Ninety-Eight) 216.7 inches. Front tread: 59 inches. Rear tread: 58 inches.

OPTIONS: Hydra-Matic transmission ($215). Heater/defroster ($85). Power steering ($100). Deluxe radio ($96). Electric antenna ($22). Rear speakers ($16). Super Deluxe signal seeking radio ($121). Back-up lights ($15). Windshield washer ($11). Padded dash ($20). Power brakes ($37). Electric clock ($19). Air conditioning ($430). Autronic eye ($46). Deluxe wheelcov-

ers ($30). Remote-control mirror ($9). Seat belts ($23). Cadet visor ($33). J-2 induction system (300 hp) with three two-barrel carburetors ($83). Special J-2 induction system (312 hp) not recommended for street use and offered to drag racers and stock car racers for off-road use ($395). Note: The Jetaway Hydra-matic was standard on Ninety-Eights and optional on all other models.

HISTORICAL FOOTNOTES: The 1957 Oldsmobiles were introduced Nov. 9, 1956. Model year production was 384,390 units and calendar year sales were 390,091 cars, including 21,840 ragtops, 98,300 two-door hardtops, 104,930 four-door hardtops and 19,500 wagons. This made Oldsmobile the fifth best-selling American automaker with a 6.2 percent share of market. J.F. Wolfram was the chief executive officer of the division. The Oldsmobile Mona Lisa show car toured the auto show circuit during 1957. Richard Petty drove Oldsmobiles in NASCAR stock car races, joining the Olds team with his father Lee Petty. Their aim was to win races with Oldsmobile's hot J-2 engine option. However, NASCAR ultimately banned multi-carbureted engines and Olds wound up with only five Grand National wins, before pulling out of factory-backed racing efforts. Oldsmobile reverted to 1954-style side trim.

1958

1958 Oldsmobile, 88 Holiday two-door hardtop (DC)

DYNAMIC EIGHTY-EIGHT - A major styling change was made in 1958 and the three series format was again retained. Since the Seventy-Six designation was dropped in 1951, the entry level series had been called the Eight-Eight. In 1958, the entry series designation became the Dynamic Eighty-Eight with seven models. Seventeen standard colors were available with five extra cost, metallic colors offered. Upholstery choices spanned a variety of colored morocceen and cloth combinations. Standard series equipment included: four headlights, oil filter, turn signals, printed circuit instrument cluster and aluminum anodized grille. Standard tire size was 8.50 x 14 inches.

1958 Oldsmobile, Dynamic 88 four-door sedan, OCW

OLDSMOBILE I.D. NUMBERS: Serial number located on left front door pillar on right side of cowl; on cowl under hood; on flange on left frame, just ahead of cowl; on metal plate on top of left front end of frame; on engine number plate. Engine number on block above water pump; and on plate on floor inside right door; on left corner of block above generator; and on

front of left cylinder head at negative battery terminal. Oldsmobile 88 numbers took the form 587( )1001 to 587( )ending number. Olds Super 88 numbers took the form 588( )1001 to 588( )ending number. The Oldsmobile 98 numbers took the form 589( )1001 to 589( )ending number. First two symbols indicate model year: 58=1958. Third symbol indicates series: 7=88; 8=Super 88; 9=98. Fourth symbol in ( ) indicated assembly plant as follows: A=Atlanta; B=Boston (Framingham); K=Kansas City; M=Michigan (Lansing); L=Linden (New Jersey); C=California (Los Angeles/Southgate); T=Texas (Arlington); and W=Wilmington, Del. Remaining symbols were the unit's sequential production number. Starting number at each assembly plant was 1001 took the above format. Ending numbers, by series, at each coded plant not available. Engine numbers were B00-1001 and up were for engineering purposes only and no longer useful for identification.

DYNAMIC EIGHTY-EIGHT SERIES

Model Number	Body/Style Number	Body Type & Seating	Factory Price	Shipping Weight	Production Total
88	58-3611	2-dr Sed-5P	2772	4102	11,833
88	58-3637	2-dr Hol HT-7P	2893	4112	35,036
88	58-3669	4-dr Sed-5P	2837	4161	60,429
88	48-3639	4-dr Hol HT-5P	2971	4185	28,241
88	58-3667TX	2-dr Conv-6P	3221	4198	4,456
88	58-3693	4-dr Sta Wag-6P	3284	4441	3,249
88	58-3695	4-dr HT Sta Wag -6P	3395	4417	3,323

NOTE 1: All 1958 Oldsmobile station wagons are Fiestas.

NOTE 2: The Holiday Fiesta was a four-door hardtop wagon.

1958 Oldsmobile, Super 88 Fiesta four-door hardtop station wagon (AA)

SUPER EIGHTY-EIGHT - The middle Oldsmobile series again was the Super Eighty-Eight with five body styles. It shared its wheelbase with the Dynamic Eighty-Eight and its engine with the Ninety-Eight. Upholstery choices included various combinations of leather, cloth and morocceen. Standard equipment included all Dynamic Eighty-Eight items plus: padded dash, foam rubber padded seat cushions, courtesy lights, parking brake light, special side moldings and chrome rocker panel moldings. Standard tire size was 8.50 x 14 inches.

1958 Oldsmobile, Super 88 Holiday four-door hardtop, OCW

SUPER EIGHT-EIGHT SERIES

Model Number	Body/Style Number	Body Type & Seating	Factory Price	Shipping Weight	Production Total
S-88	58-3637D	2-dr Hol HT-5P	3262	4153	18,653
S-88	58-3667DTX	2-dr Conv-5P	3529	4217	3,799
S-88	58-3669D	4-dr Sed-5P	3112	4185	33,844
S-88	58-3639SD	4-dr Hol HT-5P	3339	4223	27,521
S-88	58-3695	4-dr Sta Wag-6P	3623	4471	5,175

1958 Oldsmobile, Super 88 two-door convertible, OCW

1958 Oldsmobile, 98 two-door convertible (DC)

NINETY-EIGHT - The Ninety-Eight series had its own exclusive wheelbase of 126-1/2 inches, while sharing the more powerful Rocket V-8 engine with the Super Eighty-Eights. Four body styles were available. Standard series equipment included all items standard on the two Eighty-Eight series plus Hydra-Matic transmission, power steering and brakes, dual exhausts, electric clock, color accented wheel discs and chrome wheel frames. Interiors could be ordered in a variety of colored leathers, cloth and morocceen. Standard tires were 8.50 x 14 inches.

1958 Oldsmobile, 98 Holiday two-door hardtop, OCW

NINETY-EIGHT SERIES

Model Number	Body/Style Number	Body Type & Seating	Factory Price	Shipping Weight	Production Total
98	58-3037SDX	2-dr Hol HT-5P	4020	4454	11,012
98	58-3069D	4-dr Sed-5P	3824	4474	16,595
98	58-3039SDX	4-dr Hol HT-5P	4096	4559	27,063
98	48-3067DX	2-dr Conv-5P	4300	4504	5,605

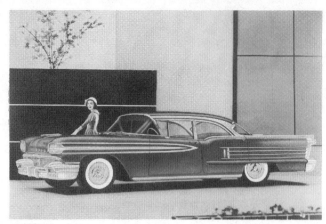

1958 Oldsmobile, 98 four-door sedan, OCW

ENGINES

(DYNAMIC 88 SERIES) Cast-iron overhead valve V-8 engine. Bore and stroke: 4 x 3-11/16 inches. Displacement: 371 cid. Hydraulic valve lifters. Compression ratio: 10.0:1. Torque: 390 pound feet at 2400 rpm. Brake hp: 265 at 4400 rpm. Carburetor: "Economy" two-barrel. Super Eighty-Eight or J-2 engine optional in series.

(SUPER 88/98 SERIES) Cast-iron overhead valve V-8 engine. Bore and stroke: 4 x 3-11/16 inches. Displacement: 371 cid. Hydraulic valve lifters. Compression ratio: 10.0:1. Brake hp: 305 at 4600 rpm. Torque: 410 pound feet at 2800 rpm. Carburetor: Quadra-Jet four-barrel.

CHASSIS FEATURES: Wheelbase: (Dynamic Eighty-Eight and Super Eighty-Eight) 122.5 inches; (Ninety-Eight) 126.5 inches. Overall length: (Dynamic Eighty-Eight and Super Eighty-Eight) 208.2 inches; (Ninety-Eight) 216.7 inches. Front tread: 59 inches. Rear tread: 58 inches.

OPTIONS: Jetaway Hydra-Matic drive. Heater/defroster. Power steering. Power brakes. Deluxe radio. Electric antenna. Rear radio speaker. Super Deluxe signal seeking radio. Trans-Portable radio. Windshield washer. Back-up lights. E-Z-Eye tinted glass. Cadet sun visor. Electric clock. Air conditioning. Autronic eye. Power seat. Seat belts. Power windows. New-Matic air suspension. Dealer kit to convert air suspension back to standard suspension. All 1958 Oldsmobiles were powered by a Rocket V-8 engine. The 265-hp version was standard on Dynamic Eighty-Eights; the 305-hp engine was optional on any Dynamic Eighty-Eight, standard on all other models. A triple carbureted J-2 engine option could be ordered on any other 1958 Olds. It boosted power to 312 hp. Other engine options were a heavy-duty air cleaner and a heavy-duty crankcase ventilation system. A three-speed manual transmission was standard on cars in the Eighty-Eight and Super Eighty-Eight series. The Jetaway Hydra-Matic was standard on all Ninety-Eights, optional on all other models.

HISTORICAL FOOTNOTES: Factory announcements took place Oct. 30, 1957 and the 1958 models were introduced Nov. 8, 1957. Model year production totaled 296,374 units for a seven percent market share. Calendar year sales of 310,795 cars were recorded, for a fourth place in the sales race. J.F. Wolfram was the chief executive officer of the division. Oldsmobile was solidly established as the sales leader in the medium-price class of the U.S. auto market. Its calendar year output included 13,705 convertibles; 63,259 two-door hardtops, 95,577 four-door hardtops and 13,265 station wagons. The 305-hp J-2-equipped Oldsmobile Super 88 Holiday four-door hardtop was capable of 0-60 mph in 8.7 seconds and 17.3 second quarter-miles. The four millionth Hydra-Matic was built on April 8, 1958. Some Oldsmobile options and accessories with low installation rates included: air suspension (6.1 percent); limited slip differential (2.3 percent); air conditioning (12.5 percent); power windows (17.7 percent) and power seat (19.5 percent).

1959

1959 Oldsmobile, Dynamic 88 two-door convertible (DC)

DYNAMIC EIGHTY-EIGHT - For the second consecutive year new styling greeted Oldsmobile buyers. The Dynamic Eight-Eight series offered six body styles, the most of any Olds series. Olds offered a smaller displacement engine on the Dynamic Eighty-Eight models. Standard series equipment included: oil filter, turn signals, air scoop brakes and Safety spectrum speedometer. Upholstery was available in a variety of cloth and morocceen combinations. Standard tire size was 8.50 x 14 inches.

1959 Oldsmobile, Dynamic 88 four-door sedan, OCW

OLDSMOBILE I.D. NUMBERS: Serial number located on left front door pillar on right side of cowl; on cowl under hood; on flange on left frame, just ahead of cowl; on metal plate on top of left front end of frame; on engine number plate. Engine number on block above water pump; and on plate on floor inside right door; on left corner of block above generator; and on front of left cylinder head at negative battery terminal. Oldsmobile 88 numbers took the form 597( )1001 to 597( )ending number. Olds Super 88 numbers took the form 598( )1001 to 598( )ending number. The Oldsmobile 98 numbers took the form 599( )1001 to 599( )ending number. First two symbols indicate model year: 59=1959. Third symbol indicates series: 7=88; 8=Super 88; 9=98. Fourth symbol in ( ) indicated assembly plant as follows: A=Atlanta; B=Boston (Framingham); K=Kansas City; M=Michigan (Lansing); L=Linden (New Jersey); C=California (Los Angeles/Southgate); T=Texas (Arlington); and W=Wilmington, Del. Remaining symbols were the unit's sequential production number. Starting number at each assembly plant was 1001 took the above format. Ending numbers, by series, at each coded plant not available. Engine numbers were C00-1001 for the 371-cid V-8 and D00-1001 for the 394-cid V-8. Engine numbers were for engineering purposes only and no longer useful for identification.

1959 Oldsmobile, Dynamic 88 four-door hardtop, OCW

DYNAMIC EIGHTY-EIGHT SERIES

Model Number	Body/Style Number	Body Type & Seating	Factory Price	Curb Weight	Production Total
88	59-3211	2-dr Cpe-5P	2837	4214	16,123
88	59-3237	2-dr Hol HT-5P	2958	4235	38,488
88	59-3267	2-dr Conv-5P	3286	4279	8,491
88	59-3219	4-dr Sed-5P	2902	4281	70,995
88	59-3239	4-dr Hol HT-5P	3036	4231	48,707
88	59-3235	4-dr Sta Wag-6P	3365	4619	11,298

NOTE 1: All 1959 Oldsmobile station wagons are called Fiestas.

NOTE 2: All 1959 Oldsmobile hardtops are called Holidays.

1959 Oldsmobile, Super 88 Holiday two-door hardtop, OCW

SUPER EIGHTY-EIGHT - The middle series Oldsmobile was again the Super Eighty-Eight, which offered five body styles. Standard equipment included all items from the Dynamic Eighty-Eight series plus rocker panel moldings, special emblems, parking brake light, sponge vinyl headliner and deep twist carpeting. Upholstery was in a variety of colored leather, morocceen or cloth. Standard tire size was 9.00 x 14 inches.

1959 Oldsmobile, Super 88 Holiday four-door hardtop (DC)

SUPER EIGHTY-EIGHT SERIES

Model Number	Body/Style Number	Body Type & Seating	Factory Price	Shipping Weight	Production Total
S-88	59-3537	2-dr Hol HT-5P	3328	4260	20,259
S-88	59-3519	4-dr Sed-5P	3178	4280	37,024
S-88	59-3539	4-dr Hol HT-5P	3405	4274	38,467
S-88	59-3567	2-dr Conv-5P	3595	4340	4,895
S-88	59-3535	4-dr Sta Wag-6P	3669	4470	7,015

1959 Oldsmobile, Super 88 Fiesta four-door station wagon, OCW

1959 Oldsmobile, 98 two-door convertible, OCW

NINETY-EIGHT - Olds stayed with its successful top series format by offering a limited number of body styles (four) on an exclusive (126.3 inch) wheelbase. All items standard on the Super Eighty-Eight were found on the Ninety-Eight as well as special emblems and moldings, electric clock, wheel trim moldings, power steering, power brakes and Jetaway Hydra-Matic Drive. Interiors were selected from leather, morocceen or cloth in different colors. Standard tire size was 9.00 x 14 inches.

1959 Oldsmobile, 98 four-door sedan, OCW

NINETY-EIGHT SERIES

Model Number	Body/Style Number	Body Type & Seating	Factory Price	Shipping Weight	Production Total
98	59-3837	2-dr Hol HT-5P	4086	4505	13,699
98	59-3867	2-dr Conv-5P	4366	4545	7,514
98	59-3819	4-dr Sed-5P	3890	4530	23,106
98	59-3839	4-dr Hol HT-5P	4163	4538	36,813

1959 Oldsmobile, 98 Holiday two-door hardtop, OCW

ENGINES

(DYNAMIC 88 SERIES) Cast-iron overhead valve V-8 engine. Bore and stroke: 4 x 3-11/16 inches. Displacement: 371 cid. Hydraulic lifters. Compression ratio: 9.75:1. Torque: 390 pound feet. Brake hp: 270 at 4600 rpm. Carburetor: Rochester 2GC "Econ-o-way" two-barrel.

(SUPER 88/98 SERIES) Cast-iron overhead valve V-8. Bore and stroke: 4-1/8 x 3-11/16 inches. Displacement: 394 cid. Hydraulic valve lifters. Compression ratio: 9.75:1. Torque: 435 pound feet. Brake hp: 315 at 4600 rpm. Carburetor: Rochester 4GC Quadra-jet.

CHASSIS FEATURES: Wheelbase: (Dynamic Eighty-Eight and Super Eighty-Eight) 123 inches; (Ninety-Eight) 126.3 inches. Overall length: (Dynamic Eighty-Eight and Super Eighty-Eight) 218.4 inches; (Ninety-Eight) 223 inches. Front tread: 61 inches. Rear tread: 61 inches.

CONVENIENCE OPTIONS: Power steering ($107). Power brakes ($43). Power windows ($107). Six-Way power seat ($102). Heater/defroster ($101). Deluxe radio ($129). Air conditioning ($430). Seat belts. Deluxe horns. Tinted glass. Electric clock. Autronic eye. Deluxe wheel discs. All 1959 Oldsmobiles were powered by Rocket V-8 engines. The Dynamic Eighty-Eight models were powered by a 371 cubic inch version, the other two series with a slightly larger bore 394 cubic inch engine. The Quadri-Jet carburetor was standard on 394 cubic inch engines, optional on 371 cubic inch engines. Dual exhausts and heavy-duty air cleaner were optional on cars not fitted with that equipment standard. The Jetaway Hydra-Matic was standard on all Ninety-Eight models, optional on all other series. Another drivetrain option was an anti-spin differential.

HISTORICAL FOOTNOTES: The 1959 Oldsmobiles were introduced Oct. 3, 1958. Model year production totaled 382,865 units or a 6.9 percent market share. Calendar year production totaled 366,305 cars. J.F. Wolfram was the chief executive officer of the division. The sleek, "flat-top" Holiday four-door hardtop styles were the company's second most popular offering. A total of 116,064 four-door Oldsmobiles were built. Two-door hardtops (Holidays) accounted for 65,926 units or 18 percent of total output. Six percent of all 1959 Oldsmobiles were convertibles. A retractable rear window was introduced on station wagons. Rare options and their installation rates included air suspension (0.5 percent), limited slip differential (5.2 percent), dual exhausts (5.3 percent) and air conditioning (15.2 percent). Racing without open factory support, Lee Petty drove a 1959 Oldsmobile two-door hardtop to a photo finish in the first Daytona 500-Mile stock car race.

1960

1960 Oldsmobile, Dynamic 88 four-door sedan, OCW

DYNAMIC EIGHTY-EIGHT - This marked the final year Oldsmobile would stay with its traditional three series format of only full-size cars. The Dynamic Eighty-Eight had seven models. Standard equipment included safety-vee steering wheel, turn signals, air scoop brakes, electric windshield wipers, Safety-spectrum speedometer and carpets with rubber inserts. Upholstery choices included cloth, morocceen or leather in an assortment of colors. Standard tire size was 8.50 x 14 inches.

OLDSMOBILE I.D. NUMBERS: Serial number located on left front door pillar on right side of cowl; on cowl under hood; on flange on left frame, just ahead of cowl; on metal plate on top of left front end of frame; on engine number plate. Engine number on block above water pump; and on plate on floor inside right door; on left corner of block above generator; and on front

of left cylinder head at negative battery terminal. Oldsmobile 88 numbers took the form 607( )1001 to 607( )ending number. Olds Super 88 numbers took the form 608( )1001 to 608( )ending number. The Oldsmobile 98 numbers took the form 609( )1001 to 609( )ending number. First two symbols indicate model year: 60=1960. Third symbol indicates series: 7=88; 8=Super 88; 9=98. Fourth symbol in ( ) indicated assembly plant as follows: A=Atlanta; B=Boston (Framingham); K=Kansas City; M=Michigan (Lansing); L=Linden (New Jersey); C=California (Los Angeles/Southgate); T=Texas (Arlington); and W=Wilmington, Del. Remaining symbols were the unit's sequential production number. Starting number at each assembly plant was 1001 took the above format. Ending numbers, by series, at each coded plant not available. Engine numbers were C00-1001 or H00-1001 for the 371-cid V-8 and D00-1001 for the 394-cid V-8. Engine numbers were for engineering purposes only and no longer useful for identification.

1960 Oldsmobile, Dynamic 88 two-door sedan, OCW

DYNAMIC EIGHTY-EIGHT SERIES

Model Number	Body/Style Number	Body Type & Seating	Factory Price	Shipping Weight	Production Total
88	60-3211	2-dr Sed-5P	2835	4052	13,545
88	60-3237	2-dr Hol HT-5P	2956	4061	29,368
88	60-3219	4-dr Sed-5P	2900	4109	76,377
88	60-3239	4-dr Hol HT-5P	3034	4067	43,761
88	60-3267	2-dr Conv-5P	3284	4184	12,271
88	60-3235	4-dr Sta Wag-5P	3363	4278	8,834
88	60-3245	4-dr Sta Wag-7P	3471	4299	5,708

NOTE 1: All 1960 Oldsmobile station wagons are called Fiestas.

NOTE 2: All 1960 Oldsmobile hardtops are called Holidays.

1960 Oldsmobile, Dynamic 88 two-door convertible, OCW

1960 Oldsmobile, Dynamic 88 Holiday four-door hardtop, OCW

1960 Oldsmobile, Super 88 two-door hardtop (AA)

SUPER EIGHTY-EIGHT - The middle Olds series again combined the wheelbase of the Dynamic Eighty-Eight with the more powerful engine from the Ninety-Eight. Standard equipment included all items from the Dynamic Eighty-Eighty plus padded dash, courtesy lamps, wheel trim rings, Star-lite headliner, two-speed windshield wipers and chrome roof side moldings. Interiors were cloth, leather or moroceen. Standard tire size was 8.50 x 14 inches.

1960 Oldsmobile, Super 88 two-door convertible, OCW

SUPER EIGHTY-EIGHT SERIES

Model Number	Body/Style Number	Body Type & Seating	Factory Price	Shipping Weight	Production Total
S-88	60-3537	2-dr Hol HT-5P	3325	4080	16,464
S-88	60-3519	4-dr Sed-5P	3176	4128	35,094
S-88	60-3539	4-dr Hol HT-5P	3402	4086	33,285
S-88	60-3567	2-dr Conv-5P	3592	4203	5,830
S-88	60-3535	4-dr Sta Wag-5P	3665	4298	3,765
S-88	60-3545	4-dr Sta Wag-7P	3773	4306	3,475

1960 Oldsmobile, Super 88 four-door sedan, OCWO

NINETY-EIGHT - Once again the top-of-the-line Oldsmobile series was the Ninety-Eight. Standard equipment included all items from the Super Eighty-Eight series plus: Jetaway Hydra-Matic transmission, power steering, power brakes, windshield washers, electric clock and deep twist carpeting. Upholstery was fabric, leather or moroceen in a variety of colors. Tire size was 9.00 x 14 inches.

1960 Oldsmobile, 98 two-door convertible, (IMS)

NINETY-EIGHT SERIES

Model Number	Body/Style Number	Body Type & Seating	Factory Price	Shipping Weight	Production Total
98	60-3837	2-dr Hol HT-5P	4083	4312	7,635
98	60-3819	4-dr Sed-5P	3887	4353	17,188
98	60-3839	4-dr Hol HT-5P	4159	4364	27,257
98	60-3867	2-dr Conv-5P	4362	4412	7,284

1960 Oldsmobile, 98 Holiday four-door hardtop, OCW

ENGINES

(DYNAMIC 88 SERIES) Cast-iron overhead valve V-8 engine. Bore and stroke: 4 x 3-11/16 inches. Displacement: 371 cid. Hydraulic valve lifters. Compression ratio: 8.75:1. Torque: 375 pound feet at 2400 rpm. Brake hp: 240 at 4600 rpm. Carburetor: Two-barrel Econ-o-way Rochester Model 2GC.

1960 Oldsmobile, 98 Holiday two-door hardtop, OCW

(SUPER 88/98) Cast-iron overhead valve V-8 engine. Bore and stroke: 4-1/8 x 3-11/16 inches. Displacement: 394 cid. Hydraulic valve lifters. Compression ratio: 9.75:1. Torque: 435 pound feet at 2800 rpm. Brake hp: 315 at 4600 rpm. Carburetor: Multi-jet Rochester 4GC four-barrel.

CHASSIS FEATURES: Wheelbase: (Dynamic Eighty-Eight and Super Eighty-Eight) 123 inches; (Ninety-Eight) 126.3 inches. Overall length: (Dynamic Eighty-Eight and Super Eighty-Eight) 217.6 inches; (Ninety-Eight) 220.9 inches. Front tread: 61 inches. Rear tread: 61 inches.

OPTIONS: Heater/defroster ($97). Power steering ($107). Deluxe radio ($88). Electric antenna ($23). Deluxe radio ($124). Back-up lamps ($9). Parking brake light ($4). Windshield washer ($11). Deluxe tri-tone horns ($11). Padded dash ($15). Power brakes ($43). Electric clock ($19). Outside rear view mirror ($4). Power windows ($106). Power seat ($68). Fiesta luggage carrier ($98). Dual exhausts ($26). Heavy-duty air cleaner/breather system ($5). Jetaway Hydra-Matic Drive, optional on 88s only ($231). Anti-Spin differential ($47).

HISTORICAL FOOTNOTES: The 1960 Oldsmobiles were introduced Oct. 1, 1959. Model year production was 347,141 units. Calendar year sales were 363,300 cars. The pace car for the Memorial Day Indianapolis 500 was a 1960 Oldsmobile 98 convertible. J.F. Wolfram was chief executive officer of the division. The aforementioned calendar year sales figure includes 19,800 F-85s, built late in the 1960 calendar year. Installation rates on rare options included: Dual exhausts (3.1 percent); limited slip differential (5.3 percent); air conditioning (18.8 percent); power seats (19 percent) and power windows (18 percent).

1961

1961 Oldsmobile, F-85 four-door sedan (DC)

F-85 - For the first time Oldsmobile broke with its three series format in 1961. The new entry-level Oldsmobile was the all new F-85 compact car. Smaller than any postwar Oldsmobile, the F-85 was powered by a unique aluminum 215-cid V-8. It joined small-car offerings from Buick and Pontiac. Standard equipment included foam-cushioned front seat, front armrests, dual sun visors, turn signals, stablizer bar and self-energizing brakes. Cloth or vinyl interiors were offered. Standard tire size was 6.50 x 11 inches. The F-85 was built in the Lansing and Southgate assembly plants.

OLDSMOBILE I.D. NUMBERS: Serial number located on left front door pillar on right side of cowl; on cowl under hood; on flange on left frame, just ahead of cowl; on metal plate on top of left front end of frame; on engine number plate. Engine number on block above water pump; and on plate on floor inside right door; on left corner of block above generator; and on front of left cylinder head at negative battery terminal. Olds F-85 numbers took the form 610( )01001 and up. Oldsmobile 88 numbers took the form 612( )01001 and up. Olds Super 88 numbers took the form 615( )01001 and up. Olds Starfire numbers took the form 616( )01001 and up. Oldsmobile 98 numbers took the form 618( )01001 and up. First two symbols indicate model year: 61=1961. Starting this year, the third symbol indicating series is the same as the second digit of the Body/Style Numbers in the second column of the charts below (i.e., 0=F-85; 2=88, etc.). Fourth symbol in ( ) indicated assembly plant as follows: A=Atlanta; K=Kansas City; M=Michigan (Lansing); L=Linden (New Jersey); C=California (Los Angeles/Southgate); T=Texas (Arlington); and W=Wilmington, Del. Remaining symbols were the unit's sequential production number. Starting number at each assembly plant was 1001 took the above format. Ending numbers, by series, at each coded plant not available. Engine numbers started with a prefix indicating displacement: S001001 for 215-cid V-8; F001001 for

394-cid /250-hp V-8; G001001 for 394-cid/325-hp V-8 and D001001 for 394-cid/330-hp Starfire V-8. Engine numbers were for engineering purposes only and not designed to aid in vehicle identification. Hydra-Matic Drive was standard equipment on the Ninety-Eights and a $231 option on the Eighty-Eights. Option S-1 was $47 anti-spin differential.

1961 Oldsmobile, F-85 Cutlass two-door sports coupe, OCW

F-85 SERIES

Model Number	Body/Style Number	Body Type & Seating	Factory Price	Shipping Weight	Production Total
85	61-3027	2-dr Cpe-5P	2502	2712	2,336
85	61-3019	4-dr Sed-5P	2384	2666	19,192
85	61-3035	4-dr Sta Wag-5P	2654	2742	6,677
85	61-3045	4-dr Sta Wag-7P	2694	2816	10,087

DELUXE

Model Number	Body/Style Number	Body Type & Seating	Factory Price	Shipping Weight	Production Total
85	61-3119	4-dr Sed-5P	2519	2798	26,311
85	61-3135	4-dr Sta Wag-5P	2789	2815	526
85	61-3117	2-dr Cut Spt Cpe -4P	2753	2712	9935
85	61-3145	4-dr Sta Wag-7P	3091	2837	757

1961 Oldsmobile, Dynamic 88 two-door hardtop, OCW

DYNAMIC EIGHTY-EIGHT - With the addition of the compact F-85 car line the Dynamic Eighty-Eight series was moved up a notch. This remained Oldsmobile's most diverse series with seven models offered. Standard equipment included padded dash, Safety spectrum speedometer, floating propeller shaft and air scoop brakes. Interiors were vinyl or cloth. Standard tire size was 8.00 x 14 inches.

1961 Oldsmobile, Dynamic 88 four-door sedan, OCW

DYNAMIC EIGHTY-EIGHT

Model Number	Body/Style Number	Body Type & Seating	Factory Price	Shipping Weight	Production Total
D88	61-3211	2-dr Sed-5P	2835	4152	4,920
D88	61-3237	2-dr Hol HT-5P	2956	3969	19,878
D88	61-3269	4-dr Sed-5P	2900	4024	42,584
D88	51-3239	4-dr Hol HT-5P	3034	4037	51,562
D88	61-3267	2-dr Conv-5P	3284	4244	9,049
D88	61-3235	4-dr Sta Wag-5P	3663	4317	5,374
D88	61-3245	4-dr Sta Wag-7P	3471	4334	4,013

1961 Oldsmobile, Super 88 four-door station wagon (DC)

SUPER EIGHTY-EIGHT - The Super Eighty-Eight combined the lighter 88 body with the more powerful 325-hp engine from the heavier Ninety-Eight. Standard equipment included all items from the Dynamic Eighty-Eight plus two-speed windshield wipers, Safety-Vee steering wheel, parking brake lamp, courtesy lamps and oil filter. Upholstery was vinyl or fabric. Standard tire size was 8.00 x 14 inches.

SUPER EIGHTY-EIGHT

Model Number	Body/Style Number	Body Type & Seating	Factory Price	Shipping Weight	Production Total
S88	61-3537	2-dr Hol HT-5P	3325	4003	7,009
S88	61-3569	4-dr Sed-5P	3176	4063	15,328
S88	61-3539	4-dr Hol HT-5P	3402	4092	23,272
S88	61-3567	2-dr Conv-5P	3592	4275	2,624
S88	61-3535	4-dr Sta Wag-5P	3665	4357	2,761
S88	61-3545	4-dr Stat Wag-7P	3773	4378	2,170

1961 Oldsmobile, Super 88 Holiday four-door hardtop, OCW

STARFIRE - Oldsmobile bolstered its top line coverage of the market with an offering in the personal luxury category -- the Starfire. This model was late coming to the Olds lineup. It was not available until Jan. 1, 1961. It came as a convertible, sharing its wheelbase with the Eighty-Eight, and was powered by a slightly more potent Rocket V-8. Standard equipment included all items from the Super Eighty-Eight plus brushed aluminum side panels, bucket seats, console, tachometer, power seats and a special dual exhaust system. Upholstery was leather. Standard tire size was 8.50 x 14 inches. Starfires were built only in Lansing.

1961 Oldsmobile, Starfire two-door convertible, OCW

STARFIRE

Model Number	Body/Style Number	Body Type & Seating	Factory Price	Shipping Weight	Production Total
ST	61-3667	2-dr Starfire Conv -5P	4647	4305	7,800

1961 Oldsmobile, 98 two-door convertible, OCW

CLASSIC NINETY-EIGHT - The Olds top-of-the-line series was the Ninety-Eight, this year with the misnomer Classic prefix. It offered five body styles. The all-new Starfires series probably cut into Ninety-Eight sales. Standard equipment included all items from the Super Eighty-Eight plus windshield washer, electric clock, Hydra-Matic transmission, power steering and power brakes. Upholstery was vinyl, cloth or leather. Standard tire size was 8.50 x 14 inches.

1961 Oldsmobile, 98 Sport Sedan four-door hardtop, OCW

CLASSIC NINETY-EIGHT

Model Number	Body/Style Number	Body Type & Seating	Factory Price	Shipping Weight	Production Total
98	61-3837	2-dr Hol HT-5P	4072	4156	4,445
98	61-3819	4-dr Twn Sed-5P	3887	4208	9,087
98	61-3839	4-dr Spt Sed-5P	4083	4187	12,343
98	61-3829	4-dr Hol HT-5P	4021	4179	13,331
98	61-3867	2-dr Conv-5P	4363	4224	3,804

ENGINES

(F-85 SERIES) Aluminum block V-8. Overhead valve. Liquid cooled. Bore and stroke: 3.5 x 2.8 inches. Displacement: 215 cid. Hydraulic valve lifters. Compression ratio: 8.75:1. Torque: 210 pound feet at 3200 rpm. Brake hp: 155 at 3200 rpm. Carburetor: two-barrel, Rochester 2GC.

(DYNAMIC 88 SERIES) Cast-iron V-8. Overhead valve. Bore and stroke: 4-1/8 x 3-11/16 inches. Displacement: 394 cid. Hydraulic valve lifters. Compression ratio: 8.75:1. Torque: 405 pound feet at 2400 rpm. Brake hp: 250 at 4400 rpm. Carburetor: Econ-o-way Rochester Model 2GC.

1961 Oldsmobile, 98 Holiday four-door hardtop, OCW

(SUPER 88/98) Cast-iron V-8. Overhead valve. Bore and stroke: 4-1/8 x 3-11/16 inches. Displacement: 394 cid. Hydraulic valve lifters. Compression ratio: 10.0:1. Brake hp: 325 at 4600 rpm. Torque: 435 pound feet at 2800 rpm. Carburetor: Rochester four-barrel 4GC.

(STARFIRE) Cast-iron V-8. Overhead valves. Bore and stroke: 4-1/8 x 3-11/16 inches. Displacement: 394 cid. Hydraulic valve lifters. Compression ratio: 10.25:1. Brake hp: 330 at 4600 rpm. Torque: 440 pound feet at 2800 rpm. Carburetor: four-barrel Rochester 4GC.

CHASSIS FEATURES: Wheelbase: (F-85) 112 inches; (Dynamic Eighty-Eight, Super Eighty-Eight and Starfire) 123 inches; (Classic Ninety-Eight) 126 inches. Overall length: (F-85) 188.2 inches; (Dynamic Eighty-Eight, Super Eighty-Eight and Starfire) 212 inches; (Classic Ninety-Eight) 218 inches. Front tread: (F-85) 56 inches; (all others) 61 inches. Rear tread: (F-85) 56 inches; (all others) 61 inches.

OPTIONS: [F-85] Heater/defroster ($74). Power steering ($86). Deluxe radio ($65). Back-up lights ($7). Windshield washer ($11). Padded dash ($12). Electric clock ($16). Air conditioning ($378). Outside mirror ($4). All F-85s were powered by the aluminum block "Rockette" V-8 engine. A power pack option consisted of high-compression heads, four-barrel carburetor and dual exhausts. It boosted horsepower by 30 to 185. Other engine options were heavy-duty air cleaner, full-flow oil filter and positive crankcase ventilation system. All F-85s came standard with a three-speed manual transmission with Hydra-Matic a popular $189 option. [OLDSMOBILE] Heater/defroster ($97). Rear window defroster ($21). Power steering ($107). Deluxe radio ($88). Electric antenna ($23). Super Deluxe signal seeking radio ($124). Back-up lights ($9). Courtesy lamps ($5). Windshield washer ($12). Padded dash ($12). Power brakes ($43). Electric clock ($19). Air conditioning ($430). Power windows ($106). Fiesta wagon luggage carrier ($98). All full-sized Oldsmobiles were powered by one of the three versions of the 394-cid Rocket V-8. The 250-hp version was standard equipment on Dynamic Eighty-Eights. The 325-hp engine was standard on Classic Ninety-Eights and Super Eighty-Eights, optional on Dynamic Eighty-Eights. A 330-hp V-8 was exclusive to the Starfire series. Other engine options included dual exhaust, heavy-duty oil filter and positive crankcase ventilation system. Hydra-Matic was standard on all Classic Ninety-Eights, optional on all other models for $231. Option S-1 was the $47 anti-spin differential.

HISTORICAL FOOTNOTES: The full-sized Oldsmobiles and the F-85 were introduced Oct. 6, 1960. Model year production was 242,323 full-size Oldsmobiles and 76,446 F-85s. Calendar year sales were 321,838 cars. J.F. Wolfram was the chief executive officer of the division.

1962

F-85 - Oldsmobile expanded its compact models in 1962 by adding a Cutlass coupe and convertible plus several Deluxe models. In an effort to get back into the high-performance mainstream a special turbocharged Jetfire coupe was introduced. Standard F-85 equipment included heater, defroster, coil springs, foam cushion seats and three-speed synchromesh transmission. Upholstery was cloth or vinyl. Standard tire size was 6.50 x 13 inches.

1962 Oldsmobile, F-85 two-door convertible, OCW

OLDSMOBILE I.D. NUMBERS: Serial number located on left front door pillar on right side of cowl; on cowl under hood; on flange on left frame, just ahead of cowl; on metal plate on top of left front end of frame; on engine number plate. Engine number on block above water pump; and on plate on floor inside right door; on left corner of block above generator; and on front of left cylinder head at negative battery terminal. Olds F-85 numbers took the form 620( )01001 and up. Olds F-85 Deluxe numbers took the form 621( )010001 and up. Oldsmobile 88 numbers took the form 622( )01001 and up. Olds Super 88 numbers took the form 625( )01001 and up. Olds Starfire numbers took the form 626( )01001 and up. Oldsmobile 98 numbers took the form 628( )01001 and up. First two symbols indicate model year: 62=1962. Third symbol indicating series is the same as the second digit of the Body/Style Numbers in the second column of the charts below (i.e., 0=F-85; 1=F-85 Deluxe, etc.). Fourth symbol in ( ) indicated assembly plant as follows: A=Atlanta; K=Kansas City; M=Michigan (Lansing); L=Linden (New Jersey); C=California (Los Angeles/Southgate); T=Texas (Arlington); and W=Wilmington, Del. Remaining symbols were the unit's sequential production number. Starting number at each assembly plant was 1001 took the above format. Ending numbers, by series, at each coded plant not available. Engine numbers started with a prefix indicating displacement: S=215-cid/155-hp V-8; SG=215-cid/185-hp V-8; ST=215-cid/215-hp Jetfire V-8; F=394-cid/280-hp V-8; FL=394-cid/260-hp V-8; G=394-cid/330-hp V-8; GS=394-cid/345-hp V-8. (Notes: Engines with G as second letter of code are high-compression. Engines with E or H as second letter behind the above symbols are low-compression versions for export. Engine numbers for each type started at 1001001 and up and were for engineering purposes only.

1962 Oldsmobile, Cutlass F-85 two-door convertible, OCW

F-85 SERIES

Model Number	Body/Style Number	Body Type & Seating	Factory Price	Shipping Weight	Production Total
STANDARD					
F-85	3027	2-dr Clb Cpe-5P	2403	2691	7,909
F-85	3019	4-dr Sed-5P	2457	2719	8,074
F-85	3067	2-dr Conv-5P	2760	2780	3,660
F-85	3035	4-dr Sta Wag-6P	2754	2805	3,204
F-85	3045	4-dr Sta Wag-9p	2835	2820	1,887
DELUXE					
F-85	3117	2-dr Cpe-5P	2694	2698	32,461
F-85	3119	4-dr Sed-5P	2592	2725	18,736
F-85	3167	2-dr Conv-5P	2971	2785	9,898
F-85	3135	4-dr Sta Wag-5P	2889	2815	4,974
JETFIRE TURBOCHARGED					
F-85	3147	2-dr Spt Cpe-5P	3045	2744	3,765

1962 Oldsmobile, F-85 Jetfire two-door sport coupe, OCW

DYNAMIC EIGHTY-EIGHT - The Eighty-Eights received evolutionary restyling with attention focused on the front and rear. The Dynamic Eighty-Eight offered the largest model selection in full-size Oldsmobiles. Standard equipment included padded dash, guard beam frame, live rubber body cushions, coil springs and foam rubber seats. Interiors were fabric or cloth. Standard tire size was 8.00 x 14 inches.

DYNAMIC EIGHTY-EIGHT

Model Number	Body/Style Number	Body Type & Seating	Factory Price	Shipping Weight	Production Total
D-88	3247	2-dr Hol HT-6P	3054	4165	39,676
D-88	3269	4-dr Sed-6P	2997	4179	68,467
D-88	3239	4-dr Hol HT-6P	3131	4173	53,438
D-88	3235	4-dr Sta Wag-6P	3460	4305	8,527
D-88	3245	4-dr Sta Wag-9P	3568	4325	6,417
D-88	3267	2-dr Conv-6P	3381	4255	12,212

NOTE 1: Oldsmobile station wagons are called Fiestas.

1962 Oldsmobile, Super 88 four-door sedan (DC)

SUPER EIGHTY-EIGHT - The Super Eighty-Eight shared its 123-inch wheelbase with the Dynamic Eighty-Eight and Starfire models and used the same engine as the Ninety-Eights. Standard equipment included all Dynamic Eighty-Eight items plus two-speed windshield wipers, parking brake lights, courtesy lamp package and special moldings. Upholstery was fabric, vinyl or leather. Standard tire size was 8.00 x 14 inches.

SUPER EIGHTY-EIGHT

Model Number	Body/Style Number	Body Type & Seating	Factory Price	Shipping Weight	Production Total
S88	3547	2-dr Hol HT-6P	3422	4182	9,010
S88	3569	4-dr Sed-6P	3273	4199	24,125
S88	3539	4-dr Hol HT-6P	3499	4197	21,175
S88	3535	4-dr Sta Wag-6P	3763	4312	3,837

1962 Oldsmobile, Starfire two-door hardtop, OCW

STARFIRE - After a midyear 1961 introduction, a second Starfire model, the two-door hardtop, joined the convertible. Oldsmobile attempted to capture a greater share of the personal/luxury car market. The Starfire was well-equipped with all Super Eighty-Eight items standard plus sports console, tachometer, Hydra-Matic with console shifter, power brakes, power steering, brushed aluminum side trim, dual exhaust with fiberglass packed mufflers and leather upholstery. Standard tire size was 8.00 x 14 inches.

STARFIRE

Model Number	Body/Style Number	Body Type & Seating	Factory Price	Shipping Weight	Production Total
SF	62-3647	2-dr Hol HT-5P	4131	4335	34,839
SF	62-3667	2-dr Conv-5P	4744	4488	7,149

1962 Oldsmobile, 98 four-door hardtop, OCW

NINETY-EIGHT - The largest 1962 Oldsmobiles were the Ninety-Eights. Five models were available including three four-doors plus an open and closed two-door. Ninety-Eights were well-appointed with all equipment from the Super Eighty-Eights plus Hydra-Matic, power brakes, power steering, power windows and power seat. Interiors were leather, vinyl or cloth. Standard tire size was 8.50 x 14 inches.

1962 Oldsmobile, 98 two-door convertible, OCW

NINETY-EIGHT

Model Number	Body/Style Number	Body Type & Seating	Factory Price	Shipping Weight	Production Total
98	62-3847	2-dr Hol HT-5P	4180	4375	7,546
98	62-3819	4-dr Twn Sed-5P	3984	4392	12,167
98	62-3839	4-dr Spts Sed-5P	4256	4384	33,095
98	62-3829	4-dr Hol HT-5P	4118	4399	7,653
98	62-3867	2-dr Conv-5P	4459	4488	3,693

ENGINES

(F-85 SERIES) Aluminum block V-8. Overhead valve. Liquid-cooled. Bore and stroke: 3.5 x 2.8 inches. Displacement: 215 cid. Hydraulic valve lifters. Compression ratio: (F-85) 8.75:1; (Cutlass and Jetfire) 10.25:1. Torque: (F-85) 210 pound feet at 4800 rpm; (Cutlass) 230 pound feet at 4800 rpm; (Jetfire) 300 pound feet at 3200 rpm. Brake hp: (F-85) 155 at 4800 rpm.; (Cutlass) 185 at 4800 rpm.; (Jetfire) 215 at 4800 rpm. Carburetor: (F-85) Rochester 2GC; (Cutlass) Rochester 4GC; (Jetfire) Turbocharged and fluid-injected.

(DYNAMIC 88) Cast-iron V-8. Overhead valve. Bore and stroke: 4-1/8 x 3-11/16 inches. Displacement: 394 cid. Hydraulic valve lifters. Compression ratio: 10.25:1. Torque: 430 pound feet at 2400 rpm. Brake hp: 280 at 4400 rpm. Carburetor: Econ-o-way Rochester 2GC.

(SUPER 88/98) Cast-iron V-8. Overhead valve. Bore and stroke: 4-1/8 x 3-11/16 inches. Displacement: 394 cid. Hydraulic valve lifters. Compression ratio: 10.25:1. Brake hp: 330 at 4600 rpm. Torque: 440 pound feet at 2800 rpm. Carburetor: Rochester 4GC four-barrel.

(STARFIRE) Cast-iron V-8. Overhead valve. Bore and stroke: 4-1/8 x 3-11/16 inches. Displacement: 394 cid. Hydraulic valve lifters. Compression ratio: 10.50:1. Torque: 440 pound feet at 3200 rpm. Brake hp: 345 at 4600 rpm. Carburetor: Rochester 4GC four-barrel.

CHASSIS FEATURES: Wheelbase: (F-85) 112 inches; (Dynamic Eighty-Eight, Super Eighty-Eight and Starfire) 123 inches; (Ninety-Eight) 126 inches. Overall length: (F-85) 188.2 inches; (Dynamic Eighty-Eight, Super Eighty-Eight and Starfire) 213.9 inches; (Ninety-Eight) 220 inches. Front tread: (F-85) 56 inches; (All others) 61 inches. Rear tread: (F-85) 56 inches; (All others) 61 inches.

1962 Oldsmobile, Starfire two-door convertible, OCW

OPTIONS: [F-85]: Power steering ($89). Deluxe radio ($65). Back-up lights ($7). Windshield washer ($12). Padded dash ($13). Electric clock ($15). Air conditioning ($385). Outside mirror ($5). All F-85s were powered by the aluminum block "Rockette" V-8 engine. This engine produced 155 hp in standard form and 185 hp in the higher powered option version. A 215 hp turbo-charged, liquid injected V-8 was exclusive to the Jetfire. Standard transmission was a manual three-speed with Hydra-Matic optional on all models. [OLDSMOBILE] Rear window defroster ($22). Power steering ($109). Deluxe radio ($91). Electric antenna ($23). Super Deluxe signal seeking radio ($126). back-up lights ($10). Courtesy lamps ($5). Wind-

shield washer ($13). Power brakes ($44). Electric clock. ($20). Air conditioning ($435). Power windows ($108). All full-sized Oldsmobiles were powered by one of four versions of the 394-cid Rocket V-8. The base Dynamic Eighty-Eight engine was a 280-hp V-8 with a 260-hp, lower compression ratio V-8 as a no cost option. Standard engine on the Super Eighty-Eight and Ninety-Eight was the 330-hp V-8 and this engine was optional on the Dynamic Eighty-Eight. A 345-hp V-8 was standard on the Starfire and optional on the Super Eighty-Eight and Ninety-Eight.

HISTORICAL FOOTNOTES: Full-sized Oldsmobiles and the F-85 were introduced Sept. 22, 1961. Model year production was 447,594 units. Calendar year sales were 458,359 cars. J.F. Wolfram was chief executive officer of the division. The turbocharged F-85 Jetfire was announced in April 1962. Oldsmobile claimed this to be the first car in the U.S. industry to offer one horsepower per cubic inch. Interestingly, Chrysler had made the same claim for its 1956 300-B and Chevrolet for its fuel-injected 1957 V-8. The Jetfire, however, was the first car to qualify as both a regular production model and as a one-to-one ratio car. For the 1962 model year, only 4.7 percent of all full-sized Oldsmobiles had power tailgate windows; 11.9 percent had bucket seats; 13.1 percent had dual exhaust and 7.8 percent had limited-slip rear axles. For F-85s, 2.1 percent had power windows; 2.6 percent had power brakes; 2.4 percent four-speed manual gear boxes and 4.8 percent bucket seats.

1963

1963 Oldsmobile, Jetfire two-door hardtop, OCW

F-85 - After a two-year run with its initial design, the F-85 got all new sheet metal below the belt line. Its length increased four inches. There were three standard models, two Deluxe models, two Cutlass models and the turbocharged Jetfire coupe. Standard F-85 items included: aluminized muffler; self-adjusting brakes; tubeless tires; front stabilizer bar; fiberglass hood insulation; and cigarette lighter. Deluxe equipment added carpets, front and rear foam seat cushions, special chrome moldings, rocker panel moldings and Deluxe steering wheel. F-85s were made in the Lansing, Kansas City and Southgate assembly plants.

1963 Oldsmobile, F-85 four-door sedan, OCW

1963 Oldsmobile, F-85 Cutlass two-door convertible, OCW

OLDSMOBILE I.D. NUMBERS: VIN located on left front door pillar. Engine unit number on left cylinder head. Serial number takes the form of four symbols, plus sequential production number. First two symbols identify year: 63=1963. Third symbol indicates series and matches second digit in Body/Style Number column of charts below. Fourth symbol indicates assembly plant: T=Texas (Arlington); A=Atlanta, Ga.; B=Boston (Framingham), Mass.; K=Kansas City, Kan.; M=Michigan (Lansing); L=Linden, N.J.; C=California (Southgate); W=Wilmington, Del. Remaining symbols are the sequential production number starting at 001001 at each factory. Ending VINs were not available. Engine numbers consisted of a alphabetical prefix and a production sequence number starting at 200001 for F-85 and 001001 for all other models. Prefixes for 1963 engines were: [215-cid V-8] S=155 hp; SE=export; SG=195 hp or 185 hp; SH=export; ST=215 hp turbocharged. [394-cid Dynamic 88 V-8] H=280 hp; HE=export; HL=260 hp; J=330 hp; JE=export; JS=345 hp. Ending engine numbers were not available.

Model Number	Body/Style Number	Body Type & Seating	Factory Price	Shipping Weight	Production Total
STANDARD LINE					
F-85	3019	4-dr Sed-6P	2512	2747	8,937
F-85	3027	2-dr Clb Cpe-6P	2403	2684	11,276
F-85	3035	4-dr Sta Wag-6P	2889	2814	3,348
DELUXE LINE					
F-85	3119	4-dr Sed-6P	2592	2767	29,269
F-85	3117	2-dr Cut Cpe-5P	2694	2704	41,343
F-85	3167	2-dr Cut Conv-5P	2971	2784	12,149
F-85	3135	4-dr Sta Wag-6P	2889	2846	6,647

1963 Oldsmobile, F-85 Cutlass two-door coupe, OCW

Model Number	Body/Style Number	Body Type & Seating	Factory Price	Shipping Weight	Production Total
JETFIRE LINE					
F-85	3147	2-dr HT-5P	3048	2884	5,842

DYNAMIC EIGHTY-EIGHT - The full-size Oldsmobiles also received all new sheet metal below the belt line. A total of six Dynamic 88 models were available. Standard equipment included: die-cast grille, deep pile carpeting, 21-gallon fuel tank, full-flow oil filter, foam seat cushions and foot-operated parking brake. Upholstery was a variety of vinyl, leather and cloth combinations. Standard tire size was 8.00 x 14 inches. Dynamic 88s were built in Lansing, Atlanta, Kansas City, Linden, Southgate, Wilmington and Arlington.

1963 Oldsmobile, Dynamic 88 two-door convertible, (DC)

1963 Oldsmobile, Dynamic 88 four-door sedan, OCW

DYNAMIC EIGHTY-EIGHT

Model Number	Body/Style Number	Body Type & Seating	Factory Price	Shipping Weight	Production Total
D88	3247	2-dr Hol HT-6P	3052	4165	39,071
D88	3269	4-dr Sed-6P	2995	4184	68,611
D88	3239	4-dr Hol HT-6P	3130	4172	62,351
D88	3267	2-dr Conv-5P	3379	4240	12,551
D88	3235	4-dr Sta Wag-6P	3459	4280	9,615
D88	3245	4-dr Sta Wag-9P	3566	4292	7,116

SUPER EIGHTY-EIGHT - The Super 88 combined the smaller 123-inch Dynamic 88 wheelbase with the larger 98 Sky Rocket V-8 engine. Four body styles were available. Standard equipment included all Dynamic Eighty-Eight items plus two-speed windshield wipers, special molding package, Deluxe steering wheel, map light, heavy-duty air cleaner and courtesy lights. Interiors were cloth, vinyl or leather in a variety of colors. Standard tire size was 8.00 x 14 inches. Super Eighty-Eights were made at the Lansing, Kansas City, Atlanta, Linden, Southgate, Wilmington and Arlington assembly plants.

1963 Oldsmobile, Super 88 Holiday four-door hardtop, OCW

SUPER EIGHTY-EIGHT

Model Number	Body/Style Number	Body Type & Seating	Factory Price	Shipping Weight	Production Total
S88	3547	2-dr Hol HT-6P	3408	4184	8,930
S88	3569	4-dr Sed-6P	3246	4196	24,575
S88	3539	4-dr Hol HT-6P	3473	4202	25,387
S88	3535	4-dr Sta Wag-6P	3748	4314	3,878

STARFIRE - The Starfire was in its third year as a two-model series situated between the Eighty-Eight and Ninety-Eight. Starfires were well-appointed automobiles with all items from the Super Eighty-Eight Series plus special moldings and trim, windshield washer, Hydra-Matic, dual exhaust, power steering, special wheel covers, courtesy lights, electric clock and power brakes. Interiors were leather or vinyl in several colors. Standard tire size was 8.00 x 14 inches.

1963 Oldsmobile, Starfire two-door convertible, OCW

STARFIRE

Model Number	Body/Style Number	Body Type & Seating	Factory Price	Shipping Weight	Production Total
SF	3657	2-dr Hol HT-5P	4129	4349	21,489
SF	3667	2-dr Conv-5P	4742	4492	4,401

1963 Oldsmobile, 98 Luxury Sedan four-door hardtop, OCW

NINETY-EIGHT - Again the top of line Oldsmobiles had an exclusive 126-inch wheelbase. In a rather unusual move the Ninety-Eight Custom Sports Coupe was the only model offered with the Starfire engine. Standard equipment included all Super Eighty-Eight items plus Hydra-Matic, power brakes, power steering, special rocker panel moldings, self-regulating electric clock, dual rear seat cigarette lighters and special headliner. Interiors were cloth, leather or vinyl. Standard tire size was 8.50 x 14 inches. Ninety-Eights were made at Lansing, Kansas City, Linden, South Gate and Wilmington.

1963 Oldsmobile, 98 Holiday Sports Sedan four-door hardtop, OCW

1963 Oldsmobile, 98 Holiday two-door hardtop, OCW

NINETY-EIGHT

Model Number	Body/Style Number	Body Type & Seating	Factory Price	Shipping Weight	Production Total
98	3847	2-dr Hol HT-6P	4178	4390	4,984
98	3819	4-dr Twn Sed-6P	3982	4395	11,053
98	3829	4-dr Lux Sed-6P	4332	4411	19,252
98	3839	4-dr Hol HT-6P	4254	4396	23,330
98	3867	2-dr Conv-5P	4457	4465	4,267
98	3947	2-dr Cust Spt Cpe -5P	4381	4384	7,422

ENGINES

(F-85 SERIES) Aluminum block V-8. Overhead valve. Liquid-cooled. Bore and stroke: 3.5 x 2.8 inches. Displacement: 215 cid. Hydraulic valve lifters. Compression ratio (F-85) 8.75:1; (Cutlass) 10.25:1; (Jetfire) 10.75:1. Torque (F-85) 210 pound feet; (Cutlass) 230 pound feet; (Jetfire) 300 pound feet. Brake hp: (F-85) 155; (Cutlass) 185; (Jetfire) 215. Carburetor: (F-85) two-barrel model 2GC; (Cutlass) four-barrel model 4GC; (Jetfire) Turbocharged, fluid-injected Model RC.

(88 SERIES) Cast iron block V-8. Overhead valve. Bore and stroke: 4-1/8 x 3-11/16 inches. Displacement: 394 cid. Hydraulic valve lifters. Compression ratio: 10.25:1. Torque: 430 pound feet. Brake hp: 280. Carburetor: two-barrel Rochester 2 GC.

(SUPER 88/98 SERIES) Cast iron block V-8. Overhead valve. Bore and stroke: 4-1/8 x 3-11/16 inches. Displacement: 394 cid. Hydraulic valve lifters. Compression ratio: 10.25:1. Torque: 440 pound feet. Brake hp: 330. Carburetor: Rochester four-barrel Model 4GC.

(98 CUSTOM/STARFIRE SERIES) Cast iron block V-8. Overhead valve. Bore and stroke: 4-1/8 x 3-11/16 inches. Displacement: 394 cid. Hydraulic valve lifters. Compression ratio: 10.50:1. Torque: 440 pound feet. Brake hp: 345. Carburetor Rochester four-barrel Model 4GC.

CHASSIS FEATURES: Wheelbase: (F-85) 112 inches, (Dynamic Eighty-Eight, Super Eighty-Eight and Starfire) 123 inches; (Ninety-Eight) 126 inches. Overall Length: (F-85) 192.2 inches; (Dynamic Eighty-Eight, Super Eighty-Eight and Starfire) 214.4 inches, (Ninety-Eight) 221.5 inches. Front tread: (F-85) 56 inches; (all others) 62.2 inches. Rear tread: (F-85) 56 inches; (all others) 61 inches.

OPTIONS [F-85]: Tinted glass ($31). Electric windows. ($102). Seat belts. Power trunk release. Vinyl top. Air conditioning ($378). Remote control outside mirror. Power brakes. Power steering ($86). Back-up lights ($11). Electric clock ($19). Station wagon luggage carrier ($65). All F-85's were powered by an aluminum block Rockette engine producing 155 hp in standard form, 185 hp in the optional Cutlass version. This was the last year for the 215-hp turbocharged, liquid-injected V-8 Jetfire coupe. All F-85s came standard with a three-speed manual transmission. A four-speed manual or Hydra-Matic were optional. [OLDSMOBILE] Tinted glass ($43). Electric windows ($106). Seat belts. Electric seats ($97). Vinyl roof. Windshield washer ($5). Air conditioning ($430). Remote control outside mirror. Power steering ($108). Tilt steering wheel. Back-up lights ($11). AM/FM radio ($124). Deluxe radio ($89). Super Deluxe signal seeking radio ($124). Electric antenna ($26). Bi-phonic radio speakers. All full-sized Oldsmobiles were

powered by one of three versions of the 394 cubic inch V-8. Exclusive to the Dynamic Eighty-Eight series was the 280-hp Rocket V-8. The Super Eight-Eight and Ninety-Eight series shared the 330-hp Sky Rocket engine. Exclusive to the Ninety-Eight Custom Sports Coupe and two Starfire models was the 345-hp Starfire engine. Other drivetrain options for full-sized cars included: G-80 anti-spin differential, G-90 mountain axle package; G-96 expressway axle package and VOI special engine cooling package. The Ninety-Eights and Starfires came with Hydra-Matic as standard equipment. All others had three-speed manual transmissions as standard equipment.

1963 Oldsmobile, 98 two-door convertible, OCW

HISTORICAL FOOTNOTES: Full-size Oldsmobiles and the F-85 line were introduced Oct. 4, 1962. Model year production was 476,753 units. Calendar year sales totaled 504,555 cars. J.F. Wolfram was the chief executive officer of the division. Optional tilt-type steering wheels, crankcase ventilation systems, self-adjusting brakes and Delcotron generators for all models were highly promoted. Because of a new 'sway control' feature, Oldsmobiles had a three-foot smaller turn circle. For the model year, 99.5 percent of all full-size Oldsmobiles had automatic transmissions, 91.7 percent had radios and 98.5 percent had power steering, but only 8.5 percent had posi-traction and 9.2 percent had bucket seats. In the F-85 Series, 88.5 percent had automatic transmission (4.3 percent had manual four-speed); 1.8 percent had power windows; 50.2 percent had bucket seats and 19 percent had seat belts.

1964

1964 Oldsmobile, F-85 Cutlass 4-4-2 two-door hardtop, (DC)

F-85 - The F-85/Cutlass was completely redesigned and gained 11 inches in length. It was transformed from a compact into an intermediate. The wheelbase was increased three inches. Gone was the aluminum block 215-cid V-8. In its place was a V-6 or cast-iron V-8 Rocket engine. This was also the first season for the midyear 4-4-2 option package. This $136 option package carried the RPO code B09. The name (in 1964) translated as 4=four-barrel; 4=four-speed; and 2=dual exhaust. Other 4-4-2 equipment included a heavy-duty suspension, dual-snorkel air cleaner, oversized redline tires and special 4-4-2 badges. F-85s could be ordered in either standard or Deluxe trim. Standard

equipment included: heater/defroster, self-adjusting brakes, oil filter, front stabilizer and dual sun visors. Deluxe and Cutlass equipment added Deluxe steering wheel, padded dash and carpets. Interiors were vinyl or cloth. Standard tire size was 6.50 x 14 inches. F-85s were built in Lansing, Atlanta, Kansas City, Linden, Southgate and Arlington.

OLDSMOBILE I.D. NUMBERS: VIN located on left front door pillar. Engine number (V-8) stamped on machined pad on left cylinder head above center exhaust port; (V-6) on front of right cylinder head. Serial number takes the form of four symbols, plus sequential production number. First symbol identifies engine type: 6=six; 8=V-8. Second symbol indicates series and matches second digit in Body/Style Number column of charts below. Third symbol identifies model year: 4=1964. Fourth symbol indicates assembly plant: T=Texas (Arlington); A=Atlanta, Ga.; B=Boston (Framingham), Mass.; K=Kansas City, Kan.; M=Michigan (Lansing); L=Linden, N.J.; C=California (Southgate); W=Wilmington, Del. Remaining symbols are the sequential production number starting at 001001 at each factory. Ending VINs were not available. Engine numbers consisted of a alphabetical prefix and a production sequence number. Prefixes for 1964 engines were: [225-cid V-6] KH=155 hp; KJ=export. [330-cid V-8] T=230 hp; TE=export; TG=290 hp; TH=export; V or TV=442 high-performance 310 hp; TK=245 hp. [394-cid V-8] H=280 hp; HE=export; HL=260 hp; J=330 hp; JE=export; JS=345 hp. Ending engine numbers were not available.

1964 Oldsmobile, F-85 two-door club coupe, OCW\

F-85 SERIES

F-85

Model Number	Body/Style Number	Body Type & Seating	Factory Price	Shipping Weight	Production Total
F-85 STANDARD					
F-85	64-3027	2-dr Clb Cpe-6P	2332	2875	16,298
F-85	64-3035	4-dr Sta Wag-6P	2688	3254	4,047
F-84	64-3069	4-dr Sed-6P	2386	2980	12,106
F-85 DELUXE					
F-85	64-3127	2-dr Spts Cpe-6P	2404	3025	6,594
F-85	64-3135	4-dr Sta Wag-6P	2876	3290	10,793
F-85	64-3169	4-dr Sed-6P	2663	3140	42,237
F-85 CUTLASS					
F-85	64-3227	2-dr Cpe-5P	2663	3140	15,440
F-85	64-3237	2-dr Hol HT-5P	2773	3155	36,153
F-85	64-3267	2-dr Conv-5P	2973	3307	12,822

1964 Oldsmobile, F-85 four-door sedan, OCW

1964 Oldsmobile, F-85 Cutlass two-door convertible, OCW

1964 Oldsmobile, F-85 Cutlass Holiday two-door coupe, OCW

VISTA CRUISER - Most Oldsmobile enthusiasts tend to think of the Vista Cruiser as an F-85 model, but it was a larger vehicle with a five inch longer wheelbase. This was the first year for the stylish station wagon and it was a late introduction. The Vista Cruiser had an elevated roof over the cargo area. The roof windows in the elevated section resembled the 1954 GM/Greyhound Scenicruiser. Standard equipment included coil springs, three-speed manual transmission, self-adjusting air scoop brakes and aluminized exhaust system. Either cloth or vinyl upholstery was offered. Standard tire size was 7.50 x 14 inches. Vista Cruisers were built in Lansing, Atlanta, Kansas City, Linden, Southgate and Arlington.

1964 Oldsmobile, Vista Cruiser four-door station wagon, OCW

VISTA CRUISER

Model Number	Body/Style Number	Body Type & Seating	Factory Price	Shipping Weight	Production Total
VC	64-3055	4-dr Sta Wag-6P	2938	3553	1,305
VC	64-3065	4-dr Sta Wag-9P	3072	3658	2,089

VISTA CRUISER CUSTOM

Model Number	Body/Style Number	Body Type & Seating	Factory Price	Shipping Weight	Production Total
VC	64-3255	4-dr Sta Wag-6P	3055	3582	3,320
VC	64-3265	4-dr Sta Wag-9P	3122	3687	7,286

JETSTAR EIGHTY-EIGHT - A pair of Jetstar nameplates were added to the Oldsmobile lineup in 1964. The new entry-level Eight-Eight was now the Jetstar Eighty-Eight. Four body styles were included in the series. Standard equipment included: foam padded front seat, carpeting, padded dash, wheel opening and rocker panel moldings and automatic dome light. Upholstery was vinyl or leather. These cars were made in the same assembly plant that built Vista Cruisers. Standard tire size was 7.50 x 14 inches.

1964 Oldsmobile, Jetstar 88 Holiday four-door hardtop, (DC)

JETSTAR EIGHTY-EIGHT

Model Number	Body/Style Number	Body Type & Seating	Factory Price	Shipping Weight	Production Total
J88	64-3347	2-dr Hol HT-6P	2981	3720	14,663
J88	64-3367	2-dr Conv-6P	3308	3817	3,903
J88	64-3369	4-dr Sed-6P	2924	3739	24,614
J88	64-3339	4-dr Hol HT-6P	3058	3758	19,325

1964 Oldsmobile, Jetstar 88 four-door sedan, OCW

DYNAMIC EIGHTY-EIGHT - With the introduction of the Jetstar Eighty-Eight, the Dynamic Eighty-Eight moved up a rung on the Oldsmobile ladder. This series had six models. Standard equipment included: foam rubber padded front seat, chrome side moldings, carpeting, padded dash, automatic dome light, courtesy and map lights and electric rear window on the Fiesta station wagon. Upholstery was in a variety of colored cloth, vinyl and leather. Standard tire size was 8.00 x 14 inches. Dynamic 88s were built at the Lansing, Atlanta, Kansas City, Linden, Southgate and Arlington plants.

1964 Oldsmobile, Dynamic 88 Holiday two-door hardtop, OCW

1964 Oldsmobile, Dynamic 88 Fiesta four-door station wagon, OCW

1964 Oldsmobile, Dynamic 88 two-door convertible, OCW

DYNAMIC EIGHTY-EIGHT

Model Number	Body/Style Number	Body Type & Seating	Factory Price	Shipping Weight	Production Total
D88	64-3447	2-dr Hol HT-6P	3051	3912	32,369
D88	64-3469	4-dr Sed-6P	2924	3952	57,590
D88	64-3467	2-dr Conv-6P	3378	4005	10,042
D88	64-3439	4-dr Hol HT-6P	3129	3980	50,327
D88	64-3435	4-dr Sta Wag-6P	3458	4155	10,747
D88	64-3445	4-dr Sta Wag-9P	3565	4180	6,599

SUPER EIGHTY-EIGHT - Following the introduction of the new Jetstar 88, the Super 88 was left with only two models. Standard equipment on the remaining 'Supers' included all items from the Dynamic Eighty-Eight plus special chrome molding package, chrome window frames, parking brake light and rear fold-down armrest. Upholstery was cloth, leather or vinyl. Standard tire size was 8.00 x 14 inches. Super 88s were made in the same plants as Dynamic 88s.

1964 Oldsmobile, Super 88 Holiday four-door hardtop, OCW

SUPER EIGHTY-EIGHT

Model Number	Body/Style Number	Body Type & Seating	Factory Price	Shipping Weight	Production Total
S88	64-3539	4-dr Hol HT-5P	3472	4054	17,778
S88	64-3569	4-dr Sed-5P	3250	4021	19,736

1964 Oldsmobile, Jetstar I two-door hardtop, OCW

JETSTAR I - The Jetstar I was introduced as a low-priced companion to the Starfire. It was a single model series. Standard equipment included: bucket seats, center console, foam padded front seats, padded dash, carpets, special molding package and windshield washer. Upholstery was vinyl, cloth or leather. Standard tire size was 8.00 x 14 inches. Jetstar Is were built with Dynamic 88s.

JETSTAR I

Model Number	Body/Style Number	Body Type & Seating	Factory Price	Shipping Weight	Production Total
J1	64-3457	2-dr Spts Cpe-5P	3592	4028	16,084

1964 Oldsmobile, Starfire two-door hardtop, OCW

STARFIRE - The two-model Starfire series continued for 1964. Starfires continued to be powered by the most powerful Olds V-8 engine. Standard equipment included: Hydra-Matic; power windows, seat, steering and brakes; whitewall tires; windshield washer; Deluxe steering wheel and wheel disc; bucket seats; console and tachometer. Interiors were cloth, vinyl or leather. Standard tire size was 8.00 x 14 inches.

STARFIRE

Model Number	Body/Style Number	Body Type & Seating	Factory Price	Shipping Weight	Production Total
SF	64-3667	2-dr Conv-5P	4742	4275	2,410
SF	64-3657	2-dr Cpe-5P	4128	4153	13,753

NINETY-EIGHT - The top-of-the-line Ninety-Eight series offered six models in two-door, four-door and convertible configurations. Standard equipment included: Hydra-Matic; power steering, brakes, windows and seats; windshield washer; special wheel discs; clock; courtesy and map lights and padded dash. Upholstery was a variety of colored cloth, vinyl or leather. Standard tire size was 8.50 x 14 inches. All Ninety-Eights were now built in Lansing, Mich.

1964 Oldsmobile, Starfire two-door convertible, (DC)

NINETY-EIGHT

Model Number	Body/Style Number	Body Type & Seating	Factory Price	Shipping Weight	Production Total
98	64-3847	2-dr Hol HT-6P	4177	4175	6,139
98	64-3947	2-dr Spt Cpe-6P	4391	4254	4,594
98	64-3867	2-dr Conv-6P	4457	4315	4,004
98	64-3829	4-dr Lux Sed-6P	4331	4238	17,346
98	64-3819	4-dr Twn Sed-6P	3982	4189	11,380
98	64-3839	4-dr Spts Sed-6P	4254	4231	24,791

ENGINES

(F-85/VISTA CRUISER SIX) Inline Six. Overhead valves. Cast-iron block. Displacement: 225 cid. Bore and stroke: 3.75 x 3.4 inches. Compression ratio: 9.0:1. Brake hp: 155 at 4400 rpm. Carburetor: Rochester one-barrel Model BC.

(F-85/VISTA CRUISER V-8) V-8. Overhead valves. Cast-iron block. Displacement: 330 cid. Bore and stroke: 3.93 x 3.38 inches. Compression ratio: 9.0:1. Brake hp: 210 at 4400 rpm. Hydraulic valve lifters. Carburetor: Rochester two-barrel Model 2GC.

(JETSTAR SERIES) V-8. Overhead valves. Cast-iron block. Displacement: 330 cid. Bore and stroke: 3.93 x 3.38 inches. Compression ratio: 10.25:1. Brake hp: 245 at 4600 rpm. Carburetor: two-barrel Rochester Model 2GC.

(DYNAMIC 88 SERIES) V-8. Cast-iron block. Displacement: 394 cid. Bore and stroke: 4-1/8 x 3-11/16 inches. Compression ratio: 10.25:1. Brake hp: 280 at 4400 rpm. Carburetor: Rochester two-barrel Model 2GC.

1964 Oldsmobile, 98 Holiday Sports Sedan four-door hardtop, OCW

(SUPER 88/98 SERIES) V-8. Cast-iron block. Displacement: 394 cid. Bore and stroke: 4-1/8 x 3-11/16 inches. Compression ratio: 10.25:1. Brake hp: 330 at 4600 rpm. Carburetor: Rochester four-barrel Model 4GC.

(JETSTAR I/STARFIRE/98 CUSTOM SERIES) V-8. Cast iron block. Displacement: 394 cid. Bore and stroke: 4-1/8 x 3-11/16 inches. Compression ratio: 10.50:1. Brake hp: 345 at 4800 rpm. Carburetor: Rochester four-barrel Model 4GC.

CHASSIS FEATURES: Wheelbase: (F-85) 115 inches; (Vista Cruiser) 120 inches; (Jetstar 88, Jetstar I, Dynamic 88, Super 88 and Starfire) 123 inches; (Ninety-Eight) 126 inches. Overall length: (F-85) 203 inches; (Vista Cruiser) 208 inches; (Jetstar 88, Jetstar I, Dynamic 88, Super 88 and Starfire) 215.3 inches; (Ninety-Eight) 222.3 inches. Front tread: (F-85 and Vista Cruiser) 58 inches; (All others) 62.2 inches. Rear tread: (F-85 and Vista Cruiser) 58 inches; (All others) 61 inches.

OPTIONS: Power brakes ($43). Power steering ($107). Air conditioning ($430). Power seats ($71). Clock ($16). Convenience lamps ($8). Outside mirror ($4). Two-tone paint ($17). AM/FM radio ($150). Deluxe push-button radio ($88). Super Deluxe signal seeking radio ($124). Power antenna ($26). Rear speaker ($16). Cruise Control ($91). Tilt steering ($43). Trunk release ($10). Rear window defroster ($21). Tinted glass ($43). Automatic transmission ($231). Three-speed manual floor shift transmission ($43). Four-speed manual floor shift transmission ($188). F-85 V-8: 330-cid/290-hp Cutlass engine ($34). Jetstar 88 V-8: 330-cid/290-hp Jetfire engine ($37). Dynamic 88 V-8: 394-cid/330-hp Rocket engine ($37). All 88 and 98 models V-8: 394-cid/345-hp Starfire engine ($64). Positive traction rear axle ($47). Midyear: 4-4-2 package as F-85 option with RPO B09 code ($136).

HISTORICAL FOOTNOTES: Oldsmobile's 1964 line was introduced Sept. 24, 1963. Model year sales included 177,600 'senior-compact' F-85s and 368,500 full-size Oldsmobiles. Sales of 546,112 units was 6.3 percent ahead of the 486,410 mark achieved in 1963. F-85, in its fourth season, maintained its uninterrupted climb with sales of 173,816 units, 38.5 percent above 1963's 125,514. H.N. Metzel was general manager of the division.

1965

1965 Oldsmobile, F-85 Cutlass convertible with 4-4-2 option, (DC)

F-85 - The F-85 series was mildly restyled and it continued to grow in popularity within the Oldsmobile model mix. In mid-1964, the 4-4-2 package was introduced to the F-85. By 1965, the optional handling and performance package gained greater recognition from automotive enthusiasts. The engine in the 442 was a 400-cid/345-hp V-8. The "442" now translated as 4=400 cid; 4=four-barrel carburetor and 2=dual exhaust. Three types of F-85s were offered this year: standard, Deluxe and the increasingly popular Cutlass. Standard F-85 equipment consisted of: heater/defroster, self-adjusting brakes, aluminized muffler, front seat belts, electric windshield wipers, dual sun visors and oil filter. Standard on the Deluxe and Cutlass models were F-85 items plus Deluxe steering wheel, padded dash and carpeting. Interiors could be ordered in vinyl or cloth. Standard tire size was 7.35 x 14 inches. F-85s were built in the Lansing, Baltimore, Kansas City and Fremont assembly plants.

OLDSMOBILE I.D. NUMBERS: VIN located on left front door pillar. Engine number on right cylinder head of V-6 and V-8. Serial number takes the form of seven symbols, plus sequential production number. First symbol identifies GM division: 3=Oldsmobile. Second to fifth symbols indicate series and match the last four digits in Body/Style Number column of charts below. Sixth symbol identifies model year: 5=-1965. Seventh symbol indicates assembly plant: C=Southgate, Calif.; D=Atlanta, Ga.; E=Linden, N.J.; G=Framingham, Mass.; M=Lansing, Mich.; Z=Fremont, Calif.; X=Kansas City, Kan.; R=Arlington, Texas. Remaining symbols are the sequential production number starting at 100001 at each factory. Ending VINs were not available. Engine numbers consisted of a alphabetical prefix and a production sequence number. Prefixes for 1965 engines were: [225-cid V-6] LH=155 hp; LJ=export. [330-cid V-8] T=250 hp; TE=export; TG=315 hp; TH=export. [330-cid JETSTAR 88] U=260 hp; UL=250 hp; UE=export two-barrel; UH=export four-barrel; UG=315 hp. [400-cid high-performance 4-4-2 V-8] V=345 hp four-barrel. [425-cid V-8] M=310 hp; ME=export two-barrel; ML=300 hp; N=360 hp; NE=export four-barrel; NS=370 hp. Ending engine numbers were not available.

F-85

Model Number	Body/Style Number	Body Type & Seating	Factory Price	Shipping Weight	Production Total
STANDARD WITH V-6					
F-85	65-3327	2-dr Clb Cpe-6P	2344	2655	5,289
F-85	65-3335	4-dr Sta Wag-6P	2689	3236	714
F-85	65-3369	4-dr Sed-6P	2505	2991	3,089
STANDARD WITH V-8					
F-85	65-3427	2-dr Spts Cpe-6P	2415	2789	7,720
F-85	65-3435	4-dr Sta Wag-6P	2797	3258	2,496
F-85	65-3469	4-dr Sed-6P	2465	3167	5,661
DELUXE WITH V-6					
F-85	65-3527	2-dr Spts Cpe-6P	2538	2984	6,141
F-85	65-3535	4-dr Sta Wag-6P	2797	3274	659
F-85	65-3569	4-dr Sed-6P	2505	3024	4,989
DELUXE WITH V-8					
F-85	65-3635	4-dr Sta Wag-6P	2868	3456	10,365
F-85	65-3669	4-dr Sed-6P	2576	3209	47,767

1965 Oldsmobile, F-85 Cutlass two-door sports coupe, OCW

CUTLASS

F-85	65-3827	2-dr Spts Cpe-6P	2643	2784	26,441
F-85	65-3837	2-dr Hol HT-6P	2784	2799	46,138
F-85	65-3867	2-dr Conv-6P	2983	2901	12,628

1965 Oldsmobile, F-85 Cutlass two-door convertible, OCW

VISTA CRUISER - Now in its first full year, the Oldsmobile Vista Cruiser and its Buick companion, the Skylark Sport Wagon, featured a "Scenic-Cruiser" style raised roof. Oldsmobile would retain this unique roof through 1972. Sheet metal came from the Cutlass/F-85, but the wheelbase and overall length were longer than standard wagons in those series. Standard equipment included: tinted Vista roof glass, underfloor luggage compartment, electric windshield wipers and self-adjusting brakes. Custom equipment included: Deluxe steering wheel, padded dash, chrome window frames and foam padded seat cushions. Interiors were vinyl or cloth. Tire size was 7.75 x 14 inches. Vista Cruisers were built in the same plants as F-85s.

VISTA CRUISER

Model Number	Body/Style Number	Body Type & Seating	Factory Price	Shipping Weight	Production Total
VC	65-3455	4-dr Sta Wag-6P	2937	3685	2,110
VC	65-3855	4-dr Cus Sta Wag-6P	3146	3747	9,335
VC	65-3465	4-dr Sta Wag-9P	3072	3762	3,335
VC	65-3865	4-dr Cus Sta Wag-9P	3270	3814	17,205

1965 Oldsmobile, Jetstar I two-door hardtop, OCW

JETSTAR EIGHTY-EIGHT - The Jetstar continued to be the entry-level Eighty-Eight. All full-size Oldsmobiles introduced completely new bodies. Standard equipment included: foam padded front seats, padded dash, rocker panel moldings, automatic dome light, electric windshield wipers, carpeting and parking brake light. Interiors were vinyl or cloth. Standard tire size was 7.75 x 14 inches. Code letters for Jetstar 88 assembly plants were: M, R, T, D, X, E and C.

1965 Oldsmobile, Jetstar 88 Holiday four-door hardtop, OCW

JETSTAR EIGHTY-EIGHT

Model Number	Body/Style Number	Body Type & Seating	Factory Price	Shipping Weight	Production Total
J88	65-5237	2-dr Hol HT-6P	2995	3701	13,911
J88	65-5267	2-dr Conv-6P	3337	3853	2,879
J88	65-5267	4-dr Sed-6P	2938	3734	22,725
J88	65-5239	4-dr Hol HT-6P	3072	3755	15,922

1965 Oldsmobile, Jetstar 88 two-door convertible, OCW

JETSTAR I - Jetstar I continued as a single model series. It featured the smaller 88 body with the big Starfire V-8 engine. It was a budget version of the expensive Starfire. Standard equipment included: bucket seats, console, carpeting, parking brake light, courtesy lamps, padded dash, windshield washer, Deluxe steering wheel, special wheel covers and clock. Interiors were vinyl. Standard tire size was 8.25 x 14 inches. Code letters for Jetstar I assembly plants were: M, R, T, D, X, E and C.

JETSTAR I

Model Number	Body/Style Number	Body Type & Seating	Factory Price	Shipping Weight	Production Total
J-1	65-5457	2-dr Spts Cpe-5P	3602	3936	6,552

1965 Oldsmobile, Dynamic 88 Holiday four-door hardtop, OCW

DYNAMIC EIGHTY-EIGHT - The Dynamic Eighty-Eight continued to be a popular full-size Oldsmobile series. The upscale subseries Delta models were added to the standard Dynamic offerings. Seven models were available. Standard Dynamic 88 equipment included: padded dash, foam front seat cushion, carpeting, parking brake light and electric windshield wipers. The Delta package added special moldings, chrome door frames, Deluxe interior trim, folding center armrest and courtesy lamps. Upholstery was cloth, vinyl or leather. Standard tire size was 8.25 x 14 inches. For city assembly plant code letters see 1965 Jetstar 88.

1965 Oldsmobile, Dynamic 88 Holiday two-door hardtop, OCW

1965 Oldsmobile, Dynamic 88 two-door convertible, OCW

DYNAMIC EIGHTY-EIGHT

Model Number	Body/Style Number	Body Type & Seating	Factory Price	Shipping Weight	Production Total
D88	65-5637	2-dr Hol HT-6P	3065	3847	24,746
D88	65-5669	4-dr Cel Sed-6P	3088	3914	47,030
D88	65-5639	4-dr Hol HT-6P	3143	3942	38,889
D88	65-5667	2-dr Conv-6P	3408	4036	8,832
DELTA					
D88	65-5837	2-dr Hol HT-6P	3253	3907	23,194
D88	65-5869	4-dr Cel Sed-6P	3158	3948	29,915
D88	65-5839	4-dr Hol HT-6P	3330	3959	37,358

1965 Oldsmobile, Delta 88 Holiday two-door hardtop, OCW

STARFIRE - This was the final year for the Starfire to carry the Oldsmobile personal luxury banner by itself. Next year the Toronado would join the team. Meanwhile, this series continued to offer two well-equipped models. Standard equipment on both the coupe and convertible included: T-stick controlled Turbo Hydra-Matic transmission, power steering and brakes, courtesy lamps, bucket seats, console, tachometer, padded dash, parking brake light, Deluxe steering wheel, special wheel covers, windshield washers and electric wipers and power windows and seat. Upholstery was vinyl, leather or cloth. Standard tire size 8.25 x 14 inches.

1965 Oldsmobile, Starfire two-door hardtop, OCW

STARFIRE

Model Number	Body/Style Number	Body Type & Seating	Factory Price	Shipping Weight	Production Total
SF	65-6657	2-dr Cpe-5P	4148	4132	13,024
SF	65-6667	2-dr Conv-5P	4778	4347	2,236

NINETY-EIGHT - The exclusive Ninety-Eight wheelbase had five models. It shared the new higher displacement 425-cid engine with most other full-size Oldsmobiles. Standard equipment included: Turbo Hydra-Matic transmission, power steering and brakes, power windows, clock, padded dash, foam padded seats, parking brake light, Deluxe steering wheel, special wheel covers, windshield washer and two-speed electric wipers, courtesy and glovebox lamps and front seat belts. Upholstery was leather, vinyl or cloth. Standard tire size was 8.55 x 14 inches. Ninety-Eights were built only in Lansing, Mich.

1965 Oldsmobile, 98 Luxury four-door sedan, OCW

NINETY-EIGHT

Model Number	Body/Style Number	Body Type & Seating	Factory Price	Shipping Weight	Production Total
98	65-8437	2-dr Spts Cpe-6P	4197	4164	12,166
98	65-8467	2-dr Conv-6P	4493	4335	4,903
98	65-8469	4-dr Twn Sed-6P	4001	4201	13,266
98	65-8439	4-dr Hol HT-6P	4273	4232	28,480
98	65-8669	4-dr Lux Sed-6P	4351	4249	33,591

ENGINES

(F-85 & VISTA CRUISER SERIES/SIX) V-6. Overhead valves. Cast iron block. Displacement: 225 cid. Bore and stroke: 3.75 x 3.40 inches. Compression ratio: 9.0:1. Brake hp: 155 at 4400 rpm. Four main bearings. Hydraulic valve lifters. Carburetor: Rochester Type BC one-barrel.

(F-85 & VISTA CRUISER SERIES/V-8) V-8. Overhead valves. Cast iron block. Displacement: 330 cid. Bore and stroke: 3.939 x 3.39 inches. Compression ratio: 9.0:1. Brake hp: 250 at 4800 rpm. Five main bearings. Hydraulic valve lifters. Carburetor: Rochester Type 2GC two-barrel.

(JETSTAR SERIES) V-8. Overhead valves. Cast iron block. Displacement: 330 cid. Bore and stroke: 3.939 x 3.385 inches. Compression ratio: 10.25:1. Brake hp: 260 at 4800 rpm. Five main bearings. Hydraulic valve lifters. Carburetor: Rochester Type 4GC four-barrel.

(JETSTAR I/STARFIRE SERIES) V-8. Overhead valves. Cast iron block. Displacement: 425 cid. Bore and stroke: 4.125 x 3.975 inches. Compression ratio: 10.25:1. Brake hp: 370 at 4800 rpm. Five main bearings. Hydraulic valve lifters. Carburetor: Rochester Type 4GC four-barrel.

(DYNAMIC 88 SERIES) V-8. Overhead valves. Cast iron block. Displacement: 425 cid. Bore and stroke: 4.125 x 3.975 inches. Compression ratio: 9.0:1. Brake hp: 300 at 4400 rpm. Five main bearings. Hydraulic valve lifters. Carburetor: Rochester Type 2GC two-barrel.

(98 SERIES) V-8. Overhead valves. Cast iron block. Displacement: 425 cid. Bore and stroke: 4.125 x 3.975 inches. Compression ratio: 10.25:1. Brake hp: 360 at 4800 rpm. Five main bearings. Hydraulic valve lifters. Carburetor: Rochester Type 4GC four-barrel.

CHASSIS FEATURES: Wheelbase: (F-85) 115 inches; (Vista Cruiser) 120 inches; (Jetstar 88, Jetstar I, Dynamic 88 and Starfire) 123 inches; (Ninety-Eight) 126 inches. Overall length: (F-85) 204.3 inches; (Vista Cruiser) 207.7 inches; (Jetstar 88, Jetstar I, Dynamic 88 and Starfire) 216.9 inches; (Ninety-Eight) 222.9 inches. Front tread: (F-85 and Vista Cruiser) 58 inches; (all others) 62 inches. Rear tread: (F-85 and Vista Cruiser) 58 inches; (all others) 64 inches.

OPTIONS: Power brakes ($45). Power steering ($109). Air conditioning ($441). Power seats ($71). Clock ($16). Courtesy lamps ($9). Outside mirror ($5). AM/FM radio ($165). Push-button radio ($88). Power antenna ($27). Rear speaker ($21). Cruise control ($91). Tilt steering ($44). Rear window defogger ($22). High-performance 4-4-2 Handling and Performance Package ($156). Three-speed manual transmission was standard on all except Ninety-Eight and Starfire. Automatic transmission ($245). Three-speed manual floor shift transmission ($45). Four-speed manual floor shift transmission ($205). V-8 330-cid/260-hp Jetfire engine ($30). V-8 330-cid/315-hp Jetfire engine ($55). V-8 425-cid/360-hp Super engine ($60). V-8 425-cid/370-hp Starfire engine ($78). Positive traction rear axle ($51).

HISTORICAL FOOTNOTES: The full-size Oldsmobiles and the F-85 models were introduced Sept. 24, 1964. Model year production was 592,804 units. Calendar year production totaled 650,801 cars. H.N. Metzel was the chief executive officer of the division. Oldsmobile achieved record sales this season.

1966

1966 Oldsmobile, F-85 Cutlass two-door convertible, OCW

F-85 - The F-85 continued to grow in popularity. Traditional full-size car buyers began looking to the Oldsmobile intermediate series. This year there were several sub-groups under the F-85 heading: Standard, Deluxe, Cutlass and 4-4-2. New to the series was the first inline six since 1950. F-85 standard equipment consisted of front and rear seat belts, padded dash, windshield washer, two-speed wipers, back-up lights, outside rear view mirror and vinyl floor covering. Deluxe equipment consisted of all standard items plus foam padded seat cushions, carpeting, chrome roof moldings and Deluxe steering wheel. Cutlass models included all items from the Deluxe list plus bucket or Custom seats, Deluxe armrests and courtesy lamp package. Upholstery was vinyl or cloth. Standard tire size was 7.35 x 14. F-85s built in Lansing, Mich., were coded with an M, while those built in Fremont, Calif., were coded with a Z.

OLDSMOBILE I.D. NUMBERS: VIN located on left front door pillar. Engine number on inline six on right side of block behind distributor. Engine number for V-8 on machined pad on front of right cylinder head. Serial number takes the form of seven symbols, plus sequential production number. First symbol identifies GM division: 3=Oldsmobile. Second to fifth symbols indicate series and match the four digits in Body/Style Number column of charts below. Sixth symbol identifies model year: 6=1966.

Seventh symbol indicates assembly plant: C=Southgate, Calif.; D=Atlanta, Ga.; E=Linden, N.J.; G=Framingham, Mass.; M=Lansing, Mich.; Z=Fremont, Calif.; X=Kansas City, Kan.; R=Arlington, Texas. Remaining symbols are the sequential production number starting at 100001 at each factory. Ending VINs were not available. Engine numbers consist of a alphabetical prefix and a production sequence number. Prefixes for 1966 engines were: [250-cid I6] VA/VB/VC=155 hp; VJ=export; VE/VF/VG=155 hp (automatic); VK=export. [330-cid F-85/Cutlass V-8] W=250 hp; WE=export two-barrel; WL=310 hp; WG=320 hp; WH=export four-barrel. [Jetstar 88 330-cid V-8] X=260 hp; XE=export two-barrel; XG=320 hp; XH=export four-barrel; XL=250 hp. [400-cid high-performance 4-4-2 V-8] V=350 hp four-barrel and 360 hp Tri-Carb. [425-cid Dynamic 88/Delta 88/Ninety-Eight V-8] M=310 hp; ME=export two-barrel; ML=300 hp; N=365 hp; NS=375 hp. [425-cid 98 only] NE=four-barrel export. [425-cid Toronado only V-8] NT=385 hp. Ending engine numbers were not available.

F-85 SERIES

Model Number	Body/Style Number	Body Type & Seating	Factory Price	Shipping Weight	Production Total
STANDARD 6-CYLINDER					
F-85	66-3335	4-dr Sta Wag-6P	2605	3350	2,160
F-85	66-3307	2-dr Clb Cpe-6P	2322	2855	12,694
F-85	66-3369	4-dr Sed-6P	2384	3023	6,616
STANDARD 8-CYLINDER					
F-85	66-3407	2-dr Clb Cpe-6P	2418	3150	6,353
F-85	66-3435	4-dr Sta Wag-6P	2764	3437	1,652
F-85	66-3469	4-dr Sed-6P	2471	3185	3,754
DELUXE 6-CYLINDER					
F-85	66-3517	2-dr Hol HT-6P	2495	2955	19,942
F-85	66-3569	4-dr Sed-6P	2479	3058	31,020
F-85	66-3539	4-dr Hol HT-6P	2610	3043	7,013
F-85	66-3535	4-dr Sta Wag-6P	2773	3386	8,492

1966 Oldsmobile, F-85 Deluxe Holiday two-door hardtop, OCW

Model Number	Body/Style Number	Body Type & Seating	Factory Price	Shipping Weight	Production Total
DELUXE 8-CYLINDER					
F-85	66-3617	2-dr Hol HT-6P	2583	3188	16,968
F-85	66-3669	4-dr Sed-6P	2567	3207	27,452
F-85	66-3639	4-dr Hol HT-6P	2699	3273	6,911
F-85	66-3635	4-dr Sta Wag-6P	2793	3458	8,058

1966 Oldsmobile, F-85 Cutlass 4-4-2 Holiday two-door hardtop, OCW

Model Number	Body/Style Number	Body Type & Seating	Factory Price	Shipping Weight	Production Total
CUTLASS					
F-85	66-3807	2-dr Spts Cpe-5P	2614	3185	17,455
F-85	66-3817	2-dr Hol HT-6P	2750	3197	44,633
F-85	66-3867	2-dr Conv-5P	2944	3197	12,154
F-85	66-3839	4-dr Sup HT-6P	2895	3255	30,871

1966 Oldsmobile, Cutlass Supreme four-door hardtop, OCW

1966 Oldsmobile, Cutlass two-door convertible, OCW

VISTA CRUISER - The demand for family station wagons continued this year and families wanting a little more space could find it in the stylish Vista Cruiser line. Standard equipment included: foam padded seats, padded dash, windshield washer, two-speed wipers, heavy-duty clutch, back-up lamps and left outside rear view mirror. Custom equipment added carpets, special chrome moldings, Deluxe steering wheel and Deluxe armrests. Upholstery was cloth or vinyl. Standard tire size was 8.25 x 14 inches. Vista Cruisers were built in F-85 plants.

VISTA CRUISER SERIES

Model Number	Body/Style Number	Body Type & Seating	Factory Price	Shipping Weight	Production Total
STANDARD					
VC	66-3455	4-dr Sta Wag-6P	2914	3753	1,660
VC	66-3465	4-dr Sta Wag-9P	3065	3787	1,869
CUSTOM					
VC	66-3855	4-dr Sta Wag-6P	3114	3769	8,910
VC	66-3865	4-dr Sta Wag-9P	3278	3804	14,167

1966 Oldsmobile, Jetstar 88 Holiday four-door hardtop, OCW

JETSTAR EIGHTY-EIGHT - The Jetstar 88 began its final year as an Oldsmobile series and was the entry-level full-size series. Three body styles were offered in 1966. Standard equipment included: front and rear seat belts, special chrome moldings, padded instrument panel, windshield washer, two-speed wipers, carpeting, back-up lamps, Deluxe armrests, left outside rear view mirror and parking brake light. Upholstery was cloth or vinyl. Standard tire size was 7.75 x 14 inches. Plant codes for Jetstar 88s were M, D, X, E and C.

JETSTAR EIGHTY-EIGHT SERIES

Model Number	Body/Style Number	Body Type & Seating	Factory Price	Shipping Weight	Production Total
J88	66-5237	2-dr Hol HT-6P	2962	3752	8,575
J88	66-5269	4-dr Cel Sed-6P	2907	3776	13,734
J88	66-5239	4-dr Hol HT-6P	3038	3752	7,938

1966 Oldsmobile, Dynamic 88 four-door sedan, OCW

DYNAMIC EIGHTY-EIGHT - The Delta Eighty-Eight was pulled out as a sub-series within this group and stood on its own. Four Dynamic Eighty-Eight models were available in the overpopulated Eighty-Eight group. Standard equipment included: Deluxe wheel discs, front and rear seat belts, carpeting, padded dash, windshield washer and two-speed wipers, foam seat cushions, chrome window moldings, back-up lamps, courtesy lamps and parking brake light. Interiors were vinyl, leather or cloth. Standard tire size was 8.25 x 14 inches. Assembly plant codes were the same as those listed for Jetstar Eighty-Eights.

1966 Oldsmobile, Dynamic 88 two-door convertible, OCW

DYNAMIC EIGHTY-EIGHT

Model Number	Body/Style Number	Body Type & Seating	Factory Price	Shipping Weight	Production Total
D88	66-5637	2-dr Hol HT-6P	3048	4913	20,857
D88	66-5667	2-dr Conv-6P	3381	4017	5,540
D88	66-5669	4-dr Cel Sed-6P	2992	3930	38,742
D88	66-5639	4-dr Hol HT-6P	3123	3945	30,784

DELTA EIGHTY-EIGHT - For the first time the Delta Eighty-Eight stood alone as a separate series. Four models were available in this top-of-the-line Eighty-Eight. Standard equipment included: special wheel discs, front and rear seat belts, carpeting, padded dash, windshield washer and two-speed wipers, Deluxe steering wheel, foam seat cushions, back-up lamps, courtesy and map lights, special armrests and parking brake light. Upholstery was vinyl, leather or cloth. Standard tire size was 8.25 x 14 inches. These cars were built in the same plants as Dynamic 88s.

1966 Oldsmobile, Delta 88 Holiday two-door hardtop, OCW

DELTA EIGHTY-EIGHT

Model Number	Body/Style Number	Body Type & Seating	Factory Price	Shipping Weight	Production Total
D88	66-5837	2-dr Hol HT-6P	3230	3917	20,587
D88	66-5857	2-dr Conv-6P	3564	4055	4,303
D88	66-5839	4-dr Hol HT-6P	3306	3984	33,326
D88	66-5869	4-dr Cel Sed-6P	3138	3963	30,140

STARFIRE - The Starfire saw its personal luxury market cramped increasingly by the Ninety-Eight two-door models and the introduction of the all-new Toronado. This was the final year for the Starfire, which was introduced in 1961. Only the hardtop remained. Standard equipment included: sports console, bucket seats, foam seat cushions, front and rear seat belts, carpeting, windshield washers and two-speed wipers, special wheel discs, electric clock, chrome molding package, courtesy lamps, outside rear view mirror and back-up lamps. Interiors were vinyl, leather or cloth. Standard tire size was 8.25 x 14 inches.

1966 Oldsmobile, Starfire two-door hardtop, OCW

STARFIRE

Model Number	Body/Style Number	Body Type & Seating	Factory Price	Shipping Weight	Production Total
SF	66-5457	2-dr HT-5P	3540	4013	13,019

NINETY-EIGHT - Some luxury market buyers purchased either Starfires or the new Toronados, but the Ninety-Eight remained the full-size top-of-the-line Oldsmobile. Five models, including a trio of four-doors, were available. Standard equipment included: Turbo Hydra-Matic transmission; power steering, brakes, windows and seats; special wheel covers; front and rear seat belts; carpeting; windshield washer and two-speed wipers; foam seat cushions; electric clock and special armrests on selected models. Upholstery was cloth, vinyl or leather. Standard tire size was 8.55 x 14 inches. Ninety-Eights were built in the same plants as Dynamic 88s and Delta 88s.

1966 Oldsmobile, 98 Luxury four-door sedan, OCW

NINETY-EIGHT

Model Number	Body/Style Number	Body Type & Seating	Factory Price	Shipping Weight	Production Total
98	66-8437	2-dr Hol HT-6P	4129	4140	11,488
98	66-8467	2-dr Conv-6P	4413	4245	4,568
98	66-8439	4-dr Hol HT-6P	4204	4184	23,048
98	66-8469	4-dr Twn Sed-6P	4001	4197	10,892
98	66-8669	4-dr Lux Sed-6P	4279	4197	38,123

TORONADO - Ranked with such blockbuster Oldsmobile introductions as the Hydra-Matic transmission in 1940 and the Rocket V-8 in 1949, Oldsmobile introduced its front-wheel-drive Toronado in 1966. The first practical, domestic, full-size front-wheel-drive car since the 1936 Cord, the Toronado offered a number of engineering innovations. Like the Ninety-Eights of the previous few years, the early "Toros" were built exclusively in Lansing, Mich. Standard equipment was extensive and included: Turbo-Hydra-Matic transmission; power steering and power brakes; Strato-bench front seat; foam seat cushions; special chrome molding package; carpeting; electric clock; back-up lamps; Deluxe armrests, instrument panel and courtesy lamps; outside rear view mirror and parking brake light. Interiors were vinyl, leather or cloth. Standard tire size was 8.85 x 15 inches.

1966 Oldsmobile, Toronado two-door coupe, OCW

TORONADO SERIES

Model Number	Body/Style Number	Body Type & Seating	Factory Price	Shipping Weight	Production Total
STANDARD					
T	66-9487	2-dr Cpe-5P	4585	4366	6,333
DELUXE					
T	66-9687	2-dr Cpe-5P	4779	4410	34,630

ENGINES

(F-85 SERIES) Inline Six. Overhead valves. Cast iron block. Displacement: 250 cid. Bore and stroke: 3.875 x 3.53 inches. Compression ratio: 8.5:1. Brake hp: 155 at 4200 rpm. Seven main bearings. Hydraulic valve lifters. Carburetor: Rochester Type BV, one-barrel.

(F-85 SERIES) V-8. Overhead valves. Cast iron block. Displacement: 330 cid. Bore and stroke: 3.985 x 3.385 inches. Compression ratio: 10.25:1. Brake hp: 310. Five main bearings. Hydraulic valve lifters. Carburetor: Rochester Type 2GC, two-barrel.

(VISTA CRUISER/JETSTAR SERIES) V-8. Cast iron block. Overhead valves. Displacement: 330 cid. Bore and stroke: 3.985 x 3.385 inches. Compression ratio: 10.25:1. Brake hp: 250. Five main bearings. Hydraulic valve lifters. Carburetor: Rochester Type 2GC, two-barrel.

(DYNAMIC 88/DELTA 88 SERIES) V-8. Overhead valves. Cast iron block. Displacement: 425 cid. Bore and stroke: 4.125 x 3.975 inches. Compression ratio: 10.25:1. Brake hp: 310. Five main bearings. Hydraulic valve lifters. Carburetor: Rochester 2GC, two-barrel.

(STARFIRE SERIES) V-8. Overhead valves. Cast iron block. Displacement: 425 cid. Bore and stroke: 4.125 x 3.975 inches. Compression ratio: 10.5:1. Brake hp: 375. Five main bearings. Hydraulic valve lifters. Carburetor: Rochester 4GC, four-barrel.

(NINETY-EIGHT SERIES) V-8. Overhead valves. Cast iron block. Displacement: 425 cid. Bore and stroke: 4.125 x 3.975 inches. Compression ratio: 10.25:1. Brake hp: 365. Five main bearings. Hydraulic valve lifters. Carburetor: Rochester 4GC, four-barrel.

(TORONADO SERIES) V-8. Overhead valve. Cast iron block. Displacement: 425 cid. Bore and stroke: 4.125 x 3.975 inches. Compression ratio: 10.5:1. Brake hp: 385. Five main bearings. Hydraulic valve lifters. Carburetor: Rochester 4GC, four-barrel.

CHASSIS FEATURES: Wheelbase: (F-85) 115 inches; (Vista Cruiser) 120 inches; (Toronado) 119 inches; (Jetstar 88/Dynamic 88) 123 inches; (Delta 88/Starfire) 123 inches; (Ninety-Eight) 126 inches. Overall length: (F-85) 204.2 inches; (Vista Cruiser) 209.1 inches; (Toronado) 211 inches; (Jetstar 88/Dynamic 88) 217 inches; (Delta 88/Starfire) 217 inches; (Ninety-Eight) 223 inches. Front tread: (F-85/Vista Cruiser) 58 inches; (Jetstar 88) 61.8 inches; (Toronado) 63.5 inches; (all others) 62.5 inches. Rear tread: (F-85/Vista Cruiser) 59 inches; (all others) 63 inches.

OPTIONS: Power brakes ($41). Power steering ($94). Air conditioning ($343). Tinted windows ($30). Power seat ($69). Head rests ($52). Power trunk ($12). Floor mats ($7). Vinyl roof ($74). Sports console ($68). Cruise control ($41). Tilt steering column ($41). Wire wheel discs ($61). Tachometer ($52). Electric clock ($15). Radio ($64). Power antenna ($29). Rear radio speaker ($15). AM/FM radio ($147). Power door locks ($68). Rear defroster ($21). The 4-4-2 package consisted of a special 400-cid/350-hp V-8, heavy-duty chassis items and special internal and external trim. It was offered on F-85 and Cutlass two-door models ($152). Three-speed manual transmission was standard on all models, except Olds 98 and Toronado. Automatic transmission ($23). Three-speed manual floor shift transmission ($84). Hurst shifter, F-85. Four-speed manual floor shift transmission ($184). Close-ratio four-speed manual transmission with floor shift ($184). V-8: 330-cid/310-hp Cutlass engine ($33). V-8: 425-cid/365-hp Super Rocket engine ($36). V-8: 425-cid/375-hp Starfire engine ($100). Positive traction rear axle ($46). Heavy-duty clutch ($5). Available rear axle gear ratios: 2.73:1; 3.93:1; 3.08:1; 3.23:1; 3.42:1; 3.90:1.

HISTORICAL FOOTNOTES: Model year sales were 586,381 cars. Calendar year sales were 594,069 units. *Motor Trend* magazine selected Toronado as its 'Car of the Year'. Oldsmobile Division got a new administration building. A total of 21,997 F-85/Cutlass models were sold with the optional 4-4-2 performance package.

1967

F-85 - The F-85 continued to be the base model of the F-85 series, but Olds intermediate buyers were ordering more luxury with their cars and Cutlass models became more popular. Three basic F-85s were offered with either the L-head six-cylinder or a Rocket V-8. Standard equipment included: vinyl floor covering, seat belts, electric windshield wipers, heater/defroster and back-up lights. Standard tire size was 7.75 x 14 inches. Interiors were cloth or vinyl. F-85s were made at Lansing, Bloomfield, N.J., and Fremont, Calif.

OLDSMOBILE I.D. NUMBERS: VIN located on left front door pillar. Engine number on right side of six-cylinder block; front of right cylinder head on V-8. Serial number takes the form of seven symbols, plus sequential production number. First symbol identifies GM division: 3=Oldsmobile. Second to fifth symbols indicate series and match the four digits in Body/Style Number column of charts below. Sixth symbol identifies model year: 7=1967. Seventh symbol indicates assembly plant: C=Southgate, Calif.; D=Atlanta, Ga.; E=Linden, N.J.; G=Framingham, Mass.; M=Lansing, Mich.; Z=Fremont, Calif.; X=Kansas City, Kan.; R=Arlington, Texas. Remaining symbols are the sequential production number starting at 100001 at each factory. Ending VINs were not available. Engine numbers consist of a alphabetical prefix and a production sequence number. Prefixes for 1967 engines were: [250-cid inline six-cylinder] FVA/FVB/FVC/FVD/FVE/FVF/FVG/FVH=155 hp; FVJ=export [330-cid F-

85/Cutlass V-8] W=260 hp; WE=250 hp. [330-cid Delmont 88 V-8] XE=250 hp; X=260 hp; XG=320 hp. [350-cid F-85/Cutlass/Cutlass Supreme V-8] WG/WH=320 hp. [400-cid high-performance 4-4-2 V-8] VG=350 hp four-barrel and 360 hp Force-Air. [400-cid Turnpike Cruiser V-8] V=300 hp; [425-cid Dynamic 88/Delta 88/Delta 88 Custom/Ninety-Eight V-8] PL=300 hp; P=310 hp; R=365 hp; RS=375 hp; PE= export two-barrel; RE=export four-barrel. [425-cid Toronado only V-8] RT=385 hp. Ending engine numbers were not available.

F-85 SERIES

Model Number	Body/Style Number	Body Type & Seating	Factory Price	Shipping Weight	Production Total
6-CYLINDER					
F-85	67-3307	2-dr Clb Cpe-6P	2410	2965	5,349
F-85	67-3369	4-dr Sed-6P	2457	3015	2,458
F-85	67-3335	4-dr Sta Wag-6P	2749	3200	2,749
8-CYLINDER					
F-85	67-3407	2-dr Clb Cpe-6P	2480	3184	6,700
F-85	67-3369	4-dr Sed-6P	2527	3211	5,126
F-85	67-3335	4-dr Sta Wag-6P	2818	3463	1,625

1967 Oldsmobile, Custom Vista Cruiser four-door station wagon, OCW

VISTA CRUISER - Two and three-seat versions of the Vista Cruiser were offered. This was again the biggest Oldsmobile station wagon. Sheet metal was nearly identical to the Cutlass/F-85 models, but the Vista Cruiser had a five-inch longer wheelbase. Standard equipment included: heavy-duty clutch, heavy-duty vinyl floor covering and foam padded seats. Custom equipment included: Deluxe armrests, carpeting, special interior light package, special moldings and Deluxe steering wheel. Upholstery was cloth or vinyl. Standard tire size was 8.25 x 14 inches. Vista Cruisers were assembled in F-85 factories.

VISTA CRUISER

Model Number	Body/Style Number	Body Type & Seating	Factory Price	Shipping Weight	Production Total
VC	67-3465	4-dr Sta Wag-8P	3135	3820	2,748
CUSTOM					
VC	67-3855	4-dr Sta Wag-6P	3228	3789	9,513
VC	67-3865	4-dr Sta Wag-8P	3339	3897	15,293

CUTLASS - The fancier version of the F-85, the Cutlass had now attained series status of its own and began a climb that would eventually make it the most popular nameplate for a U.S. built car. Either six-cylinder or V-8 power could be had in any of five Cutlass models. Upholstery was cloth or vinyl. Standard equipment included: carpeting, courtesy lamps, chrome molding package, foam seat cushions and Deluxe steering wheel. Standard tire size was 7.75 x 15 inches. Cutlasses were also assembled in F-85 factories.

CUTLASS SERIES

Model Number	Body/Style Number	Body Type & Seating	Factory Price	Shipping Weight	Production Total
6-CYLINDER					
Cut	67-3517	2-dr Hol HT-6P	2574	2965	2,564
Cut	67-3567	2-dr Conv-6P	2770	3145	567
Cut	67-3569	4-dr Twn Sed-6P	2552	3054	2,219
Cut	67-3539	4-dr Hol HT-6P	2683	3074	644
Cut	67-3535	4-dr Sta Wag-6P	2848	3200	365

1967 Oldsmobile, Cutlass Supreme 4-4-2 two-door hardtop, OCW

1967 Oldsmobile, Cutlass Supreme 4-4-2 two-door convertible, OCW

8-CYLINDER					
Cut	67-3617	2-dr Hol HT-6P	2644	3216	29,799
Cut	67-3667	2-dr Conv-6P	2839	3304	3,777
Cut	67-3669	4-dr Twn Sed-6P	2622	3229	29,062
Cut	67-3639	4-dr Hol HT-6P	2753	3298	7,344
Cut	67-3635	4-dr Sta Wag-6P	2917	3478	8,130

CUTLASS SUPREME - The Cutlass Supreme was another new Olds series, introduced as a single model in 1966. The Supreme was the only series in which the popular 4-4-2 and the high-mileage Turnpike Cruising package option could be ordered. The 4-4-2 performance packages were sold with 24,829 cars. The new 400 cid "Force-Air" engine optionally available for 4-4-2s was a ram-induction system. Its horsepower was advertised as the same as the 1966 Tri-Carb engine. Five models were in this top-of-the-line F-85. Standard equipment included: Deluxe armrests, carpeting, courtesy lamp package, special molding group, foam seats and Deluxe steering wheel. Upholstery was vinyl or cloth. Standard tire size was 7.75 x 14 inches. Cutlass Supremes were assembled in F-85 factories.

CUTLASS SUPREME SERIES

Model Number	Body/Style Number	Body Type & Seating	Factory Price	Shipping Weight	Production Total
CS	67-3807	2-dr Spt Cpe-6P	2694	3140	18,256
CS	67-3867	2-dr Conv-6P	3067	3385	10,897
CS	67-3869	4-dr Twn Sed-6P	2726	3262	8,346
CS	67-3839	4-dr Hol HT-6P	2900	3284	22,571
CS	67-3817	2-dr Hol HT-6P	2831	3152	57,858

1967 Oldsmobile, Cutlass Supreme Holiday four-door hardtop, OCW

1967 Oldsmobile, Cutlass Supreme two-door hardtop with Turnpike Cruising (TC) package, OCW

1967 Oldsmobile, Cutlass Supreme two-door convertible, OCW

DELMONT EIGHTY-EIGHT - A new prefix was used with Eighty-Eights in 1967: Delmont 88. Two sub-series were offered: the 330 and the 425. The numbers referred to the engine displacement, either 330 cid or 425 cid, depending on which engine was standard. Three models could be ordered with either engine, but the convertible came only as a 425. Standard equipment included: Deluxe armrests, carpeting, interior lamp package, special wheel covers and chrome body moldings. Interiors were vinyl, leather or cloth. Standard tire size was 8.55 x 14 inches. Full-size Oldsmobiles were made in the Lansing, Linden, Kansas City and Southgate assembly plants.

1967 Oldsmobile, Delmont 88 425 Holiday four-door hardtop, OCW

DELMONT EIGHTY-EIGHT SERIES

Model Number	Body/Style Number	Body Type & Seating	Factory Price	Shipping Weight	Production Total
330 MODELS					
88	67-5287	2-dr Hol HT-6P	3063	3876	10,786
88	67-5239	4-dr Hol HT-6P	3139	3894	10,600
88	67-5269	4-dr Twn Sed-6P	3008	3850	15,076
425 MODELS					
88	67-5687	2-dr Hol HT-6P	3126	3781	16,669
88	67-5639	4-dr Hol HT-6P	3202	3987	21,909
88	67-5669	4-dr Twn Sed-5P	3071	3955	21,511
88	67-5667	2-dr Conv-6P	3462	4058	3,525

1967 Oldsmobile, Delmont 88 425 two-door convertible, OCW

DELTA EIGHTY-EIGHT - The Delta 88 continued the proliferation of Eighty-Eight models. It now had two sub-series: the standard Delta Eighty-Eight and the Delta Eighty-Eight Custom. Four models were offered as standard Deltas, while two were available as Customs. Standard trim consisted of Deluxe armrests, carpeting, lamp package, molding package, foam seat cushions, special wheelcovers and Deluxe steering wheel. Interiors were vinyl, cloth or leather. Standard tire size was 8.55 x 14 inches.

1967 Oldsmobile, Delta 88 four-door sedan, OCW

1967 Oldsmobile, Delta 88 two-door convertible, OCW

DELTA EIGHTY-EIGHT SERIES

Model Number	Body/Style Number	Body Type & Seating	Factory Price	Shipping Weight	Production Total
STANDARD					
D88	67-5887	2-dr Hol HT-6P	3310	3915	2,447
D88	67-5867	2-dr Conv-6P	3646	4178	14,471
D88	67-5869	4-dr Twn Sed-6P	3218	3993	21,909
D88	67-5839	4-dr Hol HT-6P	3386	3951	22,270

1967 Oldsmobile, Delta Custom Holiday four-door hardtop, OCW

1967 Oldsmobile, Delta Custom Holiday two-door hardtop, OCW

CUSTOM

Model Number	Body/Style Number	Body Type & Seating	Factory Price	Shipping Weight	Production Total
D88	67-5487	2-dr Hol HT-6P	3522	3975	12,192
D88	67-5439	4-dr Hol HT-6P	3582	4027	14,306

1967 Oldsmobile, 98 two-door convertible, OCW

NINETY-EIGHT - Gone was the sporty elegance of the Starfire. The Ninety-Eight and Toronado series were now Oldsmobile's remaining luxury cars. There were five models available. Standard Ninety-Eight trim included: armrests, power brakes, dual cigarette lighters, electric clock, carpeting, lamp package, molding package, seat belts, power seats, power steering, Turbo Hydra-Matic and power windows. Upholstery was cloth, vinyl or leather. Standard tire size was 8.85 x 14 inches. Ninety-Eight models were built in Lansing.

1967 Oldsmobile, 98 Luxury four-door sedan, OCW

NINETY-EIGHT SERIES

Model Number	Body/Style Number	Body Type & Seating	Factory Price	Shipping Weight	Production Total
98	67-8457	2-dr Hol HT-6P	4214	4184	10,476
98	67-8467	2-dr Conv-6P	4498	4405	3,769
98	67-8469	4-dr Twn Sed-6P	4009	4222	8,900
98	67-8439	4-dr Hol HT-6P	4276	4285	17,533
98	67-8669	4-dr Lux Sed-6P	4351	4247	35,511

TORONADO - Changes were few from the 1966 introductory model, but there were subtle improvements. Standard equipment included: power brakes, rear cigarette lighters, electric clock, carpeting, interior lamp package, chrome molding package, foam seat cushions, Deluxe steering wheel and Turbo-Hydramatic transmission. The Deluxe package added center front seat armrests, Strato bench seat and special wheel trim rings. Upholstery was vinyl, cloth or leather. Standard tire size was 8.85 x 15 inches. Toronado engines had the letter code RT. All Toronado models were built in Lansing, Mich., and carried the letter M in the Vehicle Identification Number.

TORONADO SERIES

Model Number	Body/Style Number	Body Type & Seating	Factory Price	Shipping Weight	Production Total
T	67-9487	2-dr Cpe-5P	4674	4330	1,770
T	67-9687	2-dr Del Cpe-5P	4869	4357	20,020

1967 Oldsmobile, Toronado two-door coupe, OCW

ENGINES

(F-85) Inline Six. Overhead valves. Cast iron block. Displacement: 250 cid. Bore and stroke: 3.875 x 3.53 inches. Compression ratio: 8.5:1. Brake hp: 155 at 4200 rpm. Seven main bearings. Hydraulic valve lifters. Carburetor: Rochester Type BV, one-barrel.

(F-85/CUTLASS) Inline Six. Overhead valves. Cast iron block. Displacement: 250 cid. Bore and stroke: 3.875 x 3.53 inches. Compression ratio: 8.5:1. Brake hp: 155 at 4200 rpm. Seven main bearings. Hydraulic valve lifters. Carburetor: Rochester Type BV, one-barrel.

(F-85/CUTLASS/VISTA CRUISER SERIES) V-8. Overhead valves. Cast iron block. Displacement: 330 cid. Bore and stroke: 3.985 x 3.385 inches. Compression ratio: 9.0:1. Brake hp: 250. Five main bearings. Hydraulic valve lifters. Carburetor: Rochester Type 2GC, two-barrel.

(CUTLASS SUPREME SERIES) V-8. Overhead valves. Cast iron block. Displacement: 330 cid. Bore and stroke: 3.9385 x 3.385 inches. Compression ratio: 10.25:1. Brake hp: 320 at 4800 rpm. Five main bearings. Hydraulic valve lifters. Carburetor: Rochester 4GC, four-barrel.

(DELMONT "330" EIGHTY-EIGHT SERIES) V-8. Overhead valves. Displacement: 330 cid. Bore and stroke: 3.9385 x 3.385 inches. Compression ratio: 9.0:1. Brake hp: 250 at 4800 rpm. Five main bearings. Hydraulic valve lifters. Carburetor: Rochester 2GC, two-barrel.

(DELMONT "425" EIGHTY-EIGHT/TURNPIKE CRUISER SERIES) V-8. Overhead valves. Displacement: 425 cid. Bore and stroke: 4.125 x 3.975 inches. Compression ratio: 9.0:1. Brake hp: 300 at 4800 rpm. Five main bearings. Carburetor: Rochester 2GC, two-barrel.

1967 Oldsmobile, 98 Holiday four-door hardtop, OCW

(NINETY-EIGHT SERIES) V-8. Overhead valves. Cast iron block. Displacement: 425 cid. Bore and stroke: 4.125 x 3.975 inches. Compression ratio: 10.25:1. Brake hp: 365 at 4800

rpm. Five main bearings. Hydraulic valve lifters. Carburetor: Rochester 4GC, four-barrel.

(TORONADO/TORONADO DELUXE SERIES) V-8. Overhead valves. Cast iron block. Displacement: 425 cid. Bore and stroke: 4.125 x 3.975 inches. Compression ratio: 10.5:1. Brake hp: 385 at 4800 rpm. Five main bearings. Hydraulic valve lifters. Carburetor: Rochester 4GC, four-barrel.

CHASSIS FEATURES: Wheelbase: (F-85/Cutlass/Cutlass Supreme) 115 inches; (Vista Cruiser) 120 inches; (Toronado) 119 inches; (Delmont/Delta 88) 123 inches; (Ninety-Eight) 126 inches. Overall length: (F-85/Cutlass/Cutlass Supreme) 204.2 inches; (Vista Cruiser) 209.5 inches; (Toronado) 211 inches; (Delmont/Delta 88) 217 inches; (Ninety-Eight) 223 inches. Front tread: (F-85/Cutlass/Cutlass Supreme/Vista Cruiser) 58 inches; (Toronado) 63.5 inches; (all others) 62.5 inches. Rear tread: (F-85/Cutlass/Cutlass Supreme/Vista Cruiser) 59 inches; (all others) 63 inches.

OPTIONS: Power brakes ($104). Power steering ($94). Air conditioning ($343). Tinted windshield ($21). Shoulder belts ($23). Floor mats ($7). Power trunk lid ($12). Vinyl roof ($84). Remote-control outside mirror ($8). Sports console ($54). Cruise Control ($44). Tilt steering wheel ($24). Rocket rallye packet instruments ($84). Electric clock ($35). AM/FM radio ($133). Rear speaker ($16). Push-button AM radio ($64). Stereo tape player ($124). AM/FM stereo ($238). Tach/clock ($84). Cornering lights ($38). Wire wheel discs ($68). Power windows ($104). Power seats ($94). Power door locks ($44). Rear window defogger ($21). GT paint stripe ($10). The 4-4-2 package was available only on Cutlass Supreme series. It consisted of a special 400-cid/350-hp engine and special redline tires, special handling package and 4-4-2 emblems. Three-speed manual transmission was standard on all but Toronado and Olds 98. Automatic transmission ($236). Three-speed manual floor shift transmission ($84). Four-speed manual floor shift transmission ($184). Wide-ratio four-speed manual transmission with floor shift ($184). V-8: 330-cid/310-hp Jetfire engine ($33). V-8: 330-cid/320-hp Jetfire engine ($33). V-8: 425-cid/365-hp Super Rocket engine ($36). V-8: 425-cid/375-hp Starfire engine ($100). High-Energy ignition ($100). Air induction package ($33). Positive traction rear axle ($42). Axle ratios: 2.41:1; 2.73:1; 2.78:1; 2.93:1; 3.08:1; 3.21:1; 3.23:1; 3.42:1; 3.55:1; 3.90:1; 3.91:1.

HISTORICAL FOOTNOTES: Model year sales were 548,390 cars. Calendar year sales were 558,762 cars. The division became America's sixth ranked automobile manufacturer. The 4-4-2 performance packages were sold with 24,829 cars. The 400-cid "Force-Air" engine optionally available for 4-4-2s had a ram-induction system. Its horsepower was advertised as the same as the 1966 Tri-Carb engine.

1968

F-85 - The growth in the F-85 series was in the fancier intermediate lines such as the Cutlass, Cutlass Supreme and 4-4-2. This year, however, a two-model base F-85 series remained. Power came from either a Chevy inline six-cylinder or an Olds Rocket V-8. Standard equipment was sparse and included: dual master brake cylinder, four-way flashers, padded dash, back-up lights, chrome hubcaps and seat belts. Interiors were cloth or vinyl. Standard tire size was 7.75 x 14 inches. Production of the F-85 and other Oldsmobile intermediates was quartered at the Lansing, Fremont, Linden, Framingham and Oshawa (Canada) assembly plants.

OLDSMOBILE I.D. NUMBERS: VIN located on top left of dashboard viewable through windshield. Engine number on right of block (I-6) or right cylinder head (V-8). Serial number takes the form of seven symbols, plus sequential production number. First symbol identifies GM division: 3=Oldsmobile. Second to fifth symbols indicate series and match the four digits in Body/Style Number column of charts below. Sixth symbol identifies model year: 8=1968. Seventh symbol indicates assembly plant: C=Southgate, Calif.; D=Doraville (Atlanta), Ga.; E=Linden, N.J.; G=Framingham, Mass.; M=Lansing, Mich.; Z=Fremont, Calif.; X=Fairfax (Kansas City), Kan.; R=Arlington, Texas; 1=Oshawa, Canada. Remaining symbols are the sequential production number starting at 100001 at each factory. Ending VINs were not available. Engine numbers consist of a alphabetical prefix and a production sequence number. Prefixes for 1967 engines were: [250-cid/155-hp inline six-cylinder] VA/VB/VF/VE; [350-cid F-85/Cutlass/Cutlass Supreme V-8] QI/QJ=250 hp manual; QA/QB=250 hp automatic; QV;QX=310 hp manual; QN/QP=310 hp automatic; T=250 hp; TB/TD=250 hp automatic; TN=310 hp. [400-cid V-8] QL=290 hp; QR/QS/QT=325 hp; QW/QU=350 hp; QT=360 hp "W-30" optional V-8. [455-cid V-8] UC/UC=310 hp; UN/UO=365 hp; UA/UB=320 hp; US/UT=375 hp; UW=400 hp (Toronado only) and UX=390 hp (Toronado only). Ending engine numbers were not available.

F-85 SERIES

Model Number	Body/Style Number	Body Type & Seating	Factory Price	Shipping Weight	Production Total
SIX-CYLINDER					
F-85	3177	2-dr Clb Cpe-6P	2512	3065	4,052
F-85	3169	4-dr Sed-6P	2560	3115	1,847
V-8					
F-85	3277	2-dr Clb Cpe-6P	2617	3277	5,426
F-85	3269	4-dr Twn Sed-6P	2665	3206	3,984

CUTLASS - Just as Olds had a proliferation of full-size models several years before, the same tactic was now used on Cutlass models. Four-doors in the Olds intermediate series now had a longer wheelbase than two-door models. Olds took its midsize four-doors for 1968 and named them Cutlass models, while the two-doors were called Cutlass 'S' models. Completely new styling was introduced on 1968 Olds intermediates. Standard Cutlass equipment included: dual master cylinder, four-way flashers, energy-absorbing steering column, padded dash, back-up lights, full fiberglass hood insulation and Deluxe steering wheel. Interiors were vinyl or cloth. Standard tire size was 7.75 x 14 inches.

CUTLASS SERIES

Model Number	Body/Style Number	Body Type & Seating	Factory Price	Shipping Weight	Production Total
SIX CYLINDER					
C	3539	4-dr Hol HT-6P	2804	3174	265
C	3569	4-dr Twn Sed-6P	2674	3154	1,305
C	3535	4-dr Sta Wag-6P	2969	3345	354
V-8					
C	3639	4-dr Hol HT-6P	2909	3351	7,839
C	3669	4-dr Twn Sed-6P	2779	3328	25,994
C	3635	4-dr Sta Wag-6P	3074	3562	9,291

1968 Oldsmobile, Cutlass 'S' two-door hardtop, OCW

CUTLASS S - The new nameplates of Custlass 'S' applied to the shorter wheelbase Cutlass coupes. A total of three Cutlass 'S' models were offered. They carried the same standard equipment as Cutlass models. Also, the same tire sizes and upholstery were used.

CUTLASS 'S' SERIES

Model Number	Body/Style Number	Body Type & Seating	Factory Price	Shipping Weight	Production Total
SIX-CYLINDER					
C	3577	2-dr Spts Cpe-6P	2632	3216	1,181
C	3587	2-dr Hol HT-6P	2696	3099	1,492
C	3567	2-dr Conv-6P	2949	3245	410
V-8					
C	3677	2-dr Spts Cpe-6P	2737	3412	14,586
C	3687	2-dr Hol HT-6P	2801	3294	59,577
C	3667	2-dr Conv-6P	3055	3415	13,667

1968 Oldsmobile, Cutlass Supreme Holiday four-door hardtop, OCW

CUTLASS SUPREME - The ultimate in intermediate-size Oldsmobile luxury for 1968 was the three-model Cutlass Supreme series. A slightly more powerful version of the new 350 Rocket V-8 was standard equipment. Other regular features were: dual master cylinder, four-way flasher, back-up lights, side marker lights, seat belts, new high-performance starter, fiberglass hood insulation and Deluxe steering wheel. Upholstery was vinyl or cloth. Standard tire size was 7.75 x 14 inches.

CUTLASS SUPREME SERIES

Model Number	Body Style Number	Body Type & Seating	Factory Price	Shipping Weight	Production Total
CS	4287	2-dr Cpe-6P	2982	3335	33,518
CS	4269	4-dr Twn Sed-6P	2884	3334	5,524
CS	4239	4-dr Hol HT-6P	3057	3240	15,067

4-4-2 - Since 1964, the 4-4-2 had been a high-performance option, which continued to grow in popularity. In 1968, the 4-4-2 was made a series. Standard equipment included all Cutlass items plus heavy-duty springs, stabilizer bar, special shock absorbers and wheels, special emblems, hood louvers, paint stripe, special tires and a high output engine. Upholstery was vinyl or cloth. Standard tire size was F70-14. The Hurst/Olds option was introduced. It consisted of special Black and Silver paint, special handling package, various luxury options and a special 455-cid V-8. A total of 515 were made, all based on 4-4-2 models.

1968 Oldsmobile, 4-4-2 two-door hardtop, OCW

4-4-2 SERIES

Model Number	Body/Style Number	Body Type & Seating	Factory Price	Shipping Weight	Production Total
442	4477	2-dr Spts Cpe-5P	3087	3450	4,282
442	4487	2-dr Hol HT-5P	3150	3470	24,183
442	4467	2-dr Conv-5P	3341	3540	5,142

1968 Oldsmobile, 4-4-2 two-door convertible, OCW

VISTA CRUISER - The Vista Cruiser was again the largest Oldsmobile station wagon. It came in both a two-seat and three-seat version. Standard equipment included: dual master cylinder, four-way flasher, padded dash, back-up lights, seat belts, cross-flow radiator, folding second seat, fiberglass hood insulation, underfloor compartment and Deluxe steering wheel. Upholstery was cloth or vinyl. Standard tire size was 8.25 x 14 inches.

1968 Oldsmobile, Custom Vista Cruiser four-door station wagon, OCW

VISTA CRUISER SERIES

Model Number	Body/Style Number	Body Type & Seating	Factory Price	Shipping Weight	Production Total
VC	4855	4-dr Sta Wag-6P	3367	3842	13,375
VC	4865	4-dr Sta Wag-8P	3508	3957	22,768

1968 Oldsmobile, Delmont 88 Holiday two-door hardtop, OCW

DELMONT EIGHTY-EIGHT - Entry level for full-size Oldsmobiles was the Delmont Eighty-Eight. Four models were offered. Like all big cars, they were mildly restyled. Standard Delmont Eighty-Eight equipment included: dual master cylinder, four-way flashers, back-up lights, fiberglass hood insulation, cross-flow radiator, map lights, molding package and central dome light. Upholstery was vinyl, cloth or leather. Tire size was 8.55 x 14 inches. Factory codes were M, X, E, C and D.

1968 Oldsmobile, Delmont 88 two-door convertible, OCW

DELMONT EIGHTY-EIGHT SERIES

Model Number	Body/Style Number	Body Type & Seating	Factory Price	Shipping Weight	Production Total
88	5487	2-dr Hol HT-6P	3202	3874	18,391
88	5469	4-dr Twn Sed-6P	3146	3922	24,365
88	5439	4-dr Hol HT-6P	3278	3977	21,056
88	5467	2-dr Conv-6P	3515	3964	2,812

1968 Oldsmobile, Delta 88 Holiday two-door hardtop, OCW

DELTA EIGHTY-EIGHT - The Delta Eighty-Eight series was the heart of the Eighty-Eight sales picture. Three models were offered in standard trim, plus two additional Custom models. Standard equipment included: dual master cylinder, four-way flasher, energy-absorbing steering column, padded dash, extra sound deadening, back-up lights, larger battery, fiberglass hood insulation and chrome wheel discs. Custom models added electric clock, courtesy lamp package, molding package, special speedometer and Deluxe steering wheel. Upholstery was vinyl, cloth or leather. Standard tire size was 8.55 x 14 inches.

1968 Oldsmobile, Delta 88 four-door sedan, OCW

DELTA EIGHTY-EIGHT SERIES

Model Number	Body/Style Number	Body Type & Seating	Factory Price	Shipping Weight	Production Total
STANDARD					
D88	6487	2-dr Hol HT-6P	3449	3990	18,501
D88	6469	4-dr Twn Sed-6P	3357	3998	33,689
D88	6439	4-dr Hol HT-6P	3525	4080	30,048

1968 Oldsmobile, Delta Custom Holiday two-door hardtop, OCW

1968 Oldsmobile, 98 Holiday four-door hardtop, OCW

CUSTOM					
D88	6687	2-dr Hol HT-6P	3661	4055	9,540
D88	6639	4-dr Hol HT-6P	3721	4155	10,727

NINETY-EIGHT - Oldsmobile introduced five well-appointed Ninety-Eights. Standard equipment included: dual master cylinder, four-way flasher, energy-absorbing steering column, back-up lights, side marker lights, seat belts, cross-flow radiator, rear armrest ashtrays, power brakes, electric clock, special moldings, shoulder belts, Deluxe steering wheel, power steering, carpeted trunk and Turbo-Hydramatic transmission. Upholstery was vinyl, cloth or leather. Standard tire size was 8.85 x 14 inches. Ninety-Eight production was in Lansing, Mich.

1968 Oldsmobile, 98 two-door convertible, OCW

NINETY-EIGHT SERIES

Model Number	Body/Style Number	Body Type & Seating	Factory Price	Shipping Weight	Production Total
98	8457	2-dr Hol HT-6P	4360	4247	15,319
98	8467	2-dr Conv-6P	4618	4295	3,942
98	8439	4-dr Hol HT-6P	4422	4347	21,147
98	8469	4-dr Twn Sed-6P	4155	4258	10,584
98	8669	4-dr Lux Sed-6P	4497	4318	40,755

1968 Oldsmobile, 98 Holiday two-door hardtop, OCW

TORONADO - In its third year, the Toronado received a mild restyling. There was also an optional, high-performance version. This special extra-cost package, RPO W34, included: 455-cid/400-hp V-8 with special cam and valve springs, performance-calibrated Turbo-Hydra-Matic 425, cold air induction, low restriction exhaust and RPO Y70 paint stripes. Standard Toronado equipment included: Turbo-Hydramatic transmission, electric clock, carpets, concealed headlamps, special headliner, fiberglass hood insulation, courtesy lamp package, chrome molding package, foam padded seat cushions, rolling dial speedometer, power steering, Deluxe steering wheel, power brakes, trunk floor carpeting, torsion bar front suspension and door-opening assist springs. Upholstery was vinyl, leather or cloth. Standard tire size was 8.85 x 15 inches. All Toronados were built in Lansing, Mich., and contained the letter code M in the Vehicle Identification Number.

1968 Oldsmobile, Toronado two-door coupe, OCW

TORONADO SERIES

Model Number	Body/Style Number	Body Type & Seating	Factory Price	Shipping Weight	Production Total
T	9487	2-dr Cpe-5P	4750	4280	3,957
CUSTOM					
T	9687	2-dr Cpe-5P	-	4328	22,497

ENGINES

(F-85) Inline Six. Overhead valves. Cast iron block. Displacement: 250 cid. Bore and stroke: 3.875 x 3.53 inches. Compression ratio: 8.5:1. Brake hp: 155 at 4200 rpm. Seven main bearings. Hydraulic valve lifters. Carburetor: Rochester Type BV, one-barrel model 7026028.

(F-85/CUTLASS) Inline Six. Overhead valves. Cast iron block. Displacement: 250 cid. Bore and stroke: 3.875 x 3.53 inches. Compression ratio: 8.5:1. Brake hp: 155 at 4200 rpm. Seven main bearings. Hydraulic valve lifters. Carburetor: Rochester Type BV, one-barrel model 7026028.

(F-85/CUTLASS) V-8. Overhead valves. Cast iron block. Displacement: 350 cid. Bore and stroke: 4.057 x 3.385 inches. Compression ratio: 9.0:1. Brake hp: 250 at 4400 rpm. Five main bearings. Hydraulic valve lifters. Carburetor: Rochester 4GC, four-barrel model 7028250.

(CUTLASS SUPREME/VISTA CRUISER SERIES) V-8. Overhead valves. Cast iron block. Displacement: 350 cid. Bore and stroke: 4.057 x 3.385 inches. Compression ratio: 10.25:1. Brake hp: 310 at 4800 rpm. Five main bearings. Hydraulic valve lifters. Carburetor: Rochester 4GC, four-barrel model 7028250.

(4-4-2 SERIES) V-8. Overhead valves. Cast iron block. Displacement: 400 cid. Bore and stroke: 3.870 x 4.25 inches. Compression ratio: 10.5:1. Brake hp: 350 at 4800 rpm. Five main bearings. Hydraulic valve lifters. Carburetor: Rochester 4GC, four-barrel model 7028251.

(DELMONT EIGHTY-EIGHT SERIES) V-8. Overhead valves. Cast iron block. Displacement: 350 cid. Bore and stroke: 4.057 x 3.385 inches. Compression ratio: 9.0:1. Brake hp: 250 at 4400 rpm. Five main bearings. Hydraulic valve lifters. Carburetor: Rochester 2GC, two-barrel model 7029250.

(DELTA EIGHTY-EIGHT SERIES) V-8. Overhead valves. Cast iron block. Displacement: 455 cid. Bore and stroke: 4.126 x 4.250 inches. Compression ratio: 9.0:1. Brake hp: 310 at 4200 rpm. Five main bearings. Hydraulic valve lifters. Carburetor: Rochester 2GC, two-barrel model 709250.

(NINETY-EIGHT SERIES) V-8. Overhead valves. Cast iron block. Displacement: 455 cid. Bore and stroke: 4.126 x 4.250 inches. Compression ratio: 10.25:1. Brake hp: 365 at 4600 rpm. Five main bearings. Hydraulic valve lifters. Carburetor: Rochester 4GC, four-barrel model 7029250.

(TORONADO SERIES) V-8. Overhead valves. Cast iron block. Displacement: 455 cid. Bore and stroke: 4.126 x 4.250 inches. Compression ratio: 10.25:1. 375 hp at 4600 rpm. Five main bearings. Hydraulic valve lifters. Carburetor: Rochester 4MV, four-barrel.

CHASSIS FEATURES: Wheelbase: (Cutlass 'S'/4-4-2/Cutlass Supreme, two-doors) 112 inches; (F-85/Cutlass/Cutlass Supreme, four-doors) 116 inches; (Delmont/Delta 88) 123 inches; (Vista Cruiser) 121 inches; (Toronado) 119 inches; (Ninety-Eight) 126 inches. Overall length: (Cutlass 'S'/4-4-2/Cutlass Supreme, two-doors) 201.6 inches; (F-85/Cutlass/Cutlass Supreme, four-doors) 205.6 inches; (Delmont/Delta 88) 217.8 inches; (Vista Cruiser) 217.5 inches; (Toronado) 211.4 inches; (Ninety-Eight) 223.7 inches. Front tread: (F-85/Cutlass/Cutlass 'S'/4-4-2/Cutlass Supreme/Vista Cruiser) 59 inches; (all others) 62.5 inches. Rear tread: (F-85/Cutlass/Cutlass 'S'/4-4-2/Cutlass Supreme/Vista Cruiser) 59 inches; (all others) 63 inches.

1968 Oldsmobile, 4-4-2-based Hurst/Olds two-door sports coupe, OCW

OPTIONS: Power brakes ($53). Power steering ($98). Air conditioning ($411). Power antenna ($35). Electric clock ($17). Cruise Control ($79). Air deflector, station wagons ($17). Rear defogger ($17). Wire wheel covers ($89). Tissue dispenser ($5). Lamp package ($8). Guidematic headlamp control ($46). Rooftop luggage carrier, wagons ($52). Rooftop ski carrier ($36). Floor mats ($7). Remote-control mirror ($12). Door edge moldings ($8). Push-button AM radio ($78). AM/FM radio ($134). AM/FM stereo radio ($219). Stereo tape player ($116). Rear radio speaker ($13). Power trunk lid release ($12). Three-speed manual transmission was standard except for Toronado and Olds 98. Automatic transmission was optional except for Olds 98 and Toronado. Automatic transmission ($158). Three-speed manual floor shift transmission ($43). Four-speed manual floor shift transmission ($189). V-8: 350-cid/310-hp Rocket engine ($38). V-8: 400-cid/290-hp Turnpike Cruiser engine ($98). V-8: 400-cid/325-hp Rocket engine ($89). V-8: 455-cid/365-hp Rocket engine ($57). V-8: 455-cid/400-hp Rocket engine ($190).

HISTORICAL FOOTNOTES: Model year sales of 562,459 enabled Oldsmobile to retain sixth place in the industry. *CARS* magazine picked the 4-4-2 as its 'Performance Car of the Year.' Toronado was also 'hot' in competition, taking one-two-three in the Pikes Peak Hill Climb. The RPO W34 high performance Toronado production was 111 cars (of which the Toronado Chapter of the Oldsmobile Club of America has documented 12 survivors). Lansing also emphasized performance in advertising. 'Dr. Oldsmobile' played a starring role in the lead-footed media blitz. The 290-hp Olds 4-4-2 had a top speed of 116 mph. The 360-hp Olds 4-4-2 could reach 123 mph. The 390-hp Olds 4-4-2 needed 6.5 seconds to reach 60 mph and did the quarter-mile in 12.97 seconds. Hurst-Olds were assembled on an "off-line" basis by Hurst Performance Products, Co.

1969

F-85 - For 1969, the F-85 series was reduced to a single coupe model. Most of the sales activity for the Olds intermediates had moved to the high-performance and upscale models. Standard F-85 equipment included: four-way flashers, front armrests, cigarette lighter, vinyl floor covering, seat belts and shoulder harnesses, outside rear view mirror and chrome hubcaps. Interiors were vinyl. Standard tire size was 7.75 x 14 inches. The 1969 Olds intermediates had M, Z and E assembly plant codes.

OLDSMOBILE I.D. NUMBERS: VIN located on top left of dashboard viewable through windshield. Engine number (six-cylinder) right side of block; (V-8) front of right cylinder head. Serial number in the form of seven symbols, plus sequential production number. First symbol identifies GM division: 3=Oldsmobile. Second to fifth symbols indicate series and match the four digits in Body/Style Number column of charts below. Sixth symbol identifies model year: 9=1969. Seventh symbol indicates assembly plant: C=Southgate, Calif.; D=Doraville (Atlanta), Ga.; E=Linden, N.J.; G=Framingham, Mass.; M=Lansing, Mich.; Z=Fremont, Calif.; X=Fairfax (Kansas City), Kan.; R=Arlington, Texas; 1=Oshawa, Canada. Remaining symbols are the sequential production number starting at 100001 at each factory. Ending VINs were not available. Engine numbers consist of a alphabetical prefix and a production sequence number. Prefixes for 1969 engines were: [250-cid inline six] VD/VJ=export; VA/VB/VF/VE;=155 hp [350-cid V-8] QI=250 hp manual; QA/QB/QJ=250 hp automatic; QV/QN/QP=310 hp manual; QX="W-31" with 325 hp; TL/TB/TO/TC=250 hp. [400-cid V-8] QW=350 hp; QR/QS=325 hp; QU/QT="W-30" with 360 hp; [455-cid V-8] UC/UD/UJ=310 hp; UN/UO=365 hp; UL=390 hp; US/UT/UV=Toronado 375 hp; UW=Toronado 400 hp; UX=380 hp in Hurst-Olds. Ending engine numbers were not available.

F-85

Model Number	Body/Style Number	Body Type & Seating	Factory Price	Shipping Weight	Production Total
SIX-CYLINDER					
F-85	3177	2-dr Spts Cpe-5P	2561	3221	2,899
V-8					
F-85	3277	2-dr Spts Cpe-5P	2672	3421	5,541

CUTLASS - The next step up the Oldsmobile ladder in 1969 was the Cutlass series. Two-door models had a shorter wheelbase than four-doors. Cutlass two-door models were also tagged Cutlass S. High performance became more important for Olds intermediate buyers and this trend now extended beyond the 4-4-2 buyer. A potent "W-31" package was available in Cutlass and Cutlass Supreme models. It was based on a "Force-Air" inducted 350-cid V-8 with special equipment. Standard Cutlass features included all F-85 items plus hood louvers, insulated fiberglass hood blanket, nylon blend carpeting, special molding package and Deluxe steering wheel. Standard tire size was 7.75 x 14 inches. Upholstery was vinyl or cloth.

1969 Oldsmobile, Cutlass S two-door hardtop, OCW

CUTLASS

Model Number	Body Style Number	Body Type & Seating	Factory Price	Shipping Weight	Production Total
SIX-CYLINDER					
C	3577	2-dr Spts Cpe-5P	2681	3327	483
C	3587	2-dr Hol HT-5P	2742	3277	566
C	3567	2-dr Conv-5P	2998	3336	236
C	3569	4-dr Twn Sed-5P	2772	3300	137
C	3539	4-dr Hol HT-5P	2853	3353	236
C	3535	4-dr Sta Wag-5P	3055	3701	180

V-8					
C	3677	2-dr Spts Cpe-5P	2792	3437	10,682
C	3687	2-dr Hol HT-5P	2855	3465	66,495
C	3667	2-dr Conv-5P	3109	3534	13,498
C	3669	4-dr Twn Sed-5P	2883	3489	24,251
C	3639	4-dr Hol HT-5P	2964	3548	7046
C	3635	4-dr Sta Wag-5P	3157	3900	8,559

CUTLASS SUPREME - The ultimate luxury in Oldsmobile's intermediate line was embodied in the Cutlass Supreme. This three-model series remained one of Oldsmobile's best sellers. Standard Supreme equipment included all Cutlass items plus loop-pile carpeting, oval outside rear view mirror, molding package, inside day/night mirror, front stabilizer bar and dual-latched hood. Upholstery was vinyl or cloth. Standard tire size was 7.75 x 14 inches.

1969 Oldsmobile, Cutlass Supreme Holiday four-door hardtop, OCW

CUTLASS SUPREME

Model Number	Body/Style Number	Body Type & Seating	Factory Price	Shipping Weight	Production Total
CS	4287	2-dr Hol HT-5P	3036	3496	24,193
CS	4269	4-dr Twn Sed-5P	2938	3509	4,522
CS	4239	4-dr Hol HT-5P	3111	3586	8,714

1969 Oldsmobile, Cutlass 4-4-2 two-door hardtop, OCW

4-4-2 - Available in its second year as a series, three basic models were available. A 4-4-2 buyer could order more performance from a special "W-30" package. It was based on a special "Force-Air" inducted 360-hp version of the 400-cid V-8. A well-tuned, factory blue-printed 4-4-2 with the 400-cid V-8 was one of the fastest stock showroom domestic cars available to the public in 1969. Stock 4-4-2 equipment included all Cutlass items plus special grille, special stripes and emblems, bucket seats, heavy-duty driveshaft, special handling package, heavy-duty wheels and straight-through exhaust system. Interiors were vinyl or cloth. Tire size was F-70-14.

1969 Oldsmobile, 4-4-2-based Hurst/Olds two-door hardtop, OCW

108

4-4-2

Model Number	Body/Style Number	Body Type & Seating	Factory Price	Shipping Weight	Production Total
442	4477	2-dr Spts Cpe-5P	3141	3665	2,475
442	4487	2-dr Hol HT-5P	3204	3675	19,587
442	4467	2-dr Conv-5P	3395	3743	4,295
442/HO	4487H	2-dr Hurst/Olds-5P	4500-4900	3705	906

VISTA CRUISER - Cutlass continued to offer station wagons on both a standard 116-inch wheelbase and a stretched 121-inch wheelbase for the Vista Cruiser. Although the Vista Cruiser was a longer car, it shared Cutlass sheet metal from the B-pillar forward. Standard equipment included: Deluxe armrests, cigar lighter, dome light, molding package, foam seat cushions, dual front head restraints, Vista roof treatment and recessed windshield wipers. Standard tire size was 8.25 x 14 inches. Upholstery was vinyl or cloth.

VISTA CRUISER

Model Number	Body/Style Number	Body Type & Seating	Factory Price	Shipping Weight	Production Total
VC	4855	4-dr Sta Wag-5P	3457	4101	11,879
VC	4865	4-dr Sta Wag-7P	3600	4237	21,508

1969 Oldsmobile, Delta 88 Holiday four-door hardtop, OCW

DELTA EIGHTY-EIGHT - Three different series of full-size Eighty-Eight models were available starting with the Delta 88. Four body styles were available. Standard Delta equipment included: armrests front and rear, cigar lighter, carpeting, woodgrain instrument panel trim, lamp package, chrome molding package, front head restraints and Flo-Thru body ventilation. Upholstery was vinyl or cloth. Standard tire size was 8.55 x 15 inches. Assembly plant codes were M, X, E, C and D on full-size 1969 Oldsmobiles, with some models produced in only one factory.

1969 Oldsmobile, Delta 88 Royale Holiday two-door hardtop, OCW

DELTA EIGHTY-EIGHT

Model Number	Body/Style Number	Body Type & Seating	Factory Price	Shipping Weight	Production Total
D88	5437	2-dr Hol HT-5P	3277	4070	41,947
D88	5469	4-dr Twn Sed-5P	3222	4098	49,995
D88	5439	4-dr Hol HT-5P	3353	4148	42,690
D88	5467	2-dr Conv-5P	3590	4129	5,294

DELTA EIGHTY-EIGHT CUSTOM - The next series was the Delta Eighty-Eight Custom. Three models were available and the convertible was not available as a Custom. Later in the model year, the larger 455-cid engine became standard. Standard equipment also included all Delta Eighty-Eight items plus foam seats, seat molding package, lamp switches at all doors and a special interior lamp package. Standard tire size was 8.55 x 15 inches. Interiors were cloth or vinyl.

DELTA EIGHTY-EIGHT CUSTOM

Model Number	Body/Style Number	Body Type & Seating	Factory Price	Shipping Weight	Production Total
DC88	6437	2-dr Hol HT-5P	3525	4169	22,083
DC88	6469	4-dr Twn Sed-5P	3432	4189	31,012
DC88	6439	4-dr Hol HT-5P	3600	4254	36,502

DELTA EIGHTY-EIGHT ROYALE - The Delta Eighty-Eight Royale was a single car series. It's interesting to note that Oldsmobile picked this name from Reo, which was named for Ransom E. Olds. Reo used the Royale name on a classic 1930s model it built. Standard Delta Eighty-Eight Royale equipment included all Delta Eighty-Eight Custom items plus body paint stripes, vinyl roof, Custom Sport front seat, front center armrest and electric clock. Standard tire size was 8.55 x 15 inches. Upholstery was vinyl or leather.

DELTA EIGHTY-EIGHT ROYALE

Model Number	Body/Style Number	Body Type & Seating	Factory Price	Shipping Weight	Production Total
DR88	6647	2-dr Hol HT-5P	3836	4197	22,564

1969 Oldsmobile, 98 Luxury four-door sedan, OCW

NINETY-EIGHT - The Ninety-Eight conventional front engine/rear drive car remained the top-of-the-line Oldsmobile. It was the largest Olds product offered and had a 127-inch wheelbase. Six body styles were available. Standard equipment included: power brakes, electric clock, full carpeting, courtesy lamps, paint stripes, power seat adjuster, seat belts and shoulder harnesses, power steering, Deluxe steering wheel, power windows and Turbo-Hydramatic transmission. Standard tire size was 8.85 x 15 inches. Upholstery was vinyl, cloth or leather. All Ninety-Eights were built in Lansing, Mich., and had the letter code M.

NINETY-EIGHT

Model Number	Body/Style Number	Body Type & Seating	Factory Price	Shipping Weight	Production Total
98	8457	2-dr Hol HT-5P	4462	4359	27,041
98	8469	4-dr Twn Sed-5P	4256	4372	11,169
98	8639	4-dr Lux Sed-5P	4693	4447	25,973
98	8439	4-dr Hol HT-5P	4524	4456	17,294
98	8467	2-dr Conv-5P	4729	4457	4,288
98	8669	4-dr Lux Sed-5P	4599	4515	30,643

1969 Oldsmobile, 98 Holiday two-door hardtop, OCW

1969 Oldsmobile, Toronado two-door coupe, OCW

TORONADO - The Olds Toronado was less "unique" now, sharing honors with the Cadillac Eldorado as a full-sized front-wheel-drive automobile. Two body styles were offered. The standard equipment list included: power brakes, electric clock, full carpeting, courtesy lamps, power steering, Flo-Thru ventilation and Turbo-Hydramatic transmission. The RPO W34 high-performance Toronado option was again available. Standard tire size was 8.85 x 15 inches. Upholstery was vinyl, leather or cloth.

TORONADO

Model Number	Body/Style Number	Body Type & Seating	Factory Price	Shipping Weight	Production Total
T	9487	2-dr Cpe-5P	4836	4478	3,421
CUSTOM					
T	9687	2-dr Cpe-5P	—	4505	25,073

ENGINES

(F-85/CUTLASS SERIES) Inline six-cylinder. Overhead valves. Cast iron block. Displacement: 250 cid. Bore and stroke: 3.87 x 3.53 inches. Compression ratio: 8.5:1. Brake hp: 155 at 4200 rpm. Seven main bearings. Hydraulic valve lifters. Carburetor: Rochester MV, one-barrel.

(F-85/CUTLASS SERIES) V-8. Overhead valves. Cast iron block. Displacement: 350 cid. Bore and stroke: 4.057 x 3.385 inches. Compression ratio: 9.0:1. Brake hp: 250 at 4400 rpm. Five main bearings. Hydraulic valve lifters. Carburetor: Rochester: 2GC, two-barrel.

(CUTLASS SUPREME/VISTA CRUISER SERIES) V-8. Overhead valves. Cast iron block. Displacement: 350 cid. Bore and stroke: 4.057 x 3.385 inches. Compression ratio: 10.25:1. Brake hp: 310 at 4800 rpm. Five main bearings. Hydraulic valve lifters. Carburetor: Rochester 4GC, four-barrel.

(4-4-2 SERIES) V-8. Overhead valves. Cast iron block. Displacement: 350 cid. Bore and stroke: 3.87 x 4.25 inches. Compression ratio: 10.5:1. Brake hp: 325 (automatic transmission); 350 (manual transmission) at 4800 rpm. (W31). Five main bearings. Hydraulic valve lifters. Carburetor: Rochester 4GC, four-barrel.

(DELTA EIGHTY-EIGHT SERIES) V-8. Overhead valves. Cast iron block. Displacement: 350 cid. Bore and stroke: 4.057 x 3.385 inches. Compression ratio: 9.0:1. Brake hp: 250 at 4400 rpm. Five main bearings. Hydraulic valve lifters. Carburetor: Rochester 4GC, four-barrel.

(DELTA EIGHTY-EIGHT CUSTOM/ROYALE SERIES) V-8. Overhead valves. Cast iron block. Displacement: 455 cid. Bore and stroke: 4.125 x 4.250 inches. Compression ratio: 9.0:1. Brake hp: 310 hp at 4400 rpm. Five main bearings. Hydraulic valve lifters. Rochester 2GC, two-barrel.

(NINETY-EIGHT SERIES) V-8. Overhead valves. Cast iron block. Displacement: 455 cid. Bore and stroke: 4.125 x 4.250 inches. Compression ratio: 10.25:1. Brake hp: 365 at 4600 rpm. Five main bearings. Hydraulic valve lifters. Carburetion: Rochester 4GC, four-barrel.

(TORONADO SERIES) V-8. Overhead valves. Cast iron block. Displacement: 455 cid. Bore and stroke: 4.125 x 4.250 inches. Compression ratio: 10.25:1. Brake hp: 375 at 4600 rpm. Five main bearings. Hydraulic valve lifters. Carburetor: Rochester 4GC, four-barrel.

CHASSIS FEATURES: Wheelbase: (Cutlass/Cutlass Supreme four-doors) 116 inches; (4-4-2/Cutlass S/F-85 two-doors) 112 inches; (Vista Cruiser) 121 inches; (Delta/Delta Custom/Royale 88s) 124 inches; (Ninety-Eight) 127 inches; (Toronado) 119 inches. Overall length: (Cutlass/Supreme sedans) 205.9 inches; (4-4-2/Cutlass S/F-85 two-doors) 201.9 inches; (Vista Cruiser) 217.6 inches; (Delta/Delta Custom/Royale 88s) 218.6 inches; (Ninety-Eight) 224.4 inches; (Toronado) 214.8 inches. Front tread: (F-85/Cutlass S/Supreme/4-4-2/Vista Cruiser) 59 inches. (Toronados) 63.5 inches; (all others) 62.5 inches. Rear tread: (F-85/Cutlass S/Supreme/4-4-2/Vista Cruiser) 59 inches; (all others) 63 inches.

OPTIONS: Power brakes ($41). Power steering ($100). Air conditioning ($375). Tinted glass ($38). Power trunk release ($17). Power door locks ($44). Floor mats ($7). Rear defogger ($44). Sports console ($61). Super-Stock wheels ($73). Tilt steering wheel ($46). Rallye instruments ($84). Stereo tape player ($133). AM/FM radio ($238). Power antenna ($31). Rear speakers ($16). Vinyl roof ($121). Power seats ($100). Cornering lamps ($38). Special order paint ($83). W-31 package including special Force-Air 350 cid engine option for Cutlass ($310). W-30 special 400 cid Force-Air engine package for 4-4-2 ($264). Three-speed manual transmission was standard on all except 98 and Toronado. Automatic transmission ($227). Three-speed manual floor shift transmission ($84). Wide-ratio four-speed manual transmission with floor shift ($184). Close-ratio four-speed manual transmission with floor shift ($184). V-8: 350-cid/310-hp Rocket engine ($47). V-8: 400-cid/325-hp Rocket engine ($47). V-8: 455-cid/365-hp Rocket engine ($110). V-8: 455-cid/390-hp High-Performance Rocket engine ($141). V-8: 455-cid/400-hp Toronado engine ($47). Force-Air induction package ($42). Positive traction rear axle ($43). Cruise control ($57).

HISTORICAL FOOTNOTES: The 1969 Oldsmobiles, F-85s and Toronados were introduced Sept. 12, 1968. Oldsmobile moved ahead of Plymouth to take fifth place in the industry with sales of 655,241 units. The 12-millionth Oldsmobile was built in November 1969. In the F-85 line, 82 percent of the cars had standard V-8s; 15.5 percent had optional V-8s; 4.9 percent had four-speed transmission; nine percent had AM/FM; 26.3 percent had bucket seats and 39.3 percent had vinyl tops. On full-size Oldsmobiles, 77.3 percent of the cars had standard V-8s and the rest had optional V-8s. Only 1.9 percent of the big Olds had bucket seats; 8.1 percent had Posi-Traction and 6.6 percent had Cruise Control. Option installation rates for Toronados included 7.2 percent with bucket seats, 88.9 percent with power windows, 53.2 percent with front disc brakes, 22 percent with power door locks and 19.2 percent with Cruise Control. The Toronado Chapter of the Oldsmobile Club of America estimates have 2,800 Toronados produced with the RPO W34 high-performance option. During the year, John Beltz replaced Harold Metzel as general manager of Oldsmobile. Metzel held the job for five years.

1970

F-85 - The entry-level Oldsmobile offering contined as a single model F-85 sports coupe. Standard equipment included: padded head restraints, seat and shoulder belts, anti-theft steering column, locking glovebox and heavy-duty three-speed manual transmission. Standard tire size was F78-14. Upholstery was cloth or vinyl. Option W-45 was the Rallye 350 Package, which was installed on 3,547 Cutlass 'S' coupes and F-85 coupes. The package included Sebring yellow paint, special decals and a special 350-cid engine. Assembly plant codes on mid-size Oldsmobiles were M, Z, E and G.

OLDSMOBILE I.D. NUMBERS: VIN located on top left of dashboard viewable through windshield. Engine production code number indicating approximate production date and an engine serial number matching the VIN located on engine. Serial num-

ber takes the form of seven symbols, plus sequential production number. First symbol identifies GM division: 3=Oldsmobile. Second to fifth symbols indicate series and match the four digits in Body/Style Number column of charts below. Sixth symbol identifies model year: 0=1970. Seventh symbol indicates assembly plant: C=Southgate, Calif.; D=Doraville (Atlanta), Ga.; E=Linden, N.J.; G=Framingham, Mass.; M=Lansing, Mich.; Z=Fremont, Calif.; X=Fairfax (Kansas City), Kan. Remaining symbols are the sequential production number starting at 100001 at each factory. Ending VINs were not available. Engine numbers consist of a alphabetical prefix and a production sequence number. Prefixes for 1970 engines were: [250-cid in-line six] VB/VF=155 hp; [350-cid V-8] QI/QA/QJ/TC/TD/TL=250 hp; QN/QP/QV=310 hp; QD/QX=325 hp. [455-cid V-8] UC/UD/UJ=310 hp; TX/TY=320 hp; TP/TQ/TU/TV/TW/UN/UO=365 hp; TS/TT=370 hp; US/UT=375 hp; UL=390 hp; UV/UW=400 hp. Ending engine numbers were not available.

F-85

Model Number	Body/Style Number	Body Type & Seating	Factory Price	Shipping Weight	Production Total
SIX-CYLINDER					
F-85	3177	2-dr Spts Cpe-5P	2676	3294	2,836
V-8					
F-85	3277	2-dr Spts Cpe-5P	2787	3505	8,274

CUTLASS - The next level Oldsmobile intermediate was the Cutlass. Again, the two-door Cutlass models had a shorter wheelbase and carried the Cutlass S name. Only closed cars were found in this series for 1970, including a pair of two-doors, a pair of four-doors and a four-door station wagon. Standard equipment included all F-85 items plus special chrome molding package, Deluxe steering wheel, interior light package and special hood design. Standard tire size was G78-14. Interiors were vinyl or cloth. Option W-45 was the Rallye 350 Package, which was installed on 3,547 Cutlass 'S' coupes and F-85 coupes. The package included Sebring yellow paint, special decals and a special 350 engine.

1970 Oldsmobile, Cutlass S Holiday two-door hardtop, OCW

CUTLASS

Model Number	Body/Style Number	Body Type & Seating	Factory Price	Shipping Weight	Production Total
SIX-CYLINDER					
C	3535	4-dr Sta Wag-5P	3234	3749	85
C	3587	2-dr Hol HT-5P	2859	3342	729
C	3577	2-dr Spts Cpe-5P	2796	3305	484
C	3539	4-dr Hol HT-5P	2968	3430	238
C	3569	4-dr Twn Sed-5P	2837	3361	1,171

1970 Oldsmobile, Cutlass Supreme Holiday two-door hardtop, OCW

1970 Oldsmobile, Cutlass S Rallye 350 two-door hardtop, OCW

Model Number	Body/Style Number	Body Type & Seating	Factory Price	Shipping Weight	Production Total
V-8					
C	3635	4-dr Sta Wag-5P	3334	3956	7,680
C	3687	2-dr Hol HT-5P	2970	3556	88,578
C	3677	2-dr Spt Cpe-5P	2907	3520	10,677
C	3639	4-dr Hol HT-5P	3079	3641	9,427
C	3669	4-dr Twn Sed-5P	2948	3572	35,239

1970 Oldsmobile, Cutlass Supreme Holiday two-door hardtop, OCW

CUTLASS SUPREME - Three models were available under the Cutlass Supreme name, including a convertible. Also available, exclusively in this series, was the new 'SX' package. It included special engine items, coupled with distinct internal and external markings. Standard equipment included all Cutlass items plus Flo-Thru ventilation, special dash, V-8 engine, Deluxe steering wheel and Custom Sport seat. Standard tire size was G-78-14. Interiors were cloth or vinyl.

1970 Oldsmobile, Cutlass Supreme two-door convertible, OCW

CUTLASS SUPREME

Model Number	Body/Style Number	Body Type & Seating	Factory Price	Shipping Weight	Production Total
CS	4257	2-dr Hol HT-5P	3151	3574	11,354
CS	4267	2-dr Conv-5P	3335	3614	4,867
CS	4239	4-dr Hol HT-5P	3226	3662	10,762

4-4-2 - The 4-4-2 continued as a series. High-performance continued to sell well for Oldsmobile and this series was the division's performance leader. Three models, all two-doors, were available as 4-4-2s. Standard equipment included all Cutlass items plus foam padded seats, special handling package, external and internal emblems, Deluxe steering wheel, special engine, low-restriction exhaust system and special paint stripes. Standard tires were G70-14 raised white letter (RWL). Upholstery was vinyl or cloth.

1970 Oldsmobile, 4-4-2 two-door hardtop with W-30 package, OCW

4-4-2

Model Number	Body/Style Number	Body Type & Seating	Factory Price	Shipping Weight	Production Total
442	4487	2-dr Hol HT-5P	3376	3817	14,709
442	4477	2-dr Spts Cpe-5P	3312	3801	1,688
442	4467	2-dr Conv-5P	3567	3844	2,933

1970 Oldsmobile, 4-4-2 two-door convertible, OCW

VISTA CRUISER - The Oldsmobile Vista Cruiser station wagon came in both a two-seat and three-seat version. The Vista Cruiser continued to have a five-inch longer wheelbase than the Cutlass Cruiser. Standard equipment included: special underfloor storage compartment, seat belts and shoulder harness, energy-absorbing steering column, side marker lights, anti-theft ignition system, divided front seat, V-8 engine, tinted rooftop vista window and Deluxe steering wheel. Standard tire size was H78-14. Upholstery was vinyl or cloth.

1970 Oldsmobile, Vista Cruiser four-door station wagon, OCW

VISTA CRUISER

Model Number	Body/Style Number	Body Type & Seating	Factory Price	Shipping Weight	Production Total
VC	4855	4-dr Sta Wag-5P	3636	4183	10,758
VC	4865	4-dr Sta Wag-7P	3778	4284	23,336

DELTA EIGHTY-EIGHT - The Delta 88 line remained the basic full-line series for Oldsmobile. Four body styles were offered: two-door hardtop, convertible and two four-doors. Four-door models included a pillared Town Sedan and the other a pillarless Holiday hardtop. Standard equipment included: seat belts and shoulder harnesses, energy-absorbing steering column, anti-theft ignition, side marker lights, four-way flashers, dual hood latches, Deluxe steering wheel and full wheel discs. Standard tire size was H78-15. Upholstery was vinyl or cloth. The full-size Olds assembly plant codes were: M, X, E, C and D.

DELTA EIGHTY-EIGHT

Model Number	Body/Style Number	Body Type & Seating	Factory Price	Shipping Weight	Production Total
88	5437	2-dr Hol HT-5P	3590	4034	33,017
88	5439	4-dr Hol HT-5P	3666	4120	37,695
88	5467	2-dr Conv-5P	3903	4119	3,095
88	5469	4-dr Twn Sed-5P	3534	4078	47,067

1970 Oldsmobile Delta 88 Royale Holiday two-door hardtop, OCW

DELTA EIGHTY-EIGHT CUSTOM - The next step in the full-sized Oldsmobile line was the Delta Eighty-Eight Custom, which offered three models. The Custom was not available as a convertible. Standard equipment included all Delta Eighty-Eight items plus Custom sport seat, special moldings, interior light package and special wheel discs. Standard tire size was H78-15. Interiors were vinyl or leather.

1970 Oldsmobile, Delta 88 two-door convertible, OCW

DELTA EIGHTY-EIGHT CUSTOM

Model Number	Body/Style Number	Body Type & Seating	Factory Price	Shipping Weight	Production Total
D88C	6437	2-dr Hol HT-5P	3848	4133	16,149
D88C	6469	4-dr Twn Sed-5P	3755	4174	24,727
D88C	6439	4-dr Hol HT-5P	3924	4221	28,432

1970 Oldsmobile, Delta 88 Custom Holiday four-door hardtop, OCW

DELTA EIGHTY-EIGHT ROYALE - Oldsmobile again topped-off Eighty-Eight group with a single model Delta Eighty-Eight Royale series. Standard equipment here included all items from the Custom series plus vinyl roof covering, electric clock, double padded seats, special front fender trim and paint stripes. Standard tire size was H78-15. Interiors were vinyl or cloth.

1970 Oldsmobile, Delta 88 Royale Holiday two-door hardtop, OCW

DELTA EIGHTY-EIGHTY ROYALE

Model Number	Body/Style Number	Body Type & Seating	Factory Price	Shipping Weight	Production Total
D88R	6647	2-dr Hol HT-5P	4159	4136	13,249

1970 Oldsmobile, 98 Luxury four-door sedan, OCW

NINETY-EIGHT - Once again, the Ninety-Eight models were the largest Oldsmobiles. They still shared the luxury side of Oldsmobile's business with the Toronado. Standard equipment included: Turbo-Hydramatic 400 transmission, power steering, power brakes with front discs, power windows, power seats, Deluxe steering wheel, electric clock and full wheel discs. Standard tire size was J78-15. Interiors were vinyl, cloth or leather. All Ninety-Eights were built in Lansing, Mich., indicated by the letter code M in the Vehicle Identification Number.

1970 Oldsmobile, 98 Holiday two-door hardtop, OCW

NINETY-EIGHT

Model Number	Body/Style Number	Body Type & Seating	Factory Price	Shipping Weight	Production Total
98	8457	2-dr Hol HT-5P	4565	4391	21,111
98	8467	2-dr Conv-5P	4914	4423	3,161
98	8669	4-dr Lux Sed-5P	4793	4490	29,005
98	8639	4-dr Lux HT-5P	4888	4535	19,377
98	8439	4-dr Hol HT-5P	4582	4463	14,098
98	8469	4-dr Twn Sed-5P	4451	4397	9,092

1970 Oldsmobile, Toronado two-door coupe, OCW

TORONADO - The top-of-the-line Oldsmobile was again the front-wheel-drive Toronado. Standard equipment included: Turbo-Hydramatic transmission, power steering, power brakes, foam-padded front seat, special V-8 engine, Deluxe steering wheel and electric clock. For 1970, RPO W34 was the Toronado GT option. Standard tire size was J78-15. Interiors were vinyl, cloth or leather.

TORONADO

Model Number	Body/Style Number	Body Type & Seating	Factory Price	Shipping Weight	Production Total
T	9487	2-dr Cpe-5P	5023	4459	2,351

CUSTOM

Model Number	Body/Style Number	Body Type & Seating	Factory Price	Shipping Weight	Production Total
T	9687	2-dr Cpe-5P	5216	4498	23,082

ENGINES

(F-85/CUTLASS SERIES) Inline six-cylinder. Overhead valves. Cast iron block. Displacement: 250 cid. Bore and stroke: 3.875 x 3.530 inches. Compression ratio: 8.5:1. Brake hp: 155 at 4200 rpm. Seven main bearings. Hydraulic valve lifters. Carburetor: Rochester Model MV, one-barrel.

(F-85/CUTLASS SERIES) V-8. Overhead valves. Cast iron block. Displacement: 350 cid. Bore and stroke: 4.057 x 3.385 inches. Compression ratio: 9.0:1. Brake hp: 250 at 4400 rpm. Five main bearings. Hydraulic valve lifters. Carburetor: Rochester Model 2GC, two-barrel.

(CUTLASS SUPREME SERIES) V-8. Overhead valves. Cast iron block. Displacement: 350 cid. Bore and stroke: 4.057 x 3.385 inches. Compression ratio: 10.25:1. Brake hp: 310 at 4600 rpm. Five main bearings. Hydraulic valve lifters. Carburetor: Rochester Model 4GC, four-barrel.

(4-4-2 SERIES) V-8. Overhead valves. Cast iron block. Displacement: 455 cid. Bore and stroke: 4.125 x 4.250 inches. Compression ratio: 10.50:1. Brake hp: 365 at 5000 rpm. Five main bearings. Hydraulic valve lifters. Carburetor: Rochester Model 4GC, four-barrel.

(VISTA CRUISER SERIES) V-8. Overhead valves. Cast iron block. Displacement: 350 cid. Bore and stroke: 4.057 x 3.385 inches. Compression ratio: 9.0:1. Brake hp: 250 at 4400 rpm. Five main bearings. Hydraulic valve lifters. Carburetor: Rochester Model 2GC, two-barrel.

(DELTA 88/CUSTOM/ROYALE SERIES) V-8. Overhead valves. Cast iron block. Displacement: 350 cid. Bore and stroke: 4.125 x 4.250 inches. Compression ratio: 9.0:1. Brake hp: 310 at 4200 rpm. Five main bearings. Hydraulic valve lifters. Carburetion: Rochester Model 2GC, two-barrel.

(NINETY-EIGHT SERIES) V-8. Overhead valves. Displacement: 455 cid. Bore and stroke: 4.125 x 4.250 inches. Compression ratio: 10.25:1. Brake hp: 365 at 4600 rpm. Five main bearings. Hydraulic valve lifters. Rochester Model 4GC, four-barrel.

(TORONADO SERIES) V-8. Overhead valves. Cast iron block. Displacement: 455 cid. Bore and stroke: 4.125 x 4.250 inches. Compression ratio: 10.25:1. Brake hp: 375 hp at 4600 rpm. Five main bearings. Hydraulic valve lifters. Carburetion: Rochester Model 4GC, four-barrel.

CHASSIS FEATURES: Wheelbase: (Cutlass/F-85/4-4-2 two-door) 112 inches; (Cutlass/Cutlass Supreme four-door) 116 inches; (Vista Cruiser) 121 inches; (Delta 88) 124 inches; (Ninety-Eight) 127 inches; (Toronado) 119 inches. Overall length: (F-85/Cutlass/4-4-2 two-door) 203.2 inches; (Cutlass/Cutlass Supreme four-door) 207.2 inches; (Vista Cruiser) 218.2 inches; (Delta 88) 219.1 inches; (Ninety-Eight) 225.2 inches; (Toronado) 214.3 inches. Front tread: (all F-85/Cutlass/Supreme/Vista Cruiser) 59 inches; (Toronado) 63.5 inches; (all others) 62.5 inches. Rear tread: (all F-85/Cutlass/Supreme/Vista Cruiser) 59 inches; (all others) 63 inches.

OPTIONS: Power brakes ($55). Power steering ($109). Air conditioning ($431). Aluminum axle carrier ($157). AM radio ($69). AM/FM stereo ($238). Stereo tape player ($138). Rear speaker ($16). Deck lid spoiler ($73). Rear air deflector/station wagons ($20). Superlift rear shocks ($42). Roof luggage rack ($64). Power windows ($110). Tilt steering wheel ($46). Electric clock ($16). Cruise control ($62). Three-speed manual transmission was standard on all except 98 and Toronado. Option W-45 was the Rallye 350 Package. Three-speed manual floor shift transmission ($51). Four-speed manual floor shift transmission ($137). V-8: 350-cid/310-hp Rocket engine

($81). V-8: 350-cid/325-hp W-31 engine ($585). V-8: 455-cid/320-hp Rocket engine ($87). V-8: 455-cid/365-hp Rocket engine ($115). V-8: 455-cid/370-hp W-30 engine ($597). V-8: 455-cid/400-hp Toronado engine ($212). Air-induction package with W-30 or W-31. Positive traction rear axle ($42).

HISTORICAL FOOTNOTES: In 1970, Oldsmobile sales were 633,981 units, ranking the division fifth in the industry. In the intermediate (F-85) lines, 96 percent of all cars had automatic transmission; three percent had four-speed manual transmission; 75 percent had V-8s; 89 percent had AM radios; six percent had AM/FM; four percent had stereos; 26 percent had bucket seats; 48 percent had a vinyl roof; 10 percent had a limited-slip axle and 18 percent had styled wheels. In the full-size Oldsmobile lines, all cars had automatic transmission; 12 percent had power door locks; 41 percent had power windows; one percent had bucket seats; 71 percent had vinyl tops; 86 percent had air conditioning and 23 percent had option full wheel discs. Only seven percent of Toronados had bucket seats; 73 percent had a movable steering column and 28 percent had Cruise Control. Toronado GT production, according to the Toronado Chapter of the Oldsmobile Club of America, was over 5,000 cars. An Olds 4-4-2 convertible was the pace car for the Indianapolis 500.

1971

F-85 - The F-85 continued as a one-model series with only a four-door sedan. Standard equipment included: front door armrests, cigarette lighter, dome lamp, dual head restraints, seat belts with shoulder harnesses and chrome hubcaps. Standard tire size was F78-14. Interiors were vinyl or cloth. Assembly plant codes were G, M, R and Z.

OLDSMOBILE I.D. NUMBERS: VIN located on top left of dashboard viewable through windshield. Engine production code number indicating approximate production date and an engine serial number matching the VIN located on engine. Serial number takes the form of seven symbols, plus sequential production number. First symbol identifies GM division: 3=Oldsmobile. Second to fifth symbols indicate series and match the four digits in Body/Style Number column of charts below. Sixth symbol identifies model year: 1=1971. Seventh symbol indicates assembly plant: E=Linden, N.J.; G=Framingham, Mass.; M=Lansing, Mich.; Z=Fremont, Calif.; X=Fairfax (Kansas City) Kan.; R=Arlington, Texas. Remaining symbols are the sequential production number starting at 100001 at each factory. Ending VINs were not available. Engine numbers consist of a alphabetical prefix and a production sequence number. Prefixes for 1970 engines were: [250-cid inline six] ZB/ZG/VB/VF=145 hp; [350-cid V-8] QI/QA/QJ/TC/TD/TE=240 hp; QN/QP/QB/QD=260 hp. [455-cid V-8] UC/UD/UE/TY/TX=280 hp; TA/TN/TP/TQ/TU/TV/TW/UN/UO=320 hp; TT/TL/TS/TB=340 hp; US/UT=350 hp. Ending engine numbers were not available.

F-85 SERIES

Model Number	Body/Style Number	Body Type & Seating	Factory Price	Shipping Weight	Production Total
SIX-CYLINDER					
F-85	3169	4-dr Twn Sed-5P	2884	3358	769
V-8					
F-85	3269	4-dr Twn Sed-5P	3005	3569	3,650

CUTLASS - Oldsmobile intermediates received a mild restyling. The Cutlass series consisted of three body styles with either six-cylinder or V-8 engines. Standard equipment included all F-85 items plus Deluxe armrests, carpeting, molding packages, Flo-Thru ventilation and recessed windshield wipers. Standard tire size was F78-14. Upholstery was cloth or vinyl.

1971 Oldsmobile, Cutlass Holiday two-door hardtop, OCW

CUTLASS

Model Number	Body/Style Number	Body Type & Seating	Factory Price	Shipping Weight	Production Total
SIX-CYLINDER					
C	3536	4-dr Sta Wag-5P	3453	3680	47
C	3569	4-dr Twn Sed-5P	2998	3358	618
C	3187	2-dr Hol HT-5P	2900	3339	1,345
V-8					
C	3636	4-dr Sta Wag-5P	3574	4054	6,742
C	3669	4-dr Twn Sed-5P	3119	3598	31,904
C	3287	2-dr Hol HT-5P	3021	3552	32,278

1971 Oldsmobile, Cutlass 'S' two-door hardtop, OCW

CUTLASS 'S' - The Cutlass 'S' series had two coupe models with a six-cylinder or V-8 engine. Standard equipment included: front and rear armrests, cigarette lighter, carpeting, dome light, chrome molding package, radio antenna in windshield, seat belts with shoulder harnesses and Deluxe steering wheel. Standard tire size was F78-14. Upholstery was cloth or vinyl.

CUTLASS 'S'

Model Number	Body/Style Number	Body Type & Seating	Factory Price	Shipping Weight.	Production Total
SIX-CYLINDER					
CS	3587	2-dr Hol HT-5P	3020	3346	297
CS	3577	2-dr Spts Cpe-5P	2957	3334	113
V-8					
CS	3687	2-dr Hol HT-5P	3141	3561	63,145
CS	3677	2-dr Spts Cpe-5P	3078	3550	4339

1971 Oldsmobile, Cutlass Supreme two-door convertible, OCW

CUTLASS SUPREME - The top Oldsmobile intermediate was the Cutlass Supreme. Three body styles were available including a convertible, in its next to last year as a Cutlass offering. Standard equipment included: armrests, cigarette lighter, V-8 engine, carpeting, woodgrain dash, interior light package, moldings, seat belts with shoulder harnesses, Deluxe steering wheel and chrome hubcaps. Standard tire size was F78-14. Upholstery was vinyl or cloth.

1971 Oldsmobile, Cutlass Supreme Holiday two-door hardtop, OCW

CUTLASS SUPREME

Model Number	Body/Style Number	Body Type & Seating	Factory Price	Shipping Weight	Production Total
CSU	4267	Conv-5P	3506	3631	10,255
CSU	4239	4-dr Hol HT-5P	3397	3690	10,458
CSU	4257	2-dr Hol HT-5P	3332	3562	60,599

4-4-2 - High performance at Oldsmobile and most other manufacturers started to decline in 1971. This was the final year the 4-4-2 would have model status at Oldsmobile. Standard equipment included: special 455-cid engine, dual exhaust, carpeting, special springs, stabilizer bars, special engine mounts, strato bucket seats, heavy-duty wheels, special emblems and Deluxe steering wheel. Standard tire size was G70-14. Upholstery was vinyl or cloth.

1971 Oldsmobile, 4-4-2 two-door convertible, OCW

4-4-2

Model Number	Body/Style Number	Body Type & Seating	Factory Price	Shipping Weight	Production Total
442	4487	2-dr Hol HT-5P	3551	3835	6,285
442	4467	2-dr Conv-5P	3742	3792	1,304

VISTA CRUISER - For the first time since 1965, the Vista Cruiser was not the largest Olds wagon. The honor went this year to the new Custom Cruiser. The Vista Cruiser now filled the middle slot in the Olds wagon line and it was available as a two- or three-seat model. Standard equipment included: woodgrain trim, cigarette lighter, V-8 engine, carpeting, moldings, windshield radio antenna, seat belts with shoulder harnesses, raised vista roof and chrome hubcaps. Upholstery was vinyl or cloth. Standard tire size was H78-14.

VISTA CRUISER

Model Number	Body/Style Number	Body Type & Seating	Factory Price	Shipping Weight	Production Total
VC	4856	4-dr Sta Wag-5P	3865	4293	9,317
VC	4866	4-dr Sta Wag-7P	4007	4414	20,566

1971 Oldsmobile, Vista Cruiser four-door station wagon, OCW

DELTA EIGHTY-EIGHT - Again, the basic full-size series for Oldsmobile was the Delta Eighty-Eight. Three models were available. This new body was the last until 1977's downsized models. Standard equipment included: front and rear armrests, power front disc brakes, carpeting, inside hood release, dome light, lamp package, windshield antenna, seat belts with shoulder harnesses and Flo-Thru ventilation. Standard tire size was H78-15. Upholstery was vinyl or cloth. Full-size Oldsmobiles had assembly plant codes X, M and E, with production of high trim level models limited to specific factories.

DELTA EIGHTY-EIGHT

Model Number	Body/Style Number	Body Type & Seating	Factory Price	Shipping Weight	Production Total
88	5457	2-dr Hol HT-5P	3826	4165	27,031
88	5439	4-dr Hol HT-5P	3888	4221	31,420
88	5469	4-dr Twn Sed-5P	3770	4198	38,298

DELTA EIGHTY-EIGHT CUSTOM - The second step up the full-sized Oldsmobile line was the Delta Eighty-Eight Custom series. Three models were available. Standard equipment included: front and rear armrests, power front disc brakes, cigarette lighter, carpeting, inside hood release, lamp package, seat belt with shoulder harnesses, power steering and chrome hubcaps. Standard tire size was H78-15. Upholstery was vinyl or cloth.

1971 Oldsmobile, Delta 88 Holiday two-door hardtop, OCW

1971 Oldsmobile, Delta 88 Royale Holiday two-door hardtop, OCW

DELTA EIGHTY-EIGHT CUSTOM

Model Number	Body/Style Number	Body Type & Seating	Factory Price	Shipping Weight	Production Total
88C	6439	4-dr Hol HT-5P	4134	4335	24,251
88C	6457	2-dr Hol HT-5P	4059	4277	14,067
88C	6469	4-dr Twn Sed-5P	3966	4308	22,209

1971 Oldsmobile, Delta 88 Royale two-door convertible, OCW

DELTA EIGHTY-EIGHT ROYALE - The top-of-the line 88 was the Delta Eighty-Eight Royale. Two body styles were available, convertible and two-door hardtop. Standard equipment included: power front disc brakes, electric clock, carpeting, interior hood release, courtesy lamps, moldings, body paint stripes, vinyl top (on hardtop model), power steering, Deluxe steering wheel, Flo-Thru ventilation and special wheel discs. Standard tire size was H78-15. Upholstery was vinyl, cloth or leather.

DELTA EIGHTY-EIGHT ROYALE

Model Number	Body/Style Number	Body Type & Seating	Factory Price	Shipping Weight	Production Total
88R	6647	2-dr Hol HT-5P	4317	4254	8,397
88R	6667	2-dr Conv-5P	4325	4233	2,883

1971 Oldsmobile, Custom Cruiser four-door station wagon, OCW

CUSTOM CRUISER - This station wagon was the new addition to Oldsmobile's full-size line. It used Eighty-Eight sheet metal, but shared the Ninety-Eight wheelbase. Both two- and three-seat versions were offered. Standard equipment included: power front disc brakes, carpeting, V-8 engine, moldings, windshield radio antenna, power steering, Deluxe steering wheel and heavy-duty wheels. Standard tire size was L78-15. Upholstery was vinyl or leather.

1971 Oldsmobile, 98 Luxury four-door hardtop, OCW

CUSTOM CRUISER

Model Number	Body/Style Number	Body Type & Seating	Factory Price	Shipping Weight	Production Total
CC	6835	4-dr Sta Wag-5P	4539	4888	4,049
CC	6845	4-dr Sta Wag-7P	4680	5008	9,932

NINETY-EIGHT - Again the largest and most luxurious Oldsmobile was the Ninety-Eight. This year offerings were reduced to four models. Standard equipment included: armrests front and rear, power brakes with front discs, electric clock, V-8 engine, carpeting, inside hood release, lamp package, power seat, power steering and Turbo-Hydramatic transmission. Standard tire size was J78-15. Interiors were vinyl, cloth or leather. Ninety-Eights were built at both Linden and Lansing.

1971 Oldsmobile, 98 Holiday two-door hardtop, OCW

NINETY-EIGHT

Model Number	Body/Style Number	Body Type & Seating	Factory Price	Shipping Weight	Production Total
98	8437	2-dr Hol HT-5P	4828	4482	8,335
98	8637	2-dr Lux Cpe-5P	5103	4582	14,876
98	8439	4-dr Hol HT-5P	4890	4548	15,025
98	8639	4-dr Lux Sed-5P	5197	4598	45,055

1971 Oldsmobile, Toronado two-door coupe, OCW

TORONADO - The front-drive Toronado continued as Oldsmobile's personal/luxury model. Two coupe models were available. Standard equipment included: power brakes, cigarette lighter, electric clock, dual exhaust, remote control outside mirror, custom seats, power steering, Deluxe steering wheel and Turbo-Hydramatic transmission. Standard tire size was J78-15. Upholstery was cloth, vinyl or leather. Toronados were built exclusively at Lansing, Mich. only.

TORONADO

Model Number	Body/Style Number	Body Type & Seating	Factory Price	Shipping Weight	Production Total
T	9657	2-dr Cpe-5P	5449	4532	20,184

BROUGHAM TRIM

Model Number	Body/Style Number	Body Type & Seating	Factory Price	Shipping Weight	Production Total
T	9857	2-dr Cpe-5P	—	4551	8,796

ENGINES (This was the final year for gross horsepower figures. Starting in 1972, the industry used net horsepower figures, which are significantly lower for the same engine output.)

(F-85/CUTLASS/CUTLASS 'S' SERIES) Inline six-cylinder. Overhead valves. Cast iron block. Displacement: 250 cid. Bore and stroke: 3.875 x 3.530 inches. Compression ratio: 8.5:1. Brake hp: 145 at 4200 rpm. Seven main bearings. Carburetor: Rochester MV, one-barrel.

(F-85/CUTLASS/CUTLASS 'S' SERIES) V-8. Overhead valves. Cast iron block. Displacement: 350 cid. Bore and stroke: 4.057 x 3.385 inches. Compression ratio: 8.5:1. Brake hp: 240 at 4400 rpm. Five main bearings. Hydraulic valve lifters. Carburetor: Rochester 2GC, two-barrel.

(CUTLASS SUPREME SERIES) V-8. Overhead valves. Cast iron block. Displacement: 350 cid. Bore and stroke: 4.057 x 3.385 inches. Compression ratio: 8.5:1. Brake hp: 260 at 4600 rpm. Five main bearings. Hydraulic valve lifters. Carburetor: Rochester 4MC, four-barrel.

(4-4-2 SERIES) V-8. Overhead valves. Cast iron block. Displacement: 455 cid. Bore and stroke: 4.125 x 4.250 inches. Compression ratio: 8.5:1. Brake hp: 340 at 4600 rpm. Five main bearings. Hydraulic valve lifters. Carburetor: Rochester 4MC, four-barrel.

(VISTA CRUISER/DELTA 88 SERIES) V-8. Overhead valves. Cast iron block. Displacement: 350 cid. Bore and stroke: 4.057 x 3.385 inches. Compression ratio: 8.5:1. Brake hp: 240 at 4200 rpm. Five main bearings. Hydraulic valve lifters. Carburetor: Rochester 2GC, two-barrel.

(DELTA 88 CUSTOM/ROYALE/CUSTOM CRUISER SERIES) V-8. Overhead valves. Cast iron block. Displacement: 455 cid. Bore and stroke: 4.125 x 4.250 inches. Compression ratio: 8.5:1. Brake hp: 280 at 4400 rpm. Carburetor: Rochester 2GC, two-barrel.

(NINETY-EIGHT SERIES) V-8. Overhead valves. Cast iron block. Displacement: 445 cid. Bore and stroke: 4.125 x 4.250 inches. Compression ratio: 8.5:1. Brake hp: 320 at 4400 rpm. Five main bearings. Hydraulic valve lifters. Carburetor: Rochester 4MC, four-barrel.

(TORONADO SERIES) V-8. Overhead valves. Cast iron block. Displacement: 455 cid. Bore and stroke: 4.125 x 4.250 inches. Compression ratio: 8.5:1. Brake hp: 350 at 4400 rpm. Five main bearings. Hydraulic valve lifters. Carburetor: Rochester 4MC, four-barrel.

CHASSIS FEATURES: Wheelbase: (intermediate two-doors) 112 inches; (intermediate four-doors) 116 inches; (all 88s) 124 inches; (98 and Custom Cruiser) 127 inches; (Vista Cruiser) 121 inches; (Toronado) 122.3 inches. Overall length: (intermediate two-doors) 203.6 inches; (intermediate four-doors) 207.6 inches; (all 88s) 220.2 inches; (98s) 226.1 inches; (Toronados) 219.9 inches; (Vista Cruiser) 218.3 inches; (Custom Cruisers) 225.3 inches. Front tread: (all intermediates and Vista Cruisers) 59.7 inches; (all 88s and 98s) 64.1 inches; (Toronado) 63.1 inches. Rear tread: (all intermediates and Vista Cruiser) 59 inches; (all 88s and 98s) 64 inches; (Toronados) 63.3 inches.

OPTIONS: Power brakes ($69). Power steering ($115). Air conditioning ($407). Power windows ($115). Tinted windows ($43). Power trunk latch ($14). Floor mats ($7). Power door locks ($47). Windshield washer ($17). Remote control mirror ($12). Sports mirrors ($22). Vinyl roof ($102). Rear window defogger ($63). Sports console ($61). Two-tone finish ($36). Tilt steering wheel ($45). Super stock wheels ($75). Rallye pack instruments ($84). Stereo tape player ($133). AM/FM stereo radio ($239). AM radio ($74). Rear speaker ($16). Rear deck spoiler ($73). Power seat ($105). Headlamp off delay system ($12). Bumper guards ($47). Three-speed manual transmission was standard on all but 98s and Toronados. Automatic transmission ($242). Three-speed manual floor shift transmission ($84). Four-speed manual floor shift transmission ($195). Wide-ratio four-speed manual transmission with floor shift ($195). V-8: 350-cid/260-hp Rocket engine ($47). V-8: 455-cid/320-hp Rocket engine ($47). V-8: 455-cid/335-hp Rocket engine ($138). V-8: 455-cid/350-hp W-30 engine ($369). Positive traction rear axle ($44).

HISTORICAL FOOTNOTES: The 1971 Oldsmobiles were introduced on Sept. 10, 1970. Production of 558,889 units put Olds in sixth place. On full-size Oldsmobiles, 72.9 percent had vinyl roofs; 81.3 percent had air conditioning and 8.7 percent had a special automatic air conditioning system; 1.6 percent had styled wheels and 2.1 percent had dual exhaust. On F-85s, 0.8 percent had a four-speed manual transmission; 4.7 percent had dual exhaust; 2.3 percent had power door locks; 18.6 percent had power windows and 19.2 percent had bucket seats. On Toronados, 93.5 percent had vinyl tops; 36.8 percent had Cruise Control; 74.6 percent had a tilt steering column and 65.6 percent had tape decks.

1972

F-85 - The F-85 four-door sedan remained the entry-level, single model in the Oldsmobile intermediate line. The only F-85 offered his model year was a four-door Town Sedan. The Chevrolet-built inline six-cylinder engine was gone. Now an F-85 had a 350-cid or 455-cid Rocket V-8. Standard equipment included: plastic fender inner liners, fiberglass hood insulation, side reflector markers, four-way flashers, left outside mirror, cigarette lighter, head restraints and aluminized exhaust system. Standard tire size was F78-14. Interiors were vinyl or cloth. Oldsmobile intermediates had plant codes M, Z, G and R.

OLDSMOBILE I.D. NUMBERS: VIN located on top left of dashboard viewable through windshield. Engine production code number indicating approximate production date and an engine serial number matching the VIN located on engine. Serial number takes the form of seven symbols, plus sequential production number. First symbol identifies GM division: 3=Oldsmobile. Second symbol changed to a letter indicating series: D=F-85; F=Cutlass hardtop; G=Cutlass 'S'; J=Cutlass Supreme; K=Vista Cruiser; L=Delta 88; N=Delta 88 Royale; R=Custom Cruiser; U=98; V=Luxury; Y=Toronado; X=Toronado chassis. Third and fourth symbols indicate body style and match second two digits of Body/Style Number in charts below. Fifth symbol indicates type of engine: [350-cid V-8] H, J, K, M; [455-cid V-8] S,T,U,V,W,X. Sixth symbol identifies model year: 2=1972. Seventh symbol indicates assembly plant: E=Linden, N.J.; G=Framingham, Mass.; M=Lansing, Mich.; Z=Fremont, Calif.; X=Fairfax (Kansas City), Kan.; R=Arlington, Texas. Remaining symbols are the sequential production number starting at 100001 at each factory. Ending VINs were not available. Engine numbers consist of a alphabetical prefix and a production sequence number. Prefixes for 1972 engines were: [350-cid V-8] QA=160 hp; QB/QC/QN=175 hp; QD/QE/QJ/QK/QP=180 hp. QM=200 hp; [455-cid V-8] WX=250 hp; UD/UE/UA/UB=270 hp; US/UT=225 hp; UL/UN/UO=300 hp. Ending engine numbers were not available.

F-85

Model Number	Body/Style Number	Body Type & Seating	Factory Price	Shipping Weight	Production Total
F-85	D69	4-dr Twn Sed-5P	2958	3536	3,792

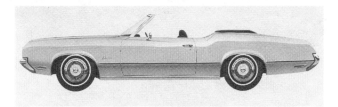

1972 Oldsmobile, Cutlass Supreme two-door convertible, OCW

CUTLASS - The Cutlass, once Oldsmobile's top intermediate, was now at the bottom of the line. Two body styles, a sedan and coupe, were in the Cutlass series. All F-85 items were standard on the Cutlass plus front and rear armrests, rear armrest ashtrays, full carpeting, fiberglass hood insulation, special molding package and Deluxe steering wheel. Standard tire size was F78-14. Upholstery was vinyl or cloth.

CUTLASS

Model Number	Body/Style Number	Body Type & Seating	Factory Price	Shipping Weight	Production Total
C	F87	2-dr Cpe-5P	2973	3509	37,790
C	G69	4-dr Twn Sed-5P	3066	3549	38,893

1972 Oldsmobile, Cutlass 4-4-2 two-door hardtop, OCW

CUTLASS 'S' - A pair of two-door models made up the Cutlass 'S' series. The 4-4-2's former full series status returned to optional status. Many Olds in this series were 4-4-2 optioned, but the package had been reduced to a handling and appearance item. Standard equipment included all Cutlass items plus simulated chrome hood louvers, Deluxe bench seats and special foam seat cushions. Standard tire size was F78-14. Upholstery was cloth or vinyl.

1972 Oldsmobile, Cutlass S Holiday two-door hardtop, OCW

CUTLASS 'S'

Model Number	Body/Style Number	Body Type & Seating	Factory Price	Shipping Weight	Production Total
CS	G87	2-dr Hol HT-5P	3087	3509	78,461
CS	G77	2-dr Spts Cpe-5P	3027	3503	4,141

1972 Oldsmobile, Cutlass Supreme Holiday two-door hardtop, OCW

CUTLASS SUPREME - The Cutlass Supreme was the top Olds intermediate. This series had a two-door hardtop, four-door hardtop and a convertible. This was the final year for a true Cutlass convertible. Standard equipment included all Cutlass items plus a higher output 350-cid engine, a special die-cast grille, woodgrain dash treatment and strato bucket seats. Standard tire size was F78-14. Upholstery was vinyl or cloth.

CUTLASS SUPREME

Model Number	Body/Style Number	Body Type & Seating	Factory Price	Shipping Weight	Production Total
CSU	J57	2-dr Hol HT-5P	3258	3520	105,087
CSU	J67	2-dr Conv-5P	3433	3614	11,571
CSU	J39	4-dr Hol HT-5P	3329	3582	14,955

CUTLASS CRUISER - Oldsmobile again offered three station wagons and the smallest was the Cutlass Cruiser. Standard equipment was identical to that of the Cutlass. Upholstery was vinyl or cloth. Standard tire size was H78-14.

1972 Oldsmobile, Cutlass Cruiser four-door station wagon, OCW

CUTLASS CRUISER

Model Number	Body/Style Number	Body Type & Seating	Factory Price	Shipping Weight	Production Total
CC	G36	4-dr Sta Wag-5P	3498	4049	7,979

VISTA CRUISER - This year the midsize Oldsmobile station wagon was the Vista Cruiser, which was in its ninth and final year for the trademark raised-roof vista greenhouse. Cutlass sheet metal was used, but the Vista Cruiser had a five-inch longer wheelbase than other four-door Oldsmobile intermediates. Standard equipment included: front and rear armrests, woodgrain decals, carpeting, V-8 engine, moldings, foam seat cushions, Deluxe steering wheel, drop or swing tailgate, heavy-duty wheels and vista roof treatment. Standard tire size was H78-14. Interiors were cloth or vinyl.

1972 Oldsmobile, Vista Cruiser four-door station wagon, OCW

VISTA CRUISER

Model Number	Body/Style Number	Body Type & Seating	Factory Price	Shipping Weight	Production Total
VC	K56	4-dr Sta Wag-5P	3774	4285	10,573
VC	K66	4-dr Sta Wag-7P	3908	4373	21,340

DELTA EIGHTY-EIGHT - Two Eighty-Eight series were offered in 1972, as the Custom was no longer an Eighty-Eight. Three body styles were available: a sedan, a coupe and a four-door hardtop. Standard equipment included: cigarette lighter, carpeting, 350-cid V-8, lamp package, moldings, windshield radio antenna, power steering, Deluxe steering wheel, Turbo-

Hydramatic transmission, power brakes (with front discs) and chrome wheelcovers. Upholstery was vinyl or cloth. Standard tire size was H78-15. Full-size Oldsmobiles had assembly plant codes M, E or X, with production of some trim levels limited to particular plants.

1972 Oldsmobile, Delta 88 two-door hardtop, OCW

DELTA EIGHTY-EIGHT

Model Number	Body/Style Number	Body Type & Seating	Factory Price	Shipping Weight	Production Total
D88	L57	2-dr Cpe-5P	4001	4296	32,036
D88	L39	4-dr Hol HT-5P	4060	4375	35,538
D88	L69	4-dr Twn Sed-5P	3948	4324	46,092

1972 Oldsmobile, Delta 88 Royale two-door convertible, OCW

DELTA EIGHTY-EIGHT ROYALE - This was the fancier of the two Eighty-Eight series and had the only full-size convertible. There were four body styles. Standard equipment included all Delta Eighty-Eight items plus Deluxe carpeting, special grille, interior light package and side moldings. Upholstery was vinyl, leather or cloth. Standard tire size was H78-15.

1972 Oldsmobile, Delta 88 Royale Holiday four-door hardtop, OCW

DELTA EIGHTY-EIGHT ROYALE

Model Number	Body/Style Number	Body Type & Seating	Factory Price	Shipping Weight	Production Total
D88R	N57	2-dr Cpe-5P	4179	4316	34,345
D88R	N39	4-dr Hol HT-5P	4238	4404	42,606
D88R	N69	4-dr Twn Sed-5P	4101	4369	34,150
D88R	N67	2-dr Conv-5P	4387	4442	3,900

CUSTOM CRUISER - The Custom Cruiser was at the top of the Oldsmobile station wagon line. It was available as a two- or three-seater. Standard equipment included: woodgrain trim, power brakes with front discs, 455-cid engine, interior hood release, interior lamp package, molding package, windshield radio antenna, foam seat cushions, power steering and Turbo-Hydramatic transmission.

1972 Oldsmobile, Custom Cruiser four-door station wagon, OCW

CUSTOM CRUISER

Model Number	Body/Style Number	Body Type & Seating	Factory Price	Shipping Weight	Production Total
CC	R35	4-dr Sta Wag-5P	4700	5109	6,907
CC	R45	4-dr Sta Wag-7P	4834	5204	18,087

1972 Oldsmobile, 98 Luxury four-door hardtop, OCW

NINETY-EIGHT - Four body styles were offered in the Ninety-Eight series for 1972. Standard equipment included: Deluxe armrests, dual ashtrays, power brakes with front discs, electric clock, carpeting, interior hood release, remote control outside mirror, molding package, interior light package, windshield radio antenna, power seat, power steering, spare tire cover and Turbo-Hydramatic transmission.

1972 Oldsmobile, 98 Holiday two-door hardtop, OCW

NINETY-EIGHT

Model Number	Body/Style Number	Body Type & Seating	Factory Price	Shipping Weight	Production Total
98	U37	2-dr Hol HT-5P	4748	4537	9,624
98	V37	2-dr Lux Cpe-5P	5009	4459	24,452
98	U39	4-dr Sed-5P	4807	4608	17,572
98	V39	4-dr Lux Sed-5P	5098	4658	69,920

NOTE 1: A midyear version of style 8639 named the Regency was produced to commemorate Oldsmobile's 75th year as an automaker.

TORONADO - The division's entry in the personal/luxury category continued to be the front-drive Toronado. Two models were offered. Standard equipment included: Deluxe armrests, dual ashtrays, power brakes with front discs, cigarette lighter, electric clock, special 455-cid engine, carpets, dual exhaust, interior hood release, molding package, remote mirror, windshield radio antenna, power steering and Turbo-Hydramatic transmission. Interiors were vinyl, cloth or leather. Standard tire size was J78-15. All Toronados were produced in Lansing.

1972 Oldsmobile, Toronado two-door coupe, OCW

TORONADO

Model Number	Body/Style Number	Body Type & Seating	Factory Price	Shipping Weight	Production Total
T	Y57	2-dr Cpe-5P	5341	4540	31,076

BROUGHAM

Model Number	Body/Style Number	Body Type & Seating	Factory Price	Shipping Weight	Production Total
T	9857	2-dr Cpe-5P	5494	4570	17,824

ENGINES

(F-85/CUTLASS/CUTLASS 'S'/CUTLASS CRUISER/DELTA 88 & DELTA 88 ROYALE SERIES) V-8. Overhead valves. Cast iron block. Displacement: 350 cid. Bore and stoke: 4.057 x 3.385 inches. Compression ratio: 8.5:1. Brake hp: 160 at 4000 rpm. Five main bearings. Hydraulic valve lifters. Carburetor: Rochester 2GC, two-barrel.

(CUTLASS SUPREME SERIES) V-8. Overhead valves. Cast iron block. Displacement: 350 cid. Bore and stroke: 4.057 x 3.385 inches. Compression ratio: 8.5:1. Brake hp: 180 at 4000 rpm. Five main bearings. Hydraulic valve lifters. Carburetor: Rochester 4MC, four-barrel.

(CUSTOM CRUISER/NINETY-EIGHT SERIES) V-8. Overhead valves. Cast iron block. Displacement: 455 cid. Bore and stroke: 4.125 x 4.250 inches. Compression ratio: 8.5:1. Brake hp: 225 at 4000 rpm. Five main bearings. Hydraulic valve lifters. Carburetor: Rochester 4MC, four-barrel.

(TORONADO SERIES) V-8. Overhead valves. Cast iron block. Displacement: 455 cid. Bore and stroke: 4.125 x 4.250 inches. Compression ratio: 8.5:1. Brake hp: 250 at 4000 rpm. Five main bearings. Hydraulic valve lifters. Carburetor: Rochester 4MC, four-barrel.

CHASSIS FEATURES: Wheelbase: (F-85/Cutlass/Cutlass Supreme four-doors) 116 inches; (Cutlass 'S'/Cutlass Supreme two-doors) 112 inches; (Vista Cruiser) 121 inches; (Toronado) 122 inches; (All 88 models) 124 inches; (Custom Cruiser/98) 127 inches. Overall length: F-85/Cutlass/Supreme four-doors) 207.6 inches; (Cutlass 'S'/Supreme two-doors) 203.6 inches; (Vista Cruiser) 218.3 inches; (Toronado) 220.6 inches; (all 88 models) 221 inches; (98) 227.8 inches; (Custom Cruiser) 227 inches. Front tread: (all intermediates) 59.3 inches; (all 88/98 models) 63.6 inches; (Toronado) 63.7 inches. Rear tread: (all intermediates) 59 inches; (Toronado) 63.6 inches; (all others) 64 inches.

OPTIONS: Power brakes ($69). Power steering ($115). Air conditioning ($407). Tinted window ($43). Power seats ($78). Window defogger ($63). Cruise control ($64). Tilt steering wheel ($45). Super stock wheels ($73). Wire wheel discs ($115). AM radio ($73). AM/FM radio ($139). Stereo tape player ($133). Electric clock ($19). Rallye pack instruments ($84). Power trunk lid ($14). Headlamp-off delay ($12). Cornering lamps ($36). Bumper guards ($16). Outside thermometer ($12). Three-speed manual transmission was standard in all intermediates. Automatic transmission ($221). Four-speed manual floor shift transmission ($195). V-8: 350-cid/180-hp L34 engine ($47). V-8: 455-cid/270-hp L-75 engine ($188). V-8: 455-cid/300-hp W-30 engine ($648). Force-Air induction package with W-30.

1972 Oldsmobile, Cutlass-based Hurst/Olds two-door hardtop, OCW

HISTORICAL FOOTNOTES: A Hurst/Olds performance package was offered in 1972 on Cutlass coupes and convertibles. A total of 629 were made. A Hurst/Olds 4-4-2 convertible was the pace car for the Indianapolis 500.

1973

1973 Oldsmobile, Omega two-door hatchback coupe, OCW

OMEGA - The new Omega compact line debuted, as the smallest and least expensive Oldsmobile. It used the Chevy Nova body, which had remained essentially unchanged since its 1968 introduction. Standard equipment included: armrests, cigarette lighter, carpeting, dome light, moldings, space saver spare tire and Deluxe steering wheel. Upholstery was cloth or vinyl. Standard tire size was E78-14. The Omega's assembly plant letter codes were L and W.

OLDSMOBILE I.D. NUMBERS: VIN located on top left of dashboard viewable through windshield. Engine production code number indicating approximate production date and an engine serial number matching the VIN located on engine. Serial number takes the form of seven symbols, plus sequential production number. First symbol identifies GM division: 3=Oldsmobile. Second symbol is a letter indicating series: F=Cutlass hardtop; G=Cutlass 'S'; J=Cutlass Supreme; K=Vista Cruiser; B=Omega; L=Delta 88; N=Delta 88 Royale; Q=Custom Cruiser; R=Custom Cruiser with woodgrain; T=98; V=98 Luxury; X=98 Regency; Y=Toronado Custom. Third and fourth symbols indicate body style and match second two digits of Body/Style Number in charts below. Fifth symbol indicates type of engine: [250-cid six]=D; [350-cid V-8]=H,K,M; [455-cid V-8]=T,U,V,W. Sixth symbol identifies model year: 3=1973. Seventh symbol indicates assembly plant: L=Van Nuys; E=Linden, N.J.; G=Framingham, Mass.; M=Lansing, Mich.; X=Fairfax (Kansas City), Kan.; R=Arlington, Texas; W=Willow Run. Remaining symbols are the sequential production number starting at 100001 at each factory. Ending VINs were not available.

Engine numbers consist of a alphabetical prefix and a production sequence number. Prefixes for 1973 engines were: [250-cid six] CCC/CCD/CCA/CCB=100 nhp; [350-cid V-8] QN/QO/QP/QQ/QS/QT=160 nhp; QA/QB/QJ/QK/QU/QV/QC/QD/QE/QL=180 nhp. [455-cid V-8] UA/UB/UD/US/UT/UU/UV=225 nhp; T=250 nhp; W=270 nhp. Ending engine numbers were not available.

OMEGA

Model Number	Body/Style Number	Body Type & Seating	Factory Price	Shipping Weight	Production Total
O	B27	2-dr Cpe-5P	2612	3094	26,126
O	B17	2-dr Hatch-5P	2761	3283	21,433
O	B69	4-dr Sed-5P	2640	3117	12,804

1973 Oldsmobile, Cutlass four-door sedan, OCW

CUTLASS - The all new 1973 body was introduced one year late due to a strike at General Motors. All two-door models had fixed rear side windows that could not be rolled down. The Cutlass was the entry-level intermediate, which had two models: a coupe and a sedan. Standard equipment included: armrests, front disc brakes, cigarette lighter, dome light, interior hood release, moldings, windshield radio antenna, Deluxe steering wheel and chrome hubcaps. Upholstery was cloth or vinyl. Standard tire size was F78-14. Intermediate Oldsmobiles had assembly plant codes M, G and R.

CUTLASS

Model Number	Body/Style Number	Body Type & Seating	Factory Price	Shipping Weight	Production Total
C	F37	2-dr Cpe-5P	3048	3905	22,002
C	G29	4-dr Sed-5P	3136	3917	35,578

CUTLASS 'S' - The newly styled Cutlass 'S' was offered in a single body style. The 4-4-2 option was again available in 1973, but it was only a handling and appearance package. Standard equipment included: armrests, ashtrays, cigarette lighter, carpeting, dome light, special hood treatment, moldings, windshield radio antenna, seat belts with shoulder harness, Deluxe steering wheel and chrome hubcaps. Standard tire size was F78-14. Upholstery was vinyl or leather.

1973 Oldsmobile, Cutlass S-based Hurst/Olds two-door coupe, OCW

CUTLASS 'S'

Model Number	Body/Style Number	Body Type & Seating	Factory Price	Shipping Weight	Production Total
CS	G37	2-dr Cpe-5P	3158	3840	77,558

1973 Oldsmobile, Cutlass 'S' Colonnade two-door coupe, OCW

CUTLASS SUPREME - The all-new Cutlass Supreme was at the top of the Olds intermediate line. It was a hands-down favorite with the intermediate buying public. A popular styling feature was its formal roof. Standard equipment included: armrests, ashtrays, front disc brakes, carpeting, interior hood release, dome light, molding package, windshield radio antenna, seat belts with shoulder harness, Deluxe steering wheel and chrome hubcaps. Upholstery was vinyl or cloth. Standard tire size was F78-14.

1973 Oldsmobile, Cutlass Supreme two-door coupe, OCW

CUTLASS SUPREME

Model Number	Body/Style Number	Body Type & Seating	Factory Price	Shipping Weight	Production Total
CSU	J57	2-dr Cpe-5P	3323	3920	219,857
CSU	J29	4-dr Sed-5P	3394	3824	26,099

1973 Oldsmobile, Cutlass Salon (option Y-78) four-door sedan, OCW

VISTA CRUISER - The Vista Cruiser series was realigned. For nine years the Vista Cruiser's wheelbase was longer than that of the Cutlass, but for 1973 its 116-inch wheelbase was shared with intermediate four-doors. The Vista Cruiser's trademark elevated rear roof was discontinued. In its place was a glass sun roof. Gone this year were the Cutlass Cruiser station wagons. Standard equipment included: ashtrays, woodgrain trim, power brakes with front discs, cigarette lighter, carpeting, interior hood release, moldings, windshield radio antenna, Deluxe steering wheel and special roof ventilator. Standard tire size was H78-14. Upholstery was vinyl or leather.

VISTA CRUISER

Model Number	Body/Style Number	Body Type & Seating	Factory Price	Shipping Weight	Production Total
VC	J35	2S Sta Wag-5P	3788	4357	10,894
VC	J45	3S Sta Wag-7P	3901	4392	13,531

DELTA EIGHTY-EIGHT - Again two Eighty-Eight four-door models were available with the entry-offering three-model Delta Eighty-Eight series. Standard equipment included: power brakes with front discs, cigarette lighter, carpeting, dome light, molding package, windshield radio antenna, power steering, Deluxe steering wheel and Turbo-Hydramatic transmission. Standard tire size was H78-15. Upholstery was vinyl or cloth. Eighty-Eights had factory codes M, E and X in their serial numbers.

1973 Oldsmobile, Vista Cruiser four-door station wagon, OCW

DELTA EIGHTY-EIGHT

Model Number	Body/Style Number	Body Type & Seating	Factory Price	Shipping Weight	Production Total
D88	L57	2-dr Cpe-5P	4047	4313	27,096
D88	L39	4-dr Hol HT-5P	4108	4420	27,986
D88	L69	4-dr Twn Sed-5P	3991	4379	42,476

1973 Oldsmobile, Delta 88 Royale two-door hardtop, OCW

DELTA EIGHTY-EIGHT ROYALE - The Delta Eighty-Eight was a bit fancier than the Delta Eighty-Eight Royale. This series offered the only convertible for 1973. Also available were two sedans and a coupe. Standard equipment included: power brakes with front discs, cigarette lighter, carpeting, interior hood release, dome light, light package, molding package, windshield radio antenna, power steering, Deluxe steering wheel, Turbo-Hydramatic transmission and Flo-Thru ventilation. Standard tire size was H78-15. Upholstery was vinyl, cloth or leather.

DELTA EIGHTY-EIGHT ROYALE

Model Number	Body/Style Number	Body Type & Seating	Factory Price	Shipping Weight	Production Total
D88R	N57	2-dr Cpe-5P	4221	4341	43,315
D88R	N39	4-dr HT Sed-5P	4293	4448	49,145
D88R	N69	4-dr Twn Sed-5P	4156	4379	42,672
D88R	N67	2-dr Conv-5P	4442	4430	7,088

CUSTOM CRUISER - The Custom Cruiser continued as the largest Oldsmobile station wagon. Both two- and three-seat models were available. Standard equipment included: armrests, power brakes with front discs, cigarette lighter, carpeting, inside hood release, dome light, molding package, windshield radio antenna, foam seat cushions, power steering, Deluxe steering wheel, Turbo-Hydramatic transmission and wheel opening covers. Standard tire size was L78-15. Upholstery was vinyl or cloth.

1973 Oldsmobile, Delta 88 Royale two-door convertible, OCW

CUSTOM CRUISER

Model Number	Body/Style Number	Body Type & Seating	Factory Price	Shipping Weight	Production Total
CC	Q35	2S Sta Wag-5P	4630	5002	5,275
CC	Q45	3S Sta Wag-7P	4769	5070	7,341

WITH WOODGRAIN TRIM

Model Number	Body/Style Number	Body Type & Seating	Factory Price	Shipping Weight	Production Total
CC	R35	2S Sta Wag-5P	4785	5005	7,142
CC	R45	3S Sta Wag-7P	4924	5072	19,163

NINETY-EIGHT - A five model Ninety-Eight series was at the upper end of the Oldsmobile line. The 75th Anniversary Regency four-door hardtop continued in 1973, following its successful mid-1972 introduction. Standard equipment included: Deluxe armrests, dual ashtrays, power brakes with front discs, interior hood release, lamp package, molding package, windshield radio antenna, power seats, power steering, Deluxe steering wheel, spare tire cover and Turbo-Hydramatic transmission. Standard tire size was J78-15. Upholstery was vinyl, cloth or leather.

NINETY-EIGHT

Model Number	Body/Style Number	Body Type & Seating	Factory Price	Shipping Weight	Production Total
98	T37	2-dr Cpe-5P	4798	4545	7,850
98	V37	2-dr Lux Cpe-5P	5070	4601	26,925
98	T39	4-dr Sed-5P	4859	4611	13,989
98	V39	4-dr Lux Sed-5P	5163	4686	55,695
98	X39	4-dr Reg Sed-5P	5417	4659	34,009

1973 Oldsmobile, Toronado two-door coupe, OCW

TORONADO - Oldsmobile continued the Toronado personal/luxury model in 1973. The Toronado was well appointed in standard trim, which included: armrests, ashtrays, power brakes with front discs, bumper guards, cigarette lighter, electric clock, door-pull handles, dual exhaust, interior hood release, molding package, windshield radio antenna, power steering, Deluxe steering wheel and Turbo-Hydramatic transmission. Standard tire size was J78-15. Upholstery was vinyl, cloth or leather. All Toronados had the M plant code in their serial numbers.

TORONADO

Model Number	Body/Style Number	Body Type & Seating	Factory Price	Shipping Weight	Production Total
T	Y57	2-dr Cpe-5P	5440	4654	28,193

BROUGHAM

Model Number	Body/Style Number	Body Type & Seating	Factory Price	Shipping Weight	Production Total
T	Z57	2-dr Cpe-5P	5594	4676	27,728

ENGINES (This is the first year of net horsepower figures. Gross horsepower figures were used through 1971. Net horsepower figures are significantly lower for the same engine output.)

(OMEGA SERIES) Inline six-cylinder. Overhead valves. Cast iron block. Displacement: 250 cid. Bore and stroke: 3.88 x 3.53 inches. Compression ratio: 8.25:1. Brake hp: 100 at 3600 rpm. Seven main bearings. Hydraulic valve lifters. Carburetor: Rochester MV, one-barrel.

(CUTLASS/CUTLASS 'S'/CUTLASS SUPREME/VISTA CRUISER SERIES) V-8. Overhead valves. Cast iron block. Displacement: 350 cid. Bore and stroke: 4.057 x 3.385 inches. Compression ratio: 8.5:1. Brake hp: 180 at 3800 rpm. Five main bearings. Hydraulic valve lifters. Carburetor: Rochester 4MC, four-barrel.

(DELTA 88/DELTA 88 ROYALE SERIES) V-8. Overhead valves. Cast iron block. Displacement: 350 cid. Bore and stroke: 4.057 x 3.385 inches. Compression ratio: 8.5:1. Brake hp: 160 at 3800 rpm. Five main bearings. Hydraulic valve lifters. Carburetor: Rochester 2GC, two-barrel.

1973 Oldsmobile, 98 Luxury two-door hardtop, OCW

(CUSTOM CRUISER/NINETY-EIGHT SERIES) V-8. Overhead valves. Cast iron block. Displacement: 455 cid. Bore and stroke: 4.125 x 4.250 inches. Compression ratio: 8.5:1. Brake hp: 275 at 3600 rpm. Five main bearings. Hydraulic valve lifters. Carburetor: Rochester 4MC, four-barrel.

(TORONADO SERIES) V-8. Overhead valves. Cast iron block. Displacement: 455 cid. Bore and stroke: 4.125 x 4.250 inches. Compression ratio: 8.5:1. Brake hp: 250 at 4000 rpm. Five main bearings. Hydraulic valve lifters. Carburetor: Rochester 4MC, four-barrel.

CHASSIS FEATURES: Wheelbase: (Omega) 111 inches; (intermediate two-doors) 112 inches; (intermediate four-doors/Vista Cruiser) 116 inches; (Eighty-Eights) 124 inches; (Ninety-Eights/Custom Cruiser) 127 inches; (Toronados) 122 inches. Overall length: (Omega) 197.5 inches; (intermediate two-doors) 207 inches; (intermediate four-doors/Vista Cruiser) 211 inches; (Eighty-Eights) 225 inches; (Ninety-Eights/Custom Cruiser) 230.2 inches; (Toronados) 226.8 inches. Front tread: (Omega) 59.1 inches; (all Cutlass) 61.4 inches;, (Eighty-Eights/Ninety-Eights) 63.7 inches; (Toronados) 63.5 inches. Rear tread: (Omega) 58.8 inches; (all Cutlass) 60.7 inches; (Eighty-Eights/Ninety-Eights) 64 inches; (Toronados) 63.6 inches.

OPTIONS: Power brakes ($46). Power steering ($113). Air conditioning ($397). Tinted windows ($30). Trunk release ($14). Power windows ($75). Power door locks ($69). Floor mats ($7). Vinyl roof ($99). Rear window defogger ($62). Sport mirrors ($22). Cruise-Control ($62). Super stock wheels ($72). Instrument gauges ($31). Electric clock ($18). AM radio ($73). AM/FM radio ($135). Rear speaker ($18). AM/FM stereo radio ($233). Paint stripe ($21). Power seat ($103). Litter container ($5). Wire wheel disc ($82). Power antenna ($32). Three-speed manual transmission was standard on all Cutlass and Omega. Automatic transmission was standard on all others. 4-4-2 appearance and handling option ($121). Automatic transmission ($215). Four-speed manual floor shift transmission

($190). V-8: 350-cid/180-hp L-34 engine ($164). V-8: 455-cid/250-hp L-75 engine ($137). V-8: 455-cid/275-hp L-74 engine ($169). Positive traction rear axle ($43).

HISTORICAL FOOTNOTES: Option W-45 was the Hurst/Olds package installed on Cutlass 'S' coupes. A total of 1,097 were produced.

1974

1974 Oldsmobile, Omega two-door hatchback coupe, OCW

OMEGA - In its second year, the Oldsmobile Omega continued as the smallest and least expensive Oldsmobile. Again in 1974, it had three body styles. Standard equipment included: armrests, ashtrays, cigarette lighter, carpeting, dome light, molding package, space saver spare tire and chrome hubcaps. Standard tire size was E-78-14. Upholstery was vinyl or cloth. Omegas had L and W plant codes in their serial numbers.

OLDSMOBILE I.D. NUMBERS: VIN located on top left of dashboard viewable through windshield. Engine production code number indicating approximate production date and an engine serial number matching the VIN located on engine. Serial number takes the form of seven symbols, plus sequential production number. First symbol identifies GM division: 3=Oldsmobile. Second symbol is a letter indicating series: B=Omega; F=Cutlass hardtop; G=Cutlass 'S'; H=Cutlass wagon; J=Cutlass Supreme; K=Vista Cruiser; L=Delta 88; N=Delta 88 Royale; Q=Custom Cruiser; R=Custom Cruiser with woodgrain; T=98; V=98 Luxury; X=98 Regency; Y=Toronado Custom; Toronado Brougham. Third and fourth symbols indicate body style and match second two digits of Body/Style Number in charts below. Fifth symbol indicates type of engine: [250-cid six]=D; [350-cid V-8]=K,M; [455-cid V-8]=T,U,W. Sixth symbol identifies model year: 4=1974. Seventh symbol indicates assembly plant: D=Doraville (Atlanta), Ga.; L=Van Nuys; E=Linden, N.J.; G=Framingham, Mass.; M=Lansing, Mich.; X=Fairfax (Kansas City), Kan.; R=Arlington, Texas; W=Willow Run. Remaining symbols are the sequential production number starting at 100001 at each factory. Ending VINs were not available. Engine numbers consist of a alphabetical prefix and a production sequence number. Prefixes for 1974 engines were: [250-cid six] DCC/DCD/DCA/DCB=100 nhp; [350-cid V-8] KB/KC/KL/KO/KU/KW/MB/MC/ML/MO=180 hp. [455-cid V-8] UC/UD/UL/UN/UP/UO/UR/UV/UX=225 nhp; T=250 nhp; W=270 nhp. Ending engine numbers were not available.

OMEGA

Model Number	Body/Style Number	Body Type & Seating	Factory Price	Shipping Weight	Production Total
O	B27	2-dr Cpe-5P	2762	3334	27,075
O	B17	2-dr Hatch-5P	2911	3438	12,449
O	B69	4-dr Twn Sed-5P	2790	3382	10,756

CUTLASS - The Cutlass was the base Oldsmobile intermediate. Minor trim changes followed the previous year's complete redesign. Standard equipment included: armrests, ashtrays, front

disc brakes, V-8 engine, carpeting, dome light, molding package, windshield radio antenna, power steering, Deluxe steering wheel and Turbo-Hydramatic transmission. Standard tire size was G78-14. Upholstery was vinyl or cloth. The Cutlass had plant codes M, G and R.

CUTLASS

Model Number	Body/Style Number	Body Type & Seating	Factory Price	Shipping Weight	Production Total
C	F37	2-dr Cpe-5P	3453	3984	16,063
C	G29	4-dr Sed-5P	3528	4040	25,718

1974 Oldsmobile, Cutlass S Colonnade two-door coupe, OCW

CUTLASS 'S' - Remaining as a single model series was the Cutlass 'S.' Standard equipment included: armrests, ashtrays, cigarette lighter, carpeting, interior hood release, dome light, molding package, windshield radio antenna, Deluxe steering wheel, front disc brakes, power steering and Turbo-Hydramatic transmission. Standard tire size was F78-14. Upholstery was vinyl or cloth.

CUTLASS 'S'

Model Number	Body/Style Number	Body Type & Seating	Factory Price	Shipping Weight	Production Total
CS	G37	2-dr Cpe-5P	3550	3993	50,860

1974 Oldsmobile, Cutlass Supreme two-door coupe, OCW

CUTLASS SUPREME - Two body styles were offered in this popular Oldsmobile series. The new Salon package attempted to bring European touring sedan influence to the Oldsmobile line. Cutlass Supreme standard equipment included: front disc brakes, cigarette lighter, carpeting, interior hood release, dome light, molding package, windshield radio antenna, power steering, Deluxe steering wheel and Turbo-Hydramatic transmission. Standard tire size was F78-14. Upholstery was vinyl or cloth.

CUTLASS SUPREME

Model Number	Body/Style Number	Body Type & Seating	Factory Price	Shipping Weight	Production Total
CSU	J29	4-dr Sed-5P	3816	4085	12,525
CSU	J57	2-dr Cpe-5P	3745	3998	172,360

CUTLASS SUPREME CRUISER/VISTA CRUISER - Oldsmobile reintroduced the Cutlass name to station wagons. The official name was the Cutlass Supreme Cruiser and it was coupled with

the long-running Vista Cruiser to form one series. The Vista Cruiser added woodgrain paneling and a glass sun roof. Standard equipment included: power brakes with front discs, cigarette lighter, carpeting, bumper impact strips, interior hood release, lamp package, molding package, windshield radio antenna, power steering, Deluxe steering wheel and Turbo-Hydramatic transmission. Standard tire size was H78-14. Upholstery was vinyl or cloth.

CUTLASS SUPREME CRUISER/VISTA CRUISER

Model Number	Body/Style Number	Body Type & Seating	Factory Price	Shipping Weight	Production Total
CSUC	H35	4-dr Sta Wag-6P	3970	4485	3,437
CSUC	H45	4-dr Sta Wag-8P	4083	4521	3,101
VC	J35	4-dr Sta Wag-6P	4180	4496	4,191
VC	J45	4-dr Sta Wag-8P	4293	4532	7,013

DELTA EIGHTY-EIGHT - Again the basic full-size model was the long-running Delta Eighty-Eight. It had three body styles: two sedans and a coupe. Two-door hardtops were transformed into coupes with a large "opera" window. Standard equipment included: armrests, ashtrays, power brakes with front discs, cigarette lighter, interior hood release, dome light, molding package, windshield radio antenna and Turbo-Hydramatic transmission. Standard tire size was H78-15. Interiors were vinyl or cloth. The Eighty-Eight used plant codes D, E, M and X.

1974 Oldsmobile, Delta 88 Royale two-door coupe, OCW

DELTA EIGHTY-EIGHT

Model Number	Body/Style Number	Body Type & Seating	Factory Price	Shipping Weight	Production Total
D88	L57	2-dr Cpe-5P	4120	4515	11,615
D88	L39	4-dr HT Sed-5P	4181	4568	11,941
D88	L69	4-dr Twn Sed-5P	4064	4536	17,939

DELTA EIGHTY-EIGHT ROYALE - The upscale Eighty-Eight model was the Royale. Two sedans and a coupe joined the only convertible that remained in the Olds line. Standard equipment included: armrests, ashtrays, cigarette lighter, carpeting, power brakes with front discs, molding package, lamp package, windshield radio antenna, power steering, Deluxe steering wheel and Turbo-Hydramatic transmission. Standard tire size was H78-15. Upholstery was vinyl, cloth or leather.

1974 Oldsmobile, Delta 88 Royale two-door convertible, OCW

DELTA EIGHTY-EIGHT ROYALE

Model Number	Body/Style Number	Body Type & Seating	Factory Price	Shipping Weight	Production Total
D88R	N57	2-dr Cpe-5P	4275	4537	27,515
D88R	N69	4-dr Twn Sed-5P	4204	4554	22,504
D88R	N39	4-dr HT Sed-5P	4341	4602	26,363
D88R	N67	2-dr Conv-5P	4490	4594	3,716

CUSTOM CRUISER - The big wagon continued in the Oldsmobile series for 1974 under the Custom Cruiser name. It was available with two or three seats. Standard equipment included: armrests, ashtrays, bodyside moldings, cigarette lighter, power brakes with front discs, carpeting, interior hood release, lamp package, windshield radio antenna, power steering, Deluxe steering wheel, heavy-duty wheels and Turbo-Hydramatic transmission. Standard tires were L78-15. Upholstery was vinyl or cloth.

CUSTOM CRUISER

Model Number	Body/Style Number	Body Type & Seating	Factory Price	Shipping Weight	Production Total
CC	Q35	4-dr Sta Wag-6P	4665	5110	1,481
CC	Q45	4-dr Sta Wag-8P	4804	5161	2,528
WITH WOODGRAIN PANELING					
CC	R35	4-dr Sta Wag-6P	4820	5122	2,960
CC	R45	4-dr Sta Wag-8P	4959	5186	8,947

1974 Oldsmobile, 98 Regency two-door hardtop, OCW

NINETY-EIGHT - The Ninety-Eight was Oldsmobile's longest running series, dating back to the 1940s, and it was still popular. Five models were offered with the Regency coupe a new addition. Standard equipment included: power brakes with front disc, cigarette lighter, electric clock, interior hood release, lamp package, molding package, remote control outside mirror, windshield radio antenna, power steering, Deluxe steering wheel, spare tire cover, power windows, power seat and Turbo-Hydramatic transmission. Standard tire size was J78-15. Upholstery was vinyl, cloth or leather.

NINETY-EIGHT

Model Number	Body/Style Number	Body Type & Seating	Factory Price	Shipping Weight	Production Total
98	V37	2-dr Cpe-5P	5141	4778	9,236
98	X37	2-dr Reg Cpe-5P	5403	4789	10,719
98	T39	4-dr Sed-5P	4930	4870	4,395
98	V39	4-dr Lux Sed-5P	5234	4892	21,896
98	X39	4-dr Reg Sed-5P	5496	4802	24,310

1974 Oldsmobile, Toronado Brougham two-door coupe, OCW

TORONADO - Once again the front-wheel-drive Toronado was the highest priced Oldsmobile. Two models -- the Custom coupe and Brougham -- were offered. Standard equipment included: armrests, ashtrays, power brakes with front discs, electric digital clock, door-pull handles, dual exhaust, carpeting, headlamp warning system, windshield radio antenna, power steering, Deluxe steering wheel, moldings and Turbo-Hydramatic transmission. All Toronados had the M factory code.

TORONADO

Model Number	Body/Style Number	Body Type & Seating	Factory Price	Shipping Weight	Production Total
T	Y57	2-dr Cpe-5P	5559	4726	8,094
BROUGHAM					
T	Z57	2-dr Cpe-5P	5713	4770	19,488

ENGINES

(OMEGA SERIES) Inline six. Overhead valves. Cast iron block. Displacement: 250 cid. Bore and stroke: 3.87 x 3.53 inches. Compression ratio: 8.0:1. Brake hp: 100 at 3600 rpm. Seven main bearings. Hydraulic valve lifters. Carburetor: Rochester MV, one-barrel.

(CUTLASS/CUTLASS 'S'/CUTLASS SUPREME/VISTA CRUISER/DELTA 88/DELTA 88 ROYALE SERIES) V-8. Overhead valves. Cast iron block. Displacement: 350 cid. Bore and stroke: 4.057 x 3.385 inches. Compression ratio: 8.5:1. Brake hp: 180 at 3800 rpm. Five main bearings. Hydraulic valve lifters. Carburetor: Rochester 4MC, four-barrel.

(CUSTOM CRUISER/NINETY-EIGHT SERIES) V-8. Overhead valves. Cast iron block. Displacement: 455 cid. Bore and stroke: 4.125 x 4.250 inches. Compression ratio: 8.5:1. Brake hp: 210 at 4000 rpm. Five main bearings. Hydraulic valve lifters. Carburetor: Rochester 4MC, four-barrel.

(TORONADO SERIES) V-8. Overhead valves. Cast iron block. Displacement: 455 cid. Bore and stroke: 4.125 x 4.250 inches. Compression ratio: 8.5:1. Brake hp: 230 at 4000 rpm. Five main bearings. Hydraulic valve lifters. Carburetors: Rochester 4MC, four-barrel.

CHASSIS FEATURES: Wheelbase (Omega) 111 inches; (intermediate two-doors) 112 inches; (intermediate four-doors) 116 inches; (all 88s) 124 inches; (Toronados) 122 inches; (98/Custom Cruiser) 127 inches. Overall length: (Omega) 199.5 inches; (intermediate two-doors) 211.5 inches; (intermediate four-doors) 214.6 inches; (all 88s) 226.91 inches; (Toronado) 228 inches; (98) 232.4 inches; (Custom Cruiser) 231.2 inches. Front tread: (Omega) 59.1 inches; (all intermediates) 61.4 inches; (88/98) 63.7 inches; (Toronado) 63.5 inches. Rear tread: (Omega) 58.8 inches; (all intermediates) 60.7 inches; (98/88) 64 inches; (Toronado) 63.6 inches.

OPTIONS: Power brakes ($48). Power steering ($114). Air conditioning ($411). Super stock wheels ($72). Sports console ($59). Sport steering wheel ($31). Sport mirrors ($22). Salon option ($361). Vinyl roof ($123). Cruise control ($67). Tilt steering wheel ($44). Electric digital clock ($38). Power trunk release ($14). Station wagon luggage rack ($63). Power antenna ($32). AM/FM stereo radio with tape player ($342). Engine block heater ($10). True track braking system ($192). AM radio ($74). AM/FM radio ($135). Three-speed manual transmission was standard on Omega. Automatic transmission was standard on all others. Automatic transmission ($237). Four-speed manual floor shift transmission ($197). V-8: 350-cid/180-hp L-34 engine ($111). V-8: 455-cid/230-hp L-75 engine ($98).

HISTORICAL FOOTNOTES: In 1974 a Hurst/Olds was offered. A H/O 4-4-2 W-30 convertible was the pace car for the 1974 Indianapolis 500.

1975

STARFIRE - Oldsmobile introduced the subcompact Starfire, smaller than the compact Omega introduced in 1973. The Starfire was based on the Chevrolet Monza. Rolling on a 97-inch wheelbase, the Starfire was the smallest postwar Oldsmobile. Standard equipment included: armrests, power brakes with front discs, cigarette lighter, bumper rub strips, V-6 engine, carpeting, electronic ignition, stowaway spare tire, custom sport steering wheel and four-speed transmission. Standard tire size was BR78-13. Upholstery was vinyl or cloth. All Starfires were made in the General Motors plant at St. Therese in Quebec, Canada.

1975 Oldsmobile, Starfire two-door hatchback coupe, OCW

OLDSMOBILE I.D. NUMBERS: VIN located on top left of dashboard viewable through windshield. Engine production code number indicating approximate production date and an engine serial number matching the VIN located on engine. Serial number takes the form of seven symbols, plus sequential production number. First symbol identifies GM division: 3=Oldsmobile. Second symbol is a letter indicating series: D=Starfire; B=Omega; C=Omega Salon; F=Cutlass hardtop; G=Cutlass 'S'; H=Cutlass Supreme Cruiser; J=Cutlass Supreme/Vista Cruiser; K=Cutlass Salon; L=Delta 88; N=Delta 88 Royale; Q=Custom Cruiser; R=Custom Cruiser with woodgrain; V=98 Luxury; X=98 Regency; Y=Toronado Custom; Z=Toronado Brougham. Third and fourth symbols indicate body style and match second two digits of Body/Style Number in charts below. Fifth symbol indicates type of engine: [231-cid V-6]=C; [250-cid six]=D; [260-cid V-8]=F; [350-cid V-8]=H,J,K,M. [400-cid V-8]=R,S. [455-cid V-8]=T,W. Sixth symbol identifies model year: 4=1974. Seventh symbol indicates assembly plant: D=Doraville (Atlanta), Ga.; 2=St. Therese; L=Van Nuys; E=Linden, N.J.; G=Framingham, Mass.; M=Lansing, Mich.; X=Fairfax (Kansas City), Kan.; R=Arlington, Texas; W=Willow Run. Remaining symbols are the sequential production number starting at 100001 at each factory. Ending VINs were not available. Engine numbers consist of a alphabetical prefix and a production sequence number. Prefixes for 1974 engines were: [250-cid six] CJU/CJT/CJL=105 nhp. [231-cid V-6] FP/FR/FS=110 nhp; [350-cid V-8] RS/RT=145 nhp; [260-cid V-8] QA/QB/QC/QD/QE/QJ/QK/QN/QP/QQ/TA/TE/TD/TN/TP/TQ=110 nhp; [350-cid V-8] PA/PB/Q2/Q3/Q4/Q5/QL/QO/QX/RN/RW/RX/TL/TO/TX=165 nhp; M=170 nhp dual exhaust. [400-cid V-8] YH/YJ=170/175 nhp; YM/YT=190 nhp. [455-cid V-8] UB/UC/UD/UE/UP/VB/VC/VD/VE/VP/YM/YT=190 nhp; W=215 nhp dual exhaust.

STARFIRE

Model Number	Body/Style Number	Body Type & Seating	Factory Price	Shipping Weight	Production Total
SF	DO7	2-dr Cpe-4P	4156	2937	28,131
SF	TO7	2-dr Cpe-4P	3872	3601	2,950

OMEGA - For the first time there were two Omega series. The standard Omega had three body styles: two coupes and a four-door sedan. Standard equipment included: armrests, front disc brakes, cigarette lighter, electronic ignition, carpeting, dome light, molding package, three-speed manual transmission and inline six-cylinder engine. Standard tire size was FR78-14. Interiors were vinyl or cloth. Omegas used plant codes W and L in their serial numbers.

OMEGA

Model Number	Body/Style Number	Body Type & Seating	Factory Price	Shipping Weight	Production Total
O	B17	2-dr Hatch-5P	3558	3426	6,287
O	B27	2-dr Cpe-5P	3435	3518	14,306
O	B69	4-dr Sed-5P	3463	3471	13,971

OMEGA SALON - The addition of the Salon package was successful in the Cutlass line, so Oldsmobile decided to do the same thing for Omega. All three Omega body styles were available as Salons. Standard equipment included all Omega items plus a console, remote control outside mirror, reclining bucket seats and Turbo-Hydramatic transmission. Standard radial tire size was FR78-14. Upholstery was vinyl or cloth.

1975 Oldsmobile, Omega Salon four-door sedan, OCW

OMEGA SALON

Model Number	Body/Style Number	Body Type & Seating	Factory Price	Shipping Weight	Production Total
OS	C17	2-dr Hatch-5P	4310	3601	1,636
OS	C27	2-dr Cpe-5P	4194	3512	2,176
OS	C69	4-dr Sed-5P	4205	3651	1,758

CUTLASS - The base Oldsmobile intermediate remained the two-model Cutlass series. A coupe and sedan were available. Standard equipment included: front disc brakes, inline six-cylinder engine, carpeting, inside hood release, dome light, molding package, lamp package, power steering, Deluxe steering wheel and three-speed manual transmission. Standard tire size was FR78-14. Upholstery was vinyl or cloth. Cutlass factory codes were M, R, D and Z, plus K for the new factory in Leeds, Mo.

CUTLASS

Model Number	Body/Style Number	Body Type & Seating	Factory Price	Shipping Weight	Production Total
C	F37	2-dr Cpe-5P	3755	3773	12,797
C	G29	4-dr Sed-5P	3830	3845	30,144

1975 Oldsmobile, Cutlass 'S' Colonnade two-door coupe, OCW

CUTLASS 'S' - The Cutlass 'S' remained a single model series with only a coupe available. Standard equipment included: armrests, ashtrays, cigarette lighter, carpeting, inside hood release, bumper impact strips, lamp package, molding package, dome light, power steering, front disc brakes, Deluxe steering wheel, three-speed manual transmission and inline six-cylinder engine. Standard radial tire size was FR78-14. Upholstery was vinyl or cloth.

CUTLASS 'S'

Model Number	Body/Style Number	Body Type & Seating	Factory Price	Shipping Weight	Production Total
CS	G37	2-dr Cpe-5P	3852	3779	42,921

CUTLASS SUPREME - Again near the top of the intermediate line was the Cutlass Supreme with two models: a coupe and a sedan. Standard equipment included: front disc brakes, cigarette lighter, inline six-cylinder engine, carpeting, inside hood release, bumper impact strips, lamp package, molding package, power steering, Deluxe steering wheel and three-speed manual transmission. Standard tire size was FR78-14. Upholstery was vinyl or cloth.

1975 Oldsmobile, Cutlass Supreme-based Hurst/Olds two-door coupe with W-30 package, OCW

CUTLASS SUPREME

Model Number	Body/Style Number	Body Type & Seating	Factory Price	Shipping Weight	Production Total
CSU	J57	2-dr Cpe-5P	4047	3793	150,874
CSU	J29	4-dr Sed-5P	4104	3891	15,517

CUTLASS SALON - The Cutlass Salon continued to be popular with Oldsmobile intermediate buyers. This was the only Cutlass model in 1975 to come standard with V-8 power, using the 260-cid engine. Standard equipment included: front disc brakes, electronic ignition system, carpeting, spring-loaded hood ornament, inside hood release, lamp package, molding package, power steering, Deluxe steering wheel and Turbo-Hydramatic transmission.

CUTLASS SALON

Model Number	Body/Style Number	Body Type & Seating	Factory Price	Shipping Weight	Production Total
CSA	K57	2-dr Cpe-5P	4654	4033	39,050
CSA	K29	4-dr Sed-5P	4726	4133	5,810

CUTLASS SUPREME CRUISER/VISTA CRUISER - Again Oldsmobile offered two intermediate station wagons. Both were available as two- or three-seat models. The Vista Cruiser added wood grain paneling and glass sun roof. Standard equipment for both included: power front disc brakes, 350-cid engine, cigarette lighter, carpeting, inside hood release, lamp package, molding package, spare tire extractor, power steering, Deluxe steering wheel, heavy-duty wheels and Turbo-Hydramatic transmission. Standard tire size was HR78-15. Upholstery was vinyl or cloth.

CUTLASS SUPREME CRUISER/VISTA CRUISER

Model Number	Body/Style Number	Body Type & Seating	Factory Price	Shipping Weight	Production Total
CSC	H35	4-dr Sta Wag-5P	4678	4492	4,490
CSU	H45	4-dr Sta Wag-7P	4791	4594	3,739
VC	J35	4-dr Sta Wag-5P	4888	4517	4,963
VC	J45	4-dr Sta Wag-7P	5001	4619	9,226

DELTA EIGHTY-EIGHT - Oldsmobile offered two Eighty-Eight series. The Delta Eighty-Eight had three models: two sedans and a coupe. Standard equipment included: power brakes with front discs, cigarette lighter, 350-cid engine, High-Energy ignition system, inside hood release, dome lamp, lamp package, molding package, power steering and Turbo-Hydramatic transmission. Standard tire size was HR78-15. Upholstery was vinyl or cloth. Delta Eighty-Eight factory codes were M, E and X.

1975 Oldsmobile, Delta 88 four-door town sedan, OCW

DELTA EIGHTY-EIGHT

Model Number	Body/Style Number	Body Type & Seating	Factory Price	Shipping Weight	Production Total
D88	L57	2-dr Cpe-5P	4843	4483	8,522
D88	L39	4-dr HT Sed-5P	4904	4544	9,283
D88	L69	4-dr Twn Sed-5P	4787	4496	16,112

1975 Oldsmobile, Delta 88 Royale four-door hardtop, OCW

DELTA EIGHTY-EIGHT ROYALE - The only series that retained a convertible for the Oldsmobile line was the Delta Eighty-Eight Royale. It joined the coupe and two four-door sedans. Standard equipment included: power brakes with front discs, cigarette lighter, electronic ignition system, 350-cid engine, carpeting, inside hood release, bumper impact strips, dome light, lamp package, molding package, power steering, Deluxe steering wheel and Turbo-Hydramatic transmission. Standard tire size was HR78-15. Upholstery was vinyl, cloth or leather.

1975 Oldsmobile, Delta 88 Royale two-door convertible, OCW

DELTA EIGHTY-EIGHT ROYALE

Model Number	Body/Style Number	Body Type & Seating	Factory Price	Shipping Weight	Production Total
D88R	N57	2-dr Cpe-5P	4998	4525	23,465
D88R	N69	4-dr Twn Sed-5P	4927	4578	21,038
D88R	N39	4-dr HT Sed-5P	5064	4546	32,481
D88R	N67	2-dr Conv-5P	5213	4595	7,181

CUSTOM CRUISER - Oldsmobile continued offering big wagons with two- and three-seat versions of its 231-inch long Custom Cruiser. Woodgrain paneling was optional. Standard equipment included: power brakes, bumper guards, cigarette lighter, electronic ignition, 455-cid engine, carpeting, lamp package, molding package, spare tire extractor, Deluxe steering wheel, power steering and Turbo-Hydramatic transmission. Standard tire size was LR78-15. Upholstery was vinyl or cloth.

CUSTOM CRUISER

Model Number	Body/Style Number	Body Type & Seating	Factory Price	Shipping Weight	Production Total
CC	Q35	4-dr Sta Wag-5P	5426	5059	1,458
CC	Q45	4-dr Sta Wag-7P	5565	5119	2,315

WITH WOODGRAIN PANELING

Model Number	Body/Style Number	Body Type & Seating	Factory Price	Shipping Weight	Production Total
CC	R35	4-dr Sta Wag-5P	5581	5072	2,837
CC	R45	4-dr Sta Wag-7P	5720	5129	9,458

1975 Oldsmobile, 98 Regency four-door hardtop, OCW

NINETY-EIGHT - The number of Ninety-Eight models offered was reduced for 1975. Four models were available consisting of coupes and sedans in Luxury and Regency trim. Standard equipment included: power brakes with front discs, cigarette lighter, electric clock, electronic ignition, hood release, bumper impact strips, lamp package, 455-cid engine, molding package, remote-controlled outside mirror, power seat, power windows, power steering, Deluxe steering wheel, chrome wheel discs and Turbo-Hydramatic transmission. Standard size tires were JR78-15. Upholstery was vinyl, cloth or leather.

1975 Oldsmobile, 98 Regency two-door coupe, OCW

NINETY-EIGHT

Model Number	Body/Style Number	Body Type & Seating	Factory Price	Shipping Weight	Production Total
98	V37	2-dr Lux Cpe-5P	5963	4731	8,798
98	X37	2-dr Reg Cpe-5P	6225	4761	16,697
98	V39	4-dr Lux Sed-5P	6104	4883	18,091
98	X39	4-dr Reg Sed-5P	6366	4895	35,264

TORONADO - Toronado remained Oldsmobile's entry in the personal/luxury market and one of the few full-size, front-wheel-drive cars built domestically. The two Toronado models were the Custom and the Brougham. Standard equipment included: Deluxe armrests, power brakes with front discs, cigarette lighter, electric digital clock, High-Energy ignition, carpeting, inside hood release, molding package, light package, power windows, power seat, power steering, Deluxe steering wheel and Turbo-Hydramatic transmission. Standard tire size was JR78-15. Upholstery was vinyl, cloth or leather. All Toronados were assembled in Lansing, Mich., and had the M factory code in their serial numbers.

TORONADO

Model Number	Body/Style Number	Body Type & Seating	Factory Price	Shipping Weight	Production Total
T	Y57	2-dr Cus Cpe-5P	6536	4787	4,419
T	Z57	2-dr Brgm Cpe-5P	6766	4793	18,882

ENGINES

(STARFIRE SERIES) V-6. Overhead valves. Cast iron block. Displacement: 231 cid. Bore and stroke: 3.8 x 3.4 inches. Compression ratio: 8.0:1. Brake hp: 110 at 3500 rpm. Five main bearings. Hydraulic valve lifters. Carburetor: Rochester 2GC, two-barrel.

(OMEGA/OMEGA SALON/CUTLASS/CUTLASS 'S'/ SERIES) In-line. Six cylinder. Overhead valves. Cast iron block. Displacement: 250 cid. Bore and stroke: 3.87 x 3.53 inches. Compression ratio: 8.0:1. Brake hp: 105 at 3400 rpm. Seven main bearings. Hydraulic valve lifters. Carburetor: Rochester MV, one-barrel.

(CUTLASS SALON SERIES) V-8. Overhead valves. Cast iron block. Displacement: 260 cid. Bore and stroke: 3.50 x 3.385 inches. Compression ratio: 8.0:1. Brake hp: 150 at 3800 rpm. Five main bearings. Hydraulic valve lifters. Carburetor: Rochester Model 2GC, two-barrel.

(CUTLASS SUPREME CRUISER/VISTA CRUISER/DELTA 88/ DELTA 88 ROYALE SERIES) V-8. Overhead valves. Cast iron block. Displacement: 350 cid. Bore and stroke: 4.057 x 3.385 inches. Compression ratio: 8.5:1. Brake hp: 180 at 4000 rpm. Five main bearings. Hydraulic valve lifters. Carburetor: M4MC, four-barrel.

(CUSTOM CRUISER/NINETY-EIGHT SERIES) V-8. Overhead valves. Cast iron block. Displacement: 455 cid. Bore and stroke: 4.125 x 4.250 inches. Compression ratio: 8.5:1. Brake hp: 210 at 4000 rpm. Five main bearings. Hydraulic valve lifters. Carburetor: M4MC, four-barrel.

(TORONADO SERIES) V-8. Overhead valves. Cast iron block. Displacement: 455 cid. Bore and stroke: 4.125 x 4.250 inches. Compression ratio: 8.5:1. Brake hp: 230 at 4000 rpm. Five main bearings. Hydraulic valve lifters. Carburetor: M4MC, four-barrel.

CHASSIS FEATURES: Wheelbase: (Starfire) 97 inches; (Omega) 111 inches; (intermediate two-door) 112 inches; (intermediate four-door) 116 inches; (88) 124 inches; (98/Custom Cruiser) 127 inches; (Toronado) 122 inches. Overall length: (Starfire) 179.3 inches; (Omega) 196.6 inches; (intermediate two-door) 211.7 inches; (intermediate four-door) 215.7 inches; (88) 226.9 inches; (98) 232.4 inches; (Toronado) 227.6 inches; (Custom Cruiser) 231.2 inches. Front tread: (Starfire) 54.7 inches; (Omega) 61.3 inches; (all intermediates) 61.1 inches; (Toronado) 63.6 inches; (all others) 63.7 inches. Rear tread: (Starfire) 53.6 inches; (Omega) 59 inches; (all intermediates) 60.7 inches; (Toronado) 63.5 inches; (all others) 63.7 inches.

OPTIONS: Power brakes ($55). Power steering ($129). Air conditioning ($487). Power trunk release ($16). Door locks ($56). Floor mats ($7). Vinyl roof ($107). Sports mirrors ($25). Two-tone finish ($38). Super stock wheel ($79). Gauges ($33). AM radio ($73). AM/ FM stereo radio ($329). Rear speaker

($19). Fuel economy meter ($24). 4-4-2 package ($128). Power seat ($116). Power windows ($149). Electric clock ($19). Locking gas cap ($6). Opera roof ($142). Pulse wipers ($26). Four-speed manual transmission was standard on Starfire. Three-speed manual transmission was standard on Omega and Cutlass. Automatic transmission was standard on others. Automatic transmission ($237). V-8: 350-cid/180-hp L-77 engine ($180). V-8: 455-cid/210-hp L-74 engine ($298). V-8: 260-cid/150-hp engine ($78). Positive traction rear axle ($49).

HISTORICAL FOOTNOTES: The 1975 Oldsmobiles were introduced Sept. 27, 1974. The division achieved third in industry sales with 628,720 units sold for the calendar year. The 'last' Oldsmobile convertible was a red Delta 88 Royale ragtop built on July 11, 1975. A Hurst/Olds package, priced at $1,095 over the base cost of the J57 Cutlass Supreme was available. Of 7,181 Delta 88 Royale convertibles built this year, 245 had a 400-cid V-8. Also, 212 Cutlass style F37 coupes and 6,015 Cutlass 'S' style G37 coupes with the 4-4-2 package installed were produced. Oldsmobile also built 32 Toronado chassis that were specially packaged for mobile homes and 150 Oldsmobile Ninety-Eight chassis with a 150-inch wheelbase for the professional car building firm Cotner-Bevington. R.J. Cook was the general manager of Oldsmobile.

1977 Oldsmobile, Cutlass 442 colonnade coupe, (O)

Heralding a trend toward smaller scale and efficiency that soon would become universal, Olds had introduced a small-block 260 cubic inch V-8 in 1975 for the compact Omega. Still, the luxury Ninety-Eight and front-drive Toronado carried a standard 455 cubic inch V-8 in 1976. That one wouldn't last another year, but the 403 V-8 hung on through 1979. The old inline six disappeared after 1976, replaced by V-6 engines. Full-size Delta 88 and Ninety-Eight models were cut down to "family size" in 1977, and the mid-size Cutlass line endured similar shrinkage the following year.

1978 Oldsmobile, Ninety-Eight Regency sedan, (O)

Even more than its General Motors mates, Oldsmobile presented a curious mixture of family-car comforts and performance-model possibilities. Ranking third in the sales race through the late 1970s, no one could deny Oldsmobile's popularity in the marketplace -- especially as the mid-size Cutlass edged out Chevrolet to become America's best seller. Nearly half a million people purchased a Cutlass in 1976. Not as widely known, or thought about, was the Olds relation to the NASCAR circuit, and its penchant for producing an occasional uniquely memorable (and collectible) model.

1982 Oldsmobile, Cutlass Ciera coupe, (JG)

Cutlass offered a rather bewildering model lineup of Supremes, Broughams, Salons and Calais coupes through these years. Fuel-efficiency improvements included the use of a four-cylinder engine in the subcompact Starfire, and a V-6 in Omega, Cutlass and Delta 88. Only Toronado carried the biggest (403) V-8 as standard equipment, in both its Brougham and upscale XS/XSR edition.

With the arrival of its 350 cubic inch diesel V-8 in 1978 (a little later than expected), Oldsmobile soon became king of diesel power in America. The gasoline crisis of 1973-74 still smoldered in motorists' minds, and diesel fuel seemed a likely candidate to help ease any future shortages. Unfortunately, the diesel was not an original creation, but derived from a conventional gasoline-powered V-8. And while its internal components and seals were beefed up, it seemed that not quite enough "beef" was used.

1983 Oldsmobile, Ninety-Eight Regency Brougham sedan, (AA)

Diesels sold well in their early years, and were adopted by all the other GM makes before too long. V-6 versions also were placed on the market. Eventually, though, customers began to complain about mechanical problems, which led to legal actions and horrid publicity. Diesels hung on until 1985, but sales diminished steadily. If new-car buyers at the time were advised to steer clear of diesels (once their flaws had been noted), the same advice generally holds for collectible models today. Diesels have long been listed at sharply reduced prices in the used-car price guides, and for good reason. On the other hand, accepting a diesel under the hood could be one way to obtain an attractive model that would otherwise be well out of pocketbook reach. Providing you don't wish to drive it regularly, at any rate.

1984 Oldsmobile, Custom Cruiser station wagon, (AA)

On the gas-engine front, Oldsmobiles, like other GM divisions, came with a number of non-Olds engines in the late 1970s. Later on, this fact too would lead to lawsuits from customers who felt they'd been cheated by a Chevrolet-powered Olds.

Toronado had hung on in full-size form through 1977-78, but finally couldn't avoid a smaller-scale body transplant. Though smaller on the outside, the resized Toronado still offered plenty of room inside. Over a million Oldsmobiles were sold in the 1979 model year, which was the second best total ever. Cutlass again ranked as America's best seller, but the fastback Cutlass models never achieved nearly the popularity of the conventional notchback design.

Omega turned to front-wheel drive for 1980 as the Olds version of Chevrolet's Citation X-car. Engine shrinkage continued, with a 307 cubic inch V-8 now standard in Ninety-Eight and Toronado instead of the former 350. Tightening emissions standards were becoming a problem for the diesel engines, especially in California.

1984 Oldsmobile, Hurst/Olds coupe, (AA)

Hefty price rises in the early years of the 1980s decade came despite the fact that sales had slumped badly. Inflationary pressures, it seemed, took precedence over the previous year's sales total, at Oldsmobile and elsewhere. Gas mileage concerns remained prominent in 1981, which brought a new four-speed (overdrive fourth) automatic transmission, as well as more use of lock-up torque converter clutches that minimized slippage. Full-size models had a more aerodynamic look. Ninety-Eight and Toronado no longer carried a standard V-8 at all, but switched to a base V-6. Nearly one in five Oldsmobiles was diesel-powered.

Going along with the rising popularity of front-wheel drive, Oldsmobile introduced a much different Cutlass for 1982: the Ciera. Rear-drive Cutlasses remained in the lineup, however. A subcompact front-drive Firenza also joined up. Of greatest interest to enthusiasts, then and now, is the Hurst/Olds variant of the rear-drive Cutlass coupe, offered in 1983-84. Its appearance marked the 15th anniversary of the first Hurst/Olds pairing,

back in 1968. Not everyone had kind words to say about the car's "Lightning Rod" shifter for the automatic transmission, which some considered gimmicky. Even so, a Hurst/Olds is one model worth seeking out. Far more available than a Hurst/Olds, if less dramatic, is one of the 4-4-2 option packages offered on Cutlass coupes in the late 1970s.

For 1984, fans who wanted extra handling qualities as well as styling had a selection of ES models to choose from. Toronado offered a Caliente option; Cutlass Ciera, a Holiday coupe. In its efforts to attract younger (presumably the most desirable) customers, Olds turned to a front-drive Calais for 1985. Luxury-minded buyers had a far different and contemporary Ninety-Eight available. A year later, both Toronado and Delta 88 also switched to front-drive. Despite a few weak years earlier in the decade, Olds generally kept a strong hold on the No. 3 spot in sales, which topped a million in each year from 1984 to '86.

1986 Oldsmobile, Calais sedan, (AA)

At first glance, apart from the relatively rare Hurst/Olds and more familiar 4-4-2, Oldsmobile doesn't seem to offer a wide variety to collectors. A closer look at the option packages reveals a slightly different story, highlighted by the Toronado XS options at the upper end, Starfire GT and Firenza packages at the small end, and Delta 88 Holiday Coupes in the middle. Then too, there's the Indy Pace Car edition of Delta 88, of which 2,401 were built in 1977.

1976

Six car lines made up the 1976 Oldsmobile lineup: 34 models in all. The new Omega Brougham and Cutlass Supreme Brougham series were introduced. The Omega Salon, base Cutlass and Delta 88 Royale convertible were dropped. To boost economy, engines included an improved 260 cubic inch V-8 and a recalibrated Toronado engine. A lighter weight (7.5 inch) axle became standard on Omega, and a five-speed overdrive gearbox optional on some models. Body colors for 1976 Oldsmobile included: silver, light or dark blue, lime, red, mahogany, saddle, or dark green metallic; white; buckskin; cream; and black. All models except Starfire and Omega could have yellow or red. Starfire and Omega could have bright yellow or red-orange.

1976 Oldsmobile, Starfire hatchback coupe, (O)

1976 Oldsmobile, Starfire hatchback coupe, (O)

STARFIRE -- SERIES 3H -- V-6 -- The subcompact four-passenger Starfire came in a base and SX sport coupe. It had a 97-inch wheelbase and was 179.3 inches long. As in 1975, quad rectangular headlamps stood in a soft plastic front-end panel that flexed with the energy-absorbing front bumper, returning to original shape after minor impact. Starfire's grille was just two small slots, side-by-side, with 'Oldsmobile' script on the driver's side (just above the grille opening). An Oldsmobile insignia adorned the center of the sloping front panel. Another (larger) grille slot was below the bumper rub strip. Park/signal lights were below the bumper, alongside the bumper slot. Starfire's rear hatchback door opened to a carpeted load floor, which could be extended

by folding the back seat forward. It had standard high-back front bucket seats with vinyl trim and a new instrument panel. Standard again was the 231 cubic inch (3.8-liter) V-6, with floor-shift four-speed manual gearbox. Optional: Turbo Hydra-matic and new manual five-speed (overdrive). Starfire tires were B78 x 13 blackwalls. SX offered a higher trim level, with cloth or vinyl upholstery, along with BR78 x 13 steel-belted radial tires, wheel opening moldings, and custom sport steering wheel. The Starfire GT option (introduced in mid-1975) included special hood and side stripes to complement the body color, Starfire Rallye wheels, raised-white-letter tires, tachometer, clock and gauges. Doors had a large 'Starfire GT' decal, as part of the striping that extended from the front to the rear of the car.

1976 Oldsmobile, Omega Brougham coupe, (O)

1976 Oldsmobile, Omega Brougham sedan, (O)

OMEGA/F85 -- SERIES 3X -- SIX/V-8 -- Joining the low-budget F85 and base compact Omega this year was a new Brougham (replacing the former Salon). Vertical rectangular parking lamps were now mounted outboard of a new full-width, chrome-plated grille. That grille had many narrow vertical bars, split into four side-by-side sections. A wider bright vertical bar in the center had an Oldsmobile emblem, and script went on lower driver's side of the grille. Single round headlamps had square housings. A bumper slot was visible between the front guards. On the cowl was 'Omega' script. Omega SX had an 'SX' decal on the lower cowl. The rear-end panel between the taillamps was restyled to give a full-width look (except F85). Omegas carried six passengers. Brougham had new interior fabrics and trim, with choice of standard bench seat or optional front buckets, in cloth or vinyl upholstery, along with a special stand-up hood emblem. The sporty SX option (on standard coupe or hatchback) included special wheel opening and bodyside decals, rocker panel and wheel opening moldings, sports-styled mirrors, Rallye suspension, and custom sport steering wheel. Base engine was a 250 cubic inch inline six; optional, a 260 two-barrel V-8 and a 350 V-8 with either two- or four-barrel carburetor. Three-speed manual shift was standard. A new five-speed overdrive floor-shift manual gearbox was available in all Omegas with the 260 V-8. Its higher (numerical) first gear ratio and overdrive fifth gear increased mileage.

CUTLASS S/SUPREME -- SERIES 3A -- SIX/V-8 -- The Cutlass name encompassed quite a few midsize Oldsmobile models, with varying appearances and characteristics. The list included Cutlass S, Cutlass Supreme, Cutlass Salon and new Cutlass Supreme Brougham. The 1975 base model was dropped, making

1976 Oldsmobile, Cutlass Supreme coupe, (O)

S the base level. Two distinct coupe styles were available: sporty fastback Cutlass S, with new sloping front end; and formal-look Cutlass Supreme, Supreme Brougham and Salon. New front ends featured wide horizontal parking/signal lamps below the quad rectangular headlamps. Hoods and front fenders also were new. Bodies were referred to as "Colonnade" hardtops. Cutlass S had a bold, vertical-bar twin-section grille design in the sloping front-end panel. The grille had a vertical appearance at the base, sweeping back at roughly a 45-degree angle, following the slope of the front-end panel, with fewer segments than the other Cutlass grilles. On the panel between the grille sections was an emblem. Quad headlamps were recessed. A wide slot in the front bumper was roughly grille-width. Coupes had large triangular quarter windows. Cutlass S again offered the 4-4-2 appearance/handling option, with distinctive new stripes and decals, large '4-4-2' decals at the forward portion of lower doors, and FE2 rally suspension. Salon/Supreme/Brougham used a wrapover twin grille with narrow vertical bars to give a more formal appearance. The grille pattern continued up over the top, back toward the hood). Following Olds custom, the grille was split into two sections with a body-color vertical divider between them. Each section was also divided into two segments. 'Oldsmobile' script went on the driver's side of the grille. Quad rectangular headlamps stood over wide, clear parking lamps. The bumper had a wide, grille-width slot. 'Cutlass Supreme Brougham' script decorated the lower cowl. Standard Cutlass equipment included a 250 cubic inch (3.3-liter) inline six-cylinder engine, three-speed column-shift manual transmission, front disc/rear drum brakes, power steering, woodgrain vinyl instrument panel trim, and FR78 x 15 blackwall steel-belted radial tires. Salon had a 260 cubic inch V-8 and Turbo Hydramatic, and GR78 x 15 whitewalls. All models except S coupe/sedan and Supreme coupe had power brakes. Supreme Broughams had 60/40 divided front bench seats, with the loose-pillow look introduced on the 98 Regency. A new five-speed overdrive floor-shift manual gearbox became available on S, Supreme, Salon and Brougham models with the small-block (260) V-8. The V-8 was recalibrated to boost mileage, including a new spark switching valve to better match spark advance to engine speed and load. A new removable hatch roof option was offered on Supreme, Salon and Brougham coupes. Twin tinted glass roof panels could be removed and stored in the trunk.

1976 Oldsmobile, Cutlass S-based 4-4-2 coupe, (O)

1976 Oldsmobile, Cutlass S Colonnade sedan, (O)

CUTLASS SUPREME AND VISTA CRUISER -- SERIES 3A -- V-8 -- Styled along the same lines as Cutlass coupes and sedans, the Supreme Cruiser and Vista Cruiser had a standard 350 cubic inch (5.7-liter) four-barrel V-8 and Turbo Hydra-matic. Options extended to the 455 cubic inch four-barrel V-8. Two seats were standard, with a third seat optional. Wagon tires were HR78 x 15 blackwalls.

1976 Oldsmobile, Delta 88 Royale Crown Landau coupe, (O)

1976 Oldsmobile, Vista Cruiser station wagon, (O)

1976 Oldsmobile, Delta 88 four-door hardtop, (O)

DELTA 88 -- SERIES 3B -- V-8 -- Like other full-size models, Delta 88 had a 124-inch wheelbase. Two models were offered: base and Royale, both in two- or four-door hardtop body styles (a style that soon would disappear). Design was similar to 1975, with a few refinements, led by new quad rectangular headlamps. A four-opening aluminum grille consisted of two sections on each side of a wide body-color divider, which held a rectangular emblem. Each section contained vertical bars. 'Oldsmobile' script went on the driver's side of the grille. Wide rectangular park/sig-

nal lamps were below the headlamps, which continued into amber side marker lenses. Parking lamps wrapped around the front fenders. The front bumper had two slots. 'Delta 88' script was on the cowl. Wraparound taillamps were square shaped, with a bright square trim element and emblem in each lens center. Across the panel below the decklid were 'Oldsmobile' block letters. Base Delta 88 engine was the 350 cubic inch (5.7-liter) four-barrel V-8, with Turbo Hydra-matic. Optional: a 455 cubic inch V-8. Standard equipment also included vari-ratio power steering, power brakes, electronic message center, chrome wheel covers, inside hood release, plush-pile carpeting, ashtray and overhead courtesy lamps, HR78 x 15 BSW SBR tires, and automatic front-door courtesy switches. Bright metal moldings were used for rocker panels, drip rails and wheel openings. Royale added velour interior, color-coordinated protective bodyside moldings, courtesy and glovebox lights, and bright metal brake and gas pedal accents. A new Crown Landau option for the Delta Royale coupe included a padded landau vinyl roof with six-inch wide stainless steel band across the top. Crown Landau also had color-keyed wheel covers, a stand-up hood ornament and Royale emblem on the rear-quarter inner panel.

1976 Oldsmobile, Custom Cruiser station wagon, (O)

CUSTOM CRUISER -- SERIES 3B -- V-8 -- Full-size wagons looked like Ninety-Eights up front, with a two-section upright grille. Each section contained a checkered pattern, separated by the body-color panel with emblem. 'Oldsmobile' script stood at the lower driver's side of the grille. Quad rectangular headlamps went above wide rectangular park/signal lamps. Twin bumper slots were alongside the license plate. 'Custom Cruiser' script decorated the cowl. Backup lenses were separate, mounted inboard of the upright taillamps. Two-seat wagons held six passengers, and a third seat increased capacity to nine. Custom Cruiser carried standard a 455 cubic inch V-8 with Turbo Hydra-matic, new semi-automatic load leveling and LR78 x 15 BSW SBR tires.

1976 Oldsmobile, Ninety-Eight Regency four-door hardtop, (O)

NINETY-EIGHT -- SERIES 3C -- V-8 -- Luxury and Regency editions of the full-size Ninety-Eight were offered, in two-door hardtop coupe or four-door hardtop. Four-doors had an extra window (like an opera window) in the C-pillar. A landau roof option for the coupe gave it a huge-looking opera window. Like the Custom Cruiser, Ninety-Eights had a dual-section eggcrate-design grille, with new front-end panel, front bumper and wraparound horizontal parking lamps. Amber marker lenses aligned with the headlamps wrapped around the fender sides. Separate clear cornering

lamps had horizontal ribs. Vertical taillamps were decorated with a small emblem in each lens. Tiny backup lamps stood alongside the license plate, on a panel that also contained small red lenses next to the taillamps. Standard Ninety-Eight equipment included a 455 cubic inch Rocket V-8 engine with four-barrel carb, Turbo Hydra-matic, vari-ratio power steering, power brakes, power driver's seat, driver's door armrest control console, electronic message center, electric clock, fold-down center armrests, front ashtray, and JR78 x 15 blackwall steel-belted radials. Rear fender skirts and bumper impact strips also were standard. A new 2.41:1 axle ratio became available, to boost highway gas mileage.

1976 Oldsmobile, Toronado coupe, (O)

TORONADO -- SERIES 3E -- V-8 -- The front-wheel-drive Toronado's revised look included grille bars with a wide chrome face, new gold/black stand-up hood ornament, and bodyside moldings to complement the body color. Toro's carburetion, ignition and EGR systems were calibrated to improve economy and driveability. New this year: a semi-automatic leveling system. The grille consisted of just two horizontal bars, low on the front end, below a deep hood front panel with 'Toronado' block lettering. Vertical park/signal lamps stood at fender tips, separate from the quad rectangular headlamps. Twin bumper slots were below the headlamps, outboard of the guards. At the rear tips of quarter panels, where taillamp lenses seemed appropriate, were body-color segments and an ornamental emblem. Instead, the taillamps were horizontal, one set of lenses along a trim strip at the decklid's lower edge (three lenses on each side), with small backup lenses on the same strip next to the license plate mounting. Two additional wide red lenses were positioned forward of the decklid, next to the back window. Standard engine was the four-barrel 455 cubic inch Rocket V-8, with Turbo Hydra-matic. Equipment included JR78 x 15 steel-belted radials, vari-ratio power steering, power front disc/rear drum brakes with new semi-metallic pads and linings, power windows, message center, driver's door console, digital clock, front ashtray, glovebox lights and inside hood release. Brougham or Custom interiors were available.

I.D. DATA: The 13-symbol Vehicle Identification Number (VIN) was located on the upper left surface of the instrument panel, visible through the windshield. The first digit is '3', indicating Oldsmobile division. Next is a letter indicating series: 'T' = Starfire; 'D' = Starfire SX; 'S' = Omega F85; 'B' = Omega; 'E' = Omega Brougham; 'G' = Cutlass S; 'J' = Cutlass Supreme or Vista Cruiser; 'M' = Cutlass Supreme Brougham; 'K' = Cutlass Salon; 'H' = Cutlass Supreme Cruiser; 'L' = Delta 88; 'N' = Delta 88 Royale; 'Q' = Custom Cruiser; 'R' = Custom Cruiser (woodgrain trim); 'V' = Ninety-Eight Luxury; 'X' = Ninety-Eight Regency; 'Y' = Toronado Custom; 'Z' = Toronado Brougham. Next come two digits that denote body type: '07' = Starfire coupe; '17' = Omega 2-dr. hatchback coupe; '27' = Omega 2-dr. pillar coupe; '37' = 2-dr. Colonnade or HT coupe; '57' = 2-dr. Colonnade coupe or HT coupe; '29' = 4-dr. Colonnade HT sedan; '39' = 4-dr. HT (4-window) sedan; '69' = 4-dr. thin-pillar (4-window) sedan; '35' = 4-dr. 2-seat wagon; '45' = 4-dr. 3-seat wagon. The fifth symbol is a letter indicating engine code: 'C' = V-6-231 2Bbl.; 'D' = L6-250 1Bbl.; 'F' = V-8-260 2Bbl.; 'X' = V-8-350 2Bbl.; 'H', 'J' or 'R' V-8-350 4Bbl.; 'S' = V-8-455 4Bbl.; 'T' = V-8-455 4Bbl. The sixth symbol denotes model year ('6' = 1976). Next is a plant code: '2' = Ste. Therese, Quebec (Canada); 'L' =

Van Nuys, Calif.; 'G' = Framingham, Mass.; 'D' = Doraville, Georgia; 'M' = Lansing, Mich.; 'W' = Willow Run, Mich.; 'R' = Arlington, Texas; 'C' = Southgate, Calif.; 'X' = Fairfax, Kansas; 'E' = Linden, New Jersey. The final six digits are the sequential serial number, which began with 100001. Engine numbers were stamped on the right front of the block (Buick-built V-8-350), on the block next to the distributor (Chevrolet inline six), or on the oil filler tube (Oldsmobile engines). A body number plate on the shroud identified model year, car division, series, style, body assembly plant, body number, trim combination, modular seat code, paint code and date built code.

STARFIRE SPORT (V-6)

Model Number	Body/Style Number	Body Type & Seating	Factory Price	Shipping Weight	Production Total
3H	T07	2-dr. Hatch Cpe-4P	3882	2888	8,305

STARFIRE SX (V-6)

Model Number	Body/Style Number	Body Type & Seating	Factory Price	Shipping Weight	Production Total
3H	D07	2-dr. Hatch Cpe-4P	4062	2919	20,854

OMEGA F-85 (SIX/V-8)

Model Number	Body/Style Number	Body Type & Seating	Factory Price	Shipping Weight	Production Total
3X	S27	2-dr. Cpe-6P	3390/3480	3171/3320	3,918

OMEGA (SIX/V-8)

3X	B27	2-dr. Cpe-6P	3485/3575	3174/3323	15,347
3X	B17	2-dr. Hatch Cpe-6P	3627/3717	3248/3397	4,497
3X	B69	4-dr. Sed-6P	3514/3604	3196/3345	20,221

OMEGA BROUGHAM (SIX/V-8)

3X	E27	2-dr. Cpe-6P	3675/3765	3178/3327	5,363
3X	E17	2-dr. Hatch Cpe-6P	3817/3907	3258/3407	1,235
3X	E69	4-dr. Sed-6P	3704/3794	3212/3361	7,587

CUTLASS 'S' (SIX/V-8)

Model Number	Body/Style Number	Body Type & Seating	Factory Price	Shipping Weight	Production Total
3A	G37	2-dr. Col Cpe-6P	3999/4194	3608/3771	59,179
3A	G29	4-dr. Col Sed-6P	4033/4228	3690/3853	34,994

Production Note: A total of 964 'S' coupes had the 260 cubic inch V-8 and five-speed manual transmission.

CUTLASS SUPREME (SIX/V-8)

3A	J57	2-dr. Col Cpe-6P	4291/4486	3637/3800	186,647
3A	J29	4-dr. Col Sed-6P	4415/4610	3730/3893	37,112

Production Note: A total of 862 Supreme coupes had the 260 cubic inch V-8 and five-speed manual transmission.

CUTLASS SUPREME CRUISER (V-8)

3A	H35	4-dr. 2S Sta Wag-6P	4923	4333	13,964
3A	H35	4-dr. 3S Sta Wag-8P	5056	4370	Note 1

CUTLASS VISTA CRUISER (V-8)

3A	J35	4-dr. 2S Sta Wag-6P	5041	4333	20,560
3A	J35	4-dr. 3S Sta Wag-8P	5174	4370	Note 1

Note 1: Three-seat wagon production is included in two-seat totals.

CUTLASS SUPREME BROUGHAM (SIX/V-8)

3A	M57	2-dr. Col Cpe-5P	4580/4775	3668/3831	91,312

CUTLASS SALON (V-8)

3A	K57	2-dr. Col Cpe-5P	4890	3829	48,440
3A	K29	4-dr. Col Sed-5P	4965	3949	7,921

DELTA 88 (V-8)

Model Number	Body/Style Number	Body Type & Seating	Factory Price	Shipping Weight	Production Total
3B	L57	2-dr. Cpe-6P	4975	4243	7,204
3B	L39	4-dr. Sed-6P	5038	4336	9,759
3B	L69	4-dr. Town Sed-6P	4918	4279	17,115

DELTA 88 ROYALE (V-8)

3B	N57	2-dr. Cpe-6P	5146	4263	33,364
3B	N39	4-dr. Sed-6P	5217	4368	52,103
3B	N69	4-dr. Town Sed-6P	5078	4294	33,268

Production Note: A total of 4,360 Royales had the Crown Landau option (code Y61).

CUSTOM CRUISER (V-8)

Model Number	Body/Style Number	Body Type & Seating	Factory Price	Shipping Weight	Production Total
3B	Q35	4-dr. 2S Sta Wag-6P	5563	5002	2,572
3B	Q45	4-dr. 3S Sta Wag-9P	5705	5062	3,626

CUSTOM CRUISER—Woodgrain Trim (V-8)

Model Number	Body/Style Number	Body Type & Seating	Factory Price	Shipping Weight	Production Total
3B	R35	4-dr. 2S Sta Wag-6P	5719	5009	3,849
3B	R45	4-dr. 3S Sta Wag-9P	5861	5071	12,269

NINETY-EIGHT LUXURY (V-8)

Model Number	Body/Style Number	Body Type & Seating	Factory Price	Shipping Weight	Production Total
3C	V37	2-dr. Cpe-6P	6271	4501	6,056
3C	V39	4-dr. Sed-6P	6419	4633	16,802

NINETY-EIGHT REGENCY (V-8)

Model Number	Body/Style Number	Body Type & Seating	Factory Price	Shipping Weight	Production Total
3C	X37	2-dr. Cpe-6P	6544	4535	26,282
3C	X39	4-dr. Sed-6P	6691	4673	55,339

TORONADO CUSTOM (V-8)

Model Number	Body/Style Number	Body Type & Seating	Factory Price	Shipping Weight	Production Total
3E	Y57	2-dr. Cpe-6P	6891	4620	2,555

TORONADO BROUGHAM (V-8)

Model Number	Body/Style Number	Body Type & Seating	Factory Price	Shipping Weight	Production Total
3E	Z57	2-dr. Cpe-6P	7137	4729	21,749

Production Note: 140 Toronado motorhome chassis also were produced.

FACTORY PRICE AND WEIGHT NOTE: For Omega and Cutlass, prices and weights to left of slash are for six-cylinder, to right for V-8 engine.

ENGINE DATA: BASE V-6 (Starfire): 90-degree, overhead-valve V-6. Cast iron block and head. Displacement: 231 cu. in. (3.8 liters). Bore & stroke: 3.80 x 3.40 in. Compression ratio: 8.0:1. Brake horsepower: 105 at 3400 rpm. Torque: 185 lb.-ft. at 2000 rpm. Four main bearings. Hydraulic valve lifters. Carburetor: 2Bbl. Rochester 2GC. VIN Code: C. BASE SIX (Omega, Cutlass): Inline. OHV. Six-cylinder. Cast iron block and head. Displacement: 250 cu. in. (4.1 liters). Bore & stroke: 3.88 x 3.53 in. Compression ratio: 8.25:1. Brake horsepower: 105 at 3800 rpm. Torque: 185 lb.-ft. at 1200 rpm. Seven main bearings. Hydraulic valve lifters. Carburetor: 1Bbl. Rochester. VIN Code: D. BASE V-8 (Cutlass Salon); OPTIONAL (Omega, Cutlass): 90-degree, overhead valve V-8. Cast iron block and head. Displacement: 260 cu. in. (4.3 liters). Bore & stroke: 3.50 x 3.39 in. Compression ratio: 8.0:1. Brake horsepower: 110 at 3400 rpm. Torque: 205 lb.-ft. at 1600 rpm. Five main bearings. Hydraulic valve lifters. Carburetor: 2Bbl. Rochester. VIN Code: F. OPTIONAL V-8 (Omega): 90-degree, overhead valve V-8. Cast iron block and head. Displacement: 350 cu. in. (5.7 liters). Bore & stroke: 3.80 x 3.85 in. Compression ratio: 8.0:1. Brake horsepower: 140 at 3200 rpm. Torque: 280 lb.-ft. at 1800 rpm. Five main bearings. Hydraulic valve lifters. Carburetor: 2Bbl. Rochester 2GC. OPTIONAL V-8 (Omega):Same as 350 cubic inch V-8 above, with 4Bbl. Rochester 4MV carburetor—Horsepower: 155 at 3400 rpm. BASE V-8 (Delta 88, Cutlass Supreme/Vista Cruiser wagon); OPTIONAL (Cutlass): 90-degree, overhead valve V-8. Cast iron block and head. Displacement: 350 cu. in. (5.7 liters). Bore & stroke: 4.06 x 3.39 in. Compression ratio: 8.5:1. Brake horsepower: 170 at 3800 rpm. Torque: 275 lb.-ft. at 2400 rpm. Five main bearings. Hydraulic valve lifters. Carburetor: 4Bbl. Rochester. VIN Code: R. BASE V-8 (Ninety-Eight, Custom Cruiser); OPTIONAL (Cutlass, Delta 88): 90-degree, overhead valve V-8. Cast iron block and head. Displacement: 455 cu. in. (7.5 liters). Bore & stroke: 4.13 x 4.25 in. Compression ratio: 8.5:1. Brake horsepower: 190 at 3400 rpm. Torque: 350 lb.-ft. at 2000 rpm. Five main bearings. Hydraulic valve lifters. Carburetor: 4Bbl. Rochester. VIN Code: S. BASE V-8 (Toronado): Same as 455 cu. in. V-8 above, except—B.H.P.: 215 at 3600 rpm. Torque: 370 lb.-ft. at 2400 rpm. Carburetor: 4Bbl. Rochester. VIN Code: T.

CHASSIS DATA: Wheelbase: (Starfire) 97.0 in.; (Omega) 111.0 in.; (Cutlass 2-dr.) 112.0 in.; (Cutlass 4-dr.) 116.0 in.; (Cutlass Supreme wag) 116.0 in.; (Delta 88) 124.0 in.; (Ninety-Eight) 127.0 in.; (Custom Crsr) 127.0 in.; (Toronado) 122.0 in. Overall Length: (Starfire) 179.3 in.; (Omega) 199.6 in.; (Cutlass 2-dr.) 211.7 in.; (Cutlass 4-dr.) 215.7 in.; (Cutlass Supreme wag) 219.9 in.; (Delta 88) 226.7 in.; (Ninety-Eight) 232.2 in.; (Custom Crsr) 231.0 in.; (Toro) 227.6 in. Height: (Starfire) 50.2 in.; (Omega 2-dr.) 53.4 in.; (Omega 4-dr.) 54.3 in.; (Cutlass 2-dr.) 53.4 in.; (Cutlass 4-dr.) 54.1 in.; (Cutlass Supreme wag) 55.5 in.; (Delta 88 2-dr.) 53.4 in.; (Delta 88 4-dr.) 54.5 in.; (Ninety-Eight 2-dr.) 54.2 in.; (Ninety-Eight 4-dr.) 54.7 in.; (Custom Crsr) 57.1 in.; (Toro) 53.2 in. Width: (Starfire) 65.4 in.; (Omega) 72.9 in.; (Cutlass 2-dr.) 76.2 in.; (Cutlass 4-dr.) 76.7 in.; (Cutlass Supreme wag) 77.7 in.; (Delta 88) 80.0 in.; (Ninety-Eight) 80.0 in.; (Custom Crsr) 80.0 in.; (Toro) 79.7 in. Front Tread: (Starfire) 54.7 in.; (Omega) 61.3 in.; (Cutlass) 61.1 in.; (Delta 88/Ninety-Eight) 63.7 in.; (Custom Crsr) 63.3 in.; (Toro) 63.6 in. Rear Tread: (Starfire) 53.6 in.; (Omega) 59.0 in.; (Cutlass) 60.7 in.; (Delta 88/Ninety-Eight) 64.0 in.; (Custom Crsr) 63.7 in.; (Toro) 63.5 in. Standard Tires: (Starfire) B78 x 13; (Starfire SX) BR78 x 13; (Omega) E78 x 14; (Cutlass) FR78 x 15; (Cutlass Supreme wag) HR78 x 15; (Cutlass Salon) GR78 x 15; (Delta 88) HR78 x 15; (Ninety-Eight) JR78 x 15; (Custom Crsr) LR78 x 15; (Toronado) JR78 x 15.

TECHNICAL: Transmission: Three-speed manual transmission (column shift) standard on Omega/Cutlass six or V-8-260. Gear ratios: (1st) 3.11:1; (2nd) 1.84:1; (3rd) 1.00:1; (Rev) 3.22:1. Four-speed floor shift standard on Starfire: (1st) 3.11:1; (2nd) 2.20:1; (3rd) 1.47:1; (4th) 1.00:1; (Rev) 3.11:1. Five-speed manual optional on Starfire, and on Omega/Cutlass coupe with V-8-260. Three-speed Turbo Hydra-matic standard on other models, optional on all. Floor selector lever available on Omega/Cutlass. Starfire, Omega/Cutlass six or V-8-260/350 THM gear ratios: (1st) 2.52:1; (2nd) 1.52:1; (3rd) 1.00:1; (Rev) 1.93:1. Cutlass (V-8-455)/Delta 88/Ninety-Eight/Toro THM: (1st) 2.48:1; (2nd) 1.48:1; (3rd) 1.00:1; (Rev) 2.08:1. Standard final drive ratio: (Starfire) 2.56:1; (Omega) 2.73:1 exc. 2.56:1 w/V-8-350; (Cutlass) 2.73:1 w/six, 3.08:1 w/V-8-260, 2.56:1 w/V-8-350 or V-8-455; (Cutlass Crsr) 2.73:1 w/V-8-350, 2.56:1 w/V-8-455; (Delta 88) 2.73:1 exc. 2.56:1 w/V-8-455; (Custom Crsr) 2.73:1; (Ninety-Eight) 2.56:1; (Toronado) 2.73:1. Steering: Recirculating ball. Front Suspension: (Starfire) coil springs w/lower trailing links and anti-sway bar; (Toronado); longitudinal torsion bars w/anti-sway bar; (others) coil springs w/control arms and anti-sway bar. Rear Suspension: (Starfire) rigid axle w/coil springs, lower trailing radius arms, upper torque arms, transverse linkage bar and anti-sway bar; (Omega) rigid axle w/semi-elliptic leaf springs; (others) rigid axle w/coil springs, lower trailing radius arms and upper torque arms. Semi-automatic leveling on Toronado. Brakes: Front disc, rear drum. Ignition: Electronic. Body construction: (Starfire) unibody; (Omega) unibody w/separate front partial frame; (others) separate body on perimeter frame. Fuel tank: (Starfire) 18.5 gal.; (Omega) 21 gal.; (Cutlass) 22 gal.; (Cutlass Supreme wag) 22 gal.; (Delta 88) 26 gal.; (Ninety-Eight) 26 gal.; (Custom Crsr wag) 22 gal.; (Toronado) 26 gal.

DRIVETRAIN OPTIONS: Engines: 260 cu. in. V-8: Omega/Cutlass ($90). 350 cu. in. 2Bbl. V-8: Omega ($140). 350 cu. in. 4Bbl. V-8: Omega ($195); Cutlass ($195) exc. Salon ($112). 455 cu. in. V-8: Cutlass ($321) exc. Salon ($238); Cutlass wag ($126); Delta 88 ($147). Transmission/Differential: Five-speed manual floor shift: Starfire ($244); Omega ($262). Turbo Hydra-matic: Starfire ($244); Omega ($262); Cutlass ($262-$286) exc. Salon/wag ($24). Floor shift lever, three-speed manual: Omega ($28). Anti-spin axle: Starfire/Omega/Cutlass ($51); full-size ($54). Brakes/Steering: Power disc brakes: Starfire ($55); Omega, Cutlass S ($58); Power steering: Starfire ($120); Omega ($136). Suspension: Driver-controlled leveling system: Cutlass ($85); full-size ($86). Rallye susp. pkg.: Ome-

ga ($15-$20). H.D. susp.: Cutlass ($23); full-size ($23). Firm ride shock absorbers: Cutlass/88/98 ($6). Superlift rear shocks: Cutlass ($45); full-size ($46). Rear stabilizer bar: Starfire ($16). Other: High-capacity cooling: Cutlass ($18). High-capacity radiator: Starfire/Omega ($18). H.D. battery: Starfire ($15). Maintenance-free battery: full-size ($28). High-capacity alternator: full-size ($43). Engine block heater ($12) exc. Starfire. California emissions equipment: Starfire/Omega/Cutlass ($50).

STARFIRE CONVENIENCE/APPEARANCE OPTIONS: Option Packages: GT pkg. ($290-$391). Aux. lighting group ($12). Comfort/Convenience: Four season air cond. ($452). Rear defogger ($66). Soft ray tinted glass ($44). Tilt steering ($48). Fuel economy meter ($25). Electric clock ($16). Sport mirrors ($27). Entertainment: AM radio ($71). AM radio w/stereo tape player ($197). AM/FM radio ($134). AM/FM stereo radio ($219). Rear speakers ($20). Exterior: Accent stripe ($24). Protective bodyside moldings ($39). Bright door edge moldings ($8). Bright wheel opening moldings: base ($18). Roof luggage rack ($54). Interior: Sports console ($73). Driver's seatback adjuster ($17). Front/rear floor mats ($14). Deluxe seatbelts ($15). Wheels and Tires: Super stock III wheels ($74-$84). Deluxe wheel covers ($39). Wheel trim rings ($33). B78 x 13 WSW. BR78 x 13 BSW/WSW/RWL.

OMEGA CONVENIENCE/APPEARANCE OPTIONS: Option Packages: SX pkg.: base hatch/cpe ($171). Convenience group ($26-$28). Comfort/Convenience: Four season air cond. ($452). Forced-air defogger ($43). Cruise control ($73). Soft ray tinted glass ($46). Power windows ($99-$140). Power door locks ($62-$89). Custom sport steering wheel ($34). Tilt steering ($52). Tachometer/voltage/temp gauges ($6). Fuel economy meter ($25). Electric clock ($18). Lighter: F85 ($5). Locking gas cap ($7). Horns and Mirrors: Dual horns ($6). Remote driver's mirror ($14). Sport mirrors ($26). Entertainment: AM radio ($75). AM radio w/stereo tape player ($209). AM/FM radio ($137). AM/FM stereo radio ($233); w/tape player ($337). Rear speakers ($20). Exterior: Vinyl roof ($91). Landau vinyl roof ($150). Two-tone paint ($35). Accent stripe ($23). Swing-out rear quarter vent windows ($48). Bright roof drip moldings ($16). Rocker panel moldings ($15). Protective bodyside moldings ($37). Bright wheel opening moldings ($17). Bright door edge moldings ($8-$12). Bright window frame moldings: F85 ($20). Bumper guards ($63). Bumper rub strips ($29). Roof luggage rack: wag ($71). Interior: Sports console ($71). Bucket seats ($79). Aux. front or rear floor mats ($7). Deluxe seatbelts ($15). Wheels and Tires: Super stock III wheels ($78-$89). Deluxe wheel covers ($32). Wire wheel covers ($111). E78 x 14 WSW. ER78 x 14 BSW/WSW. FR78 x 14 RWL SBR.

CUTLASS CONVENIENCE/APPEARANCE OPTIONS: Option Packages: 4-4-2 appearance/handling package: S cpe ($134). Special option pkg.: S cpe ($239-$250). Convenience group ($25-$31). Comfort/Convenience: Four season air cond. ($476); tempmatic ($513). Rear defogger ($77). Cruise control ($73). Twilight sentinel ($45). Soft ray tinted glass ($50). Six-way power seat ($124). Power windows ($99-$140). Power door locks ($62-$89). Power trunk release ($17). Custom sport steering wheel ($34). Tilt steering ($52). Instrument panel cluster ($35). Pulse wipers ($28). Fuel economy meter ($25). Electric clock ($20). Locking gas cap ($7). Lighting, Horns and Mirrors: Dome reading lamps ($15). Sport mirrors ($26). Remote driver's mirror ($14). Remote passenger mirror ($28). Lighted visor vanity mirror ($39). Entertainment: AM radio ($79). AM radio w/stereo tape player ($213). AM/FM radio ($142). AM/FM stereo radio ($233); w/tape player ($337). Rear speakers ($20). Exterior: Hatch roof ($550). Vinyl roof ($109). Landau vinyl roof: cpe ($109). Special solid-color paint ($125-$171). Two-tone paint ($31-$40); special ($154-$208); Firemist ($216). Accent stripe ($23). Swing-out rear quarter vent windows: wag ($48). Protective bodyside moldings ($44). Bright rocker panel and wheel opening moldings: S

($34). Bright door edge moldings ($8-$12). Special front bumper ($18). Special rear bumper: wag ($18). Bumper guards ($36); front only ($18). Rear air deflector: wag ($24). Rear storage lock/trim: wag ($14). Interior: Sports console ($71). Divided front seat: Supreme, Vista ($86). Swivel bucket seat: S cpe ($79). Aux. front or rear floor mats ($8). Trunk mat ($10). Cargo floor carpeting: Crsr ($22). Deluxe seatbelts ($15-$18). Wheels and Tires: Super stock II or III wheels ($64-$89). H.D. wheels ($10-$12). Deluxe wheel covers ($32). Wire wheel covers ($103-$120). FR78 x 15 WSW. GR78 x 15 BSW/WSW. HR78 x 15 WSW (wagon).

FULL SIZE (DELTA 88/NINETY-EIGHT/CUSTOM CRUISER/TORONADO) CONVENIENCE/APPEARANCE OPTIONS: Option Packages: Crown Landau pkg.: 88 Royale cpe ($598). Appearance option: Toro ($281). Illumination pkg. ($49). Comfort/Convenience: Air cushion restraint system (N/A). Four season air cond. ($512); tempmatic ($549). Rear defogger, electric ($78). Cruise control ($79). Theft-deterrent system ($115). Soft ray tinted glass ($64). Six-way power seat ($126) exc. 98 bench or driver's seat ($98). Power door locks ($63-$90). Power windows: 88/wag ($159). Powerglide-away tailgate: wag ($52). Power trunk lid release ($17). Tilt steering ($53). Tilt/telescope steering wheel: 98/Toro ($95). Trip odometer/safety sentinel ($19). Electric clock ($20) exc. 98/Toro. Digital clock ($22-$43). Pulse wiper ($28). Locking gas cap ($7). Lighting, Horns and Mirrors: Cornering lamps ($41). Twilight sentinel ($41-$46). Electric monitoring lamp ($43). Courtesy/warning front-door lamps: 88 Royale ($25). Dome/reading lamps ($15). Sports mirrors: 88/wag ($26). Remote driver's mirror: 88/wag ($14). Remote passenger mirror ($28). Lighted visor vanity mirror ($40). Entertainment: AM radio ($92). AM radio w/stereo tape player ($228). AM/FM radio ($153). AM/FM stereo radio ($236); w/tape player ($341). Exterior: Vinyl roof ($136-$150). Landau vinyl roof: 98 cpe ($150). Halo vinyl roof: 98 cpe ($162). Special paint ($128-$173). Two-tone paint: 88/wag ($35-$48); special ($203-$216). Shadow-tone paint: Toro ($239). Protective bodyside moldings ($29-$45). Bright window frame moldings: 88 twn sed ($26). Bright door edge moldings ($8-$12). Bumper guards: 88/98 ($36). Front bumper guards: wag ($18). Roof luggage carrier: wag ($94). Rear storage area lock: wag ($14). Interior: Divided front seat w/twin controls: Royale/Luxury cpe/sed ($87); Royale twn sed/Cust Crsr ($126). Aux. floor mats, front or rear ($8-$11). Aux. front/mats w/carpet inserts ($36-$43). Nylon carpeting ($61). Litter container ($6). Trunk mat ($10). Deluxe seatbelts: wag ($15-$18). Wheels and Tires: Wire wheel covers: 88 ($69-$104). H.D. wheels: 88 ($12). HR78 x 15 WSW: 88 ($41). JR78 x 15 WSW: 98/Toro ($38-$44). JR78 x 15 wide WSW: 98/Toro ($48-$60). LR78 x 15 WSW: wag ($47).

HISTORY: Introduced: September 25, 1975. Model year production: 874,618. Calendar year production: 964,425. Calendar year sales by U.S. dealers: 900,611. Model year sales by U.S. dealers: 851,433.

HISTORICAL FOOTNOTES: Cutlass managed to become the best-selling American automobile in 1976, pulling ahead of Chevrolet. Close to half a million customers chose a Cutlass (486,845 to be precise). Total Oldsmobile sales rose dramatically, markedly exceeding the company's early prediction, with each model posting an increase (though Starfire and Toronado rose only slightly). Overall, Oldsmobile ranked No. 3 in sales.

1977

Although the same six series appeared in Oldsmobile's lineup for 1977, the total number of models declined by six. A V-6 engine replaced the familiar inline six. As in much of the industry, fuel-efficiency got considerable attention this year, along with engineering improvements. Most notable, though, was the first wave

of downsizing: this time of full-size models, reduced to "family size." A four-door sedan was added to the Cutlass Supreme Brougham line, but taken away from Cutlass Salon. The basic Cutlass Supreme Cruiser was discontinued, leaving only one model. Toronado announced an XSR model, which changed its name to XS as production began. A number of smaller, more fuel-efficient engines were introduced: a 140 cubic inch four in Starfire; 231 cubic inch V-6 in Omega/Cutlass/Delta; 260 cubic inch V-8 in Cutlass Salon; 350 V-8 in wagons and 98; and a 403 in Toronado. The big 455 cubic inch V-8 was discontinued. Lighter blocks and heads were used, too, along with lighter Turbo Hydramatic 200 transmissions on some Starfires, Omegas and Delta 88s. Delta 88/98 models had new diagnostic electrical-system analysis. Full-size model instruments could be removed from the passenger side by taking off a trim cover. Oldsmobile bodies carried more wax coating, zinc plating, zinc-rich primers, zincrometal and improved paints for better corrosion resistance.

1977 Oldsmobile, Starfire SX hatchback coupe, (O)

STARFIRE -- SERIES 3H -- FOUR/V-6 -- The Starfire had a new grille with vertical ports, along with a larger emblem between grille sections. Vertical slots made up the grille pattern in the sloping body-color front panel, which was upright at the front. Block lettering replaced the former Oldsmobile script. Deeply recessed, quad rectangular headlamps again were mounted in a soft plastic front-end panel, which flexed with the energy-absorbing front bumper. Amber park/signal lamps were below the bumper. Wide wraparound taillamps came to a sharp point on quarter panels, with small backup lenses at inner ends of each taillamp. The rear hatchback lifted to reveal a carpeted load floor. A space-saver spare tire (with inflator bottle) fit in the right rear quarter well, concealed by a soft trim tire cover. Base engine was now the 140 cubic inch (2.3-liter) four; optional, the 231 cubic inch (3.8-liter) V-6. Four-speed manual gearbox with floor shift was standard. Only one body style was offered: a four-passenger sport coupe with high-back front bucket seats. Base Starfires had vinyl trim and a new interior door design. Carpeting and woodgrain moldings replaced the former map pockets. SX had upgraded trim in cloth or vinyl, with SBR tires, wheel opening moldings, and custom sport steering wheel. Bias-belted tires remained standard on the base model. Starfire's GT option

1977 Oldsmobile, Omega coupe, (O)

was available again, including the V-6 engine, Rallye wheels, raised-white-letter tires, and tachometer, clock and gauges on the dash. Special hood and bodyside stripes (black, white or gold) complemented the body color.

OMEGA/F85 -- SERIES 3X -- V-6/V-8 -- Omega's front end design was similar to 1976, but the grille now displayed an eggcrate (crosshatch) pattern instead of vertical bars. Single headlamps appeared again, with parking lamps in the grille's outboard ends. A body-color bumper center filler was used. Model lineup was the same: F85, standard Omega and Brougham. New taillamps had a flush, full-width appearance. They stretched from the recessed license plate to the outside and wrapped around onto the quarter panel. Square backup lenses were at the center of each lens set. Inside was a new instrument panel and steering wheel. Standard engine was the 231 cubic inch (3.8-liter) V-6, with 260 cubic inch (4.3-liter) V-8 optional. In California and high-altitude areas, the option was a 350 cubic inch V-8 instead. As before, the sporty SX option was available on coupe and hatchback coupe, including special bodyside and wheel opening decals, rocker panel and wheel opening moldings, sports styled mirrors, Rallye suspension and padded-rim custom sport steering wheel.

1977 Oldsmobile, Cutlass Supreme coupe, (O)

1977 Oldsmobile, Cutlass S Colonnade coupe, (O)

CUTLASS S/SUPREME/SALON -- SERIES 3A -- V-6/V-8 -- As in 1976, quad rectangular headlamps on the Cutlass midsize stood above horizontal parking lamps with bright bezel. Once again, different grilles were used on S and Supreme/Salon models, accenting the sportiness of Cutlass S and the more formal image of Supreme and Salon. Cutlass S had a front end with vertical-bar twin-section wrapover grille style similar in concept to the 1976 version, with bold, bright dividers forming eight wide "holes" on each side. But the front vertical segment was taller, wrapping back nearly horizontally along the top. The former version followed an angled front panel. At the rear again were dual stacked taillamps. Once again, Cutlass S could have the 4-4-2 appearance/handling option, with special striping, specific front-end panel, and dual grilles with a series of narrow horizontal bars that carried upward and rearward into the front-end panel. Cutlass Supreme/Brougham/Salon (and Vista Cruiser) had a new grille with vertical bars similar to 1976, but accented with four heavier divider bars on each side. Coupes added a bright molding to the lower part of the rear-end panel. Coupe/sedan taillamps had new vertical lenses and bezels. All Cutlasses had a restyled instrument panel. The clock moved to the right side and a rectangular air outlet replaced the former round units on the passenger side. Base engine was the 231 cubic inch (3.8-liter)

V-6, but the Salon (except in California and high-altitude) had the 260 cubic inch (4.3-liter) V-8 instead. The 4.3-liter engine was optional on other models. The removable hatch roof was optional again on coupes, redesigned with improved latching. Two tinted glass roof panels could be stored in the trunk.

1977 Oldsmobile, Cutlass S-based 4-4-2 coupe, (O)

1977 Oldsmobile, Cutlass Salon coupe with optional hatch roof, (O)

CUTLASS VISTA CRUISER -- SERIES 3A -- V-8 -- Vista Cruisers had the 350 cubic inch (5.7-liter) V-8, optional on other Cutlass models, as standard equipment. Like the others, the 403 cubic inch (6.6-liter) V-8 was optional. Front-end styling was the same as Supreme.

1977 Oldsmobile, Delta 88 Royale coupe, (O)

1977 Oldsmobile, Delta 88 Royale sedan, (O)

DELTA 88 -- SERIES 3B -- V-6/V-8 -- The Delta 88 was totally redesigned and downsized. It now qualified as "family-size" (whatever that might mean). The new version made more efficient use of interior space. Redesigned front/rear seats actually increased back-seat knee and leg room, even though the car was smaller on the outside. Models included the base Delta 88

and Royale, in two-door coupe and four-door town sedan body styles. Front-end design was similar to the former full-size appearance, with twin-segment grille. But each of the four grille sections now contained thin horizontal strips. An Olds emblem decorated the center divider panel. Quad rectangular headlamps stood above matching clear quad horizontal park/turn lamps. Headlamps didn't quite reach the fender tips, and no wraparound markers were used. A separate small amber lens (and clear cornering lens) went ahead of the front wheel: amber above the molding, clear below. Royale kept its standard colored bodyside molding, with extended rocker molding on the rear quarter; but the sail panel emblem was new this year. Royales also had a stand-up Rocket emblem. Both models had wide horizontal taillamps that extended to the license plate opening, with backup and side marker lamps forming an integral, brightly-framed unit at the outer ends (backups at quarter-panel tips). New Oldsmobile block lettering went on the deck lid. Royale models had a swing lock cover. Inside was a new instrument panel, seats, steering wheels and door trim panels. Standard engine was the 231 cubic inch (3.8-liter) V-6 with Turbo Hydra-matic. Three V-8s were optional: 260 cubic inch (4.3-liter), 350 cubic inch (5.7-liter) and 403 cubic inch (6.6-liter). The small-block V-8 was not available in California or high-altitude regions. Standard equipment included power front disc/rear drum brakes, power steering, FR78 x 15 fiberglass-belted radial tires, ashtray and overhead courtesy lamps, electronic message center, carpeted lower doors and chrome wheel covers. Royale added a custom sport bench front seat with fold-down center armrest, velour upholstery, glovebox lamp, bright metal pedal accents, stand-up hood ornament, protective bodyside moldings and bumper impact strips.

1977 Oldsmobile, Custom Cruiser station wagon, (O)

CUSTOM CRUISER -- SERIES 3B -- V-8 -- Cruiser wagons had the same front end and wheelbase as Delta 88 Royale (11 inches shorter in wheelbase than 1976). The floor and lower side-walls in the cargo area had carpeting. A new tailgate could be opened like a regular door, with the glass either up or down; or hinged down after the glass was lowered, to produce a flat area for easier loading. An electric tailgate window was standard. Engines were the same as Ninety-Eight. Custom Cruiser wagons came with two seats, or with optional rear-facing third seat. Either model could have bodyside moldings, or deluxe woodgrain.

NINETY-EIGHT -- SERIES 3C -- V-8 -- Like the Delta 88, the posher Ninety-Eight was sharply downsized, but to a 119 inch wheelbase (three inches longer than the 88). Four models were again offered: two-door coupe and four-door sedan, in Luxury

1977 Oldsmobile, Ninety-Eight Regency coupe, (O)

and Regency series. The grille had a bright, chrome-plated look with broad framework and bright center divider with recessed Ninety-Eight emblem. Each of the two sections contained a tight eggcrate (crosshatch) pattern. As before, quad rectangular headlamps stood above quad park/turn lamps. Separate marker lenses were used. Both models had specific sail panel identification. Regency sedans included an exterior sail panel light. Vertical taillamps in rear-quarter end caps included a Rocket emblem in each lens, and vertical divider. Long horizontal back-up lights with rear reflex, at the decklid's lower edge, extended to the license plate opening on each side. Decklids had new Oldsmobile block lettering. The all-new instrument panel had relocated controls and gauges. New 55/45 divided front seating with dual controls was standard on Regency, available on Luxury models. The 350 cubic inch (5.7-liter) four-barrel V-8 with Turbo Hydra-matic was standard; optional was the 403 cubic inch (6.6-liter) V-8. Standard equipment included power brakes, steering and windows, two-way power seat, GR78 x 15 blackwall steel-belted radial tires, driver's door armrest control console, electronic message centers, electric clock, fold-down center armrests and bumper impact strips. Regency added velour upholstery, a divided front seat with dual controls, digital clock and front seatback pouches.

1977 Oldsmobile, Toronado XSR coupe, (O)

1977 Oldsmobile, 98 Regency sedan, (O)

TORONADO -- SERIES 3E -- V-8 -- Appearance of the front-drive Oldsmobile was similar to 1976, but the grille had a different look. Still squat, it was nonetheless taller than before, now displaying a wide-hole rectangular eggcrate pattern (10 x 4 hole) instead of the former horizontal strips. Quad headlamps now stood above quad park/signal lamps, and identifying lamps instead of parking lights went into each front fender tip. Small slots were inboard of bumper guards. A small 'Oldsmobile' nameplate went above the grille on the driver's side, replacing the former full-width lettering. Horizontal amber/clear marker/cornering lenses were mounted ahead of the front wheel panel. In addition to the basic Brougham, Toronado offered a new XSR (changed to XS) model that had a restyled roof with panoramic wraparound back window. Twin electrically-operated glass panels were above the driver and passenger seats, which slid inboard and could be stowed (one above the other) in the center roof section. XS/XSR had special identification and wheel covers. A 403 cubic inch (6.6-liter) V-8 with Turbo Hydra-matic was standard. All Toronados had electronic spark timing (EST) with an on-board microprocessor that continuously adjusted ignition timing, and monitored engine vacuum, coolant temperature and engine speed. Standard equipment included power front disc/rear drum brakes, power steering, electric windows,

air conditioning, maintenance-free battery, velour upholstery, digital clock, Four Season air conditioning, cornering lamps, inside day/night mirror, lower front bumper guards and bumper impact strips. Bright metal moldings decorated the roof, window sill, rocker panel and wheel openings. Bodies had color-coordinated protective moldings. Tires were JR78 x 15 blackwall steel-belted radials.

1977 Oldsmobile, Toronado Brougham coupe, (O)

I.D. DATA: The 13-symbol Vehicle Identification Number (VIN) was located on the upper left surface of the instrument panel, visible through the windshield. The first digit is '3', indicating Oldsmobile division. Next is a letter indicating series: 'T' = Starfire; 'D' = Starfire SX; 'S' = Omega F85; 'B' = Omega; 'E' = Omega Brougham; 'G' = Cutlass S; 'J' = Cutlass Supreme or Vista Cruiser; 'M' = Cutlass Supreme Brougham; 'K' = Cutlass Salon; 'H' = Cutlass Supreme Cruiser; 'L' = Delta 88; 'N' = Delta 88 Royale; 'Q' = Custom Cruiser; 'V' = Ninety-Eight Luxury; 'X' = Ninety-Eight Regency; 'Z' = Toronado Brougham; 'W' = Toronado XS/XSR. Next come two digits that denote body type: '07' = Starfire coupe; '17' = Omega 2-dr. hatchback coupe; '27' = Omega 2-dr. pillar coupe; '37' = 2-dr. Colonnade or HT coupe; '57' = 2-dr. Colonnade coupe or HT coupe; '29' = 4-dr. HT sedan; '39' = 4-dr. HT (4-window) sedan; '69' = 4-dr. thin-pillar (4-window) sedan; '35' = 4-dr. 2-seat wagon; '45' = 4-dr. 3-seat wagon. The fifth symbol is a letter indicating engine code: 'B' = L4-140 2Bbl.; 'A' or 'C' = V-6-231 2Bbl.; 'F' = V-8-260 2Bbl.; 'U' = V-8-305 2Bbl.; 'R' = V-8-350 4Bbl.; 'L' = Omega V-8-350 4Bbl.; 'K' = V-8-403 4Bbl. The sixth symbol denotes model year ('7' = 1977). Next is a plant code: '2' = Ste. Therese, Quebec (Canada); 'L' = Van Nuys, Calif.; 'G' = Framingham, Mass.; 'D' = Doraville, Georgia; 'M' = Lansing, Mich.; 'W' = Willow Run, Mich.; 'R' = Arlington, Texas; 'C' = Southgate, Calif.; 'X' = Fairfax, Kansas; 'E' = Linden, New Jersey. The final six digits are the sequential serial number, which began with 100001. Engine numbers were stamped on the right front of the block (Buick-built engines), on the right side (Chevrolet-built V-8), or on the oil filler tube (Oldsmobile engines). Four-cylinder engine numbers were on a pad at right of block, above the starter. A body number plate on the shroud identified model year, car division, series, style, body assembly plant, body number, trim combination, modular seat code, paint code and date built code.

STARFIRE (FOUR/V-6)

Model Number	Body/Style Number	Body Type & Seating	Factory Price	Shipping Weight	Production Total
3H	T07	2-dr. Hatch Cpe-4P	3802/3942	—/2808	4,910

STARFIRE SX (FOUR/V-6)

Model Number	Body/Style Number	Body Type & Seating	Factory Price	Shipping Weight	Production Total
3H	D07	2-dr. Hatch Cpe-4P	3999/4139	—/2836	14,181

OMEGA F-85 (V-6/V-8)

Model Number	Body/Style Number	Body Type & Seating	Factory Price	Shipping Weight	Production Total
3X	S27	2-dr. Cpe-6P	3653/3998	3109/3258	2,241

OMEGA (V-6/V-8)

Model Number	Body/Style Number	Body Type & Seating	Factory Price	Shipping Weight	Production Total
3X	B27	2-dr. Cpe-6P	3740/3785	3127/3276	18,611
3X	B17	2-dr. Hatch Cpe-6P	3904/3949	3196/3345	4,739
3X	B69	4-dr. Sed-6P	3797/3842	3162/3311	21,723

OMEGA BROUGHAM (V-6V-8)

Model Number	Body/Style Number	Body Type & Seating	Factory Price	Shipping Weight	Production Total
3X	E27	2-dr. Cpe-6P	3934/3979	3151/3300	6,478
3X	E17	2-dr. Hatch Cpe-6P	4104/4149	3228/3377	1,189
3X	E69	4-dr. Sed-6P	3994/4039	3188/3337	9,003

CUTLASS 'S' (V-6/V-8)

Model Number	Body/Style Number	Body Type & Seating	Factory Price	Shipping Weight	Production Total
3A	G37	2-dr. Col Cpe-6P	4350/4395	3535/3680	70,155
3A	G29	4-dr. Col Sed-6P	4386/4431	3618/3763	42,923

CUTLASS SUPREME (V-6/V-8)

Model Number	Body/Style Number	Body Type & Seating	Factory Price	Shipping Weight	Production Total
3A	J57	2-dr. Col Cpe-6P	4609/4714	3565/3710	242,874
3A	J29	4-dr. Col Sed-6P	4733/4778	3666/3811	37,929

CUTLASS SUPREME CRUISER (V-8)

Model Number	Body/Style Number	Body Type & Seating	Factory Price	Shipping Weight	Production Total
3A	H35	4-dr. 2S Sta Wag-6P	N/A	4218	14,838

CUTLASS VISTA CRUISER (V-8)

Model Number	Body/Style Number	Body Type & Seating	Factory Price	Shipping Weight	Production Total
3A	J35	4-dr. 2S Sta Wag-6P	5242	4273	25,816

CUTLASS SUPREME BROUGHAM (V-6/V-8)

Model Number	Body/Style Number	Body Type & Seating	Factory Price	Shipping Weight	Production Total
3A	M57	2-dr. Cpe-5P	4968/5013	3584/3729	124,712
3A	M29	4-dr. Sed-6P	5032/5077	3692/3837	16,738

CUTLASS SALON (V-8)

Model Number	Body/Style Number	Body Type & Seating	Factory Price	Shipping Weight	Production Total
3A	K57	2-dr. Col Cpe-5P	5268	3787	56,757

DELTA 88 (V-6/V-8)

Model Number	Body/Style Number	Body Type & Seating	Factory Price	Shipping Weight	Production Total
3B	L37	2-dr. Cpe-6P	5144/5189	3431/3561	8,788
3B	L69	4-dr. Town Sed-6P	5204/5249	3472/3602	26,084

DELTA 88 ROYALE (V-6/V-8)

Model Number	Body/Style Number	Body Type & Seating	Factory Price	Shipping Weight	Production Total
3B	N37	2-dr. Cpe-6P	5362/5407	3440/3570	61,138
3B	N69	4-dr. Town Sed-6P	5432/5477	3496/3626	117,571

Production Note: A total of 2,401 Indy Pace Car replicas (W44) were built, which cost $914 more than the base model.

CUSTOM CRUISER (V-8)

Model Number	Body/Style Number	Body Type & Seating	Factory Price	Shipping Weight	Production Total
3B	Q35	4-dr. 2S Sta Wag-6P	5922	4064	32,827
3B	N/A	4-dr. 3S Sta Wag-8P	N/A	4095	Note 1

Note 1: Three-seat production is included in two-seat total.

NINETY-EIGHT LUXURY (V-8)

Model Number	Body/Style Number	Body Type & Seating	Factory Price	Shipping Weight	Production Total
3C	V37	2-dr. Cpe-6P	6808	3753	5,058
3C	V69	4-dr. Town Sedan-6P	6785	3807	14,323

NINETY-EIGHT REGENCY (V-8)

Model Number	Body/Style Number	Body Type & Seating	Factory Price	Shipping Weight	Production Total
3C	X37	2-dr. Cpe-6P	6948	3767	32,072
3C	X69	4-dr. Town Sedan-6P	7132	3840	87,970

TORONADO BROUGHAM (V-8)

Model Number	Body/Style Number	Body Type & Seating	Factory Price	Shipping Weight	Production Total
3E	Z57	2-dr. Cpe-6P	8133	4634	31,371

TORONADO XS/XSR (V-8)

Model Number	Body/Style Number	Body Type & Seating	Factory Price	Shipping Weight	Production Total
3E	W57	2-dr. Cpe-6P	11132	4688	2,713

Production Note: 176 Toronado chassis also were produced. Oldsmobile production totals listed separately one XSR coupe (W57).

FACTORY PRICE AND WEIGHT NOTE: For Omega, Cutlass and Delta 88, prices and weights to left of slash are for six-cylinder, to right for V-8 engine. For Starfire, prices/weights to left are for four-cylinder, to right for V-6.

ENGINE DATA: BASE FOUR (Starfire): Inline, overhead-cam four-cylinder. Aluminum block. Displacement: 140 cu. in. (2.3 liters). Bore & stroke: 3.50 x 3.63 in. Compression ratio: 8.0:1. Brake horsepower: 84 at 4400 rpm. Torque: 117 lb.-ft. at 2400 rpm. Five main bearings. Hydraulic valve lifters. Carburetor: 2Bbl. Holley 5210C. VIN Code: B. BASE V-6 (Omega, Cutlass, Delta 88); OPTIONAL (Starfire): 90-degree, overhead-valve V-6. Cast iron block and head. Displacement: 231 cu. in. (3.8 liters). Bore & stroke: 3.80 x 3.40 in. Compression ratio: 8.0:1. Brake horsepower: 105 at 3400 rpm. Torque: 185 lb.-ft. at 2000 rpm. Four main bearings. Hydraulic valve lifters. Carburetor: 2Bbl. Rochester 2GC. VIN Code: A or C. BASE V-8 (Cutlass Salon); OPTIONAL (Omega, Cutlass, Delta 88): 90-degree, overhead valve V-8. Cast iron block and head. Displacement: 260 cu. in. (4.3 liters). Bore & stroke: 3.50 x 3.39 in. Compression ratio: 7.5:1. Brake horsepower: 110 at 3400 rpm. Torque: 205 lb.-ft. at 1800 rpm. Five main bearings. Hydraulic valve lifters. Carburetor: 2Bbl. Rochester. VIN Code: F. OPTIONAL V-8 (Omega): 90-degree, overhead valve V-8. Cast iron block and head. Displacement: 305 cu. in. (5.0 liters). Bore & stroke: 3.74 x 3.48 in. Compression ratio: 8.5:1. Brake horsepower: 145 at 3800 rpm. Torque: 245 lb.-ft. at 2400 rpm. Five main bearings. Hydraulic valve lifters. Carburetor: 2Bbl. VIN Code: U. OPTIONAL V-8 (Omega): 90-degree, overhead valve V-8. Cast iron block and head. Displacement: 350 cu. in. (5.7 liters). Bore & stroke: 4.00 x 3.48 in. Compression ratio: 8.5:1. Brake horsepower: 170 at 3800 rpm. Torque: 270 lb.-ft. at 2400 rpm. Five main bearings. Hydraulic valve lifters. Carburetor: 4Bbl. Rochester M4MC. VIN Code: L. BASE V-8 (98, Vista/Custom Cruiser wagon); OPTIONAL (Cutlass, Delta 88): 90-degree, overhead valve V-8. Cast iron block and head. Displacement: 350 cu. in. (5.7 liters). Bore & stroke: 4.06 x 3.39 in. Compression ratio: 8.0:1. Brake horsepower: 170 at 3800 rpm. Torque: 275 lb.-ft. at 2000 rpm. Five main bearings. Hydraulic valve lifters. Carburetor: 4Bbl. Rochester. VIN Code: R. BASE V-8 (Toronado); OPTIONAL (Cutlass, Delta 88, 98): 90-degree, overhead valve V-8. Cast iron block and head. Displacement: 403 cu. in. (6.6 liters). Bore & stroke: 4.35 x 3.39 in. Compression ratio: 8.0:1. Brake horsepower: 185 at 3600 rpm. (Toronado, 200 at 3600). Torque: 320 lb.-ft. at 2200 rpm. (Toronado, 330 at 2400). Five main bearings. Hydraulic valve lifters. Carburetor: 4Bbl. Rochester. VIN Code: K.

CHASSIS DATA: Wheelbase: (Starfire) 97.0 in.; (Omega) 111.0 in.; (Cutlass cpe) 112.0 in.; (Cutlass sed) 116.0 in.; (Cutlass wag) 116.0 in.; (Delta 88) 116.0 in.; (Ninety-Eight) 119.0 in.; (Custom Crsr) 116.0 in.; (Toronado) 122.0 in. Overall Length: (Starfire) 179.3 in.; (Omega) 199.6 in.; (Cutlass cpe) 209.6 in.; (Cutlass sed) 215.2 in.; (Cutlass wag) 219.9 in.; (Delta 88) 217.5 in.; (Ninety-Eight) 220.4 in.; (Custom Crsr) 217.1 in.; (Toronado) 227.5 in. Height: (Starfire) 50.2 in.; (Omega cpe) 53.8 in.; (Omega sed) 54.7 in.; (Cutlass cpe) 53.4 in.; (Cutlass sed) 54.1 in.; (Cutlass wag) 55.5 in.; (Delta 88 cpe) 54.5 in.; (Delta 88 sed) 55.7 in.; (Ninety-Eight cpe) 55.5 in.; (Ninety-Eight sed) 56.6 in.; (Custom Crsr) 58.0 in.; (Toronado) 53.2 in. Width: (Starfire) 65.4 in.; (Omega) 72.9 in.; (Cutlass cpe) 76.2 in.; (Cutlass sed) 76.7 in.; (Cutlass wag) 77.7 in.; (Delta 88) 76.8 in.; (Ninety-Eight) 76.8 in.; (Custom Crsr) 79.8 in.; (Toronado) 80.0 in. Front Tread: (Starfire) 54.7 in.; (Omega) 61.3 in.; (Cutlass) 61.0-61.1 in.; (Delta 88/Ninety-Eight) 61.7 in.; (Custom Crsr) 62.1 in.; (Toronado) 63.6 in. Rear Tread: (Starfire) 53.6 in.; (Omega) 59.0 in.; (Cutlass) 60.7 in.; (Delta 88/Ninety-Eight) 60.7 in.; (Custom Crsr) 64.1 in.; (Toronado) 63.5 in. Standard Tires: (Starfire) A78 x 13; (Starfire SX) BR78 x 13; (Omega) E78 x 14; (Cutlass) FR78 x 15; (Cutlass wag) HR78 x 15; (Cutlass Salon) GR78 x 15; (Delta 88) FR78 x 15; (Ninety-Eight) GR78 x 15; (Custom Crsr) HR78 x 15; (Toronado) JR78 x 15.

TECHNICAL: Transmission: Three-speed manual transmission (column shift) standard on Omega/Cutlass V-6. Gear ratios: (1st) 3.11:1; (2nd) 1.84:1; (3rd) 1.00:1; (Rev) 3.22:1. Four-speed floor shift standard on Starfire, and on Cutlass V-6 or V-8-260: (1st) 3.11:1; (2nd) 2.20:1; (3rd) 1.47:1; (4th) 1.00:1; (Rev) 3.11:1. Five-speed manual optional on Starfire: (1st) 3.40:1; (2nd) 2.08:1; (3rd) 1.39:1; (4th) 1.00:1; (5th) 0.80:1; (Rev) 3.36:1. Five-speed manual on Omega with V-8-260 and Cutlass coupe with V-6: (1st) 3.10:1; (2nd) 1.89:1;

(3rd) 1.27:1; (4th) 1.00:1; (5th) 0.84:1; (Rev) 3.06:1. Three-speed Turbo Hydra-matic standard on other models, optional on all. Standard final drive ratio: (Starfire) 3.42:1; (Omega) 3.08:1; (Cutlass S/Supreme) 3.08:1; (Cutlass Salon/Brghm) 2.73:1; (Cutlass Cruiser) 2.73:1; (Delta 88) 2.73:1; (Custom Crsr) 2.73:1; (Ninety-Eight) 2.41:1; (Toronado) 2.73:1. Steering: Recirculating ball. Front Suspension: (Starfire) coil springs w/lower trailing links and anti-sway bar; (Toronado); longitudinal torsion bars w/anti-sway bar; (others) coil springs w/control arms and anti-sway bar. Rear Suspension: (Starfire) rigid axle w/coil springs, lower trailing radius arms, upper torque arms, transverse linkage bar and anti-sway bar; (Omega) rigid axle w/ semi-elliptic leaf springs; (others) rigid axle w/coil springs, lower trailing radius arms and upper torque arms. Brakes: Front disc, rear drum. Ignition: Electronic. Body construction: (Starfire) unibody; (Omega) unibody w/separate front partial frame; (others) separate body on perimeter frame. Fuel Tank: (Starfire) 18.5 gal.; (Omega) 21 gal.; (Cutlass) 22 gal.; (Cutlass wag) 22 gal.; (Delta 88) 21 gal.; (Ninety-Eight) 24.5 gal.; (Custom Crsr wag) 22 gal.; (Toronado) 26 gal.

DRIVETRAIN OPTIONS: Engines: 231 cu. in. V-6: Starfire ($140). 260 cu. in. V-8: Omega/Cutlass/88 ($45). 305 cu. in. 2Bbl. V-8: Omega ($65). 350 cu. in. 4Bbl. V-8: Omega/Cutlass/88 ($155) exc. Vista ($110). 403 cu. in. V-8: Cutlass ($220) exc. Salon ($175); Cutlass Vista wag ($65); Delta 88 ($220); 98/Custom Crsr ($65). Transmission/Differential: Five-speed manual floor shift: Starfire ($248); Cutlass ($282). Turbo Hydra-matic: Starfire ($248); Omega/Cutlass ($282). Anti-spin axle: Starfire ($51); Omega/Cutlass ($54); full-size ($57). Brakes/Steering: Power brakes: Starfire ($58); Omega ($61). Power steering: Starfire ($127); Omega ($144). Suspension: Driver-controlled leveling system: Cutlass/Vista ($90); full-size ($91). Rallye susp. pkg.: Omega/Cutlass ($27). H.D. susp.: Cutlass ($24); 88/98 ($24); Vista/Toronado ($18). Firm ride shock absorbers: Cutlass/88/98 ($7). Superlift rear shocks: Cutlass/Vista ($48); full-size ($49). Rear stabilizer bar: Starfire ($17). Other: High-capacity cooling: Omega ($19-$54); Cutlass ($19-$66); full-size ($6-$24). High-capacity radiator: Starfire ($18). H.D. battery: Starfire ($16); full-size ($18). High-capacity alternator: Cutlass/Vista/full-size ($46). Trailer wiring: Cutlass/full-size ($20-$32). Engine block heater ($13) exc. Starfire. California emissions equipment ($70). High-altitude emissions ($22).

STARFIRE CONVENIENCE/APPEARANCE OPTIONS: Option Packages: GT pkg. ($451-$567). Aux. lighting group ($13). Comfort/Convenience: Air cond. ($442). Rear defogger, electric ($71). Tinted glass ($48). Tilt steering ($50). Tach/volt/temp gauges ($56). Electric clock ($18). Sport mirrors ($29). Tilt inside mirror ($8). Entertainment: AM radio ($71). AM/FM radio ($134). AM/FM stereo radio ($219); w/tape player ($316). Rear speakers ($20). Windshield antenna ($23). Exterior: Accent stripe ($25). Protective bodyside moldings ($40). Door edge moldings ($9). Wheel opening moldings: base ($19). Interior: Sports console ($77). Driver's seatback adjuster ($18). Front/rear floor mats ($15). Deluxe seatbelts ($15). Wheels and Tires: Super stock III wheels ($74-$84). Deluxe wheel covers ($41). A78 x 13 WSW. B78 x 13 WSW. BR78 x 13 BSW/WSW/RWL. Conventional spare (NC).

OMEGA CONVENIENCE/APPEARANCE OPTIONS: Option Packages: SX pkg.: base hatch/cpe ($187). Convenience group ($28-$29). Comfort/Convenience: Air cond. ($478). Forced-air rear defogger ($48). Cruise control ($80). Tinted glass ($50). Power windows ($108-$151). Power door locks ($68-$96). Custom sport steering wheel ($36). Tilt steering ($57). Tachometer/voltage/temp gauges ($98). Electric clock ($21). Lighter: F85 ($6). Pulse wipers ($30). Horns and Mirrors: Dual horns ($7). Remote driver's mirror ($15). Sport mirrors ($28). Tilt inside mirror: F85 ($8). Entertainment: AM radio ($75). AM/FM radio ($137). AM/FM stereo radio ($233); w/tape player ($337). Rear speakers ($20). Windshield antenna ($23). Exterior: Full vinyl roof ($93). Landau vinyl roof: cpe ($162). Two-

tone paint ($42). Accent stripe ($24). Swing-out rear quarter vent windows ($51). Roof drip moldings ($17). Rocker panel moldings ($16). Protective bodyside moldings ($38). Wheel opening moldings ($18). Door edge moldings ($9-$13). Window frame moldings: F85 ($21). Bumper guards ($67). Bumper rub strips ($29). Interior: Sports console ($75). Bucket seats ($84). Aux. front or rear floor mats ($8). Deluxe seatbelts ($15). Wheels and Tires: Custom sport wheels ($78-$89). E78 x 14 WSW. ER78 x 14 BSW/WSW. FR78 x 14 RWL SBR. Stowaway spare ($17).

CUTLASS CONVENIENCE/APPEARANCE OPTIONS: Option Packages: 4-4-2 appearance/handling package: S cpe ($169). Convenience group ($24-$34). Comfort/Convenience: Four season air cond. ($499); tempmatic ($538). Rear defogger, electric ($82). Cruise control ($80). Tinted glass ($54). Six-way power driver's or bench seat ($137). Power windows ($108-$151). Power door locks ($68-$96). Power trunk release ($18). Tilt steering ($57). Instrument panel cluster ($37). Fuel economy meter ($27). Trip odometer ($11). Electric clock ($21). Digital clock ($46). Pulse wipers ($30). Lighting and Mirrors: Dome reading lamps ($16). Sport mirrors ($28). Remote driver's mirror ($15). Remote passenger mirror ($30). Lighted visor vanity mirror ($41). Entertainment: AM radio ($79). AM/FM radio ($142). AM/FM stereo radio ($233); w/ tape player ($337); w/CB radio ($453). CB radio ($195). Rear speakers ($21). Windshield antenna ($23). Power antenna ($42). Exterior: Hatch roof w/removable glass panels ($587). Full vinyl roof ($111). Landau vinyl roof: cpe ($111). Special solid-color paint ($133-$182). Two-tone paint ($42); special ($175-$219); Firemist ($229). Woodgrain paneling: Vista ($134). Accent stripe ($24). Swing-out rear quarter vent windows: wag ($51). Protective bodyside moldings ($45). Rocker panel and wheel opening moldings: S ($36). Door edge moldings ($9-$13). Special front or rear bumper ($19). Bumper guards ($38); front only ($19). Rear air deflector: wag ($25). Rear storage lock/trim: wag ($15). Roof luggage rack: wag ($75). Interior: Sports console ($75). Rear-facing third seat: wagon ($152). Divided front seat: Supreme, Vista ($91). Bucket seats: S cpe ($84). Aux. front or rear floor mats ($9). Carpeted front mats ($21); rear ($17). Litter container ($7). Trunk mat ($11). Cargo floor carpeting: Vista ($23). Deluxe seatbelts ($15-$19). Wheels and Tires: Super stock II or III wheels ($64-$89). H.D. wheels ($10-$13). Deluxe wheel covers ($34). Wire wheel covers ($103-$120). FR78 x 15 BSW/WSW SBR. FR78 x 15 WSW GBR. GR78 x 15 BSW/WSW SBR. GR70 x 15 RWL SBR. Stowaway spare ($17).

1977 Oldsmobile, Delta 88 Targa coupe Indianapolis 500 Pace Car, (IMS)

FULL SIZE (DELTA 88/NINETY-EIGHT/CUSTOM CRUISER/ TORONADO) CONVENIENCE/APPEARANCE OPTIONS: Option Packages: Appearance option: Toronado ($300). Illumination pkg. ($52) exc. Toronado. Convenience group ($10-$35). Reminder pkg. ($44). Comfort/Convenience: Four season air cond. ($539); tempmatic ($578) exc. Toronado ($39). Rear defogger, electric ($83). Cruise control ($84). Tinted glass ($69). Six-way power bench or driver's seat: 88/wag ($139); 98 ($109). Six-way power passenger seat ($139) except 88.

Power door locks ($70-$98) exc. wag ($131). Power door locks w/seatback release: Toronado ($96). Power windows: 88/wag ($114-$171). Power trunk lid release ($18). Tilt steering ($58). Tilt/telescope steering wheel: 98/Toronado ($101). Special instrument cluster: Toronado ($37). Trip odometer ($11) exc. Toronado. Fuel economy meter ($27) exc. Toronado. Electric clock: 88/wag ($21). Digital clock: 88/wag ($46); 98 ($23). Pulse wiper ($30). Lighting and Mirrors: Cornering lamps ($44) exc. Toronado. Twilight sentinel ($42). Electric monitoring lamp: 98/Toronado ($46). Courtesy/warning lamps: 88 Royale ($27). Dome/reading lamps ($16). Sport mirrors: 88/wag ($23-$28). Remote driver's mirror: 88/wag ($15). remote driver's mirror w/thermometer ($25-$39). Remote passenger mirror ($25-$30). Lighted visor vanity mirror ($42) exc. Toronado. Entertainment: AM radio ($92) ex. Toronado. AM/FM radio ($153). AM/FM stereo radio ($236); w/tape player ($341). AM/FM stereo radio w/digital clock: 98/Toronado ($341-$364). AM/FM stereo w/CB ($459); N/A on wagon. CB radio ($197); N/A on wagon. Windshield antenna ($23). Power antenna ($42). Rear speaker ($21). Exterior: Electric astroroof ($898). Electric sunroof ($734). Full vinyl roof ($138-$179). Landau vinyl roof: 88/98 cpe ($166-$179); Toronado XSR ($258). Special paint ($135-$184). Two-tone magic mirror paint: 88 cpe ($51). Firemist paint ($232). Lower bodyside paint: 88 ($100). Accent striping: 88/98 ($24). Woodgrain paneling: wag ($172). Protective bodyside moldings ($40-$46). Door edge moldings ($9-$13). Bumper guards: 88/98/wag ($38). Special rear bumper: Toronado ($13). Rear bumper step: wag ($15). Roof luggage carrier: wag ($125). Tailgate lock release: wag ($30). Interior: Divided front seat w/twin controls: Royale/Luxury ($92); wag ($134). Third seat: wagon ($175). Reclining passenger seat ($55-$79) exc. Toronado. Custom leather trim: 98 Regency ($204). Aux. floor mats, front or rear ($9-$12). Aux. mats w/carpet inserts: front ($21); rear ($17). Aux. floor mats w/carpet inserts: Toronado ($46). Litter container ($7). Trunk mat ($11). Deluxe seatbelts: 88/wag ($16-$19). Wheels and Tires: Deluxe wheel covers ($39) exc. Toronado. Wire wheel covers ($104) exc. Toronado. Custom chrome wheels: 88/98 ($100-$117). Custom sport chrome wheels: 88 ($100-$117). H.D. wheels: 88/98 ($10-$13). FR78 x 15 BSW: 88 ($36-$45); WSW ($69-$86). FR78 x 15 WSW GBR: 88 ($33-$41). GR78 x 15 WSW: 98 ($34-$43); wide WSW ($48-$60). HR78 x 15 WSW: wag ($47). JR78 x 15 WSW: Toronado ($40-$50). JR78 x 15 wide WSW: Toronado ($54-$67). Stowaway spare (NC) exc. Toronado.

HISTORY: Introduced: September 30, 1976. Model year production: 1,135,909. Calendar year production: 1,079,836. Calendar year sales by U.S. dealers: 977,046. Model year sales by U.S. dealers: 1,135,909.

HISTORICAL FOOTNOTES: Once again, Oldsmobile hit the No. 3 position in sales, exceeding one million for the first time. Cutlass again led the pack, and also played a role in NASCAR racing. Like other GM divisions, Oldsmobile promoted its freshly downsized big cars for their space- and fuel-efficiency. Diesel power was expected to become available in midyear, but delayed until model year 1978 so the current state of emissions standards could be evaluated. Abandonment of the 455 cubic inch V-8 would be just the beginning of a continual reduction of engine displacement in the years ahead.

1978

Following the full-size downsizing of 1977, the midsize Cutlass line followed, reduced to a 108.1-inch wheelbase. Cutlass coupes and sedans were an average of 657 pounds lighter, (60 pounds saved by a new frame design). Certain 260 cubic inch V-8s lost 38 pounds by switching to an aluminum intake manifold and lighter weight exhaust manifolds. Many Cutlass and 88 hoods had aluminum panels. Some Cutlass models used alumi-

num brake drums. Cutlass also had new plug-in instrument panel components. In other major news, a diesel engine of 350 cubic inch (5.7-liter) displacement became available as an option on Delta 88, Ninety-Eight and Custom Cruiser models. Derived from the gas fueled 350, many components were strengthened to handle the higher diesel compression -- but not strengthened enough, in view of problems that developed later with General Motors' diesels. Tests revealed a fuel mileage gain of up to 25 percent with the diesel over comparable gas engines. That was no small matter at a time when memories of the gas crisis were still quite fresh, and further crises seemed imminent.

1978 Oldsmobile, Starfire GT hatchback coupe, (O)

1978 Oldsmobile, Starfire hatchback coupe, (O)

STARFIRE -- SERIES 3H -- FOUR/V-6/V-8 -- The appearance of the Starfire was similar to 1977. The grille was made up of vertical bars, with soft front end and quad rectangular headlamps. At the rear: a lift-up hatchback, opening to a carpeted load floor. Base engine was Pontiac's "Iron Duke" 151 cubic inch (2.5-liter) four; optional, either a 231 cubic inch (3.8-liter) V-6 or 305 cubic inch (5.0-liter) V-8. Both base and SX models had the GT option (RPO code Y74). It came with V-6 engine, GT stripe (black, white or metallic gold) to complement the body color, Rallye wheels, raised-white-letter tires and a tachometer. A total of 905 GT options were installed on base Starfires, 2,299 on SX. New was a Firenza package (RPO code Y65),

1978 Oldsmobile, Omega coupe, (O)

2,523 were installed on Starfire SX models. Intended to deliver a "sports car" look, this package included a special front air dam, rear spoiler, front/rear wheel opening flares, sport mirrors, wide-oval tires on star spoke wheels, rally suspension and large 'Firenza' decal lettering on the door. Special paint treatment consisted of black lower bodysides with red accent striping that continued into the front and rear bumper. Firenza came in white, black, silver or bright red body colors.

OMEGA -- SERIES 3X -- V-6/V-8 -- Five models remained in the compact Omega line, as both the budget F85 and Brougham hatchback dropped out. Omega's front end displayed a new single-unit, six-section horizontal-bar (three sections on each side) grille with large surround moldings. Each section contained thin horizontal strips. Parking lamps again were mounted in outboard ends of the grille, within the same framework. Single headlamps appeared, as did the flush taillamps for a full-length look. Bumper rub strips were optional. The 231 cubic inch V-6 with three-speed column shift was standard. Optional was the 305 cubic inch V-8 (in California and high-altitude, the 350 V-8). Both the standard and hatchback coupe again could have the SX sporty option, with special bodyside decals, rocker panel and wheel opening moldings, sports mirrors, Rallye suspension and custom sport steering wheel. Topping the line was the LS option, billed as "Oldsmobile's small luxury limousine." It was a Brougham sedan option, including the V-6 engine, automatic transmission, air conditioning, AM/FM stereo, painted wheel covers, special lower bodyside accent paint and 'LS' sail panel emblems. A total of 1,198 LS packages (RPO code Y61) went into four-door Broughams.

1978 Oldsmobile, Cutlass Supreme Brougham coupe, (O)

1978 Oldsmobile, Cutlass Salon slantback coupe, (O)

CUTLASS -- SERIES 3A -- V-6/V-8 -- The resized Cutlass mid-size series had eight models: coupe and sedan in the fastback Salon and Salon Brougham, Supreme, Calais and Supreme Brougham coupe and two-seat Cruiser wagon. Styling differed, especially in the grille pattern and shape. Cutlass used an independent front suspension with wishbone-type upper and lower control arms, coil springs and link-type stabilizer. At the rear was a conventional four-link design with coil springs mounted atop the axle tube, and shock absorbers behind the axle. All Cutlass models had a standard 231 cubic inch (3.8-liter) V-6 with two-barrel carb. Three-speed manual shift was standard. Options included 260 and 305 cubic inch V-8s. Wagons had

standard automatic transmission, and high-altitude versions could get a 350 cubic inch V-8. Gas tanks shrunk to 17.5 gallons (18.2 on wagons) and trunks had a new compact spare tire. Restyled instrument panels put the speedometer, gauges and other items in a driver's side pod. The headlamp dimmer was now part of the turn signal lever. All had single rectangular headlamps alongside clear vertical park/turn lamps (in the same housing). Cutlass Salon used a four-section eggcrate (cross-hatch-pattern) upright grille surrounded by bright moldings. Coupes had frameless door glass; sedans had door frames with bright window frame scalp moldings. Large square taillamps had integrated backup lamps in the lower portion. The decklid had a full-length lower molding. Salon Brougham's grille was an eight-section upright vertical eggcrate design (four sections on each side). A stand-up Olds emblem went on the front end panel. Hoods had a center molding. Wide lower moldings were used on front fenders, doors, quarter panels, and behind the rear quarters. Sedan window frames were black. Brougham looked the same as Salon at the rear, except for a wide lower decklid molding with horizontal simulated reflex band. As before, the sporty 4-4-2 appearance/handling option on Salon and Salon Brougham coupes was available. It had a blacked-out grille and wide '4-4-2' stripe along the lower sides and decklid bottom. Supreme had a traditional Olds dual vertical six-element grille that wrapped over the front-end panel. Thin vertical bars were split into three sections on each side of the body-colored center divider. A molding extended below the headlamp housing, across the bottom of the front-end panel, to give a full-width look. Standard features included a stand-up Olds emblem and hood center molding. No bumper slots were used. At Supreme's rear, single-unit vertical taillamps at protruding quarter-panel tips were surrounded by bright moldings, with a lighted center Oldsmobile emblem and backup lights at each side of the license plate opening. The decklid held a narrow full-width lower molding. Supreme Brougham had the regular Supreme front end, but with a Brougham name on brushed chrome background of the front-end panel. Broughams had wide belt moldings, bright drip moldings, wheel opening and rocker panel

1978 Oldsmobile, Delta 88 coupe, (O)

1978 Oldsmobile, Cutlass Salon Brougham slantback sedan, (O)

143

moldings, and wide lower moldings on front fenders, doors, quarters, and rear of rear quarters. Cutlass Calais was built on a Supreme body, but with its own wrapover vertical eggcrate-style grille and stand-up hood ornament. Vertical bars appeared dominant in the crosshatch grille pattern. Calais features included wide belt moldings and wide lower moldings on front fenders, doors, quarters and rear of rear quarters, plus a body lock pillar appliqué. Cutlass Cruiser had the same front-end look as Salon Brougham, with standard wheel opening, rocker panel, drip and window moldings. Optional woodgrained vinyl had bright surrounding moldings as well as wide lower moldings on front fenders, doors and quarter panels. Cutlass standard equipment included a heater/defroster, lighter, day/night mirror and rocker panel and wheel opening moldings (except base Salon). Cutlass Cruiser had power brakes and automatic transmission. Salon models had chrome wheels and P185/75R14 glass-belted radial tires; Salon Brougham, P195/75R14. Supreme and Calais had P195/75R14 steel-belted radials.

1978 Oldsmobile, Cutlass Calais coupe, (O)

1978 Oldsmobile, Cutlass Cruiser station wagon, (O)

DELTA 88 -- SERIES 3B -- V-6/V-8 -- A new 88 dual three-segment eggcrate grille used two horizontal divider bars in each section to form three rows, all over a crosshatch pattern. A stand-up front-end emblem was standard. The Royale had a hood center molding. The new front-end panel included amber wraparound front side markers, in the same frame as the quad headlamps and quad park/signal lamps. Coupe and four-door town sedan bodies were offered, in base and Royale trim. Re-

1978 Oldsmobile, Custom Cruiser station wagon, (O)

1978 Oldsmobile, Delta 88 Royale diesel sedan, (O)

styled wide wraparound taillamps put tiny narrow backup lights at the center of each lamp section, rather than at the outboard end. Each taillamp unit continued around and onto the quarter panel side. The small lenses at quarter-panel tips contained small emblems. The 231 cubic inch V-6 with automatic transmission was standard. Optional was a 260 cubic inch or 350 cubic inch V-8, 350 cubic inch diesel V-8 and 403 gas fueled V-8. Standard equipment included chrome wheel covers, power steering and brakes, front/rear ashtrays, lighter, day/night mirror, bench front seat and moldings for rocker panels, wheel openings and roof drip. The Royale also had protective bodyside moldings, sport front seat with center armrest and front/rear bumper rub strips with white stripes.

CUSTOM CRUISER -- SERIES 3B -- V-8 -- The full-size Cruiser wagon had the Delta 88 grille and wheelbase, but its own front-end panel. The 350 V-8 was standard; diesel or 403 V-8 optional. Equipment included automatic transmission, power tailgate window, power brakes and steering, spare tire extractor, lighter, bumper impact strips, bench front seat with center armrest and cargo area carpeting.

1978 Oldsmobile, Ninety-Eight Regency diesel sedan, (O)

NINETY-EIGHT -- SERIES 3C -- V-8 -- The Ninety-Eight's appearance was similar to 1977, but the grille had a looser crosshatch pattern (wider-spaced bars forming larger holes). New amber wraparound side marker lenses went into leading edges of front fenders, in the same frame as quad headlamps and parking/signal lamps. Regency had a new stand-up front-end emblem. A hood center molding was standard. New dual paint striping including a full-length upper and lower stripe was available. Redesigned taillamps eliminated the former red reflex from around the backup lights, and had no vertical divider. On the Regency, bright lower moldings now ran from the license plate opening to the taillamp bezels. Four models were offered again: coupe and sedan in Luxury or Regency trim. Regency had two leather and vinyl interiors available. Base engine was the 350 cubic inch (5.7-liter) V-8 with automatic; optional, either a 350 diesel or 403 gas fueled V-8. Standard equipment also included power steering and brakes, GR78 x 15 blackwall steel-belted radial tires, bumper impact strips, bench seats with center armrest, power windows, lighter, electric clock and two-way power driver's seat. Regency added a digital clock and 55/45 front bench seat with dual controls.

1978 Oldsmobile, Toronado Brougham coupe, (O)

1978 Oldsmobile, 98 Luxury sedan, (O)

TORONADO -- SERIES 3E -- V-8 -- Front-end appearance of the front-drive Olds was similar to 1977, but the grille now contained a vertical-bar design instead of an eggcrate pattern, with a bright bead around each grille opening. Gray bumper rub strips with twin white stripes were standard. Rear quarter side markers were part of the standard color-coordinated bodyside moldings. Rear bumper vertical pads had a simulated reflex with Olds emblems. Toronado's XS model became an option package. A standard microprocessor sensing and automatic regulation (MISAR) system monitored and adjusted ignition timing in response to engine vacuum and speed and coolant temperature. Standard engine was the 403 cubic inch four-barrel V-8. Also standard: Turbo Hydra-matic, power brakes/steering, power windows, velour upholstery, digital clock, Four Season air conditioning and cornering lamps.

I.D. DATA: Oldsmobile's 13-symbol Vehicle Identification Number (VIN) was located on the upper left surface of the instrument panel, visible through the windshield. The first digit is '3', indicating Oldsmobile division. Next is a letter indicating series: 'T' = Starfire; 'D' = Starfire SX; 'B' = Omega; 'E' = Omega Brougham; 'G' = Cutlass Salon; 'J' = Cutlass Salon Brougham; 'R' = Cutlass Supreme; 'M' = Cutlass Supreme Brougham; 'K' = Cutlass Calais; 'H' = Cutlass Cruiser; 'L' = Delta 88; 'N' = Delta 88 Royale; 'Q' = Custom Cruiser; 'V' = Ninety-Eight Luxury; 'X' = Ninety-Eight Regency; 'Z' = Toronado Brougham; 'W' = Toronado XS. Next come two digits that denote body type: '07' = Starfire coupe; '17' = Omega 2-dr. hatchback coupe; '27' = Omega 2-dr. pillar coupe; '37' = 2-dr. coupe; '47' = 2-dr. coupe; '57' = 2-dr. coupe; '87' = 2-dr. coupe; '09' = 4-dr. sedan; '69' = 4-dr. sedan; '35' = 4-dr. 2-seat wagon. The fifth symbol is a letter indicating engine code: 'V' = L4-151 2Bbl.; 'A' = V-6-231 2Bbl.; 'F' = V-8-260 2Bbl.; 'U' = V-8-305 2Bbl.; 'H' = V-8-305 4Bbl.; 'R' = V-8-350 4Bbl.; 'L' = Omega V-8-350 4Bbl.; 'N' = diesel V-8-350; 'K' = V-8-403 4Bbl. The sixth symbol denotes model year ('8' = 1978). Next is a plant code: '2' = Ste. Therese, Quebec (Canada); 'G' = Framingham, Mass.; 'D' = Doraville, Georgia; 'M' = Lansing, Mich.; 'W' = Willow Run, Mich.; 'R' = Arlington, Texas; 'C' = Southgate, Calif.; 'X' = Fairfax, Kansas; 'E' = Linden, New Jersey; '7' = Lordstown, Ohio. The final six digits are the sequential serial number, which began with 100,001. Engine numbers were stamped on the right front of the block (Buick-built engines), on the right side (Chevrolet-built V-8), or on the oil filler tube or left valve cover (Oldsmobile engines). Four-cylinder engine numbers were on a pad at right front, near the distributor shaft. A

body number plate on the shroud identified model year, car division, series, style, body assembly plant, body number, trim combination, modular seat code, paint code and date built code.

STARFIRE (FOUR/V-6)

Model Number	Body/Style Number	Body Type & Seating	Factory Price	Shipping Weight	Production Total
3H	T07	2-dr. Hatch Cpe-4P	3925/4095	—/2786	9,265

STARFIRE SX (FOUR/V-6)

3H	D07	2-dr. Hatch Cpe-4P	4131/4301	—/2790	8,056

OMEGA (V-6/V-8)

Model Number	Body/Style Number	Body Type & Seating	Factory Price	Shipping Weight	Production Total
3X	B27	2-dr. Cpe-6P	3973/4123	3105/3262	15,632
3X	B17	2-dr. Hatch Cpe-6P	4138/4288	3171/3328	4,084
3X	B69	4-dr. Sed-6P	4048/4198	3143/3300	19,478

OMEGA BROUGHAM (V-6/V-8)

3X	E27	2-dr. Cpe-6P	4179/4329	3126/3283	3,798
3X	E69	4-dr. Sed-6P	4254/4404	3167/3324	7,125

CUTLASS SALON (V-6/V-8)

Model Number	Body/Style Number	Body Type & Seating	Factory Price	Shipping Weight	Production Total
3A	G87	2-dr. Cpe-6P	4408/4508	3056/3187	21,198
3A	G09	4-dr. Sed-6P	4508/4608	3070/3201	29,509

CUTLASS SALON BROUGHAM (V-6/V-8)

3A	J87	2-dr. Cpe-6P	4696/4796	3017/3148	10,741
3A	J09	4-dr. Sed-6P	4796/4896	3121/3252	21,902

CUTLASS SUPREME (V-6/V-8)

3A	R47	2-dr. Cpe-6P	4842/4942	3161/3295	240,917

CUTLASS CRUISER (V-6/V-8)

3A	H35	4-dr. 2S Sta Wag-6P	5242/5342	3213/3402	44,617

CUTLASS SUPREME BROUGHAM (V-6/V-8)

3A	M47	2-dr. Cpe-6P	5247/5347	3138/3269	117,880

CUTLASS (SUPREME) CALAIS (V-6/V-8)

3A	K47	2-dr. Cpe-5P	5195/5295	3146/3277	40,842

DELTA 88 (V-6/V-8)

Model Number	Body/Style Number	Body Type & Seating	Factory Price	Shipping Weight	Production Total
3B	L37	2-dr. Cpe-6P	5483/5583	3404/3588	17,469
3B	L69	4-dr. Town Sed-6P	5559/5659	3449/3633	25,322

DELTA 88 ROYALE (V-6/V-8)

3B	N37	2-dr. Cpe-6P	5707/5807	3415/3599	68,469
3B	N69	4-dr. Town Sed-6P	5807/5907	3477/3661	131,430

CUSTOM CRUISER (V-8)

Model Number	Body/Style Number	Body Type & Seating	Factory Price	Shipping Weight	Production Total
3B	Q35	4-dr. 2S Sta Wag-6P	6324	4045	34,491
3B	Q35	4-dr. 3S Sta Wag-8P	N/A	4095	Note 1

Note 1: Three-seat production is included in two-seat total.

NINETY-EIGHT LUXURY (V-8)

Model Number	Body/Style Number	Body Type & Seating	Factory Price	Shipping Weight	Production Total
3C	V37	2-dr. Cpe-6P	7064	3753	2,956
3C	V69	4-dr. Sedan-6P	7241	3805	9,136

NINETY-EIGHT REGENCY (V-8)

3C	X37	2-dr. Cpe-6P	7427	3767	28,573
3C	X69	4-dr. Sedan-6P	7611	3836	78,100

TORONADO BROUGHAM (V-8)

Model Number	Body/Style Number	Body Type & Seating	Factory Price	Shipping Weight	Production Total
3E	Z57	2-dr. Cpe-6P	8889	4624	22,362

TORONADO XS (V-8)

3E	W57	2-dr. Cpe-6P	N/A	N/A	2,453

Production Note: Toronado XS was actually an option package. 545 Toronado chassis were also produced.

FACTORY PRICE AND WEIGHT NOTE: For Omega, Cutlass and Delta 88, prices and weights to left of slash are for six-cylinder, to right for V-8 engine. For Starfire, prices/weights to left are for four-cylinder, to right for V-6.

ENGINE DATA: BASE FOUR (Starfire): Inline, overhead-valve four-cylinder. Cast iron block and head. Displacement: 151 cu. in. (2.5 liters). Bore & stroke: 4.00 x 3.00 in. Compression ratio: 8.3:1. Brake horsepower: 85 at 4400 rpm. Torque: 123 lb.-ft. at 2800 rpm. Five main bearings. Hydraulic valve lifters. Carburetor: 2Bbl. Holley 5210C. Pontiac-built. VIN Code: V. BASE V-6 (Omega, Cutlass, Cutlass wagon, Delta 88); OPTIONAL (Starfire): 90-degree, overhead-valve V-6. Cast iron block and head. Displacement: 231 cu. in. (3.8 liters). Bore & stroke: 3.80 x 3.40 in. Compression ratio: 8.0:1. Brake horsepower: 105 at 3400 rpm. Torque: 185 lb.-ft. at 2000 rpm. Four main bearings. Hydraulic valve lifters. Carburetor: 2Bbl. Rochester 2GE. Buick-built. VIN Code: A. OPTIONAL V-8 (Cutlass, Cutlass wagon, Delta 88): 90-degree, overhead valve V-8. Cast iron block and head. Displacement: 260 cu. in. (4.3 liters). Bore & stroke: 3.50 x 3.39 in. Compression ratio: 7.5:1. Brake horsepower: 110 at 3400 rpm. Torque: 205 lb.-ft. at 1800 rpm. Five main bearings. Hydraulic valve lifters. Carburetor: 2Bbl. Rochester 2GC. VIN Code: F. OPTIONAL V-8 (Starfire, Omega, Cutlass): 90-degree, overhead valve V-8. Cast iron block and head. Displacement: 305 cu. in. (5.0 liters). Bore & stroke: 3.74 x 3.48 in. Compression ratio: 8.4:1. Brake horsepower: 145 at 3800 rpm. Torque: 245 lb.-ft. at 2400 rpm. Five main bearings. Hydraulic valve lifters. Carburetor: 2Bbl Rochester 2GC. Chevrolet-built. VIN Code: U. OPTIONAL V-8 (Cutlass): Same as 305 cu. in. V-8 above, with four-barrel carburetor -- Horsepower: 160 at 4000 rpm. Torque: 235 lb.-ft. at 2400 rpm. VIN Code: H. OPTIONAL V-8 (California/high-altitude Omega, Cutlass Cruiser): 90-degree, overhead valve V-8. Cast iron block and head. Displacement: 350 cu. in. (5.7 liters). Bore & stroke: 4.00 x 3.48 in. Compression ratio: 8.2:1. Brake horsepower: 160 at 3800 rpm. Torque: 260 lb.-ft. at 2400 rpm. Five main bearings. Hydraulic valve lifters. Carburetor: 4Bbl. Rochester M4MC. Chevrolet-built. VIN Code: L. BASE V-8 (98, Custom Cruiser wagon); OPTIONAL (Delta 88): 90-degree, overhead valve V-8. Cast iron block and head. Displacement: 350 cu. in. (5.7 liters). Bore & stroke: 4.06 x 3.39 in. Compression ratio: 7.9:1. Brake horsepower: 170 at 3800 rpm. Torque: 275 lb.-ft. at 2000 rpm. Five main bearings. Hydraulic valve lifters. Carburetor: 4Bbl. Rochester M4MC. VIN Code: R. BASE V-8 (Toronado); OPTIONAL (Delta 88, 98, Custom Cruiser): 90-degree, overhead valve V-8. Cast iron block and head. Displacement: 403 cu. in. (6.6 liters). Bore & stroke: 4.35 x 3.39 in. Compression ratio: 7.9:1. Brake horsepower: 185 at 3600 rpm. (Toronado, 190 at 3600). Torque: 320 lb.-ft. at 2000 rpm. (Toronado, 325 at 2000). Five main bearings. Hydraulic valve lifters. Carburetor: 4Bbl. Rochester M4MC. VIN Code: K. DIESEL V-8 (Delta 88, 98, Custom Cruiser): 90-degree, overhead valve V-8. Cast iron block and head. Displacement: 350 cu. in. (5.7 liters). Bore & stroke: 4.06 x 3.39 in. Compression ratio: 22.5:1. Brake horsepower: 120 at 3600 rpm. Torque: 220 lb.-ft. at 1600 rpm. Five main bearings. Hydraulic valve lifters. Fuel injection. VIN Code: N.

1978 Oldsmobile, Delta 88 Royale sedan, (O)

CHASSIS DATA: Wheelbase: (Starfire) 97.0 in.; (Omega) 111.0 in.; (Cutlass) 108.1 in.; (Delta 88) 116.0 in.; (98) 119.0 in.; (Custom Crsr) 116.0 in.; (Toronado) 122.0 in. Overall Length: (Starfire) 179.3 in.; (Omega) 199.6 in.; (Cutlass Supreme cpe) 200.1 in.; (Cutlass Salon) 197.7 in.; (Cutlass wag) 197.6 in.; (Delta 88) 217.5 in.; (98) 220.4 in.; (Custom Crsr) 217.1 in.; (Toronado) 227.5 in. Height: (Starfire) 50.2 in.; (Omega cpe) 53.8 in.; (Omega sed) 54.7 in.; (Cutlass cpe) 53.4 in.; (Cutlass sed) 54.2 in.; (Cutlass wag) 54.5 in.; (Delta 88 cpe) 54.5 in.; (Delta 88 4-dr.) 55.2 in.; (98) 55.5 in.; (Custom Crsr) 57.2 in.; (Toronado) 53.2 in. Width: (Starfire) 65.4 in.; (Omega) 72.9 in.; (Cutlass cpe) 71.3 in.; (Cutlass sed) 71.9 in.; (Cutlass wag) 71.7 in.; (Delta 88) 76.8 in.; (98) 76.8 in.; (Custom Crsr) 79.8 in.; (Toronado) 80.0 in. Front Tread: (Starfire) 54.7 in.; (Omega) 61.9 in.; (Cutlass) 58.5 in.; (Delta 88/98) 61.7 in.; (Custom Crsr) 62.1 in.; (Toronado) 63.7 in. Rear Tread: (Starfire) 53.6 in.; (Omega) 59.6 in.; (Cutlass) 57.7 in.; (Delta 88/98) 60.7 in.; (Custom Crsr) 64.1 in.; (Toronado) 63.6 in. Standard Tires: (Starfire) A78 x 13; (Starfire SX) BR78 x 13; (Omega) E78 x 14; (Cutlass Supreme/Calais) P195/75R14; (Cutlass Salon) P185/75R14; (Cutlass wag) P195/75R14; (Delta 88) FR78 x 15; (98) GR78 x 15; (Custom Crsr) HR78 x 15; (Toronado) JR78 x 15.

TECHNICAL: Transmission: Three-speed manual transmission standard on Omega and Cutlass V-6. Four-speed floor shift standard on Starfire V-6 and Omega/Cutlass V-8-305. Five-speed manual optional on Starfire, and Omega/Cutlass V-6 and V-8-260. Three-speed Turbo Hydra-matic standard on other models, optional on all. Standard final drive ratio: (Starfire) 2.73:1; (Omega) 3.08:1; (Cutlass) 2.93:1; (Cutlass Cruiser) 2.73:1; (Delta 88) 2.73:1; (Custom Crsr) 2.73:1; (98) 2.41:1; (Toronado) 2.73:1. Steering: Recirculating ball. Front Suspension: (Starfire) coil springs w/lower trailing links and anti-sway bar; (Toronado); longitudinal torsion bars w/anti-sway bar; (others) coil springs w/control arms and anti-sway bar. Rear Suspension: (Starfire) rigid axle w/coil springs, lower trailing radius arms, upper torque arms, transverse linkage bar and anti-sway bar; (Omega) rigid axle w/semi-elliptic leaf springs; (others) rigid axle w/coil springs, lower trailing radius arms and upper torque arms. Semi-automatic leveling on Toronado. Brakes: Front disc, rear drum. Ignition: Electronic. Body construction: (Starfire) unibody; (Omega) unibody w/separate front partial frame; (others) separate body on perimeter frame. Fuel Tank: (Starfire) 18.5 gal.; (Omega) 21 gal.; (Cutlass) 17.5 gal.; (Cutlass wag) 18.2 gal.; (Delta 88) 21 or 25.3 gal.; (98) 25.3 gal.; (Custom Crsr wag) 22 gal.; (Toronado) 26 gal.

DRIVETRAIN OPTIONS: Engines: 231 cu. in. V-6: Starfire ($170). 260 cu. in. V-8: Cutlass/88 ($100). 305 cu. in. 2Bbl. V-8: Starfire ($320): Starfire w/GT pkg. ($150): Omega/Cutlass ($150). 305 cu. in. 4Bbl. V-8: Cutlass ($200). 350 cu. in. 4Bbl. V-8: Omega ($265); Cutlass Crsr/88 ($265). 403 cu. in. V-8: Delta 88 ($330); 98/Custom Crsr ($65). Diesel 350 cu. in. V-8: 88 ($850); 98/Custom Crsr ($740). Transmission/Differential: Four-speed floor shift: Omega/Cutlass ($125). Five-speed manual floor shift: Starfire ($175). Turbo Hydra-matic: Starfire (N/A); Omega/Cutlass ($307). Limited-slip differential: Starfire ($56); Omega/Cutlass ($60); 88 ($64). Brakes/Steering: Power brakes: Starfire ($66); Omega ($69). Power steering: Starfire (N/A); Omega/Cutlass ($152). Power disc brakes: Omega/Cutlass ($69-$300). Suspension: Rallye susp. pkg.: Omega/Cutlass ($29). H.D. susp.: Cutlass/full-size ($19-$25). Firm ride shock absorbers: Cutlass/88/98 ($7). Superlift rear shocks: Cutlass/88/98 ($52). Rear stabilizer bar: Starfire ($18). Automatic load leveling: Cutlass/88/98 ($116). Load leveling: Toronado ($96). Other: High-capacity cooling ($20-$72). High-capacity radiator: Starfire ($19). H.D. battery ($17-$20). High-capacity alternator: Cutlass/full-size ($49). Trailer wiring: Cutlass/full-size ($21-$34). Engine block heater ($14) exc. Starfire. California emissions equipment ($75-$100). High-altitude emissions ($33).

1978 Oldsmobile, Cutlass-based 4-4-2 coupe (W-29 package), (O)

OPTION PACKAGES: Starfire GT pkg. ($504-$627). Omega LS pkg.: Brougham sedan ($1943). Omega SX pkg.: base hatch/cpe ($201). Cutlass 4-4-2 appearance/handling pkg.: Salon cpe ($260); Salon Brghm ($111). Toronado XS pkg. ($2700).

MAJOR CONVENIENCE/APPEARANCE OPTIONS: Four Season air conditioner ($470-$581). Tempmatic air conditioning: Cutlass/88/98 ($584-$626); Toronado ($45). Power seat ($120-$151); N/A Starfire. Power windows ($118-$190); N/A Starfire. Cornering lamps: Cutlass/88/98 ($45). Twilight sentinel: 88/98/Toronado ($45). Power astroroof: Cutlass/88/98/Toronado ($699-$978). Power sliding metal sunroof: Cutlass/88/98/Toronado ($499-$778). Removable glass panel roof: Cutlass ($625). Sliding glass panel roof: Starfire ($215). Landau vinyl roof ($168-$268); N/A Starfire. Full vinyl roof ($79-$187); N/A Starfire. Firemist paint: Cutlass/88/98/Toronado ($165). Rear-facing third seat: Custom Cruiser ($186).

HISTORY: Introduced: October 6, 1977. Model year production: 1,015,805. Calendar year production (U.S.): 910,254. Calendar year sales by U.S. dealers: 1,006,344. Model year sales by U.S. dealers: 952,151. A total of 33,841 diesel-powered Oldsmobiles were produced in the model year.

HISTORICAL FOOTNOTES: Olds again captured the No. 3 spot in sales. Oldsmobiles came with a variety of engines, from Buick, Chevrolet and Pontiac as well as its own powerplants. This phenomenon, which pervaded the GM camp, eventually led to some consumer dissatisfaction and even lawsuits from those who felt cheated. The new diesel V-8 engine proved popular, and would soon equip many other GM cars, making Olds a leader in diesel power. In a continuing attempt to improve rust resistance, one-side electro-galvanized steel was used on Oldsmobile door outer panels and outer quarter panels.

1979

A redesigned front-drive Toronado was the year's major news, downsized but with more head/leg room. A new 260 cubic inch (4.3-liter) diesel V-8 joined the original 350 diesel, making diesel power available on 19 of Oldsmobile's 26 models. It was available with either automatic transmission or five-speed manual. Both diesel V-8 engines adopted a fast-start system that "nearly eliminates the need to wait while the glow plugs warm the air in the pre-chamber." The car was expected to start in six seconds at zero degrees, compared to a full minute in 1978.

STARFIRE -- SERIES 3H -- FOUR/V-6 -- Not only did the Olds subcompact look a little different this year, it felt somewhat different. Up front was a new four-element vertical-bar grille in body color, in a new hard fiberglass-reinforced sloping front-end panel. And a hard rear end replaced the soft one of 1978. The new grille contained four sections of thin vertical bars. Park/signal lamps were now behind the outer grille segments. Single quad recessed headlamps provided the illumination, and small horizontal amber marker lenses went ahead of each front wheel. Base and SX two-door sport coupes had a hatchback rear and fold-down back seat. Standard engine was the 151 cubic inch (2.5-liter) four. The GT package was optional again, with bodyside and hood paint stripes (black, white or metallic gold) and 'GT' lettering. That package included a 231 cubic inch (3.8-liter) V-6 engine, Rallye wheels, raised-white-letter tires, tachometer, clock and temperature gauge. The Firenza option, introduced late in the 1978 model year, also reappeared, installed on 3,873 Starfire SX models. It included a special front air dam, rear spoiler, flared front/rear wheel openings, sport mirrors, wide oval tires on sport wheels, and Rallye suspension. Firenzas had special paint, with Firenza identification on the lower paint stripe.

1979 Oldsmobile, Omega Brougham coupe, (O)

1979 Oldsmobile, Omega Brougham sedan, (O)

OMEGA -- SERIES 3X -- V-6/V-8 -- Not many Oldsmobiles entered a new year without at least a revised grille, and Omega was no exception. This one had four sections on each side, each contained a set of thin vertical bars. Amber vertical park/signal lamps stood at the outboard ends of the grille (in the same framework). Single round headlamps were used again. Base Omegas came in notchback coupe, hatchback coupe and four-door sedan; Brougham as a coupe and sedan. Standard engine was a 231 cubic inch (3.8-liter) V-6. The SX option on base Omega coupe and hatchback included rocker panel and wheel opening moldings, special wheel opening and bodyside decals, sport styled mirrors, Rallye suspension and custom sport steering wheel. An LS option package for Brougham sedans included automatic transmission, Four Season air conditioner, 'LS' sail-panel emblem, painted wheel covers and special paint scheme with accent stripes.

1979 Oldsmobile, Starfire hatchback coupe, (O)

147

1979 Oldsmobile, Cutlass Calais coupe, (O)

1979 Oldsmobile, Cutlass Salon diesel slantback sedan, (O)

1979 Oldsmobile, Cutlass Salon Brougham slantback coupe, (O)

CUTLASS -- SERIES 3A -- V-6/V-8 -- As usual, Cutlass models could be identified mainly by their grilles. Nine models included a Salon and Salon Brougham coupe and sedan; Supreme, Calais and Supreme Brougham coupe; Cutlass Cruiser wagon; and new Cruiser Brougham. The standard Cutlass engine was the 231 cubic inch (3.8-liter) V-6. Coupes and sedans could have a 260 cubic inch (4.3-liter) diesel V-8. Cutlass Cruisers could get the larger 350 cubic inch diesel V-8. Cutlass Salon had a six-segment grille; Salon Brougham 12 segments. Both back ends had dual vertical taillamps. The Salon grille had three sections on each side, and amber vertical (formerly clear) park/signal lamps in the same frame as single rectangular headlamps. Salon Brougham's grille had six side-by-side sections on each side of the body-color divider, instead of four as in 1978. Supreme and Supreme Brougham had a four-element vertical-bar grille that wrapped over the front-end panel. Calais now sported an upright twin rectangular-bar type grille with eggcrate pattern, replacing the former wrapover design. All three formal coupes had the same back end with vertical taillamps divided by a bright center. Cutlass Cruiser had the same front end as Cutlass Salon, while Cruiser Brougham shared grilles with the Salon Brougham. Salon and Salon Brougham coupes could again have the 442 appearance/handling package, which included '442' paint striping and lettering on lower bodyside and decklid, bucket seats, sports console, Rallye suspension, and blacked-out grille. 409 Supremes had a five-speed gearbox and the LV-8 engine; 267 had the five-speed and LF7 engine. A total of 38,672 Cutlass diesels were produced. Cutlass Calais announced a Hurst/Olds option (RPO code W30). It included a 350 cubic inch (5.7-liter) four-barrel V-8 and automatic transmission. The body had special black and gold (or white and gold) paint, gold aluminum sport wheels and gold sport mirrors. Also included: raised-white-letter tires, sport console with Hurst shifter, power steering and brakes, digital clock, ride/handling package, sport steering wheel, full instrumentation and contour reclining front bucket seats. A total of 2,499 were built.

1979 Oldsmobile, Delta 88 coupe, (AA)

1979 Oldsmobile, Cutlass Supreme Brougham coupe, (O)

1979 Oldsmobile, Cutlass Cruiser Brougham diesel station wagon, (O)

1979 Oldsmobile, Delta 88 Royale sedan, (O)

DELTA 88 -- SERIES 3B -- V-6/V-8 -- Overall Delta 88 appearance was similar to 1978, and the front end had the same basic design. But this year's grille contained thin horizontal strips along with three vertical divider bars on each side, to form four sections. Wraparound side markers carried a new design. Base and Royale models were offered again, in two-door coupe and four-door sedan. Base engine was a 231 cubic inch (3.8-liter)

V-6 with automatic; optional was the 350 cubic inch diesel V-8. A total of 48,879 diesels were produced. Reviving an old name, a sporty Holiday 88 coupe was offered this year on the base model. It included a T-handle floor shifter, Rallye suspension, sports console, sport steering wheel, front bucket seats, dual sport mirrors, custom wheel covers and special Holiday 88 emblem on the sail panel.

1979 Oldsmobile, Custom Cruiser station wagon, (O)

CUSTOM CRUISER -- SERIES 3B -- V-8 -- The full-size wagon was available in base form, or with a deluxe option that included woodgrain trim. Two seats were standard, with rear-facing third seat optional. The 350 cubic inch (5.7-liter) gas fueled V-8 was standard; optional was the 350 diesel.

1979 Oldsmobile, Ninety-Eight Regency sedan, (O)

NINETY-EIGHT -- SERIES 3C -- V-8 -- Even though the Ninety-Eight front end looked basically the same as before, each grille side now contained a solid crosshatch pattern (with no dividers). The rear was similar too, but backup lenses were much smaller, now mounted alongside the license plate at inner ends of a decorative panel. The two-door coupe and four-door sedan came in Luxury and Regency series. A 350 cubic inch (5.7-liter) V-8 was standard; optional was the 350 diesel (21,231 were produced). A total of 1,999 models came with an LS package (RPO code Y68). Standard Ninety-Eight equipment included: power brakes/steering, power windows, two-way power driver's seat, clock, fold-down center armrests, and courtesy lamps. The Regency had a loose-cushion-look interior with velour upholstery, divided front seat with dual controls, digital clock and front seatback pouches.

1979 Oldsmobile, Toronado diesel coupe, (O)

TORONADO -- SERIES 3E -- V-8 -- Toronado received a substantial downsizing as well as a substantial price hike. Wheelbase dropped to 114 inches, length to 205.6 (down from 122 and 227.5, respectively, in 1978). Even the car's width was reduced by nearly nine inches. Still front-drive, Toronado had a new steering linkage and power steering gear to improve tight maneuvering. Turning diameter was cut by over three feet. The downsized model weighed about 900 pounds less than its predecessor, and carried four passengers. A 350 cubic inch (5.7-liter) V-8 was standard; optional was the 350 diesel. A total of 8,040 diesel Toronados were produced. Gas mileage was estimated to be about three mpg better than before (city). The rectangular shape of grille openings was repeated in the quad headlamps, and balanced by long horizontal park and turn signal lamps. 'Toronado' lettering extended across the front-end panel, above the grille. Toronado featured a formal roofline. Small, fixed rear quarter windows were covered when the landau or full vinyl roof was ordered. A Toronado emblem went on the sail panel (except when replaced by optional opera lamps). Long horizontal taillamps and backup lamps extended from the decklid's edge to the license plate opening. 'Toronado' lettering stretched across the decklid. A flush-mounted windshield produced smooth airflow. The back window was flush-fitted, installed from inside the car, allowing smaller reveal moldings. A fiber optic system lit the center Toronado namplate, ashtray and lighter, cruise control, rear defogger and light switches. The steering column held a combination dimmer/signal control. The new instrument panel had a vinyl pad that offered "the look and feel of leather." Standard automatic leveling adjusted car height by electric compression, with an electronic height sensor controlling air pressure in the rear shock absorbers. A rear stabilizer bar was standard. Other standard Toronado equipment included air conditioning, automatic transmission, six-way power driver's seat, divided front seat, side window defogers, power windows, remote driver's mirror, automatic level control, AM/FM stereo radio, digital clock, stowaway spare tire, power antenna, SBR whitewall tires, cornering lamps, power brakes/steering, door courtesy/warning lights and a temperature gauge. New options included reclining front seats, opera lamps, illuminated door locks and interior, Rallye suspension and fiber-optic lamp monitors.

I.D. DATA: Oldsmobile's 13-symbol Vehicle Identification Number (VIN) was located on the upper left surface of the instrument panel, visible through the windshield. The first digit is '3', indicating Oldsmobile division. Next is a letter indicating series: 'T' = Starfire; 'D' = Starfire SX; 'B' = Omega; 'E' = Omega Brougham; 'G' = Cutlass Salon; 'J' = Cutlass Salon Brougham; 'R' = Cutlass Supreme; 'M' = Cutlass Supreme Brougham; 'K' = Cutlass Calais; 'G' = Cutlass Cruiser; 'H' = Cutlass Cruiser Brougham; 'L' = Delta 88; 'N' = Delta 88 Royale; 'Q' = Custom Cruiser; 'V' = Ninety-Eight Luxury; 'X' = Ninety-Eight Regency; 'Z' = Toronado Brougham. Next come two digits that denote body type: '07' = Starfire hatch coupe; '17' = Omega 2-dr. hatchback coupe; '27' = Omega 2-dr. notch coupe; '37' = 2-dr. coupe; '47' = 2-dr. coupe; '57' = 2-dr. coupe; '87' = 2-dr. plain-back coupe; '09' = 4-dr. 6-window sedan; '69' = 4-dr. 4-window notch sedan; '35' = 4-dr. 2-seat wagon. The fifth symbol is a letter indicating engine code: 'V' = L4-151 2Bbl.; 'A' = V-6-231 2Bbl.; 'F' = V-8-260 2Bbl.; 'P' = diesel V-8-260; 'Y' = V-8-301 2Bbl.; 'G' = V-8-305 2Bbl.; 'H' = V-8-305 4Bbl.; 'R' = V-8-350 4Bbl.; 'L' = Omega V-8-350 4Bbl.; 'N' = diesel V-8-350; 'K' = V-8-403 4Bbl. The sixth symbol denotes model year ('9' = 1979). Next is a plant code: '2' = Ste. Therese, Quebec (Canada); 'G' = Framingham, Mass.; 'D' = Doraville, Georgia; 'M' = Lansing, Mich.; 'W' = Willow Run, Mich.; 'R' = Arlington, Texas; 'X' = Fairfax, Kansas; 'E' = Linden, New Jersey; '7' = Lordstown, Ohio. The final six digits are the sequential serial number, which began with 100,001. Engine numbers were stamped on the front of the right rocker cover, or top of left cover (Buick-built engines), on the front of the right cover (Chevrolet-built V-8), at the front of

either rocker cover (Pontiac V-8), or on the left rocker cover (Oldsmobile engines). Four-cylinder engine numbers were on a pad at right front, near the distributor shaft. A body number plate on the shroud identified model year, car division, series, style, body assembly plant, body number, trim combination, modular seat code, paint code and date built code.

STARFIRE (FOUR/V-6)

Model Number	Body/Style Number	Body Type & Seating	Factory Price	Shipping Weight	Production Total
3H	T07	2-dr. Hatch Cpe-4P	4095/4295	2690/----	13,144

STARFIRE SX (FOUR/V-6)

Model Number	Body/Style Number	Body Type & Seating	Factory Price	Shipping Weight	Production Total
3H	D07	2-dr. Hatch Cpe-4P	4295/4495	2703/----	7,155

Starfire Engine Note: A V-8 engine cost $195 more than the V-6.

OMEGA (V-6/V-8)

Model Number	Body/Style Number	Body Type & Seating	Factory Price	Shipping Weight	Production Total
3X	B27	2-dr. Cpe-6P	4181/4376	3080/3210	4,806
3X	B17	2-dr. Hatch Cpe-6P	4345/4540	3157/3287	956
3X	B69	4-dr. Sed-6P	4281/4476	3118/3248	5,826

OMEGA BROUGHAM (V-6/V-8)

3X	E27	2-dr. Cpe-6P	4387/4582	3091/3221	1,078
3X	E69	4-dr. Sed-6P	4487/4682	3149/3279	2,145

CUTLASS SALON (V-6/V-8)

Model Number	Body/Style Number	Body Type & Seating	Factory Price	Shipping Weight	Production Total
3A	G87	2-dr. Cpe-6P	4623/4763	3060/3175	8,399
3A	G09	4-dr. Sed-6P	4723/4863	3080/3195	20,266

CUTLASS SALON BROUGHAM (V-6/V-8)

3A	J87	2-dr. Cpe-6P	4907/5047	3100/3215	3,617
3A	J09	4-dr. Sed-6P	5032/5172	3127/3242	18,714

1979 Oldsmobile, Hurst/Olds coupe with W-30 package (gold over white version), (O)

CUTLASS SUPREME (V-6/V-8)

Model Number	Body/Style Number	Body Type & Seating	Factory Price	Shipping Weight	Production Total
3A	R47	2-dr. Cpe-6P	5063/5203	3091/3206	277,944

CUTLASS SUPREME BROUGHAM (V-6/V-8)

3A	M47	2-dr. Cpe-6P	5492/5632	3116/3231	137,323

CUTLASS CALAIS (V-6/V-8)

3A	K47	2-dr. Cpe-5P	5491/5631	3122/3237	43,780

CUTLASS CRUISER (V-6/V-8)

3A	G35	4-dr. 2S Sta Wag-6P	4980/5120	3201/3361	10,755
3A	H35	4-dr. Brghm Wag-6P	5517/5657	3245/3405	42,953

DELTA 88 (V-6/V-8)

Model Number	Body/Style Number	Body Type & Seating	Factory Price	Shipping Weight	Production Total
3B	L37	2-dr. Cpe-6P	5782/5922	3462/3639	16,202
3B	L69	4-dr. Sed-6P	5882/6022	3488/3665	25,424

DELTA 88 ROYALE (V-6/V-8)

3B	N37	2-dr. Cpe-6P	6029/6169	3471/3648	60,687
3B	N69	4-dr. Sed-6P	6154/6294	3513/3690	152,626

1979 Oldsmobile, Delta 88 Royale sedan, (O)

CUSTOM CRUISER (V-8)

Model Number	Body/Style Number	Body Type & Seating	Factory Price	Shipping Weight	Production Total
3B	Q35	4-dr. 2S Sta Wag-6P	6742	4042	36,648
3B	Q35	4-dr. 3S Sta Wag-8P	6935	N/A	Note 1

Note 1: Three-seat production is included in two-seat total.

NINETY-EIGHT LUXURY (V-8)

Model Number	Body/Style Number	Body Type & Seating	Factory Price	Shipping Weight	Production Total
3C	V37	2-dr. Cpe-6P	7492	3806	2,104
3C	V-69	4-dr. Sed-6P	7673	3850	6,720

NINETY-EIGHT REGENCY (V-8)

3C	X37	2-dr. Cpe-6P	7875	3810	29,965
3C	X69	4-dr. Sed-6P	8063	3885	91,862

TORONADO BROUGHAM (V-8)

Model Number	Body/Style Number	Body Type & Seating	Factory Price	Shipping Weight	Production Total
3E	Z57	2-dr. Cpe-4P	10112	3731	50,056

FACTORY PRICE AND WEIGHT NOTE: For Omega, Cutlass and Delta 88, prices and weights to left of slash are for six-cylinder, to right for V-8 engine. For Starfire, prices/weights to left are for four-cylinder, to right for V-6.

1979 Oldsmobile, Hurst/Olds coupe with W-30 package (gold over black version), (O)

ENGINE DATA: BASE FOUR (Starfire): Inline, overhead-valve four-cylinder. Cast iron block and head. Displacement: 151 cu. in. (2.5 liters). Bore & stroke: 4.00 x 3.00 in. Compression ratio: 8.3:1. Brake horsepower: 85 at 4400 rpm. Torque: 123 lb.-ft. at 2800 rpm. Five main bearings. Hydraulic valve lifters. Carburetor: 2Bbl. Rochester 2SE. Pontiac-built. VIN Code: V. BASE V-6 (Omega, Cutlass, Cutlass wagon, Delta 88); OPTIONAL (Starfire): 90-degree, overhead-valve V-6. Cast iron block and head. Displacement: 231 cu. in. (3.8 liters). Bore & stroke: 3.80 x 3.40 in. Compression ratio: 8.0:1. Brake horsepower: 115 at 3800 rpm. Torque: 190 lb.-ft. at 2000 rpm. Four main bearings. Hydraulic valve lifters. Carburetor: 2Bbl. Rochester M2ME. Buick-built. VIN Code: A. OPTIONAL V-8 (Cutlass, Cutlass wagon, Delta 88): 90-degree, overhead valve V-8. Cast iron block and head. Displacement: 260 cu. in. (4.3 liters). Bore & stroke:

3.50 x 3.39 in. Compression ratio: 7.5:1. Brake horsepower: 105 at 3600 rpm. Torque: 205 lb.-ft. at 1800 rpm. Five main bearings. Hydraulic valve lifters. Carburetor: 2Bbl. Rochester M2MC. VIN Code: F. DIESEL V-8 (Cutlass): 90-degree, overhead valve V-8. Cast iron block and head. Displacement: 260 cu. in. (4.3 liters). Bore & stroke: 3.50 x 3.39 in. Compression ratio: 22.5:1. Brake horsepower: 90 at 3600 rpm. Torque: 160 lb.-ft. at 1600 rpm. Five main bearings. Hydraulic valve lifters. Fuel injection. VIN Code: P. OPTIONAL V-8 (Delta 88): 90-degree, overhead valve V-8. Cast iron block and head. Displacement: 301 cu. in. (4.9 liters). Bore & stroke: 4.00 x 3.00 in. Compression ratio: 8.2:1. Brake horsepower: 135 at 3800 rpm. Torque: 240 lb.-ft. at 1600 rpm. Five main bearings. Hydraulic valve lifters. Carburetor: 2Bbl. Rochester M2MC. Pontiac-built. VIN Code: Y. OPTIONAL V-8 (Starfire, Omega): 90-degree, overhead valve V-8. Cast iron block and head. Displacement: 305 cu. in. (5.0 liters). Bore & stroke: 3.74 x 3.48 in. Compression ratio: 8.4:1. Brake horsepower: 130 at 3200 rpm. Torque: 245 lb.-ft. at 2000 rpm. Five main bearings. Hydraulic valve lifters. Carburetor: 2Bbl. Rochester M2MC. Chevrolet-built. VIN Code: G. OPTIONAL V-8 (Cutlass): Same as 305 cu. in. V-8 above, with four-barrel Rochester M4MC carburetor Horsepower: 160 at 4000 rpm. Torque: 235 lb.-ft. at 2400 rpm. VIN Code: H. OPTIONAL V-8 (California/high-altitude Omega, Cutlass Cruiser): 90-degree, overhead valve V-8. Cast iron block and head. Displacement: 350 cu. in. (5.7 liters). Bore & stroke: 4.00 x 3.48 in. Compression ratio: 8.5:1. Brake horsepower: 160 at 3800 rpm. Torque: 260 lb.-ft. at 2400 rpm. Five main bearings. Hydraulic valve lifters. Carburetor: 4Bbl. Rochester M4MC. Chevrolet-built. VIN Code: L. BASE V-8 (98, Custom Cruiser wagon, Toronado); OPTIONAL (Delta 88): 90-degree, overhead valve V-8. Cast iron block and head. Displacement: 350 cu. in. (5.7 liters). Bore & stroke: 4.06 x 3.39 in. Compression ratio: 8.0:1. Brake horsepower: 160-165 at 3800 rpm. Torque: 270-275 lb.-ft. at 2000 rpm. Five main bearings. Hydraulic valve lifters. Carburetor: 4Bbl. Rochester M4MC. VIN Code: R. OPTIONAL V-8 (98, Custom Cruiser): 90-degree, overhead valve V-8. Cast iron block and head. Displacement: 403 cu. in. (6.6 liters). Bore & stroke: 4.35 x 3.39 in. Compression ratio: 7.8:1. Brake horsepower: 175 at 3600 rpm. Torque: 310 lb.-ft. at 2000 rpm. Five main bearings. Hydraulic valve lifters. Carburetor: 4Bbl. Rochester M4MC. VIN Code: K. DIESEL V-8 (Cutlass Cruiser, Delta 88, 98, Custom Cruiser, Toronado): 90-degree, overhead valve V-8. Cast iron block and head. Displacement: 350 cu. in. (5.7 liters). Bore & stroke: 4.06 x 3.39 in. Compression ratio: 22.5:1. Brake horsepower: 125 at 3600 rpm. Torque: 225 lb.-ft. at 1600 rpm. Five main bearings. Hydraulic valve lifters. Fuel injection. VIN Code: N.

CHASSIS DATA: Wheelbase: (Starfire) 97.0 in.; (Omega) 111.0 in.; (Cutlass) 108.1 in.; (Delta 88) 116.0 in.; (98) 119.0 in.; (Custom Crsr) 116.0 in.; (Toronado) 114.0 in. Overall Length: (Starfire) 179.6 in.; (Omega) 199.6 in.; (Cutlass Supreme/Calais cpe) 200.1 in.; (Cutlass Salon) 197.7 in.; (Cutlass wag) 197.6 in.; (Delta 88) 217.5 in.; (98) 220.4 in.; (Custom Crsr) 217.1 in.; (Toronado) 205.6 in. Height: (Starfire) 50.2 in.; (Omega cpe) 53.8 in.; (Omega sed) 54.7 in.; (Cutlass) 53.4-54.2 in.; (Cutlass wag) 54.5 in.; (Delta 88 cpe) 54.5 in.; (Delta 88 4dr.) 55.2 in.; (98 cpe) 55.5 in.; (98 sed) 55.5 in.; (Custom Crsr) 57.2 in.; (Toronado) 54.2 in. Width: (Starfire) 65.4 in.; (Omega) 72.9 in.; (Cutlass) 71.3-71.9 in.; (Cutlass wag) 71.7 in.; (Delta 88) 76.8 in.; (98) 76.8 in.; (Custom Crsr) 79.8 in.; (Toronado) 71.4 in. Front Tread: (Starfire) 54.7 in.; (Omega) 61.9 in.; (Cutlass) 58.5 in.; (Delta 88/98) 61.7 in.; (Custom Crsr) 62.1 in.; (Toronado) 59.3 in. Rear Tread: (Starfire) 53.6 in.; (Omega) 59.6 in.; (Cutlass) 57.7 in.; (Delta 88/98) 60.7 in.; (Custom Crsr) 64.1 in.; (Toronado) 60.0 in. Standard Tires: (Starfire) A78 x 13; (Starfire SX) BR78 x 13; (Omega) E78 x 14; (Cutlass Supreme/Calais) P195/75R14; (Cutlass Salon) P185/75R14; (Cutlass wag) P195/75R14; (Delta 88) FR78 x 15; (98) GR78 x 15; (Custom Crsr) HR78 x 15; (Toronado) P205/75R15.

TECHNICAL: Transmission: Three-speed manual transmission standard on Omega and Cutlass. Four-speed floor shift standard on Starfire, Omega V-8-305 and Cutlass. Five-speed manual optional on Starfire/Cutlass. Three-speed Turbo Hydra-matic standard on other models, optional on all. Standard final drive ratio: (Starfire) 2.73:1; (Omega) 3.08:1; (Cutlass) 2.93:1; (Cutlass Cruiser) 2.73:1; (Delta 88) 2.73:1; (Custom Crsr) 2.41:1; (98) 2.41:1; (Toronado) 2.41:1. Steering: Recirculating ball. Front Suspension: (Starfire) coil springs w/lower trailing links and anti-sway bar; (Toronado); longitudinal torsion bars w/anti-sway bar; (others) coil springs w/control arms and anti-sway bar. Rear Suspension: (Starfire) rigid axle w/coil springs, lower trailing radius arms, upper torque arms, transverse linkage bar and anti-sway bar; (Omega) rigid axle w/semi-elliptic leaf springs; (Toronado) independent with coil springs, longitudinal trailing arms and automatic leveling; (others) rigid axle w/coil springs, lower trailing radius arms and upper torque arms. Brakes: Front disc, rear drum. Ignition: Electronic. Body construction: (Starfire) unibody; (Omega) unibody w/separate front partial frame; (others) separate body on perimeter frame. Fuel Tank: (Starfire) 18.5 gal.; (Omega) 20.3 gal.; (Cutlass) 18.1 gal.; (Cutlass wag) 18.2 gal.; (Delta 88) 20.7 or 25 gal.; (98) 25.0 gal.; (Custom Crsr wag) 22 gal.; (Toronado) 20 gal.

1979 Oldsmobile, Starfire Firenza hatchback coupe, (O)

DRIVETRAIN OPTIONS: Engines: 231 cu. in. V-6: Starfire ($200). 260 cu. in. V-8: Cutlass/88 ($140). Diesel 260 cu. in. V-8: Cutlass ($735). 301 cu. in. 2Bbl. V-8: Delta 88 ($195). 305 cu. in. 2Bbl. V-8: Starfire ($395): Starfire w/GT pkg. ($195); Omega ($195). 305 cu. in. 4Bbl. V-8: Cutlass ($255). 350 cu. in. 4Bbl. V-8: Omega/Cutlass Crsr/88 ($320). 403 cu. in. V-8: 98/Custom Crsr ($70). Diesel 350 cu. in. V-8: Cutlass Crsr/88 ($895); 98/Custom Crsr ($785); Toronado ($395). Engine oil cooler: Cutlass ($40). Transmission/Differential: Four-speed floor shift: Omega/Cutlass ($135). Five-speed manual floor shift: Starfire ($175); Cutlass ($310). Turbo Hydra-matic: Starfire ($295); Omega/Cutlass ($335). Limited-slip differential: Starfire ($60); Omega/Cutlass ($64); 88/98 ($68). Brakes/Steering: Power brakes: Starfire ($71); Omega/Cutlass ($76). Power four-wheel disc brakes: Toronado ($205). Power steering: Starfire/Omega/Cutlass ($163). Suspension: Rallye susp. pkg.: Omega ($43); Cutlass ($37); Toronado ($28). H.D. susp.: Cutlass/88/98 ($25); Custom Crsr ($10). Firm ride shock absorbers: Cutlass/88/98 ($7). Superlift rear shocks: Cutlass/88/98 ($54-$55). Automatic load leveling: Cutlass/88/98 ($120). Other: High-capacity cooling ($21-$92). High-capacity radiator: Starfire ($20); Omega ($21). H.D. battery ($18-$21). High-capacity alternator: Cutlass/full-size ($49). Trailer wiring: Cutlass/full-size ($22-$35). Engine block heater ($15). California emissions equipment ($83). High-altitude emissions ($35).

OPTION PACKAGES: Starfire GT pkg. ($447-$577). Firenza sport pkg.: Starfire ($375). Omega LS pkg.: Brougham sedan ($2078). Omega SX pkg.: base hatch/cpe ($231). Cutlass 442 appearance/handling pkg.: Salon cpe ($276); Salon Brghm ($122). Delta 88 Holiday coupe pkg.: base ($288). Sport paint pkg.: Cutlass Supreme/Calais cpe ($181).

MAJOR CONVENIENCE/APPEARANCE OPTIONS: Four Season air conditioner ($496-$605). Tempmatic air conditioning: Cutlass/88/98 ($602-$650); Toronado ($45). Power seat ($135-$166); N/A Starfire. Power windows ($126-$205); N/A Starfire. Twilight sentinel: Cutlass/88/98/Toronado ($47). Cornering lamps: Cutlass/88/98 ($49). Power astroroof: Cutlass/88/98/Toronado ($729-$998). Power sliding metal sunroof: Cutlass/88/98/Toronado ($529-$798). Removable glass panel roof: Cutlass ($655). Removable glass panel sunroof: Starfire ($180). Landau vinyl roof ($178-$200); N/A Starfire. Full vinyl roof ($79-$145); N/A Starfire. Woodgrain vinyl bodyside/tailgate paneling: Cutlass/Custom Cruiser wagon ($243-$261). Rear-facing third seat: Custom Cruiser ($193).

HISTORY: Introduced: September 28, 1978. Model year production: 1,068,155. Calendar year production (U.S.): 1,007,996. Calendar year sales by U.S. dealers: 949,488. Model year sales by U.S. dealers: 1,000,673.

HISTORICAL FOOTNOTES: Sales topped the million mark, making 1979 the second biggest model year ever for Oldsmobile. Cutlass accounted for well over half the total, reaching more than 536,000 units. Again, Cutlass was America's best seller, with Supreme alone taking over four-fifths of the sales. The fastback Cutlass models did not sell nearly as well. Full-size sales dropped, but not nearly as much as some other makes. Part of the reason was the availability of the diesel engine, which gained popularity before its durability problems surfaced.

1980

The 1980 model year was highlighted by eye-popping price increases and a new front-drive Omega. A new 5.0-liter gas fueled V-8 was the standard engine in Ninety-Eight and Toronado, and optional in Eighty-Eight. It was derived from the 350 cubic inch (5.7-liter) engine, with a smaller bore. The 403 cubic inch (6.6-liter V-8) was dropped. New poppet-type injector nozzles on diesels were smaller and did not require fuel return lines, and delivered a finer spray.

1980 Oldsmobile, Starfire Firenza hatchback coupe, (AA)

STARFIRE -- SERIES 3H -- FOUR/V-6 -- Oldsmobile's subcompact barely qualified for this year's lineup, as it was dropped in December 1979. For its brief final season, little change was evident, and no V-8 engine was available.

1980 Oldsmobile, Omega Brougham coupe, (AA)

1980 Oldsmobile, Omega Brougham sedan, (O)

OMEGA -- SERIES 3X -- FOUR/V-6 -- A far different GM X-body Omega -- much lighter (and more expensive) -- joined the Olds line this year. It featured front-wheel-drive, with a transverse-mounted 151 cubic inch (2.5-liter) four-cylinder engine. Wheelbase was six inches shorter than the former Omega, 18.5 inches shorter overall. Omega carried five passengers. Weighing 750 pounds less than prior Omegas, it was a clone of the Chevrolet Citation, thus closely related to Buick and Pontiac models as well. Four models were offered: coupe and sedan, in base or Brougham trim. Unlike Chevrolet and Pontiac, Oldsmobile did not offer a hatchback. A sporty SX option was available. A dual vertical-bar grille extended above and below the headlamps, wrapping up into the front-end panel. Vertical park/turn signal lamps stood between the single rectangular headlamps and the grille. Centered on the front-end panel was a red Oldsmobile emblem. 'Oldsmobile' block letters went on the left grille section. Anodized aluminum bumpers had optional bumper guards and rub strips. 'Omega' block letters were on the sail panel of all models, while Broughams added a sail panel emblem. Omega Brougham had a stand-up hood ornament and hood center molding, as well as rocker panel and wheel opening moldings. Hood, rocker, wheel and front-end panel moldings were optional on base Omegas. Wide lower rocker panel moldings were optional on both. Large chrome-bordered vertical wrap-over taillamps had a center Oldsmobile emblem. Backup lamps were at the bottom of taillamps. 'Oldsmobile' block letters went on the lower right corner of the rear-end panel. Broughams had a bright lower rear-end panel molding and license plate opening molding and a decklid lock ornament. Four-door Broughams had a bright brushed center pillar appliqué, which was optional on base models. All Omegas had bright side window frame moldings. Base Omegas had a narrow bead belt molding, while Broughams had a wide belt molding. Sedan rear-quarter windows rolled down; coupes had fixed rear quarter windows. Base models had hubcaps; Broughams had wheel covers. Fourteen body colors were offered. Speedometer, clock and light switch were plug-in type for easier servicing. The glovebox top snapped out to service the right side of the instrument panel. Doors locked via a sliding lever below the door handle, to improve theft-resistance. Standard equipment included four-speed manual floor shift, rack-and-pinion steering, low-drag front disc brakes, maintenance-free wheel bearings, P185/80R13 glass-belted radial tires, self-adjusting clutch, Freedom battery, AM radio, inside hood release, day/night mirror, and bench seats. Brougham added a custom sport bench seat with fold-down center armrest. Options included a 2.8-liter V-6, six-way seat adjusters (for either bucket or bench seats), reclining front seatbacks, removable glass sunroof, electric rear window defogger, combination dome and dual-lens reading lamp, digital clock, push-button AM/FM stereo with cassette player (or with 40-channnel CB transceiver). Coupes could have an optional landau top, and all could get a full vinyl roof with bright back window reveal moldings. Omega's SX option came in 10 colors on the base coupe and sedan. The package included black grille bars; black lower body color; blacked-out window frames, headlamp doors, taillamp bezels and side markers and black bumpers and fillers. Also included: a one-piece body-color decklid spoiler, sport mirrors, special wheel trim and decal stripes.

1980 Oldsmobile, Omega coupe with SX option, (O)

1980 Oldsmobile, Cutlass Supreme coupe, (AA)

1980 Oldsmobile, Cutlass sedan, (O)

1980 Oldsmobile, Cutlass Salon slantback coupe, (O)

CUTLASS -- SERIES 3A -- V-6/V-8 -- Ten Cutlass models were available this year, including three new notchback sedans. They replaced the unpopular Cutlass Salon and Salon Brougham four-door slantback models. The lineup included Cutlass Salon and Salon Brougham coupe, Cutlass sedan, Cutlass LS sedan, Cutlass Supreme and Supreme Brougham coupe, Cutlass Brougham sedan, Cutlass Calais coupe, Cutlass Cruiser and Cruiser Brougham wagon. For the first time, opera lamps were optional on LS and Brougham sedans. Each side of Salon's grille contained three vertical bars over a series of horizontal bars. Single headlamps were outboard of park/signal lamps. Salon continued the slantback styling on a two-door coupe. The Calais grille was an eggcrate design (5 x 4 hole pattern on each side)

similar to 1979, but with a narrower center divider segment. This year's version also featured quad rectangular headlamps, along with wide park/signal lamps mounted in the bumper. Cutlass Brougham and LS carried a grille similar to Calais, but with single headlamps. Cutlass Calais could get the 4-4-2 (W-30) option with either black or white body paint, W-30 and 4-4-2 identification, gold accent stripes, and gold-painted grille, pillar, hood and top. The package also included sport aluminum wheels with raised-white-letter tires, sport mirrors and the 350 cubic inch (5.7-liter) four-barrel V-8 with automatic transmission. The 350 V-8 was not available in any other Cutlass. A total of 886 4-4-2 packages installed. A total of 6,000 custom appearance packages (RPO code Y68) from American Sunroof were installed on Supremes. Oldsmobile has also estimated that as many as eight simulated convertible tops (code W44) were installed. This year, 46,990 Cutlass diesels were produced.

1980 Oldsmobile, Delta 88 Royale coupe, (AA)

1980 Oldsmobile, Cutlass Brougham sedan, (O)

1980 Oldsmobile, Cutlass Calais coupe, (O)

1980 Oldsmobile, Cutlass Cruiser Brougham station wagon, (O)

DELTA 88 -- SERIES 3B -- V-6/V-8 -- The Delta 88 was substantially restyled, including softer side feature lines, a longer front end and shorter back end. Park/turn signal lamps went into the bumper, allowing a lower front end (and reduced drag). Other aerodynamic improvements included flatter wheel covers, rounded front corners and a small spoiler added to the decklid. A straighter backlight angle gave a more formal appearance. This year's grille had four sections on each side, with three vertical dividers over a pattern of narrow vertical bars. Quad headlamps and wraparound front side marker lenses were used. At the rear were large wraparound taillamps with emblems in their lenses. Base, Royale and Royale Brougham models were offered in two body styles: two-door coupe or four-door sedan. A Holiday 88 coupe option (RPO code Y78) was installed in 3,547 vehicles. It included contour bucket front seats, a sports console with shifter, sport mirrors, custom sport steering wheel, special emblems and special color-keyed wheel covers. A total of 49,087 diesel 88s were built. Standard equipment included a 231 cubic inch (3.8-liter) V-6 with automatic transmission, P205/75R15 steel-belted radial tires, bumper guards and impact strips, wheel covers, rocker panel and wheel opening moldings, lighter, day/night mirror and power brakes/steering.

1980 Oldsmobile, Delta 88 sedan, (O)

1980 Oldsmobile, Custom Cruiser diesel station wagon, (O)

CUSTOM CRUISER -- SERIES 3B -- V-8 -- This year's full-size wagon adopted the Delta 88's grille and front-end. The 307 cubic inch (5.0-liter) four-barrel V-8 with automatic transmission was standard.

1980 Oldsmobile, Ninety-Eight Regency sedan, (AA)

NINETY-EIGHT -- SERIES 3C -- V-8 -- Ninety-Eight restyling paralleled the Delta 88, with softened side feature lines and aerodynamic improvements. Each side of the split eggcrate grille contained a 5 x 4 pattern. Quad headlamps extended outward into wraparound marker lenses. Wide park/signal lamps were bumper-mounted. Cornering lamps were mounted low on the front fenders. 'Ninety Eight' script went on the cowl, just below the bodyside molding. Vertical taillamps sat at quarter-panel tips. Three models were offered: Luxury sedan, and Regency coupe and sedan. Standard equipment included fender skirts, a 307 cubic inch (5.0-liter) V-8 engine with four-barrel carb, automatic transmission, P215/75R15 steel-belted radial tires, bumper guards and impact strips, dual remote-control mirrors, power windows and driver's seat, rocker panel and wheel opening moldings and electric clock. Regency added an AM/FM stereo radio and digital clock. A total of 18,446 diesels were produced.

1980 Oldsmobile, Toronado coupe, (O)

TORONADO -- SERIES 3E -- V-8 -- A new grille gave Toronado a slightly different appearance for its second season in downsized form. The front end was similar to 1979, but the grille consisted only of horizontal bars (no vertical dividers). Moreover, those bars extended outward to the fender tips and contained the parking/signal lamps. Quad rectangular headlamps were used. 'Toronado' block letters reached across the upper grille panel and the decklid. Horizontal taillamps had small backup lenses next to the rear license plate. Standard equipment included a 307 cubic inch (5.0-liter) V-8 with automatic transmission, AM/FM stereo radio, power antenna, rocker panel and wheel opening moldings, level control, power six-way driver's seat, and power windows. Tires were P205/75R15 steel-belted radial whitewalls. Also standard: power door locks, air conditioning, digital clock, and side window defrosters. Toronado's weight was cut by over 100 pounds through the use of many lighter weight components, including the alternator, aluminum intake manifold, compact spare tire, and aluminum bumper reinforcements. A new sport coupe option, Toronado XSC, included a special ride/handling package, bucket seats with console, leather-wrapped steering wheel, voltmeter and oil pressure gauge. A total of 12,362 diesel models were built.

I.D. DATA: Oldsmobile's 13-symbol Vehicle Identification Number (VIN) was located on the upper left surface of the instrument panel, visible through the windshield. The first digit is '3', indicating Oldsmobile division. Next is a letter indicating series: 'T' = Starfire; 'D' = Starfire SX; 'B' = Omega; 'E' = Omega Brougham; 'G' = Cutlass/Salon; 'J' = Cutlass Salon Brougham; 'R' = Cutlass Supreme; 'M' = Cutlass Supreme Brougham; 'K' = Cutlass Calais; 'G' = Cutlass Cruiser; 'H' = Cutlass Cruiser Brougham; 'L' = Delta 88; 'N' = Delta 88 Royale; 'Y' = Delta 88 Royale Brougham; 'P' = Custom Cruiser; 'V' = Ninety-Eight Luxury; 'X' = Ninety-Eight Regency; 'Z' = Toronado Brougham. Next come two digits that denote body type: '07' = Starfire hatch coupe; '37' = 2-dr. coupe; '47' = 2-dr. coupe; '57' = 2-dr. coupe; '87' = 2-dr. plain-back coupe; '69' = 4-dr. 4-window notch sedan; '35' = 4-dr. 2-seat wagon. The fifth symbol is a letter indicating engine code: '5' = L4-151 2Bbl.; '7' = V-6-173 2Bbl.; 'A' = V-6-231 2Bbl.; 'F' = V-8-260 2Bbl.; 'S' =

V-8-265 2Bbl.; 'H' = V-8-305 4Bbl.; 'Y' = V-8-307 4Bbl.; 'R' = V-8-350 4Bbl.; 'N' = diesel V-8-350. The sixth symbol denotes model year ('A' = 1980). Next is a plant code: '2' = Ste. Therese, Quebec (Canada); 'G' = Framingham, Mass.; 'D' = Doraville, Georgia; 'M' = Lansing, Mich.; 'W' = Willow Run, Mich.; 'R' = Arlington, Texas; 'X' = Fairfax, Kansas; 'E' = Linden, New Jersey; '7' = Lordstown, Ohio. The final six digits are the sequential serial number, which began with 100,001. Engine numbers were stamped on the front of the right rocker cover, or top of left cover (Buick-built engines), on the front of the right rocker cover (Chevrolet-built V-8), on label at front or rear of right rocker cover (Chevrolet V-6), or on the left rocker cover (Oldsmobile engines). Four-cylinder engine numbers were on a pad at right front of block, near the distributor shaft; or left front, below cylinder head. A body number plate on the shroud identified model year, car division, series, style, body assembly plant, body number, trim combination, modular seat code, paint code and date built code.

STARFIRE (FOUR/V-6)

Model Number	Body/Style Number	Body Type & Seating	Factory Price	Shipping Weight	Production Total
3H	T07	2-dr. Hatch Cpe-4P	4750/4975	2656/----	Note 1

STARFIRE SX (FOUR/V-6)

3H	D07	2-dr. Hatch Cpe-4P	4950/5175	2668/----	8,237

Note 1: Production included in SX total.

OMEGA (FOUR/V-6)

Model Number	Body/Style Number	Body Type & Seating	Factory Price	Shipping Weight	Production Total
3X	B37	2-dr. Cpe-5P	5100/5325	2400/2439	28,267
3X	B69	4-dr. Sed-5P	5266/5491	2427/2466	42,172

OMEGA BROUGHAM (FOUR/V-6)

3X	E37	2-dr. Cpe-5P	5380/5605	2432/2471	21,595
3X	E69	4-dr. Sed-5P	5530/5755	2459/2498	42,289

CUTLASS/SALON (V-6/V-8)

Model Number	Body/Style Number	Body Type & Seating	Factory Price	Shipping Weight	Production Total
3A	G87	2-dr. Salon Cpe-6P	5372/5552	3065/3214	3,429
3A	G69	4-dr. Sed-6P	5532/5712	3069/3218	36,923

CUTLASS SALON BROUGHAM (V-6/V-8)

3A	J87	2-dr. Cpe-6P	5662/5842	3065/3214	965

CUTLASS SUPREME (V-6/V-8)

3A	R47	2-dr. Cpe-6P	6252/6432	3190/3339	169,597
3A	R69	4-dr. LS Sed-6P	6353/6533	3179/3328	86,868

CUTLASS SUPREME BROUGHAM (V-6/V-8)

3A	M47	2-dr. Cpe-6P	6691/6871	3201/3350	77,875
3A	M69	4-dr. Sed-6P	6776/6956	3206/3355	52,462

CUTLASS CALAIS (V-6/V-8)

3A	K47	2-dr. Cpe-5P	6716/6896	3201/3350	26,269

CUTLASS CRUISER (V-6/V-8)

3A	G35	4-dr. 2S Sta Wag-6P	5978/6158	3263/3423	7,815
3A	H35	4-dr. Brghm Wag-6P	6377/6557	3300/3460	22,791

DELTA 88 (V-6/V-8)

Model Number	Body/Style Number	Body Type & Seating	Factory Price	Shipping Weight	Production Total
3B	L37	2-dr. Cpe-6P	6457/6637	3325/3465	6,845
3B	L69	4-dr. Sed-6P	6552/6732	3358/3498	15,285

DELTA 88 ROYALE (V-6/V-8)

3B	N37	2-dr. Cpe-6P	6716/6896	3333/3473	39,303
3B	N69	4-dr. Sed-6P	6864/7044	3336/3476	87,178

DELTA 88 ROYALE BROUGHAM (V-6/V-8)

3B	Y37	2-dr. Cpe-6P	7079/7259	3333/3473	Note 2
3B	Y69	4-dr. Sed-6P	7160/7340	3336/3476	Note 2

Note 2: Production included in 88 Royale totals above.

CUSTOM CRUISER (V-8)

Model Number	Body/Style Number	Body Type & Seating	Factory Price	Shipping Weight	Production Total
3B	P35	4-dr. 2S Sta Wag-6P	7443	3910	17,067
3B	P35	4-dr. 3S Sta Wag-8P	7651	3940	Note 3

Note 3: Three-seat production is included in two-seat total.

NINETY-EIGHT LUXURY (V-8)

Model Number	Body/Style Number	Body Type & Seating	Factory Price	Shipping Weight	Production Total
3C	V69	4-dr. Sed-6P	9113	3789	2,640

NINETY-EIGHT REGENCY (V-8)

3C	X37	2-dr. Cpe-6P	9620	3811	12,391
3C	X69	4-dr. Sed-6P	9742	3832	58,603

TORONADO BROUGHAM (V-8)

Model Number	Body/Style Number	Body Type & Seating	Factory Price	Shipping Weight	Production Total
3E	Z57	2-dr. Cpe-4P	11361	3627	43,440

FACTORY PRICE AND WEIGHT NOTE: For Cutlass and Delta 88, prices and weights to left of slash are for six-cylinder, to right for V-8 engine. For Starfire/Omega, prices/weights to left are for four-cylinder, to right for V-6.

ENGINE DATA: BASE FOUR (Starfire, Omega): Inline, overhead-valve four-cylinder. Cast iron block and head. Displacement: 151 cu. in. (2.5 liters). Bore & stroke: 4.00 x 3.00 in. Compression ratio: 8.2:1. Brake horsepower: 85 at 4400 rpm. (Omega, 90 at 4000). Torque: 128 lb.-ft. at 2400 rpm. (Omega, 134 at 2400). Five main bearings. Hydraulic valve lifters. Carburetor: 2Bbl. Rochester 2SE. Pontiac-built. VIN Code: 5. OPTIONAL V-6 (Omega): 60-degree, overhead-valve V-6. Cast iron block and aluminum head. Displacement: 173 cu. in. (2.8 liters). Bore & stroke: 3.50 x 3.00 in. Compression ratio: 8.5:1. Brake horsepower: 115 at 4800 rpm. Torque: 145 lb.-ft. at 2400 rpm. Four main bearings. Hydraulic valve lifters. Carburetor: 2Bbl. Rochester 2SE. Chevrolet-built. VIN Code: 7. BASE V-6 (Cutlass, Delta 88); OPTIONAL (Starfire): 90-degree, overhead-valve V-6. Cast iron block and head. Displacement: 231 cu. in. (3.8 liters). Bore & stroke: 3.80 x 3.40 in. Compression ratio: 8.0:1. Brake horsepower: 110 at 3800 rpm. Torque: 190 lb.-ft. at 1600 rpm. Four main bearings. Hydraulic valve lifters. Carburetor: 2Bbl. Rochester M2ME. Buick-built. VIN Code: A. OPTIONAL V-8 (Cutlass): 90-degree, overhead valve V-8. Cast iron block and head. Displacement: 260 cu. in. (4.3 liters). Bore & stroke: 3.50 x 3.39 in. Compression ratio: 7.5:1. Brake horsepower: 105 at 3400 rpm. Torque: 195 lb.-ft. at 1600 rpm. Five main bearings. Hydraulic valve lifters. Carburetor: 2Bbl. Rochester M2MC. VIN Code: F. OPTIONAL V-8 (Delta 88): 90-degree, overhead valve V-8. Cast iron block and head. Displacement: 265 cu. in. (4.3 liters). Bore & stroke: 3.75 x 3.00 in. Compression ratio: 8.3:1. Brake horsepower: 120 at 3600 rpm. Torque: 210 lb.-ft. at 1800 rpm. Five main bearings. Hydraulic valve lifters. Carburetor: 2Bbl. VIN Code: S. BASE V-8 (98, Toronado); OPTIONAL (Delta 88): 90-degree, overhead valve V-8. Cast iron block and head. Displacement: 307 cu. in. (5.0 liters). Bore & stroke: 3.80 x 3.39 in. Compression ratio: 8.0:1. Brake horsepower: 150 at 3600 rpm. Torque: 245 lb.-ft. at 1600 rpm. Five main bearings. Hydraulic valve lifters. Carburetor: 4Bbl. Rochester M4MC. VIN Code: Y. OPTIONAL V-8 (Cutlass): 90-degree, overhead valve V-8. Cast iron block and head. Displacement: 305 cu. in. (5.0 liters). Bore & stroke: 3.74 x 3.48 in. Compression ratio: 8.6:1. Brake horsepower: 155 at 4000 rpm. Torque: 240 lb.-ft. at 1600 rpm. Five main bearings. Hydraulic valve lifters. Carburetor: 4Bbl. Rochester M4MC. Chevrolet-built. VIN Code: H. OPTIONAL V-8 (Delta 88, 98, Toronado): 90-degree, overhead valve V-8. Cast iron block and head. Displacement: 350 cu. in. (5.7 liters). Bore & stroke: 4.06 x 3.39 in. Compression ratio: 8.0:1. Brake horsepower: 160 at 3600 rpm. Torque: 270 lb.-ft. at 1600 rpm. Five main bearings. Hydraulic valve lifters. Carbure-

tor: 4Bbl. Rochester E4MC. VIN Code: R. DIESEL V-8 (Cutlass, Delta 88, 98, Custom Cruiser, Toronado): 90-degree, overhead valve V-8. Cast iron block and head. Displacement: 350 cu. in. (5.7 liters). Bore & stroke: 4.06 x 3.39 in. Compression ratio: 22.5:1. Brake horsepower: 105 at 3200 rpm. Torque: 205 lb.-ft. at 1600 rpm. Five main bearings. Hydraulic valve lifters. Fuel injection. VIN Code: N.

CHASSIS DATA: Wheelbase: (Starfire) 97.0 in.; (Omega) 104.9 in.; (Cutlass) 108.1 in.; (Delta 88) 116.0 in.; (98) 119.0 in.; (Custom Crsr) 116.0 in.; (Toronado) 114.0 in. Overall Length: (Starfire) 179.6 in.; (Omega) 181.8 in.; (Cutlass) 199.1 in.; (Cutlass Supreme) 200.9 in.; (Cutlass wag) 198.4 in.; (Delta 88) 218.4 in.; (98) 221.4 in.; (Custom Crsr) 219.4 in.; (Toronado) 206.0 in. Height: (Starfire) 50.2 in.; (Omega) 51.9 in.; (Cutlass) 53.0-54.1 in.; (Cutlass wag) 54.3 in.; (Delta 88 cpe) 54.1 in.; (Delta 88 sed) 54.7 in.; (98) 55.3 in.; (Custom Crsr) 56.6 in.; (Toronado) 52.5 in. Width: (Starfire) 65.4 in.; (Omega) 69.8 in.; (Cutlass) 71.3-71.9 in.; (Cutlass wag) 71.8 in.; (Delta 88) 76.3 in.; (98) 76.3 in.; (Custom Crsr) 79.8 in.; (Toronado) 71.4 in. Front Tread: (Starfire) 54.7 in.; (Omega) 58.7 in.; (Cutlass) 58.5 in.; (Delta 88/98) 61.7 in.; (Custom Crsr) 62.1 in.; (Toronado) 59.3 in. Rear Tread: (Starfire) 53.6 in.; (Omega) 57.0 in.; (Cutlass) 57.7 in.; (Delta 88/98) 60.7 in.; (Custom Crsr) 64.1 in.; (Toronado) 60.0 in. Standard Tires: (Starfire) A78 x 13; (Starfire SX) BR78 x 13; (Omega) P185/80R13; (Cutlass) P185/75R14; (Cutlass Supreme/Brghm/Calais) P195/75R14; (Cutlass wag) P195/75R14; (Delta 88) P205/75R15; (98) P215/75R15; (Custom Crsr) P225/75R15; (Toronado) P205/75R15.

TECHNICAL: Transmission: Three-speed manual transmission standard on Cutlass (except LS/Brougham/Calais, automatic standard). Four-speed floor shift standard on Starfire/Omega. Three-speed Turbo Hydra-matic standard on other models, optional on all. Standard final drive ratio: Axle ratios not available. Steering: (Omega) rack and pinion; (others) recirculating ball. Front Suspension: (Starfire) coil springs w/lower trailing links and anti-sway bar; (Omega) MacPherson struts w/lower controls arms and coil springs; (Toronado); longitudinal torsion bars w/anti-sway bar; (others) coil springs w/control arms and anti-sway bar. Rear Suspension: (Starfire) rigid axle w/coil springs, lower trailing radius arms, upper torque arms, transverse linkage bar and anti-sway bar; (Omega) coil springs and lower control arms; (Toronado) independent with coil springs, longitudinal trailing arms and automatic leveling; (others) rigid axle w/coil springs, lower trailing radius arms and upper torque arms. Brakes: Front disc, rear drum. Ignition: Electronic. Body construction: (Starfire/Omega) unibody; (others) separate body on perimeter frame. Fuel Tank: (Starfire) 18.5 gal.; (Omega) 14 gal.; (Cutlass) 18.0 gal.; (Cutlass wag) 18.2 gal.; (Delta 88) 25 gal.; (98) 25 gal.; (Custom Crsr wag) 22 gal.; (Toronado) 21 gal.

DRIVETRAIN OPTIONS: Engines: 173 cu. in. V-6: Omega ($225). 231 cu. in. V-6: Starfire ($225). 260 cu. in. V-8: Cutlass ($180). 265 cu. in. V-8: Cutlass ($180). 307 cu. in. 2Bbl. V-8: Cutlass ($295). 305 cu. in. 4Bbl. V-8: Cutlass ($295). 350 cu. in. 4Bbl. V-8: 88 ($425); Custom Crsr/98/Toronado ($130). Diesel 350 cu. in. V-8: Cutlass/88 ($960); 98/Custom Crsr ($860); Toronado ($860). Transmission/Differential: Turbo Hydra-matic: Starfire ($320); Omega ($337); Cutlass ($358). Limited-slip differential: Starfire ($65); Cutlass ($70); 88/98 ($74). Brakes/Steering: Power brakes: Starfire/Omega ($76). Power four-wheel disc brakes: Toronado ($232). Power steering: Starfire ($158); Omega ($164); Cutlass ($174). Suspension: Rallye susp. pkg.: Cutlass/88 ($40); Toronado ($28). H.D. susp.: Omega ($20). Performance H.D. susp.: Omega/Cutlass/88/98 ($27); Custom Crsr ($12). Superlift rear shocks: Omega ($55). Automatic load leveling: Cutlass/88/98 ($145). Other: High-capacity cooling ($22-$75). High-capacity radiator ($15-$52). H.D. battery ($20-$21) exc. diesel ($42). Engine block heater ($16).

OPTION PACKAGES: Starfire GT pkg. ($496-$644). Firenza sport pkg.: Starfire ($427). Omega SX pkg.: base ($262-$303). Cutlass 4-4-2 appearance/handling pkg.: Calais ($1425). Delta 88 Holiday coupe pkg.: base ($295). Toronado XSC sport pkg. ($331). Designer interior pkg.: Cutlass Supreme/Brghm ($181).

MAJOR CONVENIENCE/APPEARANCE OPTIONS: Four Season air conditioner ($531-$647). Tempmatic air conditioning: Cutlass/88/98 ($651-$697); Toronado ($50). Power seat ($148-$179). Power windows ($133-$221); N/A Starfire. Twilight sentinel: Cutlass/88/98/Toronado ($50). Cornering lamps: Cutlass/88/98 ($53). Power astroroof w/sliding glass panel: Cutlass/88/98/Toronado ($773-$1058). Power sliding metal sunroof: Cutlass/88/98/Toronado ($561-$848). Removable glass roof panels: Cutlass ($695). Removable glass panel sunroof: Starfire/Omega ($193-$240). Landau vinyl roof ($175-$213); N/A Starfire. Full vinyl roof: Omega/Cutlass/88/98 ($116-$174). Rear-facing third seat: Custom Cruiser ($208).

HISTORY: Introduced: October 11, 1979 except Omega, April 19, 1979. Model year production: 910,306. Calendar year production (U.S.): 783,230. Calendar year sales by U.S. dealers: 820,681. Model year sales by U.S. dealers: 825,526.

HISTORICAL FOOTNOTES: Oldsmobile's fleet fuel economy average was 21.1 MPG (35 percent better than the 15.6 MPG in 1975). Diesel engine prospects were impacted by shifting emissions regulations. Federal standards were relaxed a bit as the model year began, but California presented more of a problem. The smaller (4.2-liter) diesel was discontinued after a brief life in some 1979 models. Still, diesel V-8 production increased sharply this year, up some 73 percent over 1979. Production of the gasoline fueled 350 V-8, on the other hand, declined sharply and it was soon phased out. Oldsmobile slipped considerably for 1980 following excellent 1979 model year sales. But then, so did most other makes. Cutlass remained America's most popular car.

1981

Substantial price increases greeted Oldsmobile buyers once again. With the phaseout of Starfire early in the 1980 model year, only five lines were offered. Cutlass Salon and Salon Brougham coupes were dropped. Cutlass Supreme was restyled to cut drag 15 percent. Fuel mileage gains came from a new four-speed automatic transmission, expanded use of lock-up torque converter clutches, low-drag brakes, higher-pressure tires, better aerodynamics (especially full-size), more on-board computers, and engine downsizing. Lock-up torque converter clutches were standard on all Olds models with automatic except Omega and Toronado. Four-speed automatic was standard on Ninety-Eight and Custom Cruiser, and Delta 88 with 5.0-liter V-8; optional on 88s with 4.3-liter engine. It had 0.67:1 overdrive fourth gear. All gas engines now had computer command control, with an electronic carburetor control to maintain constant air/fuel ratio. Only seven engines were available this year, versus ten in 1980 (and many more in prior years, when a proliferation of 49-state, California and high-altitude powerplants had been the rule). Only 88/98, Toronado and Custom Cruiser had the 5.0-liter V-8. A 4.1-liter V-6 was now standard in Ninety-Eight and Toronado -- the first V-6 in either of those models. This year, 19 of the 23 Olds models could have 5.7-liter diesel (but 5.0-liter was the biggest gas engine). Diesels added roller valve lifters, among other internal changes. An electronic control module (ECM), a little black box in the passenger compartment, controlled the engine of all gas fueled models. It monitored coolant temperature, manifold pressure, transmission gear, rpm, idle speed, oxygen in exhaust and other functions. A diagnostic system and "Check Engine" warning light were part of the computerized system. The Sport Omega was the first use of flex injected-molded fenders on an Oldsmobile. That model also used a soft front and rear fascia, as did the newly restyled Cutlass Supreme coupe bumpers.

1981 Oldsmobile, Omega sedan, (AA)

1981 Oldsmobile, Omega ES2800 sedan, (O)

1981 Oldsmobile, Sport Omega coupe, (O)

OMEGA -- SERIES 3X -- FOUR/V-6 -- New options were the biggest news for the front-drive Omega in its second year. Four special styling options were announced: SX, Sport Omega, ES-2500 and ES-2800. A total 696 sport packages (RPO code Y78) were installed. As before, a coupe and sedan came in base or Brougham trim. This year's grille was a curious wrapover design. Not only did the pattern wrap slightly over onto the hood area, but the wrapover portion extended outward, above the single headlamps. The style was similar to before, but with a pattern of thin vertical bars accented by three horizontal dividers instead of vertical elements alone. Park/signal lamps were bumper-mounted. The sporty ES version carried a non-wrapover blacked-out grille.

CUTLASS -- SERIES 3A -- V-6/V-8 -- Eight models this year included Cutlass and Cutlass LS sedan, Cutlass Supreme and Supreme Brougham coupe, Brougham sedan, Calais, Cruiser, and Cruiser Brougham. Cutlass Supreme had all-new styling and improved aerodynamics. A soft-fascia front end extended to the bumper rub strip. The new swing-away grille displayed an egg-

1981 Oldsmobile, Cutlass Calais T-top coupe, (AA)

1979 Oldsmobile, Cutlass LS sedan, (O)

crate pattern on each side (4 x 6 hole arrangement). But the bottom two rows of the grille angled forward at the base, toward the bumper. Quad headlamps were used. Park and turn signal lamps were in the lower bumper, which also had twin slots. Supreme's profile had a tapered look, with a lowered front and slightly higher decklid. The side feature line was softened and covered the body's length, with a flush-mounted quarter window. Wheel opening moldings were standard. Supreme's rear-end panel wrapped down to provide a soft covering for the upper bumper, with a chrome lower bar. Narrow two-section vertical taillamps wrapped up and over in typical Oldsmobile style. The base Cutlass sedan and Cutlass Cruiser had the same new grille. Cutlass LS, Brougham and Cruiser Brougham had their own grille and new quad headlamps with park/signal lamps in the bumper. This upright grille had five vertical bars on each side of a wide, bright center divider. Headlamp framing extended to wraparound side marker lights. Identifying script went on the cowl. Taillamps were wider than Supreme's and didn't reach the top of the quarter panel. Standard equipment included a 231 cubic inch (3.8-liter) V-6, column-shift automatic transmission, power brakes and stand-up hood ornament. Calais had specially painted wheel covers and front/rear stabilizer bars. Supreme coupes included rocker panel moldings. Tires were P195/75R14 steel-belted blackwalls. A total of 15,000 appearance packages (RPO code Y68) were installed.

1981 Oldsmobile, Cutlass Supreme coupe, (O)

1981 Oldsmobile, Cutlass Brougham sedan, (O)

DELTA 88 -- SERIES 3B -- V-6/V-8 -- Each side of 88's new rectangular segmented grille contained an 8 x 2 pattern of bold holes. Quad rectangular headlamps led into side marker lenses. Park/signal lamps were set into the bumper. Rear ends had a small decklid spoiler, as on all full-size Olds models. Large angular wraparound taillamps displayed two horizontal trim strips. Six models were offered: coupe or sedan in base, Royale or Roy-

ale Brougham trim. Standard Delta 88 equipment included a 231 cubic inch (3.8-liter) V-6 with automatic transmission, power brakes and steering, front/rear armrests, bumper guards, stand-up hood ornament, bumper impact strips, rocker panel and wheel opening moldings, lighter, walnut-grained instrument panel, dome lamp, wheel covers and P205/75R15 steel-belted radial blackwalls. Royale added bodyside moldings and a custom sport bench seat with center armrest. Brougham coupes had opera lamps; both Broughams had belt reveal moldings. A total 1,637 Holiday coupe packages (RPO code Y78) equipped base 88 models.

1981 Oldsmobile, Delta 88 Royale Brougham coupe, (AA)

1981 Oldsmobile, Custom Cruiser station wagon, (O)

CUSTOM CRUISER -- SERIES 3B -- V-8 -- The full-size wagon had the same grille as the Delta 88, but had the V-8 only. The 5.0-liter V-8 with four-speed overdrive automatic transmission was standard.

1981 Oldsmobile, Ninety-Eight Regency Brougham sedan, (AA)

NINETY-EIGHT -- SERIES 3C -- V-6/V-8 -- The Ninety-Eight's front-end appearance was similar to Delta 88, but the grille had two vertical and one horizontal bar on each side, over a tight crosshatch pattern. That gave each side six major sections, with a recessed eggcrate design. The rear end carried a small decklid spoiler. Taillamps were much narrower than 88's. Three models were available: Luxury sedan, and Regency coupe or sedan. Standard Ninety-Eight equipment included a 252 cubic inch (4.1-liter) V-8 and four-speed automatic overdrive transmission, power brakes and steering, power windows, bumper guards and impact strips, electric clock, fender skirts, dome reading lamp and remote-control outside mirrors. Also standard: rocker panel and wheel opening moldings, belt reveal and roof drip moldings, two-way power seat, and P215/75R15 steel-belted radial whitewalls. Regency added an AM/FM stereo radio, digital clock, opera lamps and divided front seat with twin controls.

1981 Oldsmobile, Toronado coupe, (AA)

TORONADO -- SERIES 3E -- V-6/V-8 -- The front-drive Toronado was little changed. The Brougham coupe was the standard model, with sporty XSC package available. As before, the grille extended the entire width of the car. Park and turn lamps were hidden behind the grille, below the quad rectangular headlamps. Long horizontal taillamps and backup lamps extended from the decklid's edge to the license plate opening. A total of 3,959 XSC packages (RPO code Y78) were installed. Toronado's standard equipment included a 252 cubic inch (4.1-liter) V-8 and automatic transmission, automatic level control, power brakes and steering, air conditioning, bumper guards and impact strips, digital clock, side window defogger, power windows and door locks and halogen headlamps. Also included: cornering lamps, rocker panel and wheel opening moldings, AM/FM stereo radio, power antenna, six-way power driver's seat, remote-control mirrors, tinted glass and P205/75R15 steel-belted whitewalls.

I.D. DATA: A new 17-symbol Vehicle Identification Number (VIN) was located on the upper left surface of the instrument panel, visible through the windshield. The first three symbols ('1G3') indicate Oldsmobile division. Symbol four denotes restraint type: 'A' = manual (active) belts. Symbol five is car line/series: 'B' = Omega; 'E' = Omega Brougham; 'G' = Cutlass Salon; 'J' = Cutlass Salon Brougham; 'R' = Cutlass Supreme; 'M' = Cutlass Supreme Brougham; 'K' = Cutlass Calais; 'G' = Cutlass Cruiser; 'H' = Cutlass Cruiser Brougham; 'L' = Delta 88; 'N' = Delta 88 Royale; 'Y' = Delta 88 Royale Brougham; 'P' = Custom Cruiser; 'V' = Ninety-Eight Luxury; 'X' = Ninety-Eight Regency; 'Z' = Toronado Brougham. Next come two digits that denote body type: '37' = 2-dr. coupe; '47' = 2-dr. coupe; '57' = 2-dr. coupe; '69' = 4-dr. 4-window notch sedan; '35' = 4-dr. 2-seat wagon. Symbol eight is a letter for engine code: '5' = L4-151 2Bbl.; 'X' = V-6-173 2Bbl.; 'A' = V-6-231 2Bbl.; '4' = V-6-252 4Bbl.; 'F' = V-8-260 2Bbl.; 'Y' = V-8-307 4Bbl.; 'N' = diesel V-8-350. Next comes a check digit, followed by a code for model year: ('B' = 1981). Symbol eleven is the assembly plant code: '2' = Ste. Therese, Quebec (Canada); 'G' = Framingham, Mass.; 'D' = Doraville, Georgia; 'M' = Lansing, Mich.; 'W' = Willow Run, Mich.; 'R' = Arlington, Texas; 'X' = Fairfax, Kansas; 'E' = Linden, New Jersey. The final six digits are the sequential serial number, starting with 100,001. Engine numbers were stamped on the front of the right rocker cover, or top of left cover (Buick-built engines), on label at front or rear of right rocker cover (Chevrolet V-6), or on the left rocker cover (Oldsmobile engines). Four-cylinder engine numbers were on a pad at left or right front of block. A body number plate on the upper right cowl identified model year, series, style, body assembly plant, body number, trim combination, modular seat code, paint code, date built code and option codes.

OMEGA (FOUR/V-6)

Model Number	Body/Style Number	Body Type & Seating	Factory Price	Shipping Weight	Production Total
3X	B37	2-dr. Cpe-5P	6343/6468	2414/2464	27,323
3X	B69	4-dr. Sed-5P	6514/6639	2444/2494	51,715

OMEGA BROUGHAM (FOUR/V-6)

Model Number	Body/Style Number	Body Type & Seating	Factory Price	Shipping Weight	Production Total
3X	E37	2-dr. Cpe-5P	6700/6825	2437/2487	19,260
3X	E69	4-dr. Sed-5P	6855/6980	2474/2524	49,620

CUTLASS (V-6/V-8)

Model Number	Body/Style Number	Body Type & Seating	Factory Price	Shipping Weight	Production Total
3A	G69	4-dr. Sed-6P	6955/7005	3127/3283	25,580

CUTLASS SUPREME (V-6/V-8)

Model Number	Body/Style Number	Body Type & Seating	Factory Price	Shipping Weight	Production Total
3A	R47	2-dr. Cpe-6P	7484/7534	3137/3290	187,875

CUTLASS LS (V-6/V-8)

Model Number	Body/Style Number	Body Type & Seating	Factory Price	Shipping Weight	Production Total
3A	R69	4-dr. Sed-6P	7652/7702	3160/3313	84,272

CUTLASS SUPREME BROUGHAM (V-6/V-8)

Model Number	Body/Style Number	Body Type & Seating	Factory Price	Shipping Weight	Production Total
3A	M47	2-dr. Cpe-6P	7969/8019	3162/3315	93,855
3A	M69	4-dr. Sed-6P	8100/8150	3166/3319	53,952

CUTLASS CALAIS (V-6/V-8)

Model Number	Body/Style Number	Body Type & Seating	Factory Price	Shipping Weight	Production Total
3A	K47	2-dr. Cpe-5P	8004/8054	3151/3304	4,105

CUTLASS CRUISER (V-6/V-8)

Model Number	Body/Style Number	Body Type & Seating	Factory Price	Shipping Weight	Production Total
3A	G35	4-dr. 2S Sta Wag-6P	7418/7468	3293/3445	31,926
3A	H35	4-dr. Brghm Wag-6P	7725/7775	3286/3448	Note 1

Note 1: Brougham production included in basic total.

DELTA 88 (V-6/V-8)

Model Number	Body/Style Number	Body Type & Seating	Factory Price	Shipping Weight	Production Total
3B	L37	2-dr. Cpe-6P	7429/7479	3401/3570	3,330
3B	L69	4-dr. Sed-6P	7524/7574	3427/3596	10,806

DELTA 88 ROYALE (V-6/V-8)

Model Number	Body/Style Number	Body Type & Seating	Factory Price	Shipping Weight	Production Total
3B	N37	2-dr. Cpe-6P	7693/7743	3405/3574	41,682
3B	N69	4-dr. Sed-6P	7842/7892	3446/3615	104,124

DELTA 88 ROYALE BROUGHAM (V-6/V-8)

Model Number	Body/Style Number	Body Type & Seating	Factory Price	Shipping Weight	Production Total
3B	Y37	2-dr. Cpe-6P	8058/8108	3435/3604	Note 2
3B	Y69	4-dr. Sed-6P	8141/8191	3480/3649	Note 2

Note 2: Production included in 88 Royale totals above.

CUSTOM CRUISER (V-8)

Model Number	Body/Style Number	Body Type & Seating	Factory Price	Shipping Weight	Production Total
3B	P35	4-dr. 2S Sta Wag-6P	8452	3950	18,956

NINETY-EIGHT LUXURY (V-6/V-8)

Model Number	Body/Style Number	Body Type & Seating	Factory Price	Shipping Weight	Production Total
3C	V69	4-dr. Sed-6P	9951/9951	3661/3822	1,957

NINETY-EIGHT REGENCY (V-6/V-8)

Model Number	Body/Style Number	Body Type & Seating	Factory Price	Shipping Weight	Production Total
3C	X37	2-dr. Cpe-6P	10440/10440	3655/3816	13,696
3C	X69	4-dr. Sed-6P	10558/10558	3714/3875	74,017

TORONADO BROUGHAM (V-6/V-8)

Model Number	Body/Style Number	Body Type & Seating	Factory Price	Shipping Weight	Production Total
3E	Z57	2-dr. Cpe-5P	12148/12148	3567/3696	42,604

FACTORY PRICE AND WEIGHT NOTE: Prices and weights to left of slash are for six-cylinder, to right for V-8 engine except Omega, to left for four-cylinder and to right for V-6.

ENGINE DATA: BASE FOUR (Omega): Inline, overhead-valve four-cylinder. Cast iron block and head. Displacement: 151 cu. in. (2.5 liters). Bore & stroke: 4.00 x 3.00 in. Compression ratio: 8.2:1. Brake horsepower: 90 at 4000 rpm. Torque: 125 lb.-ft. at 2400 rpm. Five main bearings. Hydraulic valve lifters. Carburetor: 2Bbl. Rochester. Pontiac-built. VIN Code: 5. OPTIONAL V-6 (Omega): 60-degree, overhead-valve V-6. Cast iron block and aluminum head. Displacement: 173 cu. in. (2.8 liters). Bore & stroke: 3.50 x 3.00 in. Compression ratio: 8.5:1. Brake horsepower: 110 at 4800 rpm. Torque: 145 lb.-ft. at 2400 rpm. Four main bearings. Hydraulic valve lifters. Carburetor: 2Bbl. Rochester. Chevrolet-built. VIN Code: X. BASE V-6 (Cutlass, Delta 88): 90-degree, overhead-valve V-6. Cast iron block and head. Displacement: 231 cu. in. (3.8 liters). Bore & stroke: 3.80 x 3.40 in. Compression ratio: 8.0:1. Brake horsepower: 110 at 3800 rpm. Torque: 190 lb.-ft. at 1600 rpm. Four main bearings. Hydraulic valve lifters. Carburetor: 2Bbl. Rochester 2ME. Buick-built. VIN Code: A. BASE V-6 (98, Toronado): 90-degree, overhead-valve V-6. Cast iron block and head. Displacement: 252 cu. in. (4.1 liters). Bore & stroke: 3.96 x 3.40 in. Compression ratio: 8.0:1. Brake horsepower: 125 at 4000 rpm. Torque: 205 lb.-ft. at 2000 rpm. Four main bearings. Hydraulic valve lifters. Carburetor: 4Bbl. Rochester M4MC. Buick-built. VIN Code: 4. OPTIONAL V-8 (Cutlass, Delta 88): 90-degree, overhead valve V-8. Cast iron block and head. Displacement: 260 cu. in. (4.3 liters). Bore & stroke: 3.50 x 3.39 in. Compression ratio: 7.5:1. Brake horsepower: 105 at 3600 rpm. Torque: 190 lb.-ft. at 1600 rpm. Five main bearings. Hydraulic valve lifters. Carburetor: 2Bbl. Rochester 2MC. VIN Code: F. OPTIONAL V-8 (Delta 88, 98, Toronado): 90-degree, overhead valve V-8. Cast iron block and head. Displacement: 307 cu. in. (5.0 liters). Bore & stroke: 3.80 x 3.38 in. Compression ratio: 8.0:1. Brake horsepower: 140 at 3800 rpm. Torque: 240 lb.-ft. at 1600 rpm. Five main bearings. Hydraulic valve lifters. Carburetor: 4Bbl. Rochester M4ME. VIN Code: Y. DIESEL V-8 (Cutlass, Delta 88, 98, Custom Cruiser, Toronado): 90-degree, overhead valve V-8. Cast iron block and head. Displacement: 350 cu. in. (5.7 liters). Bore & stroke: 4.06 x 3.39 in. Compression ratio: 22.5:1. Brake horsepower: 105 at 3200 rpm. Torque: 200 lb.-ft. at 1600 rpm. Five main bearings. Hydraulic valve lifters. Fuel injection. VIN Code: N.

CHASSIS DATA: Wheelbase: (Omega) 104.9 in.; (Cutlass) 108.1 in.; (Delta 88) 116.0 in.; (98) 119.0 in.; (Custom Crsr) 116.0 in.; (Toronado) 114.0 in. Overall Length: (Omega) 181.8 in.; (Cutlass sed) 199.1 in.; (Cutlass Calais/Supreme) 200.0 in.; (Cutlass wag) 198.2 in.; (Delta 88) 218.1 in.; (98) 221.1 in.; (Custom Crsr) 220.3 in.; (Toronado) 206.0 in. Height: (Omega) 53.7 in.; (Cutlass) 54.9-55.9 in.; (Cutlass wag) 56.2 in.; (Delta 88 cpe) 56.0 in.; (Delta 88 sed) 56.7 in.; (98) 57.2 in.; (Custom Crsr) 58.5 in.; (Toronado) 54.6 in. Width: (Omega) 69.8 in.; (Cutlass) 71.9 in.; (Cutlass wag) 71.9 in.; (Delta 88) 76.3 in.; (98) 76.3 in.; (Custom Crsr) 79.8 in.; (Toronado) 71.4 in. Front Tread: (Omega) 58.7 in.; (Cutlass) 58.5 in.; (Delta 88/98) 61.7 in.; (Custom Crsr) 62.1 in.; (Toronado) 59.3 in. Rear Tread: (Omega) 57.0 in.; (Cutlass) 57.7 in.; (Delta 88/98) 60.7 in.; (Custom Crsr) 64.1 in.; (Toronado) 60.0 in. Standard Tires: (Omega) P185/80R13; (Cutlass) P185/75R14; (Cutlass Supreme/Brghm/Calais) P195/75R14; (Cutlass wag) P195/75R14; (Delta 88) P205/75R15; (98) P215/75R15; (Custom Crsr) N/A; (Toronado) P205/75R15.

TECHNICAL: Transmission: Three-speed manual transmission standard on Cutlass sedan (except LS/Brougham/, automatic standard). Four-speed floor shift standard on Omega. Three-speed Turbo Hydra-matic standard on other models, optional on all. Four-speed automatic overdrive standard on 98, optional on 88. Standard final drive ratio: (Omega) 3.32:1 w/4-spd, 2.53:1 w/auto.; (Cutlass V-6) 3.08:1 w/3-spd, 2.41:1 w/auto.; (Cutlass V-8) 2.29:1; (Cutlass Cruiser) 2.73:1 w/V-6, 2.41:1 w/V-8-260, 2.29:1 w/V-8-307; (Delta 88) 2.73:1 w/V-6, 2.56:1 w/V-8-260, 2.41:1 w/V-8-307 or diesel; (Custom Crsr) 2.73:1; (98) 3.23:1 w/V-6, 2.73:1 w/V-8-307, 2.41:1 w/diesel; (Toronado) 2.93:1 w/V-6, 2.41:1 w/V-8. Steering: (Omega) rack and pinion; (others) recirculating ball. Front Suspension: (Omega) MacPherson struts w/coil springs and lower control arms; (Toronado); longitudinal torsion bars w/anti-sway bar; (others) coil springs w/control arms and anti-sway bar. Rear Suspension: (Omega) rigid axle w/lower control arms, trailing arm and coil springs; (Toronado) independent with coil springs, longitudinal swinging trailing arms and automatic leveling; (others) rigid axle w/coil springs, lower trailing radius arms and upper torque arms. Brakes: Front disc, rear drum. Ignition: Electronic. Body construction: (Omega) unibody; (others) separate body on perimeter frame. Fuel Tank: (Omega) 14 gal.; (Cutlass) 18.1 gal.; (Cutlass wag) 18.1 gal.; (Delta 88) 25 gal.; (98) 25 gal.; (Custom Crsr wag) 22 gal.; (Toronado) 21 gal.

DRIVETRAIN OPTIONS: Engines: 173 cu. in. V-6: Omega ($125). 260 cu. in. V-8: Cutlass/88 ($50). 307 cu. in. 4Bbl. V-8: Cutlass wag ($50); 88 ($203); 98/Toronado (NC). Diesel 350 cu. in. V-8: Cutlass/88 ($695); 98/Custom Crsr ($542);

Toronado ($695). Transmission/Differential: Turbo Hydra-matic: Omega/Cutlass ($349). Overdrive automatic: 88 (NC). Limited-slip differential: Cutlass/88/98 ($69). Brakes/Steering: Power brakes: Omega ($69). Power four-wheel disc brakes: Toronado ($215). Power steering: Omega ($168). Suspension: Firm ride/handling pkg.: Omega ($32); Cutlass/88/Toronado ($24-$39); 98 ($24). Superlift rear shocks: Omega ($54). Automatic load leveling: 88/98 ($142). Other: High-capacity cooling ($24-$74). High-capacity radiator: Cutlass/88 ($21); 98/Toronado ($21-$32). High-capacity alternator: Omega ($49); Cutlass/88 ($27-$75); 98/Toronado ($27). H.D. battery ($20) exc. diesel ($40). Engine block heater ($16). Trailer wiring harness ($23-$24). California emissions ($46) exc. diesel ($182).

OPTION PACKAGES: Omega ES pkg.: Brghm sedan ($895-$1020). Omega sport pkg.: base cpe ($669). Omega SX pkg.: base cpe ($358). Delta 88 Holiday coupe pkg.: base ($271). Toronado XSC sport pkg. ($310).

MAJOR CONVENIENCE/APPEARANCE OPTIONS: Four Season air conditioner ($585-$625). Tempmatic air conditioning: Cutlass/88 ($635-$675); 98/Toronado ($50). Cruise control ($132-$135). Power seat ($146-$173). Power windows ($140-$221). Cornering lamps: 88/98 ($51). Twilight sentinel: 98/Toronado ($49). Power astroroof w/sliding glass panel: Cutlass/88/98/Toronado ($773-$995). Power sliding metal sunroof: Cutlass/Toronado ($561-$848). Removable glass roof panels: Cutlass ($695). Glass panel sunroof: Omega ($246). Landau vinyl roof ($173-$195). Full vinyl roof: Omega/88/98 ($115-$159). Rear-facing third seat: Custom Cruiser ($190).

HISTORY: Introduced: September 25, 1980. Model year production: 940,655. Calendar year production (U.S.): 838,333. Calendar year sales by U.S. dealers: 848,739. Model year sales by U.S. dealers: 882,505.

HISTORICAL FOOTNOTES: Sales increased again this year, but still fell far short of the million level achieved two years earlier. Cutlass, however, continued as the most popular car in the country. Diesel engine production rose dramatically, but not all of them were installed in Oldsmobiles. Still, over 18 percent of Oldsmobiles sold were now diesel-powered. A steady decline in engine sizes meant the gas V-6 was now dominant over the V-8 at the production level. Over half of the engines built in 1980 had been gas V-8s, compared to less than one-third this year. Fleet fuel economy reached 22.5 mpg (1.2 mpg higher than 1980).

1982

In addition to five returning models, a new front-drive Cutlass Cieras joined the Olds line in late fall, displaying a contemporary aero appearance. Fleet fuel economy achieved 25.3 mpg (up nearly three mpg from 1981). To further boost mileage, Oldsmobile took several steps, starting with greater use of torque converter lock-up clutches (on all V-6 engines, and on all fours by mid-year). Throttle-body fuel injection became standard on the 151 cubic inch (2.5-liter) four. Automatic overdrive transmissions were standard on 98 and Toronado, and 88 with V-8 power. A new 181 cubic inch (3.0-liter) V-6 engine was optional in Cutlass Ciera. A new V-6 diesel weighed over 150 pounds less than the V-8 diesel, and was estimated to give Cutlass Supreme fuel mileage of 36 mpg on the highway. All models except the compact Omega had diesel power available.

FIRENZA -- SERIES 3J -- FOUR -- The subcompact front-drive, five-passenger Firenza hatchback had a transverse-mounted 112 cubic inch (1.8-liter) four-cylinder engine and four-speed manual transaxle. It was introduced in March 1982, to replace the discontinued Starfire as Oldsmobile's subcompact. Coupes and sedans were offered, in base or SX/LX trim. Coupes had swing-out rear quarter windows. A 121 cubic inch (2.0-liter) four-cylinder engine was optional. Firenza had no conventional

1982 Oldsmobile, Firenza hatchback coupe, (AA)

grille above the bumper, but only a sloping solid center panel between deeply recessed quad headlamps. Parking/signal lamps were positioned between each headlamp pair. Below the bumper were sets of vertical ribbed slots on both sides. A 'Firenza' nameplate stood high on the cowl. Large taillamps with Olds emblems wrapped just slightly onto quarter panels. Hatchbacks had a small decklid spoiler. Standard Firenza equipment included an AM radio, side window defogger, sport console, passenger assist grips, power brakes, day/night mirror, reclining cloth/vinyl front bucket seats and compact spare tire. Coupes had a folding back seat and Rallye wheels with stainless steel trim rings. Sedans included deluxe wheel covers. The SX coupe added a Rallye instrument cluster. Both LX and SX included bodyside moldings, velour bucket seats, power steering and color-keyed outside mirrors (driver's remote-controlled).

1982 Oldsmobile, Firenza sedan, (O)

1982 Oldsmobile, Omega sedan, (JAG)

OMEGA -- SERIES 3X -- FOUR/V-6 -- Four compact Omega models were offered: base and Brougham coupe and sedan, along with ES-2500 and ES-2800 options. Styling changes included a new, slightly sloping front end with a grille containing 5 x 4 eggcrate-patterned segments on each side of the divider. Park and turn signal lamps were recessed behind the grille, with single headlamps at the outboard sides. Dual-lens taillamps contained integral vertical backup lights with Olds emblem. Taillamps had a lower appearance, not reaching the decklid top. A new ESC option on Brougham coupe featured "continental" styling and lightweight flex fenders. Omega had new fluidic windshield wipers, a larger gas tank and match-mounted tires with pressure increased to 35 psi. A new high-output 2.8-liter

160

V-6 became optional in Omega ES, with free-flow exhaust, improved cylinder head port design, and high-output camshaft. The base 151 cubic inch (2.5-liter) four switched to throttle-body fuel injection. A standard 173 cubic inch (2.8-liter) V-6 was optional. Four-speed manual or automatic transmissions were available with each engine.

1982 Oldsmobile, Cutlass Ciera sedan, (JG)

CUTLASS CIERA -- SERIES 3A -- FOUR/V-6 -- As advertised, this aerodynamically-styled GM A-body compact was the first Cutlass model with front-wheel drive. Ciera's twin-section grille had an eggcrate pattern (5 x 6 hole arrangement) similar to Omega's on each side of the wide center divider panel, which held an Oldsmobile emblem. Framework around the recessed quad rectangular headlamps continued around the front fender sides to enclose clear/amber marker lenses. Thin horizontal park/signal lamps were mounted right along the bumper rub strip. At the rear were large wraparound taillamps. Ciera came in base, Brougham and LS trim. Brougham coupes and sedans had a divided front seat with loose-pillow look. At the cowl was a small multi-color international-style decorative panel, below a 'Cutlass Ciera' nameplate. A 151 cubic inch (2.5-liter) four-cylinder engine was standard, with a 181 cubic inch (3.0-liter) V-6 optional. Also optional: a 4.3-liter diesel. Ciera standard equipment included an AM radio, four-speed manual transaxle, P185/80R13 blackwall glass-belted radial tires, deluxe wheel covers, power steering, and bench seat. Brougham added lower bodyside moldings, pillar appliqué moldings (on sedan) and sport bench seat with fold-down armrest. Base models had rocker panel moldings. All except the base coupe had wheel opening moldings and rocker panel moldings.

1982 Oldsmobile, Cutlass Ciera coupe, (JAG)

CUTLASS SUPREME -- SERIES 3G -- V-6/V-8 -- The midsize line included Cutlass Supreme coupe and sedan, Supreme Brougham coupe and sedan, Calais coupe and Cruiser wagon. As usual, Cutlass grilles varied according to the model. Sedans and wagons had a new square eggcrate grille. Cutlass Supreme coupes displayed a specific vertical grille with body-colored dividers. Supreme Brougham and Calais coupes had an eggcrate grille with two vertical body-colored bars in each side. Coupes had a sloping front end with soft fascia front panel that extended to the rub strip. Their rear end panel wrapped down to provide a soft covering for the upper bumper. Sedans had a different rear-end look, including three-segment taillamps at outboard sides of the back panel. Each model had quad headlamps, and

park/turn signal lamps were mounted in the lower bumper. The 231 cubic inch (3.8-liter) V-6 was standard; optional was the 260 cubic inch (4.3-liter) V-8 or 5.7-liter diesel. Coupes and sedans could get the new 4.3-liter diesel V-6, while wagons came with an optional 5.0-liter V-8 engine.

DELTA 88 -- SERIES 3B -- V-6/V-8 -- A new grille made of thin horizontal bars was the major change on the 88. Framework around the quad rectangular headlamps extended into wraparound side markers. Large wraparound taillamps had single lenses divided into three segments, with horizontal ribbing. Backup lenses stood alongside the license plate mounting. Five models were offered: Delta 88 sedan, Royale coupe and sedan, and Royale Brougham coupe and sedan. A multi-function lever controlled the turn signal, wiper, dimmer and optional cruise control (with resume). The 231 cubic inch (3.8-liter) V-6 was standard; optional was a 260 cubic inch (4.3-liter) V-8, 5.0-liter V-8 and 5.7-liter diesel.

CUSTOM CRUISER -- SERIES 3B -- V-8 -- With few changes, full-size wagons had a standard 307 cubic inch (5.0-liter) V-8 with four-barrel carburetor, and optional 350 cubic inch diesel V-8.

1982 Oldsmobile, Ninety-Eight Regency Brougham sedan, (JG)

NINETY-EIGHT REGENCY -- SERIES 3C -- V-6/V-8 -- The Ninety-Eight changed little, apart from a new checkered lattice-design grille, divided as usual into two separate sections. Three models were available: Regency coupe and sedan, and new Regency Brougham sedan. Regency Brougham had lower body and bodyside moldings, sail panel emblem, a vinyl padded roof, locking wire wheel covers, convenience group, halogen headlamps, cornering lamps and deluxe interior components. A multi-function lever controlled the turn signal, wiper, dimmer and optional cruise control (with resume). A 252 cubic inch (4.1-liter) V-6 was standard, with 307 cubic inch (5.0-liter) gas fueled V-8 and 5.7-liter diesel optional.

1982 Oldsmobile, Toronado coupe, (JG)

TORONADO -- SERIES 3E -- V-6/V-8 -- Toronado's new chrome/argent grille was similar to the previous design, stretching to the fender tips, but had extra horizontal bars this year. A single-piece nameplate emblem replaced the former individual letters. Only one model was offered: the Brougham coupe, with standard 252 cubic inch (4.1-liter) V-6. Optional: a 307 cubic inch (5.0-liter) V-8 or 350 diesel. A new memory seat option (on no other model) offered two memory positions on the six-way power seat. Pushing a button moved the seat to one of its pre-set locations. The new optional 2000 series radio had separate bass and treble controls, balance and fade controls, automatic loudness and increased power output.

I.D. DATA: Oldsmobile's 17-symbol Vehicle Identification Number (VIN) again was located on the upper left surface of the instrument panel, visible through the windshield. The first three symbols ('1G3') indicate Oldsmobile division. Symbol four denotes restraint type: 'A' = manual (active) belts. Symbol five is car line/series: 'C' = Firenza; 'D' = Firenza SX/LX; 'B' = Omega; 'E' = Omega Brougham; 'G' = Cutlass Ciera; 'J' = Cutlass Ciera LS; ''M'' = Cutlass Ciera Brougham; R' = Cutlass Supreme; 'M' = Cutlass Supreme Brougham; 'K' = Cutlass Calais; 'H' = Cutlass Cruiser; 'L' = Delta 88; 'N' = Delta 88 Royale; 'Y' = Delta 88 Royale Brougham; 'P' = Custom Cruiser; 'X' = Ninety-Eight Regency; 'W' = Ninety-Eight Regency Brougham; 'Z' = Toronado Brougham. Next come two digits that denote body type: '27' = 2-dr. coupe; '37' = 2-dr. coupe; '47' = 2-dr. coupe; '57' = 2-dr. coupe; '77' = 2-dr. coupe; '19' = 4-dr. sedan; '69' = 4-dr. 4-window notch sedan; '35' = 4-dr. 2-seat wagon. Symbol eight is a letter for engine code: 'G' = L4-112 2Bbl.; 'B' = L4-122 2Bbl.; 'R' = L4-151 FI; 'X' = V-6-173 2Bbl.; 'E' = V-6-181 2Bbl.; 'A' = V-6-231 2Bbl.; '4' = V-6-252 4Bbl.; '8' = V-8-260 2Bbl.; 'T' or 'V' = diesel V-6-262; 'Y' = V-8-307 4Bbl.; 'N' = diesel V-8-350. Next comes a check digit, followed by a code for model year: ('C' = 1982). Symbol eleven is the assembly plant code: '2' = Ste. Therese, Quebec (Canada); 'D' = Doraville, Georgia; 'M' = Lansing, Mich.; 'W' = Willow Run, Mich.; 'X' = Fairfax, Kansas; 'E' = Linden, New Jersey; 'Z' = Fremont. The final six digits are the sequential serial number, starting with 100,001. Engine numbers were stamped on the front of the right rocker cover, or top of left cover (Buick-built engines), on label at front or rear of right rocker cover (Chevrolet V-6), or on the left rocker cover (Oldsmobile engines). Four-cylinder engine numbers were on a pad at left or right front of block. A body number plate on the upper right cowl identified model year, series, style, body assembly plant, body number, trim combination, modular seat code, paint code, date built code and option codes.

FIRENZA (FOUR)

Model Number	Body/Style Number	Body Type & Seating	Factory Price	Shipping Weight	Production Total
3J	C77	2-dr. S Cpe-5P	7413	N/A	8,894
3J	C69	4-dr. Sed-5P	7448	N/A	9,256
3J	D77	2-dr. SX Cpe-5P	8159	N/A	6,017
3J	D69	4-dr. LX Sed-5P	8080	N/A	5,941

OMEGA (FOUR/V-6)

Model Number	Body/Style Number	Body Type & Seating	Factory Price	Shipping Weight	Production Total
3X	B37	2-dr. Cpe-5P	7388/7513	2437/2489	12,140
3X	B69	4-dr. Sed-5P	7574/7699	2470/2522	29,548

OMEGA BROUGHAM (FOUR/V-6)

Model Number	Body/Style Number	Body Type & Seating	Factory Price	Shipping Weight	Production Total
3X	E37	2-dr. Cpe-5P	7722/7847	2461/2513	9,430
3X	E69	4-dr. Sed-5P	7891/8016	2501/2553	26,351

CUTLASS CIERA (FOUR/V-6)

Model Number	Body/Style Number	Body Type & Seating	Factory Price	Shipping Weight	Production Total
3A	G27	2-dr. Cpe-5P	8847/8972	2577/2660	5,185
3A	G19	4-dr. Sed-5P	8997/9122	2596/2679	9,717
3A	J27	2-dr. LS Cpe-5P	8968/9093	2583/2666	10,702
3A	J19	4-dr. LS Sed-5P	9157/9282	2587/2652	29,322

CUTLASS CIERA BROUGHAM (FOUR/V-6)

Model Number	Body/Style Number	Body Type & Seating	Factory Price	Shipping Weight	Production Total
3A	M27	2-dr. Cpe-5P	9397/9522	2585/2668	12,518
3A	M19	4-dr. Sed-5P	9599/9724	2588/2653	33,876

CUTLASS SUPREME (V-6/V-8)

Model Number	Body/Style Number	Body Type & Seating	Factory Price	Shipping Weight	Production Total
3G	R47	2-dr. Cpe-6P	8588/8658	3136/3232	89,617
3G	R69	4-dr. Sed-6P	8712/8782	3197/3252	60,053

CUTLASS SUPREME BROUGHAM (V-6/V-8)

Model Number	Body/Style Number	Body Type & Seating	Factory Price	Shipping Weight	Production Total
3G	M47	2-dr. Cpe-6P	9160/9230	3163/3259	59,592
3G	M69	4-dr. Sed-6P	9255/9325	3222/3277	34,717

CUTLASS CALAIS (V-6/V-8)

Model Number	Body/Style Number	Body Type & Seating	Factory Price	Shipping Weight	Production Total
3G	K47	2-dr. Cpe-5P	9379/9449	3198/3273	17,109

CUTLASS CRUISER (V-6/V-8)

Model Number	Body/Style Number	Body Type & Seating	Factory Price	Shipping Weight	Production Total
3G	H35	4-dr. Sta Wag-6P	8905/8975	3338/3479	20,363

DELTA 88 (V-6/V-8)

Model Number	Body/Style Number	Body Type & Seating	Factory Price	Shipping Weight	Production Total
3B	L69	4-dr. Sed-6P	8603/8673	3425/3556	8,278

DELTA 88 ROYALE (V-6/V-8)

Model Number	Body/Style Number	Body Type & Seating	Factory Price	Shipping Weight	Production Total
3B	N37	2-dr. Cpe-6P	8733/8803	3402/3533	41,382
3B	N69	4-dr. Sed-6P	8894/8964	3440/3571	105,184

DELTA 88 ROYALE BROUGHAM (V-6/V-8)

Model Number	Body/Style Number	Body Type & Seating	Factory Price	Shipping Weight	Production Total
3B	Y37	2-dr. Cpe-6P	9202/9272	3437/3568	Note 1
3B	Y69	4-dr. Sed-6P	9293/9363	3473/3604	Note 1

Note 1: Production included in 88 Royale totals above.

CUSTOM CRUISER (V-8)

Model Number	Body/Style Number	Body Type & Seating	Factory Price	Shipping Weight	Production Total
3B	P35	4-dr. Sta Wag-6P	9614	3909	19,367

NINETY-EIGHT REGENCY (V-6/V-8)

Model Number	Body/Style Number	Body Type & Seating	Factory Price	Shipping Weight	Production Total
3C	X37	2-dr. Cpe-6P	12117/12117	3648/3817	11,832
3C	X69	4-dr. Sed-6P	12294/12294	3705/3821	79,135
3C	W69	4-dr. Brghm-6P	13344/13344	3751/3867	Note 2

Note 2: Production included in basic sedan total.

TORONADO BROUGHAM (V-6/V-8)

Model Number	Body/Style Number	Body Type & Seating	Factory Price	Shipping Weight	Production Total
3E	Z57	2-dr. Cpe-5P	14462/14462	3584/3705	33,928

FACTORY PRICE AND WEIGHT NOTE: Prices and weights to left of slash are for six-cylinder, to right for V-8 engine except Omega/Ciera, to left for four-cylinder and to right for V-6.

ENGINE DATA: BASE FOUR (Firenza): Inline, overhead-valve four-cylinder. Cast iron block and head. Displacement: 112 cu. in. (1.8 liters). Bore & stroke: 3.50 x 2.91 in. Compression ratio: 9.0:1. Brake horsepower: 88 at 5100 rpm. Torque: 100 lb.-ft. at 2800 rpm. Five main bearings. Hydraulic valve lifters. Carburetor: 2Bbl. Rochester E2SE. VIN Code: G. **OPTIONAL FOUR** (Firenza): Inline, overhead-valve four-cylinder. Cast iron block and head. Displacement: 122 cu. in. (2.0 liters). Bore & stroke: 3.50 x 3.14 in. Compression ratio: 9.0:1. Brake horsepower: 90 at 5100 rpm. Torque: 111 lb.-ft. at 2700 rpm. Five main bearings. Hydraulic valve lifters. Carburetor: 2Bbl. Rochester E2SE. VIN Code: B. **BASE FOUR** (Omega, Cutlass Ciera): Inline, overhead-valve four-cylinder. Cast iron block and head. Displacement: 151 cu. in. (2.5 liters). Bore & stroke: 4.00 x 3.00 in. Compression ratio: 8.2:1. Brake horsepower: 90 at 4000 rpm. Torque: 134 lb.-ft. at 2400 rpm. Five main bearings. Hydraulic valve lifters. Fuel injection (TBI). Pontiac-built. VIN Code: R. **OPTIONAL V-6** (Omega): 60-degree, overhead-valve V-6. Cast iron block and aluminum head. Displacement: 173 cu. in. (2.8 liters). Bore & stroke: 3.50 x 3.00 in. Compression ratio: 8.5:1. Brake horsepower: 112 at 5100 rpm. Torque: 148 lb.-ft. at 2400 rpm. Four main bearings. Hydraulic valve lifters. Carburetor: 2Bbl. Rochester E2SE. Chevrolet-built. VIN Code: X. NOTE: A high-output 173 cu. in. V-6 was available -- Compression ratio: 8.9:1. Horsepower: 130 at 5400 rpm. Torque: 145 lb.-ft. at 2400 rpm. **OPTIONAL V-6** (Cutlass Ciera): 90-degree, overhead-valve V-6. Cast iron block and head. Displacement: 181 cu. in. (3.0 liters). Bore & stroke: 3.80 x 2.66 in. Compression ratio: 8.45:1. Brake horsepower: 110 at 4800 rpm. Torque: 145 lb.-ft. at 2000 rpm. Four main bearings. Hydraulic valve lifters. Carburetor: 2Bbl. Rochester E2ME. VIN Code: E. **BASE V-6** (Cutlass Supreme, Delta 88): 90-degree, overhead-valve V-6. Cast iron block and head. Displacement: 231 cu. in. (3.8 liters). Bore & stroke: 3.80 x 3.40 in. Compression ratio: 8.0:1. Brake horsepower: 110 at 3800 rpm. Torque: 190 lb.-ft. at 1600 rpm. Four main bearings. Hydraulic valve lifters. Carburetor: 2Bbl. Rochester E2ME. Buick-built. VIN Code: A. **BASE V-6** (98, Toronado): 90-degree, over-

head-valve V-6. Cast iron block and head. Displacement: 252 cu. in. (4.1 liters). Bore & stroke: 3.96 x 3.40 in. Compression ratio: 8.0:1. Brake horsepower: 125 at 4000 rpm. Torque: 205 lb.-ft. at 2000 rpm. Four main bearings. Hydraulic valve lifters. Carburetor: 4Bbl. Rochester E4ME. Buick-built. VIN Code: 4. OPTIONAL V-8 (Cutlass, Delta 88): 90-degree, overhead valve V-8. Cast iron block and head. Displacement: 260 cu. in. (4.3 liters). Bore & stroke: 3.50 x 3.38 in. Compression ratio: 7.5:1. Brake horsepower: 100 at 3600 rpm. Torque: 190 lb.-ft. at 1600 rpm. Five main bearings. Hydraulic valve lifters. Carburetor: 2Bbl. Rochester E2ME. VIN Code: 8. DIESEL V-6 (Cutlass Ciera, Cutlass Supreme): 90-degree, overhead valve V-8. Cast iron block and head. Displacement: 262 cu. in. (4.3 liters). Bore & stroke: 4.06 x 3.38 in. Compression ratio: 21.6:1. Brake horsepower: 85 at 3600 rpm. Torque: 165 lb.-ft. at 1600 rpm. Five main bearings. Hydraulic valve lifters. Fuel injection. VIN Code: T or V. BASE V-8 (Custom Cruiser); OPTIONAL (Cutlass Supreme, Delta 88, 98, Toronado): 90-degree, overhead valve V-8. Cast iron block and head. Displacement: 307 cu. in. (5.0 liters). Bore & stroke: 3.80 x 3.38 in. Compression ratio: 8.0:1. Brake horsepower: 140 at 3600 rpm. Torque: 240 lb.-ft. at 1600 rpm. Five main bearings. Hydraulic valve lifters. Carburetor: 4Bbl. Rochester M4MC. VIN Code: Y. DIESEL V-8 (Cutlass Supreme, Delta 88, 98, Custom Cruiser, Toronado): 90-degree, overhead valve V-8. Cast iron block and head. Displacement: 350 cu. in. (5.7 liters). Bore & stroke: 4.06 x 3.39 in. Compression ratio: 21.6:1. Brake horsepower: 105 at 3200 rpm. Torque: 200 lb.-ft. at 1600 rpm. Five main bearings. Hydraulic valve lifters. Fuel injection. VIN Code: N.

CHASSIS DATA: Wheelbase: (Firenza) 101.2 in.; (Omega/Ciera) 104.9 in.; (Cutlass) 108.1 in.; (Delta 88) 116.0 in.; (98) 119.0 in.; (Custom Crsr) 116.0 in.; (Toronado) 114.0 in. Overall Length: (Firenza cpe) 174.3 in.; (Firenza sed) 176.2 in.; (Omega) 182.8 in.; (Ciera) 188.4 in.; (Cutlass sed) 199.1 in.; (Cutlass Supreme cpe) 200.0 in.; (Cutlass wag) 200.4 in.; (Delta 88) 218.1 in.; (98) 221.1 in.; (Custom Crsr) 220.3 in.; (Toronado) 206.0 in. Height: (Firenza cpe) 51.7 in.; (Firenza sed) 53.7 in.; (Omega) 53.7 in.; (Ciera) 54.1 in.; (Cutlass Supreme) 54.9-55.9 in.; (Cutlass wag) 56.2 in.; (Delta 88 cpe) 56.0 in.; (Delta 88 sed) 56.7 in.; (98) 57.2 in.; (Custom Crsr) 58.5 in.; (Toronado) 54.6 in. Width: (Firenza) 65.0 in.; (Omega) 69.8 in.; (Ciera) 69.5 in.; (Cutlass) 71.6-71.9 in.; (Cutlass wag) 71.8 in.; (Delta 88) 76.3 in.; (98) 76.3 in.; (Custom Crsr) 79.8 in.; (Toronado) 71.4 in. Front Tread: (Firenza) 55.4 in.; (Omega/Ciera) 58.7 in.; (Cutlass) 58.5 in.; (Delta 88/98) 61.7 in.; (Custom Crsr) 62.1 in.; (Toronado) 59.3 in. Rear Tread: (Firenza) 55.2 in.; (Omega/Ciera) 57.0 in.; (Cutlass) 57.7 in.; (Delta 88/98) 60.7 in.; (Custom Crsr) 64.1 in.; (Toronado) 60.0 in. Standard Tires: (Firenza) P175/80R13; (Omega/Ciera) P185/80R13; (Cutlass) P185/75R14; (Cutlass Supreme) P195/75R14; (Delta 88) P205/75R15; (98) P215/75R15; (Custom Crsr) P225/75R15; (Toronado) P205/75R15.

TECHNICAL: Transmission: Four-speed floor shift standard on Firenza/Omega. Gear ratios: (1st) 3.53:1; (2nd) 1.95:1; (3rd) 1.24:1; (4th) 0.73:1 or 0.81:1; (Rev) 3.42:1. Three-speed Turbo Hydra-matic standard on Ciera/Cutlass/88. Four-speed automatic overdrive standard on Custom Cruiser/98/Toronado. Standard final drive ratio: (Firenza) 3.65:1; (Omega) 3.32:1 w/ 4-spd, 2.39:1 w/auto.; (Omega V-6) 3.32:1 w/4-spd, 2.53:1 w/auto.; (Ciera) 2.39:1 or 2.53:1; (Cutlass) 2.41:1 w/V-6, 2.29:1 w/V-8, 2.41:1 w/V-6 diesel; (Cutlass Cruiser) 2.73:1 w/ V-6, 2.41:1 w/V-8-260, 2.29:1 w/V-8-307 or diesel; (Delta 88) 2.73:1 w/V-6, 2.56:1 w/V-8-260, 2.41:1 w/V-8-307, 2.93:1 w/diesel; (Custom Crsr) 2.73:1 exc. 2.93:1 w/diesel; (98) 3.23:1 w/V-6, 2.73:1 w/V-8-307, 2.93:1 w/diesel; (Toronado) 3.15:1 w/V-6, 2.73:1 w/V-8, 2.93:1 w/diesel. Steering: (Firenza/Omega/Ciera) rack and pinion; (others) recirculating ball. Front Suspension: (Firenza) MacPherson struts w/coil springs and anti-sway bar; (Omega/Ciera) MacPherson struts w/ coil springs; (Toronado); longitudinal torsion bars w/anti-sway bar; (others) coil springs w/control arms and anti-sway bar.

Rear Suspension: (Firenza) coil springs w/trailing crank arms; (Omega/Ciera) coil springs w/trailing arms; (Toronado) independent with coil springs, longitudinal trailing arms and automatic leveling; (others) rigid axle w/coil springs, lower trailing radius arms and upper torque arms. Brakes: Front disc, rear drum. Ignition: Electronic. Body construction: (Firenza/Omega/Ciera) unibody; (others) separate body and frame. Fuel tank: (Firenza) 14 gal.; (Omega) 14.2 gal.; (Ciera) 14.5 or 15.7 gal.; (Cutlass) 18.1 gal.; (Cutlass wag) 18.2 gal.; (Delta 88) 25 gal.; (98) 25 gal.; (Custom Crsr wag) 22 gal.; (Toronado) 21.1 gal.

DRIVETRAIN OPTIONS: Engines: 121 cu. in. four: Firenza ($50). 173 cu. in. V-6: Omega ($125). 181 cu. in. V-6: Ciera ($125). 260 cu. in. V-8: Cutlass/88 ($70). Diesel 262 cu. in. V-6: Cutlass/Ciera ($775). 307 cu. in. 4Bbl. V-8: Cutlass wag ($70); 88 ($70); 98/Toronado (NC). Diesel 350 cu. in. V-8: Cutlass/88/98/Custom Crsr/Toronado ($825). Transmission/ Differential: Turbo Hydra-matic: Firenza ($370); Omega ($396). Limited-slip differential: Cutlass/88/98 ($80). Brakes/ Steering: Power steering: Firenza ($180). Suspension: Firm ride/handling pkg. ($28-$46). Automatic load leveling: Ciera/ 88/98 ($165). Other: High-capacity cooling ($30-$83). High-capacity radiator ($24) exc. Firenza/Omega. High-capacity alternator ($35-$85) exc. Firenza. H.D. battery ($22-$25) exc. diesel ($50). Engine block heater ($19). Block/fuel line heater ($49). Trailer wiring ($28) exc. Firenza/Omega. California emissions ($46) exc. diesel ($205).

OPTION PACKAGES: Omega ES pkg.: Brghm sedan ($896-$1146).

MAJOR CONVENIENCE/APPEARANCE OPTIONS: Four Season air conditioner ($675-$695). Tempmatic air conditioning: Cutlass/88 ($730-$750); 98/Toronado ($50). Cruise control ($155-$165). Power seat ($178-$197). Power windows ($165-$240). Twilight sentinel: 98/Toronado ($57). Cornering lamps: 88/98 ($57). Power astroroof w/sliding glass panel: Cutlass/88/98/Toronado ($875-$1125). Removable glass roof panels: Cutlass ($790). Glass panel sunroof: Omega/Ciera ($275). Landau vinyl roof ($195-$225). Full vinyl roof: Omega/ Ciera/88/98 ($140-$180). Rear-facing third seat: Custom Cruiser ($215).

HISTORY: Introduced: September 24, 1981, except Omega, December 12, 1981; Cutlass Ciera, January 14, 1982; and Firenza, March 4, 1982. Model year production: 789,454. Calendar year production (U.S.): 759,637. Calendar year sales by U.S. dealers: 799,585. Model year sales by U.S. dealers: 759,000.

HISTORICAL FOOTNOTES: Sales fell for the 1982 model year, even below the depressed 1980 level. Only 88 and 98 sold better than in 1981, and not by much.

1983

For later enthusiasts, if not for the ordinary buyer at the time, the biggest Oldsmobile news of 1983 was the reappearance of a Hurst/Olds option on a Cutlass coupe. The lineup consisted of 30 models, including two new Firenza wagons. Four special appearance options were also available. A new 1.8-liter OHC four (with new five-speed manual shift) became available for Firenza, which otherwise had a standard 2.0-liter with four-speed manual. Both had optional automatic. The 260 cubic inch (4.3-liter) gas fueled V-8 offered in 1982 on Cutlass Supreme and 88 was dropped. Four-speed automatic transmissions proliferated, available now on Cutlass Ciera with a 3.0-liter V-6 or 4.3 diesel V-6 after midyear. Three-speed automatic with diesel engine was dropped for Custom Cruiser and 98, making four-speed automatic standard in all full-size wagons and the 98. Mechanical changes to cut weight included a smaller alternator with plastic fan on diesels and the 5.0-liter gas fueled V-8, and a stainless steel exhaust manifold and aluminum water pump on the transverse-mounted V-6 diesel.

1983 Oldsmobile, Firenza hatchback coupe, (O)

1983 Oldsmobile, Firenza Cruiser station wagon, (O)

FIRENZA -- SERIES 3J -- FOUR -- Appearance changed little in Firenza's second season. The five-passenger, front-wheel-drive GM J-body subcompact came in six models, including two new wagons: Cruiser and LX Cruiser. Standard wagon equipment included a tailgate-ajar warning lamp. Wagon options included rear wiper/washer, two-tone paint, simulated woodgrain and accent stripe. All Firenzas had a standard floor console and reclining front bucket seats, as well as a fold-down rear seat. Split-folding rear seats were available in coupe or wagon. Standard seat trim was vinyl or cloth, with deluxe trim available in velour. New standard engine was the 122 cubic inch (2.0-liter) four with TBI, with four-speed manual transmission. It was actually the original 1.8-liter powerplant from Chevrolet, but stroked to reach the larger displacement. Five-speed manual and three-speed automatic were available. Optional was the new 1.8-liter OHC four with fuel injection, from GM of Brazil, with either automatic or five-speed. Firenza equipment included four-speed manual transaxle, power brakes, bumper moldings, sport console, side window defogger, wheel opening and belt reveal moldings, AM radio and P175/80R13 glass-belted blackwalls. SX added a Rallye instrument cluster and Rallye trim wheels. SX and LS (and Cruiser Brougham) included power steering, velour reclining front bucket seats, rocker panel moldings and color-keyed mirrors (driver's remote).

1983 Oldsmobile, Omega coupe, (AA)

OMEGA -- SERIES 3X -- FOUR/V-6 -- A tighter crosshatch pattern (6 x 12 hole arrangement) replaced the former looser design on Omega's eggcrate grille, but otherwise appearance was similar to 1982. Aerodynamic patch mirrors, with housings faired into the door window surrounds, replaced chrome mir-

rors. The standard driver's mirror was black; optional dual mirrors were body-color. Rear-end appearance was the same as 1982. Four models were offered: coupe and sedan, in base or Brougham trim. Inside was a new two-tone instrument panel. Brushed pewter or brushed bronze complemented the interior color. New side-window defoggers went in the radio speaker grilles and front defroster grilles. A rocker headlamp control replaced the former push-pull switch, and a headlamp-on warning was standard. Standard bench seats now had low backs and separate headrests, and a fold-down armrest. The 151 cubic inch (2.5-liter) four-cylinder engine with standard four-speed manual or optional automatic was standard. Optional: a 173 cubic inch (2.8-liter) V-6, manual or automatic shift. A high-output 2.8 V-6 was available with the ES option, expected to reach 60 mph in about 11 seconds. The high-output engine had optional a four-speed manual transmission, for extra acceleration. An ES or ESC (European Sport Coupe) appearance package added a "continental" look with blacked-out grille; wraparound bumpers with integral scoop; and black headlamp bezels, taillamp bezels, door frames, quarter window and rocker panel moldings. The package also included a firm ride/handling package, custom sport steering wheel, styled polycast wheels with trim rings and blackwall tires.

1983 Oldsmobile, Cutlass Ciera sedan, (AA)

CUTLASS CIERA -- SERIES 3A -- FOUR/V-6 -- Appearance of the front-drive midsize, introduced in early 1982, was similar this year except for a revised rear-end panel molding and taillamp treatment. Coupe and sedan bodies were offered, in LS and Brougham series. The former base models were dropped. New optional electro-luminescent opera lamps were available on either coupe or sedan. An optional console now included a coin holder and T-shifter lever. An electronic instrument cluster was available (Oldsmobile's first). It included a digital speedometer, bar-graph fuel and temperature gauges, low fuel indicator, trip odometer, and English/metric switch. The 151 cubic inch (2.5-liter) four-cylinder engine with automatic was standard. Optional was a 181 cubic inch (3.0-liter) V-6 or 4.3-liter diesel V-6. Optional engines came with either three- or four-speed automatic (the latter available later in the model year). Cutlass Ciera offered an ES package, similar to Omega's, on any model. It included blacked-out grille bars, headlamp housings and rear-end treatment, as well as black bumper rub strips and bodyside moldings. Oversize SBR blackwall tires were used, with specially-designed wheel covers. Reclining bucket seats, console with floor shifter, sport steering and gauge package with tachometer were standard plus an F41 firm ride/handling suspension package. The ES package came in five body colors.

1983 Oldsmobile, Cutlass Supreme coupe, (O)

CUTLASS SUPREME -- SERIES 3G -- V-6/V-8 -- Changes on the midsize rear-drive Cutlass focused on the grille, which, as usual, differed from model to model. Coupes had new sloping-forward rectangular-patterned grilles with bright vertical bars and recessed horizontal bars. The grille followed the sharply-split angle of the front panel, which contained an identification nameplate below the left headlamp. Sedans and wagons had a new upright square-pattern grille, and their rectangular headlamp framing extended outward to meet wraparound marker lenses. Coupes had no such side markers. Six models were offered: Supreme and Supreme Brougham coupe and sedan, Calais coupe and Cutlass Cruiser wagon. Calais had a unique look with black headlamp doors, amber parking lamp lenses and standard paint striping. Optional Calais bodyside moldings were black. Supreme and Cruiser standard engine was the 231 cubic inch (3.8-liter) V-6, with either a 307 cubic inch (5.0-liter) gas fueled V-8 or 5.7-liter diesel V-8 optional. Supreme coupes and sedans could also get the 4.3-liter diesel V-6. All models had a three-speed automatic transmission. The 260 cubic inch gas fueled V-8 was dropped. Cutlass Supreme standard equipment included automatic transmission, power brakes and steering, bright wheel covers, P195/75R14 blackwall SBR tires, bumper rub strips with integral guards and cloth or vinyl custom sport bench seat with fold-down center armrest. Moldings highlighted wheel openings, rocker panels, roof drip and hood center. Supreme Brougham added a convenience group, velour divided front seat, wide door/fender moldings and woodgrain dash. Calais came with front and rear stabilizer bars, bodyside accent stripes, color-keyed Super Stock wheels, sport mirrors (left remote), halogen headlamps, sport console with floor shift lever and contour reclining front bucket seats. Saving the best for last, about 2,500 Hurst/Olds options equipped Cutlass Calais coupes, painted black/silver. Red and silver stripes went on upper bodysides and the front-end panel. A specially-tuned 307 cubic inch (5.0-liter V-8) produced 180 horsepower and 245 pound-feet of torque. It had a dual-snorkel air cleaner with chrome cover, special 70-degree secondary air valve travel and dual exhaust. Four-speed automatic with special shift calibration and torque converter ratio, plus a Hurst "Lightning Rod" shifter, turned a 3.73:1 rear axle. The grille was black/argent. Shadow-lettered Hurst/Olds decals decorated doors and decklid. C-pillars and dash carried a 15th anniversary Hurst/Olds medallion. Fifteen inch chrome/argent wheels held Goodyear Eagle GT tires. Inside extras included reclining bucket seats, quartz clock and tachometer. Also on Hurst/Olds: air conditioning with wide-open-throttle lockout, front lower air dam, decklid spoiler and hood scoop. Hurst/Olds, according to the factory, could accelerate to 60 mph in 8.5 seconds.

1983 Oldsmobile, Hurst/Olds 15th Anniversary coupe, (O)

DELTA 88 -- SERIES 3B -- V-6/V-8 -- Hardly a year went by without a grille change on most Oldsmobiles, and that was the extent of the change for the Delta 88. The new grille consisted of horizontal bars divided into three sections on each side of the traditional wide divider. Six models were offered: base sedan, Royale coupe and sedan and Royale Brougham coupe and sedan. The 231 cubic inch (3.8-liter) V-6 was standard, with the 307 cubic inch (5.0-liter) gas fueled V-8 or 5.7-liter diesel optional. Both gas and diesel V-8s could have either three- or four-speed automatic. Base 88 standard equipment included power steering and brakes, driver's remote mirror, bumper guards and rub strips, lighter, P205/75R15 blackwall SBR tires and compact spare tire. Standard trim included rocker panel, wheel opening and roof drip moldings. Royale added a velour custom sport bench seat with center armrest and color-keyed bodyside moldings. The Brougham added a divided velour bench seat, belt reveal molding, convenience group and opera lamps (on coupe).

CUSTOM CRUISER -- SERIES 3B -- V-8 -- The full-size wagon was similar to Ninety-Eight, but had an exclusive grille with 3 x 3 segments on each side, and horizontal strips within each segment. Custom Cruiser had a 307 cubic inch (5.0-liter) V-8 with four-speed automatic standard.

1983 Oldsmobile, Delta 88 Royale Brougham coupe, (AA)

1983 Oldsmobile, 98 Regency sedan, (O)

NINETY-EIGHT REGENCY -- SERIES 3C -- V-6/V-8 -- This year's Ninety-Eight grille had a tighter crosshatch pattern but maintained the traditional Olds look, similar to 1982. The nameplate was now on the driver's side of the grille, not above it. Three models were offered: Regency coupe and sedan and Regency Brougham sedan. The 252 cubic inch (4.1-liter) V-6 with four-speed overdrive automatic was standard. Optional was a 307 cubic inch (5.0-liter) gas fueled V-8 or 5.7-liter diesel V-8. Four-speed automatic was standard with both V-8s. Standard Ninety-Eight equipment included power brakes and steering, tinted glass, Four Season air conditioner, bumper guards and impact strips, digital clock, power windows and door locks, fender skirts, dual remote-control mirrors, P215/75R15 whitewalls and compact spare tire. A divided front seat had dual controls, velour upholstery and two-way power driver's side. Regency Brougham added a fully padded vinyl roof, tilt steering, locking wire wheel covers, lower bodyside moldings, and halogen high-beam headlamps and cornering lamps.

TORONADO -- SERIES 3E -- V-6/V-8 -- Engine selection on the personal-luxury front-drive coupe was the same as Ninety-Eight. Essentially a carryover, the grille was slightly revised. The panel above the full-width grille added a center emblem and lost its nameplate (which moved onto the grille itself). A new optional

1983 Oldsmobile, Toronado Brougham coupe, (AA)

sound system from Delco/Bose, rated 100 watts, included an electronic-tuning radio/cassette player with Dolby noise reduction, dynamic noise reduction, and custom-equalized sound. Toronado standard equipment included the 252 cubic inch (4.1-liter) V-6 with four-speed automatic overdrive, power steering and brakes, AM/FM electronic-tuning stereo radio, speed control (with resume feature), tilt steering wheel, power windows, Four Season air conditioning, power antenna (in front fender) and digital clock. Also standard: power door locks, side window defoggers, automatic leveling, dual remote-control mirrors and P205/75R15 steel-belted radial whitewalls.

I.D. DATA: Oldsmobile's 17-symbol Vehicle Identification Number (VIN) again was located on the upper left surface of the instrument panel, visible through the windshield. The first three symbols ('1G3') indicate Oldsmobile division. Symbol four denotes restraint type: 'A' = manual (active) belts. Symbol five is car line/series: 'C' = Firenza; 'D' = Firenza SX/LX; 'B' = Omega; 'E' = Omega Brougham; 'J' = Cutlass Ciera LS; 'M' = Cutlass Ciera Brougham; 'R' = Cutlass Supreme; 'M' = Cutlass Supreme Brougham; 'K' = Cutlass Calais; 'H' = Cutlass Cruiser; 'L' = Delta 88; 'N' = Delta 88 Royale; 'Y' = Delta 88 Royale Brougham; 'P' = Custom Cruiser; 'X' = Ninety-Eight Regency; 'W' = Ninety-Eight Regency Brougham; 'Z' = Toronado Brougham. Next come two digits that denote body type: '27' = 2-dr. coupe; '37' = 2-dr. coupe; '47' = 2-dr. coupe; '57' = 2-dr. coupe; '77' = 2-dr. coupe; '19' = 4-dr. sedan; '69' = 4-dr. 4-window notch sedan; '35' = 4-dr. 2-seat wagon. Symbol eight is a letter for engine code: '0' = L4-112 FI; 'P' = L4-121 FI; 'R' = L4-151 FI; 'X' = V-6-173 2Bbl.; 'Z' = H.O. V-6-173 2Bbl.; 'E' = V-6-181 2Bbl.; 'A' = V-6-231 2Bbl.; '4' = V-6-252 4Bbl.; 'T' or 'V' = diesel V-6-262; 'Y' = V-8-307 4Bbl.; '9' = Hurst/Olds V-8-307 4Bbl.; 'N' = diesel V-8-350. Next comes a check digit, followed by a code for model year: ('D' = 1983). Symbol eleven is the assembly plant code: '2' = Ste. Therese, Quebec (Canada); 'D' = Doraville, Georgia; 'M' = Lansing, Mich.; 'W' = Willow Run, Mich.; 'X' = Fairfax, Kansas; 'E' = Linden, New Jersey; 'K' = Leeds, Missouri. The final six digits are the sequential serial number, starting with 300,001 (except 88/98 built at Lansing, 700,001). Engine numbers were stamped on the front of the right rocker cover, or top of left cover (Buick-built engines), on label at front or rear of right rocker cover (Chevrolet V-6), or on the left rocker cover (Oldsmobile engines). Four-cylinder engine numbers were on a pad at left or right front of block. A body number plate on the upper right cowl identified model year, series, style, body assembly plant, body number, trim combination, modular seat code, paint code, date built code and option codes.

FIRENZA (FOUR)

Model Number	Body/Style Number	Body Type & Seating	Factory Price	Shipping Weight	Production Total
3J	C77	2-dr. S Cpe-5P	7007	2374	8,208
3J	C69	4-dr. S Sed-5P	7094	2353	11,278
3J	D77	2-dr. SX Cpe-5P	7750	2410	3,767
3J	D69	4-dr. LX Sed-5P	7646	2372	5,067

FIRENZA CRUISER (FOUR)

Model Number	Body/Style Number	Body Type & Seating	Factory Price	Shipping Weight	Production Total
3J	C35	4-dr. Sta Wag-5P	7314	2429	7,460
3J	D35	4-dr. LX Sta Wag-5P	7866	2453	4,972

OMEGA (FOUR/V-6)

Model Number	Body/Style Number	Body Type & Seating	Factory Price	Shipping Weight	Production Total
3X	B37	2-dr. Cpe-5P	7478/7628	2423/2487	6,448
3X	B69	4-dr. Sed-5P	7676/7826	2461/2533	24,287

OMEGA BROUGHAM (FOUR/V-6)

| 3X | E37 | 2-dr. Cpe-5P | 7767/7917 | 2454/2518 | 5,177 |
| 3X | E69 | 4-dr. Sed-5P | 7948/8098 | 2486/2558 | 18,014 |

CUTLASS CIERA LS (FOUR/V-6)

Model Number	Body/Style Number	Body Type & Seating	Factory Price	Shipping Weight	Production Total
3A	J27	2-dr. Cpe-5P	8703/8853	2596/2698	12,612
3A	J19	4-dr. Sed-5P	8892/9042	2630/2733	66,731

CUTLASS CIERA BROUGHAM (FOUR/V-6)

| 3A | M27 | 2-dr. Cpe-5P | 9183/9333 | 2621/2723 | 17,088 |
| 3A | M19 | 4-dr. Sed-5P | 9385/9535 | 2655/2758 | 73,219 |

CUTLASS SUPREME (V-6/V-8)

| 3G | R47 | 2-dr. Cpe-6P | 8950/9175 | 3155/3339 | 107,946 |
| 3G | R69 | 4-dr. Sed-6P | 9103/9328 | 3196/3380 | 56,347 |

CUTLASS SUPREME BROUGHAM (V-6/V-8)

| 3G | M47 | 2-dr. Cpe-6P | 9589/9814 | 3192/3376 | 60,025 |
| 3G | M69 | 4-dr. Sed-6P | 9719/9944 | 3230/3414 | 28,451 |

CUTLASS CALAIS (V-6/V-8)

| 3G | K47 | 2-dr. Cpe-5P | 9848/10073 | 3237/3421 | 19,660 |

CUTLASS CRUISER (V-6/V-8)

| 3G | H35 | 4-dr. Sta Wag-6P | 9381/9606 | 3342/3537 | 22,037 |

DELTA 88 (V-6/V-8)

Model Number	Body/Style Number	Body Type & Seating	Factory Price	Shipping Weight	Production Total
3B	L69	4-dr. Sed-6P	9084/9309	3426/3537	8,297

DELTA 88 ROYALE (V-6/V-8)

| 3B | N37 | 2-dr. Cpe-6P | 9202/9427 | 3403/3511 | 54,771 |
| 3B | N69 | 4-dr. Sed-6P | 9363/9588 | 3466/3623 | 132,683 |

DELTA 88 ROYALE BROUGHAM (V-6/V-8)

| 3B | Y37 | 2-dr. Cpe-6P | 9671/9896 | 3428/3539 | Note 1 |
| 3B | Y69 | 4-dr. Sed-6P | 9762/9987 | 3466/3648 | Note 1 |

Note 1: Production included in 88 Royale totals above.

CUSTOM CRUISER (V-8)

Model Number	Body/Style Number	Body Type & Seating	Factory Price	Shipping Weight	Production Total
3B	P35	4-dr. Sta Wag-6P	10083	3932	25,243

NINETY-EIGHT REGENCY (V-6/V-8)

Model Number	Body/Style Number	Body Type & Seating	Factory Price	Shipping Weight	Production Total
3C	X37	2-dr. Cpe-6P	12943/13018	3655/3814	13,816
3C	X69	4-dr. Sed-6P	13120/13195	3708/3867	105,948
3C	W69	4-dr. Brghm-6P	14170/14245	3748/3907	Note 2

Note 2: Production included in basic sedan total.

TORONADO BROUGHAM (V-6/V-8)

Model Number	Body/Style Number	Body Type & Seating	Factory Price	Shipping Weight	Production Total
3E	Z57	2-dr. Cpe-5P	15252/15327	3593/3758	39,605

FACTORY PRICE AND WEIGHT NOTE: Prices and weights to left of slash are for six-cylinder, to right for V-8 engine except Omega/Ciera, to left for four-cylinder and to right for V-6.

ENGINE DATA: BASE FOUR (Firenza): Inline, overhead-valve four-cylinder. Cast iron block and head. Displacement: 121 cu. in. (2.0 liters). Bore & stroke: 3.50 x 3.14 in. Compression ratio: 9.3:1. Brake horsepower: 86 at 4900 rpm. Torque: 110 lb.-ft. at 3000 rpm. Five main bearings. Hydraulic valve lifters. Electronic fuel injection. VIN Code: P. OPTIONAL FOUR (Firenza): Inline, overhead-cam four-cylinder. Cast iron block and head. Displacement: 112 cu. in. (1.8 liters). Bore & stroke: 3.34 x 3.11 in. Compression ratio: 9.0:1. Brake horsepower: 84 at 5200 rpm. Torque: 102 lb.-ft. at 2800 rpm. Five main

bearings. Hydraulic valve lifters. Electronic fuel injection. VIN Code: O. BASE FOUR (Omega, Cutlass Ciera): Inline, overhead-valve four-cylinder. Cast iron block and head. Displacement: 151 cu. in. (2.5 liters). Bore & stroke: 4.00 x 3.00 in. Compression ratio: 8.2:1. Brake horsepower: 90 at 4000 rpm. Torque: 134 lb.-ft. at 2400 rpm. Five main bearings. Hydraulic valve lifters. Fuel injection (TBI). Pontiac-built. VIN Code: R. OPTIONAL V-6 (Omega): 60-degree, overhead-valve V-6. Cast iron block and aluminum head. Displacement: 173 cu. in. (2.8 liters). Bore & stroke: 3.50 x 3.00 in. Compression ratio: 8.5:1. Brake horsepower: 112 at 4800 rpm. Torque: 145 lb.-ft. at 2100 rpm. Four main bearings. Hydraulic valve lifters. Carburetor: 2Bbl. Rochester E2SE. Chevrolet-built. VIN Code: X. OPTIONAL V-6 (Omega): High-output version of 173 cu. in. V-6 above -- Compression ratio: 8.9:1. Horsepower: 130 at 5400 rpm. Torque: 145 lb.-ft. at 2400 rpm. VIN Code: Z. OPTIONAL V-6 (Cutlass Ciera): 90-degree, overhead-valve V-6. Cast iron block and head. Displacement: 181 cu. in. (3.0 liters). Bore & stroke: 3.80 x 2.66 in. Compression ratio: 8.45:1. Brake horsepower: 110 at 4800 rpm. Torque: 145 lb.-ft. at 2000 rpm. Four main bearings. Hydraulic valve lifters. Carburetor: 2Bbl. Rochester E2ME. VIN Code: E. BASE V-6 (Cutlass Supreme, Delta 88): 90-degree, overhead-valve V-6. Cast iron block and head. Displacement: 231 cu. in. (3.8 liters). Bore & stroke: 3.80 x 3.40 in. Compression ratio: 8.0:1. Brake horsepower: 110 at 3800 rpm. Torque: 190 lb.-ft. at 1600 rpm. Four main bearings. Hydraulic valve lifters. Carburetor: 2Bbl. Rochester. Buick-built. VIN Code: A. BASE V-6 (98, Toronado): 90-degree, overhead-valve V-6. Cast iron block and head. Displacement: 252 cu. in. (4.1 liters). Bore & stroke: 3.96 x 3.40 in. Compression ratio: 8.0:1. Brake horsepower: 125 at 4000 rpm. Torque: 205 lb.-ft. at 2000 rpm. Four main bearings. Hydraulic valve lifters. Carburetor: 4Bbl. Rochester. Buick-built. VIN Code: 4. DIESEL V-6 (Cutlass Ciera, Cutlass Supreme): 90-degree, overhead valve V-8. Cast iron block and head. Displacement: 262 cu. in. (4.3 liters). Bore & stroke: 4.06 x 3.38 in. Compression ratio: 22.5:1. Brake horsepower: 85 at 3600 rpm. Torque: 165 lb.-ft. at 1600 rpm. Five main bearings. Hydraulic valve lifters. Fuel injection. VIN Code: T or V. BASE V-8 (Custom Cruiser); OPTIONAL (Cutlass Supreme, Delta 88, 98, Toronado): 90-degree, overhead valve V-8. Cast iron block and head. Displacement: 307 cu. in. (5.0 liters). Bore & stroke: 3.80 x 3.38 in. Compression ratio: 8.0:1. Brake horsepower: 140 at 3600 rpm. Torque: 240 lb.-ft. at 1600 rpm. Five main bearings. Hydraulic valve lifters. Carburetor: 4Bbl. Rochester. VIN Code: Y. OPTIONAL HURST/OLDS V-8 (Cutlass Calais): Same as 307 cu. in. V-8 above, but -- Compression ratio: 8.0:1. Horsepower: 180 at 4000 rpm. Torque: 245 lb.-ft. at 3200 rpm. VIN Code: 9. DIESEL V-8 (Cutlass Supreme, Delta 88, 98, Custom Cruiser, Toronado): 90-degree, overhead valve V-8. Cast iron block and head. Displacement: 350 cu. in. (5.7 liters). Bore & stroke: 4.06 x 3.39 in. Compression ratio: 22.5:1. Brake horsepower: 105 at 3200 rpm. Torque: 200 lb.-ft. at 1600 rpm. Five main bearings. Hydraulic valve lifters. Fuel injection. VIN Code: N.

CHASSIS DATA: Wheelbase: (Firenza) 101.2 in.; (Omega/Ciera) 104.9 in.; (Cutlass) 108.1 in.; (Delta 88) 116.0 in.; (98) 119.0 in.; (Custom Crsr) 116.0 in.; (Toronado) 114.0 in. Overall Length: (Firenza cpe) 174.3 in.; (Firenza sed) 176.2 in.; (Firenza wag) 175.7 in.; (Omega) 182.8 in.; (Ciera) 188.4 in.; (Cutlass Supreme) 200.0-200.4 in.; (Cutlass wag) 200.4 in.; (Delta 88) 218.1 in.; (98) 221.1 in.; (Custom Crsr) 220.3 in.; (Toronado) 206.0 in. Height: (Firenza cpe) 50.8 in.; (Firenza sed) 52.8 in.; (Firenza wag) 53.9 in.; (Omega) 54.8 in.; (Ciera) 55.1 in.; (Cutlass Supreme cpe) 55.6 in.; (Cutlass Supreme sed) 56.6 in.; (Cutlass wag) 56.9 in.; (Delta 88 cpe) 56.8 in.; (Delta 88 sed) 57.5 in.; (98) 58.0 in.; (Custom Crsr) 59.1 in.; (Toronado) 55.2 in. Width: (Firenza) 65.0 in.; (Omega) 69.8 in.; (Ciera) 69.5 in.; (Cutlass cpe) 71.6 in.; (Cutlass sed) 71.9 in.; (Cutlass wag) 71.8 in.; (Delta 88) 76.3 in.; (98) 76.3 in.; (Custom Crsr) 79.8 in.; (Toronado) 71.4 in. Front Tread: (Firenza) 55.4 in.; (Omega/Ciera) 58.7 in.; (Cutlass) 58.5 in.; (Delta 88/98) 61.7 in.; (Custom Crsr) 62.1 in.; (Toronado) 59.3 in. Rear Tread: (Firenza) 55.2 in.; (Omega/Ciera) 57.0 in.; (Cutlass) 57.7 in.; (Delta 88/98) 60.7 in.; (Custom Crsr) 64.1 in.; (Toronado) 60.0 in. Standard Tires: (Firenza) P175/80R13; (Omega/Ciera) P185/80R13; (Cutlass Supreme) P195/75R14; (Delta 88) P205/75R15; (98) P215/75R15; (Custom Crsr) P225/75R15; (Toronado) P205/75R15.

TECHNICAL: Transmission: Four-speed floor shift standard on Firenza/Omega. Gear ratios: (1st) 3.53:1; (2nd) 1.95:1; (3rd) 1.24:1; (4th) 0.73:1 or 0.81:1; (Rev) 3.42:1 or 3.50:1. Five-speed manual trans. optional on Firenza: (1st) 3.91:1; (2nd) 2.15:1; (3rd) 1.45:1; (4th) 1.03:1; (5th) 0.74:1; (Rev) 3.50:1. Three-speed Turbo Hydra-matic standard on Cutlass/Ciera/88. Four-speed automatic overdrive standard on Custom Cruiser/98/Toronado. Standard final drive ratio: (Firenza) 4.10:1 w/4-spd, 3.83:1 w/5-spd, 3.18:1 w/auto.; (Omega) 3.32:1 w/4-spd, 2.39:1 w/auto.; (Omega V-6) 3.32:1 w/4-spd, 2.53:1 w/auto.; (Omega H.O. V-6) 3.65:1 w/4-spd, 3.06:1 w/auto.; (Ciera) 2.39:1 w/four, 2.53:1 w/V-6; (Cutlass) 2.41:1 except 2.29:1 w/diesel V-8, 3.73:1 with Hurst/Olds option; (Cutlass Cruiser) 2.73:1 w/V-6, 2.29:1 w/V-8-307 or diesel; (Delta 88) 2.73:1 w/V-6, 2.41:1 w/V-8; (98) 3.23:1 w/V-6, 2.73:1 w/V-8-307, 2.93:1 w/diesel; (Toronado) 3.00:1 w/V-6, 2.73:1 w/V-8, 2.93:1 w/diesel. Steering: (Firenza/Omega/Ciera) rack and pinion; (others) recirculating ball. Front Suspension: (Firenza/Omega/Ciera) MacPherson struts w/coil springs, lower control arms and anti-sway bar; (Toronado); torsion bars w/anti-sway bar; (others) coil springs with upper/lower control arms and anti-sway bar. Rear Suspension: (Firenza) beam axle w/coil springs, trailing arms and anti-sway bar; (Omega/Ciera) beam axle with integral anti-sway, coil springs and Panhard rod; (Toronado) independent with coil springs, semi-trailing arms, anti-sway bar and automatic leveling; (others) rigid axle w/coil springs, lower trailing radius arms and upper torque arms (four-link). Brakes: Front disc, rear drum. Ignition: Electronic. Body construction: (Firenza/Omega/Ciera) unibody; (others) separate body and frame. Fuel tank: (Firenza) 14 gal.; (Omega) 14.6 gal.; (Ciera) 15.7 gal.; (Cutlass) 18.1 gal.; (Cutlass wag) 18.2 gal.; (Delta 88) 25 gal.; (98) 25 gal.; (Custom Crsr wag) 22 gal.; (Toronado) 21.1 gal.

DRIVETRAIN OPTIONS: Engines: 112 cu. in. four: Firenza ($50). 173 cu. in. V-6: Omega ($150). 181 cu. in. V-6: Ciera ($150). Diesel 262 cu. in. V-6: Cutlass/Ciera ($500). 307 cu. in. 4Bbl. V-8: Cutlass/88 ($225); 98/Toronado ($75). Diesel 350 cu. in. V-8: Cutlass/88/98/Custom Crsr/Toronado ($700). Transmission/Differential: Five-speed manual trans.: Firenza ($75). Turbo Hydra-matic: Firenza ($395); Omega ($425). Four-speed overdrive auto.: 88 ($175). Limited-slip differential: Cutlass/88/98 ($95). Limited-slip differential w/air shocks: Hurst/Olds Calais ($159). Steering/Suspension: Power steering: base Firenza ($199). Firm ride/handling pkg. ($30-$49). Automatic load leveling: Ciera/88/98 ($165). Other: High-capacity cooling ($40-$70). High-capacity radiator ($30) exc. Firenza/Omega. H.D. battery ($25) exc. diesel ($50). Engine block heater ($18). Block/fuel line heater ($49). Trailer wiring ($30) exc. Firenza/Omega. California emissions ($75) exc. diesel ($215).

OPTION PACKAGES: Omega ESC pkg.: Brghm coupe ($851-$1151). Omega ES pkg.: Brghm coupe ($896-$1196). Ciera ES pkg. ($752-$897). Hurst/Olds pkg.: Calais coupe ($1997).

MAJOR CONVENIENCE/APPEARANCE OPTIONS: Four Season air conditioner ($625-$725). Tempmatic air conditioning: 88 ($780); 98/Toronado ($55). Cruise control ($170). Power seat ($185-$210). Power windows ($180-$255). Twilight sentinel: 98/Toronado ($60). Cornering lamps: 88/98 ($60). Power astroroof w/sliding glass panel: Cutlass/88/98/Toronado ($895-$1195). Removable glass roof panels: Cutlass ($825). Glass panel sunroof: Firenza/Omega/Ciera ($295). Landau vinyl roof ($215-$240). Full vinyl roof: Omega/Ciera/Cutlass/88 ($155-$180). Rear-facing third seat: Custom Cruiser ($220).

HISTORY: Introduced: September 23, 1982. Model year production: 939,157. Calendar year production (U.S.): 1,050,846. Calendar year sales by U.S. dealers: 1,007,559. Model year sales by U.S. dealers: 955,243.

HISTORICAL FOOTNOTES: The first Hurst/Olds model was introduced 15 years earlier, in 1968. The Hurst/Olds would return for 1984.

1984

ES models were promoted this year for their styling and handling. One more ES option was offered: on Firenza sedan. Toronado had a new Caliente option, and Cutlass Ciera had a Holiday coupe. A new barometric sensor in the 5.0-liter V-8 altered spark advance, air/fuel ratio, air and EGR. A similar sensor in diesels adjusted injection timing and EGR calibration. Other improvements were made to diesels, although their popularity continued to dwindle. Oldsmobile still promoted the 4.3-liter diesel, though, for its relative quiet running and economy. Diesel V-8s were no longer available in California, but the V-6 was.

1984 Oldsmobile, Firenza GT hatchback coupe, (AA)

1984 Oldsmobile, Firenza S hatchback coupe, (O)

1984 Oldsmobile, Firenza LX sedan, (O)

FIRENZA -- SERIES 3J -- FOUR -- A new front-end look, intended to add more Olds "character," introduced full-width air intake strips below the bumper. A new color-matched grille, urethane-molded, could deform in a minor impact, yet return to original shape. Wraparound side marker lenses now connected to the headlamp frames. Firenza was promoted to younger customers for its sporty, fun-to-drive qualities. Manual-shift models included an upshift indicator light, to help drivers attain maxi-

mum gas mileage. Wagons added an optional cargo area cover that stored behind the back seat. Six models were offered: S hatchback coupe, base four-door sedan, SX hatchback coupe, LX four-door sedan, Cruiser wagon and LX Cruiser wagon. SX and LX were identified by wide bumper fascia moldings. The S hatchback coupe could get a GT package (RPO code WJ4), and 2,312 were produced. A total of 1,125 ES packages (code W47) were installed on base sedans, 1,008 on LX sedans. Chevrolet's 2.0-liter four-cylinder engine was standard; optional was a 1.8-liter OHC four from GM of Brazil. Firenza ES offered "international" styling with blacked-out moldings and minimal brightwork. Black appliqués went on the C-pillars, with black sport mirrors. Wide black bumper fascia moldings (front/rear) and black rocker panel moldings were used. Polycast wheels were standard. Three ES body colors were offered: silver, light royal blue, or light maple metallic. GT had the same updated front end as other Firenzas. This year, GT included not only the spectra red and silver paint scheme offered in 1983, but also a white and silver version. Polycast sport wheels and black accents were included. The GT's instrument panel was highlighted by red beading, which also accented the subtle checkered gray fabric seat inserts.

OMEGA -- SERIES 3X -- FOUR/V-6 -- Changes were modest for the compact front-drive. A new flush-look bumper treatment was possible through use of thermoplastic olifin bumper end caps. Omega's new grille consisted of horizontal strips. Park/signal lamps were now vertical, mounted between the grille and headlamps. Manual-shift models included an upshift indicator

1984 Oldsmobile, Omega ES sedan, (AA)

1984 Oldsmobile, Firenza ES sedan, (O)

1984 Oldsmobile, Firenza Cruiser LX station wagon, (O)

light. New tread design on standard SBR all-season tires improved snow/wet traction, but kept noise down. Four models were available: base and Brougham, coupe and sedan. Engines were the same as 1983: base 151 cubic inch (2.5-liter) four; optional 2.8 V-6 (standard or high-output). Brougham sedans could have an ES package (RPO code W48), featuring an "international" theme similar to Firenza's. The revised grille had a blacked-out treatment. Three colors were available: silver, light royal blue and light maple metallic. Only 224 of the ES packages were installed.

1984 Oldsmobile, Cutlass Ciera coupe, (AA)

1984 Oldsmobile, Cutlass Ciera Holiday coupe, (O)

CUTLASS CIERA -- SERIES 3A -- FOUR/V-6 -- The Ciera was updated front and rear. This year's grille was changed little, but the twin sections now consisted of thin vertical bars. Each model now had six-passenger capacity, with divided bench and custom bench seats. New 14-inch wheels had larger standard tires. Coupes had a wide B-pillar. Inside, a new center console contained a storage area under the armrest. An optional auto calculator could be installed in the console. Four-speed automatic became standard with the 231 cubic inch (3.8-liter) V-6 and optional with the V-6 diesel after production started. This transmission was specifically designed for transverse-mounted front-drive models. It had an integral four-speed design, using two planetary gear sets instead of the usual three in rear-drives. Five models were offered: LS coupe and four-door sedan, Brougham coupe and sedan and new Cruiser two-seat wagon. The new wagon actually had more cargo capacity than rear-drive Cutlass wagons, and could hold 4 x 8 foot plywood sheets. The entire tailgate opened upward with one motion, and the back window was separately hinged. Wagon options included accent striping or two-tone paint, sunroof, simulated woodgrain trim and roof rack. A rear-facing third seat option gave eight-passenger capacity, and included a D-pillar assist handle. Wagons had opening rear vent windows and a rear step pad. Coupes and sedans could have an ES package with new, larger 14 inch SBR BSW tires and a decklid luggage rack. ES also had black belt reveal and drip moldings and black door handle accents. Brougham coupes could have a Holiday coupe package, which offered a unique profile with padded vinyl landau top and opera windows. The option was identified by special script and emblem on the C-pillar. Opera lamps were available. The 151 cubic inch (2.5-liter) four-cylinder engine with automatic was standard; optional was a 3.0-liter gas fueled V-6 or 4.3-liter V-6. Four-speed automatic was available with either V-6. Newly optional this year: Buick's 3.8-liter V-6 with multi-port fuel injection.

1984 Oldsmobile, Cutlass Supreme coupe, (AA)

1984 Oldsmobile, Cutlass Ciera ES sedan, (O)

1984 Oldsmobile, Cutlass Supreme sedan, (O)

CUTLASS SUPREME -- SERIES 3G -- V-6/V-8 -- New grilles and revised taillamps were the most noticeable changes on rear-drive midsize models. This year's coupe grille had a sweep-forward design similar to before, but with seven sections of vertical bars on each side of the divider. Sedan grilles had large openings in a 4 x 3 pattern, with the same headlamp design as 1983: quad headlamps meeting wraparound side marker lenses. All-season SBR tires had a new tread design. Joining the option list: chrome sport wheels. Five models were offered: Supreme and Brougham coupe and four-door sedan, and Calais coupe (which could get the Hurst/Olds package). The Cutlass Cruiser wagon was dropped, since Cutlass Ciera introduced a competing wagon. Four-speed overdrive automatic was available with all engines except the base 231 cubic inch (3.8-liter) V-6. A total of 3,500 Hurst/Olds limited-edition options (RPO code W40) were installed on Calais. Bodies were silver with black lower body paint, with red and black accent stripes on up-

1984 Oldsmobile, Cutlass Calais-based Hurst/Olds coupe, (O)

169

1984 Oldsmobile, Ciera-based Cutlass Cruiser station wagon, (O)

1984 Oldsmobile, Custom Cruiser station wagon, (O)

per bodysides and the front-end panel. Silver, red and black accent stripes separated the two-tone paint, and also appeared on bumper rub strips. Hurst/Olds included a black front lower air dam, a hood scoop and a silver decklid spoiler. The modified 5.0-liter V-8 had specific carburetion, a dual-snorkel, chrome-covered air cleaner and low-restriction dual-outlet mufflers. The engine produced 180 horsepower at 4000 rpm, and 245 pound-feet. of torque at 3200 rpm. Four-speed overdrive automatic was used, linked to the Hurst Lightning Rod shifter, which allowed control of upshifts and downshifts. Hurst/Olds' firm ride/handling package included unequal-length front control arms with 1.25 inch diameter anti-sway bar. At the rear was a rigid axle with trailing links and 7/8-inch anti-sway bar. Super-lift air shocks were used. Tires were 15 inch Goodyear Eagle GT, on chrome/argent wheels with red accent stripes.

1984 Oldsmobile, Delta 88 Royale coupe, (AA)

DELTA 88 -- SERIES 3B -- V-6/V-8 -- Promoted as the best selling full-size domestic, and as a family car, Delta 88 featured a new grille (as usual) and restyled taillamps, but was otherwise little changed. Five models made the lineup: Royale and Royale Brougham coupe and sedan, plus the Custom Cruiser wagon (two-seat or optional rear-facing third seat). The 231 cubic inch (3.8-liter) V-6 was standard. Grille sections contained short horizontal strips to form eight segments on each side. As before, the quad rectangular headlamps extended to meet wraparound side marker lenses, with park/signal lamps down in the bumper. Wraparound taillamps had vertical ribbings, divided into upper and lower segments.

1984 Oldsmobile, Ninety-Eight Regency Brougham sedan, (AA)

NINETY-EIGHT REGENCY -- SERIES 3C -- V-8 -- A tightly-patterned crosshatch grille was the major change for Ninety-Eight, along with new wire wheel cover designs and new bodyside

moldings. Vertical taillamps had emblems on their lenses. Wide twin-section backup lamps were used. Models included the Regency coupe and sedan and Regency Brougham sedan. The 4.1-liter V-6 was dropped, making the 307 cubic inch (5.0-liter) V-8 standard. No diesel V-8 was available in California.

TORONADO -- SERIES 3E -- V-6/V-8 -- A new Caliente package was available for upscale Toronado customers. Caliente had a padded landau roof and stainless steel crown molding, accented with Toronado emblem. A full-length, bright bodyside molding highlighted the car's feature line. Bodysides also had a wide, ridged lower molding. Standard equipment included dual electric remote mirrors, locking wire wheel covers, leather-wrapped sport steering wheel and electronic instrument panel cluster. Leather seat trim was standard, sheepskin inserts optional. A total of 5,007 Caliente (RPO code WJ8) packages were installed. All Toronados had a revised front end. The new grille contained bright horizontal bars, with a color-coordinated band running the full width of the front end. Unlike earlier models, park and turn signal lamps were exposed this year. Optional electronic instruments had blue fluorescent digital speed displays, plus bar graphs for fuel level and temperature. An Optional voice system warned of problems in overheating, low oil pressure and charging failures, and gave advice. The 252 cubic inch (4.1-liter) V-6 was standard; optional was a 307 cubic inch (5.0-liter) gas fueled V-8 or 350 cubic inch diesel V-8.

I.D. DATA: Oldsmobile's 17-symbol Vehicle Identification Number (VIN) again was located on the upper left surface of the instrument panel, visible through the windshield. The first three symbols ('1G3') indicate Oldsmobile division. Symbol four denotes restraint type: 'A' = manual (active) belts. Symbol five is car line/series: 'C' = Firenza; 'D' = Firenza SX/LX; 'B' = Omega; 'E' = Omega Brougham; 'J' = Cutlass Ciera LS; "M = Cutlass Ciera Brougham; 'J' = Cutlass Ciera LS Cruiser; 'R' = Cutlass Supreme; 'M' = Cutlass Supreme Brougham; 'K' = Cutlass Calais; 'L' = Delta 88; 'N' = Delta 88 Royale; 'Y' = Delta 88 Royale Brougham; 'V' = Delta 88 Royale Brougham LS; 'P' = Custom Cruiser; 'G' = Ninety-Eight Regency; 'H' = Ninety-Eight Regency Brougham; 'Z' = Toronado Brougham. Next come two digits that denote body type: '27' = 2-dr. coupe; '37' = 2-dr. coupe; '47' = 2-dr. coupe; '57' = 2-dr. coupe; '77' = 2-dr. coupe; '19' = 4-dr. sedan; '69' = 4-dr. 4-window notch sedan; '35' = 4-dr. 2-seat wagon. Symbol eight is a letter for engine code: 'O' = L4-112 FI; 'P' = L4-121 FI; 'R' = L4-151 FI; 'X' = V-6-173 2Bbl.; 'Z' = H.O. V-6-173 2Bbl.; 'E' = V-6-181 2Bbl.; 'A' = V-6-231 2Bbl.; '4' = V-6-252 4Bbl.; 'T' or 'V' = diesel V-6-262; 'Y' = V-8-307 4Bbl.; '9' = Hurst/Olds V-8-307 4Bbl.; 'N' = diesel V-8-350. Next comes a check digit, followed by a code for model year: ('E' = 1984). Symbol eleven is the assembly plant code: '2' = Ste. Therese, Quebec (Canada); 'D' = Doraville, Georgia; 'G' = Framingham, Mass.; 'M' = Lansing, Mich.; 'W' = Willow Run, Mich.; 'X' = Fairfax, Kansas; 'E' = Linden, New Jersey; 'R' = Arlington, Texas; 'K' = Leeds, Missouri; and Detroit. The final six digits are the sequential serial number, starting with 300,001 (except 88/98 built at Lansing, 700,001). Engine numbers were stamped on the front of the right rocker cover, or top of left cover (Buick-built engines), on label at front or rear of right rocker cover (Chevrolet V-6), or on the left rocker cover (Oldsmobile engines). Four-cylinder engine

numbers were on a pad at left or right front of block. A body number plate on the upper right cowl identified model year, series, style, body assembly plant, body number, trim combination, modular seat code, paint code, date built code and option codes.

FIRENZA (FOUR)

Model Number	Body/Style Number	Body Type & Seating	Factory Price	Shipping Weight	Production Total
3J	C77	2-dr. S Cpe-5P	7214	2390	13,811
3J	C69	4-dr. Sed-5P	7301	2393	34,564
3J	D77	2-dr. SX Cpe-5P	7957	2437	4,179
3J	D69	4-dr. LX Sed-5P	7853	2438	11,761

FIRENZA CRUISER (FOUR)

Model Number	Body/Style Number	Body Type & Seating	Factory Price	Shipping Weight	Production Total
3J	C35	4-dr. Sta Wag-5P	7521	2439	12,389
3J	D35	4-dr. LX Sta Wag-5P	8073	2457	5,771

OMEGA (FOUR/V-6)

Model Number	Body/Style Number	Body Type & Seating	Factory Price	Shipping Weight	Production Total
3X	B37	2-dr. Cpe-5P	7634/7884	2431/2503	5,242
3X	B69	4-dr. Sed-5P	7832/8082	2461/2540	21,571

OMEGA BROUGHAM (FOUR/V-6)

| 3X | E37 | 2-dr. Cpe-5P | 7923/8173 | 2448/2520 | 5,870 |
| 3X | E69 | 4-dr. Sed-5P | 8104/8354 | 2482/2561 | 20,303 |

CUTLASS CIERA LS (FOUR/V-6)

Model Number	Body/Style Number	Body Type & Seating	Factory Price	Shipping Weight	Production Total
3A	J27	2-dr. Cpe-5P	9014/9264	2611/2714	14,887
3A	J19	4-dr. Sed-5P	9203/9453	2650/2753	99,182

CUTLASS CIERA BROUGHAM (FOUR/V-6)

| 3A | M27 | 2-dr. Cpe-5P | 9519/9769 | 2637/2740 | 22,687 |
| 3A | M19 | 4-dr. Sed-5P | 9721/9971 | 2676/2779 | 102,667 |

CUTLASS SUPREME (V-6/V-8)

| 3G | R47 | 2-dr. Cpe-6P | 9376/9751 | 3133/3328 | 132,913 |
| 3G | R69 | 4-dr. Sed-6P | 9529/9904 | 3184/3361 | 62,136 |

CUTLASS SUPREME BROUGHAM (V-6/V-8)

| 3G | M47 | 2-dr. Cpe-6P | 10015/10390 | 3171/3366 | 87,207 |
| 3G | M69 | 4-dr. Sed-6P | 10145/10520 | 3214/3391 | 37,406 |

CUTLASS CALAIS (V-6/V-8)

| 3G | K47 | 2-dr. Cpe-5P | 10274/10649 | 3209/3404 | 24,893 |

Production Note: Cutlass Supreme and Calais totals include Canadian production for U.S. market.

CUTLASS CIERA LS CRUISER (FOUR/V-6)

Model Number	Body/Style Number	Body Type & Seating	Factory Price	Shipping Weight	Production Total
3G	J35	4-dr. Sta Wag-5P	9551/9801	2824/2927	41,816

DELTA 88 ROYALE (V-6/V-8)

Model Number	Body/Style Number	Body Type & Seating	Factory Price	Shipping Weight	Production Total
3B	N37	2-dr. Cpe-6P	9939/10314	3380/3566	23,387
3B	N69	4-dr. Sed-6P	10051/10426	3419/3605	87,993

DELTA 88 ROYALE BROUGHAM (V-6/V-8)

3B	Y37	2-dr. Cpe-6P	10408/10783	3413/3599	41,913
3B	Y69	4-dr. Sed-6P	10499/10874	3449/3635	89,450
3B	V69	4-dr. LS Sed-6P	13854/14229	N/A	17,064

CUSTOM CRUISER (V-8)

Model Number	Body/Style Number	Body Type & Seating	Factory Price	Shipping Weight	Production Total
3B	P35	4-dr. Sta Wag-6P	10839	4033	34,061

NINETY-EIGHT REGENCY (V-8)

Model Number	Body/Style Number	Body Type & Seating	Factory Price	Shipping Weight	Production Total
3C	G37	2-dr. Cpe-6P	13974	3829	7,855
3C	G69	4-dr. Sed-6P	14151	3886	26,919
3C	H69	4-dr. Brghm-6P	15201	3937	42,059

TORONADO BROUGHAM (V-6/V-8)

Model Number	Body/Style Number	Body Type & Seating	Factory Price	Shipping Weight	Production Total
3E	Z57	2-dr. Cpe-6P	16107/16332	3612/3795	48,100

FACTORY PRICE AND WEIGHT NOTE: Prices and weights to left of slash are for six-cylinder, to right for V-8 engine except Omega/Ciera, to left for four-cylinder and to right for V-6.

ENGINE DATA: BASE FOUR (Firenza): Inline, overhead-valve four-cylinder. Cast iron block and head. Displacement: 121 cu. in. (2.0 liters). Bore & stroke: 3.50 x 3.14 in. Compression ratio: 9.3:1. Brake horsepower: 88 at 4800 rpm. Torque: 110 lb.-ft. at 2400 rpm. Five main bearings. Hydraulic valve lifters. Electronic fuel injection. VIN Code: P. OPTIONAL FOUR (Firenza): Inline, overhead-cam four-cylinder. Cast iron block and head. Displacement: 112 cu. in. (1.8 liters). Bore & stroke: 3.34 x 3.11 in. Compression ratio: 9.0:1. Brake horsepower: 82 at 5200 rpm. Torque: 102 lb.-ft. at 2800 rpm. Five main bearings. Hydraulic valve lifters. Electronic fuel injection. VIN Code: O. BASE FOUR (Omega, Cutlass Ciera): Inline, overhead-valve four-cylinder. Cast iron block and head. Displacement: 151 cu. in. (2.5 liters). Bore & stroke: 4.00 x 3.00 in. Compression ratio: 8.2:1. Brake horsepower: 92 at 4000 rpm. Torque: 134 lb.-ft. at 2800 rpm. Five main bearings. Hydraulic valve lifters. Fuel injection (TBI). Pontiac-built. VIN Code: R. OPTIONAL V-6 (Omega): 60-degree, overhead-valve V-6. Cast iron block and aluminum head. Displacement: 173 cu. in. (2.8 liters). Bore & stroke: 3.50 x 3.00 in. Compression ratio: 8.5:1. Brake horsepower: 112 at 4800 rpm. Torque: 145 lb.-ft. at 2100 rpm. Four main bearings. Hydraulic valve lifters. Carburetor: 2Bbl. Chevrolet-built. VIN Code: X. OPTIONAL V-6 (Omega): High-output version of 173 cu. in. V-6 above -- Compression ratio: 8.9:1. Horsepower: 130 at 5400 rpm. Torque: 145 lb.-ft. at 2400 rpm. VIN Code: Z. OPTIONAL V-6 (Cutlass Ciera): 90-degree, overhead-valve V-6. Cast iron block and head. Displacement: 181 cu. in. (3.0 liters). Bore & stroke: 3.80 x 2.66 in. Compression ratio: 8.4:1. Brake horsepower: 110 at 4800 rpm. Torque: 145 lb.-ft. at 2600 rpm. Four main bearings. Hydraulic valve lifters. Carburetor: 2Bbl. VIN Code: E. BASE V-6 (Cutlass Supreme, Delta 88): 90-degree, overhead-valve V-6. Cast iron block and head. Displacement: 231 cu. in. (3.8 liters). Bore & stroke: 3.80 x 3.40 in. Compression ratio: 8.0:1. Brake horsepower: 110 at 3800 rpm. Torque: 190 lb.-ft. at 1600 rpm. Four main bearings. Hydraulic valve lifters. Carburetor: 2Bbl. Buick-built. VIN Code: A. BASE V-6 (Toronado): 90-degree, overhead-valve V-6. Cast iron block and head. Displacement: 252 cu. in. (4.1 liters). Bore & stroke: 3.96 x 3.40 in. Compression ratio: 8.0:1. Brake horsepower: 125 at 4000 rpm. Torque: 205 lb.-ft. at 2000 rpm. Four main bearings. Hydraulic valve lifters. Carburetor: 4Bbl. Buick-built. VIN Code: 4. DIESEL V-6 (Cutlass Ciera, Cutlass Supreme): 90-degree, overhead valve V-8. Cast iron block and head. Displacement: 262 cu. in. (4.3 liters). Bore & stroke: 4.06 x 3.38 in. Compression ratio: 22.8:1. Brake horsepower: 85 at 3600 rpm. Torque: 165 lb.-ft. at 1600 rpm. Five main bearings. Hydraulic valve lifters. Fuel injection. VIN Code: T or V. BASE V-8 (Custom Cruiser); OPTIONAL (Cutlass Supreme, Delta 88, Toronado): 90-degree, overhead valve V-8. Cast iron block and head. Displacement: 307 cu. in. (5.0 liters). Bore & stroke: 3.80 x 3.38 in. Compression ratio: 8.0:1. Brake horsepower: 140 at 3600 rpm. Torque: 240 lb.-ft. at 1600 rpm. Five main bearings. Hydraulic valve lifters. Carburetor: 4Bbl. Rochester. VIN Code: Y. OPTIONAL HURST/OLDS V-8 (Cutlass Calais): Same as 307 cu. in. V-8 above, but -- Compression ratio: 8.0:1. Horsepower: 180 at 4000 rpm. Torque: 245 lb.-ft. at 3200 rpm. VIN Code: 9. DIESEL V-8 (Cutlass Supreme, Delta 88, 98, Custom Cruiser, Toronado): 90-degree, overhead valve V-8. Cast iron block and head. Displacement: 350 cu. in. (5.7 liters). Bore & stroke: 4.06 x 3.39 in. Compression ratio: 22.7:1. Brake horsepower: 105 at 3200 rpm. Torque: 200 lb.-ft. at 1600 rpm. Five main bearings. Hydraulic valve lifters. Fuel injection. VIN Code: N.

CHASSIS DATA: Wheelbase: (Firenza) 101.2 in.; (Omega/Ciera) 104.9 in.; (Cutlass) 108.1 in.; (Delta 88) 115.9 in.; (98) 119.0 in.; (Custom Crsr) 115.9 in.; (Toronado) 114.0 in. Overall Length: (Firenza cpe) 173.3 in.; (Firenza sed) 176.1 in.; (Firenza wag) N/A; (Omega) 182.8 in.; (Ciera) 188.4 in.; (Ciera wag) 191.0 in.; (Cutlass Supreme) 200.0-200.4 in.; (Delta 88) 218.1 in.; (98) 221.1 in.; (Custom Crsr) 220.3 in.; (Toronado) 206.0 in. Height: (Firenza cpe) 51.1 in.; (Firenza sed) 53.7 in.; (Firenza wag) 55.2 in.; (Omega) 53.7 in.; (Ciera) 54.1 in.; (Cutlass Supreme cpe) 54.9 in.; (Cutlass Supreme sed) 55.9 in.; (Delta 88 cpe) 56.0 in.; (Delta 88 sed) 56.7 in.; (98) 57.2 in.; (Custom Crsr) 58.5 in.; (Toronado) 54.6 in. Width: (Firenza) 65.0 in.; (Omega) 69.8 in.; (Ciera) 69.5 in.; (Cutlass cpe) 71.6; (Cutlass sed) 71.9 in.; (Delta 88) 76.3 in.; (98) 76.3 in.; (Custom Crsr) 79.8 in.; (Toronado) 71.4 in. Front Tread: (Firenza) 55.3 in.; (Omega/Ciera) 58.7 in.; (Cutlass) 58.5 in.; (Delta 88/98) 61.7 in.; (Custom Crsr) 62.1 in.; (Toronado) 59.3 in. Rear Tread: (Firenza) 55.1 in.; (Omega/Ciera) 57.0 in.; (Cutlass) 57.7 in.; (Delta 88/98) 60.7 in.; (Custom Crsr) 64.1 in.; (Toronado) 60.0 in. Standard Tires: (Firenza) P175/80R13; (Omega) P185/80R13; (Ciera) P185/75R14; (Cutlass Supreme) P195/75R14; (Delta 88) P205/75R15; (98) P215/75R15; (Custom Crsr) P225/75R15; (Toronado) P205/75R15.

TECHNICAL: Transmission: Four-speed floor shift standard on Firenza/Omega. Gear ratios: (1st) 3.53:1; (2nd) 1.95:1; (3rd) 1.24:1; (4th) 0.73:1 or 0.81:1; (Rev) 3.42:1 or 3.50:1. Five-speed manual trans. optional on Firenza: (1st) 3.91:1; (2nd) 2.15:1; (3rd) 1.45:1; (4th) 1.03:1; (5th) 0.74:1; (Rev) 3.50:1. Three-speed Turbo Hydra-matic standard on Cutlass/Ciera/88. Four-speed automatic overdrive standard on Custom Cruiser/98/Toronado. Standard final drive ratio: (Firenza) 4.10:1 w/4-spd, 3.45:1 w/5-spd, 3.18:1 w/auto.; (Omega) 3.32:1 w/4-spd, 2.39:1 w/auto.; (Omega V-6) 3.32:1 w/4-spd, 2.53:1 w/auto.; (Omega H.O. V-6) 3.65:1 w/4-spd, 3.33:1 w/auto.; (Ciera) 2.84:1 w/four, 2.53:1 w/V-6, 3.06:1 or 2.84:1 w/V-6 and 4-spd auto.; (Cutlass) 2.41:1 except 2.56:1 w/V-8 and 4-spd auto., 3.73:1 with Hurst/Olds option; (Delta 88) 2.73:1 w/V-6, 2.41:1 w/V-8; (98) 2.73:1 exc. 2.93:1 w/diesel; (Toronado) 3.15:1 w/V-6, 2.73:1 w/V-8, 2.93:1 w/diesel. Steering: (Firenza/Omega/Ciera) rack and pinion; (others) recirculating ball. Front Suspension: (Firenza/Omega/Ciera) MacPherson struts w/coil springs, lower control arms and anti-sway bar; (Toronado); torsion bars w/anti-sway bar; (others) coil springs with upper/lower control arms and anti-sway bar. Rear Suspension: (Firenza) beam axle w/coil springs, trailing arms and anti-sway bar; (Omega/Ciera) beam axle with integral anti-sway, coil springs and Panhard rod; (Toronado) independent with coil springs, semi-trailing arms, anti-sway bar and automatic leveling; (others) rigid axle w/coil springs, lower trailing radius arms and upper torque arms (four-link). Brakes: Front disc, rear drum. Ignition: Electronic. Body construction: (Firenza/Omega/Ciera) unibody; (others) separate body and frame. Fuel tank: (Firenza) 14 gal.; (Omega) 14.6 or 15.1 gal.; (Ciera) 15.7 gal.; (Cutlass) 18.2 or 19.8 gal.; (Delta 88) 25 gal.; (98) 25 gal.; (Custom Crsr wag) 22 gal.; (Toronado) 21 gal.

1984 Oldsmobile, Toronado Caliente coupe, (AA)

DRIVETRAIN OPTIONS: Engines: 112 cu. in. four: Firenza

($50). 173 cu. in. V-6: Omega ($250). H.O. 173 cu. in. V-6: Omega Brghm sed ($400). 181 cu. in. V-6: Ciera ($250). Diesel 262 cu. in. V-6: Cutlass/Ciera ($500). 307 cu. in. 4Bbl. V-8: Cutlass/88 ($375); Toronado ($225). Diesel 350 cu. in. V-8: Cutlass/88/98/Toronado ($700). Transmission/Differential: Five-speed manual trans.: Firenza ($75). Turbo Hydra-matic: Firenza ($395); Omega ($425). Four-speed automatic overdrive: Cutlass/88 ($175). Limited-slip differential: Cutlass/88/98 ($95). Steering/Suspension: Power steering: base Firenza ($204). Firm ride/handling pkg. ($30-$49). Automatic load leveling: Ciera/88/98 ($175). Other: High-capacity cooling ($40-$70) except Firenza. High-capacity radiator: Cutlass/88/98/Toronado ($30). H.D. battery ($26) exc. diesel ($52). Engine block heater ($18). Block/fuel line heater ($49). Trailer wiring: 88/98/Toronado ($30). California emissions ($99).

OPTION PACKAGES: Firenza GT pkg.: S cpe ($695). Firenza ES pkg.: base sedan ($450); LX sedan ($375). Omega ES pkg.: Brghm sedan ($675). Ciera Holiday coupe pkg.: Brghm ($565). Ciera ES pkg. ($696-$851). Hurst/Olds pkg.: Calais coupe ($1997). Toronado Caliente pkg. ($2195).

MAJOR CONVENIENCE/APPEARANCE OPTIONS: Four Season air conditioner ($630-$730). Tempmatic air conditioning: 88 ($785); 98/Toronado ($55). Cruise control ($175). Power seat ($178-$215). Power windows ($185-$260). Twilight sentinel: Toronado ($60). Cornering lamps: 88/98 ($60). Power astroroof w/sliding glass panel: Cutlass ($895); 88/98/Toronado ($1195). Removable glass roof panels: Cutlass ($825). Glass panel sunroof: Firenza/Omega/Ciera ($300). Landau vinyl roof ($215-$245). Full vinyl roof: Omega/Ciera/Cutlass/88 ($160-$185). Full padded vinyl roof: Cutlass ($245). Rear-facing third seat: Cutlass/Custom Cruiser ($215-$220).

HISTORY: Introduced: September 22, 1983. Model year production: 1,179,656. Calendar year production (U.S.): 1,065,528. Calendar year sales by U.S. dealers: 1,056,053. Model year sales by U.S. dealers: 1,098,685.

HISTORICAL FOOTNOTES: A "special feel in an Oldsmobile" was the promotional theme, suggesting quality, value, prestige, pride of ownership and confidence in the name. Also emphasized was the "Oldsmobile difference."

1985

One new model was introduced this year: the Calais, positioned between the subcompact (Firenza) and Cutlass Ciera, intended to attract younger drivers. Omega was discontinued, a victim of the X-car recalls and problems. Anticipating the federal standard of 1986, a high-mount brakelight was optional on Cutlass Ciera, Calais and Ninety-Eight Regency.

1985 Oldsmobile, Firenza LX sedan, (O)

FIRENZA -- SERIES 3J -- FOUR/V-6 -- Firenza looked the same in front, but gained a revised look at the rear. It also received an optional V-6, a multi-port fuel-injected 173 cubic inch (2.8-liter) V-6 from Chevrolet in addition to the base 2.0-liter four (also Chevrolet's). The 130-horsepower V-6 was standard on GT. The GT delivered a 0-60 mph time of 9 seconds with four-speed

1985 Oldsmobile, Firenza GT hatchback coupe, (O)

manual, 9.5 seconds with automatic. To fit the V-6 into the Firenza, a serpentine belt system was used, along with a bubble hood. The grille area was expanded to improve cooling. Also optional was a 1.8-liter four from GM of Brazil. Coupe, sedan and wagons were available, along with sporty GT and sophisticated ES options. A total of 498 GT packages (RPO code W54) and 863 ES packages were installed. The ES had black-out body moldings and polycast wheels.

1985 Oldsmobile, Calais convertible Indianapolis 500 Pace Car, (AA)

1985 Oldsmobile, Firenza Cruiser station wagon, (O)

1985 Oldsmobile, Calais coupe, (O)

CALAIS -- SERIES 3N -- FOUR/V-6 -- Though retaining traditional Olds styling cues, the new GM N-body Calais coupe featured a sporty, contemporary design with a formal roof. Front-drive was used, and the car held five passengers. Calais was similar to the new Buick Somerset Regal and Pontiac Grand Am. Two trim levels were offered, intended to appeal to the "style-conscious, quality-oriented, younger car buyer." Calais

featured a wedge shape with soft rounded lines. The hood extended to the windshield, eliminating the cowl panel. The grille had thin vertical bars with a smaller-than-usual center divider that contained no emblem. Rectangular headlamps were used, with park/signal lamps set into the front bumper. 'Calais' script went on the leading edges of doors, just above the bodyside molding. No "tulip" rear-end panel was used between the rear window and decklid. Door hinges were bolted on rather than welded. A zincrometal decklid outer panel was used, with a galvanized steel inner panel. Base coat/clear coat paint gave a high-gloss finish. Front bucket seats and console were standard. Light and wiper switches were in pods at steering wheel sides. Optional analog gauges and electronic instruments were available. The 151 cubic inch (2.5-liter) four-cylinder engine with TBI and roller lifters, with five-speed manual or three-speed automatic, was standard. Optional was a 3.0-liter V-6 with multiport fuel injection (automatic only). Wire wheels or all-new aluminum wheels (a Calais exclusive) were optional. A total of 2,998 "500" packages were installed on the base coupe, and 6,763 Special Edition models (code WK5) were produced.

1985 Oldsmobile, Cutlass Ciera Holiday coupe, (AA)

CUTLASS CIERA -- SERIES 3A -- FOUR/V-6 -- A more aerodynamic front was introduced on Ciera. The small-crosshatch egg-crate grille sections had greater slope, and wraparound side marker lenses a more rounded shape. As before, wide park/signal lights were in the bumper strip. Wraparound taillamps had rounded tops. Wide backup lights were mounted in a panel with center 'Oldsmobile' nameplate. An energy-absorbing back bumper used a polyethylene honeycomb with roll-form beam. The rear license was bumper-mounted. A high-mount brakelight was optional. Models included an LS and Brougham coupe and sedan and Cruiser wagon. The standard 151 cubic inch (2.5-liter) four added roller lifters. Options included a 3.0-liter carbureted V-6, new 3.8-liter PFI V-6, and diesel V-6 (with new aluminum head). Three specialty options were offered: GT, ES and Holiday Coupe. A total of 1,084 GT packages (RPO code W45), 3,101 ES packages (code W48) and 9,836 Holiday coupe packages were installed. GT models had the 3.8-liter V-6 as well as special trim and suspension. Ciera standard equipment included a 151 cubic inch (2.5-liter) fuel-injected four, power rack-and-pinion steering, power brakes, AM radio, velour custom bench seat, automatic transmission and P185/75R14 SBR all-season blackwalls. Bodies had bright belt beveal and roof drip moldings and black window frame moldings. Cruiser had wheel opening and rocker panel moldings. Ciera Brougham added a convenience group, bright rocker panel and wheel opening moldings and 55/45 divided bench seat.

1985 Oldsmobile, Cutlass Ciera sedan, (JG)

1985 Oldsmobile, Ciera-based Cutlass Cruiser station wagon, (O)

1985 Oldsmobile, Delta 88 Royale Brougham coupe, (JAG)

1985 Oldsmobile, Cutlass Supreme sedan, (O)

1985 Oldsmobile, Delta 88 Royale Brougham sedan, (O)

CUTLASS SUPREME -- SERIES 3G -- V-6/V-8 -- Replacing the Hurst/Olds option after two years was the 4-4-2 package, with high-output V-8, and special paint and suspension. The 4-4-2 name was revived. A total of 3,000 4-4-2 packages (RPO code W42) were produced. Features included a '4-4-2' door decal, 3.73:1 rear axle, super stock wheels and Eagle GT tires. The Cutlass line displayed a revised front end. Coupe grilles continued sloping forward, with crosshatch patterns on each side but split into three side-by-side segments. Sedan grilles were upright again, having thin horizontal strips divided into four side-by-side sections. Sedans continued with wraparound side marker lenses and park/signal lights in the bumper. Standard Supreme equipment included a 231 cubic inch (3.8-liter) V-6, three-speed automatic transmission, power brakes and steering, cloth/vinyl custom bench seat, AM radio, P195/75R14 blackwall SBR tires, bumper guards and rub strips and bright wheel covers. Bright moldings went on rocker panels, wheel openings, windshield, hood center and roof drip area. Brougham added 55/45 divided front seat, wide bodyside moldings, belt reveal moldings, convenience group, and reading lamp; rocker panel moldings were deleted from the Brougham coupe. The sporty Salon added front and rear stabilizer bars, color-keyed Super Stock wheels, specific bodyside accent paint stripes, leather-wrapped steering wheel, contour reclining front bucket seats, sport console (with floor shift), Rallye instruments and color-keyed sport mirrors. Salon also had wheel opening and wide bodyside moldings. Optional engines were the diesel V-6 or V-8, and 307 cubic inch (5.0-liter) gas fueled V-8, which added roller lifters plus other internal modifications.

DELTA 88 -- SERIES 3B -- V-6/V-8 -- As usual, Delta 88 featured a new grille, with four rows on each side. New at the rear were elongated backup lamps between the taillamps and license plate. Brougham and Brougham LS models were offered, the latter with a 4 x 5 "hole" eggcrate pattern grille. The Buick-built 231 cubic inch (3.8-liter) V-6 remained standard. Optional was a 307 cubic inch (5.0-liter) gas fueled V-8, now with roller lifters, and a 5.7-liter diesel. Added standard equipment included an AM/FM stereo radio and all-season SBR tires. The Custom Cruiser wagon was again available (V-8 powered). Standard 88 equipment included three-speed automatic, power brakes/steering, custom cloth bench seat, AM/FM stereo radio, bumper guards and rub strips, left remote mirror and woodgrain dash. Bright moldings were used on rocker panels, wheel openings, bodyside, windshield and roof drip rail. Royale Brougham added a 55/45 divided seat, belt reveal moldings, convenience group and opera lamps (on coupe). Delta 88 LS added a four-

speed overdrive automatic transmission, power windows, wire wheel covers (with locks), tilt steering, lower bodyside moldings, six-way power driver's seat, air conditioning, digital clock, tinted glass, opera lamps, dual color-keyed remote mirrors and power door locks. Tires were P205/75R15 blackwall SBR except LS, P215/75R15 whitewalls. Standard Cruiser equipment included a 307 cubic inch (5.0-liter) V-8, four-speed automatic, AM/FM stereo, power brakes/steering, 55/45 divided bench seat (vinyl or velour), power tailgate window, driver's remote mirror and P225/75R15 blackwall SBR tires. An all-new Delta 88 was being developed for 1986.

1985 Oldsmobile, Ninety-Eight Regency coupe, (AA)

1985 Oldsmobile, Custom Cruiser station wagon, (O)

NINETY-EIGHT REGENCY -- SERIES 3C -- V-6 -- After a long history as a big rear-drive luxury model, Ninety-Eight switched to front-drive, though still able to carry six passengers. Introduced as an early 1985, the extensively redesigned Ninety-Eight was offered in coupe and sedan form, base and Regency trim. Aero styling highlights included a sloping hood and curved decklid, rounded edges, bumpers flush to bodyside and flush-

mounted windshield and backlight. The windshield flowed into flush side door glass, with only a narrow black molding visible at the windshield (the pillar was under the glass). It was 15 inches shorter than its predecessor, weighing 570 to 635 pounds less. But inside dimensions were nearly identical to the 1984 rear-drive. Dual grilles were separated by a chrome center post with "rocket" emblem. Quad rectangular headlamps and the grille were surrounded by bright trim. Amber side marker lenses were integral with the headlamp housings. A soft fascia covered the upper portion of the bright bumpers. Crystal-lens parking lamps were horizontally-mounted in the front bumper. Both bumpers had a black rub strip with white stripe. Ninety-Eight's traditional formal roofline continued, with narrow C-pillars. Opera lamps were standard. Coupes had a landau vinyl roof; sedans, a full vinyl roof. Sedans also had a pillar appliqué. Narrow vertical taillamps held rocket emblem accents. Wide horizontal backup lamps extended from the taillamps to the license plate opening. Regency models had polished stainless steel wheel covers. Regency Brougham carried aero-profile simulated wire wheel covers. A split-bench seat had lumbar, lateral back and cushion support, with six-way power driver's seat. Two-position memory was optional, as was six-way power for the passenger seat and manual recliner. Power windows were standard. An optional auto calculator (available with the optional electronic instrument cluster) showed 12 functions including time, date, trip distance, elapsed time, estimated distance and time of arrival, distance since fill-up and average fuel economy. A voice synthesis system alert also was included. Options included an automatic day/night mirror and power remote mirrors. The standard carbureted 181 cubic inch (3.0-liter) V-6 was transverse-mounted, with four-speed automatic overdrive transmission. Broughams had a standard 3.8-liter V-6 with multi-port fuel injection. A 4.3-liter diesel V-6 was also available. Ninety-Eight's chassis featured fully independent suspension. The floor pan was galvanized for corrosion protection, and all body panels except the roof had either galvanized zinc or special pre-coatings on inside surfaces.

1985 Oldsmobile, Toronado Caliente coupe, (AA)

TORONADO -- SERIES 3E -- V-8 --

Only a V-8 engine powered Toronados this year, as the former V-6 sold poorly. Appearance changed little. Toronado's grille was little changed, a full-width dual-segment design with park/signal lamps at the outside; but tiny crosshatch patterning was visible through each center portion. The standard 307 cubic inch (5.0-liter) V-8 had new roller lifters, new exhaust manifold and other internal changes. Standard equipment included four-speed automatic overdrive, power brakes/steering, Four Season air conditioner, power windows, digital clock, tinted glass, automatic leveling, AM/FM stereo radio with electronic tuning, six-way power driver's seat and P205/75R15 whitewalls. Also standard: cornering lamps, dual remote mirrors, speed control and bright body moldings. The 350 cubic inch diesel V-8 was available for the last time. A total of 7,342 Caliente packages (RPO code WJ8) were produced. It featured a padded landau vinyl roof, stainless steel crown, bright bodyside and lower bodyside moldings, special front-end panel emblem, dual power mirrors, tempmatic air conditioning, leather-wrapped steering wheel, wire wheel covers and electronic instrument panel.

1985 Oldsmobile, 98 Regency sedan, (O)

I.D. DATA: Oldsmobile's 17-symbol Vehicle Identification Number (VIN) again was located on the upper left surface of the instrument panel, visible through the windshield. The first three symbols ('1G3') indicate Oldsmobile division. Symbol four denotes restraint type: 'A' = manual (active) belts. Symbol five is car line/series: 'C' = Firenza; 'D' = Firenza SX/LX; 'F' = Calais; 'T' = Calais Supreme; 'J' = Cutlass Ciera LS; "M' = Cutlass Ciera Brougham; 'J' = Cutlass Ciera LS Cruiser; R' = Cutlass Supreme; 'M' = Cutlass Supreme Brougham; 'K' = Cutlass Salon; 'L' = Delta 88; 'N' = Delta 88 Royale; 'Y' = Delta 88 Royale Brougham; 'V' = Delta 88 Royale Brougham LS; 'P' = Custom Cruiser; 'X' = Ninety-Eight Regency; 'W' = Ninety-Eight Regency Brougham; 'Z' = Toronado Brougham. Next come two digits that denote body type: '11' = 2-dr. notchback sedan; '27' = 2-dr. coupe; '37' = 2-dr. coupe; '47' = 2-dr. coupe; '57' = 2-dr. coupe; '77' = 2-dr. coupe; '19' = 4-dr. sedan; '69' = 4-dr. 4-window notch sedan; '35' = 4-dr. 2-seat wagon. Symbol eight is a letter for engine code: '0' = L4-112 FI; 'P' = L4-121 FI; 'R' = L4-151 FI; 'W' = V-6-173 FI; 'E' = V-6-181 2Bbl.; 'L' = V-6-181 FI; 'A' = V-6-231 2Bbl.; '3' = V-6-231 FI; 'T' = diesel V-6-262; 'Y' = V-8-307 4Bbl.; '9' = Hurst/Olds V-8-307 4Bbl.; 'N' = diesel V-8-350. Next comes a check digit, followed by a code for model year: ('F' = 1985). Symbol eleven is the assembly plant code: '2' = Ste. Therese, Quebec (Canada); 'D' = Doraville, Georgia; 'G' = Framingham, Mass.; 'M' = Lansing, Mich.; 'P' = Pontiac, Mich.; 'E' = Linden, New Jersey; 'R' = Arlington, Texas; and 'K' = Leeds, Missouri. (Oldsmobiles were also built in Detroit and Orion, Michigan; Wilmington, Delaware; and Wentzville, Missouri.) The final six digits are the sequential serial number. Engine numbers were stamped on the front of the right rocker cover, or top of left cover (Buick-built engines), on label at front or rear of right rocker cover (Chevrolet V-6), or on the left rocker cover (Oldsmobile engines). Four-cylinder engine numbers were on a pad at left or right front of block. A body number plate on the upper right cowl identified model year, series, style, body assembly plant, body number, trim combination, modular seat code, paint code, date built code and option codes.

FIRENZA (FOUR/V-6)

Model Number	Body/Style Number	Body Type & Seating	Factory Price	Shipping Weight	Production Total
3J	C77	2-dr. S Cpe-5P	7588/8148	2390/----	5,842
3J	C69	4-dr. Sed-5P	7679/8239	2393/----	25,066
3J	D77	2-dr. SX Cpe-5P	8395/8955	2437/----	1,842
3J	D69	4-dr. LX Sed-5P	8255/8815	2438/----	7,563

FIRENZA CRUISER (FOUR/V-6)

3J	C35	4-dr. Sta Wag-5P	7898/8458	2439/----	6,291
3J	D35	4-dr. LX Sta Wag-5P	8492/9052	2457/----	2,436

CALAIS (FOUR/V-6)

Model Number	Body/Style Number	Body Type & Seating	Factory Price	Shipping Weight	Production Total
3N	F27	2-dr. Cpe-5P	8499/9059	2431/2503	49,545

CALAIS SUPREME (FOUR/V-6)

3N	T27	2-dr. Cpe-5P	8844/9404	2448/2520	56,695

CUTLASS CIERA LS (FOUR/V-6)

Model Number	Body/Style Number	Body Type & Seating	Factory Price	Shipping Weight	Production Total
3A	J27	2-dr. Cpe-6P	9307/9567	2611/2714	13,396
3A	J19	4-dr. Sed-6P	9497/9757	2650/2753	118,575

CUTLASS CIERA BROUGHAM (FOUR/V-6)

3A	M27	2-dr. Cpe-6P	9787/10047	2637/2740	20,476
3A	M19	4-dr. Sed-6P	9998/10258	2676/2779	112,441

CUTLASS CIERA CRUISER (FOUR/V-6)

3G	J35	4-dr. Sta Wag-6P	9858/10118	2824/2927	38,225

CUTLASS SUPREME (V-6/V-8)

3G	R47	2-dr. Cpe-6P	9797/10087	3133/3328	75,045
3G	R69	4-dr. Sed-6P	9961/10251	3184/3361	43,085

CUTLASS SUPREME BROUGHAM (V-6/V-8)

3G	M47	2-dr. Cpe-6P	10468/10758	3171/3366	58,869
3G	M69	4-dr. Sed-6P	10602/10892	3214/3391	28,741

CUTLASS SALON (V-6/V-8)

3G	K47	2-dr. Cpe-6P	10770/11060	3209/3404	17,512

DELTA 88 ROYALE (V-6/V-8)

Model Number	Body/Style Number	Body Type & Seating	Factory Price	Shipping Weight	Production Total
3B	N37	2-dr. Cpe-6P	10488/11053	3380/3566	15,002
3B	N69	4-dr. Sed-6P	10596/11161	3419/3605	69,641

DELTA 88 ROYALE BROUGHAM (V-6/V-8)

3B	Y37	2-dr. Cpe-6P	10968/11533	3413/3599	31,891
3B	Y69	4-dr. Sed-6P	11062/11627	3449/3635	72,103
3B	V69	4-dr. LS Sed-6P	-----/14331	N/A	30,239

CUSTOM CRUISER (V-8)

Model Number	Body/Style Number	Body Type & Seating	Factory Price	Shipping Weight	Production Total
3B	P35	4-dr. Sta Wag-6P	11627	4033	22,889

NINETY-EIGHT REGENCY (V-6)

Model Number	Body/Style Number	Body Type & Seating	Factory Price	Shipping Weight	Production Total
3C	X11	2-dr. Sed-6P	14725	3684	4,734
3C	X69	4-dr. Sed-6P	14665	3733	43,697

NINETY-EIGHT REGENCY BROUGHAM (V-6)

3C	W11	2-dr. Sed-6P	15932	3784	9,704
3C	W69	4-dr. Sed-6P	15864	4059	111,297

TORONADO BROUGHAM (V-8)

Model Number	Body/Style Number	Body Type & Seating	Factory Price	Shipping Weight	Production Total
3E	Z57	2-dr. Cpe-5P	16798	3612	42,185

FACTORY PRICE AND WEIGHT NOTE: Prices and weights to left of slash are for six-cylinder, to right for V-8 engine except Firenza/Calais/Ciera, to left for four-cylinder and to right for V-6.

1985 Oldsmobile, Cutlass Supreme coupe, (JAG)

ENGINE DATA: BASE FOUR (Firenza): Inline, overhead-valve four-cylinder. Cast iron block and head. Displacement: 121 cu. in. (2.0 liters). Bore & stroke: 3.50 x 3.14 in. Compression ratio: 9.3:1. Brake horsepower: 88 at 4800 rpm. Torque: 110 lb.-ft. at 2400 rpm. Five main bearings. Hydraulic valve lifters. Electronic fuel injection. VIN Code: P. OPTIONAL FOUR (Firenza): Inline, overhead-cam four-cylinder. Cast iron block and aluminum head. Displacement: 112 cu. in. (1.8 liters). Bore & stroke: 3.34

x 3.11 in. Compression ratio: 9.0:1. Brake horsepower: 82 at 5200 rpm. Torque: 102 lb.-ft. at 2800 rpm. Five main bearings. Hydraulic valve lifters. Electronic fuel injection. VIN Code: O. BASE FOUR (Calais, Cutlass Ciera): Inline, overhead-valve four-cylinder. Cast iron block and head. Displacement: 151 cu. in. (2.5 liters). Bore & stroke: 4.00 x 3.00 in. Compression ratio: 8.2:1. Brake horsepower: 92 at 4400 rpm. Torque: 134 lb.-ft. at 2800 rpm. Five main bearings. Hydraulic valve lifters. Fuel injection (TBI). Pontiac-built. VIN Code: R. OPTIONAL V-6 (Firenza): 60-degree, overhead-valve V-6. Cast iron block and aluminum head. Displacement: 173 cu. in. (2.8 liters). Bore & stroke: 3.50 x 3.00 in. Compression ratio: 8.9:1. Brake horsepower: 130 at 4800 rpm. Torque: 150 lb.-ft. at 2400 rpm. Four main bearings. Hydraulic valve lifters. Electronic fuel injection. Chevrolet-built. VIN Code: W. BASE V-6 (98); OPTIONAL V-6 (Cutlass Ciera): 90-degree, overhead-valve V-6. Cast iron block and head. Displacement: 181 cu. in. (3.0 liters). Bore & stroke: 3.80 x 2.66 in. Compression ratio: 8.4:1. Brake horsepower: 110 at 4800 rpm. Torque: 145 lb.-ft. at 2600 rpm. Four main bearings. Hydraulic valve lifters. Carburetor: 2Bbl. Rochester E2SE. VIN Code: E. OPTIONAL V-6 (Calais): Same as 181 cu. in. V-6 above, with fuel injection -- Compression ratio: 9.0:1. Horsepower: 125 at 4900 rpm. Torque: 150 lb.-ft. at 2400 rpm. VIN Code: L. BASE V-6 (Calais, Delta 88): 90-degree, overhead-valve V-6. Cast iron block and head. Displacement: 231 cu. in. (3.8 liters). Bore & stroke: 3.80 x 3.40 in. Compression ratio: 8.0:1. Brake horsepower: 110 at 3800 rpm. Torque: 190 lb.-ft. at 1600 rpm. Four main bearings. Hydraulic valve lifters. Carburetor: 2Bbl. Rochester E2ME. Buick-built. VIN Code: A. BASE V-6 (Cutlass Supreme, Delta 88, 98 Brougham); OPTIONAL (Ciera LS/Brougham, 98): Same as 231 cu. in. V-6 above, but with fuel injection -- Horsepower: 125 at 4400 rpm. Torque: 195 lb.-ft. at 2000 rpm. VIN Code: 3. DIESEL V-6 (Cutlass Ciera, Cutlass Supreme, 98): 90-degree, overhead valve V-6. Cast iron block and head. Displacement: 262 cu. in. (4.3 liters). Bore & stroke: 4.06 x 3.38 in. Compression ratio: 22.8:1. Brake horsepower: 85 at 3600 rpm. Torque: 165 lb.-ft. at 1600 rpm. Five main bearings. Hydraulic valve lifters. Fuel injection. VIN Code: T. BASE V-8 (Delta 88 LS, Custom Cruiser, Toronado); OPTIONAL (Cutlass Supreme, Delta 88): 90-degree, overhead valve V-8. Cast iron block and head. Displacement: 307 cu. in. (5.0 liters). Bore & stroke: 3.80 x 3.38 in. Compression ratio: 8.0:1. Brake horsepower: 140 at 3600 rpm. (Cutlass, 140 at 3200). Torque: 240 lb.-ft. at 1600 rpm. (Cutlass, 255 at 2000). Five main bearings. Hydraulic valve lifters. Carburetor: 4Bbl. Rochester 4MC. VIN Code: Y. OPTIONAL HURST/OLDS V-8 (Cutlass Calais): Same as 307 cu. in. V-8 above, but -- Compression ratio: 9.0:1. Horsepower: 180 at 4000 rpm. Torque: 245 lb.-ft. at 3200 rpm. VIN Code: 9. DIESEL V-8 (Cutlass Supreme, Delta 88, Custom Cruiser, Toronado): 90-degree, overhead valve V-8. Cast iron block and head. Displacement: 350 cu. in. (5.7 liters). Bore & stroke: 4.06 x 3.39 in. Compression ratio: 22.7:1. Brake horsepower: 105 at 3200 rpm. Torque: 200 lb.-ft. at 1600 rpm. Five main bearings. Hydraulic valve lifters. Fuel injection. VIN Code: N.

CHASSIS DATA: Wheelbase: (Firenza) 101.2 in.; (Calais) 103.4 in.; (Ciera) 104.9 in.; (Cutlass) 108.1 in.; (Delta 88) 115.9 in.; (98) 110.8 in.; (Custom Crsr) 115.9 in.; (Toronado) 114.0 in. Overall Length: (Firenza cpe) 174.3 in.; (Firenza sed) 176.2 in.; (Firenza wag) 176.2 in.; (Calais) 177.5 in.; (Ciera) 190.0-190.3 in.; (Ciera wag) 194.4 in.; (Cutlass Supreme) 200.0-200.4 in.; (Delta 88) 218.1 in.; (98) 196.1 in.; (Custom Crsr) 220.3 in.; (Toronado) 206.0 in. Height: (Firenza cpe) 51.7 in.; (Firenza sed) 53.7 in.; (Firenza wag) 55.2 in.; (Calais) 52.5 in.; (Ciera) 54.1 in.; (Ciera wag) 54.5 in.; (Cutlass Supreme cpe) 54.9 in.; (Cutlass Supreme sed) 55.9 in.; (Delta 88 cpe) 56.0 in.; (Delta 88 sed) 56.7 in.; (98) 55.0 in.; (Custom Crsr) 58.5 in.; (Toronado) 54.6 in. Width: (Firenza) 65.0 in.; (Calais) 66.9 in.; (Ciera) 69.5 in.; (Cutlass cpe) 71.6; (Cutlass sed) 71.9 in.; (Delta 88) 76.3 in.; (98) 71.4 in.; (Custom Crsr) 79.8 in.; (Toronado) 71.4 in. Front Tread: (Firenza) 55.4 in.; (Calais) 55.5 in.; (Ciera) 58.7 in.; (Cutlass) 58.5 in.; (Delta 88)

61.7 in.; (98) 60.3 in.; (Custom Crsr) 62.1 in.; (Toronado) 59.3 in. Rear Tread: (Firenza) 55.2 in.; (Calais) 55.2 in.; (Ciera) 57.0 in.; (Cutlass) 57.7 in.; (Delta 88) 60.7 in.; (98) 59.8 in.; (Custom Crsr) 64.1 in.; (Toronado) 60.0 in. Standard Tires: (Firenza) P175/80R13; (Calais) P185/80R13; (Ciera) P185/75R14; (Cutlass Supreme) P195/75R14; (Delta 88) P205/75R15; (98) P205/75R14; (Custom Crsr) P225/75R15; (Toronado) P205/75R15.

TECHNICAL: Transmission: Four-speed floor shift standard on Firenza four. Gear ratios: (1st) 3.53:1; (2nd) 1.95:1; (3rd) 1.24:1; (4th) 0.81:1; (Rev) 3.42:1. Four-speed on Firenza V-6: (1st) 3.31:1; (2nd) 1.95:1; (3rd) 1.24:1; (4th) 0.90:1; (Rev) 3.42:1. Five-speed manual trans. standard on Calais: (1st) 3.73:1; (2nd) 2.04:1; (3rd) 1.45:1; (4th) 1.03:1; (5th) 0.74:1; (Rev) 3.50:1. Five-speed manual trans. optional on Firenza: (1st) 3.91:1; (2nd) 2.15:1; (3rd) 1.45:1; (4th) 1.03:1; (5th) 0.74:1; (Rev) 3.50:1. Three-speed Turbo Hydramatic standard on Cutlass/Ciera/88. Four-speed automatic overdrive standard on Custom Cruiser/98/Toronado. Standard final drive ratio: (Firenza) 3.65:1 w/4-spd, 3.45:1 w/5-spd, 3.18:1 w/auto.; (Calais) 3.35:1 w/5-spd, 2.84:1 w/auto.; (Ciera) 2.84:1 w/four, 2.53:1 w/V-6-181, 2.84:1 w/V-6-231; (Cutlass) 2.41:1 w/V-6, 2.14:1 w/V-8; (Delta 88) 2.73:1; (98) 3.06:1 w/V-6-181, 2.84:1 w/V-6-231, 3.06:1 w/diesel; (Toronado) 2.73:1 except 2.93:1 w/diesel. Steering: (Firenza/Calais/Ciera/98) rack and pinion; (others) recirculating ball. Front Suspension: (Firenza/Calais/Ciera/98) MacPherson struts w/coil springs, lower control arms and anti-sway bar; (Toronado); torsion bars w/anti-sway bar; (others) coil springs with upper/lower control arms and anti-sway bar. Rear Suspension: (Firenza) beam axle w/coil springs, trailing arms and anti-sway bar; (Calais) semi-independent w/coil springs and trailing arms; (Ciera) beam axle with integral anti-sway, coil springs and Panhard rod; (98) independent w/struts, coil springs, lower control arms, anti-sway bar and automatic level control; (Toronado) independent with coil springs, semi-trailing arms, anti-sway bar and automatic leveling; (others) rigid axle w/coil springs, lower trailing radius arms and upper torque arms (four-link). Brakes: Front disc, rear drum. Ignition: Electronic. Body construction: (Firenza/Calais/Ciera/98) unibody; (others) separate body and frame. Fuel tank: (Firenza) 14 gal.; (Calais) 13.6 gal.; (Ciera) 16.6 gal.; (Cutlass) 18.1 gal.; (Delta 88) 27 gal.; (98) 18 gal.; (Custom Crsr wag) 22 gal.; (Toronado) 21.1 gal.

DRIVETRAIN OPTIONS: Engines: 112 cu. in. four: Firenza ($50). 173 cu. in. V-6: Firenza ($560). 181 cu. in. V-6: Calais ($560); Ciera ($260). 231 cu. in. V-6: Ciera ($520); 98 ($260). Diesel 262 cu. in. V-6: Cutlass/Ciera/98 ($260); 98 Brghm (NC). 307 cu. in. 4Bbl. V-8: Cutlass/88 ($390). Diesel 350 cu. in. V-8: Cutlass/88/ ($390); Custom Crsr/Delta LS/Toronado (NC). Transmission/Differential: Five-speed manual trans.: Firenza ($75). Turbo Hydra-matic: Firenza ($425). Four-speed automatic overdrive: Ciera/88 ($175). Limited-slip differential: Cutlass/88 ($100). Steering/Suspension: Power steering: base Firenza ($215). Firm ride/handling pkg. ($30-$49). Automatic load leveling: Ciera/88 ($180). Other: High-capacity cooling ($40-$70). High-capacity radiator: Ciera/Cutlass/88/98/Toronado ($30). H.D. battery ($26) exc. diesel ($52); N/A on Calais. Engine block heater ($18). Block/fuel line heater ($49). California emissions ($99).

OPTION PACKAGES: Firenza GT pkg.: S cpe (N/A). Firenza ES pkg. ($595-$1555). Calais 500 pkg.: base ($1595). Ciera ES pkg.: LS sedan ($895). Ciera Holiday coupe pkg.: Brghm ($565). Ciera GT pkg.: LS cpe ($3295). Cutlass Salon 4-4-2 pkg. ($1175). Toronado Caliente pkg. ($1970).

MAJOR CONVENIENCE/APPEARANCE OPTIONS: Four Season air conditioner ($645-$750). Tempmatic air conditioning: 88 ($805); 98 ($125); Toronado ($55). Cruise control ($175). Power seat ($178-$225). Power windows ($195-$270). Twilight sentinel: 98/Toronado ($60). Cornering lamps: 88/98 ($60). Power astroroof w/sliding glass panel: Cutlass ($925);

88/98/Toronado ($1230). Removable glass roof panels: Cutlass ($850). Glass panel sunroof: Firenza/Calais/Ciera ($310). Landau vinyl roof: Ciera/Cutlass/88/98/Toronado ($215-$245). Full vinyl roof: Ciera/Cutlass/88 ($160-$185). Full padded vinyl roof: Cutlass/98 ($245). Rear-facing third seat: Cutlass/Custom Cruiser ($215-$220).

HISTORY: Introduced: October 2, 1984, except Firenza, November 8, 1984, and Ninety-Eight, April 5, 1984. Model year production: 1,192,549. Calendar year production (U.S.): 1,168,982. Calendar year sales by U.S. dealers: 1,066,122. Model year sales by U.S. dealers: 1,087,675.

HISTORICAL FOOTNOTES: The new Ninety-Eight was called "the most thoroughly tested vehicle ever introduced by the division." A thousand of the first production models were driven by engineers to study possible problems. Assembly included innovations such as video camera and gamma ray inspection of sheet metal parts. Front and rear outer panels were formed in the same draw die, so beltlines and feature lines would match precisely. A red Firenza concept car with metallic silver lower rocker panels was shown to the auto press, with chassis modification based on Sports Car Club of America off-road production class rally racing. It had a more rakish C-pillar angle than normal and an integral rear spoiler.

1986

All-new front-drive Delta 88 and Toronado models highlighted the year for Oldsmobile. There was also a new Firenza notchback coupe and Calais sedan. Special features included anti-lock braking (ABS) and FE3 suspension.

1986 Oldsmobile, Firenza GT hatchback coupe, (AA)

FIRENZA -- SERIES 3J -- FOUR/V-6 -- Front appearance of the Olds subcompact was similar to 1985, with a revised full-width lower grille consisting of horizontal bars. At the rear was a new body-color panel. The SX hatchback was dropped, but a new notchback coupe added. This year's lineup included a base coupe and sedan; S hatchback coupe; LC coupe; GT hatchback coupe; LX sedan; and Cruiser two-seat wagon. Firenza was promoted as an affordable entry-level car, with coupes targeted at young drivers and women. A Firenza GT replaced the upscale hatchback. The GT had a 173 cubic inch (2.8-liter) V-6 with manual shift, 14 inch low-profile Eagle GT tires and a handling package. Oldsmobile claimed a 0-60 mph time of 10 seconds. The 122 cubic inch (2.0-liter) four-cylinder engine was standard. Optional was a 112 cubic inch (1.8-liter) four or 173 cubic inch (2.8-liter) V-6. Standard Firenza equipment included the 2.0-liter four with four-speed manual transaxle, bright wheel opening moldings, swing-out rear quarter windows, full-length console, AM radio, contoured reclining front bucket seats, LX/LC added a decklid lock, bright rocker panel moldings, dual mirrors (driver's remote) and power steering. LC included leather-wrapped steering wheel and full instruments. GT hatchback added P205/60R14 Eagle GT tires on aluminum wheels, a 2.8-liter V-6 with multi-port fuel injection, two-tone paint, instrument cluster with tachometer, leather-wrapped steering wheel, FE3 handling suspension and velour interior.

1986 Oldsmobile, Firenza coupe, (O)

1986 Oldsmobile, Calais coupe, (JAG)

1986 Oldsmobile, Cutlass Ciera GT coupe, (AA)

1986 Oldsmobile, Calais ES sedan, (O)

1986 Oldsmobile, Cutlass Ciera sedan, (JAG)

CALAIS -- SERIES 3N -- FOUR/V-6 -- Introduced as a coupe in 1985, Calais now added a four-door sedan. Four models were offered: base and Supreme trim levels, in coupe and sedan. Two new specialty models arrived: a sophisticated ES sports sedan, and sporty GT coupe. The ES sedan had aero composite headlamps as well as black-out rocker panels, bumpers, moldings and mirrors. Equipment included the FE3 firm ride/handling suspension, 14-inch styled aluminum wheels and Eagle GT tires as well as rallye instrument cluster. The GT featured composite headlamps, aero rocker panels, specific front and rear fascias, two-tone paint, FE3 suspension, 14-inch styled aluminum wheels and Eagle GT tires. A 3.0-liter V-6 was optional. Both ES and GT included front bucket seats, integral rear headrests and rallye gauge cluster. This year's Calais grille had vertical bars and an Olds rocket emblem. Specialty models had a completely different front-end look with their aero headlamps, and full-width horizontal strips that extended outward below the headlamps and through the lower portion of the grille panel. (The upper center panel was solid, but GT had a center emblem.) Optional this year: column shift for the extra-cost automatic (not available on other N-cars). A fuel-injected 151 cubic inch (2.5-liter) four-cylinder engine linked to five-speed manual was standard. Optional was a 181 cubic inch (3.0-liter) V-6 with PFI (automatic required). Calais standard equipment included power brakes and steering, P185/80R13 SBR blackwall tires, stand-up hood ornament, wheel opening and rocker panel moldings, tinted glass, full-length console, electronic-tuning AM/FM stereo radio with seek/scan and digital clock and reclining front bucket seats. Supreme added deluxe bodyside moldings and body-color mirrors (driver's remote), as well as a lamp/convenience group and roof rail courtesy lamp.

CUTLASS CIERA -- SERIES 3A -- FOUR/V-6 -- Seven models comprised this year's Ciera line: base coupe and sedan, S coupe, Brougham coupe and sedan, Brougham S coupe and Cruiser two-seat wagon (available with rear-facing third seat). The GT package was available for S coupe and base sedan. GT and ES models had a new standard 231 cubic inch (3.8-liter) V-6 with sequential fuel injection, three-coil ignition and roller valve lifters. Also included: a new FE3 handling performance package. A GT equipment package was offered for Ciera S and on Ciera four-door sedan, including halogen headlamps, integral front air dam

with foglamps, and aero fascia and rocker panel treatments, as well as specially-styled leather bucket seats, leather-wrapped steering wheel and rallye gauges. GT models had a 3.8-liter V-6 with dual-outlet exhaust and console-mounted four-speed overdrive automatic transmission. Also included: the FE3 handling package with styled aluminum wheels and Eagle GT tires. Ciera's grille now had a 7 x 3 pattern of wide openings, but similar in design to the year previous. Pontiac's "Iron Duke" 151 cubic inch (2.5-liter) four-cylinder engine was standard. Newly optional was Chevrolet's 2.8-liter V-6 with MFI (replacing the former carbureted 3.0-liter V-6). The diesel 4.3-liter V-6 was dropped in spring 1985. In March 1986, a Cutlass Ciera coupe became available, along with four new midyear "specialty" models. They had an all-new roofline with sloping back window and revised C-pillar design, for a European profile. No other GM division offered this styling. Two trim levels were offered: S and SL.

1986 Oldsmobile, Cutlass Supreme sedan, (AA)

CUTLASS SUPREME -- SERIES 3G -- V-6/V-8 -- Rear-drive midsize appearance was similar to 1985, except for a 5 x 5 hole pattern in the sedan's upright eggcrate grille. Sporty Salon and 4-4-2 models had a contemporary front with aero composite headlamps. Five models were offered: Supreme coupe and sedan, Supreme Brougham coupe and sedan, and Salon coupe (with 4-4-2 package available). Buick's 231 cubic inch (3.8-liter) V-6, now with sequential fuel injection, was standard. Optional was the 307 cubic inch (5.0-liter) four-barrel V-8.

1986 Oldsmobile, Delta 88 Royale coupe, (AA)

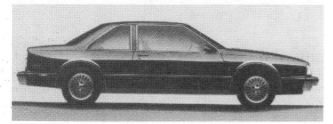

1986 Oldsmobile, Delta 88 Royale Brougham coupe, (JAG)

DELTA 88 -- SERIES 3H -- V-6 -- Ninety-Eight switched to contemporary front-drive in 1985. Now it was 88's turn. The all-new coupe and sedan bodies featured soft lines and rounded edges, but traditional Olds semi-notchback roofline and split grille. Coupes had a rounded backlight and sloping roofline, aimed at younger buyers who wanted roominess as well as style. Four models were offered: Royale coupe and sedan, and Royale Brougham coupe and sedan. Twin narrow grilles in a sloping panel stood alongside a wide center body-color divider with emblem. The nameplate was on the left grille section. Wide park/signal lamps were below the bumper strips. Also below the bumper was a single air intake slot. Recessed headlamps met shapely wraparound side marker lenses. Taillamps were flush-mounted to follow the back panels and wrapped around the quarter panel slightly, with upper and lower lens sections. Small backup lenses stood below the rear bumper strip. A 181 cubic inch (3.0-liter) V-6 was standard; optional was a 231 cubic inch (3.8-liter) V-6.

1986 Oldsmobile, Delta 88 Royale sedan, (O)

1979 Oldsmobile, Custom Cruiser station wagon, (O)

CUSTOM CRUISER -- SERIES 3B -- V-8 -- Now that Delta 88 and Ninety-Eight were front-drive, the old rear-drive wagon became its own model. Two-seat wagons with six-passenger capacity were standard, with a rear-facing third seat available for two more passengers. Wagons came only with the four-barrel 307 cubic inch (5.0-liter) V-8 and four-speed overdrive automatic. Diesel engines were no longer available. Custom Cruiser was similar to Buick Estate, Chevrolet Caprice Classic and Pontiac Parisienne wagons.

1986 Oldsmobile, 98 Regency Brougham sedan, (O)

NINETY-EIGHT REGENCY -- SERIES 3C -- V-6 -- Not much changed for the front-drive Ninety-Eight in its second season. The most notable addition was on the option list: anti-lock braking, the first such offering from Oldsmobile. Sensors at each wheel detected wheel speed changes. Then, a computer altered the pressure applied at each wheel to prevent lockup and potential skids. Ninety-Eight had recessed quad headlamps and wraparound side marker lenses, with wide park/signal lamps below the bumper strip. Twin intake slots were in the bumper. The sloping grille consisted of tight crosshatch sections. Cornering lamps stood low on the front fenders. Vertical taillamps with emblems wrapped slightly around onto each quarter panel. Four models were offered: Regency and Regency Brougham coupe and sedan. Sole engine was the 231 cubic inch (3.8-liter) V-6, now with sequential fuel injection. Options included an FE3 handling package. A new luxury Grande option package for Broughams included aero composite headlamps, classic egg-crate grille, leather interior and leather-wrapped steering wheel. Optional on Grande: suede pigskin interior with suede sport steering wheel and a storage console. About 3,000 Grandes were expected to be produced, all at Orion, Michigan.

1986 Oldsmobile, Toronado coupe, (JAG)

TORONADO -- SERIES 3E -- V-6 -- An all-new downsized design was introduced for Toronado's 20th anniversary. The sleek new front end had concealed headlamps integral with the grille for an aerodynamic look. Headlamp doors moved below the lamps when they were switched on. A 0.36 drag coefficient was 35 percent better than the 1985 model. This version was 18 inches shorter and 550 pounds lighter than its predecessor, but still carried six passengers. Toronado's wedge silhouette featured a low sloping hood, upwardly curving rear fascia and high rear deck. The lower roof sloped gently into a slightly rounded backlight. Taillamps consisted of a full-width horizontal bar. Front sheet metal panels were rounded, and all glass was flush-mounted. With headlamps closed, the front end had full-width horizontal strips on each side of the center divider (which contained an emblem). A four-section air intake was in the bumper area, with park/signal lamps in the bumper strip. Internal seals replaced drip moldings. Wheel covers were flatter and more

flush. All inner and outer body panels were now two-sided galvanized steel for corrosion protection. A new stainless steel exhaust system was introduced, with modular welded construction instead of clamps. In the engine compartment, all wires were covered (and protected) by rigid plastic channels. Toronado had rack-and-pinion steering, and four-wheel low-drag disc brakes. Front suspension was MacPherson struts with single lower control arm and microcellular urethane jounce bumpers. Standard (and only) engine was a 231 cubic inch (3.8-liter) V-6 with four-speed automatic overdrive. No engine options were available, but the V-6 actually delivered more horsepower than the former V-8. A power driver's seat was standard. Extensive electronics were used in Toronado, to provide convenience, information, safety and servicing ease. It offered the first "body computer" in an Olds, receiving information from sensors throughout the car to control instruments, message center and optional voice control system, as well as engine functions. A message center alerted the driver to problems, with 26 diagnostic and 11 trip monitor messages. A system monitor let the driver check if the car was in proper running condition. Toronado's heat/vent/air conditioning system could be fully automatic or manually controlled. A special 20th anniversary Toronado was offered at midyear. It came in a choice of two paint schemes, with specific striping, leather-wrapped steering wheel, leather seats with pigskin inserts and P215/60R15 tires on special 15 x 6 inch aluminum wheels. Multi-colored 20th anniversary emblems went on the hood and C-pillars. The model also included a personalized registration plaque.

I.D. DATA: Oldsmobile's 17-symbol Vehicle Identification Number (VIN) again was located on the upper left surface of the instrument panel, visible through the windshield. The first three symbols ('1G3') indicate Oldsmobile division. Symbol four denotes restraint type: 'A' = manual (active) belts. Symbol five is car line/series: 'C' = Firenza; 'D' = Firenza LC/LX; 'F' = Calais; 'T' = Calais Supreme; 'J' = Cutlass Ciera LS; 'M' = Cutlass Ciera Brougham; 'R' = Cutlass Supreme; 'M' = Cutlass Supreme Brougham; 'K' = Cutlass Salon; 'L' = Delta 88; 'N' = Delta 88 Royale; 'Y' = Delta 88 Royale Brougham; 'P' = Custom Cruiser; 'X' = Ninety-Eight Regency; 'W' = Ninety-Eight Regency Brougham; 'Z' = Toronado Brougham. Next come two digits that denote body type: '11' = 2-dr. notchback sedan; '27' = 2-dr. coupe; '37' = 2-dr. coupe; '47' = 2-dr. coupe; '57' = 2-dr. coupe; '77' = 2-dr. hatch coupe; '19' = 4-dr. sedan; '69' = 4-dr. 4-window notch sedan; '35' = 4-dr. 2-seat wagon. Symbol eight is a letter for engine code: '0' = L4-112 FI; 'P' = L4-121 FI; 'R' = L4-151 FI; 'X' = V-6-173 2Bbl.; 'W' = V-6-173 FI; 'L' = V-6-181 FI; 'A' = V-6-231; 'Y' = V-8-307 4Bbl. Next comes a check digit, followed by a code for model year: ('G' = 1986). Symbol eleven is the assembly plant code: 'D' = Doraville, Georgia; 'G' = Framingham, Mass.; 'M' = Lansing, Mich.; 'P' = Pontiac, Mich.; 'W' = Willow Run, Mich.; 'E' = Linden, New Jersey; 'R' = Arlington, Texas; 'K' = Leeds, Missouri; '1' = Oshawa, Ontario; '2' = Ste. Therese, Quebec. (Oldsmobiles were also built in Hamtramck, Detroit and Orion, Mich.; and at Wentzville, Missouri.) The final six digits are the sequential serial number. Engine numbers were stamped on the front of the right rocker cover, or top of left cover (Buick-built engines), on label at front or rear of right rocker cover (Chevrolet V-6), or on the left rocker cover (Oldsmobile engines). Four-cylinder engine numbers were on a pad at left front of block, below cylinder head. A body number plate on the upper right cowl identified model year, series, style, body assembly plant, body number, trim combination, modular seat code, paint code, date built code and option codes.

FIRENZA (FOUR)

Model Number	Body/Style Number	Body Type & Seating	Factory Price	Shipping Weight	Production Total
3J	C27	2-dr. Cpe-5P	7782	2276	12,003
3J	C77	2-dr. S Hatch-5P	7941	2329	2,531
3J	D27	2-dr. LC Cpe-5P	8611	2328	2,867
3J	C69	4-dr. Sed-5P	8035	2330	18,437
3J	D69	4-dr. LX Sed-5P	8626	2361	4,415

FIRENZA CRUISER (FOUR)

Model Number	Body/Style Number	Body Type & Seating	Factory Price	Shipping Weight	Production Total
3J	C35	4-dr. Sta Wag-5P	8259	2387	5,416

FIRENZA GT (V-6)

Model Number	Body/Style Number	Body Type & Seating	Factory Price	Shipping Weight	Production Total
3J	D77	2-dr. Hatch Cpe-5P	9774	2509	1,032

CALAIS (FOUR/V-6)

Model Number	Body/Style Number	Body Type & Seating	Factory Price	Shipping Weight	Production Total
3N	F27	2-dr. Cpe-5P	9283/10358	2415/2527	52,726
3N	F69	4-dr. Sed-5P	9478/10553	2481/2593	40,393

CALAIS SUPREME (FOUR/V-6)

| 3N | T27 | 2-dr. Cpe-5P | 9668/10743 | 2426/2538 | 33,060 |
| 3N | T69 | 4-dr. Sed-5P | 9863/10938 | 2484/2596 | 25,128 |

CUTLASS CIERA (FOUR/V-6)

Model Number	Body/Style Number	Body Type & Seating	Factory Price	Shipping Weight	Production Total
3A	J27	2-dr. Cpe-6P	10153/10588	2651/2708	9,233
3A	J37	2-dr. S Cpe-6P	10619/11054	N/A	16,281
3A	J19	4-dr. Sed-6P	10354/10789	2694/2751	144,466
3G	J35	4-dr. Sta Wag-6P	10734/11169	2853/2912	35,890

CUTLASS CIERA BROUGHAM (FOUR/V-6)

3A	M27	2-dr. Cpe-6P	10645/11080	2667/2724	11,534
3A	M37	2-dr. S Cpe-6P	11154/11764	2771/2829	12,525
3A	M19	4-dr. Sed-6P	10868/11303	2724/2781	123,027

CUTLASS SUPREME (V-6/V-8)

| 3G | R47 | 2-dr. Cpe-6P | 10698/11238 | 3123/3283 | 79,654 |
| 3G | R69 | 4-dr. Sed-6P | 10872/11412 | 3173/3321 | 41,973 |

CUTLASS SUPREME BROUGHAM (V-6/V-8)

| 3G | M47 | 2-dr. Cpe-6P | 11408/11948 | 3153/3313 | 55,275 |
| 3G | M69 | 4-dr. Sed-6P | 11551/12091 | 3201/3349 | 24,646 |

CUTLASS SALON (V-6/V-8)

| 3G | K47 | 2-dr. Cpe-6P | 11728/12268 | 3175/3335 | 9,608 |

DELTA 88 ROYALE (V-6)

Model Number	Body/Style Number	Body Type & Seating	Factory Price	Shipping Weight	Production Total
3H	N37	2-dr. Cpe-6P	12760	3046	13,696
3H	N69	4-dr. Sed-6P	12760	3091	88,564

DELTA 88 ROYALE BROUGHAM (V-6)

| 3H | Y37 | 2-dr. Cpe-6P | 13461 | 3075 | 23,697 |
| 3H | Y69 | 4-dr. Sed-6P | 13461 | 3116 | 108,344 |

CUSTOM CRUISER (V-8)

Model Number	Body/Style Number	Body Type & Seating	Factory Price	Shipping Weight	Production Total
3B	P35	4-dr. Sta Wag-6P	13416	4004	21,073

NINETY-EIGHT REGENCY (V-6)

Model Number	Body/Style Number	Body Type & Seating	Factory Price	Shipping Weight	Production Total
3C	X11	2-dr. Sed-6P	16062	3179	803
3C	X69	4-dr. Sed-6P	15989	3215	23,717

NINETY-EIGHT REGENCY BROUGHAM (V-6)

| 3C | W11 | 2-dr. Sed-6P | 17052 | 3196 | 5,007 |
| 3C | W69 | 4-dr. Sed-6P | 16979 | 3232 | 95,045 |

TORONADO BROUGHAM (V-6)

Model Number	Body/Style Number	Body Type & Seating	Factory Price	Shipping Weight	Production Total
3E	Z57	2-dr. Cpe-5P	19418	3216	15,924

FACTORY PRICE AND WEIGHT NOTE: Cutlass Supreme prices and weights to left of slash are for six-cylinder, to right for V-8 engine; others, to left for four-cylinder and to right for V-6.

ENGINE DATA: BASE FOUR (Firenza): Inline, overhead-valve four-cylinder. Cast iron block and head. Displacement: 121 cu. in. (2.0 liters). Bore & stroke: 3.50 x 3.14 in. Compression ratio: 9.3:1. Brake horsepower: 88 at 4800 rpm. Torque: 110 lb.-ft. at 2400 rpm. Five main bearings. Hydraulic valve lifters.

Electronic fuel injection. VIN Code: P. OPTIONAL FOUR (Firenza): Inline, overhead-cam four-cylinder. Cast iron block and aluminum head. Displacement: 112 cu. in. (1.8 liters). Bore & stroke: 3.34 x 3.11 in. Compression ratio: 9.0:1. Brake horsepower: 84 at 5200 rpm. Torque: 98 lb.-ft. at 2800 rpm. Five main bearings. Hydraulic valve lifters. Electronic fuel injection. VIN Code: O. BASE FOUR (Calais, Cutlass Ciera): Inline, overhead-valve four-cylinder. Cast iron block and head. Displacement: 151 cu. in. (2.5 liters). Bore & stroke: 4.00 x 3.00 in. Compression ratio: 8.2:1. Brake horsepower: 92 at 4400 rpm. Torque: 132-134 lb.-ft. at 2800 rpm. Five main bearings. Hydraulic valve lifters. Fuel injection (TBI). Pontiac-built. VIN Code: R. OPTIONAL V-6 (Firenza): 60-degree, overhead-valve V-6. Cast iron block and aluminum head. Displacement: 173 cu. in. (2.8 liters). Bore & stroke: 3.50 x 3.00 in. Compression ratio: 8.9:1. Brake horsepower: 130 at 4800 rpm. Torque: 160 lb.-ft. at 3600 rpm. Four main bearings. Hydraulic valve lifters. Electronic fuel injection. Chevrolet-built. VIN Code: W. OPTIONAL V-6 (Cutlass Ciera): Carbureted version of 173 cu. in. V-6 above -- Compression ratio: 8.5:1. Horsepower: 112 at 4800 rpm. Torque: 145 lb.-ft. at 2100 rpm. Carburetor: 2Bbl. VIN Code: X. BASE V-6 (Delta 88): 90-degree, overhead-valve V-6. Cast iron block and head. Displacement: 181 cu. in. (3.0 liters). Bore & stroke: 3.80 x 2.66 in. Compression ratio: 9.0:1. Brake horsepower: 125 at 4900 rpm. Torque: 150 lb.-ft. at 2400 rpm. Four main bearings. Hydraulic valve lifters. Electronic fuel injection. VIN Code: L. BASE V-6 (Cutlass Supreme): 90-degree, overhead-valve V-6. Cast iron block and head. Displacement: 231 cu. in. (3.8 liters). Bore & stroke: 3.80 x 3.40 in. Compression ratio: 8.0:1. Brake horsepower: 110 at 3800 rpm. Torque: 190 lb.-ft. at 1600 rpm. Four main bearings. Hydraulic valve lifters. Carburetor: 2Bbl. Rochester E2ME. Buick-built. VIN Code: A. BASE V-6 (Ninety-Eight, Toronado); OPTIONAL (Cutlass Ciera, Delta 88): Same as 231 cu. in. V-6 above, but with sequential fuel injection -- Horsepower: 140 at 4400 rpm. (Ciera/Delta 88, 150 at 4400). Torque: 200 lb.-ft. at 2000 rpm. BASE V-8 (Custom Cruiser); OPTIONAL (Cutlass Supreme): 90-degree, overhead valve V-8. Cast iron block and head. Displacement: 307 cu. in. (5.0 liters). Bore & stroke: 3.80 x 3.38 in. Compression ratio: 8.0:1. Brake horsepower: 140 at 3200 rpm. Torque: 255 lb.-ft. at 2000 rpm. Five main bearings. Hydraulic valve lifters. Carburetor: 4Bbl. Rochester E4MC. VIN Code: Y.

CHASSIS DATA: Wheelbase: (Firenza) 101.2 in.; (Calais) 103.4 in.; (Ciera) 104.9 in.; (Cutlass) 108.1 in.; (Delta 88) 110.8 in.; (98) 110.8 in.; (Custom Crsr) 115.9 in.; (Toronado) 108.0 in. Overall Length: (Firenza cpe) 174.3 in.; (Firenza sed) 176.2 in.; (Firenza wag) 176.2 in.; (Calais) 178.8 in.; (Ciera) 190.3 in.; (Ciera wag) 194.4 in.; (Cutlass Supreme) 200.0-200.4 in.; (Delta 88) 196.0 in.; (98) 196.4 in.; (Custom Crsr) 220.3 in.; (Toronado) 187.9 in. Height: (Firenza cpe) 51.7 in.; (Firenza sed) 53.7 in.; (Firenza wag) 55.2 in.; (Calais) 53.3 in.; (Ciera) 54.1 in.; (Ciera wag) 54.5 in.; (Cutlass Supreme cpe) 54.9 in.; (Cutlass Supreme sed) 55.9 in.; (Delta 88 cpe) 54.5-54.6 in.; (98) 55.1 in.; (Custom Crsr) 58.5 in.; (Toronado) 52.9 in. Width: (Firenza) 65.0 in.; (Calais) 66.9 in.; (Ciera) 69.5 in.; (Cutlass cpe) 71.6; (Cutlass sed) 71.9 in.; (Delta 88) 72.1 in.; (98) 71.4 in.; (Custom Crsr) 79.8 in.; (Toronado) 70.7 in. Front Tread: (Firenza) 55.4 in.; (Calais) 55.5 in.; (Ciera) 58.7 in.; (Cutlass) 58.5 in.; (Delta 88) 60.3 in.; (98) 60.3 in.; (Custom Crsr) 62.1 in.; (Toronado) 59.9 in. Rear Tread: (Firenza) 55.2 in.; (Calais) 55.2 in.; (Ciera) 57.0 in.; (Cutlass) 59.8 in.; (Delta 88) 60.7 in.; (98) 59.8 in.; (Custom Crsr) 64.1 in.; (Toronado) 59.9 in. Standard Tires: (Firenza) P175/80R13; (Calais) P185/80R13; (Ciera) P185/75R14; (Cutlass Supreme) P195/75R14; (Delta 88) P205/75R14; (98) P205/75R14; (Custom Crsr) P225/75R15; (Toronado) P205/70R14.

TECHNICAL: Transmission: Four-speed floor shift standard on Firenza. Five-speed manual trans. standard on Calais, optional on Firenza: Three-speed Turbo Hydra-matic standard on Cutlass/Ciera. Four-speed automatic overdrive standard on Delta 88/

Custom Cruiser/98/Toronado. Standard final drive ratio: (Firenza) 3.65:1 w/4-spd, 3.45:1 w/5-spd, 3.18:1 w/auto.; (Calais) 3.35:1 w/5-spd, 2.84:1 w/auto.; (Ciera) 2.84:1 except 3.06:1 w/V-6-173 and 4-spd auto.; (Cutlass) 2.41:1 w/V-6, 2.14:1 w/V-8, 3.73:1 w/V-8 and 4-spd auto.; (Delta 88) 3.06:1 w/V-6-181, 2.73:1 w/V-6-231; (98) 2.84:1; (Toronado) 2.84:1. Steering: (Cutlass/Custom Cruiser) recirculating ball; (others) rack and pinion. Front Suspension: (Firenza/Calais/Ciera/88/98) MacPherson struts w/coil springs, lower control arms and anti-sway bar; (Toronado) MacPherson struts w/link control arm and anti-sway bar; (Cutlass/Custom Crsr) coil springs with upper/lower control arms. Rear Suspension: (Firenza) beam axle w/coil springs, trailing arms and anti-sway bar; (Calais) semi-independent w/coil springs and trailing arms; (Ciera) beam axle with integral anti-sway, coil springs and Panhard rod; (88) independent w/struts, coil springs and anti-sway bar; (98) independent w/struts, coil springs, lower control arms, anti-sway bar and automatic level control; (Toronado) independent with transverse leaf spring, control arms and automatic leveling; (Cutlass/Custom Crsr) rigid axle w/coil springs, lower trailing radius arms and upper torque arms (four-link). Brakes: Front disc, rear drum except Toronado, four-wheel disc. Ignition: Electronic. Body construction: (Cutlass/Custom Cruiser) separate body and frame; (others) unibody. Fuel tank: (Firenza/Calais) 13.6 gal.; (Ciera) 16.6 gal.; (Cutlass) 18.1 gal.; (Delta 88) 18 gal.; (98) 18 gal.; (Custom Crsr wag) 22 gal.; (Toronado) 18 gal.

DRIVETRAIN OPTIONS: Engines: 112 cu. in. four: Firenza ($50). 173 cu. in. 2Bbl. V-6: Ciera ($435). 173 cu. in. FI V-6: Ciera ($560). 181 cu. in. V-6: Calais ($610). 307 cu. in. 4Bbl. V-8: Cutlass ($540). Transmission/Differential: Five-speed manual trans.: Firenza ($75). Turbo Hydra-matic: Firenza/Calais ($465). Four-speed automatic overdrive: Ciera/Cutlass ($175). Column shift: Calais ($110 credit). Limited-slip differential: Cutlass/Custom Cruiser ($100). Steering/Suspension: Power steering: base Firenza ($215). Firm ride/handling pkg. ($30-$49). Automatic load leveling: Ciera/88/Custom Crsr ($180). Other: High-capacity cooling ($40-$70). High-capacity radiator: Cutlass/Custom Crsr/88/98/Toronado ($30). Wiring harness: Custom Crsr/98 ($30). Engine block heater ($18). California emissions ($99).

OPTION PACKAGES: Calais GT pkg.: base cpe ($1350). Calais ES pkg.: base sed ($995). Calais sport appearance pkg. ($150-$195). Ciera ES pkg.: base sedan ($1992). Ciera Holiday coupe pkg.: Brghm ($680). Ciera GT pkg.: base cpe ($3330). Cutlass Salon 4-4-2 pkg. ($2075). 98 premium interior: Brghm ($975).

MAJOR CONVENIENCE/APPEARANCE OPTIONS: Four Season air conditioner ($645-$750). Tempmatic air conditioning: 88 ($805); 98 ($125); Custom Crsr ($55). Cruise control ($175). Power seat ($178-$225). Power windows ($195-$270). Electronic instrument panel: Ciera/Calais/98 ($83-$299). Twilight sentinel: 98 ($60). Cornering lamps: 98 ($60). Power astroroof w/sliding glass panel: Cutlass ($925); 98 ($1230). Removable glass roof panels: Cutlass ($850). Glass panel sunroof: Firenza/Calais/Ciera ($310). Landau vinyl roof: Ciera/Cutlass ($245). Full vinyl roof: Ciera/Cutlass ($160). Full padded vinyl roof: Cutlass/98 ($245). Rear-facing third seat: Cutlass/Custom Cruiser ($215-$220).

HISTORY: Introduced: October 3, 1985, except 88 and Toronado, November 14, 1985, and Calais, August 28, 1985. Model year production: 1,157,990. Calendar year production (U.S.): 927,173. Calendar year sales by U.S. dealers: 1,059,390. Model year sales by U.S. dealers: 1,067,819.

HISTORICAL FOOTNOTES: Olds had ranked No. 3 in sales through the past decade. Now, for the third year in-a-row, sales hit the million mark. Ciera was the best selling Oldsmobile by a comfortable margin over the new front-drive Delta 88. Sales of the downsized Toronado, however, reached only half their 1985 level. The two Cutlass lines amounted to nearly half of Olds sales.

OLDSMOBILE 1987-1997

One benefit of a history of Oldsmobile is that a study of the past management decisions and focus gives the Division's product planning, engineering and marketing groups insight for options for future product direction.

Today we see analogies of that practice. The key spin today is that with shared bodies, Oldsmobile and General Motors are attempting to develop different cars from the same platforms, which project different images and offer a different driving feel, experience and personality.

By looking back at Oldsmobile and General Motors history, we can see one of the key motivators for today's focus. General Motors was criticized in 1982 for developing five essentially cookie-cutter cars off the J-body Chevrolet Cavalier. Oldsmobile saw the effect of this policy as the Oldsmobile Firenza J-car, close-clone, was discontinued in 1988. This was in spite of the fact that the J-car was relatively successful as a Chevrolet Cavalier and Pontiac Sunbird, remaining in production with little change through 1994.

A history of Oldsmobile also has value to the corporate historian and the individual collector/restorer for direction in the important items to preserve. It points out key technological thresholds toward the development and advancement of the present automobile. A thorough and accurate history allows us to point out and properly value particular body styles, technical advances, options and give proper recognition to revolutionary breakthroughs in automotive technology and ensure they are restored and preserved.

Key examples are the 1940 automatic transmission, the 1949 short-stroke overhead valve V-8 engine and the 1953 air conditioning. It also gives the collector the opportunity to point out interesting features of his car and see how later models reinterpreted these features that were initially introduced on his particular car. These are features from an engineering standpoint and also from a style and design standpoint.

The 1976 through 1979 first-generation Cadillac Seville, becoming more collectible today, uses a modified Oldsmobile 350 cubic inch V-8. Right now the V-6 for the 1998 Oldsmobile Intrigue is being designed as a version of the Aurora V-8.

We see how the designer of the Oldsmobiles for the last years of the 20th century can look to previous design and styling features to re-incorporate them in Oldsmobile in a different manner. This allows for a fresh style based on traditional design features. A study of Oldsmobile history gives the designer options of interpreting today's styling trends with unique, recognizable Oldsmobile styling aspects, to give Oldsmobile a continuous and readily recognizable character to surpass the cookie-cutter tendency in using shared bodies.

It is a means of maintaining customer brand interest to be able to visit a showroom and see features of new Oldsmobiles taken from past Oldsmobiles, features that are being reinterpreted in creative but unmistakable form today.

According to John Meyer, editor of *Horseless Carriage Gazette*, a study of automobile history is important because automobile design has always been an evolution and builds on previous generations of design. On the other hand, there have been instances with sharp breaks from the past in automobile design that have fallen flat in the marketplace. The key concept is to build continuity.

Meyer also said that the study of automotive history is important from the standpoint of technology. He said, "Most technical advances were thought of before people think they were. For instance, front-drive was produced in 1912."

Meyer said that often a small technical advance will make a ma-

jor technological advancement more workable. For instance, from 1936 through 1966, there were technological advances that made the front-drive, adopted by the Toronado, a reliable design.

The Toronado could be called a refinement of front-drive 1936 Cord technology. A major problem with the Cord's front-drive was reliability, the Rzeppa constant-velocity universal joints failed prematurely due to inadequate lubrication. Advances during the 30 years since the Cord yielded space-age seal and lubricant technology that was adopted successfully in the 1966 Oldsmobile Toronado. This brought lasting acceptance of front-wheel drive to the U.S. market.

Many technological advances don't work the first time. Advances in related technology will then make it workable. For example, the advantages of high compression were known long before the 1949 Oldsmobile Rocket V-8. Oldsmobile was a pioneer in taking advantage of the development of higher octane gasoline that was necessary to capitalize on the concept of the high compression V-8.

In reviewing Oldsmobile history, we see a trend of Oldsmobile focusing on widely divergent market niches over the years. Oldsmobile began as a volume producer of low-priced cars in the early part of the first decade of the 1900s. From this, it went to the top-of-the-line Limited luxury model in 1910, selling as high as $5,000. Later, it went to a quality car that was lower priced.

Another Oldsmobile trend was that Oldsmobile was able to do particularly well during times of changes in the marketplace. In the middle of the Depression, Oldsmobile had a number of years of increased sales, achieving record sales. Oldsmobile also did well after the start of the 1973 energy crisis. Oldsmobile was particularly strong in intermediates and the Cutlass became the top selling automobile. Oldsmobile edged out Ford as the second best selling car line in 1985.

In the development of Oldsmobile, we see the gradual trend to increased engine displacement. In the 1920s, the six-cylinder gradually increased displacement and this continued with the introduction of the straight-8 in 1932. The big change after the war was the overhead valve V-8, which started at 303 cubic inches and increased to 394 cubic inches in 1959.

Oldsmobile V-8s finally topped out at 455 cubic inches for 1969, before the start of the energy crisis. The energy crisis necessitated smaller displacement V-8s together with four-cylinder and V-6s for increased fuel efficiency and eventually increased performance. After the energy crisis subsided, the four-cylinders and V-6s began to produce more power with the same displacement.

The V-8 rose from the ashes of the energy crises due to moderation in gasoline prices and the introduction of Japanese V-8 engines by Lexus and Infiniti. Oldsmobile introduced the 1995 Aurora V-8 to compete with the Japanese V-8s at a lower price.

As Oldsmobile nears and surpasses its 100th anniversary, there will be a number of new products. Gary White, Oldsmobile's engineering manager, said that Oldsmobile will position itself against upscale models and premium brands from Japan, following the lead of the Aurora.

In 1996 a new generation Oldsmobile Bravada was introduced. In 1997 there is a new Silhouette minivan with sliding doors on both sides plus an all-new Cutlass to replace the Cutlass Ciera. In 1998 the Intrigue will succeed the Cutlass Supreme, and the Alero will supersede the Achieva in 1998-1/2 or 1999.

1987

Oldsmobile observed its 90th model year in 1987, and changes to the lineup from 1986 were minimal. A new brougham level station wagon was offered as part of the Cutlass Ciera lineup. Midyear changes included the dropping of the 98 Regency coupe, which was replaced by the 98 Touring Sedan. The Toronado Trofeo, a specialty model, also debuted in this model year. In all, Oldsmobile offered 31 models based on nine different body styles.

1987 Oldsmobile, Calais Supreme coupe, (O)

1987 Oldsmobile, Firenza GT hatchback coupe, (O)

FIRENZA -- SERIES 3J -- FOUR/V-6 -- Available in coupe (base, LC), hatchback coupe (S, GT), sedan (base, LX) and Cruiser station wagon models a new sporty appearance was featured for 1987. Designed to appeal to more youthful buyers, the base Firenza models featured sporty black grille, exterior moldings, antenna, door handles, outside mirrors and headlamp bezels. Also offered on these models was standard wide black front and rear fascia moldings. A bright decor package was standard on the uplevel Firenza notchback coupe and sedan. Options available to enhance the Firenza lineup included a 14-inch aluminum styled wheel and four-way manual seat adjuster for the driver. All Firenza models with the exception of the Cruiser wagon were available with the FE3 suspension for firm, precise handling. Included in the FE3 package were gas pressure suspension struts and shock absorbers. Base and FE3 suspension systems received improvements comprised of new supports and dust shields for struts and larger, teflon-lined front lower control arm bushings. Firenza's standard powertrain consisted of an electronically fuel-injected 2.0-liter four-cylinder engine coupled to a manual four-speed transaxle. A 2.0-liter four-cylinder engine with overhead cam as well as an automatic transmission were also available. The Firenza GT featured a 2.8-liter V-6 with a new five-speed manual transaxle that provided higher (170 pound-feet) torque capacity. This new gearbox was designed by West Germany's Getrag AG. Standard Firenza equipment included P175/80R13 steel-belted radial tires, high energy ignition system, side window defogger and internal hood release.

CALAIS -- SERIES 3N -- FOUR/V-6 -- Calais coupe and sedan models were offered in base, Supreme and GT versions for 1987. The entire Calais lineup received composite headlamps, newly designed horizontal grille and new red and amber taillamps. A running production change was the addition of a passive restraint safety belt system. Oldsmobile offered two new wheels in the Calais lineup, which consisted of a 13-inch steel styled wheel and a 14-inch aluminum styled cross spoke wheel. The GT specialty model was available in both Calais coupe and sedan body styles. The GT package included wide aero rocker and door moldings, a specific grille with a body-colored panel between the headlamps, amber park and turn lamps and two-tone paint scheme available in four combinations. The sporting image of the Calais GT coupe and sedan was further emphasized through such standard equipment as a rallye instrument cluster, leather-wrapped sport steering wheel and P215/60R14 radial tires. The Calais GT also offered a Level III suspension that included higher rate springs, larger diameter front stabilizer bar, and higher rate control arm bushings. Standard powertrain for the Calais consisted of an electronically fuel-injected Tech IV four-cylinder engine rated at 2.5 liters. This powerplant was mated to a manual five-speed transaxle. A multiport fuel-injected 3.0-liter V-6 engine coupled to a three-speed automatic transmission was available.

1987 Oldsmobile, Calais GT coupe, (O)

1987 Oldsmobile, Firenza Cruiser station wagon, (O)

1987 Oldsmobile, Cutlass Ciera GT coupe, (O)

1987 Oldsmobile, Cutlass Ciera GT sedan, (O)

CUTLASS CIERA -- SERIES 3A -- FOUR/V-6 -- Oldsmobile's best-selling nameplate several years running, Ciera had much new to offer in 1987. S and SL trim level coupes and a Brougham Cruiser station wagon were introduced to the Ciera lineup that also featured a base sedan, Brougham sedan, GT coupe and sedan and Cutlass Cruiser station wagon. The Brougham station wagon provided an extra level of luxury and targeted mid-size market buyers. Interior appointments featured a standard 55/45 divided bench seat and lower body side moldings on the rocker panel and wheel openings. Composite halogen headlamps were offered as standard equipment on Ciera Brougham and GT models. A modified front fascia and wraparound front side marker lamps accentuated Ciera's sleek styling. Base Ciera models featured a new grille and P185/75R14 radial tires as standard equipment. Ciera's standard powertrain was the 2.5-liter Tech IV four-cylinder engine mated to an automatic transaxle. A 2.8-liter V-6 engine was available. The Ciera GT came standard with the sequential port fuel-injected 3.8-liter V-6 mated to a four-speed automatic transaxle. Also standard in the GT coupe and sedan models were reclining front bucket seats, Level III suspension, aluminum styled wheels, front air dam, dual outlet exhaust system, fog lamps and high-capacity cooling equipment.

1987 Oldsmobile, Ciera-based Cutlass Cruiser station wagon, (O)

1987 Oldsmobile, Cutlass Supreme sedan, (O)

CUTLASS SUPREME -- SERIES 3G -- V-6/V-8 -- Along with the Custom Cruiser station wagon the Cutlass Supreme coupe and sedan models were the lone rear-drive representatives in Oldsmobile's 1987 lineup. Coupe models only (base, Brougham and Salon), received composite headlamp treatment

1987 Oldsmobile, Cutlass Supreme coupe, (O)

as well as a new grille, front end panel and side marker lamps. Sedan versions included the base model and Brougham. A 442 version of the Cutlass Supreme coupe was also available. Standard powertrain in the Cutlass Supreme was the 3.8-liter carbureted V-6 coupled to a three-speed automatic transmission. A 5.0-liter V-8 powerplant was also available. The 442 coupe offered as standard the 5.0-liter high-output V-8 engine mated to a four-speed automatic transmission. Oldsmobile claimed a 0-60 mph time of 9.5 seconds.

1987 Oldsmobile, Cutlass Ciera SL coupe, (O)   (O)

1987 Oldsmobile, Delta 88 Royale Brougham sedan, (O)

DELTA 88 ROYALE -- SERIES 3H -- V-6 -- After a complete redesign in 1986, appearance changes for 1987 in Oldsmobile's Delta 88 lineup included composite headlamps, a specific front end panel, side marker lamps and a new grille. Also new were the aero outside rear view mirrors designed to limit wind noise and the amber and red taillamp design. A running production change on the Delta 88 lineup was the addition of the passive

1987 Oldsmobile, Delta 88 Royale Brougham coupe, (O)

184

restraint system. The Delta 88 Royale was available as both coupe or sedan in two trim levels, base and Brougham. The 3.0-liter fuel-injected V-6 offered the previous year was deleted. Standard powertrain for Delta 88s became the 3.8-liter sequential port fuel-injected V-6 coupled to a four-speed automatic transaxle.

1987 Oldsmobile, Custom Cruiser station wagon, (O)

CUSTOM CRUISER -- SERIES 3B -- V-8 -- Oldsmobile's luxury liner for 1987 was the Custom Cruiser station wagon, which offered 87.2 cubic feet of cargo space and seating for up to eight passengers. The Custom Cruiser was powered by a 5.0-liter carbureted V-8 engine mated to a four-speed automatic transmission. Standard equipment included high energy ignition, air conditioning, tinted glass with power tailgate and P225/75R15 radial tires mounted on 15 x 7-inch wheels featuring deluxe wheel discs.

1987 Oldsmobile, 98 Regency Brougham sedan, (O)

NINETY-EIGHT REGENCY -- SERIES 3C -- V-6 -- Ninety-Eight was Oldsmobile's luxury flagship model with a lineup that consisted of a base sedan and both Brougham and Grande coupe and sedan versions. The base coupe was dropped for 1987. Mid-year, a Touring Sedan based on the Regency four-door sedan was released. This specialty model featured subdued trim and specific ornamentation. Clear fog lamps were housed in the front valance, which also served as an air dam. Interior appointments featured a leather-wrapped steering wheel and leather-trimmed door panels with genuine walnut burl armrest trimplates. Walnut trim was also featured on the floor-mounted

1987 Oldsmobile, 98 Touring Sedan, (O)

four-speed automatic transmission and analog instrument gauge cluster. The entire Ninety-Eight lineup received a more distinctive frontal appearance comprised of a new grille, front end panel and side marker lamps. Aero external rear view mirrors were also added to reduce wind noise. The Brougham coupe received a new opera lamp. Standard powertrain was the 3.8-liter sequential port fuel-injected V-6 engine mated to a four-speed automatic transaxle.

TORONADO -- SERIES 3E -- V-6 -- After Toronado observed its 20th anniversary the previous year with a major redesign, Oldsmobile's personal luxury car retained its aerodynamic lines for 1987. Available as a coupe or by mid-year with specialty Trofeo package, Toronados were powered by a 3.8-liter sequentially fuel injected V-6 engine coupled to a four-speed automatic transmission. Level III suspension was standard equipment as were power six-way adjustable leather bucket seats, electronic-automatic air conditioning, electronic cruise control, power retractable halogen headlamps and tinted glass. Trofeos sported a black valance with fog lamps, rocker panel extensions and black wheel well, belt line and window moldings.

1987 Oldsmobile, Toronado Trofeo coupe, (O)

I.D. DATA: Oldsmobile's 17-symbol Vehicle Identification Number (VIN) again was located on the upper left surface of the instrument panel, visible through the windshield. The first three characters (1G3) indicates Oldsmobile Division. The fourth and fifth letters designate the body type/series: A/J - Cutlass Ciera LS and Cutlass Cruiser, A/M - Cutlass Ciera Brougham, B/P - Custom Cruiser, C/W - Ninety-Eight Regency Brougham, C/X - Ninety-Eight Regency, E/Z - Toronado Brougham, G/K - Cutlass Salon Coupe, G/M - Cutlass Supreme Brougham, G/R - Cutlass Supreme, H/N - Delta 88 Royale, H/Y - Delta 88 Royale Brougham, J/C - Firenza, J/D - Firenza LC/LX/GT, N/F - Calais, N/T - Calais Supreme. The sixth number identifies the body style: 1 - 2-dr coupe/sedan, 2 - 2-dr hatchback, 3 - 2-dr convertible, 5 - 4-dr sedan, 6 - 4-dr hatchback, 8 - 4-dr station wagon. The seventh number identifies the restraint code: 1 - manual belts, 4 - automatic belts. The eighth letter identifies the engine: A = 3.8-liter/231-cid 2-bbl carbureted V-6, K = 2.0-liter/121-cid fuel-injected inline four-cylinder, L = 3.0-liter/181-cid fuel-injected V-6, R = 2.5-liter/151-cid fuel-injected inline four-cylinder, U = 2.5-liter/151-cid fuel-injected inline four-cylinder, W = 2.8-liter/173-cid fuel-injected V-6, Y = 5.0-liter/307-cid 4-bbl carbureted V-8, 1 = 2.0-liter/121-cid fuel-injected inline four-cylinder, 3 = 3.8-liter/231-cid fuel-injected V-6 and 9 = 5.0-liter/307-cid 4-bbl carbureted V-8. The ninth number is the check digit. The tenth letter represents the model year (H = 1987). The eleventh character identifies the assembly plant: D - Doraville, Ga.; E - Linden, N.J.; G - Framingham, Mass.; K - Leeds, Mo.; M - Lansing, Mich.; P - Pontiac, Mich.; R - Arlington, Texas; U - Hamtramck, Mich.; W - Willow Run, Mich.; 1 - Wentzville, Mo.; 3 - Detroit, Mich.; 4 - Orion, Mich.; (Canada) 1 - Oshawa, Ontario; and 2 - Ste. Therese, Quebec. The final six digits are the sequential serial number.

FIRENZA (FOUR)

Model Number	Body/Style Number	Body Type & Seating	Factory Price	Shipping Weight	Production Total
3J	C27	2-dr. Cpe-5P	8541	2327	5335
3J	C77	2-dr. S Hatch-5P	8976	2380	991
3J	D27	2-dr. LC Cpe-5P	9639	2379	874
3J	C69	4-dr. Sed-5P	8499	2381	12597
3J	D69	4-dr. LX Sed-5P	9407	2412	2388

FIRENZA CRUISER (FOUR)

Model Number	Body/Style Number	Body Type & Seating	Factory Price	Shipping Weight	Production Total
3J	C35	4-dr. Sta Wag-5P	9146	2438	2860

FIRENZA GT (V-6)

Model Number	Body/Style Number	Body Type & Seating	Factory Price	Shipping Weight	Production Total
3J	D77	2-dr. Hatch-5P	11034	2576	783

CALAIS (FOUR/V-6)

Model Number	Body/Style Number	Body Type & Seating	Factory Price	Shipping Weight	Production Total
3N	F27	2-dr. Cpe-5P	9741/10401	2470/2551	52285
3N	F69	4-dr. Sed-5P	9741/10401	2539/2619	35166

CALAIS SUPREME (FOUR/V-6)

Model Number	Body/Style Number	Body Type & Seating	Factory Price	Shipping Weight	Production Total
3N	T27	2-dr. Cpe-5P	10397/11057	2488/2568	17883
3N	T69	4-dr. Sed-5P	10397/11057	2551/2630	11676

CUTLASS CIERA (FOUR/V-6)

Model Number	Body/Style Number	Body Type & Seating	Factory Price	Shipping Weight	Production Total
3A	J37	2-dr. S Cpe-6P	10940/11550	2769/2853	21904
3A	J19	4-dr. Sed-6P	10940/11550	2733/2817	140333
3A	J35	4-dr. Sta Wag-6P	11433/12043	2933/3017	20556

CUTLASS CIERA BROUGHAM (FOUR/V-6)

Model Number	Body/Style Number	Body Type & Seating	Factory Price	Shipping Weight	Production Total
3A	M37	2-dr. SL Cpe-6P	11747/12357	2780/2864	11960
3A	M19	4-dr. Sed-6P	11747/12357	2804/2888	94764
3A	M35	4-dr. Sta Wag-6P	12095/12705	2933/3017	7770

CUTLASS SUPREME (V-6/V-8)

Model Number	Body/Style Number	Body Type & Seating	Factory Price	Shipping Weight	Production Total
3G	R47	2-dr. Cpe-6P	11539/12129	3203/3384	50713
3G	R69	4-dr. Sed-6P	11539/12129	3260/3430	21581

CUTLASS SUPREME BROUGHAM (V-6/V-8)

Model Number	Body/Style Number	Body Type & Seating	Factory Price	Shipping Weight	Production Total
3G	M47	2-dr. Cpe-6P	12378/12968	3228/3409	30100
3G	M69	4-dr. Sed-6P	12378/12968	3276/3446	13551

CUTLASS SALON (V-6/V-8)

Model Number	Body/Style Number	Body Type & Seating	Factory Price	Shipping Weight	Production Total
3G	K47	2-dr. Cpe-6P	12697/13287	3203/3384	9221

DELTA 88 ROYALE (V-6)

Model Number	Body/Style Number	Body Type & Seating	Factory Price	Shipping Weight	Production Total
3H	N37	2-dr. Cpe-6P	13639	3176	4550
3H	N69	4-dr. Sed-6P	13639	3216	73277

DELTA 88 ROYALE BROUGHAM (V-6)

Model Number	Body/Style Number	Body Type & Seating	Factory Price	Shipping Weight	Production Total
3H	Y37	2-dr. Cpe-6P	14536	3204	8393
3H	Y69	4-dr. Sed-6P	14536	3237	84212

CUSTOM CRUISER (V-8)

Model Number	Body/Style Number	Body Type & Seating	Factory Price	Shipping Weight	Production Total
3B	P35	4-dr. Sta Wag-6P	14420	4136	17742

NINETY-EIGHT REGENCY (V-6)

Model Number	Body/Style Number	Body Type & Seating	Factory Price	Shipping Weight	Production Total
3C	X69	4-dr. Sed-6P	17371	3307	19738

NINETY-EIGHT REGENCY BROUGHAM (V-6)

Model Number	Body/Style Number	Body Type & Seating	Factory Price	Shipping Weight	Production Total
3C	W11	2-dr. Cpe-6P	18388	3285	4207
3C	W69	4-dr. Sed-6P	18388	3320	60817

TORONADO (V-6)

Model Number	Body/Style Number	Body Type & Seating	Factory Price	Shipping Weight	Production Total
3E	Z57	2-dr. Cpe-5P	19938	3352	15,040

FACTORY PRICE AND WEIGHT NOTE: Cutlass Supreme prices and weights to left of slash are for V-6, to right for V-8 engine; others, to left for four-cylinder and to right for V-6.

ENGINE DATA: BASE FOUR (Firenza): Inline, overhead-valve four-cylinder. Cast iron block and aluminum head. Displacement: 121 cu. in. (2.0 liters). Bore & stroke: 3.50 x 3.15 in. Compression ratio: 9.0:1. Net horsepower: 90 @ 5600 rpm. Torque: 108 lb. ft. @ 3200 rpm. Five main bearings. Hydraulic valve lifters. Fuel injection (TBI). VIN Code: K or 1. OPTIONAL FOUR (Firenza, Cutlass Ciera): Inline, overhead-cam four-cylinder. Cast iron block and aluminum head. Displacement: 121 cu. in. (2.0 liters). Bore & stroke: 3.50 x 3.15 in. Compression ratio: 8.8:1. Net horsepower: 102 @ 5200 rpm. Torque: 130 @ 2800 rpm. Five main bearings. Hydraulic valve lifters. Fuel injected. VIN Code: K or 1. BASE FOUR (Calais, Cutlass Ciera): Inline, overhead-valve four-cylinder. Cast iron block and aluminum head. Displacement: 151 cu. in. (2.5 liters). Bore & stroke: 4.00 x 3.00 in. Compression ratio: 9.0:1. Net horsepower: 98 @ 4800. Torque: 132 @ 2800 rpm. Five main bearings. Hydraulic valve lifters. Fuel injected (TBI). VIN Code: R or U. OPTIONAL V-6 (Firenza, Cutlass Ciera): 60-degree overhead valve V-6. Cast iron block and aluminum head. Displacement: 173 cu. in. (2.8 liters). Bore & stroke: 3.50 x 2.99 in. Compression ratio: 8.9:1. Net horsepower: 125 @ 4500 rpm. Torque: 160 lb. ft. @ 3600 rpm. Four main bearings. Hydraulic valve lifters. Fuel injection (MFI). VIN Code: W. OPTIONAL SIX (Calais): 60-degree overhead valve V-6. Cast iron block and aluminum head. Displacement: 181 cu. in. (3.0 liters). Bore & stroke: 3.80 x 2.70 in. Compression ratio: 9.0:1. Net horsepower: 125 @ 4900 rpm. Torque: 150 lb. ft. @ 2400 rpm. Four main bearings. Hydraulic valve lifters. Fuel injection (MFI). VIN Code: L. BASE V-6 (Cutlass Supreme): 90-degree overhead valve V-6. Cast iron block and head. Displacement: 231 cu. in. (3.8 liters). Bore & stroke: 3.80 x 3.40 in. Compression ratio: 8.0:1. Net horsepower: 110 @ 3800 rpm. Torque: 190 lb. ft. @ 1600 rpm. Four main bearings. Hydraulic valve lifters. 2-bbl. carb. VIN Code: A or 3. BASE V-6 (Delta 88, Ninety-Eight, Toronado): 90-degree overhead valve V-6. Cast iron block and head. Displacement: 231 cu. in. (3.8 liters). Bore & stroke: 3.80 x 3.40 in. Compression ratio: 8.5:1. Net horsepower: 150 @ 4400 rpm. Torque: 200 lb. ft. @ 2000 rpm. Four main bearings. Hydraulic valve lifters. Fuel injected (SFI - Delta 88 and Ninety-Eight/MFI - Toronado). VIN Code: A or 3. BASE V-6 (Cutlass Ciera GT): standard engine same as aforementioned 231 cu. in. (3.8-liter) V-6 with SFI fuel-injection. BASE V-8 (Custom Cruiser): 90-degree overhead valve V-8. Cast iron block and head. Displacement: 307 cu. in. (5.0 liters). Bore & stroke: 3.80 x 3.39 in. Compression ratio: 8.0:1. Net horsepower: 140 @ 3200 rpm. Torque: 255 lb. ft. @ 2000 rpm. Five main bearings. Hydraulic valve lifters. 4-bbl. carb. VIN Code: Y or 9. OPTIONAL V-8 (Cutlass Supreme) same as aforementioned base engine for Custom Cruiser. BASE V-8 (Cutlass 442): 90-degree overhead valve high output V-8. Cast iron block and head. Displacement: 307 cu. in. (5.0 liters). Bore & stroke: 3.80 x 3.39 in. Compression ratio: 9.5:1. Net horsepower: 170 @ 4000 rpm. Torque: 250 lb. ft. @ 2600 rpm. Five main bearings. Hydraulic valve lifters. 4-bbl. carb. VIN Code: Y or 9.

CHASSIS DATA: Wheelbase: (Firenza) 101.2 in.; (Calais) 103.4 in.; (Ciera) 104.9 in.; (Cutlass Supreme) 108.1 in.; (Delta 88) 110.8 in.; (Custom Cruiser) 116.0 in.; (Ninety-Eight) 110.8 in.; (Toronado) 108.0 in. Overall Length: (Firenza cpe) 174.3 in.; (Firenza sed) 176.2 in.; (Calais) 178.8 in.; (Ciera) 188.3 in.; (Ciera sta wag) 190.8 in.; (Cutlass Supreme cpe) 200.0 in.; (Cutlass Supreme sed) 200.4 in.; (Delta 88) 196.1 in.; (Custom Cruiser) 220.3 in.; (Ninety-Eight) 196.4 in.; (Toronado) 187.5 in. Height: (Firenza cpe) 51.7 in.; (Firenza sed) 53.7 in.; (Firenza sta wag) 55.2 in.; (Calais) 52.4 in.; (Ciera) 54.1 in.; (Ciera sta wag) 54.3 in.; (Cutlass Supreme cpe) 54.9 in.; (Cutlass Supreme sed) 55.9 in.; (Delta 88 cpe) 54.7 in.; (Delta 88 sed) 55.5 in.; (Custom Cruiser) 58.5 in.; (Ninety-Eight) 55.1 in.; (Toronado) 53.0 in. Width: (Firenza) 65.0 in.; (Calais) 66.6 in.; (Ciera) 69.3 in.; (Cutlass Supreme cpe) 71.6 in.; (Cutlass Supreme sed) 71.9 in.; (Delta 88) 72.4

in.; (Custom Cruiser) 79.8 in.; (Ninety-Eight) 72.4 in.; (Torado) 70.8 in. Front tread: (Firenza) 55.4 in.; (Calais) 55.5 in.; (Ciera) 58.7 in.; (Cutlass Supreme) 58.5 in.; (Delta 88) 60.3 in.; (Custom Cruiser) 62.1 in.; (Ninety-Eight) 60.3 in.; (Torado) 60.0 in. Rear tread: (Firenza) 55.2 in.; (Calais) 55.2 in.; (Ciera) 57.0 in.; (Cutlass Supreme) 58.7 in.; (Delta 88) 59.8 in.; (Custom Cruiser) 64.1 in.; (Ninety-Eight) 59.8 in.; (Torado) 60.0 in. Standard tires: (Firenza) P175/80R13; (Calais) P185/80R13; (Ciera) P185/75R14; (Cutlass Supreme) P195/75R14; (Delta 88) P205/75R14; (Custom Cruiser) P225/75R15; (Ninety-Eight) P205/75R14; (Toronado) P205/75R14.

TECHNICAL: Transmission: Five-speed manual floor shift standard on Firenza and Calais. Three-speed automatic or five-speed manual floor shift available on Firenza with GT package. Three-speed automatic standard on Cutlass Ciera/Cutlass Cruiser/Cutlass Supreme. Four-speed automatic standard on Delta 88/Custom Cruiser/Ninety-Eight/Toronado and available on Cutlass Ciera with GT package and Cutlass 442. Standard final drive ratio: (Firenza) 3.65:1 with five-speed manual trans.; (Calais) 3.35:1 with five-speed manual trans.; (Cutlass Ciera cpe and sed) 2.39:1 with three-speed automatic trans., (Cutlass Ciera sta wag) 2.84:1; (Cutlass Supreme) 2.41:1 with three-speed automatic trans.; (Delta 88/Custom Cruiser/Ninety-Eight) 2.73:1 with four-speed automatic trans.; (Toronado) 2.84:1 with four-speed automatic trans. Steering: (Cutlass/Custom Cruiser) recirculating ball; (others) rack and pinion. Front Suspension: (Firenza/Calais/Ciera/Delta 88/Ninety-Eight) MacPherson struts w/ coil springs, lower control arms and anti-sway bar; (Cutlass/Custom Cruiser) coil springs with upper/lower control arms; (Toronado) MacPherson struts w/ link control arm and anti-sway bar. Rear Suspension: (Firenza) beam axle w/ coil springs, trailing arms and anti-sway bar; (Calais) semi-independent w/ coil springs and trailing arms; (Ciera) beam axle with integral anti-sway, coil springs and Panhard rod; (Delta 88) independent w/ struts, coil springs and anti-sway bar; (Ninety-Eight) independent w/ struts, coil springs, lower control arms, anti-sway bar and automatic level control; (Cutlass/Custom Cruiser) rigid axle w/ coil springs, lower trailing radius arms and upper torque arms (four-link); (Toronado) independent w/ transverse leaf spring, control arms and automatic level control. Brakes: (All except Toronado) Front disc, rear drum; (Toronado) four-wheel disc. Ignition: electronic. Body Construction: (Cutlass/Custom Cruiser) separate body and frame; (others) unibody. Fuel tank: (Firenza/Calais) 13.6 gal.; (Ciera) 15.7 gal.; (Cutlass) 18.1 gal.; (Delta 88/Ninety-Eight/Toronado) 18.0 gal.; (Custom Cruiser) 22.0 gal.

DRIVETRAIN OPTIONS: (Firenza) 121 cu. in. FI four-cylinder ($50). (Ciera) 173 cu. in. FI V-6 ($610) and 231 cu. in. FI V-6 ($745). (Calais) 181 cu. in. FI V-6 ($660). (Cutlass Supreme) 307 cu. in. 4-bbl. V-8 ($590). Transmission/Differential: (Firenza) five-speed manual ($75). (Firenza/Calais) automatic ($490). (Ciera/Cutlass Supreme) automatic w/ overdrive ($175). (Calais) Column shift ($110 credit). (Cutlass/Custom Cruiser) Limited Slip Differential ($100). Power Steering: base Firenza ($225). Suspension: firm ride and handling package ($30-$49); touring car ride and handling package ($149-$593); (Ciera/Delta 88/Custom Cruiser) automatic load leveling ($175). Other: (Ninety-Eight) anti-lock brakes ($925). (Cutlass/Custom Cruiser/Delta 88/Ninety-Eight) high-capacity radiator ($30). High-capacity cooling ($40-$70). (Cutlass/Custom Cruiser/Delta 88/Ninety-Eight) Wiring harness ($30). California emission equipment ($99).

OPTION PACKAGES: (Calais) GT package ($1350); Sport Appearance Package ($195 - base/$150 - Supreme). (Ciera) GT package ($3060 - S coupe or sedan). (Cutlass) 442 package ($2577 - coupe). (Ninety-Eight) Grande Package ($975 - Brougham).

MAJOR CONVENIENCE/APPEARANCE OPTIONS: Four Season air conditioning a ($675-$775). Sunroof ($350). Rear facing

third seat ($215 - Ciera Cruiser and Brougham Cruiser/$220 - Custom Cruiser). Full vinyl roof ($175 - Ciera and Cutlass/$200 - Delta 88). Removable roof panels ($895 - Cutlass Supreme). Electric Sliding Glass Astroroof ($925 - Cutlass Supreme/$1230 - Ninety-Eight). Electric rear window defogger ($145). Pulse wiper system ($55). Cruise control ($175). Deluxe leather steering wheel ($54). Theft deterrent system ($159). Deluxe Mobile Telephone ($2850).

HISTORY: Introduced: October 9, 1986. Model year production: 806,915. Calendar year production (U.S.) 601,774. Calendar year sales by U.S. dealers: 714,394. Model year sales by U.S. dealers: 770,675.

Historical Footnotes: After three consecutive years of model year sales over one million units, Oldsmobile's numbers dropped 27.8 percent with 770,675 cars sold for a 7.3 percent of U.S. market share (9.5 percent the previous year). All lines decreased in sales with Ciera faring the best at 264,860 units moved compared to 330,572 the year previous.

1988

The Oldsmobile lineup underwent some significant changes from the year previous, with the major new-for-1988 change being the merger of the Calais line into the Cutlass series. The Cutlass Supreme also was revamped mid-model year to a front-wheel drive platform. The Ciera lineup offered a new International Series coupe and sedan, and two new engines debuted in Oldsmobiles this year: the 3800 V-6 for the Ninety-Eight Regency, Touring Sedan, Toronado and Trofeo (available in the Delta 88) and the 2.3-liter 16-valve Quad 4 (four-cylinder) available in the Cutlass Calais. In all, Oldsmobile offered 32 models based on 15 different body styles.

1988 Oldsmobile, Firenza sedan, (O)

1988 Oldsmobile, Firenza coupe, (O)

FIRENZA -- SERIES 3J -- FOUR -- A scaled-back lineup from the year before, the Firenza was offered in coupe, sedan and Cruiser station wagon form for 1988. Oldsmobile's most affordable offering featured a distinctive new front end appearance with composite headlamps and a new grille. New bumpers and fascias were added front and back. The lineup also received a

new look via standard wide side body moldings. One new wheel and three new tire selections were available this year. A new turbine design base wheel disc added to the stylish exterior appearance. The base tire was larger and an optional 14-inch tire was offered as part of a sport appearance package. A new 14-inch performance tire with improved mud and snow traction was standard for use with the FE3 handling package. The FE3 suspension system was part of the sport appearance package on the Firenza coupe and sedan. This package also included 14-inch aluminum styled wheels, GT+4 performance tires, a leather wrapped steering wheel and rallye gauge instrument cluster. Firenza's standard powertrain consisted of an electronically fuel-injected 2.0-liter four-cylinder engine coupled to a manual five-speed transaxle. A 2.0-liter four-cylinder engine with overhead cam as well as a three-speed automatic transaxle were also available.

1988 Oldsmobile, Firenza Cruiser station wagon, (O)

1988 Oldsmobile, Cutlass Calais coupe, (O)

CUTLASS CALAIS -- SERIES 3N -- FOUR/V-6 -- Calais became part of the Cutlass family for 1988, and was available in coupe and sedan trim as base, SL and a new International Series models. Improved utility of Calais SL and International Series interior space was offered with a new, standard 60/40 split rear folding seat, which allowed a pass through to the trunk. All or one-half of the rear seat could be folded down, and with both seat backs folded down the pass through to trunk measurement was 13 x 39 inches. The new 2.3-liter, 16-valve, dual overhead cam, multi-port fuel-injected Quad 4 engine made its debut in the Calais International Series coupe and sedan and, according to Oldsmobile, was available across the Calais lineup. The Quad 4 was offered with the Muncie-Getrag five-speed manual transaxle and three-speed automatic transaxle. Calais models housing the Quad 4 had new graphics for the front fenders to identify vehicles equipped with the engine. Zero to 60 mph performance for the Quad 4/five-speed-equipped Calais was 8.5 seconds, according to Oldsmobile. Base engine and drivetrain for the Calais was the improved 2.5-liter inline four-cylinder featuring balance shafts introduced the year previous. This powerplant was coupled to a five-speed manual transmission. Both a 3.0-liter V-6 engine and three-speed automatic transaxle were also available. Calais International Series models offered the FE3 handling package as standard equipment as well as rallye instrument cluster, air conditioning, top-of-the-line radio, pulse wipers,

trunk release and tilt steering wheel. An aggressive, styled sport steering wheel was offered mid-model year. Outside, the Calais "I package" included aero rocker panels, specific front and rear fascias, two-tone paint and 14-inch aluminum styled wheels with performance tires.

1988 Oldsmobile, Cutlass Ciera Brougham sedan, (O)

1988 Oldsmobile, Cutlass Ciera coupe, (O)

CUTLASS CIERA -- SERIES 3A -- FOUR/V-6 -- Maintaining its position as Oldsmobile's top seller, the mid-size Ciera's 1988 lineup was comprised of base and International Series coupe and sedan models as well as an SL coupe, Brougham sedan, Cutlass Cruiser station wagon and Cutlass Cruiser Brougham station wagon. Base level Ciera models received an enhanced aerodynamic appearance and composite headlamps. Ciera sedan models got a new three-function power sunroof that could be opened conventionally or tilted open from the rear to act as a vent. The sunroof also included a sliding shade to block the sun. Inside, the Ciera offered a new monochromatic instrument panel and optional storage armrest. Also available, and exclusive to Oldsmobile, was a new Driver Information System. International Series coupe and sedan models received aero front and rear panels and side rocker panels. The "I package" also included reclining front bucket seats with center console, air conditioning, rallye gauge cluster, composite halogen headlamps with black bezels, fog lamps, FE3 suspension including revised shock valving/spring rate/stabilizer bar size for improved road contact, aluminum styled wheels with performance GT+4 tires and a 3.8-liter sequential fuel-injected V-6 engine with hydraulic roller lifters. Standard powerplant for the Ciera was the 2.5-liter fuel-injected inline four-cylinder, which offered balance shafts and lighter weight pistons for smoother operation. Optional Ciera engine

1988 Oldsmobile, Ciera-based Cutlass Cruiser station wagon, (O)

was the 2.8-liter multi-port fuel-injected V-6 with three-speed or four-speed automatic transmission. The 3.8-liter V-6 engine with four-speed automatic transmission standard on the International Series Cieras was also available across-the-lineup.

1988 Oldsmobile, Cutlass Supreme Classic Brougham coupe, (O)

CUTLASS SUPREME -- SERIES 3G (through December 1987, then 3W for new front-drive platform) -- V-6/V-8 -- The Cutlass Supreme Classic, Oldsmobile's venerable rear-drive G-bodied car, gave way mid-model year in 1988 to the all-new GM10 front-drive Cutlass Supreme. The Classic was offered only in base and Brougham coupe form. The new Cutlass Supreme came in coupe version only, in base, SL and International Series models. The Classic was powered by a 5.0-liter, 4-bbl. carbureted V-8 mated to a four-speed automatic transmission. Standard powerplant on the front-drive Cutlass Supreme was a 2.8-liter multi-port fuel-injected V-6 coupled to a four-speed automatic overdrive transmission. A five-speed manual overdrive transmission was also available. The Cutlass Supreme's new design lowered its drag coefficient to .32 compared to the boxier Classic's .44 mark. Standard equipment on the Cutlass Supreme included: composite halogen headlamps, stainless steel exhaust system, four-wheel power disc brakes, "lubed-for-life" suspension, air conditioning and "wet arm" windshield wipers. The International Series coupe offered as standard gear a full vacuum fluorescent instrument cluster, front contoured bucket seats with four-way power articulation, sport tuned exhaust system and the FE3 suspension system helped by P215/65R15 steel belted radial tires mounted on 15 x 6-inch cast aluminum styled wheels. The exterior of the "I package" Cutlass Supreme was highlighted by specific front and rear fascias and lower body aero rocker moldings in gunmetal or silver trim. Also featured were specific wheel opening moldings, blacked-out grille pattern, low-gloss black moldings and pillar appliqués and accent paint stripes.

1988 Oldsmobile, Delta 88 Royale coupe, (O)

DELTA 88 ROYALE -- SERIES 3H -- V-6 -- The Delta 88 Royale lineup continued unchanged from the year previous with coupe or sedan in two trim levels, base and Brougham. Featured exclusively, although as optional equipment on both sedans was a driver's side airbag -- the only General Motors car so equipped in 1988. Also optional were anti-lock brakes. Standard powertrain for the Delta 88 was a 3.8-liter, sequential fuel-injected V-6 coupled to a four-speed automatic transaxle. Optional was the new 3800 3.8-liter, sequential fuel-injected V-6 mated to a four-speed automatic transaxle.

1988 Oldsmobile, Delta 88 Royale Brougham sedan, (O)

1988 Oldsmobile, Custom Cruiser station wagon, (O)

CUSTOM CRUISER -- SERIES 3B -- V-8 -- After the mid-model year demise of the Cutlass Supreme Classic the Custom Cruiser station wagon was the lone remaining rear-drive car Oldsmobile offered. As it did in the previous year, the Custom Cruiser offered 87.2 cubic feet of cargo space and seating for up to eight passengers. It was again powered by a 5.0-liter 4-bbl. carbureted V-8 engine with new-for-1988 electronic spark control, mated to a four-speed automatic transmission.

1988 Oldsmobile, 98 Regency sedan, (O)

1988 Oldsmobile, 98 Regency Brougham sedan, (O)

NINETY-EIGHT REGENCY -- SERIES 3C -- V-6 -- Oldsmobile's full-size luxury car, the Ninety-Eight Regency lineup for 1988 consisted of sedans only, in base and Brougham levels as well as a Touring Sedan. The Brougham coupe offered the previous year was dropped. Standard powertrain on all Ninety-Eight models was the new 3800 3.8-liter, sequential fuel-injected V-6 mated to a four-speed automatic transaxle. The 3800 featured balance shafts for smoother operation, and output was rated at 165 hp. A new power pull-down trunk lid was optional

equipment as was the Driver Information System and driver's side illuminated visor vanity mirror. The Ninety-Eight featured gas-filled and deflected disc front and rear struts to improve ride quality of the standard FE2 (and FE3 on Touring Sedan) suspension system. Introduced midway the year before, the Touring Sedan returned for its first full model year in 1988. Standard suspension was the FE3 system with P215/65R15 GT+4 performance blackwall radial tires mounted on 15-inch aluminum styled wheels. Also standard on the Touring Sedan was the Tevis anti-lock braking system and genuine walnut burl trim on the instrument panel and console.

1988 Oldsmobile, Touring Sedan, (O)

1988 Oldsmobile, Toronado Trofeo coupe, (O)

TORONADO -- SERIES 3E -- V-6 -- Oldsmobile's personal luxury car, Toronado and Trofeo models returned in 1988 with a new front end appearance to enhance its aerodynamic design. Headlamp covers were more pronounced and carried a wraparound design into the side marker lamps. New features on the Toronado included a change oil message added to the message center, a new defogger directing warm air to the windshield and floor was integrated into the climate control system, climate control and radio control buttons were enlarged and a "wet arm" windshield wiper system was added. Optional on the Toronado and Trofeo was anti-lock brakes. Standard powertrain for the Toronado and Trofeo was the 3800 3.8-liter V-6 coupled to a four-speed automatic transmission. The Trofeo's bucket seats featured a new power lumbar and power back contour function. Also new was the "wet arm" windshield wiper system similar to that found on the Toronado. Trofeo's standard equipment included the FE3 suspension with P215/65R15 GT+4 blackwall radial tires mounted on styled aluminum wheels.

I.D. DATA: Oldsmobile's 17-symbol Vehicle Identification Number (VIN) again was located on the upper left surface of the instrument panel, visible through the windshield. The first three characters (1G3) indicates Oldsmobile Division. The fourth and fifth letters designate the body type/series: A/J - Cutlass Ciera and Cutlass Cruiser, A/M - Cutlass Ciera Brougham and SL, A/S - Cutlass Ciera International Series, B/P - Custom Cruiser, C/V - Ninety-Eight Touring Sedan, C/W - Ninety-Eight Regency Brougham, C/X - Ninety-Eight Regency, E/V - Trofeo, E/Z - Toronado, G/M - Cutlass Supreme Classic Brougham, G/R - Cutlass Supreme Classic, H/N - Delta 88 Royale, H/Y - Delta 88 Royale Brougham, J/C - Firenza, N/F - Cutlass Calais, N/T - Cutlass Calais SL, W/H - Cutlass Supreme, W/S - Cutlass Brougham. The

1988 Oldsmobile, Toronado coupe, (O)

sixth number identifies the body style: 1 - 2-dr coupe/sedan, 2 - 2-dr hatchback, 3 - 2-dr convertible, 5 - 4-dr sedan, 6 - 4-dr hatchback, 8 - 4-dr station wagon. The seventh number identifies the restraint code: 1 - manual belts, 3 - manual belts with driver's side airbag, 4 - automatic belts. The eighth letter identifies the engine: C = 3.8-liter/231-cid fuel-injected V-6, D = 2.3-liter/138-cid multi-port fuel-injected inline four-cylinder, H = 5.0-liter/307-cid 4-bbl carbureted V-8, K = 2.0-liter/122-cid fuel-injected inline four-cylinder, L = 3.0-liter/181-cid fuel-injected V-6, M = 2.0-liter/122-cid fuel-injected inline four-cylinder, R = 2.5-liter/151-cid fuel-injected inline four-cylinder, U = 2.5-liter/151-cid fuel-injected inline four-cylinder, W = 2.8-liter/173-cid fuel-injected V-6, Y = 5.0-liter/307-cid 4-bbl carbureted V-8, 1 = 2.0-liter/121-cid fuel-injected inline four-cylinder and 3 = 3.8-liter/231-cid fuel-injected V-6. The ninth number is the check digit. The tenth letter represents the model year (J = 1988). The eleventh character identifies the assembly plant: D - Doraville, Ga.; E - Linden, N.J.; G - Framingham, Mass.; K - Leeds, Mo.; M - Lansing, Mich.; P - Pontiac, Mich.; R - Arlington, Texas; U - Hamtramck, Mich.; W - Willow Run, Mich.; 1 - Wentzville, Mo.; 3 - Detroit, Mich.; 4 - Orion, Mich.; (Canada) 1 - Oshawa, Ontario and 2 - Ste. Therese, Quebec. The final six digits are the sequential serial number.

FIRENZA (FOUR)

Model Number	Body/Style Number	Body Type & Seating	Factory Price	Shipping Weight	Production Total
3J	C27	2-dr. Cpe-5P	9295	2327	2724
3J	C69	4-dr. Sed-5P	9295	2381	8612

FIRENZA CRUISER (FOUR)

3J	C35	4-dr. Sta Wag-5P	9995	2438	920

CUTLASS CALAIS (FOUR/V-6)

Model Number	Body/Style Number	Body Type & Seating	Factory Price	Shipping Weight	Production Total
3N	F27	2-dr. Cpe-5P	10320/10980	2470/2531	48998
3N	F69	4-dr. Sed-5P	10320/10980	2539/2603	31867

CUTLASS CALAIS SL (FOUR/V-6)

3N	T27	2-dr. SL Cpe-5P	11195/11855	2488/2549	9458
3N	T69	4-dr. SL Sed-5P	11195/11855	2551/2615	7907

CUTLASS CALAIS INTERNATIONAL SERIES (FOUR)

3N	K27	2-dr. Cpe-5P	13695	2757	7977
3N	K69	4-dr. Sed-5P	13695	2830	4069

CUTLASS CIERA (FOUR/V-6)

Model Number	Body/Style Number	Body Type & Seating	Factory Price	Shipping Weight	Production Total
3A	J37	2-dr. Cpe-6P	10995/11605	2769/2842	12920
3A	J19	4-dr. Sed-6P	11656/12266	2733/2805	127353
3A	J35	4-dr. Sta Wag-6P	12320/12930	2933/3004	11779

CUTLASS CIERA BROUGHAM (FOUR/V-6)

3A	M37	2-dr. SL Cpe-6P	11845/12455	2780/2853	4608
3A	M19	4-dr. Sed-6P	12625/13235	2804/2876	78423
3A	M35	4-dr. Sta Wag-6P	12995/13605	3004/3075	5401

CUTLASS CIERA INTERNATIONAL SERIES (V-6)

3A	S37	2-dr. Cpe-6P	14995	2958	4564
3A	S19	4-dr. Sed-6P	15825	2913	5687

CUTLASS SUPREME CLASSIC (V-8)

Model Number	Body/Style Number	Body Type & Seating	Factory Price	Shipping Weight	Production Total
3G	R47	2-dr. Cpe-6P	13163	3180	15568

CUTLASS SUPREME CLASSIC BROUGHAM (V-8)

Model Number	Body/Style Number	Body Type & Seating	Factory Price	Shipping Weight	Production Total
3G	M47	2-dr. Cpe-6P	13995	3233	12110

CUTLASS SUPREME (V-6)

Model Number	Body/Style Number	Body Type & Seating	Factory Price	Shipping Weight	Production Total
3W	H47	2-dr. Cpe-6P	12846	2958	46448
3W	S47	2-dr. SL Cpe-6P	13495	N/A	31131

CUTLASS SUPREME INTERNATIONAL SERIES (V-6)

Model Number	Body/Style Number	Body Type & Seating	Factory Price	Shipping Weight	Production Total
3W	R47	2-dr. Cpe-6P	15644	N/A	17144

DELTA 88 ROYALE (V-6)

Model Number	Body/Style Number	Body Type & Seating	Factory Price	Shipping Weight	Production Total
3H	N37	2-dr. Cpe-6P	14498	3172	3783
3H	N69	4-dr. Sed-6P	14498	3116	85178

DELTA 88 ROYALE BROUGHAM (V-6)

3H	Y37	2-dr. Cpe-6P	15451	3187	4808
3H	Y69	4-dr. Sed-6P	15451	3220	67148

CUSTOM CRUISER (V-8)

Model Number	Body/Style Number	Body Type & Seating	Factory Price	Shipping Weight	Production Total
3B	P35	4-dr. Sta Wag-6P	15655	4136	11114

NINETY-EIGHT REGENCY (V-6)

Model Number	Body/Style Number	Body Type & Seating	Factory Price	Shipping Weight	Production Total
3C	X69	4-dr. Sed-6P	17995	3300	18793
3C	V69	4-dr. Tr. Sed-6P	24470	3421	8531

NINETY-EIGHT REGENCY BROUGHAM (V-6)

3C	W69	4-dr. Sed-6P	19371	3316	52611

TORONADO (V-6)

Model Number	Body/Style Number	Body Type & Seating	Factory Price	Shipping Weight	Production Total
3E	Z57	2-dr. Cpe-5P	20598	3364	7698
3E	V57	2-dr. Trofeo Cpe-5P	22695	3426	8798

FACTORY PRICE AND WEIGHT NOTE: Beginning with Cutlass Calais, prices and weights to left of slash are for four-cylinder models and to right for V-6.

ENGINE DATA: BASE FOUR (Firenza): Inline, overhead-valve four-cylinder. Cast iron block and aluminum head. Displacement: 121 cu. in. (2.0 liters). Bore & stroke: 3.50 x 3.15 in. Compression ratio: 9.0:1. Net horsepower: 90 @ 5600 rpm. Torque: 108 lb. ft. @ 3200 rpm. Five main bearings. Hydraulic valve lifters. Fuel injection. OPTIONAL FOUR (Firenza): Inline, overhead-cam four-cylinder. Cast iron block and aluminum head. Displacement: 121 cu. in. (2.0 liters). Bore & stroke: 3.38 x 3.38 in. Compression ratio: 8.8:1. Net horsepower: 96 @ 4800 rpm. Torque: 118 @ 3600 rpm. Five main bearings. Hydraulic valve lifters. Fuel injected. BASE FOUR (Cutlass Calais, Cutlass Ciera): Inline, overhead-valve four-cylinder. Cast iron block and aluminum head. Displacement: 151 cu. in. (2.5 liters). Bore & stroke: 4.00 x 3.00 in. Compression ratio: 9.0:1. Net horsepower: 98 @ 4800. Torque: 135 @ 3200 rpm. Five main bearings. Hydraulic valve lifters. Fuel injected. BASE FOUR (Cutlass Calais International Series) Quad 4 inline, dual overhead cam four-cylinder. Cast iron block and aluminum head. Displacement: 138 cu. in. (2.3 liters). Bore & stroke: 3.62 x 3.35 in. Compression ratio: 9.5:1. Net horsepower: 150 @ 5200 rpm. Torque: 160 @ 4000. Four valves per cylinder. Fuel injection (MFI). OPTIONAL SIX (Cutlass Calais): Overhead valve V-6. Displacement: 181 cu. in. (3.0 liters). Bore & stroke: 3.50 x 2.66 in. Compression ratio: 9.0:1. Net horsepower: 125 @ 4900 rpm. Torque: 150 lb. ft. @ 2400 rpm. Fuel injection (MFI). OPTIONAL SIX (Cutlass Ciera, Cutlass Cruiser): Overhead valve V-6. Displacement: 173 cu. in. (2.8 liters). Bore & stroke: 3.50 x 2.90 in. Compression ratio: 8.9:1. Net horsepower: 125 @ 4500 rpm. Torque: 160 lb. ft. @ 3600 rpm. Fuel injection (MFI). BASE SIX (Cutlass Supreme): Overhead valve V-6. Displacement: 173 cu. in. (2.8 liters). Bore & stroke: 3.50 x 3.00 in. Compression ratio: 8.9:1. Net horsepower: 125 @ 4500 rpm. Torque: 160 lb. ft. @ 3600 rpm. Fuel injection (MFI). BASE SIX (Delta 88): Overhead valve V-6. Displacement: 231 cu. in. (3.8 liters). Bore & stroke: 3.80 x 3.40 in. Compression ratio: 8.5:1. Net horsepower: 150 @ 4400 rpm. Torque: 200 lb. ft. @ 2000 rpm. Fuel injected (SFI). OPTIONAL SIX (Cutlass Ciera, Cutlass Cruiser): same as aforementioned 231 cu. in. (3.8-liter) V-6 with SFI. BASE SIX (Ninety-Eight, Toronado) 3800 90-degree, overhead valve V-6. Cast iron block and head. Displacement: 231 cu. in. (3.8 liters). Bore & stroke: 3.80 x 3.40 in. Compression ratio: 8.5:1. Net horsepower: 165 @ 4800 rpm. Torque: 210 lb. ft. @ 2000 rpm. Fuel injected (SFI). OPTIONAL SIX (Delta 88): same as aforementioned 3800 231 cu. in. (3.8-liter) V-6 with SFI. BASE V-8 (Cutlass Supreme Classic, Custom Cruiser): Overhead valve V-8. Cast iron block and head. Displacement: 307 cu. in. (5.0 liters). Bore & stroke: 3.80 x 3.40 in. Compression ratio: 7.9:1. Net horsepower: 140 @ 3200 rpm. Torque: 255 lb. ft. @ 2000 rpm. 4-bbl. carb.

CHASSIS DATA: Wheelbase: (Firenza) 101.2 in.; (Calais) 103.4 in.; (Ciera) 104.9 in.; (Cutlass Cruiser) 104.9 in.; (Cutlass Supreme Classic) 108.1 in.; (Cutlass Supreme) 107.5 in.; (Delta 88) 110.8 in.; (Custom Cruiser) 116.0 in.; (Ninety-Eight) 110.8 in.; (Toronado) 108.0 in. Overall Length: (Firenza cpe) 174.3 in.; (Firenza sed) 176.2 in.; (Firenza Cruiser) 175.7 in.; (Calais cpe) 178.6 in.; (Calais sed) 178.8 in.; (Ciera) 190.3 in.; (Cutlass Cruiser) 194.4 in.; (Cutlass Supreme Classic) 200.0 in.; (Cutlass Supreme) 192.1 in.; (Delta 88) 196.3 in.; (Custom Cruiser) 220.3 in.; (Ninety-Eight) 196.3 in.; (Toronado) 187.5 in. Height: (Firenza cpe) 51.7 in.; (Firenza sed) 53.7 in.; (Firenza Cruiser) 55.2 in.; (Calais) 52.3 in.; (Ciera) 54.1 in.; (Cutlass Cruiser) 54.5 in.; (Cutlass Supreme Classic) 54.9 in.; (Cutlass Supreme) 52.8 in.; (Delta 88 cpe) 54.7 in.; (Delta 88 sed) 55.5 in.; (Custom Cruiser) 58.5 in.; (Ninety-Eight) 55.1 in.; (Toronado) 53.0 in. Width: (Firenza) 65.0 in.; (Calais) 66.9 in.; (Ciera) 69.5 in.; (Cutlass Cruiser) 69.5 in.; (Cutlass Supreme Classic) 71.6 in.; (Cutlass Supreme) 71.0 in.; (Delta 88) 72.4 in.; (Custom Cruiser) 79.8 in.; (Ninety-Eight) 72.4 in.; (Toronado) 70.8 in. Front tread: (Firenza) 55.4 in.; (Calais) 55.5 in.; (Ciera) 58.7 in.; (Cutlass Cruiser) 58.7 in.; (Cutlass Supreme Classic) 58.5 in.; (Cutlass Supreme) 59.5 in.; (Delta 88) 60.3 in.; (Custom Cruiser) 62.1 in.; (Ninety-Eight) 60.3 in.; (Toronado) 60.0 in. Rear tread: (Firenza) 55.2 in.; (Calais) 55.2 in.; (Ciera) 57.0 in.; (Cutlass Cruiser) 57.0 in.; (Cutlass Supreme Classic) 57.7 in.; (Cutlass Supreme) 58.0 in.; (Delta 88) 59.8 in.; (Custom Cruiser) 64.1 in.; (Ninety-Eight) 59.8 in.; (Toronado) 60.0 in. Standard tires: (Firenza) P185/80R13; (Calais) P185/80R13; (Ciera) P185/75R14; (Cutlass Cruiser) P185/75R14; (Cutlass Supreme Classic) P195/75R14; (Cutlass Supreme) P195/75R14; (Delta 88) P205/75R14; (Custom Cruiser) P225/75R15; (Ninety-Eight) P205/75R14; (Touring Sedan) P215/65R15; (Toronado) P205/75R14.

TECHNICAL: Transmission: Five-speed manual floor shift standard on Firenza. Three-speed automatic or five-speed manual floor shift available on Firenza. Three-speed automatic standard on Cutlass Calais/Cutlass Ciera/Cutlass Cruiser. Five-speed manual floor shift available on Calais. Four-speed automatic standard on Delta 88/Custom Cruiser/Ninety-Eight/Toronado/Cutlass Ciera International Series. Four-speed automatic available on Cutlass Ciera/Cutlass Cruiser. Standard final drive ratio: (Firenza) 3.45:1 with five-speed manual trans.; (Calais) 2.84:1 with three-speed automatic trans.; (Ciera) 2.84:1 with three-speed automatic trans., (Cutlass Cruiser) 2.84:1 with three-speed automatic trans.; (Cutlass Supreme Classic) 2.56:1 with four-speed automatic trans.; (Cutlass Supreme) 3.33:1 with four-speed automatic trans.; (Delta 88/Custom Cruiser/Ninety-Eight/Toronado) 2.73:1 with four-speed automatic trans.; Steering: (Cutlass Supreme Classic/Custom Cruiser) recirculating ball; (others) rack and pinion. Brakes: (all except Cutlass Su-

preme and Toronado) front disc, rear drum; (Cutlass Supreme/Toronado) four-wheel disc. Ignition: electronic. Body Construction: (Cutlass/Custom Cruiser) separate body and frame; (others) unibody. Fuel tank: (Firenza/Calais) 13.6 gal.; (Ciera/Cutlass Cruiser) 15.7 gal.; (Cutlass Supreme) 16.6 gal.; (Cutlass Supreme Classic/Delta 88/Ninety-Eight/Toronado) 18.0 gal.; (Custom Cruiser) 22.0 gal.

DRIVETRAIN OPTIONS: (Calais) 2.3-liter Quad 4 engine ($600). (Firenza) automatic transmission ($490). (Custom Cruiser) Limited Slip Differential ($100). Other: (Ninety-Eight) anti-lock brakes ($925). (Custom Cruiser/Delta 88/Ninety-Eight) High-capacity cooling ($65). (All) California emission equipment ($99).

HISTORY: Calendar year production (U.S.): 562,920. Calendar year sales by U.S. dealers: 715,270. Model year sales by U.S. dealers: 694,464.

Historical Footnotes: After suffering an almost 28 percent drop in car sales the year previous, Oldsmobile sales dropped another 10 percent with 694,464 units moved for model year 1988. Decreases were recorded across the lineup with Ciera's 233,584 cars sold the leader. A turbocharged, intercooled 250-hp Quad 4-powered open-air Cutlass Supreme "piloted" by the legendary Chuck Yeager paced the 1988 Indianapolis 500. Also, a 20th Anniversary Hurst/Olds Cutlass based on the rear-drive Cutlass Supreme Classic was produced as a limited edition aero-appearance package by Hurst/Aero Group of Tempe, Arizona.

1989

After the previous year's worst sales performance since 1975, Oldsmobile dropped its low-selling Firenza with no small car replacement for 1989. Also, a name revision was enacted for Eighty-Eight models as the long-standing "Delta" portion was dropped. Overall, the lineup revisions were few with the Cutlass Calais adding an S series coupe and sedan, the Cutlass Ciera receiving an SL sedan (replacing the Brougham version from the year before) to go with the existing SL coupe, and the introduction of the 3300 V-6 engine (which replaced the 3.0-liter V-6 previously offered). Also, a late-year High Output Quad 4 was introduced on the Calais option list.

1989 Oldsmobile, Cutlass Calais SL sedan, (O)

1989 Oldsmobile, Cutlass Calais SL coupe, (O)

1989 Oldsmobile, Cutlass Calais International Series sedan, (O)

CUTLASS CALAIS -- SERIES 3N -- FOUR/V-6 -- As of 1989, the Calais became Oldsmobile's most compact offering. Available in two-door coupe and four-door sedan version, four model levels were offered: base (termed Value Leader by Oldsmobile), new-for-1989 S, SL and International Series. The Value Leader model was aimed at buyers seeking a high level of standard content at an affordable price. This base Calais was sold only with the 2.5-liter four-cylinder engine and limited additional equipment. The Calais lineup was restyled from the previous year, and offered a more aggressive front end treatment, new rear fascia, all-red taillamps and side body appearance. Inside, the Calais featured more black (instead of chrome) trim. The Calais SL featured new silver or dark gray lower accent color. Other new standard equipment included 14-inch Goodrich Touring T/A tires and uplevel wheel covers. The Calais International Series was fortified with new ground effects styling, standard fog lamps, monochromatic paint, tri-color emblems and high-performance 16-inch wheels and tires. Inside, the "I-package" updates included a standard Driver Information System and redesigned gear shift and parking brake handles. Standard powertrain for the Calais was the 2.5-liter four-cylinder engine, which was rated at 110 net horsepower (up from 98 the year before). The Quad 4 engine introduced the year previous was again standard in the Calais International Series and available across the lineup. A new Series 3300 3.3-liter V-6, rated at 160 net horsepower at 5200 rpm and 185 lb.-ft. of torque at 3200 rpm, was optional in the Calais S and SL editions. A High Output version of the Quad 4, rated at 180 net horsepower and 160 lb.-ft. of torque at 5200 rpm, was made optional late in the year in the Calais International Series.

1989 Oldsmobile, Cutlass Calais International Series coupe, (O)

1989 Oldsmobile, Cutlass Calais coupe with Quad 4 appearance package, (O)

1989 Oldsmobile, Cutlass Ciera International Series sedan, (O)

1989 Oldsmobile, Cutlass Supreme coupe, (O)

1989 Oldsmobile, Ciera-based Cutlass Cruiser SL station wagon, (O)

CUTLASS CIERA -- SERIES 3A -- FOUR/V-6 -- The 1989 version of the Oldsmobile Ciera entered the new model year with the most extensive styling improvements since its 1982 launch. The lineup consisted of base, SL and International Series coupes and sedans. The Cutlass Cruiser station wagon was now offered in two trim levels: base and SL (formerly the Cruiser Brougham). Updates included new grilles and front fascias, new taillamps and rear fascias (except Cruiser models) and exterior trim revisions. Windshield and backlight moldings were made black instead of the previous bright. Hood ornamentation found on the previous year's Ciera was deleted and wide body side moldings added. Sedan models featured a more rounded roofline and more steeply sloped rear window. International Series models received new black rub strips and body side moldings, minor alterations of identifying badges and a new graphite treatment for interior switches and trim. The 2.5-liter four-cylinder engine remained the standard powerplant for the Ciera and Cruiser. Optional engines were the 2.8-liter V-6, rated at 125 net horsepower, and the new Series 3300 3.3-liter V-6, which replaced the previous year's 3.8-liter V-6 offering. The Ciera SL, which replaced the Brougham offered the year before, featured new interior fabrics, dark gray instead of bright door accents and a new storage armrest with the 55/45 front seat. The Cutlass Ciera International Series was equipped with the Series 3300 3.3-liter V-6 engine, Driver Information System and 14-inch cross-spoke aluminum wheels. The six-seater Cruiser models had an EPA cargo rating of 41.6 cubic feet and nearly four feet of load floor behind the rear bench. With the back seat folded, cargo volume was 74.4 cubic feet and the load floor was over six feet long.

CUTLASS SUPREME -- SERIES 3W -- V-6 -- The front-drive Cutlass Supreme was in its first full year of production in 1989, and changes from the previous year's intro model consisted of minor refinements. A mid-model year addition of a new 3.1-liter V-6 engine mated to a four-speed automatic transaxle with across-the-lineup availability -- replacing the 2.8-liter V-6 -- headed the list. Again, the Cutlass Supreme was offered in coupe versions only, in base, SL and International Series trim. The aerodynamic design of the Cutlass Supreme offered a 0.306 drag coefficient. Also, power assisted four-wheel disc brakes were featured on all models. Air conditioning became

standard equipment across the lineup. Optional equipment included anti-lock brakes, power sunroof, extendible underhood lamp and remote lock control. A split bench seat was standard on base Cutlass Supremes. Black grilles replaced chrome grilles on base and SL Cutlass Supremes. The SL models now had cross-spoke aluminum wheels as standard equipment. Inside, the SL's electronic instrument cluster could now be bolstered with an optional Driver Information System. Steering wheel touch controls, which operated the radio and new optional electronic climate control. The Cutlass Supreme International Series new standard features included power mirrors, fog lamps, dual cooling fans, remote lock control, P215/60R16 GT+4 tires with 16-inch aluminum wheels and Driver Information System. New options consisted of steering wheel touch controls for managing sound and climate control, CD player and eight-speaker sound system and gray leather interior. Standard powertrain (until mid-model year) was the 2.8-liter V-6 coupled to a five-speed manual transaxle.

1989 Oldsmobile, Cutlass Supreme International Series coupe, (O)

1989 Oldsmobile, Eighty-Eight Royale Brougham sedan, (O)

EIGHTY-EIGHT ROYALE -- SERIES 3H -- V-6 -- As of 1989, the former Delta 88 Royale was renamed the Eighty-Eight Royale. The Eighty-Eight nameplate observed its 40th Anniversary in this year, which saw only minor refinements to Oldsmobile's family sedan. The Eighty-Eight was again offered in both coupe and sedan versions in base and Brougham trim. Identifying graphics were simplified to modernize appearance both inside and out. Other design departures included: hood ornament deleted, radio antenna relocated to right rear, new bin-type glovebox, new all-red taillamps and body color instead of bright

interior door trim. In addition, Eighty-Eight Brougham models received color coordinated rear view mirrors and trunk lid release as standard equipment. Optional equipment across-the-lineup included the Driver Information System, anti-lock brakes and driver's side airbag. Standard powertrain for all Eighty-Eight models was the Series 3800 3.8-liter V-6 mated to a four-speed automatic transaxle.

1989 Oldsmobile, Eighty-Eight Royale coupe, (O)

1989 Oldsmobile, Custom Cruiser station wagon, (O)

CUSTOM CRUISER -- SERIES 3B -- V-8 -- Called the "Rock of Ages" in Oldsmobile press material, the Custom Cruiser was Olds' sole remaining V-8-powered rear-drive model. With its rear-facing third seat erected, the Custom Cruiser accommodated eight passengers. With the third seat down, the Custom Cruiser handled six passengers and 50 EPA cubic feet of cargo. An optional towing package was available, rated for loads up to 5,000 pounds. Minor revisions included rear quarter window moldings receiving a bright finish, several new exterior paint offerings and, as with other Oldsmobile models, three-point seat belts were added to outboard rear positions. Standard powertrain remained the 5.0-liter V-8 linked to a four-speed automatic transmission.

1989 Oldsmobile, Ninety-Eight Regency Brougham sedan, (O)

NINETY-EIGHT REGENCY -- SERIES 3C -- V-6 -- Oldsmobile's luxury Ninety-Eight sedan-only lineup again consisted of base and Brougham models. The Touring Sedan based on the Ninety-Eight was also again offered in 1989. Refinements for the Ninety-Eight included passive front seat belts, a new grille, radio antenna moved to the right rear, bin-type glovebox, deletion of the hood windsplit molding from year previous, body color side moldings and door edge guards, red instead of body color back-up lamp bezel, graphic identification in block instead of script

lettering and a new lay-down hood ornament. New features on the Touring Sedan included: a new grille, body color side moldings, bin-type glovebox, revised front seat headrests and new carpeting. Standard powertrain for the Ninety-Eight and Touring Sedan models was the Series 3800 3.8-liter V-6 coupled to a four-speed automatic transaxle. The Touring Sedan featured FE3 suspension as standard while it was optional on the Ninety-Eight. Other optional equipment on the Ninety-Eight included: anti-lock brakes, driver's side airbag, electrochromic day/night mirror, steering wheel touch controls and full automatic HVAC system (standard on Brougham sedan). Standard on the Touring Sedan was the Driver Information System, anti-lock brakes, automatic door locks, twilight sentinel, steering wheel touch controls and GT+4 radial tires with 16-inch aluminum wheels.

1989 Oldsmobile, Touring Sedan, (O)

1989 Oldsmobile, Toronado Trofeo coupe, (O)

TORONADO -- SERIES 3E -- V-6 -- Oldsmobile's personal luxury car, the Toronado and its spin-off Trofeo received several revisions for 1989. The Toronado featured a new engine mounting system, new oil level sensor to monitor upkeep without raising the hood, monochromatic paint, new seat fabrics and dark trim plates. The Trofeo's new features included: four-lamp high-beam headlamp system, body color front air dam and rocker extensions, engine mounting system and oil level sensor. New standard equipment for the Toronado included: body color side moldings, bucket seats and console, floor mats and 15-inch aluminum wheels. Trofeo offered as new standard equipment anti-lock brakes, touch control steering wheel, auto-

1989 Oldsmobile, Toronado coupe, (O)

matic door locks, electrochromic day/night mirror, twilight sentinel, power trunk pull down, courtesy and reading lamps, floor mats, illumination for interior and front door locks and body color side moldings. Optional on both Toronado and Trofeo was the new color Visual Information Center and cellular mobile phone. Standard powertrain for both the Toronado and Trofeo was the Series 3800 3.8-liter V-6 mated to a four-speed automatic transaxle.

I.D. DATA: Oldsmobile's 17-symbol Vehicle Identification Number (VIN) again was located on the upper left surface of the instrument panel, visible through the windshield. The first three characters (1G3) indicates Oldsmobile Division. The fourth and fifth letters designate the body type/series: A/J - Cutlass Ciera and Cutlass Cruiser, A/M - Cutlass Ciera Brougham and SL, A/S - Cutlass Ciera International Series, B/P - Custom Cruiser, C/V - Touring Sedan, C/W - Ninety-Eight Regency Brougham, C/X - Ninety-Eight Regency, C/X - Toronado Trofeo, E/Z - Toronado, H/N - Eighty-Eight Royale, H/Y - Eighty-Eight Royale Brougham, N/F - Cutlass Calais S, N/K - Cutlass Calais International Series, N/L - Cutlass Calais, N/T - Cutlass Calais SL, W/H - Cutlass Supreme, W/R - Cutlass Supreme International Series, W/S - Cutlass Supreme SL. The sixth number identifies the body style: 1 - 2-dr coupe/sedan, 2 - 2-dr hatchback/liftback, 3 - 2-dr convertible, 5 - 4-dr sedan, 6 - 4-dr hatchback/liftback, 8 - 4-dr station wagon. The seventh number identifies the restraint code: 1 - manual belts, 3 - manual belts with driver's side airbag, 4 - automatic belts. The eighth letter identifies the engine: A = 2.3-liter multi-port fuel-injected inline four-cylinder, C = 3.8-liter multi-port fuel-injected V-6, D = 2.3-liter multi-port fuel-injected inline four-cylinder, N = 3.3-liter fuel-injected V-6, R = 2.5-liter fuel-injected inline four-cylinder, T = 3.1-liter fuel-injected V-6, U = 2.5-liter fuel-injected inline four-cylinder, W = 2.8-liter multi-port fuel-injected V-6, Y = 5.0-liter/307-cid 4-bbl carbureted V-8. The ninth number is the check digit. The tenth letter represents the model year (K = 1989). The eleventh character identifies the assembly plant: D - Doraville, Ga.; E - Linden, N.J.; G - Framingham, Mass.; K - Leeds, Mo.; M - Lansing, Mich.; P - Pontiac, Mich.; R - Arlington, Texas; U - Hamtramck, Mich.; W - Willow Run, Mich.; 1 - Wentzville, Mo.; 3 - Detroit, Mich.; 4 - Orion, Mich.; (Canada) 1 - Oshawa, Ontario; and 2 - Ste. Therese, Quebec . The final six digits are the sequential serial number.

CUTLASS CALAIS (FOUR)

Model Number	Body/Style Number	Body Type & Seating	Factory Price	Shipping Weight	Production Total
3N	L27	2-dr. Cpe-5P	9995	2512	11432
3N	L69	4-dr. Sed-5P	9995	2573	14506

CUTLASS CALAIS S (FOUR/V-6)

3N	F27	2-dr. Cpe-5P	10895/11605	2512/2596	33633
3N	F69	4-dr. Sed-5P	10995/11705	2573/2657	25592

CUTLASS CALAIS SL (FOUR/V-6)

3N	T27	2-dr. Cpe-5P	11895/12605	2538/2622	10350
3N	T69	4-dr. Sed-5P	11995/12705	2597/2681	9443

CUTLASS CALAIS INTERNATIONAL SERIES (FOUR)

3N	K27	2-dr. Cpe-5P	14395	2740	3345
3N	K69	4-dr. Sed-5P	14495	2804	1590

CUTLASS CIERA (FOUR/V-6)

Model Number	Body/Style Number	Body Type & Seating	Factory Price	Shipping Weight	Production Total
3A	J37	2-dr. Cpe-6P	11695/12305	2736/2819	7221
3A	J69	4-dr. Sed-6P	12195/12805	2764/2847	140264
3A	J35	4-dr. Sta Wag-6P	12995/13605	2913/2984	12368

CUTLASS CIERA SL (FOUR/V-6)

3A	M37	2-dr. Cpe-6P	12695/13305	2767/2848	2548
3A	M69	4-dr. Sed-6P	13495/14105	2791/2872	65725
3A	M35	4-dr. Sta Wag-6P	13995/14605	2938/3009	4431

CUTLASS CIERA INTERNATIONAL SERIES (V-6)

3A	S37	2-dr. Cpe-6P	15995	N/A	1913
3A	S69	4-dr. Sed-6P	16795	N/A	5132

CUTLASS SUPREME (V-6)

Model Number	Body/Style Number	Body Type & Seating	Factory Price	Shipping Weight	Production Total
3W	H47	2-dr. Cpe-6P	14295	3119	49895

CUTLASS SUPREME SL (V-6)

3W	S47	2-dr. Cpe-6P	15195	N/A	32015

CUTLASS SUPREME INTERNATIONAL SERIES (V-6)

3W	R47	2-dr. Cpe-6P	16995	N/A	18116

EIGHTY-EIGHT ROYALE (V-6)

Model Number	Body/Style Number	Body Type & Seating	Factory Price	Shipping Weight	Production Total
3H	N37	2-dr. Cpe-6P	15195	3219	1927
3H	N69	4-dr. Sed-6P	15295	3264	81512

EIGHTY-EIGHT ROYALE BROUGHAM (V-6)

3H	Y37	2-dr. Cpe-6P	16295	3247	3024
3H	Y69	4-dr. Sed-6P	16395	3290	65576

CUSTOM CRUISER (V-8)

Model Number	Body/Style Number	Body Type & Seating	Factory Price	Shipping Weight	Production Total
3B	P35	4-dr. Sta Wag-6P	16795	4221	8929

NINETY-EIGHT REGENCY (V-6)

Model Number	Body/Style Number	Body Type & Seating	Factory Price	Shipping Weight	Production Total
3C	X69	4-dr. Sed-6P	19295	3329	17184

NINETY-EIGHT REGENCY BROUGHAM (V-6)

3C	W69	4-dr. Sed-6P	20495	3353	48726
3C	V69	4-dr. Tour Sed-6P	25995	3501	7193

TORONADO (V-6)

Model Number	Body/Style Number	Body Type & Seating	Factory Price	Shipping Weight	Production Total
3E	Z57	2-dr. Cpe-5P	21995	3361	3734
3E	V57	2-dr. Trofeo-5P	24995	3429	6143

FACTORY PRICE AND WEIGHT NOTE: Cutlass Calais/Ciera prices and weights to left of slash are for four-cylinder engine and to right for V-6.

ENGINE DATA: BASE FOUR (Cutlass Calais): Inline, overhead-valve four-cylinder. Cast iron block and aluminum head. Displacement: 151-cid (2.5 liters). Bore & stroke: 4.00 x 3.00 in. Compression ratio: 8.3:1. Brake horsepower: 110 @ 5200 rpm. Torque: 135 lb. ft. @ 3200 rpm. Five main bearings. Fuel injection. BASE FOUR (Cutlass Calais International Series): Quad 4 inline, 16-valve, dual overhead-cam four-cylinder. Cast iron block and aluminum head. Displacement: 138 cu. in. (2.3 liters). Bore & stroke: 3.62 x 3.35 in. Compression ratio: 9.5:1. Net horsepower: 150 @ 5200 rpm. Torque: 160 lb. ft. @ 4000 rpm. Fuel injected (MFI). OPTIONAL FOUR (Cutlass Calais): same aforementioned 2.3-liter/138-cid Quad 4 with MFI. OPTIONAL FOUR (Cutlass Calais International Series): High Output Quad 4 inline, 16-valve, dual overhead-cam four-cylinder. Cast iron block and aluminum head. Displacement: 2.3 liters. Bore & stroke: 3.62 x 3.35 in. Compression ratio: 10.0:1. Net horsepower: 180 @ 6200. Torque: 160 lb. ft. @ 5200 rpm. Fuel injected (MFI). BASE FOUR (Cutlass Ciera/Cutlass Cruiser): Inline, overhead-valve four-cylinder. Cast iron block and aluminum head. Displacement: 151-cid (2.5 liters). Bore & stroke: 4.00 x 3.00 in. Compression ratio: 8.3:1. Brake horsepower: 98 @ 4800 rpm. Torque: 135 lb. ft. @ 3200 rpm. Five main bearings. Fuel injection. BASE V-6 (Cutlass Ciera International Series): Series 3300 90-degree overhead valve V-6. Displacement: 3.3 liters. Bore & stroke: 3.70 x 3.16 in. Compression ratio: 9.0:1. Brake horsepower: 160 @ 5200 rpm. Torque: 185 lb. ft. @ 3200 rpm. Fuel injection (MFI). OPTIONAL SIX (Cutlass Calais/Cutlass Ciera/Cutlass Cruiser): same aforementioned Series 3300 3.3-liter V-6 with MFI. BASE SIX (Cutlass Supreme - replaced mid-model year by 3.1-liter V-6): 60-degree overhead valve V-6. Displacement: 173

cu. in. (2.8 liters). Bore & stroke: 3.50 x 2.99 in. Compression ratio: 8.9:1. Brake horsepower: 130 @ 4500 rpm. Torque: 170 lb. ft. @ 3600 rpm. Fuel injection (MFI). BASE SIX (Cutlass Supreme - replaced 2.8-liter V-6 mid-model year): 60-degree overhead valve V-6. Displacement: 3.1 liters. Bore & stroke: 3.60 x 3.30 in. Compression ratio: 8.8:1. Brake horsepower: 140 @ 4800 rpm. Torque: 180 lb. ft. @ 3600 rpm. Fuel injection (MFI). OPTIONAL SIX (Cutlass Ciera/Cutlass Cruiser): same aforementioned 2.8-liter V-6 with MFI. BASE SIX (Eighty-Eight/Ninety-Eight/Touring Sedan/Toronado/Trofeo): Series 3800 90-degree overhead valve V-6. Displacement: 231 cu. in. (3.8 liters). Bore & stroke: 3.80 x 3.40 in. Compression ratio: 8.5:1. Brake horsepower: 165 @ 4800 rpm. Torque: 210 lb. ft. @ 2000 rpm. Fuel injected (SFI). BASE V-8 (Custom Cruiser): 90-degree overhead valve V-8. Cast iron block and head. Displacement: 307 cu. in. (5.0 liters). Bore & stroke: 3.80 x 3.39 in. Compression ratio: 8.0:1. Net horsepower: 140 @ 3200 rpm. Torque: 255 lb. ft. @ 2000 rpm. 4-bbl. carb.

CHASSIS DATA: Wheelbase: (Calais) 103.4 in.; (Ciera) 104.9 in.; (Cutlass Cruiser) 104.9 in.; (Cutlass Supreme) 107.7 in.; (Eighty-Eight) 110.8 in.; (Custom Cruiser) 115.9 in.; (Ninety-Eight) 110.8 in.; (Touring Sedan) 110.8 in.; (Toronado) 108.0 in.; (Trofeo) 108.0 in. Overall Length: (Calais) 178.8 in.; (Ciera) 190.3 in.; (Cutlass Cruiser) 194.4 in.; (Cutlass Supreme) 192.1 in.; (Eighty-Eight) 196.1 in.; (Custom Cruiser) 220.3 in.; (Ninety-Eight) 196.4 in.; (Touring Sedan) 194.6 in.; (Toronado) 187.5 in.; (Trofeo) 187.5 in. Height: (Calais) 52.4 in.; (Ciera) 54.1 in.; (Cutlass Cruiser) 54.5 in.; (Cutlass Supreme) 52.8 in.; (Eighty-Eight) 54.7 in.; (Custom Cruiser) 58.5 in.; (Ninety-Eight) 55.1 in.; (Touring Sedan) 55.1 in.; (Toronado) 53.0 in.; (Trofeo) 53.0 in. Width: (Calais) 66.7 in.; (Ciera) 69.5 in.; (Cutlass Cruiser) 69.5 in.; (Cutlass Supreme) 71.0 in.; (Eighty-Eight) 72.4 in.; (Custom Cruiser) 79.8 in.; (Ninety-Eight) 72.4 in.; (Touring Sedan) 72.4 in.; (Toronado) 70.8 in.; (Trofeo) 70.8 in. Front tread: (Calais) 55.6 in.; (Ciera) 58.7 in.; (Cutlass Cruiser) 58.7 in.; (Cutlass Supreme) 59.5 in.; (Eighty-Eight) 60.3 in.; (Custom Cruiser) 62.1 in.; (Ninety-Eight) 60.3 in.; (Touring Sedan) 60.3 in.; (Toronado) 60.0 in.; (Trofeo) 60.0 in. Rear tread: (Calais) 55.2 in.; (Ciera) 57.0 in.; (Cutlass Cruiser) 57.0 in.; (Cutlass Supreme) 58.0 in.; (Eighty-Eight) 59.8 in.; (Custom Cruiser) 64.1 in.; (Ninety-Eight) 59.8 in.; (Touring Sedan) 59.8 in.; (Toronado) 60.0 in.; (Trofeo) 60.0 in. Standard tires: (Calais) P185/80R13; (Ciera) P185/75R14; (Cutlass Cruiser) P185/75R14; (Cutlass Supreme) P195/75R14; (Cutlass Supreme International Series) P215/60R16; (Eighty-Eight) P205/75R14; (Custom Cruiser) P225/75R15; (Ninety-Eight) P205/75R14; (Touring Sedan) P215/60R16; (Toronado) P205/70R15; (Trofeo) P215/65R15.

TECHNICAL: Transmission: Five-speed manual floor shift standard on Calais. Three-speed automatic available on Calais. Three-speed automatic standard on Cutlass Ciera/Cutlass Cruiser. Four-speed automatic available on Cutlass Ciera/Cutlass Cruiser. Four-speed automatic standard on Cutlass Supreme and Cutlass Supreme SL/Eighty-Eight/Custom Cruiser/Ninety-Eight/Touring Sedan/Toronado/Trofeo. Five-speed manual floor shift standard on Cutlass Supreme International Series with 2.8-liter V-6 only. Four-speed automatic available on Cutlass Supreme International Series. Standard final drive ratio: (Calais) 3.35:1 with five-speed manual trans.; (Cutlass Ciera) 2.84:1 with three-speed automatic trans., (Cutlass Cruiser) 2.84:1; (Cutlass Supreme) 3.33 with four-speed automatic trans.; (Eighty-Eight/Ninety-Eight/Touring Sedan/Toronado/Trofeo) 2.84:1 with four-speed automatic trans.; (Custom Cruiser) 2.93:1 with four-speed automatic trans. Steering: (all except Custom Cruiser) power assisted rack and pinion; (Custom Cruiser) power assisted recirculating ball. Front Suspension: (Calais/Ciera/Cutlass Cruiser/Cutlass Supreme/Eighty-Eight/Ninety-Eight/Touring Sedan/Toronado/Trofeo) Independent, MacPherson strut w/ coil springs and anti-roll bar; (Custom Cruiser) Independent, unequal length control arms, coil springs, anti-roll bar. Rear Suspension: (Calais) Independent, trailing crank arm

w/ twist beam and coil springs; (Ciera) Twist beam integral w/ two trailing arms, coil springs, Panhard rod, anti-roll bar; (Cutlass Cruiser) Twist beam integral w/ two trailing arms, coil springs, track bar; (Cutlass Supreme) Independent, tri-link strut location, transverse leaf spring, anti-roll bar; (Eighty-Eight/Ninety-Eight) Independent, MacPherson strut, coil springs, anti-roll bar with FE2 and FE3 suspension options; (Touring Sedan) Independent, MacPherson strut, coil springs, anti-roll bar with FE3 suspension; (Custom Cruiser) Rigid axle, four locating links, coil springs; (Toronado/Trofeo) Independent, MacPherson strut, transverse leaf spring, optional anti-roll bar. Brakes: (all except Cutlass Supreme/Toronado/Trofeo) power assisted front disc, rear drum - anti-lock optional on Eighty-Eight/Ninety-Eight and standard on Touring Sedan; (Cutlass Supreme/Toronado/Trofeo) power assisted four-wheel disc, anti-lock optional on Cutlass Supreme/Toronado and standard on Trofeo. Body Construction: (all except Custom Cruiser) unibody; (Custom Cruiser) separate body and frame. Fuel tank: (Calais) 13.6 gal.; (Ciera) 15.7 gal.; (Cutlass Cruiser) 15.7 gal.; (Cutlass Supreme) 16.6 gal.; (Eighty-Eight/Ninety-Eight/Touring Sedan) 18.0 gal.; (Custom Cruiser) 22.0 gal.; (Toronado/Trofeo) 18.8 gal.

DRIVETRAIN OPTIONS: (Calais) Quad 4 2.3-liter four-cylinder ($660); Series 3300 3.3-liter V-6 ($710). (Ciera) 2.8-liter V-6 ($610); Series 3300 3.3-liter V-6 ($710). (Cutlass Cruiser) 2.8-liter V-6 ($610); Series 3300 3.3-liter V-6 ($710). Transmission/Differential: (Calais) three-speed automatic ($515 except base model at $405); column shift ($110 credit). (Ciera) four-speed automatic w/ overdrive ($200). (Cutlass Cruiser) four-speed automatic w/ overdrive ($200). (Custom Cruiser) Limited Slip Differential ($100). Suspension: (Calais) FE3 touring car ride and handling package ($447-$541). (Ciera) FE3 touring car ride and handling package ($505). (Cutlass Cruiser) FE2 firm ride and handling package ($30). (Cutlass Supreme) FE3 touring car ride and handling package ($284-$549). (Eighty-Eight) FE3 touring car ride and handling package ($779); FE2 firm ride and handling package ($271). (Ninety-Eight) FE3 touring car ride and handling package ($146-$339). (Toronado) FE3 touring car ride and handling package ($126). (Cutlass Supreme/Eighty-Eight/Ninety-Eight) anti-lock brakes ($925). (Ciera/Cutlass Cruiser/Eighty-Eight/Ninety-Eight/Toronado/Trofeo) high-capacity cooling ($40-$70). (Custom Cruiser) Trailering package ($96). (Custom Cruiser) automatic leveling system ($175). (All) California emission equipment ($100). Engine block heater ($18).

OPTION PACKAGES: (Calais S) Quad 4 appearance package ($1180).

MAJOR CONVENIENCE/APPEARANCE OPTIONS: Driver Information System ($150). Driver's side airbag ($850). Power door locks ($150 - $205). Body accent stripe ($45). Full vinyl roof ($260). Electric Sliding Glass Astroroof ($925 - $1230). Electric rear window defogger ($150). Cruise control ($185). Mobile telephone ($1795).

HISTORY: Calendar year production (U.S.) 520,981. Calendar year sales by U.S. dealers: 600,037. Model year sales by U.S. dealers: 653,127.

Historical Footnotes: A third in-a-row lackluster sales year with total units moved for model year 1989 amounting to 653,127 (8.8 percent market share). This was a six percent drop from the year before.

1990

Following another year of subpar sales performance, Oldsmobile revamped the way it did business by introducing "The Oldsmobile Edge" for 1990 as well as offering more new products than ever before launched in a single model year. The "Edge" program was the most comprehensive customer satisfaction program in General Motors history, and included a 30-day/1,500-

mile return policy for any customer not satisfied with his/her Oldsmobile. New offerings were comprised of the Silhouette minivan, High Output Quad 442 Cutlass Calais, a line of Cutlass Supreme sedans as well as a mid-model year addition of a sport sedan and convertible, and completely redesigned Toronado and Trofeo models.

1990 Oldsmobile, Cutlass Calais SL sedan, (O)

1990 Oldsmobile, Cutlass Calais International Series sedan, (O)

1990 Oldsmobile, Cutlass Calais International Series coupe, (O)

CUTLASS CALAIS -- SERIES 3N -- FOUR/V-6 -- Again Oldsmobile's most compact offering, the Calais lineup for 1990 remained intact from the year before with coupe and sedan versions offered in base, S, SL and International Series trim. A Quad 442 Sport Performance Package was offered on the Calais S coupe. The Quad 442 featured the 2.3-liter High Output Quad 4 mated to a five-speed manual transaxle, FE3 touring suspension, full instrumentation and aluminum wheels. Across the lineup, new seat de-

1990 Oldsmobile, Cutlass Calais Quad 4-4-2 coupe, (O)

1990 Oldsmobile, Cutlass Ciera SL sedan, (O)

signs and interior fabrics were featured. Optional equipment included a compact disc player on all but the base Calais models. Standard powertrain for the Calais and Calais S was the 2.5-liter four-cylinder coupled to a five-speed manual transaxle. In addition to the Quad 442, the Calais International Series used the High Output Quad 4 engine with five-speed manual transaxle as its standard powertrain. Calais SL featured the Quad 4 engine coupled to a three-speed automatic as standard, which was optional in the Calais S and Calais International Series models. Available in the Calais SL was the Series 3300 3.3-liter V-6.

1990 Oldsmobile, Cutlass Ciera International Series sedan, (O)

CUTLASS CIERA -- SERIES 3A -- FOUR/V-6 -- Oldsmobile extensively revised its Cutlass Ciera lineup, adding an S coupe and sedan while dropping its base coupe and SL coupe. The 1990 Ciera lineup consisted of a base sedan, S coupe and sedan, SL sedan and International Series coupe and sedan. The Ciera-based Cutlass Cruiser station wagon lineup was also changed with the base two-seater from the year before now called the Cruiser S in addition to the returning Cruiser SL three-seat wagon. New front shock absorbers offered an improved ride to the Ciera lineup. Engine selection was also simplified with the 2.5-liter four-cylinder engine, rated at a higher 110 horsepower due to intake and exhaust port revisions and more aggressive valve timing, standard in the base sedan, S models and Cutlass Cruiser S. Standard engine in the SL sedan, Cruiser SL and International Series models was the Series 3300 3.3-liter V-6, which was optional in the base sedan, S models and Cutlass Cruiser S.

1990 Oldsmobile, Cutlass Supreme SL sedan, (O)

197

1990 Oldsmobile, Cutlass Supreme convertible, (O)

1990 Oldsmobile, Eighty-Eight Royale Brougham sedan, (O)

CUTLASS SUPREME -- SERIES 3W -- V-6 -- The Cutlass Supreme lineup for 1990 was bolstered by the addition of three sedan models and a convertible. Offerings consisted of both coupe and sedan versions in base, SL and International Series trim as well as a mid-model year introduction of a convertible. The Cutlass Supreme sedan featured a distinct wraparound rear window design. Bucket seats were new, standard components of the base models and optional in the SL models. A split, fold-down backrest for easy access to the trunk compartment was a feature in SL and International Series Cutlass Supremes. New shock absorbers reduced impact harshness and increased rear suspension travel in both the standard and FE3 suspensions. The convertible featured a structural top bar that enhanced body integrity and reduced vibration noise as well as an electrically-operated power top with a full headliner. The convertible's interior trim was common with the SL. Its front and rear fascias and rocker panel details were shared with the Cutlass Supreme International Series models. Standard equipment included air conditioning. Standard powertrain for the base Cutlass Supreme and International Series was the 2.3-liter, 180-hp High Output Quad 4 four-cylinder engine mated to a five-speed manual transaxle. The 160-hp version of the 2.3-liter Quad 4 coupled to a three-speed automatic was optional in the base model. The 3.1-liter V-6 mated to a four-speed automatic transaxle was standard in the Cutlass Supreme SL and convertible and was available in other models.

EIGHTY-EIGHT ROYALE -- SERIES 3H -- V-6 -- Oldsmobile's 1990 Eighty-Eight Royale family coupe and sedan model lineup continued unchanged from the previous year with base and Brougham levels again offered. The Eighty-Eight's body structure was improved by stiffening key joints and engine compartment rail sections for enhanced ride quality. Design improvements included restyled grilles, headlamp bezels, taillamps, front and rear fascias and side moldings for a cleaner appearance. Inside, up-level seats and new fabrics were featured. Optional equipment included remote-activated keyless entry, driver's side airbag, anti-lock brakes and 15-inch cast aluminum wheels. Standard powertrain for all Eighty-Eight models was the Series 3800 3.8-liter V-6 mated to a four-speed automatic transaxle.

1990 Oldsmobile, Eighty-Eight Royale coupe, (O)

1990 Oldsmobile, Cutlass Supreme International Series sedan, (O)

1990 Oldsmobile, Custom Cruiser station wagon, (O)

1990 Oldsmobile, Cutlass Supreme International Series coupe, (O)

1990 Oldsmobile, Cutlass Cruiser SL station wagon, (O)

CUSTOM CRUISER -- SERIES 3B -- V-8 -- Entering its third decade of production, Oldsmobile kept things pretty much unchanged for the Custom Cruiser station wagon. New features for Oldsmobile's lone rear-drive V-8-powered offering amounted to new interior and exterior color selections, door-mounted passive seat belts for outboard front seat passengers, and an aluminum wheel option. The stalwart Custom Cruiser's standard powertrain was again the 5.0-liter V-8 linked to a four-speed automatic transmission.

1990 Oldsmobile, Silhouette minivan, (O)

SILHOUETTE -- SERIES 3U -- V-6 -- Based on GM's GMT200 composite all-purpose van, Oldsmobile's new-for-1990 Silhouette was the upscale version of both Pontiac's Trans Sport and Chevrolet's Lumina minivans. The Silhouette featured a plastic body and steeply laid back windshield that swept uninterrupted from front bumper to trailing edge of roof, providing an exceptionally low 0.30 coefficient of drag. Offered in both six- or seven-seat configurations, with the two rear rows of modular seats removed the cargo capacity was 112.6 cubic feet. Standard equipment included electrically controlled air conditioning, power steering and brakes, 14-inch aluminum wheels, tinted glass, tilt steering wheel and analog gauge instrument cluster that included a tachometer. Optional was the FE3 touring suspension including 15-inch aluminum wheels, with electronic level control. Standard powertrain for the Silhouette was the 3.1-liter V-6 engine mated to a three-speed automatic transaxle.

1990 Oldsmobile, Ninety-Eight Regency sedan, (O)

NINETY-EIGHT REGENCY -- SERIES 3C -- V-6 -- The sedan-only lineup continued for the luxury Ninety-Eight in 1990 with base and Brougham models as well as the Touring Sedan that was based on the Ninety-Eight. Minor refinements for all the sedans included improved body structure from increased beam stiffness and reinforced joints. The Ninety-Eight models also received a revised steering gear to improve on-center steering feel. The Touring Sedan received acoustic materials in the roof, trunk floor and rear seat areas to reduce interior noise as well as a switch to Goodyear GA touring tires. Front and rear headrests on the Touring Sedan were made smaller, and remote keyless entry was standard. All sedans offered the driver's window auto-down feature as standard equipment. Optional equipment on the Ninety-Eight models included remote controlled power door locks, driver's side airbag and anti-lock brakes. Standard powertrain for the Ninety-Eight and Touring Sedan models was the Series 3800 3.8-liter V-6 coupled to a four-speed automatic transaxle.

1990 Oldsmobile, Touring Sedan, (O)

TORONADO -- SERIES 3E -- V-6 -- In 1990, Toronado and Trofeo models wore all new sheet metal (except for their hoods) and featured a sleek exterior profile that was 12.4 inches longer than the previous year's offering. Both received a new interior design while their trunk volume increased by 2.5 cubic feet. The Toronado's and Trofeo's sweeping exterior was highlighted by grooved lower moldings, more integrated bumpers, hidden headlamps and one-piece taillamps. Inside, standard equipment included a driver's side airbag and full analog instruments (in the Toronado with bucket seats and a floor shifter; digital electronic instruments are fitted to Toronados equipped with the optional 55/45 split bench front seat). Toronado featured an advanced chassis design with fully independent suspension, four-wheel disc brakes, automatic leveling and 15-inch cast aluminum wheels. To distinguish itself from the Toronado, the Trofeo featured aggressive ground effects and 16-inch aluminum wheels with 65 series high-performance tires. Standard were the FE3 touring suspension and anti-lock four-wheel disc brakes. Inside, the Trofeo featured new, power-adjustable leather bucket seats. Options included Oldsmobile's unique color Visual Information Center and mobile telephone. Standard powertrain for both the Toronado and Trofeo was the Series 3800 3.8-liter V-6 mated to a four-speed automatic transaxle.

1990 Oldsmobile, Toronado Trofeo coupe, (O)

I.D. DATA: Oldsmobile's 17-symbol Vehicle Identification Number (VIN) again was located on the upper left surface of the instrument panel, visible through the windshield. The first three characters (1G3) indicates Oldsmobile Division. The fourth and fifth letters designate the body type/series: A/J - Cutlass Ciera S and Cutlass Cruiser, A/L - Cutlass Ciera, A/M - Cutlass Ciera SL and Cutlass Cruiser SL, A/S - Cutlass Ciera International Series, B/P - Custom Cruiser, C/V - Touring Sedan, C/W - Ninety-Eight Regency Brougham, C/X - Ninety-Eight Regency, E/V - Toronado Trofeo, E/Z - Toronado, H/N - Eighty-Eight Royale, H/Y - Eighty-Eight Royale Brougham, N/F - Cutlass Calais S, N/K - Cutlass Calais International Series, N/L - Cutlass Calais, N/T - Cutlass Calais SL, W/H - Cutlass Supreme, W/R - Cutlass Supreme International Series, W/S - Cutlass Supreme SL, U/M - Silhouette, W/T - Cutlass Supreme Convertible. The sixth number identifies the body style: 1 - 2-dr coupe/sedan, 2 - 2-dr hatchback/lift-

back, 3 - 2-dr convertible, 4 - 2-dr station wagon, 5 - 4-dr sedan, 6 - 4-dr hatchback/liftback, 7 - 4-dr liftback, 8 - 4-dr station wagon. The seventh number identifies the restraint code: 1 - manual belts, 3 - manual belts with driver's side airbag, 4 - automatic belts. The eighth letter identifies the engine: A = 2.3-liter fuel-injected inline four-cylinder, C = 3.8-liter fuel-injected V-6, D = 2.3-liter fuel-injected inline four-cylinder, N = 3.3-liter fuel-injected V-6, R = 2.5-liter fuel-injected inline four-cylinder, T = 3.1-liter fuel-injected V-6, U = 2.5-liter fuel-injected inline four-cylinder, Y = 5.0-liter 4-bbl carbureted V-8. The ninth number is the check digit. The tenth letter represents the model year (L = 1990). The eleventh character identifies the assembly plant: D - Doraville, Ga.; H - Flint, Mich.; M - Lansing, Mich.; T - Tarrytown, N.Y.; U - Hamtramck, Mich.; 1 - Wentzville, Mo.; 4 - Orion, Mich.; 6 - Oklahoma City, Okla.; (Canada) 2 - Ste. Therese, Quebec . The final six digits are the sequential serial number.

CUTLASS CALAIS (FOUR)

Model Number	Body/Style Number	Body Type & Seating	Factory Price	Shipping Weight	Production Total
3N	L27	2-dr. Cpe-5P	9995	2518	15846
3N	L69	4-dr. Sed-5P	9995	2585	41018

CUTLASS CALAIS S (FOUR)

| 3N | F27 | 2-dr. Cpe-5P | 10895 | 2518 | 12839 |
| 3N | F69 | 4-dr. Sed-5P | 10995 | 2585 | 12207 |

CUTLASS CALAIS SL (FOUR/V-6)

| 3N | T27 | 2-dr. Cpe-5P | 13195/13245 | 2691/2746 | 2503 |
| 3N | T69 | 4-dr. Sed-5P | 13295/13345 | 2754/2809 | 3971 |

CUTLASS CALAIS INTERNATIONAL SERIES (FOUR)

| 3N | K27 | 2-dr. Cpe-5P | 14895 | 2823 | 1454 |
| 3N | K69 | 4-dr. Sed-5P | 14995 | 2896 | 877 |

CUTLASS CIERA (FOUR/V-6)

Model Number	Body/Style Number	Body Type & Seating	Factory Price	Shipping Weight	Production Total
3A	L69	4-dr. Sed-6P	11995/12705	2733/2837	46933

CUTLASS CIERA S (FOUR/V-6)

3A	J37	2-dr. Cpe-6P	12395/13105	2785/2889	2203
3A	J69	4-dr. Sed-6P	12995/13705	2821/2925	54549
3A	J35	4-dr. Sta Wag-6P	13395/14105	2990/3087	3321

CUTLASS CIERA SL (V-6)

| 3A | M69 | 4-dr. Sed-6P | 14695 | 2966 | 33229 |
| 3A | M35 | 4-dr. Sta Wag-6P | 15295 | 3156 | 5576 |

CUTLASS CIERA INTERNATIONAL SERIES (V-6)

| 3A | S37 | 2-dr. Cpe-6P | 15995 | 2988 | 411 |
| 3A | S69 | 4-dr. Sed-6P | 16795 | 3024 | 959 |

CUTLASS SUPREME (FOUR/V-6 - Convertible V-6 only)

Model Number	Body/Style Number	Body Type & Seating	Factory Price	Shipping Weight	Production Total
3W	H47	2-dr. Cpe-6P	14495/14995	3153/3208	15848
3W	H69	4-dr. Sed-6P	14595/15095	3244/3299	47043
3W	T67	2-dr. Conv-6P	------/20995	------/3485	494

CUTLASS SUPREME SL (V-6)

| 3W | S47 | 2-dr. Cpe-6P | 16095 | 3270 | 10076 |
| 3W | S69 | 4-dr. Sed-6P | 16195 | 3355 | 32798 |

CUTLASS SUPREME INTERNATIONAL SERIES (FOUR/V-6)

| 3W | R47 | 2-dr. Cpe-6P | 17995/18495 | 3277/3277 | 5602 |
| 3W | R69 | 4-dr. Sed-6P | 17995/18495 | 3350/3350 | 7474 |

EIGHTY-EIGHT ROYALE (V-6)

Model Number	Body/Style Number	Body Type & Seating	Factory Price	Shipping Weight	Production Total
3H	N37	2-dr. Cpe-6P	15895	3234	1127
3H	N69	4-dr. Sed-6P	15995	3283	65800

EIGHTY-EIGHT ROYALE BROUGHAM (V-6)

| 3H | Y37 | 2-dr. Cpe-6P | 17295 | 3263 | 1585 |
| 3H | Y69 | 4-dr. Sed-6P | 17395 | 3308 | 48311 |

CUSTOM CRUISER (V-8)

Model Number	Body/Style Number	Body Type & Seating	Factory Price	Shipping Weight	Production Total
3B	P35	4-dr. Sta Wag-6P	17595	4327	3890

SILHOUETTE (V-6)

Model Number	Body/Style Number	Body Type & Seating	Factory Price	Shipping Weight	Production Total
3U	M06	3-dr. Minivan-7P	17195	3648	28109

NINETY-EIGHT REGENCY (V-6)

Model Number	Body/Style Number	Body Type & Seating	Factory Price	Shipping Weight	Production Total
3C	X69	4-dr. Sed-6P	19995	3325	17914

NINETY-EIGHT REGENCY BROUGHAM (V-6)

| 3C | W69 | 4-dr. Sed-6P | 21595 | 3369 | 38915 |
| 3C | V69 | 4-dr. Tour Sed-6P | 26795 | 3497 | 5566 |

TORONADO (V-6)

Model Number	Body/Style Number	Body Type & Seating	Factory Price	Shipping Weight	Production Total
3E	Z57	2-dr. Cpe-5P	21995	3464	5596
3E	V57	2-dr. Trofeo-5P	24995	3559	9426

FACTORY PRICE AND WEIGHT NOTE: Beginning with the Cutlass Calais SL, prices and weights to left of slash are for four-cylinder engine and to right for V-6.

ENGINE DATA: BASE FOUR (Cutlass Calais and Calais S): Inline, overhead-valve four-cylinder. Cast iron block and aluminum head. Displacement: 151 cu. in. (2.5 liters). Bore & stroke: 4.10 x 3.00 in. Compression ratio: 8.3:1. Net horsepower: 110 @ 5200 rpm. Torque: 135 lb. ft. @ 3200 rpm. Five main bearings. Fuel injection. BASE FOUR (Cutlass Calais Quad 442/Calais International Series): High Output Quad 4 inline, 16-valve, dual overhead-cam four-cylinder. Cast iron block and aluminum head. Displacement: 140 cu. in. (2.3 liters). Bore & stroke: 3.62 x 3.35 in. Compression ratio: 10.0:1. Net horsepower: 180 @ 6200 rpm. Torque: 160 lb. ft. @ 5200 rpm. Fuel injected (MFI). BASE FOUR (Cutlass Calais SL): Quad 4 inline, 16-valve, dual overhead-cam four-cylinder. Cast iron block and aluminum head. Displacement: 138 cu. in. (2.3 liters). Bore & stroke: 3.62 x 3.35 in. Compression ratio: 9.5:1. Net horsepower: 160 @ 6200 rpm. Torque: 155 lb. ft. @ 5200 rpm. Fuel injected (MFI). OPTIONAL FOUR (Cutlass Calais S and International Series): same aforementioned 2.3-liter/138-cid Quad 4 with MFI. BASE FOUR (Cutlass Ciera/Ciera S/Cutlass Cruiser S): Inline, overhead-valve four-cylinder. Cast iron block and aluminum head. Displacement: 151 cu. in. (2.5 liters). Bore & stroke: 4.10 x 3.00 in. Compression ratio: 8.3:1. Net horsepower: 110 @ 5200 rpm. Torque: 135 lb. ft. @ 3200 rpm. Five main bearings. Fuel injection. BASE V-6 (Cutlass Ciera SL/Ciera International Series): Series 3300 90-degree overhead valve V-6. Displacement: 204 cu. in. (3.3 liters). Bore & stroke: 3.70 x 3.16 in. Compression ratio: 9.0:1. Net horsepower: 160 @ 5200 rpm. Torque: 185 lb. ft. @ 2000 rpm. Fuel injection (MFI). OPTIONAL SIX (Cutlass Calais SL/Cutlass Ciera/Ciera S/Cutlass Cruiser S): same aforementioned Series 3300 3.3-liter/204-cid V-6 with MFI. BASE FOUR (Cutlass Supreme/Cutlass Supreme International Series): same aforementioned High Output Quad 4 2.3-liter/140-cid four-cylinder with MFI. BASE SIX (Cutlass Supreme Convertible/Cutlass Supreme SL): 60-degree overhead valve V-6. Displacement: 189 cu. in. (3.1 liters). Bore & stroke: 3.60 x 3.30 in. Compression ratio: 8.8:1. Net horsepower: 135 @ 4400 rpm. Torque: 180 lb. ft. @ 3600 rpm. Fuel injection (MFI). OPTIONAL FOUR (Cutlass Supreme): same aforementioned Quad 4 2.3-liter/138-cid four-cylinder with MFI. OPTIONAL SIX (Cutlass Supreme/Cutlass Supreme International Series): same aforementioned 3.1-liter/189-cid V-6 with MFI. BASE SIX (Eighty-Eight/Ninety-Eight/Touring Sedan/Toronado/Trofeo): Series 3800 90-degree overhead valve V-6. Displacement: 231 cu. in. (3.8 liters). Bore &

stroke: 3.80 x 3.40 in. Compression ratio: 8.5:1. Net horsepower: 165 @ 4800 rpm. Torque: 210 lb. ft. @ 2000 rpm. Fuel injected (SFI). BASE SIX (Silhouette): same aforementioned 3.1-liter/189-cid V-6 with MFI. BASE V-8 (Custom Cruiser): 90-degree overhead valve V-8. Cast iron block and head. Displacement: 307 cu. in. (5.0 liters). Bore & stroke: 3.80 x 3.39 in. Compression ratio: 8.0:1. Net horsepower: 140 @ 3200 rpm. Torque: 255 lb. ft. @ 2000 rpm. 4-bbl. carb.

CHASSIS DATA: Wheelbase: (Calais) 103.4 in.; (Ciera) 104.9 in.; (Cutlass Cruiser) 104.9 in.; (Cutlass Supreme) 107.5 in.; (Eighty-Eight) 110.8 in.; (Custom Cruiser) 116.0 in.; (Silhouette) 109.8 in.; (Ninety-Eight) 110.8 in.; (Touring Sedan) 110.8 in.; (Toronado) 108.0 in.; (Trofeo) 108.0 in. Overall Length: (Calais) 178.8 in.; (Ciera) 193.2 in.; (Cutlass Cruiser) 194.4 in.; (Cutlass Supreme Coupe and Convertible) 192.3 in.; (Cutlass Supreme Sedan) 192.2 in.; (Eighty-Eight) 196.3 in.; (Custom Cruiser) 220.0 in.; (Silhouette) 194.2 in.; (Ninety-Eight) 196.3 in.; (Touring Sedan) 196.3 in.; (Toronado) 200.3 in.; (Trofeo) 200.3 in. Height: (Calais) 52.4 in.; (Ciera) 54.1 in.; (Cutlass Cruiser) 54.5 in.; (Cutlass Supreme Coupe) 53.3 in.; (Cutlass Supreme Sedan) 54.8 in.; (Cutlass Supreme Convertible) 54.3 in.; (Eighty-Eight Coupe) 53.9 in.; (Eighty-Eight Sedan) 54.5 in.; (Custom Cruiser) 58.5 in.; (Silhouette) 65.2 in.; (Ninety-Eight) 54.8 in.; (Touring Sedan) 54.8 in.; (Toronado) 53.0 in.; (Trofeo) 53.0 in. Width: (Calais) 66.6 in.; (Ciera) 69.5 in.; (Cutlass Cruiser) 69.5 in.; (Cutlass Supreme) 71.0 in.; (Eighty-Eight) 72.6 in.; (Custom Cruiser) 79.8 in.; (Silhouette) 73.9 in.; (Ninety-Eight) 72.6 in.; (Touring Sedan) 72.6 in.; (Toronado) 72.8 in.; (Trofeo) 72.8 in. Front tread: (Calais) 55.8 in.; (Ciera) 58.7 in.; (Cutlass Cruiser) 58.7 in.; (Cutlass Supreme) 59.5 in.; (Eighty-Eight) 60.3 in.; (Custom Cruiser) 62.1 in.; (Silhouette) 59.2 in.; (Ninety-Eight) 60.3 in.; (Touring Sedan) 60.3 in.; (Toronado) 59.9 in.; (Trofeo) 59.9 in. Rear tread: (Calais) 55.2 in.; (Ciera) 57.0 in.; (Cutlass Cruiser) 57.0 in.; (Cutlass Supreme) 58.0 in.; (Eighty-Eight) 59.8 in.; (Custom Cruiser) 64.1 in.; (Silhouette) 61.4 in.; (Ninety-Eight) 59.8 in.; (Touring Sedan) 59.8 in.; (Toronado) 59.9 in.; (Trofeo) 59.9 in. Standard tires: (Calais) P185/80R13; (Ciera) P185/75R14; (Cutlass Cruiser) P185/75R14; (Cutlass Supreme) P195/75R14; (Cutlass Supreme Convertible) P215/65R15; (Eighty-Eight) P205/75R14; (Custom Cruiser) P225/75R15; (Silhouette) P205/70R14; (Ninety-Eight) P205/75R14; (Touring Sedan) P215/60R16; (Toronado) P205/70R15; (Trofeo) P215/60R16.

TECHNICAL: Transmission: Five-speed manual floor shift standard on all Cutlass Calais models except SL. Three-speed automatic standard on Calais SL, optional on all other Calais models. Three-speed automatic standard on Cutlass Ciera/Cutlass Cruiser/Silhouette. Four-speed automatic available on Cutlass Ciera/Cutlass Cruiser. Five-speed manual floor shift standard on Cutlass Supreme/Cutlass Supreme International Series. Four-speed automatic standard on Cutlass Supreme Convertible/Cutlass Supreme SL/Eighty-Eight/Custom Cruiser/Ninety-Eight/Touring Sedan/Toronado/Trofeo. Three-speed automatic available on Cutlass Supreme. Standard final drive ratio: (Calais) 3.35:1 with five-speed manual trans.; (Cutlass Ciera) 2.84:1 with three-speed automatic trans.; (Cutlass Cruiser) 2.84:1 with three-speed automatic trans.; (Cutlass Supreme) 3.61:1 with five-speed manual trans.; (Cutlass Supreme Convertible) 3.33:1 with four-speed automatic trans.; (Eighty-Eight/Ninety-Eight/Touring Sedan/Toronado/Trofeo) 2.84:1 with four-speed automatic trans.; (Custom Cruiser) 2.93:1 with four-speed automatic trans.; (Silhouette) N/A. Steering: (all except Custom Cruiser) power assisted rack and pinion; (Custom Cruiser) power assisted recirculating ball. Front Suspension: (Calais/Ciera/Cutlass Cruiser/Cutlass Supreme/Eighty-Eight/Ninety-Eight/Touring Sedan/Toronado/Trofeo) Independent, MacPherson strut w/ coil springs and anti-roll bar; (Custom Cruiser) Independent, unequal length control arms, coil springs, anti-roll bar; (Silhouette) MacPherson struts, stamped lower control arms, stabilizer bar. Rear Suspension:

(Calais) Independent, trailing crank arm w/ twist beam and coil springs; (Ciera) Twist beam integral w/ two trailing arms, coil springs, Panhard rod, anti-roll bar; (Cutlass Cruiser) Twist beam integral w/ two trailing arms, coil springs, track bar; (Cutlass Supreme) Independent, tri-link strut location, transverse leaf spring, anti-roll bar; (Eighty-Eight/Ninety-Eight) Independent, MacPherson strut, coil springs, anti-roll bar with FE2 and FE3 suspension options; (Touring Sedan) Independent, MacPherson strut, coil springs, anti-roll bar with FE3 suspension; (Custom Cruiser) Rigid axle, four locating links, coil springs; (Silhouette) open-section transverse beam on stamped steel trailing arms, tube shocks, coil springs, stabilizer bar; (Toronado/Trofeo) Independent, MacPherson strut, transverse leaf spring, optional anti-roll bar. Brakes: (all except Cutlass Supreme/Toronado/Trofeo) power assisted front disc, rear drum - anti-lock optional on Eighty-Eight/Ninety-Eight and standard on Touring Sedan; (Cutlass Supreme/Toronado/Trofeo) power assisted four-wheel disc, anti-lock optional on Cutlass Supreme/Toronado and standard on Trofeo. Body Construction: (all except Custom Cruiser and Silhouette) unibody; (Custom Cruiser) separate body and frame, (Silhouette) space frame substructure attached to ladder frame. Fuel tank: (Calais) 13.6 gal.; (Ciera) 15.7 gal.; (Cutlass Cruiser) 15.7 gal.; (Cutlass Supreme) 16.5 gal.; (Eighty-Eight/Ninety-Eight/Touring Sedan/Toronado) 18.0 gal.; (Custom Cruiser) 22.0 gal.; (Silhouette) 20.0 gal.; (Trofeo) 18.3 gal.

DRIVETRAIN OPTIONS: (Calais S) Quad 4 2.3-liter four-cylinder ($660); (Calais SL) Series 3300 3.3-liter V-6 ($50); (Calais International Series) Quad 4 2.3-liter four-cylinder ($400). (Ciera/Ciera S/Cutlass Cruiser S) Series 3300 3.3-liter V-6 ($710). (Cutlass Supreme) Quad 4 2.3-liter four-cylinder ($325). (Cutlass Supreme/Cutlass Supreme International Series) 3.1-liter V-6 ($500). Transmission/Differential: (Calais/Calais S) three-speed automatic ($540); (Calais) column shift ($110 credit). (Ciera S/Cutlass Cruiser S) four-speed automatic ($200). (Custom Cruiser) Limited Slip Differential ($100). Suspension: (Calais) FE3 touring car ride and handling package ($182-$526). (Ciera) FE3 touring car ride and handling package ($447-$505). (Cutlass Supreme) FE3 touring car ride and handling package ($549). (Eighty-Eight) FE3 touring car ride and handling package ($713-$779). (Silhouette) FE3 touring suspension ($232). (Ninety-Eight) FE3 touring car ride and handling package ($246-$339). (Toronado) FE3 touring car ride and handling package ($126). (Cutlass Supreme/Eighty-Eight/Ninety-Eight) anti-lock brakes ($925). (Ciera/Cutlass Cruiser/Eighty-Eight/Ninety-Eight/Toronado/Trofeo) high-capacity cooling ($40-$125). (Eighty-Eight) Towing package ($271). (Custom Cruiser) Trailering package ($96). (Custom Cruiser) automatic leveling system ($175). (All) California emission equipment ($100). Engine block heater ($18).

OPTION PACKAGES: (Calais S coupe) Quad 442 sport performance package ($1667). (Ciera S) XC special edition package ($489) (Cutlass Cruiser S) XC special edition package ($604). (Cutlass Supreme Convertible) sports package ($1376). (Toronado) two-tone paint scheme ($101).

MAJOR CONVENIENCE/APPEARANCE OPTIONS: Driver Information System ($150). Driver's side airbag ($850). Four-Season air conditioning ($720). Rallye interior ($355). Power door locks ($175-$215). Body accent stripe ($45). Full vinyl roof ($260). Sunroof ($350). Electric Sliding Glass Astroroof ($650 - $1230). Electric rear window defogger ($160). Mobile telephone ($995).

HISTORY: Model year production (U.S.): 580,855. Calendar year production (U.S.) 447,177. Calendar year sales by U.S. dealers: 537,856. Model year sales by U.S. dealers: 524,898.

Historical Footnotes: Due to Oldsmobile's continuing sales and market share slide, General Motors replaced Olds' General Manager William W. Lane with J. Michael Losh, who was brought over from Pontiac. The slide continued with Oldsmobile's market share slipping to 7.9 percent based on model year sales of 524,898 units compared to 8.8/653,127 the previous year.

1991

It was a banner year for anniversaries for Oldsmobile in 1991 with the Ninety-Eight observing its 50th and the Toronado reaching its 25th. It was also a big year for change. Olds joined the ranks of automakers offering "yuppie trucks" with its introduction of the Bravada, a four-door, four-wheel-drive, five-passenger sport utility vehicle. Both the Ninety-Eight and Custom Cruiser underwent massive redesigns, including getting a power boost. The International Series coupe and sedan were both axed from the Cutlass Ciera lineup after dismal sales the year before. Anti-lock brakes became standard equipment on several Oldsmobiles, while both a 4.3-liter V-6 (Bravada) and 3.4-liter twin dual overhead-cam V-6 (Cutlass Supreme International Series) joined the powerplant lineup.

1991 Oldsmobile, Cutlass Ciera SL sedan, (O)

CUTLASS CIERA -- SERIES 3A -- FOUR/V-6 -- With the aforementioned dropping of the Cutlass Ciera International Series, that model's 1991 lineup consisted of a base sedan, S coupe and sedan, SL sedan and Ciera-based Cutlass Cruiser station wagons in S and SL trim. New features included a revised full body acoustics package and an instrument panel cluster with trip odometer and temperature gauge. The Tech IV 2.5-liter four-cylinder engine coupled to a three-speed automatic transaxle was the standard powertrain on the Ciera sedan, S models and Cruiser S. The SL sedan and Cruiser SL featured the Series 3300 3.3-liter V-6 that came with a three-speed automatic transaxle.

1991 Oldsmobile, Cutlass Calais coupe, (O)

1991 Oldsmobile, Cutlass Calais International Series sedan, (O)

CUTLASS CALAIS -- SERIES 3N -- FOUR/V-6 -- Termed Oldsmobile's most affordable car, the Cutlass Calais was again Oldsmobile's most compact offering, also. The Calais lineup for 1991 continued from the year before with coupe and sedan versions offered in base, S, SL and International Series trim. Larger brakes were offered across the lineup. A Quad 442 Sport Performance Package, including the 2.3-liter High Output Quad 4 engine coupled to a five-speed manual transaxle, was again offered on the Calais S coupe. Anti-lock brakes were standard in the Calais International Series as was the High Output Quad 4 2.3-liter dual overhead-cam four-cylinder engine with a five-speed manual transaxle. Standard powertrain for the Calais and Calais S models was the Tech IV 2.5-liter four-cylinder engine mated to a five-speed manual transaxle. Calais SL models came standard with the Quad 4 2.3-liter dual overhead-cam four-cylinder engine coupled to a three-speed automatic transaxle.

1991 Oldsmobile, Cutlass Cruiser SL station wagon, (O)

1991 Oldsmobile, Cutlass Supreme SL sedan, (O)

1991 Oldsmobile, Cutlass Supreme convertible, (O)

CUTLASS SUPREME -- SERIES 3W -- V-6 -- Oldsmobile's Cutlass Supreme for 1991 was again offered in coupe and sedan versions in base, SL and International Series trim as well as a convertible, which was introduced mid-model year the year before. Across the lineup, a noise reduction package was introduced. Cutlass Supreme sedans featured lower shoulder belt anchors. The Cutlass Supreme International Series offered as standard powertrain a new 3.4-liter, twin dual overhead-cam V-6 engine coupled to an electronically controlled four-speed Turbo-Hydra-matic transaxle on the I Series sedan and five-speed

1991 Oldsmobile, Cutlass Calais International Series coupe, (O)

manual transaxle on the I Series coupe. The Cutlass Supreme offered as standard powertrain the 2.3-liter Quad 4 dual overhead-cam engine mated to a three-speed automatic transaxle, while the convertible and Cutlass Supreme SL models featured a 3.1-liter V-6 and four-speed automatic transaxle.

1991 Oldsmobile, Cutlass Supreme International Series coupe, (O)

1991 Oldsmobile, Eighty-Eight Royale Brougham sedan, (O)

EIGHTY-EIGHT ROYALE -- SERIES 3H -- V-6 -- The Eighty-Eight Royale lineup for 1991 was again the base and Brougham level coupes and sedans offered the year previous. Minor structural enhancements were a new feature as was a shift interlock feature, reclining driver's side seat back (with 55/45 divided bench seat) and pulse wipers and tilt steering being added to the standard equipment list. The Series 3800 3.8-liter V-6 with four-speed automatic transaxle remained the standard powertrain across the lineup.

1991 Oldsmobile, Custom Cruiser station wagon, (O)

CUSTOM CRUISER -- SERIES 3B -- V-8 -- Oldsmobile's veteran V-8-powered, rear-drive offering was totally revised for 1991. While it remained in the rear-drive configuration, the redesign changed just about every other aspect of this three-seat station wagon. The new bullet-shaped sheet metal featured a vista roof and flush-mounted glass. Composite halogen headlamps lit the Custom Cruiser's way. Gas struts aided the opening of the hood. Anti-lock brakes were standard equipment. Even the long-standard 5.0-liter V-8 engine received new electronic throttle body injection and put out 170 hp, a 30-hp increase over the previous year.

SILHOUETTE -- SERIES 3U -- V-6 -- In only its sophomore year, Oldsmobile's minivan received extensive improvements for 1991. Among the new features were brake system improvements, a stainless steel exhaust system, standard outside power mirrors, rear heating and air conditioning unit, a lock delay feature on the sliding door with optional power locks, and an overhead console with compass, outside thermometer, maplights and storage compartments. As in its debut year, the Silhouette's standard powertrain was the 3.1-liter V-6 engine mated to a three-speed automatic transaxle.

1991 Oldsmobile, Silhouette minivan, (O)

1991 Oldsmobile, Ninety-Eight Regency Elite sedan, (O)

NINETY-EIGHT REGENCY -- SERIES 3C -- V-6 -- Upon its 50th anniversary, a revamped lineup had the 1991 Ninety-Eight available either as a Regency Elite sedan or Touring Sedan. The Brougham sedan from the year before was dropped. Both were completely redesigned inside and out from the Ninety-Eight models offered a year earlier. The new exterior styling made the Ninety-Eight 9.5 inches longer (205.8 inches long) than the previous year's version. A driver's side airbag and anti-lock brakes were standard equipment. Optional was the Computer Command Ride System. Standard powertrain for the Ninety-Eight and Touring Sedan models was the more powerful (170 hp) Series 3800 3.8-liter V-6 coupled to a new electronically controlled four-speed Turbo-Hydra-matic transaxle.

1991 Oldsmobile, Ninety-Eight Touring Sedan, (O)

1991 Oldsmobile, Toronado Trofeo coupe, (O)

203

TORONADO -- SERIES 3E -- V-6 -- The other anniversary model, observing its 25th, the Toronado and its upscale offshoot the Trofeo received minor revisions for 1991. The biggest change was under the hood with the new 170-hp Series 3800 Tuned Port Injection 3.8-liter V-6 linked to an electronically controlled four-speed Turbo-Hydra-Matic transmission offered as the standard powertrain. Also new was the control door unlocking from trunk position mechanism and the optional heated windshield. The Trofeo featured steering wheel touch controls, driver's side airbag and anti-lock brakes as standard equipment, while the airbag was available on the Toronado.

1991 Oldsmobile, Toronado coupe, (O)

BRAVADA -- SERIES 3T -- V-6 -- Oldsmobile's new Bravada, based on the Chevrolet S-10 Blazer and GMC S-15 Jimmy, was the automaker's headline grabber for 1991. The sport utility vehicle's standard equipment list included: all-weather air conditioning, anti-lock brakes, cruiser control, remote control door locks, electric outside mirrors, tinted glass, 15-inch cast aluminum wheels and the new 160-hp, electronic fuel-injected 4.3-liter Vortec V-6 engine linked to a four-speed automatic transmission as its powertrain. Optional equipment included a heavy-duty trailering package, electronic instrument panel cluster and custom leather seating. The Bravada's towing capacity was rated at 5,500 pounds, while its cargo capacity was rated at 74.3 cubic feet.

1991 Oldsmobile, Bravada sport utility vehicle, (O)

I.D. DATA: Oldsmobile's 17-symbol Vehicle Identification Number (VIN) again was located on the upper left surface of the instrument panel, visible through the windshield. The first three characters (1G3) indicates Oldsmobile Division. The fourth and fifth letters designate the body type/series: A/J - Cutlass Ciera S and Cutlass Cruiser, A/L - Cutlass Ciera, A/M - Cutlass Ciera SL and Cutlass Cruiser SL, B/P - Custom Cruiser, C/V - Touring Sedan, C/W - Ninety-Eight Regency Elite, E/V - Toronado Trofeo, E/Z - Toronado, H/N - Eighty-Eight Royale, H/Y - Eighty-Eight Royale Brougham, N/F - Cutlass Calais S, N/K - Cutlass Calais International Series, N/L - Cutlass Calais, N/T - Cutlass Calais SL, T/V - Bravada, U/M - Silhouette, W/H - Cutlass Supreme, W/R - Cutlass Supreme International Series, W/S - Cutlass Supreme SL, W/T - Cutlass Supreme Convertible. The sixth number identifies the body style: 1 - 2-dr coupe/sedan, 2 - 2-dr hatchback/liftback, 3 - 2-dr convertible, 4 - 2-dr station wagon, 5 - 4-dr sedan, 6 - 4-dr hatchback/liftback, 8 - 4-dr station wagon. The seventh number identifies the restraint code: 1 - active (manual) belts, 3 - active (manual) belts with driver's side airbag, 4 - passive (automatic) belts. The eighth letter identifies the engine: A = 2.3-liter fuel-injected inline four-cylinder, B = 4.3-liter fuel-injected V-6, C = 3.8-liter fuel-injected V-6, D = 2.3-liter fuel-injected inline four-cylinder, E = 5.0-liter fuel-injected V-8, L = 3.8-liter fuel-injected V-6, N = 3.3-liter fuel-injected V-6, R = 2.5-liter fuel-injected inline four-cylinder, T = 3.1-liter fuel-injected V-6, U = 2.5-liter fuel-injected inline four-cylinder, X = 3.4-liter fuel-injected V-6. The ninth number is the check digit. The tenth letter represents the model year (M = 1991). The eleventh character identifies the assembly plant: D - Doraville, Ga.; H - Flint, Mich.; M - Lansing, Mich.; T - Tarrytown, N.Y.; U - Hamtramck, Mich.; W - Willow Run, Mich.; 1 - Wentzville, Mo.; 2 - Moraine, Ohio; 4 - Orion, Mich.; 6 - Oklahoma City, Okla.; (Canada) 2 - Ste. Therese, Quebec . The final six digits are the sequential serial number.

CUTLASS CALAIS (FOUR)

Model Number	Body/Style Number	Body Type & Seating	Factory Price	Shipping Weight	Production Total
3N	L27	2-dr. Cpe-5P	10295	2518	14978
3N	L69	4-dr. Sed-5P	10295	2585	41746
CUTLASS CALAIS S (FOUR)					
3N	F27	2-dr. Cpe-5P	11495	2518	6906
3N	F69	4-dr. Sed-5P	11595	2585	7267
CUTLASS CALAIS SL (FOUR/V-6)					
3N	T27	2-dr. Cpe-5P	15095/15145	2691/2852	1030
3N	T69	4-dr. Sed-5P	15195/15245	2754/2925	2437
CUTLASS CALAIS INTERNATIONAL SERIES (FOUR)					
3N	K27	2-dr. Cpe-5P	16295	2823	671
3N	K69	4-dr. Sed-5P	16395	2896	379

CUTLASS CIERA (FOUR/V-6)

Model Number	Body/Style Number	Body Type & Seating	Factory Price	Shipping Weight	Production Total
3A	L69	4-dr. Sed-6P	12495/13205	2813/2896	63888
CUTLASS CIERA S (FOUR/V-6)					
3A	J37	2-dr. Cpe-6P	13395/14105	2771/2854	1665
3A	J69	4-dr. Sed-6P	12995/13705	2813/2896	29307
3A	J35	4-dr. Sta Wag-6P	13895/14605	2975/3058	3977
CUTLASS CIERA SL (V-6)					
3A	M69	4-dr. Sed-6P	15895	2958	13700
3A	M35	4-dr. Sta Wag-6P	16595	3160	3247

CUTLASS SUPREME (FOUR/V-6 - Convertible V-6 only)

Model Number	Body/Style Number	Body Type & Seating	Factory Price	Shipping Weight	Production Total
3W	H47	2-dr. Cpe-6P	14995/15170	3187/3211	16766
3W	H69	4-dr. Sed-6P	15095/15270	3286/3310	52241
3W	T67	2-dr. Conv-6P	------/20995	------/3602	1515
CUTLASS SUPREME SL (V-6)					
3W	S47	2-dr. Cpe-6P	16895	3175	4253
3W	S69	4-dr. Sed-6P	16995	3270	15653
CUTLASS SUPREME INTERNATIONAL SERIES (V-6)					
3W	R47	2-dr. Cpe-6P	19695	3432	2304
3W	R69	4-dr. Sed-6P	19795	3512	7357

EIGHTY-EIGHT ROYALE (V-6)

Model Number	Body/Style Number	Body Type & Seating	Factory Price	Shipping Weight	Production Total
3H	N37	2-dr. Cpe-6P	17095	3248	234
3H	N69	4-dr. Sed-6P	17195	3292	33690
EIGHTY-EIGHT ROYALE BROUGHAM (V-6)					
3H	Y37	2-dr. Cpe-6P	18695	3277	458
3H	Y69	4-dr. Sed-6P	18795	3303	21865

CUSTOM CRUISER (V-8)

Model Number	Body/Style Number	Body Type & Seating	Factory Price	Shipping Weight	Production Total
3B	P35	4-dr. Sta Wag-6P	20495	4435	7663

SILHOUETTE (V-6)

Model Number	Body/Style Number	Body Type & Seating	Factory Price	Shipping Weight	Production Total
3U	M06	3-dr. Minivan-7P	18195	3648	17793

NINETY-EIGHT REGENCY ELITE (V-6)

Model Number	Body/Style Number	Body Type & Seating	Factory Price	Shipping Weight	Production Total
3C	X69	4-dr. Sed-6P	23695	3607	50625

NINETY-EIGHT TOURING SEDAN (V-6)

3C	V69	4-dr. Sed-6P	28595	3690	4280

TORONADO (V-6)

Model Number	Body/Style Number	Body Type & Seating	Factory Price	Shipping Weight	Production Total
3E	Z57	2-dr. Cpe-5P	23795	3455	2705
3E	V57	2-dr. Trofeo-5P	26495	3525	5348

BRAVADA (V-6)

3T	V06	4-dr. Sport Utility-5P	23795	3939	11145

FACTORY PRICE AND WEIGHT NOTE: Beginning with the Cutlass Calais SL, prices and weights to left of slash are for four-cylinder engine and to right for V-6.

ENGINE DATA: BASE FOUR (Cutlass Calais and Calais S): Inline, overhead-valve four-cylinder. Cast iron block and aluminum head. Displacement: 151 cu. in. (2.5 liters). Bore & stroke: 4.00 x 3.00 in. Compression ratio: 8.3:1. Net horsepower: 110 @ 5200 rpm. Torque: 135 lb. ft. @ 3200 rpm. Five main bearings. Fuel injection (EFI). BASE FOUR (Cutlass Calais SL): Quad 4 inline, 16-valve, dual overhead-cam four-cylinder. Cast iron block and aluminum head. Displacement: 138 cu. in. (2.3 liters). Bore & stroke: 3.62 x 3.35 in. Compression ratio: 9.5:1. Net horsepower: 160 @ 6200 rpm. Torque: 155 lb. ft. @ 5200 rpm. Fuel injected (MFI). BASE FOUR (Cutlass Calais Quad 442/Calais International Series): High Output Quad 4 inline, 16-valve, dual overhead-cam four-cylinder. Cast iron block and aluminum head. Displacement: 140 cu. in. (2.3 liters). Bore & stroke: 3.62 x 3.35 in. Compression ratio: 10.0:1. Net horsepower: 180 @ 6200 rpm. Torque: 160 lb. ft. @ 5200 rpm. Fuel injected (MFI). OPTIONAL FOUR (Cutlass Calais/Calais S/Calais International Series): same aforementioned 2.3-liter/138-cid Quad 4 four-cylinder with MFI. BASE FOUR (Cutlass Ciera/Ciera S/Cutlass Cruiser S): Inline, overhead-valve four-cylinder. Cast iron block and aluminum head. Displacement: 151 cu. in. (2.5 liters). Bore & stroke: 4.00 x 3.00 in. Compression ratio: 8.3:1. Net horsepower: 110 @ 5200 rpm. Torque: 135 lb. ft. @ 3200 rpm. Five main bearings. Fuel injection (EFI). BASE V-6 (Cutlass Ciera SL/Cruiser SL): Series 3300 90-degree overhead valve V-6. Displacement: 204 cu. in. (3.3 liters). Bore & stroke: 3.70 x 3.16 in. Compression ratio: 9.0:1. Net horsepower: 160 @ 5200 rpm. Torque: 185 lb. ft. @ 2000 rpm. Fuel injection (MFI). OPTIONAL SIX (Cutlass Calais SL/Cutlass Ciera/Ciera S/Cutlass Cruiser S): same aforementioned Series 3300 3.3-liter/204-cid V-6 with MFI. BASE FOUR (Cutlass Supreme): same aforementioned Quad 4 2.3-liter/138-cid four-cylinder with MFI. BASE SIX (Cutlass Supreme Convertible/Cutlass Supreme SL): 60-degree overhead valve V-6. Displacement: 189 cu. in. (3.1 liters). Bore & stroke: 3.50 x 3.31 in. Compression ratio: 8.8:1. Net horsepower: 140 @ 4400 rpm. Torque: 185 lb. ft. @ 3200 rpm. Fuel injection (MFI). BASE SIX (Cutlass Supreme International Series): Twin dual overhead cam V-6. Displacement: 207 cu. in. (3.4 liters). Bore & stroke: 3.62 x 3.31 in. Compression ratio: 9.3:1. Net horsepower: 210 @ 5200 rpm. Torque: 215 lb. ft. @ 4000. Fuel injected (MFI). OPTIONAL SIX (Cutlass Supreme): same aforementioned 3.1-liter/189-cid V-6 with MFI. OPTIONAL SIX (Cutlass Supreme/Cutlass Supreme SL): same aforementioned 3.4-liter/207-cid V-6 with MFI. BASE SIX (Eighty-Eight/Ninety-Eight/Touring Sedan/Toronado/Trofeo): Series 3800 90-degree overhead valve V-6. Displacement: 231 cu. in. (3.8 liters). Bore & stroke: 3.80 x 3.40 in. Compression ratio: 8.5:1. Net horsepower: 170 @ 4800 rpm (except Eighty-Eight - 165 @ 4800 rpm). Torque: 220 lb. ft. @ 3200 rpm (except Eighty-Eight - 210 lb. ft. @ 2000 rpm). Fuel injected (TPI) (except Eighty-Eight - SFI). BASE SIX (Silhouette): V-6. Displacement: 189 cu. in. (3.1 liters). Bore & stroke: 3.50 x 3.40 in. Compression ratio: 8.5:1. Net horsepower: 120 @ 4200 rpm. Torque: 175 lb. ft. @ 2200 rpm. Fuel injected (TBI). BASE V-8 (Custom Cruiser): 90-degree overhead valve V-8. Cast iron block and head. Displacement: 307 cu. in. (5.0 liters). Bore & stroke: 3.74 x 3.48 in. Compression ratio: 9.3:1. Net horsepower: 170 @ 4200 rpm. Torque: 255 lb. ft. @ 2500 rpm. Fuel injected (EFI). BASE SIX (Bravada): V-6. Displacement: 262 cu. in. (4.3 liters). Bore & stroke: 4.00 x 3.48 in. Compression ratio: 8.6:1. Net horsepower: 160 @ 4000 rpm. Torque: 230 lb. ft. @ 3800 rpm. Fuel injected (TBI).

CHASSIS DATA: Wheelbase: (Calais) 103.4 in.; (Ciera) 104.9 in.; (Cutlass Cruiser) 104.9 in.; (Cutlass Supreme) 107.5 in.; (Eighty-Eight) 110.8 in.; (Custom Cruiser) 115.9 in.; (Silhouette) 109.8 in.; (Ninety-Eight) 110.8 in.; (Touring Sedan) 110.8 in.; (Toronado) 108.0 in.; (Trofeo) 108.0 in.; (Bravada) 107.0 in. Overall Length: (Calais) 179.3 in.; (Ciera) 190.3 in.; (Cutlass Cruiser) 194.4 in.; (Cutlass Supreme Coupe and Convertible) 192.3 in.; (Cutlass Supreme Sedan) 192.2 in.; (Eighty-Eight) 197.6 in.; (Custom Cruiser) 217.5 in.; (Silhouette) 194.2 in.; (Ninety-Eight) 205.8 in.; (Touring Sedan) 205.8 in.; (Toronado) 200.3 in.; (Trofeo) 200.3 in.; (Bravada) 178.9 in. Height: (Calais) 52.4 in.; (Ciera) 54.1 in.; (Cutlass Cruiser) 54.5 in.; (Cutlass Supreme Coupe) 53.3 in.; (Cutlass Supreme Sedan) 54.8 in.; (Cutlass Supreme Convertible) 54.3 in.; (Eighty-Eight Coupe) 53.7 in.; (Eighty-Eight Sedan) 54.5 in.; (Custom Cruiser) 60.3 in.; (Silhouette) 65.2 in.; (Ninety-Eight) 55.1 in.; (Touring Sedan) 55.1 in.; (Toronado) 53.0 in.; (Trofeo) 53.0 in.; (Bravada) 65.5 in. Width: (Calais) 66.6 in.; (Ciera) 69.5 in.; (Cutlass Cruiser) 69.5 in.; (Cutlass Supreme) 71.0 in.; (Eighty-Eight) 73.0 in.; (Custom Cruiser) 79.7 in.; (Silhouette) 73.9 in.; (Ninety-Eight) 74.6 in.; (Touring Sedan) 74.6 in.; (Toronado) 72.8 in.; (Trofeo) 72.8 in.; (Bravada) 65.2 in. Front tread: (Calais) 55.8 in.; (Ciera) 58.7 in.; (Cutlass Cruiser) 58.7 in.; (Cutlass Supreme) 59.5 in.; (Eighty-Eight) 60.3 in.; (Custom Cruiser) 62.1 in.; (Silhouette) 59.2 in.; (Ninety-Eight) 60.5 in.; (Touring Sedan) 60.5 in.; (Toronado) 59.9 in.; (Trofeo) 59.9 in.; (Bravada) 55.6 in. Rear tread: (Calais) 55.4 in.; (Ciera) 57.0 in.; (Cutlass Cruiser) 57.0 in.; (Cutlass Supreme) 58.0 in.; (Eighty-Eight) 59.8 in.; (Custom Cruiser) 64.1 in.; (Silhouette) 61.4 in.; (Ninety-Eight) 60.2 in.; (Touring Sedan) 60.2 in.; (Toronado) 59.9 in.; (Trofeo) 59.9 in.; (Bravada) 54.1 in. Standard tires: (Calais) P185/75R14; (Ciera) P185/75R14; (Cutlass Cruiser) P185/75R14; (Cutlass Supreme) P195/75R14; (Cutlass Supreme Convertible) P205/70R15; (Eighty-Eight) P205/75R14; (Custom Cruiser) P225/75R15; (Silhouette) P205/70R14; (Ninety-Eight) P205/70R15; (Touring Sedan) P215/60R16; (Toronado) P215/65R15; (Trofeo) P215/60R16; (Bravada) P235/75R15.

TECHNICAL: Transmission: Five-speed manual floor shift standard on all Cutlass Calais models except SL. Three-speed automatic standard on Calais SL, optional on all other Calais models. Three-speed automatic standard on Cutlass Ciera/Cutlass Cruiser/Silhouette. Four-speed automatic available on Cutlass Ciera/Cutlass Cruiser. Three-speed automatic standard on Cutlass Supreme. Five-speed manual floor shift standard on Cutlass Supreme International Series coupe. Four-speed automatic standard on Cutlass Supreme Convertible/Cutlass Supreme SL/Cutlass Supreme International Series sedan/Eighty-Eight/Custom Cruiser/Ninety-Eight/Touring Sedan/Toronado/Trofeo/Bravada. Standard final drive ratio: (Calais) 3.35:1 with five-speed manual trans.; (Cutlass Ciera) 2.84:1 with three-speed automatic trans.; (Cutlass Cruiser) 2.84:1 with three-speed automatic trans.; (Cutlass Supreme) 3.18:1 with three-speed automatic trans.; (Cutlass Supreme Convertible) 3.33:1 with four-speed automatic trans.; (Eighty-Eight/Ninety-Eight/

Touring Sedan) 2.84:1 with four-speed automatic trans.; (Toronado/Trofeo) 3.06:1 with four-speed automatic trans.; (Custom Cruiser) 2.73:1 with four-speed automatic trans.; (Silhouette) N/A; (Bravada) 3.42:1 with four-speed automatic trans. Steering: (all except Custom Cruiser and Bravada) power assisted rack and pinion; (Custom Cruiser) power assisted recirculating ball; (Bravada) integral power steering variable ratio. Front Suspension: (Calais/Ciera/Cutlass Cruiser/Cutlass Supreme/Eighty-Eight/Ninety-Eight/Touring Sedan/Toronado/Trofeo) Independent, MacPherson strut w/ coil springs and anti-roll bar; (Custom Cruiser) Independent, unequal length control arms, coil springs, anti-roll bar; (Silhouette) MacPherson struts, stamped lower control arms, stabilizer bar; (Bravada) Independent driving axle w/ upper and lower control arms, torsion bar springs, front stabilizer bar and frame-mounted differential carrier. Rear Suspension: (Calais) Independent, trailing crank arm w/ twist beam and coil springs; (Ciera) Twist beam integral w/ two trailing arms, coil springs, Panhard rod, anti-roll bar; (Cutlass Cruiser) Twist beam integral w/ two trailing arms, coil springs, track bar; (Cutlass Supreme) Independent, rear fiberglass leaf spring plus shock struts; (Eighty-Eight) Independent, MacPherson strut, coil springs, anti-roll bar with FE3 suspension options; (Ninety-Eight) automatic load leveling and coil springs; (Custom Cruiser) Rigid axle, four locating links, coil springs; (Silhouette) open-section transverse beam on stamped steel trailing arms, tube shocks, coil springs, stabilizer bar; (Toronado/Trofeo) Transflex Independent Rear, plus automatic load leveling; (Bravada) Salisbury axle design with semi-elliptic leaf springs. Brakes: (Calais/Ciera/Eighty-Eight/Silhouette) power assisted front disc, rear drum; (Ninety-Eight/Custom Cruiser) anti-lock power front disc, rear drum; (Cutlass Supreme/Toronado/Trofeo) power four-wheel disc - anti-lock standard on Toronado/Trofeo and optional on Cutlass Supreme; (Bravada) front disc, rear drum, Kelsey-Hayes four-wheel anti-lock. Body Construction: (all except Custom Cruiser/Silhouette/Bravada) unibody; (Custom Cruiser/Bravada) separate body and frame, (Silhouette) space frame substructure attached to ladder frame. Fuel tank: (Calais) 13.6 gal.; (Ciera) 15.7 gal.; (Cutlass Cruiser) 15.7 gal.; (Cutlass Supreme) 16.5 gal.; (Eighty-Eight/Ninety-Eight/Touring Sedan) 18.0 gal.; (Custom Cruiser) 22.0 gal.; (Silhouette) 20.0 gal.; (Trofeo) 18.3 gal.; (Toronado) 20 gal.; (Bravada) 20.0 gal.

DRIVETRAIN OPTIONS: (Calais/Calais S) Quad 4 2.3-liter four-cylinder ($660); (Calais SL) Series 3300 3.3-liter V-6 ($50); (Calais International Series) Quad 4 2.3-liter four-cylinder ($415). (Ciera/Ciera S/Cutlass Cruiser S) Series 3300 3.3-liter V-6 ($710). (Cutlass Supreme) 3.1-liter V-6 ($175); (Cutlass Supreme) 3.4-liter V-6 ($1728 - w/ five-speed manual trans./$2003 - w/ four-speed automatic trans.); (Cutlass Supreme SL) 3.4-liter V-6 ($1200 - w/ five-speed manual trans./$1450 - w/ four-speed automatic trans.). Transmission: (Calais/Calais S) three-speed automatic ($555); (Ciera S/Cutlass Cruiser S/Ciera SL) four-speed automatic ($200). Suspension: (Calais) FE3 touring car ride and handling package ($244-$608). (Cutlass Supreme) FE3 touring car ride and handling package ($216-$569). (Eighty-Eight) FE3 touring car ride and handling package ($723-$789). (Silhouette) FE3 touring suspension ($243). (Ninety-Eight) FE3 touring car ride and handling package ($245). (Toronado) FE3 touring car ride and handling package ($60). (Cutlass Supreme/Eighty-Eight) anti-lock brakes ($925). (Ciera/Cutlass Cruiser/Cutlass Supreme/Eighty-Eight) high-capacity cooling ($40-$125). (Eighty-Eight) Towing package ($271). (Ninety-Eight) Towing package ($150). (Custom Cruiser) Towing package ($220). (Bravada) heavy-duty towing package ($409). (All) California emission equipment ($100). Engine block heater ($18).

OPTION PACKAGES: (Calais S coupe) Quad 442 sport performance package ($1721). (Cutlass Cruiser S) sport appearance package ($851). (Cutlass Supreme coupe) sport appearance package ($426). (Cutlass Supreme sedan) sport appearance package ($140). (Cutlass Supreme Convertible) sport appear-

ance package ($1540). (Cutlass/Toronado) two-tone paint scheme ($101). (Bravada) Cold Climate Package ($90).

MAJOR CONVENIENCE/APPEARANCE OPTIONS: Computer Command Ride System ($434). Cruise control ($210). Driver information system ($150). Driver's side airbag ($850). Steering wheel touch controls ($410). Self-defrosting windshield ($250). Head-Up instrument display ($295). Air conditioning ($150-$720). Power door locks ($190-$250). Body accent stripe ($45). Electric Sliding Glass Astroroof ($695-$1350). Electric rear window defogger ($190). Mobile telephone ($995).

HISTORY: Calendar year production (U.S.) 474,837. Calendar year sales by U.S. dealers: 458,124. Model year sales by U.S. dealers: 476,595.

Historical Footnotes: Oldsmobile's model year sales continued its decline to 476,595 units moved in 1991 compared to 524,898 the year before.

1992

After another lackluster sales performance and further decline of market share the year before, Oldsmobile streamlined its lineup for 1992. The most visible change was the dropping of the Cutlass Calais name and the introduction of the Achieva line of S and SL coupes and sedans. The Eighty-Eight received a redesign as well as a reduced lineup dropping both coupe models from the prior year and offering a base sedan and LS sedan. The Ciera also had its ranks thinned by the elimination of its coupe models offered previously. The revised lineup now consisted of the S and SL sedans. The Cutlass Supreme lineup was also simplified by dropping the base and SL coupes and sedans offered previously and introducing an S coupe and sedan to accompany the convertible and International Series coupe and sedan in the lineup. After a one-year hiatus, the Ninety-Eight added a base sedan to bolster its lineup, which already included both the Elite and Touring Sedans.

1992 Oldsmobile, Achieva SC coupe, (O)

ACHIEVA -- SERIES 3N -- FOUR/V-6 -- A more stylish, refined, mid-model year replacement for the Cutlass Calais, the Achieva offered Oldsmobile's typical two-tiered lineup, which in this case consisted of S and SL coupes and sedans. Standard powertrain for the Achieva S was the 120-hp 2.3-liter Quad inline

1992 Oldsmobile, Achieva SL sedan, (O)

overhead cam four-cylinder engine linked to a five-speed manual transaxle. The SL models used a three-speed automatic mated to the 160-hp dual overhead-cam Quad 4. The 180-hp High Output Quad 4 was offered in the S coupe as part of an optional W44 Sport Coupe Performance Package that dressed up the car with a black grille, rear aero wing, 16-inch aluminum wheels with P205/55R16 performance tires, dual exhaust and other accessories. Anti-lock brakes were standard across the lineup. The Series 3300 3.3-liter V-6 was optional in the Achieva SL models as well as the S coupe when the W44 package was ordered.

CUTLASS CIERA -- SERIES 3A -- FOUR/V-6 -- Even with its revised S and SL sedan-only lineup, as well as the previously offered, Ciera-based Cutlass Cruiser S and SL station wagons, the 1992 Ciera was still Oldsmobile's best selling automobile. Standard powertrain on the S models, including the Cruiser S, was the Tech IV 2.5-liter four-cylinder engine coupled to a three-speed automatic transaxle. For the SL models, including the Cruiser SL, standard powertrain was the Series 3300 3.3-liter V-6 that came with a three-speed automatic transaxle (four-speed automatic in Cruiser SL), which was the optional engine selection for the S models.

1992 Oldsmobile, Cutlass Supreme SL sedan, (O)

1992 Oldsmobile, Cutlass Supreme convertible, (O)

CUTLASS SUPREME -- SERIES 3W -- V-6 -- The new-for-1992 S coupe and sedan were the entry-level Cutlass Supremes after the demise of the previous year's base and SL coupes and sedans. The lone remaining representatives of the International Series, which debuted in 1988 on several Oldsmobile lines, was the Cutlass Supreme I Series coupe and sedan, which featured anti-lock brakes as standard equipment. The Cutlass Supreme convertible was again offered, and its standard powertrain consisted of the 3.1-liter V-6 mated to a four-speed automatic transaxle. The 3.1-liter V-6 was also the standard engine in the S models, but in those Cutlass Supremes it was linked to a three-speed automatic transaxle. The International Series utilized the

3.4-liter twin dual overhead cam V-6 and four-speed automatic. The 3.1-liter V-6 was available to I Series models, while the 3.4-liter V-6 could be ordered in the S coupe. A five-speed manual transaxle and four-speed automatic were also available to the Cutlass Supreme S models.

1992 Oldsmobile, Cutlass Supreme International Series coupe, (O)

EIGHTY-EIGHT ROYALE -- SERIES 3H -- V-6 -- Less was more concerning the Eighty-Eight Royale's lineup for 1992. With two fewer models with the demise of the coupe models offered the year before, the sedan-only offering greatly spurred Eighty-Eight sales. Featured in base and LS trim levels, standard powertrain for both was the Series 3800 3.8-liter V-6 coupled to a four-speed automatic transaxle. A driver's side airbag was standard equipment on both as was anti-lock brakes on the LS sedan, available on the base. Both also offered as standard equipment the "Pass-Key" vehicle security system.

1992 Oldsmobile, Eighty-Eight Royale LS sedan, (O)

CUSTOM CRUISER -- SERIES 3B -- V-8 -- After a total redesign the year before, Oldsmobile's rear-drive eight-passenger station wagon remained relatively unchanged for 1992. Anti-lock brakes and driver's side airbag were both standard equipment. The fuel-injected 5.0-liter V-8 with four-speed automatic transmission was again the standard powertrain. New was the optional 5.7-liter V-8 engine with 9.8:1 compression ratio and rated at 180 horsepower.

1992 Oldsmobile, Silhouette minivan, (O)

SILHOUETTE -- SERIES 3U -- V-6 -- Minor changes were made to Oldsmobile's minivan for 1992, which offered the Series 3800 3.8-liter V-6 linked to a four-speed automatic transaxle as optional equipment. The 191-hp 3.1-liter V-6 with throttle body fuel injection was standard along with a three-speed automatic transaxle. Anti-lock brakes were standard equipment along with larger than the prior year's P205/70R15 radial tires mounted on 15 x 6-inch aluminum styled wheels.

1992 Oldsmobile, Ninety-Eight Touring Sedan, (O)

NINETY-EIGHT REGENCY -- SERIES 3C -- V-6 -- The 1992 Ninety-Eight lineup grew by one over the previous year with the return (not offered in 1991) of the base Regency sedan. This Ninety-Eight model was offered along with the Regency Elite sedan and Touring Sedan. The Series 3800 3.8-liter V-6 with four-speed automatic transaxle was the standard powertrain on all Ninety-Eight models, and a supercharged version of this engine was optional on the Touring Sedan. Among the standard equipment available across the lineup were: anti-lock brakes, driver's side airbag, "Pass-Key" vehicle security system and power trunk lid lock release. A traction control system was optional on all Ninety-Eight models.

1992 Oldsmobile, Toronado Trofeo coupe, (O)

TORONADO -- SERIES 3E -- V-6 -- Anti-lock brakes and driver's side airbag were standard equipment on both the 1992 Toronado and Trofeo. "Pass-Key" vehicle security system and twilight sentinel automatic headlight control were also standard, as was the Series 3800 3.8-liter V-6 with tuned port fuel injection, linked to a four-speed automatic transaxle. The Trofeos came standard with front fascia with extended air dam, body color grille with headlamp covers and 16 x 7 aluminum styled wheels.

1992 Oldsmobile, Bravada sport utility vehicle, (O)

BRAVADA -- SERIES 3T -- V-6 -- In its second year, the Bravada for 1992 featured full-time all-wheel drive and 4.3-liter Vortec V-6 engine linked to a four-speed automatic as standard equipment. Also standard were high-pressure gas-assisted front and rear shock absorbers, anti-lock brakes with accompanying monitor light, power rear tailgate lock release, rooftop aero design luggage carrier and locking rear positraction differential.

I.D. DATA: Oldsmobile's 17-symbol Vehicle Identification Number (VIN) again was located on the upper left surface of the instrument panel, visible through the windshield. The first three characters (1G3) indicates Oldsmobile Division. The fourth and fifth letters designate the body type/series: A/J - Cutlass Ciera and Cutlass Cruiser S, A/L - Cutlass Ciera S, A/M - Cutlass Ciera SL and Cutlass Cruiser SL, B/P - Custom Cruiser, C/V - Touring Sedan, C/W - Ninety-Eight Regency Elite, C/X - Ninety-Eight Regency, E/V - Toronado Trofeo, E/Z - Toronado, H/N - Eighty-Eight Royale, H/Y - Eighty-Eight Royale LS, N/F - Achieva SL, N/L - Achieva S, T/V - Bravada, U/M - Silhouette, W/H - Cutlass Supreme S, W/R - Cutlass Supreme International Series, W/T - Cutlass Supreme Convertible. The sixth number identifies the body style: 1 - 2-dr coupe/sedan, 2 - 2-dr hatchback/liftback, 3 - 2-dr convertible, 4 - 2-dr station wagon, 5 - 4-dr sedan, 6 - 4-dr hatchback/liftback, 8 - 4-dr station wagon. The seventh number identifies the restraint code: 1 - active (manual) belts, 2 - active (manual) belts with driver's and passenger's side airbags, 3 - active (manual) belts with driver's side airbag, 4 - passive (automatic) belts, 5 - passive (automatic) belts with driver's side airbag. The eighth letter identifies the engine: A = 2.3-liter fuel-injected inline four-cylinder, D = 2.3-liter fuel-injected inline four-cylinder, E = 5.0-liter fuel-injected V-8, L = 3.8-liter fuel-injected V-6, N = 3.3-liter fuel-injected V-6, R = 2.5-liter fuel-injected inline four-cylinder, T = 3.1-liter fuel-injected V-6, W = 4.3-liter fuel-injected V-6, X = 3.4-liter fuel-injected V-6, 1 = 3.8-liter fuel-injected V-6, 3 = 2.3-liter fuel-injected inline four-cylinder, 7 = 5.7-liter fuel-injected V-8. The ninth number is the check digit. The tenth letter represents the model year (N = 1992). The eleventh character identifies the assembly plant: D - Doraville, Ga.; H - Flint, Mich.; M - Lansing, Mich.; T - Tarrytown, N.Y.; U - Hamtramck, Mich.; W - Willow Run, Mich.; 1 - Wentzville, Mo.; 2 - Moraine, Ohio; 4 - Orion, Mich.; 6 - Oklahoma City, Okla. The final six digits are the sequential serial number.

ACHIEVA S (FOUR/V-6 - coupe only)

Model Number	Body/Style Number	Body Type & Seating	Factory Price	Shipping Weight	Production Total
3N	L37	2-dr. Cpe-5P	12715/15075	2696/2751	24719
3N	L69	4-dr. Sed-5P	12815/------	2778/------	38171

ACHIEVA SL (FOUR/V-6)

3N	F37	2-dr. Cpe-5P	14495/14545	2795/2850	2892
3N	F69	4-dr. Sed-5P	14595/14645	2865/2920	11674

CUTLASS CIERA S (FOUR/V-6)

Model Number	Body/Style Number	Body Type & Seating	Factory Price	Shipping Weight	Production Total
3A	L69	4-dr. Sed-6P	12755/13465	2886/2976	123243
3A	J35	4-dr. Sta Wag-6P	13860/14570	2992/3082	5861

CUTLASS CIERA SL (V-6)

3A	M69	4-dr. Sed-6P	16895	3048	8867
3A	M35	4-dr. Sta Wag-6P	17395	3226	1932

CUTLASS SUPREME (V-6)

Model Number	Body/Style Number	Body Type & Seating	Factory Price	Shipping Weight	Production Total
3W	T67	2-dr. Conv-6P	21995	3589	4306

CUTLASS SUPREME S (V-6)

3W	H47	2-dr. Cpe-6P	15695	3221	20700
3W	H69	4-dr. Sed-6P	15795	3375	63692

CUTLASS SUPREME INTERNATIONAL SERIES (V-6)

3W	R47	2-dr. Cpe-6P	21795	3385	1181
3W	R69	4-dr. Sed-6P	21895	3498	2066

EIGHTY-EIGHT ROYALE (V-6)

Model Number	Body/Style Number	Body Type & Seating	Factory Price	Shipping Weight	Production Total
3H	N69	4-dr. Sed-6P	18495	3404	75182

EIGHTY-EIGHT ROYALE LS (V-6)

3H	Y69	4-dr. Sed-6P	21395	3468	40142

CUSTOM CRUISER (V-8)

Model Number	Body/Style Number	Body Type & Seating	Factory Price	Shipping Weight	Production Total
3B	P35	4-dr. Sta Wag-6P	20995	4435	4347

SILHOUETTE (V-6)

Model Number	Body/Style Number	Body Type & Seating	Factory Price	Shipping Weight	Production Total
3U	M06	3-dr. Minivan-7P	19095	3735	16727

NINETY-EIGHT REGENCY (V-6)

Model Number	Body/Style Number	Body Type & Seating	Factory Price	Shipping Weight	Production Total
3C	X69	4-dr. Sed-6P	24595	3512	20076

NINETY-EIGHT REGENCY ELITE (V-6)

3C	W69	4-dr. Sed-6P	26195	3527	24713

NINETY-EIGHT TOURING SEDAN (V-6)

3C	V69	4-dr. Sed-6P	28995	3697	2795

TORONADO (V-6)

Model Number	Body/Style Number	Body Type & Seating	Factory Price	Shipping Weight	Production Total
3E	Z57	2-dr. Cpe-5P	24695	3467	1239
3E	V57	2-dr. Trofeo-5P	27295	3528	5197

BRAVADA (V-6)

3T	V06	4-dr. Sport Utility-5P	24595	3939	11869

FACTORY PRICE AND WEIGHT NOTE: Beginning with the Achieva S coupe, prices and weights to left of slash are for four-cylinder engine and to right for V-6.

ENGINE DATA: BASE FOUR (Achieva S): Quad inline, overhead-cam four-cylinder. Cast iron block and aluminum head. Displacement: 138 cu. in. (2.3 liters). Bore & stroke: 3.62 x 3.35 in. Compression ratio: 9.5:1. Net horsepower: 120 @ 5200 rpm. Torque: 140 lb. ft. @ 3200 rpm. Fuel injected. **BASE FOUR** (Achieva SL): Quad 4 inline, 16-valve, dual overhead-cam four-cylinder. Cast iron block and aluminum head. Displacement: 138 cu. in. (2.3 liters). Bore & stroke: 3.62 x 3.35 in. Compression ratio: 9.5:1. Net horsepower: 160 @ 6000 rpm. Torque: 155 lb. ft. @ 4800 rpm. Fuel injected. **OPTIONAL FOUR** (Achieva S Sport Coupe): High Output Quad 4 inline, 16-valve, dual overhead-cam four-cylinder. Cast iron block and aluminum head. Displacement: 138 cu. in. (2.3 liters). Bore & stroke: 3.62 x 3.35 in. Compression ratio: 10.0:1. Net horsepower: 180 @ 6200 rpm. Torque: 160 lb. ft. @ 5200 rpm. Fuel injected. **BASE FOUR** (Cutlass Ciera S/Cutlass Cruiser S): Inline, overhead-valve four-cylinder. Cast iron block and aluminum head. Displacement: 151 cu. in. (2.5 liters). Bore & stroke: 4.00 x 3.00 in. Compression ratio: 8.3:1. Net horsepower: 105 @ 4800 rpm. Torque: 135 lb. ft. @ 3200 rpm. Five main bearings. Fuel injection (EFI). **BASE V-6** (Cutlass Ciera SL/Cruiser SL): Series 3300 90-degree overhead valve V-6. Displacement: 204 cu. in. (3.3 liters). Bore & stroke: 3.70 x 3.16 in. Compression ratio: 9.0:1. Net horsepower: 160 @ 5200 rpm. Torque: 185 lb. ft. @ 2000 rpm. Fuel injection (MPI). **OPTIONAL SIX** (Achieva SL/Achieva S Sport Coupe/Cutlass Ciera S/Cutlass Cruiser S): same aforementioned Series 3300 3.3-liter/204-cid V-6 with MPI. **BASE SIX** (Cutlass Supreme Convertible/Cutlass Supreme S): 60-degree overhead valve V-6. Displacement: 191 cu. in. (3.1 liters). Bore & stroke: 3.50 x 3.31 in. Compression ratio: 8.9:1. Net horsepower: 140 @ 4400 rpm. Torque: 185 lb. ft. @ 3200 rpm. Fuel injection (MFI). **BASE SIX** (Cutlass Supreme International Series): Twin dual overhead cam V-6. Displacement: 207 cu. in. (3.4 liters). Bore & stroke: 3.62 x 3.30 in. Compression ratio: 9.3:1. Net horsepower: 210 @ 5200 rpm. Torque: 215 lb. ft. @ 4000. Fuel injected (MFI). **OPTIONAL SIX** (Cutlass Supreme International): same aforementioned 3.1-liter/191-cid V-6 with MFI. **OPTIONAL SIX** (Cutlass Supreme S): same aforementioned 3.4-liter/207-cid V-6 with MFI. **BASE SIX** (Eighty-Eight/Ninety-

Eight/Touring Sedan/Toronado/Trofeo): Series 3800 90-degree overhead valve V-6. Displacement: 231 cu. in. (3.8 liters). Bore & stroke: 3.80 x 3.40 in. Compression ratio: 8.5:1. Net horsepower: 170 @ 4800 rpm. Torque: 220 lb. ft. @ 3200 rpm. Fuel injected (TPI). **OPTIONAL SIX** (Touring Sedan) supercharged version of the aforementioned 3.8-liter/231-cid V-6. Net horsepower: 200 @ 4400 rpm. Torque: 260 lb. ft. @ 2800 rpm. **BASE SIX** (Silhouette): V-6. Displacement: 191 cu. in. (3.1 liters). Bore & stroke: 3.50 x 3.31 in. Compression ratio: 8.9:1. Net horsepower: 120 @ 4200 rpm. Torque: 175 lb. ft. @ 2200 rpm. Fuel injected (TBI). **OPTIONAL SIX** (Silhouette): same aforementioned 3.8-liter/231-cid V-6 with TPI. **BASE V-8** (Custom Cruiser): 90-degree overhead valve V-8. Cast iron block and head. Displacement: 307 cu. in. (5.0 liters). Bore & stroke: 3.74 x 3.48 in. Compression ratio: 9.3:1. Net horsepower: 170 @ 4200 rpm. Torque: 255 lb. ft. @ 2500 rpm. Fuel injected (EFI). **OPTIONAL V-8** (Custom Cruiser): 90-degree overhead valve V-8. Cast iron block and head. Displacement: 350 cu. in. (5.7 liters). Bore & stroke: 4.00 x 3.48 in. Compression ratio: 9.8:1. Net horsepower: 180 @ 4000 rpm. Torque: 300 lb. ft. @ 2400 rpm. Fuel injected (EFI). **BASE SIX** (Bravada): V-6. Displacement: 262 cu. in. (4.3 liters). Bore & stroke: 4.00 x 3.48 in. Compression ratio: 8.6:1. Net horsepower: 200 @ 4400 rpm. Torque: 260 lb. ft. @ 3600 rpm. Fuel injected (TBI).

CHASSIS DATA: Wheelbase: (Achieva) 103.4 in.; (Ciera) 104.9 in.; (Cutlass Cruiser) 104.9 in.; (Cutlass Supreme) 107.5 in.; (Eighty-Eight) 110.8 in.; (Custom Cruiser) 115.9 in.; (Silhouette) 109.8 in.; (Ninety-Eight) 110.7 in.; (Touring Sedan) 110.7 in.; (Toronado) 108.0 in.; (Trofeo) 108.0 in.; (Bravada) 107.0 in. Overall Length: (Achieva) 187.9 in.; (Ciera) 190.3 in.; (Cutlass Cruiser) 194.4 in.; (Cutlass Supreme Coupe and Convertible) 193.9 in.; (Cutlass Supreme Sedan) 193.7 in.; (Eighty-Eight) 200.4 in.; (Custom Cruiser) 217.5 in.; (Silhouette) 194.2 in.; (Ninety-Eight) 205.5 in.; (Touring Sedan) 205.5 in.; (Toronado) 200.3 in.; (Trofeo) 200.3 in.; (Bravada) 178.9 in. Height: (Achieva) 53.2 in.; (Ciera) 54.1 in.; (Cutlass Cruiser) 54.5 in.; (Cutlass Supreme Coupe) 53.3 in.; (Cutlass Supreme Sedan) 54.8 in.; (Cutlass Supreme Convertible) 54.7 in.; (Eighty-Eight) 55.7 in.; (Custom Cruiser) 60.3 in.; (Silhouette) 65.7 in.; (Ninety-Eight) 54.8 in.; (Touring Sedan) 54.8 in.; (Toronado) 53.3 in.; (Trofeo) 53.3 in.; (Bravada) 65.5 in. Width: (Achieva) 67.5 in.; (Ciera) 69.5 in.; (Cutlass Cruiser) 69.5 in.; (Cutlass Supreme) 71.0 in.; (Eighty-Eight) 74.1 in.; (Custom Cruiser) 79.7 in.; (Silhouette) 73.9 in.; (Ninety-Eight) 74.6 in.; (Touring Sedan) 74.6 in.; (Toronado) 72.8 in.; (Trofeo) 72.8 in.; (Bravada) 65.2 in. Front tread: (Achieva) 55.9 in.; (Ciera) 58.7 in.; (Cutlass Cruiser) 58.7 in.; (Cutlass Supreme) 59.5 in.; (Eighty-Eight) 60.4 in.; (Custom Cruiser) 62.1 in.; (Silhouette) 59.2 in.; (Ninety-Eight) 61.5 in.; (Touring Sedan) 61.5 in.; (Toronado) 59.9 in.; (Trofeo) 59.9 in.; (Bravada) 55.6 in. Rear tread: (Achieva) 55.4 in.; (Ciera) 57.0 in.; (Cutlass Cruiser) 57.0 in.; (Cutlass Supreme) 58.0 in.; (Eighty-Eight) 60.4 in.; (Custom Cruiser) 64.1 in.; (Silhouette) 61.4 in.; (Ninety-Eight) 60.3 in.; (Touring Sedan) 60.3 in.; (Toronado) 59.9 in.; (Trofeo) 59.9 in.; (Bravada) 54.1 in. Standard tires: (Achieva) P185/75R14; (Ciera) P185/75R14; (Cutlass Cruiser) P185/75R14; (Cutlass Supreme) P205/70R15; (Cutlass Supreme Convertible) P225/60R16; (Eighty-Eight) P205/70R15; (Custom Cruiser) P225/75R15; (Silhouette) P205/70R15; (Ninety-Eight) P205/70R15; (Touring Sedan) P225/60R16; (Toronado) P215/65R15; (Trofeo) P215/60R16; (Bravada) P235/75R15.

TECHNICAL: Transmission: Five-speed manual floor shift standard on Achieva S. Three-speed automatic standard on Achieva SL, optional on S models. Three-speed automatic standard on Cutlass Ciera S and SL/Cutlass Cruiser S/Cutlass Supreme S/Silhouette. Four-speed automatic available on Cutlass Ciera S and SL/Cutlass Cruiser S/Cutlass Supreme S/Silhouette. Four-speed automatic standard on Cutlass Cruiser SL/Cutlass Supreme Convertible/Cutlass Supreme International Series/Eighty-Eight/

Custom Cruiser/Ninety-Eight/Touring Sedan/Toronado/Trofeo/Bravada. Five-speed manual floor shift available on Cutlass Supreme S. Standard final drive ratio: (Achieva) 3.61:1 with five-speed manual trans.; (Cutlass Ciera) 2.84:1 with three-speed automatic trans.; (Cutlass Cruiser) 2.84:1 with three-speed automatic trans.; (Cutlass Supreme) 2.84:1 with three-speed automatic trans.; (Cutlass Supreme Convertible) 3.33 with four-speed automatic trans.; (Eighty-Eight/Ninety-Eight) 2.84:1 with four-speed automatic trans.; (Touring Sedan/Toronado/Trofeo) 3.06:1 with four-speed automatic trans.; (Custom Cruiser) 2.73:1 with four-speed automatic trans.; (Silhouette) N/A; (Bravada) 3.42:1 with four-speed automatic trans. Steering: (all except Custom Cruiser and Bravada) power assisted rack and pinion; (Custom Cruiser) power assisted recirculating ball; (Bravada) integral power steering variable ratio. Front Suspension: (Achieva/Ciera/Cutlass Cruiser/Cutlass Supreme/Eighty-Eight/Ninety-Eight/Touring Sedan/Toronado/Trofeo) Independent, MacPherson strut w/ coil springs and anti-roll bar; (Custom Cruiser) Independent, unequal length control arms, coil springs, anti-roll bar; (Silhouette) MacPherson struts, stamped lower control arms, stabilizer bar; (Bravada) Independent driving axle w/ upper and lower control arms, torsion bar springs, front stabilizer bar and frame-mounted differential carrier. Rear Suspension: (Achieva) Independent, trailing crank arm w/ twist beam and coil springs; (Ciera) Twist beam integral w/ two trailing arms, coil springs, anti-roll bar; (Cutlass Cruiser) Twist beam integral w/ two trailing arms, coil springs, track bar; (Cutlass Supreme) Independent, rear fiberglass leaf spring plus shock struts; (Eighty-Eight) Independent, MacPherson strut, coil springs, anti-roll bar with FE3 suspension options; (Ninety-Eight) automatic load leveling and coil springs with FE3 suspension options; (Custom Cruiser) Rigid axle, four locating links, coil springs; (Silhouette) variable rate coil springs; (Toronado/Trofeo) Transflex Independent Rear, plus automatic load leveling; (Bravada) Salisbury axle design with semi-elliptic leaf springs. Brakes: (Achieva/Ciera) power assisted front disc, rear drum; (Eighty-Eight/Ninety-Eight/Custom Cruiser/Silhouette) anti-lock power front disc, rear drum; (Cutlass Supreme/Toronado/Trofeo) power four-wheel disc - anti-lock standard on Cutlass Supreme International Series/Toronado/Trofeo and optional on Cutlass Supreme S and Convertible; (Bravada) front disc, rear drum, Kelsey-Hayes four-wheel anti-lock. Body Construction: (all except Custom Cruiser/Silhouette/Bravada) unibody; (Custom Cruiser/Bravada) separate body and frame, (Silhouette) space frame substructure attached to ladder frame. Fuel tank: (Achieva) 15.2 gal.; (Ciera) 15.7 gal.; (Cutlass Cruiser) 15.7 gal.; (Cutlass Supreme) 16.5 gal.; (Eighty-Eight/Ninety-Eight/Touring Sedan) 18.0 gal.; (Custom Cruiser) 22.0 gal.; (Silhouette) 20.0 gal.; (Toronado/Trofeo) 18.8 gal.; (Bravada) 20.0 gal.

DRIVETRAIN OPTIONS: (Achieva S) Quad 4 2.3-liter dual overhead-cam inline four-cylinder ($410); (Achieva SL/Achieva S Sport Coupe) Series 3300 3.3-liter V-6 ($50). (Ciera S/Cutlass Cruiser S) Series 3300 3.3-liter V-6 ($710). (Cutlass Supreme S) 3.4-liter V-6 ($1083-$1570); (Cutlass Supreme International Series) 3.1-liter V-6 ($995 credit). (Ninety-Eight) supercharged 3.8-liter V-6 ($1022). (Silhouette) 3.8-liter V-6 ($800). Transmission: (Achieva S) three-speed automatic ($555); (Ciera S/Cutlass Cruiser S/Ciera SL) four-speed automatic ($200); (Cutlass Supreme S) five-speed manual (NC); four-speed automatic ($175-$200). Suspension: (Eighty-Eight) FE3 touring car ride and handling package ($718). (Silhouette) FE3 touring suspension ($205). (Ninety-Eight) FE3 touring car ride and handling package ($330-$384); (Ninety-Eight Regency Elite) FE3 touring car ride and handling package ($199-$253). (Toronado) FE3 touring car ride and handling package ($60). (Cutlass Supreme S and Convertible) anti-lock brakes ($450). (Ciera S and SL/Cutlass Cruiser S and SL/Cutlass Supreme S) high-capacity cooling ($40-$125). (Eighty-Eight) Towing package ($150-$325). (Ninety-Eight) Towing package ($150). (Custom Cruiser) Towing package ($120). (Silhouette)

Towing package ($355). (Bravada) heavy-duty towing package ($409). (All) California emission equipment ($100). Engine block heater ($18).

OPTION PACKAGES: (Achieva S Sport Coupe) W44 performance package ($1895-$2360). (Cutlass Cruiser S) sport appearance package ($851). (Cutlass Supreme S) Sport Luxury Package ($628-$988). (Eighty-Eight Royale LS) LSS Package ($1995). (Bravada) Cold Climate Package ($90).

MAJOR CONVENIENCE/APPEARANCE OPTIONS: Computer Command Ride System ($434). Cruise control ($225). traction control system ($175). Power decklid lock release ($60). Self-defrosting windshield ($250). Power antenna ($85). Pulse wiper system ($65). Body accent stripe ($45). Electric Sliding Glass Astroroof ($1350). Electric rear window defogger ($170). Mobile telephone ($995).

HISTORY: Model year production (U.S.): 482,998. Calendar year production (U.S.) 423,592. Calendar year sales by U.S. dealers: 416,126. Model year sales by U.S. dealers: 437,544

Historical Footnotes: John Rock, former GMC Truck general manager, replaced J. Michael Losh as Oldsmobile's general manager. Oldsmobile introduced its new image theme, "The Power of Intelligent Engineering," which was also the cornerstone of all Oldsmobile advertising. The Oklahoma City, Okla., assembly plant where Cieras were produced was ranked the top automotive manufacturing plant in North America in the J.D. Power and Associates 1992 Initial Quality Study. The Ciera was also ranked best in its price class in that same study, and, with the Ciera-based Cutlass Cruiser station wagon, surpassed the two-million mark in sales since its 1982 inception.

1993

The year 1993 will long be remembered by Oldsmobile enthusiasts for the loss of two long-standing models: the Custom Cruiser station wagon and the Toronado/Trofeo. Both underwent significant redesigns shortly before their demise, but continued low sales forced Oldsmobile to abandon both, which, with the Custom Cruiser, also meant the demise of the V-8 engine and rear-drive format for Oldsmobile automobiles. The remainder of the lineup was intact from the year before, with only minor modifications to select models.

1993 Oldsmobile, Achieva SL sedan, (O)

ACHIEVA -- SERIES 3N -- FOUR/V-6 -- In its first full year of production in 1993, the Achieva was again offered in coupe and sedan versions in S and SL trim. A Sport Coupe, known as Achieva SCX, was also offered as a package. It featured the 185-hp High Output Quad 4 engine with a special ratio five-speed manual transaxle, as well as aluminum wheels with V-rated tires and Computer Command Ride System. The S models came standard with the 115-hp Quad overhead-cam four-cylinder engine linked to a five-speed manual transaxle. The uplevel SL models utilized the 155-hp Quad 4 dual overhead-cam engine coupled to a three-speed automatic transaxle, which was optional for the S models. The Series 3300 3.3-liter engine was available on all models. Standard equipment included anti-lock brakes, battery run-down protection, a full set of analog instru-

ments, child comfort guide for shoulder belts, and automatically engaging door locks. Other improvements were done to the mounting system, cylinder block and induction system of Quad family engines to reduce noise and harshness through their full rpm range.

1993 Oldsmobile, Achieva SCX coupe, (O)

1993 Oldsmobile, Cutlass Ciera SL sedan, (O)

CUTLASS CIERA -- SERIES 3A -- FOUR/V-6 -- The Cutlass Ciera sedan-only and Cutlass Cruiser lineup remained unchanged from the year before with S and SL versions of each. For 1993, Ciera SL and Cruiser SL models offered a driver's side airbag as standard equipment, which was optional on Ciera S and Cruiser S models. Standard powertrain for Ciera S sedan and Cruiser S station wagon was the new 2.2-liter inline, fuel-injected four-cylinder engine mated to a three-speed automatic transaxle. The Ciera SL and Cruiser SL models had the Series 3300 3.3-liter V-6 with three-speed automatic transaxle as standard on the Ciera SL and four-speed automatic on the Cruiser SL. The Series 3300 V-6 was optional on S models, and the four-speed automatic transaxle was optional across the lineup (except Cruiser SL where it was standard equipment). Also new, Ciera and Cruiser received variable-rate springs and increased front caster to improve their ride quality.

1993 Oldsmobile, Cutlass Supreme S coupe, (O)

1993 Oldsmobile, Cutlass Supreme International Series sedan, (O)

CUTLASS SUPREME -- SERIES 3W -- V-6 -- In 1993, Cutlass Supreme came in three body styles: coupe, sedan and convertible. The coupe and sedan were offered in both S and International Series trim levels in addition to the Cutlass Supreme Convertible, this lineup unchanged from the year before. The 140-hp 3.1-liter V-6 was the standard engine in both the S models and convertible with the S cars utilizing a three-speed automatic transaxle while the convertible used a four-speed automatic. The 200-hp 3.4-liter twin dual overhead-cam V-6 engine with electronically-controlled four-speed automatic transaxle was the standard powertrain of the International Series and optional in all other Cutlass Supreme models. New-for-1993 was automatic power door locks across the lineup and a new 16-inch aluminum wheel standard on the I Series and included on the convertible when the 3.4-liter engine option was selected.

1993 Oldsmobile, Cutlass Supreme convertible, (O)

1993 Oldsmobile, Eighty-Eight Royale LSS sedan, (O)

EIGHTY-EIGHT ROYALE -- SERIES 3H -- V-6 -- Completely re-engineered the previous year, the return of the sedan-only lineup of Eighty-Eight Royales in 1993 still featured many refinements. Again offered in base and LS trim levels, the most significant change occurred under the hood. The standard Series 3800 3.8-liter V-6 received a higher compression ratio, new injectors and revised emission controls, the result being more torque (225 pound feet, up from 220 the year before), better fuel economy, cleaner exhaust and improved acceleration. This engine was linked to an electronic shift four-speed automatic transaxle. Anti-lock brakes and driver's side airbag were also standard equipment across the lineup. An LSS Package was offered on the LS sedan, which transformed the car into a sport sedan equipped with bucket seats, full instrumentation, touring suspension, variable effort steering and 16-inch aluminum wheels.

1993 Oldsmobile, Silhouette minivan, (O)

SILHOUETTE -- SERIES 3U -- V-6 -- In its fourth model year, the Silhouette received a minor exterior design change in 1993 consisting of updates to front and rear fascias and rocker moldings. Also, the standard 15-inch aluminum wheels received a new six-spoke turbine design. Inside, the steering wheel design had a self-aligning hub that automatically deformed in a collision. An improved acoustics package was installed to enhance quietness. New standard features include a locking storage compartment in the center floor console and the mid-model year addition of a power-operated sliding side door. The 3.1-liter V-6 linked to a three-speed automatic transaxle was the standard powertrain, with the Series 3800 3.8-liter V-6 and four-speed automatic optional.

1993 Oldsmobile, Ninety-Eight Regency Elite sedan, (O)

NINETY-EIGHT REGENCY -- SERIES 3C -- V-6 -- Oldsmobile's flagship, the Ninety-Eight Regency lineup for 1993 again featured sedans only in base, Elite and Touring Sedan trim. Standard powertrain consisted of the upgraded Series 3800 3.8-liter V-6 mated to an electronic shift four-speed automatic transaxle. Standard features included driver's side airbag, anti-lock brakes, shift interlock, power door locks, "Pass-Key" security system, child security lock for rear windows and power window lock-out switch. Optional are a traction control system and towing package. On the Touring Sedan, a supercharged version of the Series 3800 V-6 was available.

1993 Oldsmobile, Ninety-Eight Touring Sedan, (O)

BRAVADA -- SERIES 3T -- V-6 -- The 200-hp 4.3-liter Central Port Injection V-6 engine that powered the Bravada was the most powerful V-6 available in the sport utility class in 1993. To this potent package, Oldsmobile added a Hydra-matic 4L60-E electronic automatic four-speed overdrive transmission. Inside, the Bravada received several upgrades. These included a standard six-way power adjuster and power lumbar adjusters on both front bucket seats, an overhead console containing a digital compass and outside temperature display, and solar glass. A new special option Gold Package was offered that featured gold exterior trim and gold-tinted aluminum wheels.

1993 Oldsmobile, Bravada sport utility vehicle, (O)

I.D. DATA: Oldsmobile's 17-symbol Vehicle Identification Number (VIN) again was located on the upper left surface of the instrument panel, visible through the windshield. The first three characters (1G3) indicates Oldsmobile Division. The fourth and fifth letters designate the body type/series: A/J - Cutlass Cruiser S, A/G - Cutlass Ciera S, A/M - Cutlass Ciera SL and Cutlass Cruiser SL, C/V - Touring Sedan, C/W - Ninety-Eight Regency Elite, C/X - Ninety-Eight Regency, H/N - Eighty-Eight Royale, H/Y - Eighty-Eight Royale LS, N/F - Achieva SL, N/L - Achieva S, T/V - Bravada, U/M - Silhouette, W/H - Cutlass Supreme S, W/R - Cutlass Supreme International Series, W/T - Cutlass Supreme Convertible. The sixth number identifies the body style: 1 - 2-dr coupe, 2 - 2-dr hatchback/liftback, 3 - 2-dr convertible, 4 - 2-dr station wagon, 5 - 4-dr sedan, 6 - 4-dr hatchback/liftback, 8 - 4-dr station wagon. The seventh number identifies the restraint code: 1 - active (manual) belts, 2 - active (manual) belts with driver's and passenger's side airbags, 3 - active (manual) belts with driver's side airbag, 4 - passive (automatic) belts, 5 - passive (automatic) belts with driver's side airbag. The eighth letter identifies the engine: A = 2.3-liter fuel-injected inline four-cylinder, D = 2.3-liter fuel-injected inline four-cylinder, L = 3.8-liter fuel-injected V-6, M = 3.1-liter fuel-injected V-6, N = 3.3-liter fuel-injected V-6, T = 3.1-liter fuel-injected V-6, W = 4.3-liter fuel-injected V-6, X = 3.4-liter fuel-injected V-6, 1 = 3.8-liter fuel-injected V-6, 3 = 2.3-liter fuel-injected inline four-cylinder, 4 = 2.2-liter fuel-injected inline four-cylinder. The ninth number is the check digit. The tenth letter represents the model year (P = 1993). The eleventh character identifies the assembly plant: D - Doraville, Ga.; H - Flint, Mich.; M - Lansing, Mich.; T - Tarrytown, N.Y.; 1 - Wentzville, Mo.; 2 - Moraine, Ohio; 4 - Orion, Mich.; 6 - Oklahoma City, Okla. The final six digits are the sequential serial number.

ACHIEVA S (FOUR/V-6)

Model Number	Body/Style Number	Body Type & Seating	Factory Price	Shipping Weight	Production Total
3N	L37	2-dr. Cpe-5P	13049/13509	2716/2771	13525
3N	L69	4-dr. Sed-5P	13149/13609	2779/2834	30837

ACHIEVA SL (FOUR/V-6)

3N	F37	2-dr. Cpe-5P	14849/14899	2822/2945	590
3N	F69	4-dr. Sed-5P	14949/14999	2890/3013	3283

CUTLASS CIERA S (FOUR/V-6)

Model Number	Body/Style Number	Body Type & Seating	Factory Price	Shipping Weight	Production Total
3A	L69	4-dr. Sed-6P	14199/14859	2733/2917	142552
3A	J35	4-dr. Sta Wag-6P	14899/15559	2934/3099	5785

CUTLASS CIERA SL (V-6)

3A	M69	4-dr. Sed-6P	17899	3019	4304
3A	M35	4-dr. Sta Wag-6P	18399	3231	1084

CUTLASS SUPREME (V-6)

3W	T67	2-dr. Conv-6P	22699	3651	6751

CUTLASS SUPREME S (V-6)

3W	H47	2-dr. Cpe-6P	15695	3243	23544
3W	H69	4-dr. Sed-6P	15795	3354	51678

CUTLASS SUPREME INTERNATIONAL SERIES (V-6)

3W	R47	2-dr. Cpe-6P	22799	3243	395
3W	R69	4-dr. Sed-6P	22899	3354	645

EIGHTY-EIGHT ROYALE (V-6)

Model Number	Body/Style Number	Body Type & Seating	Factory Price	Shipping Weight	Production Total
3H	N69	4-dr. Sed-6P	19549	3404	47428

EIGHTY-EIGHT ROYALE LS (V-6)

3H	Y69	4-dr. Sed-6P	21949	3485	14903

SILHOUETTE (V-6)

Model Number	Body/Style Number	Body Type & Seating	Factory Price	Shipping Weight	Production Total
3U	M06	3-dr. Minivan-7P	19499	3689	20476

NINETY-EIGHT REGENCY (V-6)

Model Number	Body/Style Number	Body Type & Seating	Factory Price	Shipping Weight	Production Total
3C	X69	4-dr. Sed-6P	24999	3512	8906

NINETY-EIGHT REGENCY ELITE (V-6)

3C	W69	4-dr. Sed-6P	26999	3539	9900

NINETY-EIGHT TOURING SEDAN (V-6)

3C	V69	4-dr. Sed-6P	29699	3593	1885

BRAVADA (V-6)

Model Number	Body/Style Number	Body Type & Seating	Factory Price	Shipping Weight	Production Total
3T	V06	4-dr. Sport Utility-5P	25349	4041	9671

FACTORY PRICE AND WEIGHT NOTE: Beginning with the Achieva S coupe, prices and weights to left of slash are for four-cylinder engine and to right for V-6.

ENGINE DATA: BASE FOUR (Achieva S): Quad inline, overhead-cam four-cylinder. Cast iron block and aluminum head. Displacement: 138 cu. in. (2.3 liters). Bore & stroke: 3.62 x 3.35 in. Compression ratio: 9.5:1. Net horsepower: 115 @ 5200 rpm. Torque: 140 lb. ft. @ 3200 rpm. Fuel injected. **BASE FOUR (Achieva SL):** Quad 4 inline, 16-valve, dual overhead-cam four-cylinder. Cast iron block and aluminum head. Displacement: 138 cu. in. (2.3 liters). Bore & stroke: 3.62 x 3.35 in. Compression ratio: 9.5:1. Net horsepower: 155 @ 6000 rpm. Torque: 150 lb. ft. @ 4800 rpm. Fuel injected. **BASE FOUR (Achieva SCX):** High Output Quad 4 inline, 16-valve, dual overhead-cam four-cylinder. Cast iron block and aluminum head. Displacement: 138 cu. in. (2.3 liters). Bore & stroke: 3.62 x 3.35 in. Compression ratio: 10.0:1. Net horsepower: 185 @ 6200 rpm. Torque: 155 lb. ft. @ 5200 rpm. Fuel injected. **OPTIONAL FOUR (Achieva S)** same aforementioned Quad 4 2.3-liter/138-cid dual overhead-cam, fuel-injected four-cylinder. **BASE FOUR (Cutlass Ciera S/Cutlass Cruiser S):** Inline, overhead-valve four-cylinder. Cast iron block and aluminum head. Displacement: 133 cu. in. (2.2 liters). Bore & stroke: 3.50 x 3.46 in. Compression ratio: 9.0:1. Net horsepower: 110 @ 5200 rpm. Torque: 130 lb. ft. @ 3200 rpm. Fuel injection (MFI). **BASE V-6 (Cutlass Ciera SL/Cruiser SL):** Series 3300 90-degree overhead valve V-6. Displacement: 204 cu. in. (3.3 liters). Bore & stroke: 3.70 x 3.16 in. Compression ratio: 9.0:1. Net horsepower: 160 @ 5200 rpm. Torque: 185 lb. ft. @ 2000 rpm. Fuel injection (MFI). **OPTIONAL SIX (Achieva S/Achieva SL/Achieva SCX/Cutlass Ciera S/Cutlass Cruiser S):** same aforementioned Series 3300 3.3-liter/204-cid V-6 with MFI. **BASE SIX (Cutlass Supreme Convertible/Cutlass Supreme S):** 60-degree overhead valve V-6. Displacement: 191 cu. in. (3.1 liters). Bore & stroke: 3.50 x 3.31 in. Compression ratio: 8.9:1. Net horsepower: 140 @ 4200 rpm. Torque: 185 lb. ft. @ 3200 rpm. Fuel injection (MFI). **BASE SIX (Cutlass Supreme International Series):** Twin dual overhead cam V-6. Displacement: 207 cu. in. (3.4 liters). Bore & stroke: 3.62 x 3.30 in. Compression ratio: 9.3:1. Net horsepower: 200 @ 5200 rpm. Torque: 215 lb. ft. @ 4000. Fuel injected (MFI). **OPTIONAL SIX (Cutlass Supreme International):** same aforementioned 3.1-liter/191-cid V-6 with MFI. **OPTIONAL SIX (Cutlass Supreme Convertible/Cutlass Supreme S):** same aforementioned 3.4-liter/207-cid V-6 with MFI. **BASE SIX (Eighty-Eight/Ninety-Eight/Touring Sedan):** Series 3800 90-degree overhead valve V-6. Displacement: 231 cu. in. (3.8 liters). Bore & stroke: 3.80 x 3.40 in. Compression ratio: 9.0:1. Net horsepower: 170 @ 4800 rpm. Torque: 225 lb. ft. @ 3200 rpm. Fuel injected (TPI). **OPTIONAL SIX (Touring Sedan)** supercharged version of the aforementioned 3.8-liter/231-cid V-6. Net horsepower: 205 @ 4400 rpm. Torque: 260 lb. ft. @ 2800 rpm. **BASE SIX (Silhouette):** V-6. Displacement: 191 cu. in. (3.1 liters). Bore & stroke: 3.50 x 3.31 in. Compression ratio: 9.0:1. Net horsepower: 120 @ 4200 rpm. Torque: 175 lb. ft. @ 2200 rpm. Fuel injected (TBI). **OPTIONAL SIX (Silhouette):** same aforementioned 3.8-liter/231-cid V-6 with TPI. **BASE SIX (Bravada):** V-6. Displacement: 262 cu. in. (4.3 liters). Bore & stroke: 4.00 x 3.48 in. Compression ratio: 8.6:1. Net horsepower: 200 @ 4400 rpm. Torque: 260 lb. ft. @ 3600 rpm. Fuel injected (TBI).

CHASSIS DATA: Wheelbase: (Achieva) 103.4 in.; (Ciera) 104.9 in.; (Cutlass Cruiser) 104.9 in.; (Cutlass Supreme) 107.5 in.; (Eighty-Eight) 110.8 in.; (Silhouette) 109.8 in.; (Ninety-Eight) 110.7 in.; (Touring Sedan) 110.7 in.; (Bravada) 107.0 in. Overall Length: (Achieva) 187.9 in.; (Ciera) 190.3 in.; (Cutlass Cruiser) 194.4 in.; (Cutlass Supreme Coupe and Convertible) 193.9 in.; (Cutlass Supreme Sedan) 193.7 in.; (Eighty-Eight) 200.4 in.; (Silhouette) 194.2 in.; (Ninety-Eight) 205.5 in.; (Touring Sedan) 205.5 in.; (Bravada) 178.9 in. Height: (Achieva) 53.1 in.; (Ciera) 54.1 in.; (Cutlass Cruiser) 54.5 in.; (Cutlass Supreme Coupe and Convertible) 53.3 in.; (Cutlass Supreme Sedan) 54.8 in.; (Eighty-Eight) 55.7 in.; (Silhouette) 65.7 in.; (Ninety-Eight) 54.8 in.; (Touring Sedan) 54.8 in.; (Bravada) 65.5 in. Width: (Achieva) 67.2 in.; (Ciera) 69.5 in.; (Cutlass Cruiser) 69.5 in.; (Cutlass Supreme) 71.0 in.; (Eighty-Eight) 74.1 in.; (Silhouette) 73.9 in.; (Ninety-Eight) 74.6 in.; (Touring Sedan) 74.6 in.; (Bravada) 65.2 in. Front tread: (Achieva) 55.6 in.; (Ciera) 58.7 in.; (Cutlass Cruiser) 58.7 in.; (Cutlass Supreme) 59.5 in.; (Eighty-Eight) 60.4 in.; (Silhouette) 59.2 in.; (Ninety-Eight) 61.5 in.; (Touring Sedan) 61.5 in.; (Bravada) 55.6 in. Rear tread: (Achieva) 55.3 in.; (Ciera) 57.0 in.; (Cutlass Cruiser) 57.0 in.; (Cutlass Supreme) 58.0 in.; (Eighty-Eight) 60.4 in.; (Silhouette) 61.4 in.; (Ninety-Eight) 60.3 in.; (Touring Sedan) 60.3 in.; (Bravada) 54.1 in. Standard tires: (Achieva) P185/75R14; (Ciera) P185/75R14; (Cutlass Cruiser) P185/75R14; (Cutlass Supreme) P205/70R15; (Cutlass Supreme Convertible) P225/60R16; (Eighty-Eight) P205/70R15; (Silhouette) P205/70R15; (Ninety-Eight) P205/70R15; (Touring Sedan) P225/60R16; (Bravada) P235/75R15.

TECHNICAL: Transmission: Five-speed manual floor shift standard on Achieva S. Three-speed automatic standard on Achieva SL, optional on S models. Three-speed automatic standard on Cutlass Ciera S and SL/Cutlass Cruiser S/Cutlass Supreme S/Silhouette. Four-speed automatic available on Cutlass Ciera S and SL/Cutlass Cruiser S/Cutlass Supreme S/Silhouette. Four-speed automatic standard on Cutlass Cruiser SL/Cutlass Supreme Convertible/Cutlass Supreme International Series/Eighty-Eight/Ninety-Eight/Touring Sedan/Bravada. Standard final drive ratio: (Achieva) 3.58:1 with five-speed manual trans.; (Cutlass Ciera) 3.06:1 with three-speed automatic trans.; (Cutlass Cruiser) 3.06:1 with three-speed automatic trans.; (Cutlass Supreme) 2.84:1 with three-speed automatic trans.; (Cutlass Supreme Convertible) 3.33:1 with four-speed automatic trans.; (Eighty-Eight/Ninety-Eight) 2.84:1 with four-speed automatic trans.; (Touring Sedan) 3.06:1 with four-speed automatic trans.; (Silhouette) N/A; (Bravada) 3.42:1 with four-speed automatic trans. Steering: (all except Bravada) power assisted rack and pinion; (Bravada) integral power steering variable ratio. Front Suspension: (Achieva/Ciera/Cutlass Cruiser/Cutlass Supreme/Eighty-Eight/Ninety-Eight/Touring Sedan) Independent, MacPherson strut w/ coil springs and anti-roll bar; (Silhouette) MacPherson struts, stamped lower control arms, stabilizer bar; (Bravada) Independent driving axle w/ upper and lower control arms, torsion bar springs, front stabilizer bar and frame-mounted differential carrier. Rear Suspension: (Achieva) Independent, trailing crank arm w/ twist beam and coil springs; (Ciera) Variable rate coil spring; (Cutlass Cruiser) Variable rate coil spring; (Cutlass Supreme) Independent, transverse fiberglass leaf spring plus shock struts; (Eighty-Eight) Independent, MacPherson strut, coil springs, anti-roll bar with FE3 suspension options; (Ninety-Eight) automatic load leveling and coil springs with FE3 suspension options; (Silhouette) variable rate coil springs; (Bravada) Salisbury axle design with semi-elliptic leaf springs. Brakes: (Ciera) power assisted front disc, rear drum; (Achieva/Eighty-Eight/Ninety-Eight/Silhouette) anti-lock power front disc, rear drum; (Cutlass Supreme) power four-wheel disc

-- anti-lock standard on Cutlass Supreme International Series and optional on Cutlass Supreme S and Convertible; (Bravada) front disc, rear drum, Kelsey-Hayes four-wheel anti-lock. Body Construction: (all except Silhouette/Bravada) unibody; (Bravada) separate body and frame, (Silhouette) space frame substructure attached to ladder frame. Fuel tank: (Achieva) 15.2 gal.; (Ciera) 16.5 gal.; (Cutlass Cruiser) 16.5 gal.; (Cutlass Supreme) 16.5 gal.; (Eighty-Eight/Ninety-Eight/Touring Sedan) 18.0 gal.; (Silhouette) 20.0 gal.; (Bravada) 20.0 gal.

DRIVETRAIN OPTIONS: (Achieva S) Quad 4 2.3-liter dual overhead-cam inline four-cylinder ($410); (Achieva S/Achieva SL) Series 3300 3.3-liter V-6 ($460 - S;$50 - SL). (Ciera S/ Cutlass Cruiser S) Series 3300 3.3-liter V-6 ($660). (Cutlass Supreme S) 3.4-liter V-6 ($1158-$1645); (Cutlass Supreme Convertible) 3.4-liter V-6 ($995). (Cutlass Supreme International Series) 3.1-liter V-6 ($995 credit). (Ninety-Eight) supercharged 3.8-liter V-6 ($1022). (Silhouette) 3.8-liter V-6 ($800). Transmission: (Achieva S) three-speed automatic ($555); (Ciera S/Cutlass Cruiser S/Ciera SL) four-speed automatic ($200); (Cutlass Supreme S) four-speed automatic ($175). Suspension: (Eighty-Eight) FE3 Touring Suspension System ($720-$810). (Silhouette) FE3 Touring Suspension System ($205). (Ninety-Eight) FE3 Touring Suspension System ($239-$370). (Cutlass Supreme S and Convertible) anti-lock brakes ($450). (Ciera S and SL/Cutlass Cruiser S and SL/Cutlass Supreme S and International Series) high-capacity cooling ($40-$125). (Eighty-Eight) Towing package ($150-$325). (Ninety-Eight) Towing package ($150). (Silhouette) Towing package ($355). (Bravada) heavy-duty towing package ($255). (All) California emission equipment ($100). Engine block heater ($18).

OPTION PACKAGES: (Achieva S Coupe) SCX performance package ($2475). (Cutlass Supreme S) Sport Luxury Package ($628-$883). (Eighty-Eight Royale LS) LSS Package ($1995). (Bravada) Gold Package ($60).

MAJOR CONVENIENCE/APPEARANCE OPTIONS: Computer Command Ride System ($380-$470). Cruise control ($225). traction control system ($175). Driver's side airbag ($500). Tilt-away steering wheel ($145). Power decklid lock release ($60). Remote lock control package ($185). Power antenna ($85). Pulse wiper system ($65). Body accent stripe ($45). Electric Sliding Glass Astroroof ($695-$1350). Electric rear window defogger ($170).

HISTORY: Model year production (U.S.): 367,999. Calendar year production (U.S.) 433,589. Calendar year sales by U.S. dealers: 402,936. Model year sales by U.S. dealers: 382,021.

Historical Footnotes: Oldsmobile's model year sales declined to 382,021 in 1993 compared to 437,544 the year before.

1994

Oldsmobile again simplified its lineup, offering seven fewer models in 1994 than the year before. With the exception of the Bravada, every model offered by Oldsmobile came standard with a driver's side airbag. In the Eighty-Eight and Ninety-Eight, a passenger's side airbag was also standard. Anti-lock brakes were also installed on every Oldsmobile. The air conditioning refrigerant Freon was replaced in all but the Bravada with R134A, which contained no environment-harming CFCs and is non-ozone depleting. Models dropped that were offered the previous year consisted of the Achieva SL coupe, Cutlass Ciera SL sedan, Cutlass Cruiser SL, Cutlass Supreme International Series coupe and sedan and the Ninety-Eight-based Touring Sedan. A new Achieva SC coupe made its debut, as did a Special Edition line of Oldsmobiles that featured SE versions of the Achieva S coupe and sedan/ SC coupe/SL sedan, Cutlass Ciera S/Cutlass Cruiser S, Cutlass Supreme SL coupe and sedan, Eighty-Eight Royale, Eighty-Eight LSS, Ninety-Eight Regency, Silhouette and Bravada.

1994 Oldsmobile, Achieva SL Special Edition sedan, (O)

ACHIEVA -- SERIES 3N -- FOUR/V-6 -- The Achieva lineup was restructured for 1994 with Oldsmobile's least expensive, compact model offered as an S coupe and sedan, new SC sport coupe and new design SL sport sedan. New features in addition to the standard driver's side airbag included tilt steering, pulse wipers and illuminated entry system with theater dimming; a revised automatic door locking system; standard rear window defogger; new leather trim option for SC and SL models; a four-speed electronically controlled automatic transaxle standard with the Quad 4 and V-6 engines and 10 decibel reduction of Quad 4 induction noise. A new, optional 3100 sequential fuel-injected V-6 engine replaced the previous year's 3.3-liter V-6. The 3100 V-6 featured a structural aluminum oil pan, cross-bolted main bearing caps, composite plastic rocker arm covers, direct ignition and special assembled crankshaft.

CUTLASS CIERA -- SERIES 3A -- FOUR/V-6 -- With the deletion of the SL versions offered previously, the Cutlass Ciera lineup for 1994 consisted of the S sedan and Ciera-based Cutlass Cruiser S. Standard equipment on the Ciera S and Cruiser S was upgraded with the addition of a driver's side airbag, anti-lock brakes, tilt wheel, rear window defogger and pulse wipers. Automatic door locks were also improved. Powertrain changes included new features on the standard-on-S-sedans 2.2-liter four-cylinder engine, the biggest of which was a horsepower increase of 10, to 120 total. Improvements on the engine were comprised of upgraded roller lifters, new assembled camshaft, direct ignition and extended-life spark plugs. A new 3100 sequential fuel-injected V-6 engine linked to an electronically controlled three-speed automatic transaxle was the standard powertrain on the Cruiser S station wagon and optional on the S sedan.

1994 Oldsmobile, Cutlass Supreme SL Special Edition sedan, (O)

CUTLASS SUPREME -- SERIES 3W -- V-6 -- The 1994 Cutlass Supreme lineup was simplified with the elimination of the International Series coupe and sedan and upgrading of standard equipment for the S coupe and sedan as well as Cutlass Supreme Convertible. Standard equipment across the lineup included driver's side airbag, anti-lock brakes, tilt wheel, pulse wipers, rallye gauge cluster, rear window defogger and door handle-activated illuminated entry system. Brake systems were also improved with a larger booster, larger rear brake calipers,

extended-life pads and enhanced corrosion resistance. In addition, the convertible's standard equipment included programmable automatic door locks, driver's side six-way power seat and leather upholstery. Standard powertrain for all Cutlass Supreme models was the new 160-hp 3100 sequential fuel-injected V-6 mated to an electronic four-speed automatic transaxle. The 210-hp 3.4-liter twin dual overhead cam V-6 engine with four-speed automatic was optional as a performance package item accompanied by a deck spoiler (S coupe only) and five-spoke aluminum wheels.

1994 Oldsmobile, Eighty-Eight Royale LSS Special Edition sedan, (O)

EIGHTY-EIGHT ROYALE -- SERIES 3H -- V-6 -- For 1994, the Eighty-Eight Royale, offered in base and LS trim levels in sedan-only, received interior upgrades that included standard dual airbags, redesigned instruments and controls, door panels configured with built-in grips and pockets, illuminated power seat switches and all-new radio. Engineering refinements included reduced engine and exhaust noise due to a larger muffler and added resonator. Optional traction control minimized wheel spin. Standard powertrain was the Series 3800 3.8-liter V-6 coupled to an electronically controlled four-speed automatic transaxle.

1994 Oldsmobile, Silhouette Special Edition minivan, (O)

SILHOUETTE -- SERIES 3U -- V-6 -- Called Oldsmobile's "family mover," the 1994 Silhouette multipurpose minivan received refinements that included a taller axle ratio for the standard powertrain to both diminish engine noise at cruising speed and improve efficiency. New standard features included a driver's side airbag, anti-lock brakes, high-mounted center stop lamp, programmable automatic door locks, lift gate handle and child security lock on the side sliding door. Optional equipment included traction control, outboard integrated child seats on center row bench seat, leather seating and GL-20 glass to reduce the transmission of ultraviolet and infrared rays. Standard powertrain was the 3.1-liter V-6 linked to a three-speed automatic transaxle. The Series 3800 3.8-liter V-6 and four-speed automatic was optional.

1994 Oldsmobile, Ninety-Eight Regency Special Edition sedan, (O)

NINETY-EIGHT REGENCY -- SERIES 3C -- V-6 -- Offered in base and Elite sedans, the 1994 Ninety-Eight Regency received many refinements. With the deletion of the Touring Sedan offered previously, the optional, 225-hp supercharged version of the standard Series 3800 3.8-liter V-6 engine was available in the Elite. A four-speed automatic transaxle completed the standard powertrain. Across the lineup, standard equipment included driver's and passenger's side airbags, anti-lock brakes, auxiliary power outlet for use with on-board accessories and programmable automatic door locks. Improvements included new instrument panel, door panel and steering wheel designs, quieter exhaust, 15-inch radial spoke aluminum wheels (standard on Elite, optional on base sedan) and additional front seat travel. Traction control was optional.

1994 Oldsmobile, Bravada Special Edition sport utility vehicle, (O)

BRAVADA -- SERIES 3T -- V-6 -- The Bravada was made more comfortable to drive in 1994 due to a quieter engine, more effective muffler and revised shock absorber valving aimed at improving the ride. Other improvements consisted of added sideguard door beams, center high-mounted stop lamp and enhanced corrosion resistance for underhood and underbody components. Standard powertrain was the 200-hp 4.3-liter V-6 mated to an electronically controlled four-speed automatic transmission and SmartTrak (the combination of full-time all-wheel drive and anti-lock brakes).

I.D. DATA: Oldsmobile's 17-symbol Vehicle Identification Number (VIN) again was located on the upper left surface of the instrument panel, visible through the windshield. The first three characters (1G3) indicates Oldsmobile Division. The fourth and fifth letters designate the body type/series: A/G - Cutlass Ciera S, A/J - Cutlass Cruiser S, C/W - Ninety-Eight Regency Elite, C/X - Ninety-Eight Regency, H/N - Eighty-Eight Royale, H/Y - Eighty-Eight Royale LS, N/F - Achieva SL and SC, N/L - Achieva S, T/V - Bravada, U/M - Silhouette, W/H - Cutlass Supreme S, W/T - Cutlass Supreme Convertible. The sixth number identifies the body style: 1 - 2-dr coupe, 2 - 2-dr hatchback/liftback, 3 -

2-dr convertible, 4 - 2-dr station wagon, 5 - 4-dr sedan, 6 - 4-dr hatchback/liftback, 8 - 4-dr station wagon. The seventh number identifies the restraint code: 1 - active (manual) belts, 2 - active (manual) belts with driver's and passenger's side airbags, 3 - active (manual) belts with driver's side airbag, 4 - passive (automatic) belts, 5 - passive (automatic) belts with driver's side airbag, 6 - passive (automatic) belts with driver's and passenger's side airbags. The eighth letter identifies the engine: A = 2.3-liter fuel-injected inline four-cylinder, D = 2.3-liter fuel-injected inline four-cylinder, L = 3.8-liter fuel-injected V-6, M = 3.1-liter fuel-injected V-6, W = 4.3-liter fuel-injected V-6, X = 3.4-liter fuel-injected V-6, 1 = 3.8-liter fuel-injected V-6, 3 = 2.3-liter fuel-injected inline four-cylinder, 4 = 2.2-liter fuel-injected inline four-cylinder. The ninth number is the check digit. The tenth letter represents the model year (R = 1994). The eleventh character identifies the assembly plant: D - Doraville, Ga.; H - Flint, Mich.; M - Lansing, Mich.; T - Tarrytown, N.Y.; 2 - Moraine, Ohio; 4 - Orion, Mich.; 6 - Oklahoma City, Okla. The final six digits are the sequential serial number.

ACHIEVA S (FOUR/V-6)

Model Number	Body/Style Number	Body Type & Seating	Factory Price	Shipping Weight	Production Total
3N	L37	2-dr. Cpe-5P	14075/14485	2716/2734	15668
3N	L69	4-dr. Sed-5P	14175/14585	2779/2797	43329

Note: Achieva S Special Edition prices were as follows: $13,995 for two-door coupe (R7B) and four-door sedan (R7B); $14,995 for two-door coupe (R7C) and four-door sedan (R7C); and $17,295 for two-door coupe (R7D) and four-door sedan (R7D).

ACHIEVA SC (FOUR/V-6)

Model Number	Body/Style Number	Body Type & Seating	Factory Price	Shipping Weight	Production Total
3N	F37	2-dr. Cpe-5P	17475/17335	2822/2840	1555

Note: Achieva SC Special Edition price N/A.

ACHIEVA SL (FOUR/V-6)

Model Number	Body/Style Number	Body Type & Seating	Factory Price	Shipping Weight	Production Total
3N	F69	4-dr. Sed-5P	17475/17335	2890/2908	1540

Note: Achieva SL Special Edition price N/A.

CUTLASS CIERA S (FOUR - sedan only/V-6)

Model Number	Body/Style Number	Body Type & Seating	Factory Price	Shipping Weight	Production Total
3A	G69	4-dr. Sed-6P	15675/16485	2833/2936	132351
3A	J35	4-dr. Sta Wag-6P	-------/17175	------/3086	9809

Note: Cutlass Ciera S and Cruiser S Special Edition prices were as follows: $14,195 for four-door sedan (R7B); $16,195 for four-door sedan (R7C); and $17,195 for four-door station wagon (R7D).

CUTLASS SUPREME (V-6)

Model Number	Body/Style Number	Body Type & Seating	Factory Price	Shipping Weight	Production Total
3W	T67	2-dr. Conv-6P	25275	3638	8638

CUTLASS SUPREME S (V-6)

Model Number	Body/Style Number	Body Type & Seating	Factory Price	Shipping Weight	Production Total
3W	H47	2-dr. Cpe-6P	17375	3307	35757
3W	H69	4-dr. Sed-6P	17475	3405	77861

Note: Cutlass Supreme SL (Sport Luxury package) Special Edition prices were as follows: $17,195 for two-door coupe (R7B) and four-door sedan (R7B); and $18,195 for two-door coupe (R7C) and four-door sedan (R7C).

EIGHTY-EIGHT ROYALE (V-6)

Model Number	Body/Style Number	Body Type & Seating	Factory Price	Shipping Weight	Production Total
3H	N69	4-dr. Sed-6P	20875	3439	60362

Note: Eighty-Eight Royale Special Edition price was as follows: $19,995 (R7B)

EIGHTY-EIGHT ROYALE LS (V-6)

Model Number	Body/Style Number	Body Type & Seating	Factory Price	Shipping Weight	Production Total
3H	Y69	4-dr. Sed-6P	22875	3469	21664

Note: Eighty-Eight Royale LSS Special Edition price was as follows: $23,295 (R7C)

SILHOUETTE (V-6)

Model Number	Body/Style Number	Body Type & Seating	Factory Price	Shipping Weight	Production Total
3U	M06	3-dr. Minivan-7P	20465	3697	26017

Note: Silhouette Special Edition prices were as follows: $20,195 (R7B) or $21,995 (R7C).

NINETY-EIGHT REGENCY (V-6)

Model Number	Body/Style Number	Body Type & Seating	Factory Price	Shipping Weight	Production Total
3C	X69	4-dr. Sed-6P	25875	3512	20171

Note: Ninety-Eight Regency Special Edition price was as follows: $25,295.

NINETY-EIGHT REGENCY ELITE (V-6)

Model Number	Body/Style Number	Body Type & Seating	Factory Price	Shipping Weight	Production Total
3C	W69	4-dr. Sed-6P	27975	3527	6463

BRAVADA (V-6)

Model Number	Body/Style Number	Body Type & Seating	Factory Price	Shipping Weight	Production Total
3T	V06	4-dr. Sport Utility-5P	26320	4041	17681

Note: Bravada Special Edition price was as follows: $25,295.

FACTORY PRICE AND WEIGHT NOTE: Beginning with the Achieva S coupe, prices and weights to left of slash are for four-cylinder engine and to right for V-6.

ENGINE DATA: BASE FOUR (Achieva S): Quad inline, overhead-cam four-cylinder. Cast iron block and aluminum head. Displacement: 140 cu. in. (2.3 liters). Bore & stroke: 3.62 x 3.35 in. Compression ratio: 9.5:1. Net horsepower: 115 @ 5200 rpm. Torque: 140 lb. ft. @ 3200 rpm. Fuel injected (MFI). BASE FOUR (Achieva SC/Achieva SL): High Output Quad 4 inline, 16-valve, dual overhead-cam four-cylinder. Cast iron block and aluminum head. Displacement: 140 cu. in. (2.3 liters). Bore & stroke: 3.62 x 3.35 in. Compression ratio: 10.0:1. Net horsepower: 175 @ 6200 rpm. Torque: 155 lb. ft. @ 5200 rpm. Fuel injected (MFI). OPTIONAL FOUR (Achieva S/Achieva SC/Achieva SL) Quad 4 inline, 16-valve, dual overhead-cam four-cylinder. Cast iron block and aluminum head. Displacement: 140 cu. in. (2.3 liters). Bore & stroke: 3.62 x 3.35 in. Compression ratio: 9.5:1. Net horsepower: 155 @ 6000 rpm. Torque: 150 lb. ft. @ 4800 rpm. Fuel injected (MFI). BASE FOUR (Cutlass Ciera S): Inline, overhead-valve four-cylinder. Cast iron block and aluminum head. Displacement: 133 cu. in. (2.2 liters). Bore & stroke: 3.50 x 3.46 in. Compression ratio: 9.0:1. Net horsepower: 120 @ 5200 rpm. Torque: 130 lb. ft. @ 4000 rpm. Fuel injection (MFI). BASE SIX (Cutlass Cruiser S): Series 3100 60-degree overhead valve V-6. Displacement: 191 cu. in. (3.1 liters). Bore & stroke: 3.50 x 3.31 in. Compression ratio: 9.5:1. Net horsepower: 160 @ 5200 rpm. Torque: 185 lb. ft. @ 4000 rpm. Fuel injection (SFI). OPTIONAL SIX (Achieva S/Achieva SC/Achieva SL/Cutlass Ciera S): same aforementioned Series 3100 3.1-liter/191-cid V-6 with SFI. BASE SIX (Cutlass Supreme Convertible/Cutlass Supreme S): 60-degree overhead valve V-6. Displacement: 191 cu. in. (3.1 liters). Bore & stroke: 3.50 x 3.31 in. Compression ratio: 9.5:1. Net horsepower: 160 @ 5200 rpm. Torque: 185 lb. ft. @ 4000 rpm. Fuel injection (SFI). OPTIONAL SIX (Cutlass Supreme Convertible/Cutlass Supreme S): Twin dual overhead cam V-6. Displacement: 207 cu. in. (3.4 liters). Bore & stroke: 3.62 x 3.30 in. Compression ratio: 9.3:1. Net horsepower: 210 @ 5200 rpm. Torque: 215 lb. ft. @ 4000. Fuel injected (SFI). BASE SIX (Eighty-Eight/Ninety-Eight): Series 3800 90-degree overhead valve V-6. Displacement: 231 cu. in. (3.8 liters). Bore & stroke: 3.80 x 3.40 in. Compression ratio: 9.0:1. Net horsepower: 170 @ 4800 rpm. Torque: 225 lb. ft. @ 3200 rpm. Fuel injected (TPI). OPTIONAL SIX (Ninety-Eight Regency Elite) supercharged version of the aforementioned 3.8-liter/231-cid V-6. Compression ratio: 8.5:1. Net horsepower: 225 @ 5000 rpm. Torque: 275 lb. ft. @ 3200 rpm. BASE SIX (Silhouette): V-6. Displacement: 191 cu. in. (3.1 liters). Bore & stroke: 3.50 x 3.31 in.

Compression ratio: 9.0:1. Net horsepower: 120 @ 4200 rpm. Torque: 175 lb. ft. @ 2200 rpm. Fuel injected (TBI). OPTIONAL SIX (Silhouette): same aforementioned 3.8-liter/231-cid V-6 with TPI. BASE SIX (Bravada): V-6. Displacement: 262 cu. in. (4.3 liters). Bore & stroke: 4.00 x 3.48 in. Compression ratio: 8.6:1. Net horsepower: 200 @ 4400 rpm. Torque: 260 lb. ft. @ 3600 rpm. Fuel injected (CPI).

CHASSIS DATA: Wheelbase: (Achieva) 103.4 in.; (Ciera) 104.9 in.; (Cutlass Cruiser) 104.9 in.; (Cutlass Supreme) 107.5 in.; (Eighty-Eight) 110.8 in.; (Silhouette) 109.8 in.; (Ninety-Eight) 110.8 in.; (Bravada) 107.0 in. Overall Length: (Achieva) 187.9 in.; (Ciera) 190.3 in.; (Cutlass Cruiser) 194.4 in.; (Cutlass Supreme Coupe and Convertible) 193.9 in.; (Cutlass Supreme Sedan) 193.7 in.; (Eighty-Eight) 200.4 in.; (Silhouette) 194.2 in.; (Ninety-Eight) 205.7 in.; (Bravada) 178.9 in. Height: (Achieva) 53.4 in.; (Ciera) 54.1 in.; (Cutlass Cruiser) 54.5 in.; (Cutlass Supreme Coupe) 53.3 in.; (Cutlass Supreme Convertible) 54.7 in.; (Cutlass Supreme Sedan) 54.8 in.; (Eighty-Eight) 55.7 in.; (Silhouette) 65.7 in.; (Ninety-Eight) 54.8 in.; (Bravada) 65.5 in. Width: (Achieva) 67.5 in.; (Ciera) 69.5 in.; (Cutlass Cruiser) 69.5 in.; (Cutlass Supreme) 71.0 in.; (Eighty-Eight) 74.1 in.; (Silhouette) 73.9 in.; (Ninety-Eight) 74.6 in.; (Bravada) 65.2 in. Front tread: (Achieva) 55.9 in.; (Ciera) 58.7 in.; (Cutlass Cruiser) 58.7 in.; (Cutlass Supreme) 59.5 in.; (Eighty-Eight) 60.4 in.; (Silhouette) 59.2 in.; (Ninety-Eight) 60.4 in.; (Bravada) 55.6 in. Rear tread: (Achieva) 55.4 in.; (Ciera) 57.0 in.; (Cutlass Cruiser) 57.0 in.; (Cutlass Supreme) 58.0 in.; (Eighty-Eight) 60.4 in.; (Silhouette) 61.4 in.; (Ninety-Eight) 60.4 in.; (Bravada) 54.1 in. Standard tires: (Achieva) P185/75R14; (Ciera) P185/75R14; (Cutlass Cruiser) P185/75R14; (Cutlass Supreme) P205/70R15; (Cutlass Supreme Convertible) P225/60R16; (Eighty-Eight) P205/70R15; (Silhouette) P205/70R15; (Ninety-Eight) P205/70R15; (Bravada) P235/75R15.

TECHNICAL: Transmission: Five-speed manual floor shift standard on Achieva S/Achieva SC/Achieva SL. Three-speed automatic optional on S models. Four-speed automatic optional on S/SC/SL models. Three-speed automatic standard on Cutlass Ciera S and Cutlass Cruiser S/Silhouette. Four-speed automatic available on Cutlass Ciera S and Cutlass Cruiser S/Silhouette. Four-speed automatic standard on Cutlass Supreme Convertible/Cutlass Supreme S/Eighty-Eight/Ninety-Eight/Bravada. Standard final drive ratio: (Achieva) 3.58:1 with five-speed manual trans.; (Cutlass Ciera) 3.06:1 with three-speed automatic trans.; (Cutlass Cruiser) 2.97:1 with four-speed automatic trans.; (Cutlass Supreme/Cutlass Supreme Convertible) 3.33:1 with four-speed automatic trans.; (Eighty-Eight/Ninety-Eight) 2.84:1 with four-speed automatic trans.; (Silhouette) N/A; (Bravada) 3.42:1 with four-speed automatic trans. Steering: (all except Bravada) power assisted rack and pinion; (Bravada) integral power steering variable ratio. Front Suspension: (Achieva/Ciera/Cutlass Cruiser/Cutlass Supreme/Eighty-Eight/Ninety-Eight/Touring Sedan) Independent, MacPherson strut w/ coil springs and anti-roll bar; (Silhouette) MacPherson struts, stamped lower control arms, stabilizer bar; (Bravada) Independent driving axle w/ upper and lower control arms, torsion bar springs, front stabilizer bar and frame-mounted differential carrier. Rear Suspension: (Achieva) Independent, trailing crank arm w/ twist beam and coil springs; (Ciera) Variable rate coil spring; (Cutlass Cruiser) Variable rate coil spring; (Cutlass Supreme) Independent, transverse fiberglass leaf spring plus shock struts; (Eighty-Eight) Independent, coil springs, anti-roll bar; (Ninety-Eight) Independent, automatic load leveling, coil springs, anti-roll bar; (Silhouette) variable rate coil springs; (Bravada) Salisbury axle design with semi-elliptic leaf springs. Brakes: (Achieva/Ciera/Eighty-Eight/Ninety-Eight/Silhouette) anti-lock power front disc, rear drum; (Cutlass Supreme S and Convertible) anti-lock power four-wheel disc; (Bravada) front disc, rear drum, Kelsey-Hayes four-wheel anti-lock. Body Construction: (all except Silhouette/Bravada) unibody; (Bravada) separate body and frame, (Silhouette) space frame substructure attached to ladder frame. Fuel tank: (Achieva) 15.2

gal.; (Ciera) 16.5 gal.; (Cutlass Cruiser) 16.5 gal.; (Cutlass Supreme) 17.1 gal.; (Eighty-Eight/Ninety-Eight) 18.0 gal.; (Silhouette) 20.0 gal.; (Bravada) 20.0 gal.

DRIVETRAIN OPTIONS: (Achieva S) Quad 4 2.3-liter dual overhead-cam inline four-cylinder ($410); (Achieva SC/Achieva SL) Series 3100 3.1-liter V-6 ($140 credit). (Achieva SC/Achieva SL) Quad 4 2.3-liter dual overhead-cam inline four-cylinder ($140 credit). (Ciera S) Series 3100 3.1-liter V-6 ($810). (Cutlass Supreme S) 3.4-liter V-6 ($1123-$1520); (Cutlass Supreme Convertible) 3.4-liter V-6 ($1085). (Ninety-Eight) supercharged 3.8-liter V-6 ($1541-$1631). (Silhouette) 3.8-liter V-6 ($800). Transmission: (Achieva S) three-speed automatic ($555); (Achieva S/Achieva SC/Achieva SL) four-speed automatic ($755). (Ciera S/Cutlass Cruiser S) four-speed automatic ($810 as packaged with 3.1-liter V-6, separate price N/A); (Silhouette) four-speed automatic ($800 as packaged with 3.8-liter V-6, separate price N/A). Suspension: (Silhouette) FE3 Touring Suspension System ($205). (Ciera S/Cutlass Cruiser S) high-capacity cooling ($40). (Silhouette) Towing package - 3,000 pound ($355). (Bravada) heavy-duty towing package ($255). (All) California emission equipment ($100). Engine block heater ($18).

OPTION PACKAGES: (Cutlass Supreme S) Sport Luxury Package ($823-$913). (Eighty-Eight Royale LS) LSS Package ($845). (Eighty-Eight Royale LS) Comfort Package ($555). (Eighty-Eight Royale LS) Luxury/Convenience Package ($725). (Bravada) Gold Package ($60).

MAJOR CONVENIENCE/APPEARANCE OPTIONS: Computer Command Ride System ($380-$470). Traction control system ($175-$350). Four-season air conditioner ($830). Deck lid luggage carrier ($115). Trunk convenience net ($30). Custom leather trim ($425-$870). Six-way power driver's seat adjuster ($270). Power antenna ($85). Body accent stripe ($45). Electric Sliding Glass Astroroof ($595-$1350). Electric cluster with driver information center ($345).

HISTORY: Model year production (U.S.): 435,172. Calendar year production (U.S.) 481,326. Calendar year sales by U.S. dealers: 448,945. Model year sales by U.S. dealers: 438,096.

Historical Footnotes: Oldsmobile's new Aurora, listed as a 1995 model (see 1995 listings), was sold beginning in April 1994. Model year sales increased to 438,096 compared to 382,021 in the year before.

1995

While it was launched in April of the previous year, Oldsmobile's new 1995 Aurora was touted by the automaker as its leading edge product -- the company's "renaissance" automobile -- as it prepared for Oldsmobile's centennial date (August 21, 1997) and beyond. For 1995, the Bravada offered for sale through December 1994 was a carry-over of the 1994 model, with plans for an all-new Bravada to be launched in 1996. Change was again the norm in the remainder of Oldsmobile's lineup. The Achieva SC coupe and SL sedan offered the previous year were

1995 Oldsmobile, Aurora sedan, (O)

deleted leaving the Achieva S coupe and sedan. The Cutlass Ciera S and Cutlass Cruiser S offered the year before were renamed Ciera SL sedan and Ciera SL station wagon for 1995, eliminating the long-standing association with the Cutlass name. The same S to SL renaming occurred with the Cutlass Supreme coupe and sedan. The base Ninety-Eight Regency was also dropped, leaving the Regency Elite as the sole model in the Ninety-Eight lineup for 1995.

AURORA -- SERIES 3G -- V-8 -- Oldsmobile's state-of-the-art four-door front-wheel drive luxury performance sedan offered a grocery list of technological advancements and offered a powertrain anchored by the return of the V-8 engine to the Oldsmobile fold, not seen since the rear-drive Custom Cruiser was discontinued after the 1992 model. The Aurora's V-8 was a new 4.0-liter dual overhead-cam unit with die-cast aluminum block and cast-aluminum cylinder heads. The 244 cubic inch V-8 had a 10.3:1 compression ratio and was produced at General Motors' Livonia, Mich., engine plant. It was linked to a Hydra-Matic 4T80-E four-speed electronically-controlled automatic transaxle. Standard features of the Aurora included anti-lock brakes, driver's and passenger's side airbags, traction control, "Pass-Key II" anti-theft system and Goodyear Eagle GA tires mounted on 7.0 x 16-inch cast aluminum wheels. Also new was the use of recycled materials in six areas of the Aurora including the rear seat electrical module support panel, headliner supports, aluminum bumper beams, front end and radiator panels, sound insulation and trunk lining.

1995 Oldsmobile, Achieva S coupe, (O)

ACHIEVA -- SERIES 3N -- FOUR/V-6 -- For 1995, the Achieva lineup was streamlined from the year before with only the S coupe and sedan offered, but in two levels of standard equipment: Series I and Series II. The engine lineup previously available to the Achieva was simplified for 1995 with the retirement of both the Quad 2.3-liter overhead-cam four-cylinder and High Output Quad 4 2.3-liter four-cylinder engine. Standard powertrain was an improved 2.3-liter dual overhead-cam four-cylinder engine mated to a five-speed manual transaxle. The refined 2.3-liter engine featured a balance shaft system for smoother operation and platinum-tipped spark plugs for 100,000-mile tune-up-free driving. The optional powertrain was the 155-hp 3.1-liter sequential fuel-injected V-6 linked to a four-speed automatic transmission, which was also available with the standard 2.3-liter four-cylinder engine. Also refined was the suspension settings including new shock absorber valving, revised front strut design, revised "spring-on-center" rear axle assembly and the addition of a rear anti-roll bar.

CIERA -- SERIES 3A -- FOUR/V-6 -- Aside from the aforementioned disassociation with the Cutlass name and the switch from S to SL designation, the changes to the 1995 Ciera SL sedan and Ciera SL station wagon from past models were minor. The SL sedan was available in Series I and Series II levels of equipment. New standard equipment included a shift interlock system and seat and door trim fabric designs were altered. Anti-lock brakes and driver's side airbag remained standard offerings. The 2.2-liter four-cylinder engine mated to a three-speed automatic transaxle was the standard powertrain in the SL sedan. In the SL station wagon, the 3.1-liter sequential fuel-injected V-6 with four-speed automatic transaxle was standard, while this combination was optional in the SL sedan.

1995 Oldsmobile, Cutlass Supreme SL sedan, (O)

CUTLASS SUPREME -- SERIES 3W -- V-6 -- The 1995 Cutlass Supreme was again offered in coupe, sedan and convertible versions. The aforementioned S to SL name change had the SL coupe and sedan available in two levels of standard equipment while the convertible was offered one way. Standard equipment included dual front airbags, low oil sensor, power windows, cruise control, 16-inch aluminum wheels, interlock shift device and CFC-free air conditioning. Standard powertrain was the 160-hp Series 3100 3.1-liter sequential fuel-injected V-6 linked to a four-speed electronically-controlled automatic transaxle. Optional was the 210-hp 3.4-liter twin dual cam V-6 with four-speed automatic. New-for-1995 was the Cutlass Supreme's suspension, which was retuned to provide more responsive steering and reduce body roll. Included in this rework was the addition of Electronic Variable Orifice (EVO) rack and pinion steering (standard with 3.4-liter V-6/optional with 3.1-liter V-6) as well as optimization of spring rates, strut and shock absorber valving and anti-roll bar sizing. Also new was the redesigned instrument panel as well as console, interior door panels and seat fabric. Lap and shoulder belts were revised, with anchor points being the B-pillar and floor.

1995 Oldsmobile, Cutlass Supreme convertible, (O)

1995 Oldsmobile, Eighty-Eight Royale LSS sedan, (O)

EIGHTY-EIGHT ROYALE -- SERIES 3H -- V-6 -- The lineup for 1995 Eighty-Eight Royale models consisted of base, LS and LSS versions. Each came equipped one way with a limited number of options available. The big change occurred under the hood with the introduction of the Series II version of the standard Eighty-Eight engine. The 3.8-liter V-6, with 9.4:1 compression ratio, was completely redesigned to improve responsiveness and durability. New features included a low-

deck block design to save weight and cross-bolted main bearings for added strength. Cylinder heads had more efficient intake and exhaust ports and cleaner burning combustion chambers. The valvetrain was both stiffer and lighter and featured larger diameter valves for improved breathing. An innovative two-piece intake manifold with tuned runners and a larger throttle body delivered the air to the engine. Optional for the LSS was the 225-hp supercharged 3800 V-6. Both engines were mated to a four-speed automatic transaxle. Standard equipment on the LSS included the touring ride and handling suspension with electronic level control at the rear. New features for the Eighty-Eight lineup included "flash-to-pass" function added to the turn-signal stalk and rear seat belt child comfort guides.

1995 Oldsmobile, Silhouette minivan, (O)

SILHOUETTE -- SERIES 3U -- V-6 -- The Silhouette for 1995 received several upgrades over the previous year's model including a shift interlock device and 170-hp 3800 V-6 with electronically-controlled four-speed automatic transaxle as standard powertrain (replacing the 3100 V-6 offered the year before). In addition to damage-resistant composite body panels and vandal-proof antenna, the Silhouette was offered with two levels of equipment: Series I's standard items consisted of driver's side airbag, anti-lock brakes, air conditioning, power windows and door locks, cruise control, remote keyless entry and rooftop luggage carrier. The uplevel Series II model offered Series I items plus driver's side power seat, leather trim, steering wheel touch controls and power sliding side door. Optional equipment included traction control and built-in child safety seats. Mechanical improvements consisted of the oil pan being laminated to reduce noise as well as a new gasket for better sealing and integrating the oil pan baffle into one component. Oil and water pumps were spline driven to reduce noise.

1995 Oldsmobile, Ninety-Eight Regency Elite sedan, (O)

NINETY-EIGHT REGENCY -- SERIES 3C -- V-6 -- With the deletion of the previous year's base model, the Ninety-Eight for 1995 was offered only as the Regency Elite with two levels of standard equipment. Standard features included dual airbags, anti-lock brakes, automatic power door locks and 15-inch aluminum wheels. The upgraded Series II 3800 V-6 coupled to a four-speed automatic transaxle was the standard powertrain. Optional was the supercharged version of the 3800 V-6, as was traction control. New features included "flash-to-pass" function on the turn-signal stalk, a console storage headliner and rear seat belt child comfort guides. The Ninety-Eight's interior was

also updated. Map pockets and pull-to-close handles were faired into the door design, metaphoric power seat adjuster switches were located over the armrests and an electrochromic inside rear view mirror provided a compass.

BRAVADA -- SERIES 3T -- V-6 -- A new Bravada model was not offered in 1995. The model from the previous year was sold through December of 1994 (see 1994 Bravada listings for specifications of this model). A totally new Bravada was then produced for sale as a 1996 model beginning in late fall 1995 (see 1996 Bravada listings for specifications of this model).

I.D. DATA: Oldsmobile's 17-symbol Vehicle Identification Number (VIN) again was located on the upper left surface of the instrument panel, visible through the windshield. The first three characters (1G3) indicates Oldsmobile Division. The fourth and fifth letters designate the body type/series: A/J - Cutlass Ciera SL sedan and SL station wagon, C/X - Ninety-Eight Regency Elite, G/R - Aurora, H/N - Eighty-Eight Royale, H/Y - Eighty-Eight Royale LS, N/L - Achieva S, T/V - Bravada, U/M - Silhouette, W/H - Cutlass Supreme SL, W/T - Cutlass Supreme Convertible. The sixth number identifies the body style: 1 - 2-dr coupe, 2 - 2-dr hatchback/liftback, 3 - 2-dr convertible, 4 - 2-dr station wagon, 5 - 4-dr sedan, 6 - 4-dr hatchback/liftback, 8 - 4-dr station wagon. The seventh number identifies the restraint code: 1 - active (manual) belts, 2 - active (manual) belts with driver's and passenger's side airbags, 3 - active (manual) belts with driver's side airbag, 4 - passive (automatic) belts, 5 - passive (automatic) belts with driver's side airbag, 6 - passive (automatic) belts with driver's and passenger's side airbags. The eighth letter identifies the engine: C = 4.0-liter fuel-injected V-8, D = 2.3-liter fuel-injected inline four-cylinder, K = 3.8-liter fuel-injected V-6, M = 3.1-liter fuel-injected V-6, W = 4.3-liter fuel-injected V-6, X = 3.4-liter fuel-injected V-6, 1 = 3.8-liter fuel-injected V-6, 4 = 2.2-liter fuel-injected inline four-cylinder. The ninth number is the check digit. The tenth letter represents the model year (S = 1995). The eleventh character identifies the assembly plant: D - Doraville, Ga.; H - Flint, Mich.; M - Lansing, Mich.; T - Tarrytown, N.Y.; 2 - Moraine, Ohio; 4 - Orion, Mich.; 6 - Oklahoma City, Okla. The final six digits are the sequential serial number.

AURORA (V-8)

Model Number	Body/Style Number	Body Type & Seating	Factory Price	Shipping Weight	Production Total
3G	R29	4-dr. Sed-6P	31370	3967	47831

ACHIEVA S (FOUR/V-6)

3N	L37	2-dr. Cpe-5P	13500/13912	2716/2734	16078
3N	L69	4-dr. Sed-5P	13500/13912	2779/2797	41185

CIERA SL (FOUR - sedan only/V-6)

Model Number	Body/Style Number	Body Type & Seating	Factory Price	Shipping Weight	Production Total
3A	J69	4-dr. Sed-6P	14460/15270	2733/2836	126244
3A	J35	4-dr. Sta Wag-6P	------/17060	------/2986	9102

CUTLASS SUPREME (V-6)

Model Number	Body/Style Number	Body Type & Seating	Factory Price	Shipping Weight	Production Total
3W	T67	2-dr. Conv-6P	25460	3651	4490

CUTLASS SUPREME SL (V-6)

3W	H47	2-dr. Cpe-6P	17460	3243	24809
3W	H69	4-dr. Sed-6P	17460	3354	83933

EIGHTY-EIGHT ROYALE (V-6)

Model Number	Body/Style Number	Body Type & Seating	Factory Price	Shipping Weight	Production Total
3H	N69	4-dr. Sed-6P	20410	3439	56862

EIGHTY-EIGHT ROYALE LS (V-6)

3H	Y69	4-dr. Sed-6P	22710	3439	7106

EIGHTY-EIGHT ROYALE LSS (V-6)

3H	Y69	4-dr. Sed-6P	24415	3439	11513

SILHOUETTE (V-6)

Model Number	Body/Style Number	Body Type & Seating	Factory Price	Shipping Weight	Production Total
3U	M06	3-dr. Minivan-7P	20255	3689	26383

NINETY-EIGHT REGENCY ELITE (V-6)

Model Number	Body/Style Number	Body Type & Seating	Factory Price	Shipping Weight	Production Total
3C	X69	4-dr. Sed-6P	26060	3593	25444

BRAVADA (V-6)

Model Number	Body/Style Number	Body Type & Seating	Factory Price	Shipping Weight	Production Total
3T	V06	4-dr. Sport Utility-5P	26320	4041	N/A

FACTORY PRICE AND WEIGHT NOTE: Beginning with the Achieva S coupe, prices and weights to left of slash are for four-cylinder engine and to right for V-6.

ENGINE DATA: BASE FOUR (Achieva S): Quad 4 inline, dual overhead-cam four-cylinder. Cast iron block and aluminum head. Displacement: 138 cu. in. (2.3 liters). Bore & stroke: 3.62 x 3.35 in. Compression ratio: 9.5:1. Net horsepower: 150 @ 6000 rpm. Torque: 145 lb. ft. @ 4800 rpm. Fuel injected (MFI). BASE FOUR (Ciera SL sedan): Inline, overhead-valve four-cylinder. Cast iron block and aluminum head. Displacement: 133 cu. in. (2.2 liters). Bore & stroke: 3.50 x 3.46 in. Compression ratio: 9.0:1. Net horsepower: 120 @ 5200 rpm. Torque: 130 lb. ft. @ 4000 rpm. Fuel injection (MFI). BASE SIX (Ciera SL station wagon): Series 3100 60-degree overhead valve V-6. Cast iron block and aluminum heads. Displacement: 191 cu. in. (3.1 liters). Bore & stroke: 3.50 x 3.31 in. Compression ratio: 9.5:1. Net horsepower: 160 @ 5200 rpm. Torque: 185 lb. ft. @ 4000 rpm. Fuel injection (SFI). OPTIONAL SIX (Achieva S/Ciera SL sedan): same aforementioned Series 3100 3.1-liter/191-cid V-6 with SFI. BASE SIX (Cutlass Supreme Convertible/Cutlass Supreme SL): 60-degree overhead valve V-6. Displacement: 191 cu. in. (3.1 liters). Bore & stroke: 3.50 x 3.31 in. Compression ratio: 9.5:1. Net horsepower: 160 @ 5200 rpm. Torque: 185 lb. ft. @ 4000 rpm. Fuel injection (SFI). OPTIONAL SIX (Cutlass Supreme Convertible/Cutlass Supreme SL): Twin dual overhead cam V-6. Cast iron block and aluminum heads. Displacement: 207 cu. in. (3.4 liters). Bore & stroke: 3.62 x 3.31 in. Compression ratio: 9.3:1. Net horsepower: 210 @ 5200 rpm. Torque: 215 lb. ft. @ 4000. Fuel injected (SFI). BASE SIX (Eighty-Eight/Ninety-Eight): Series II 3800 90-degree overhead valve V-6. Cast iron block and cast iron heads. Displacement: 231 cu. in. (3.8 liters). Bore & stroke: 3.80 x 3.40 in. Compression ratio: 9.4:1. Net horsepower: 205 @ 5200 rpm. Torque: 230 lb. ft. @ 4000 rpm. Fuel injected (SFI). OPTIONAL SIX (Eighty-Eight LSS/Ninety-Eight Regency Elite) supercharged version of the aforementioned 3.8-liter/231-cid V-6. Compression ratio: 8.5:1. Net horsepower: 225 @ 5000 rpm. Torque: 275 lb. ft. @ 3600 rpm. BASE SIX (Silhouette): V-6. Displacement: 231 cu. in. (3.8 liters). Bore & stroke: 3.80 x 3.40 in. Compression ratio: 9.4:1. Net horsepower: 170 @ 4800 rpm. Torque: 225 lb. ft. @ 3200 rpm. Fuel injected (SFI). BASE SIX (Bravada): V-6. Displacement: 262 cu. in. (4.3 liters). Bore & stroke: 4.00 x 3.48 in. Compression ratio: 8.6:1. Net horsepower: 200 @ 4400 rpm. Torque: 260 lb. ft. @ 3600 rpm. Fuel injected (CPI). BASE EIGHT (Aurora) 90-degree dual overhead-cam V-8. Aluminum block and aluminum heads. Displacement: 244 cu. in. (4.0 liters). Bore & stroke: 3.43 x 3.31 in. Compression ratio: 10.3:1. Net horsepower: 250 @ 5600 rpm. Torque: 260 lb. ft. @ 4400 rpm. Fuel injected (SFI).

CHASSIS DATA: Wheelbase: (Aurora) 113.8 in.; (Achieva) 103.4 in.; (Ciera sedan) 104.9 in.; (Ciera station wagon) 104.9 in.; (Cutlass Supreme) 107.0 in.; (Eighty-Eight) 110.8 in.; (Silhouette) 109.8 in.; (Ninety-Eight) 110.7 in.; (Bravada) 107.0 in. Overall Length: (Aurora) 205.4 in.; (Achieva) 187.9 in.; (Ciera sedan) 190.3 in.; (Ciera station wagon) 194.4 in.; (Cutlass Supreme coupe and convertible) 193.9 in.; (Cutlass Supreme sedan) 193.7 in.; (Eighty-Eight) 200.4 in.; (Silhou-

ette) 194.7 in.; (Ninety-Eight) 205.7 in.; (Bravada) 178.9 in. Height: (Aurora) 55.4 in.; (Achieva) 53.1 in.; (Ciera sedan) 54.1 in.; (Ciera station wagon) 54.5 in.; (Cutlass Supreme coupe) 53.3 in.; (Cutlass Supreme convertible) 54.3 in.; (Cutlass Supreme sedan) 54.8 in.; (Eighty-Eight) 55.7 in.; (Silhouette) 65.7 in.; (Ninety-Eight) 54.8 in.; (Bravada) 65.5 in. Width: (Aurora) 74.4 in.; (Achieva) 67.2 in.; (Ciera sedan) 69.5 in.; (Ciera station wagon) 69.5 in.; (Cutlass Supreme) 71.0 in.; (Eighty-Eight) 74.1 in.; (Silhouette) 73.9 in.; (Ninety-Eight) 74.6 in.; (Bravada) 65.2 in. Front tread: (Aurora) 62.5 in.; (Achieva) 55.6 in.; (Ciera sedan) 58.7 in.; (Ciera station wagon) 58.7 in.; (Cutlass Supreme) 59.5 in.; (Eighty-Eight) 60.4 in.; (Silhouette) 59.2 in.; (Ninety-Eight) 60.4 in.; (Bravada) 55.6 in. Rear tread: (Aurora) 62.6 in.; (Achieva) 55.3 in.; (Ciera sedan) 57.0 in.; (Ciera station wagon) 57.0 in.; (Cutlass Supreme) 58.0 in.; (Eighty-Eight) 60.4 in.; (Silhouette) 61.4 in.; (Ninety-Eight) 60.6 in.; (Bravada) 54.1 in. Standard tires: (Aurora) P235/60R16; (Achieva) P195/70R14; (Ciera sedan) P185/75R14; (Ciera station wagon) P185/75R14; (Cutlass Supreme) P215/60R16; (Cutlass Supreme convertible) P225/60R16; (Eighty-Eight) P205/70R15; (Silhouette) P205/70R15; (Ninety-Eight) P205/70R15; (Bravada) P235/75R15.

TECHNICAL: Transmission: Five-speed manual floor shift standard on Achieva S. Three-speed automatic standard on Ciera SL sedan. Four-speed automatic standard on Aurora/Ciera SL station wagon/Cutlass Supreme/Eighty-Eight/Silhouette/Ninety-Eight/Bravada. Four-speed automatic available on Achieva S/Ciera SL sedan models. Standard final drive ratio: (Aurora) 3.48:1 with four-speed automatic trans.; (Achieva) 3.94:1 with five-speed manual trans.; (Ciera SL sedan) 3.06:1 with three-speed automatic trans.; (Ciera SL station wagon) 2.97:1 with four-speed automatic trans.; (Cutlass Supreme) 3.33:1 with four-speed automatic trans.; (Eighty-Eight/Ninety-Eight) 2.84:1 with four-speed automatic trans.; (Silhouette) 3.06:1 with four-speed automatic trans.; (Bravada) 3.42:1 with four-speed automatic trans. Steering: (all except Aurora/Bravada) power assisted rack and pinion; (Aurora) rack and pinion with magnetic speed-variable assist; (Bravada) integral power steering variable ratio. Front Suspension: (Aurora/Achieva/Ciera/Cutlass Supreme/Eighty-Eight/Silhouette/Ninety-Eight) Independent, MacPherson strut w/ coil springs and anti-roll bar; (Bravada) Independent driving axle w/ upper and lower control arms, torsion bar springs, front stabilizer bar and frame-mounted differential carrier. Rear Suspension: (Aurora) Independent, cast aluminum semi-trailing arm w/ lateral links, coil springs, anti-roll bar and automatic leveling; (Achieva) trailing crank arm w/ twist beam and coil springs; (Ciera SL sedan) semi-independent, twist beam integral with two trailing arms, coil springs, Panhard rod, anti-roll bar; (Ciera SL station wagon) twist beam integral with two trailing arms, coil springs, Panhard rod; (Cutlass Supreme) Independent, tri-link strut location, transverse fiberglass leaf spring, anti-roll bar; (Eighty-Eight) Independent, Chapman strut, coil springs, anti-roll bar; (Ninety-Eight) Independent, Chapman strut, automatic load leveling, coil springs, anti-roll bar; (Silhouette) beam axle integral with two trailing arms, Panhard rod, coil springs; (Bravada) Salisbury axle design with semi-elliptic leaf springs. Brakes: (Achieva/Ciera/Eighty-Eight/Ninety-Eight/Silhouette) anti-lock power front disc, rear drum; (Aurora/Cutlass Supreme) anti-lock power four-wheel disc; (Bravada) front disc, rear drum, Kelsey-Hayes four-wheel anti-lock. Body Construction: (all except Silhouette/Bravada) uni-body; (Bravada) separate body and frame, (Silhouette) space frame substructure attached to ladder frame. Fuel tank: (Aurora) 20.0 gal.; (Achieva) 15.2 gal.; (Ciera) 16.5 gal.; (Cutlass Supreme) 16.5 gal.; (Eighty-Eight/Ninety-Eight) 18.0 gal.; (Silhouette) 20.0 gal.; (Bravada) 20.0 gal.

DRIVETRAIN OPTIONS: (Achieva S) Series 3100 3.1-liter V-6 ($412). (Ciera SL sedan) Series 3100 3.1-liter V-6 ($810). (Cutlass Supreme SL) 3.4-liter V-6 ($1223); (Cutlass Supreme convertible) 3.4-liter V-6 ($1185-$1255). (Eighty-Eight LSS) supercharged 3.8-liter V-6 ($1022). (Ninety-Eight Regency

Elite) supercharged 3.8-liter V-6 ($1022). Transmission: (Achieva S) four-speed automatic ($755); (Achieva S Series II) five-speed manual trans. ($755 credit). (Eighty-Eight Royale and Royale LS) traction control system ($175). (Ninety-Eight Series I) traction control ($175). (Silhouette) Towing package - included FE3 touring suspension and traction control system ($705). Engine block heater ($18).

OPTION PACKAGES: (Aurora) Autobahn package ($395). (Achieva S sedan) Rear aero wing package (Series I - $224/Series II - $147). (Cutlass Supreme SL sedan) Sport Luxury Package (NC). (Bravada) Gold Package (NC).

MAJOR CONVENIENCE/APPEARANCE OPTIONS: Remote keyless entry ($125-$185). Alloy wheels ($391). Cruise control ($225). Power sunroof ($995). Heated driver and passenger front seats ($295). Power driver's seat ($270-$305). Leather seats ($515-$610). Astroroof ($995).

HISTORY: Model year production (U.S.): 480,998. Calendar year production (U.S.) 408,125. Calendar year sales by U.S. dealers: 387,545. Model year sales by U.S. dealers: 411,896.

Historical Footnotes: Oldsmobile's internationally focused Antares concept car debuted at the February 1995 Chicago Auto Show. Model year sales decreased to 411,896 compared to 438,096 the year before.

1996

Paramount among the many changes to Oldsmobile's model offerings in 1996 was the elimination of the Cutlass Supreme convertible and the return of an all-new-design Bravada. Also returning were the Achieva SC coupe and SL sedan, which were last offered in 1994 but deleted the following year. Both the SC and SL Achievas were offered with three levels of equipment: Series I through Series III. The Achieva S coupe and sedan offered with two levels of equipment in 1995 were eliminated. The Cutlass Supreme SL coupe and sedan were offered in four equipment levels (Series I through Series IV), two more than the year before. The Eighty-Eight lineup was revamped for 1996 with the long-standing Royale name deleted and the LSS model marketed as a stand-alone model with no ties to the Eighty-Eight. Also, daytime running lamps (DRLs) became standard equipment on the Aurora, Achieva, Eighty-Eight, LSS, Ninety-Eight and Bravada.

1996 Oldsmobile, Aurora sedan, (O)

AURORA -- SERIES 3G -- V-8 -- In its first full year of sales in 1995, Oldsmobile's Aurora outsold all the other makes in its market segment as well as garnering over 20 automotive awards. Not resting on those laurels, the 1996 Aurora offered several improvements over the previous year's model. Included in the upgrades were the addition of daytime running lamps, a more responsive ride and handling package, backlight glass rid of distortion, the addition of both a universal theft-deterrent system and universal garage door opener and refined keyless entry system and interior lighting system. New-for-1996 options were chrome-plated aluminum road wheels and gold graphics package. Standard powertrain was the 32-valve, dual overhead-cam 4.0-liter V-8 linked to a four-speed automatic transaxle. This V-

8 featured two 128 Kbytes computers that coordinated the engine's operation as well as regulating other systems ranging from the cooling fans to cruise control. The engine also featured a "limp-home" capability that cycled the V-8's eight cylinders between work and rest to keep them cool in the event of total coolant loss.

1996 Oldsmobile, Achieva SL sedan, (O)

ACHIEVA -- SERIES 3N -- FOUR/V-6 -- The Achieva S coupe and sedan offered the year before were eliminated for 1996, and the Achieva lineup consisted of the SC coupe and SL sedan. The SC coupe was available with three levels of equipment: Series I, Series II and Series III. The SL sedan offered Series II and Series III levels of equipment, but had no Series I. Changes were extensive with the most prominent being a new standard engine offering. The 2.3-liter dual overhead-cam four-cylinder offered previously was replaced with a 150-hp 2.4-liter (146 cu. in.) twin cam four-cylinder engine with 9.5:1 compression ratio and twin balance shafts in the oil pan. Standard transaxle was the five-speed manual, with a four-speed automatic available. Also available was the upgraded 3100 3.1-liter sequential fuel-injected V-6 engine rated at 155 hp. It featured a stiffer cylinder block and intake manifold design to reduce noise as well as long-life coolant, roller rocker arms (to go with roller lifters introduced earlier) and distributorless ignition. Achieva's new-for-1996 standard features included dual airbags, air conditioning, PASSlock theft-deterrent system, daytime running lamps and, with automatic transaxle selected, Enhanced Traction System (ETS).

1996 Oldsmobile, Achieva SC coupe, (O)

1996 Oldsmobile, Ciera SL sedan, (O)

CIERA -- SERIES 3A -- FOUR/V-6 -- The 1996 Ciera lineup received only minor refinements including more simplified exterior badging and the aforementioned upgrades to the 3.1-liter V-6, which was standard in the Ciera SL station wagon as well as the SL sedan with Series II equipment and available in the Series I

level Ciera SL sedan. The Ciera SL sedan with Series I equipment came standard with the 2200 2.2-liter (133 cu. in.) inline four-cylinder engine coupled to a column-shifted three-speed automatic transaxle. Series II level sedans and SL station wagons came standard with a four-speed automatic transaxle, also available in the Series I Ciera SL sedan. New interior features included storage armrests and sound system upgrades.

1996 Oldsmobile, Ciera SL station wagon, (O)

1996 Oldsmobile, Cutlass Supreme SL sedan, (O)

CUTLASS SUPREME -- SERIES 3W -- V-6 -- As of 1996, Oldsmobile no longer offered a convertible with the elimination of the Cutlass Supreme convertible. The remaining lineup consisted of the SL coupe and sedan, both offered with four levels of equipment: Series I, Series II, Series III and Series IV. Dual airbags, four-wheel anti-lock disc brakes and air conditioning continued as standard equipment. Standard powertrain was the 160-hp 3.1-liter V-6 with the aforementioned revisions including the strengthening of the cylinder block and intake manifold. This engine was linked to a four-speed automatic transaxle. Optional was the 3.4-liter dual overhead-cam V-6, which was also upgraded. Revisions to both intake and exhaust passages plus new cam timing and a compression ratio boost (from 9.25:1 to 9.7:1) delivered five extra horsepower at 5200 rpm and five more pound-feet of torque at 4000 rpm. Emission levels were also lowered by new reduced-crevice-volume pistons, high-efficiency spark plugs, an air-injection-reaction system and an exhaust-gas-recirculation improvement.

1996 Oldsmobile, Cutlass Supreme SL coupe, (O)

EIGHTY-EIGHT -- SERIES 3H -- V-6 -- Elimination of the long-standing Royale name and the spin-off the previous year's LSS model to a separate, non-Eighty-Eight offering left the streamlined 1996 Eighty-Eight lineup with the base sedan and LS sedan. Both received extensive exterior design revisions to bring them in line with the "Aurora look." Front and rear fascias, grille

1996 Oldsmobile, Eighty-Eight LS sedan, (O)

panel, headlamps, taillamps, fenders and badging/ornamentation were of an all-new design. Front fenders were stamped steel instead of the previous composite design. Bodyside and wheel-opening moldings were revised as were the wheel covers. The LS sedan's aluminum wheels were also redesigned. Also refined were the automatic door lock system and remote keyless accessory control package. New standard equipment included the twilight sentinel (automatic headlamp control), which was fitted with daytime running lamps. Standard powertrain remained unchanged from the year before, it being the Series II 3.8-liter V-6 mated to a four-speed automatic transaxle. The supercharged version of the original 3.8-liter V-6 was no longer offered.

1996 Oldsmobile, LSS sedan, (O)

LSS -- SERIES 3Y -- V-6 -- Marketed as a "blood brother" to the Aurora, the Oldsmobile LSS touring sedan severed its association with the Eighty-Eight family and went it alone in 1996. The LSS featured new exterior design details including foglamps and 16-inch wheels to help identify it with the Aurora. Inside, front and rear seats featured articulated head rests like the Aurora, and the LSS offered rear seat pass-through for added convenience. New features included magnetic variable-assist rack and pinion steering and refined programmable door locks and remote keyless entry system. New standard equipment included twilight sentinel and daytime running lamps. Standard powertrain was the 205-hp Series II 3.8-liter V-6 coupled to an electronically-controlled four-speed automatic transaxle. Optional was the new-for-1996 240-hp, supercharged Series II 3800 V-6 with a 6000 rpm redline. This engine featured airflow and combustion improvements in combination with a larger super-

1996 Oldsmobile, Silhouette minivan, (O)

charger (90 cubic inches compared to the former 62), stiffer block, lighter valvetrain and cross-bolted main bearing caps for enhanced reliability. Other optional equipment consisted of a power sunroof, CD player, cloth trim and engine block heater for cold climate use.

SILHOUETTE -- SERIES 3U -- V-6 -- The seven-passenger Silhouette, as it was the year before, was marketed in Series I and Series II levels of equipment for 1996. In Series I configuration, the minivan contained an airbag, air conditioning, anti-lock brakes, six-way power-adjusted driver's seat and roof-mounted luggage rack. In Series II trim, a buyer got the aforementioned equipment plus power sliding side door, steering wheel-mounted touch controls and leather seats. New-for-1996 was the standard engine for the Silhouette. Displacing 3.4-liters and rated at 180 hp, the 60-degree 3400 V-6 featured a reinforced cylinder block, aluminum cylinder heads, assembled steel camshaft, sequential electronic fuel injection, roller-type lifters and rocker arms, forged steel connecting rods, distributorless ignition and platinum-tipped spark plugs. This engine was linked to a electronically-controlled Hydra-Matic four-speed automatic transaxle that was "filled-for-life."

1996 Oldsmobile, Ninety-Eight Regency Elite sedan, (O)

NINETY-EIGHT REGENCY -- SERIES 3C -- V-6 -- The Ninety-Eight lineup for 1996 again consisted of only the Regency Elite sedan offered, as it was the year before, with two levels of equipment: Series I and Series II. In Series I trim, the Regency Elite sedan's standard offerings included air conditioning, anti-lock brakes, dual airbags and leather trim (velour upholstery was available). When Series II equipment was ordered, the Ninety-Eight also featured traction control, electronic instrumentation cluster, memory controls for the driver's seat, automatic trunk pull-down, electrochromic heated outside mirror on the driver's side and cornering lamps. Refinements were done to the interior lighting, locking and security features, and standard was twilight sentinel with daytime running lamps. Standard powertrain was the Series II 3.8-liter V-6 with four-speed automatic transaxle. The previous year's optional supercharged 3.8-liter V-6 was no longer offered.

BRAVADA -- SERIES 3T -- V-6 -- After a one-model-year hiatus, Oldsmobile's four-door sport utility vehicle was completely re-engineered for 1996 with an emphasis placed on luxury, interior space functionality and ride quality. The longer, wider Bravada was again outfitted with SmartTrak, a combination of full-time all-wheel drive, four-wheel anti-lock brakes and a locking rear differential. Convenience equipment included a split-folding rear

1996 Oldsmobile, Bravada sport utility vehicle, (O)

seat, remote keyless entry and overhead console. Safety features included daytime running lamps, driver's side airbag and integrated fog lamps. Luxury items included deep-tint solar glass, leather upholstery, compass, entertainment system, outside thermometer, trip computer and universal garage door opener. Optional equipment consisted of a 5,000-pound towing package, raised white letter tires, engine block heater, CD player and gold trim package. Standard powertrain for the Bravada was the 190-hp 4.3-liter sequential central port fuel-injected V-6 linked to an electronically-controlled four-speed automatic transmission. Bravada's ride quality was enhanced through a more rigid "boxed" frame that permitted relaxing the suspension settings. Mono-tube De Carbone high-pressure gas shock absorbers provided consistent damping over varied road surfaces.

I.D. DATA: Oldsmobile's 17-symbol Vehicle Identification Number (VIN) again was located on the upper left surface of the instrument panel, visible through the windshield. The first three characters (1G3) indicates Oldsmobile Division. The fourth and fifth letters designate the body type/series: A/J - Cutlass Ciera SL sedan and SL station wagon, C/X - Ninety-Eight Regency Elite, G/R - Aurora, H/N - Eighty-Eight and Eighty-Eight LS, H/Y - LSS, N/L - Achieva SC and Achieva SL, T/V - Bravada, U/M - Silhouette, W/H - Cutlass Supreme SL. The sixth number identifies the body style: 1 - 2-dr coupe, 2 - 2-dr hatchback/liftback, 3 - 2-dr convertible, 4 - 2-dr station wagon, 5 - 4-dr sedan, 6 - 4-dr hatchback/liftback, 8 - 4-dr station wagon. The seventh number identifies the restraint code: 1 - active (manual) belts, 2 - active (manual) belts with driver's and passenger's side airbags, 3 - active (manual) belts with driver's side airbag, 4 - passive (automatic) belts, 5 - passive (automatic) belts with driver's side airbag, 6 - passive (automatic) belts with driver's and passenger's side airbags, 7 - active (manual) belt driver and passive (automatic) belt passenger with driver's and passenger's side airbags. The eighth letter identifies the engine: C = 4.0-liter fuel-injected V-8, K = 3.8-liter fuel-injected V-6, M = 3.1-liter fuel-injected V-6, T = 2.4-liter fuel-injected inline four-cylinder, W = 4.3-liter fuel-injected V-6, X = 3.4-liter fuel-injected V-6, 1 = 3.8-liter fuel-injected V-6, 4 = 2.2-liter fuel-injected inline four-cylinder. The ninth number is the check digit. The tenth letter represents the model year (T = 1996). The eleventh character identifies the assembly plant: F - Fairfax, Kan.; M - Lansing, Mich.; T - Tarrytown, N.Y.; 2 - Moraine, Ohio; 4 - Orion, Mich.; 6 - Oklahoma City, Okla. The final six digits are the sequential serial number.

AURORA (V-8)

Model Number	Body/Style Number	Body Type & Seating	Factory Price	Shipping Weight	Prod. Total
3G	R29	4-dr. Sed-6P	34360	3967	24954 *

ACHIEVA SC (FOUR/V-6)

3N	L37	2-dr. Cpe-5P	13495/13952	2751/N/A	Note 1

ACHIEVA SL (FOUR/V-6)

3N	L69	4-dr. Sed-5P	14495/14952	2813/N/A	Note 1

Note 1: Total Achieva production was 41,068 * cars. No breakout for SC vs. SL models was available.

CIERA SL (FOUR - sedan only/V-6)

Model Number	Body/Style Number	Body Type & Seating	Factory Price	Shipping Weight	Production Total
3A	J69	4-dr. Sed-6P	14455/15265	2924/3058	Note 2
3A	J35	4-dr. Sta Wag-6P	------/17455	------/3229	Note 2

Note 2: Total Ciera production was 126,137 * cars. No breakout for sedan vs. station wagon models was available.

CUTLASS SUPREME SL (V-6)

Model Number	Body/Style Number	Body Type & Seating	Factory Price	Shipping Weight	Production Total
3W	H47	2-dr. Cpe-6P	17455	3283	Note 3
3W	H69	4-dr. Sed-6P	17455	3388	Note 3

Note 3: Total Cutlass Supreme production was 86,613 * cars. No breakout for coupe vs. sedan was available.

EIGHTY-EIGHT (V-6)

Model Number	Body/Style Number	Body Type & Seating	Factory Price	Shipping Weight	Production Total
3H	N69	4-dr. Sed-6P	20405	3455	Note 4

EIGHTY-EIGHT LS (V-6)

Model Number	Body/Style Number	Body Type & Seating	Factory Price	Shipping Weight	Production Total
3H	N69	4-dr. Sed-6P	22810	3459	Note 4

LSS (V-6)

Model Number	Body/Style Number	Body Type & Seating	Factory Price	Shipping Weight	Production Total
3H	Y69	4-dr. Sed-5P	26010	3502	Note 4

Note 4: Total Eighty-Eight and LSS production was 70,740 * cars. No breakout for base, LS and LSS models was available.

SILHOUETTE (V-6)

Model Number	Body/Style Number	Body Type & Seating	Factory Price	Shipping Weight	Production Total
3U	M06	3-dr. Minivan-7P	21900	3739	11985 *

NINETY-EIGHT REGENCY ELITE (V-6)

Model Number	Body/Style Number	Body Type & Seating	Factory Price	Shipping Weight	Production Total
3C	X69	4-dr. Sed-6P	28160	3515	15134 *

BRAVADA (V-6)

3T	V06	4-dr. Sport Utility-5P	29995	4184	17385 *

* All production figures represent cars and trucks produced through February 1996, the latest month for which figures were available at the time this book went to the printer.

FACTORY PRICE AND WEIGHT NOTE: Beginning with the Achieva SC coupe, prices and weights to left of slash are for four-cylinder engine and to right for V-6.

ENGINE DATA: BASE FOUR (Achieva SC/Achieva SL): Twin cam inline four-cylinder. Cast iron block and aluminum head. Displacement: 146 cu. in. (2.4 liters). Bore & stroke: 3.54 x 3.70 in. Compression ratio: 9.5:1. Net horsepower: 150 @ 5600 rpm. Torque: 155 lb. ft. @ 4400 rpm. Fuel injected (SFI). BASE FOUR (Ciera SL sedan): Inline, overhead-valve four-cylinder. Cast iron block and aluminum head. Displacement: 133 cu. in. (2.2 liters). Bore & stroke: 3.50 x 3.46 in. Compression ratio: 9.0:1. Net horsepower: 120 @ 5200 rpm. Torque: 130 lb. ft. @ 4000 rpm. Fuel injection (MFI). BASE SIX (Ciera SL station wagon): Series 3100 60-degree overhead valve V-6. Cast iron block and aluminum heads. Displacement: 191 cu. in. (3.1 liters). Bore & stroke: 3.50 x 3.31 in. Compression ratio: 9.5:1. Net horsepower: 160 @ 5200 rpm. Torque: 185 lb. ft. @ 4000 rpm. Fuel injection (SFI). OPTIONAL SIX (Achieva SC/Achieva SL/Ciera SL sedan): same aforementioned Series 3100 3.1-liter/191-cid V-6 with SFI. BASE SIX (Cutlass Supreme SL): 60-degree overhead valve V-6. Displacement: 191 cu. in. (3.1 liters). Bore & stroke: 3.50 x 3.31 in. Compression ratio: 9.5:1. Net horsepower: 160 @ 5200 rpm. Torque: 185 lb. ft. @ 4000 rpm. Fuel injection (SFI). OPTIONAL SIX (Cutlass Supreme SL): Twin dual overhead cam V-6. Cast iron block and aluminum heads. Displacement: 207 cu. in. (3.4 liters). Bore & stroke: 3.62 x 3.31 in. Compression ratio: 9.7:1. Net horsepower: 215 @ 5200 rpm. Torque: 220 lb. ft. @ 4000. Fuel injected (SFI). BASE SIX (Eighty-Eight/LSS/Ninety-Eight): Series II 3800 90-degree overhead valve V-6. Cast iron block and cast iron heads. Displacement: 231 cu. in. (3.8 liters). Bore & stroke: 3.80 x 3.40 in. Compression ratio: 9.4:1. Net horsepower: 205 @ 5200 rpm. Torque: 230 lb. ft. @ 4000 rpm. Fuel injected (SFI). OPTIONAL SIX (LSS) supercharged version of the aforementioned Series II 3.8-liter/231-cid V-6. Compression ratio: 8.5:1. Net horsepower: 240 @ 5200 rpm. Torque: 280 lb. ft. @ 3200 rpm. Fuel injected (SFI). BASE SIX (Silhouette): Series 3400 60-degree V-6. Displacement: 205 cu. in. (3.4 liters). Bore & stroke: 3.80 x 3.40 in. Compression ratio: 8.5:1. Net horsepower: 180 @ 5200 rpm. Torque: 205 lb. ft. @ 4000 rpm. Fuel injected (SFI).

BASE SIX (Bravada): Vortec V-6. Displacement: 262 cu. in. (4.3 liters). Bore & stroke: 4.00 x 3.48 in. Compression ratio: 9.2:1. Net horsepower: 190 @ 4400 rpm. Torque: 250 lb. ft. @ 2800 rpm. Fuel injected (CPI). BASE EIGHT (Aurora) 90-degree dual overhead-cam V-8. Aluminum block and aluminum heads. Displacement: 244 cu. in. (4.0 liters). Bore & stroke: 3.43 x 3.31 in. Compression ratio: 10.3:1. Net horsepower: 250 @ 5600 rpm. Torque: 260 lb. ft. @ 4400 rpm. Fuel injected (SFI).

CHASSIS DATA: Wheelbase: (Aurora) 113.8 in.; (Achieva) 103.4 in.; (Ciera sedan) 104.9 in.; (Ciera station wagon) 104.9 in.; (Cutlass Supreme) 107.5 in.; (Eighty-Eight) 110.8 in.; (LSS) 110.8 in.; (Silhouette) 109.8 in.; (Ninety-Eight) 110.7 in.; (Bravada) 107.0 in. Overall Length: (Aurora) 205.4 in.; (Achieva) 187.9 in.; (Ciera sedan) 193.2 in.; (Ciera station wagon) 195.4 in.; (Cutlass Supreme coupe) 193.9 in.; (Cutlass Supreme sedan) 193.7 in.; (Eighty-Eight) 201.6 in.; (LSS) 201.6 in.; (Silhouette) 194.7 in.; (Ninety-Eight) 205.7 in.; (Bravada) 180.9 in. Height: (Aurora) 55.4 in.; (Achieva) 53.5 in.; (Ciera sedan) 54.1 in.; (Ciera station wagon) 54.5 in.; (Cutlass Supreme coupe) 53.3 in.; (Cutlass Supreme sedan) 54.8 in.; (Eighty-Eight) 55.7 in.; (LSS) 55.7 in.; (Silhouette) 65.7 in.; (Ninety-Eight) 54.8 in.; (Bravada) 63.2 in. Width: (Aurora) 74.4 in.; (Achieva SC) 68.6 in.; (Achieva SL) 68.1 in.; (Ciera sedan) 69.5 in.; (Ciera station wagon) 69.5 in.; (Cutlass Supreme) 71.0 in.; (Eighty-Eight) 74.7 in.; (LSS) 74.7 in.; (Silhouette) 73.9 in.; (Ninety-Eight) 74.6 in.; (Bravada) 66.5 in. Front tread: (Aurora) 62.5 in.; (Achieva) 55.6 in.; (Ciera sedan) 58.7 in.; (Ciera station wagon) 58.7 in.; (Cutlass Supreme) 59.5 in.; (Eighty-Eight) 60.4 in.; (LSS) 60.4 in.; (Silhouette) 59.2 in.; (Ninety-Eight) 60.4 in.; (Bravada) 56.6 in. Rear tread: (Aurora) 62.6 in.; (Achieva) 55.3 in.; (Ciera sedan) 57.0 in.; (Ciera station wagon) 57.0 in.; (Cutlass Supreme) 58.0 in.; (Eighty-Eight) 60.4 in.; (LSS) 60.4 in.; (Silhouette) 61.4 in.; (Ninety-Eight) 60.6 in.; (Bravada) 55.1 in. Standard tires: (Aurora) P235/60R16; (Achieva) P195/70R14; (Ciera sedan) P185/75R14; (Ciera station wagon) P185/75R14; (Cutlass Supreme) P205/70R15; (Eighty-Eight) P205/70R15; (LSS) P225/60R16; (Silhouette) P205/70R15; (Ninety-Eight) P205/70R15; (Bravada) P235/70R15.

TECHNICAL: Transmission: Five-speed manual floor shift standard on Achieva SC and Achieva SL. Three-speed automatic standard on Ciera SL sedan. Four-speed automatic standard on Aurora/Ciera SL station wagon/Cutlass Supreme/Eighty-Eight/LSS/Silhouette/Ninety-Eight/Bravada. Four-speed automatic available on Achieva SC/Achieva SL/Ciera SL sedan models. Standard final drive ratio: (Aurora) 3.48:1 with four-speed automatic trans.; (Achieva) 3.94:1 with five-speed manual trans.; (Ciera SL sedan) 3.06:1 with three-speed automatic trans.; (Ciera SL station wagon) 2.97:1 with four-speed automatic trans.; (Cutlass Supreme) 3.33:1 with four-speed automatic trans.; (Eighty-Eight/Ninety-Eight) 2.84:1 with four-speed automatic trans.; (LSS/Silhouette) 3.06:1 with four-speed automatic trans.; (Bravada) 3.73:1 with four-speed automatic trans. Steering: (all except Aurora/Bravada) power assisted rack and pinion; (Aurora) rack and pinion with magnetic speed-variable assist; (Bravada) integral power steering variable ratio. Front Suspension: (Aurora/Achieva/Ciera/Cutlass Supreme/Eighty-Eight/LSS/Silhouette/Ninety-Eight) Independent, MacPherson strut w/ coil springs and anti-roll bar; (Bravada) Independent driving axle w/ upper and lower control arms, torsion bar springs, front stabilizer bar and frame-mounted differential carrier. Rear Suspension: (Aurora) Independent, cast aluminum semi-trailing arm w/ lateral links, coil springs, anti-roll bar and automatic leveling; (Achieva) Trailing twist axle with tubular control arms and open section transverse beam, coil springs and anti-roll bar; (Ciera SL sedan) semi-independent, twist beam integral with two trailing arms, coil springs, Panhard rod, anti-roll bar; (Ciera SL station wagon) twist beam integral with two trailing arms, coil springs, Panhard rod; (Cutlass Supreme) Independent, tri-link strut location, transverse fiberglass leaf spring,

anti-roll bar; (Eighty-Eight/LSS) Independent, Chapman strut, coil springs, anti-roll bar; (Ninety-Eight) Independent, Chapman strut, automatic load leveling, coil springs, anti-roll bar; (Silhouette) beam axle integral with two trailing arms, Panhard rod, coil springs; (Bravada) Rigid axle design with semi-elliptic leaf springs, stabilizer bar beam, coil springs and anti-roll bar. Brakes: (Achieva/Ciera/Eighty-Eight/LSS/Ninety-Eight/Silhouette) anti-lock power front disc, rear drum; (Aurora/Cutlass Supreme) anti-lock power four-wheel disc; (Bravada) front disc, rear drum, Kelsey-Hayes four-wheel anti-lock. Body Construction: (all except Silhouette/Bravada) unibody; (Bravada) separate body and frame, (Silhouette) space frame substructure attached to ladder frame. Fuel tank: (Aurora) 20.0 gal.; (Achieva) 15.2 gal.; (Ciera) 16.5 gal.; (Cutlass Supreme) 17.1 gal.; (Eighty-Eight/LSS/Ninety-Eight) 18.0 gal.; (Silhouette) 20.0 gal.; (Bravada) 18.0 gal.

DRIVETRAIN OPTIONS: (Achieva SC/Achieva SL) Series 3100 3.1-liter V-6 ($457). (Ciera SL sedan) Series 3100 3.1-liter V-6 ($810). (Cutlass Supreme SL) 3.4-liter V-6 ($1223); (LSS) supercharged Series II 3.8-liter V-6 ($1022). Transmission: (Achieva SC/Achieva SL) four-speed automatic ($975); (Achieva SC Series III/Achieva SL Series III) five-speed manual trans. ($755 credit). (Eighty-Eight and Eighty-Eight LS) traction control system ($175). (Ninety-Eight Series I) traction control ($175). Engine block heater ($18).

OPTION PACKAGES: (Aurora) Autobahn package ($395). (Aurora) Gold graphics package ($50). (Achieva SL) Rear aero wing package (Series II - $224/Series III - $147).

MAJOR CONVENIENCE/APPEARANCE OPTIONS: Remote keyless entry ($125-$185). Chrome-plated wheels ($600-$800). Cruise control ($225). Power sunroof ($695-$745). Power driver's seat ($270-$350). Astroroof ($995).

HISTORY: Model year production through February 1996 (U.S.): 394,016 (latest figure available at the time this book went to the printer).

Historical Footnotes: The Aurora's 4.0-liter V-8 engine was announced as one of two (Nissan being the other supplier) powerplants to be used (modified for racing) in the fledgling Indy Racing League, which has the Indianapolis 500 as its cornerstone event. Oldsmobile's Eighty-Eight models could have the GuideStar navigation system installed as an option for $1,995. This system utilized global positioning satellites and an onboard gyroscope to precisely ascertain a vehicle's location. A dash-mounted liquid-crystal display screen plotted a map and most efficient route to the selected destination, which was given as a voice prompt by GuideStar.

1997

Observing its centennial in 1997 (the official date was August 21), Oldsmobile did not stand on tradition nor name recognition in this banner year. Both the long-standing Ninety-Eight name and Ciera name (also Oldsmobile's best-selling car many years running) were gone from the lineup. In their places were the Regency and Cutlass, respectively, both four-door sedan offerings (the Cutlass not to be confused with the Cutlass Supreme, which was a separate line). Also, with the demise of the Ciera, it left Oldsmobile without a station wagon for the first time since 1956. Within Oldsmobile's 100 anniversary year, the Cutlass Supreme was observing its 30th anniversary. Within the Cutlass Supreme's lineup, the Series IV level of equipment offered the year before was eliminated. Also deleted were the Achieva SC and SL Series III models offered previously. And unlike the year before, the Achieva SL was offered with the Series I level of equipment in 1997. The Silhouette minivan was also completely redesigned as part of Oldsmobile's ongoing "Centennial Plan" to prepare for the automaker's second century of existence.

1997 Oldsmobile, Aurora sedan, (O)

AURORA -- SERIES 3G -- V-8 -- Even though it was touted as one of the most carefully engineered and best thought-out products launched by Oldsmobile, the 1997 Aurora received several refinements. Among the changes was the addition of an electronic compass in the rear view mirror, enlarged front brakes, redesigned exterior door handles, more "user-friendly" seat belt buckle release buttons, the right-outside mirror gained an automatic tilt-down function to aid backing and improved speakers for the CD sound system. The universal garage door opener became standard equipment. The 32-valve, 250-hp, dual overhead-cam 4.0-liter V-8 linked to an electronically-controlled Hydra-Matic 4T80-E four-speed automatic transaxle remained the Aurora's standard powertrain. To trim weight, cast aluminum was used to form the front control arms and steering knuckles. For the first time since its inception, the Aurora also carried discrete Oldsmobile badging on the right-rear corner of the car.

1997 Oldsmobile, Achieva SL sedan, (O)

ACHIEVA -- SERIES 3N -- FOUR/V-6 -- Oldsmobile's entry-level compact car, the 1997 Achieva was again available in SC coupe and SL sedan versions. The Series III level of equipment offered the year before was eliminated to simplify offerings with Series I and Series II levels of equipment available. Also, not available the previous year, the SL sedan was offered in Series I form. Standard equipment included dual airbags, enhanced traction control, anti-lock brakes, air conditioning, rear window defogger, pulse wipers, power door locks, illuminated entry/exit system, tile steering wheel and remote trunk and fuel-filler door releases. New-for-1997 standard items were a four-speed automatic transmission, 15-inch touring tires, driver's side adjustable lumbar, power mirrors and long-life brake fluid. Refinements included door system upgrades for dynamic side impact protection and cross-lace alloy wheels standard on the Series II coupe. Also, a five-speed manual transmission was available in both Series I coupe and sedan and Series II coupe. Standard powertrain was the 2.4-liter twin cam sequential fuel-injected four-cylinder mated to an electronically-controlled Hydra-Matic 4T60-E four-speed automatic transaxle. The 3100 3.1-liter V-6 was available in the Series I coupe and both Series II coupe and sedan. Standard on both Series I and Series II coupe models (and optional on Series II sedan) was a sport package comprised of rear aero wing, front fog lamps and leather-wrapped steering wheel and shift knob.

1997 Oldsmobile, Cutlass sedan, (O)

CUTLASS -- SERIES N/A -- V-6 -- Cutlass, Oldsmobile's new-for-1997 mid-size family four-door sedan offered in base and GLS trim, replaced the long-successful Ciera line. Built at the Oklahoma City, Oklahoma, assembly plant, the Cutlass was assembled using a new "doors-off" manufacturing process that allowed for continuous quality checks. Standard equipment included anti-lock brakes, air conditioning, power steering/brakes/door locks, split-folding rear seat, dual-zone rear window defogger, PASSlock II security system, daytime running lamps (with automatic activation of headlamps at dusk) and aluminized stainless-steel muffler and tailpipe. Standard powertrain was the 160-hp 3100 3.1-liter V-6 coupled to an electronically-controlled Hydra-Matic 4T40-E four-speed automatic transaxle. The Cutlass sedan's unibody construction featured a safety cage consisting of strengthened roof pillars, headers and rails, side-guard door beams and door-sill members as well as crumple zones front and rear to absorb impact energy in the event of a collision.

1997 Oldsmobile, Cutlass Supreme sedan, (O)

CUTLASS SUPREME -- SERIES 3W -- V-6 -- In its 30th year, and nearing eight million sold, the Cutlass Supreme for 1997 remained available in SL coupe and sedan versions with three levels of equipment offered: Series I, Series II and Series III. The Series IV level of equipment offered the year before was dropped to simplify sales. Also, the optional 3.4-liter dual overhead-cam V-6 offered previously was eliminated. Standard powertrain for the Cutlass Supreme SL was the 160-hp 3100 3.1-liter V-6 linked to an electronically-controlled Hydra-Matic 4T60-E four-speed automatic transaxle. The Cutlass Supreme received only minor refinements including structural side impact upgrades to comply with federal requirements. A power trunk release and 16-inch aluminum wheels became standard equipment. The

1997 Oldsmobile, Eighty-Eight LS sedan, (O)

bench seat available in previous years was deleted from the coupe model. Also, coupe models received a rear aero wing as a standard item, which caused a redesign in the taillamp so it blended with the decklid's aerodynamic spoiler surface.

EIGHTY-EIGHT -- SERIES 3H -- V-6 -- After a face lift the year before, the Eighty-Eight received minor refinements for 1997, including the addition of updated Oldsmobile logos inside and out. The Eighty-Eight again was offered only as a sedan in base and LS trim. Standard powertrain remained the 205-hp Series II 3800 3.8-liter V-6 linked to a Hydra-Matic 4T60-E four-speed automatic transaxle. Upgrades included dynamic side impact protection and a new electronically-controlled capacity clutch in the Hydra-Matic transaxle, which replaced the conventional lock-up clutch used previously. Also the powertrain's control computer's memory capacity was doubled, from 256 Kbytes to 512 Kbytes, for enhanced diagnostic capabilities. New-for-1997 features in the Eighty-Eight included a fold-down storage armrest for the bench front seat, the addition of three overhead exit-assist handles for passengers and improved seat belt buckle release buttons. For the upscale LS sedan, standard equipment included traction control, aluminum wheels, programmable power door locks, keyless entry, power mirrors, front bucket seats with a center console and eight-way power driver's seat. Larger then previous P215/65R15 tires were included in the bucket seat package. Also, the automatic shifter handle was relocated from the steering column to the console.

1997 Oldsmobile, LSS sedan, (O)

LSS -- SERIES 3Y -- V-6 -- The LSS touring sedan was again a stand-alone model for 1997, and received several upgrades including the aforementioned side impact protection, electronically-controlled capacity clutch in its Hydra-Matic transaxle and powertrain computer memory enhancement (256 Kbytes to 512 Kbytes). New-for-1997 features included a new center console, auxiliary power outlet, rear seat heat ducts, redesigned automatic shifter, overhead exit-assist handles, improved seat belt buckle release buttons and Goodyear Eagle LS P225/60R16 tires, which replaced the GA versions used the year before. Standard powertrain was the 205-hp Series II 3800 3.8-liter V-6 with electronically-controlled Hydra-Matic 4T60-E four-speed automatic transaxle. Optional was the 240-hp supercharged version of that engine. With the supercharged 3800 V-6 in place, the final drive ratio was revised from the year before, from 2.97:1 to 2.93:1.

1997 Oldsmobile, Silhouette minivan, (O)

SILHOUETTE -- SERIES 3U -- V-6 -- The 1997 Silhouette was the first from-the-ground-up redesign of Oldsmobile's minivan since its inception in 1990, and was offered in three versions: base, GL and GLS. Standard features included anti-lock brakes, daytime running lamps, front fog lamps, power windows, roof rack, air conditioning with built-in pollen filter, solar-control glass and tinted windshield, tilt steering, cruise control, programmable automatic door locks and manual lumbar adjusters on front passenger seats. In addition, the GL's standard equipment included remote keyless entry and theft deterrent system, overhead console with driver information center, power sliding door, six-way power front seats and deep tinted glass. The GLS added touring suspension package, rear air conditioner and heater, traction control system and aluminum wheels as standard items. Optional on the GLS was leather seating. The Silhouette offered 126.6 cubic feet of cargo space and had a towing capacity of 2,000 pounds. Standard powertrain was the 180-hp 3.4-liter overhead valve V-6 coupled to an electronically-controlled Hydra-Matic 4T60-E four-speed automatic transaxle. The all-new unibody Silhouette also utilized safety cage construction as well as offering dual airbags, steel guard beams built into all doors and a collapsible steering column for driver protection in the event of an accident.

1997 Oldsmobile, Regency sedan, (O)

REGENCY -- SERIES 3H -- V-6 -- Much of the Ninety-Eight's heritage lived on in the Regency, which was marketed to "mop up older more traditional customers who have demonstrated unflappable support of Oldsmobile." The list of optional equipment was short: sunroof and engine block heater. Standard items included traction control, leather upholstery, daytime running lamps with twilight sentinel, overhead storage console, power trunk lid release, electrochromic rear view mirrors, electronic compass, front and rear storage armrests, cargo-retention net for the trunk, cruise control, 15-inch aluminum wheels with whitewall radial tires, power windows, power door locks and power outside rear view mirrors. The Regency utilized safety cage construction and offered dual airbags and side impact protection. Standard powertrain was the Series II 3800 3.8-liter V-6 linked to a Hydra-Matic 4T60-E four-speed automatic transaxle that featured the aforementioned, new electronically-controlled capacity clutch. Powertrain control computer memory capacity was double that of the year before (in the Ninety-Eight's 3800 V-6), 512 Kbytes compared to 256 Kbytes, respectively. On a traditional note, one carry-over item from the Ninety-Eight to the Regency was the chrome grille treatment.

1997 Oldsmobile, Bravada sport utility vehicle, (O)

BRAVADA -- SERIES 3T -- V-6 -- After undergoing a major redesign the year before, the Bravada was further significantly changed for 1997. Among the refinements was the addition of four-wheel disc brakes, weight-saving plug-in front halfshafts, weight-saving driveshaft made of aluminum and metal-matrix composite, a more ergonomic keyless entry fob, improved one-piece liftgate with liftglass rear door and a more efficient (1.5 percent gain overall) automatic transmission. A new option was the tilt and slide electric sunroof. Standard powertrain was the 190-hp 4.3-liter sequential central port injected V-6 linked to an electronically-controlled Hydra-Matic 4L60-E four-speed automatic transmission. To diminish the amount of fuel vapor lost to the atmosphere, the Bravada featured a new composite fuel cap and filler inlet. Bravada was again outfitted with SmartTrak, a combination of full-time all-wheel drive, four-wheel anti-lock brakes and a locking rear differential. Cargo capacity was 37.3 cubic feet with the rear seat up and 74.1 cubic feet with the rear seat folded down. Standard towing capacity of the Bravada was 5,000 pounds.

I.D. DATA: Oldsmobile's 17-symbol Vehicle Identification Number (VIN) again was located on the upper left surface of the instrument panel, visible through the windshield. The first three characters (1G3) indicates Oldsmobile Division. The fourth and fifth letters designate the body type/series: G/R - Aurora, H/C - Regency, H/N - Eighty-Eight and Eighty-Eight LS, H/Y - LSS, N/B - Cutlass, N/G - Cutlass, N/L - Achieva SC and Achieva SL, T/V - Bravada, U/M - Silhouette, W/H - Cutlass Supreme SL. The sixth number identifies the body style: 1 - 2-dr coupe, 2 - 2-dr hatchback/liftback, 3 - 2-dr convertible, 5 - 4-dr sedan, 6 - 4-dr hatchback/liftback, 8 - 4-dr station wagon. The seventh number identifies the restraint code: 2 - active (manual) belts with driver's and passenger's side frontal airbags, 4 - active (manual) belts with driver's and passenger's side frontal and side airbags. The eighth letter identifies the engine: C = 4.0-liter fuel-injected V-8, K = 3.8-liter fuel-injected V-6, M = 3.1-liter fuel-injected V-6, T = 2.4-liter fuel-injected inline four-cylinder, W = 4.3-liter fuel-injected V-6, 1 = 3.8-liter fuel-injected V-6. The ninth number is the check digit. The tenth letter represents the model year (V = 1997). The eleventh character identifies the assembly plant: D - Doraville, Ga.; F - Fairfax, Kan.; M - Lansing, Mich.; T - Tarrytown, N.Y.; 2 - Moraine, Ohio; 4 - Orion, Mich.; 6 - Oklahoma City, Okla. The final six digits are the sequential serial number.

AURORA (V-8)

Model Number	Body/Style Number	Body Type & Seating	Factory Price	Shipping Weight	Production. Total
3G	R29	4-dr. Sed-6P	35735	3967	N/A

ACHIEVA SC (FOUR/V-6)

| 3N | L37 | 2-dr. Cpe-5P | 15425/16975 | 2886/N/A | N/A |

ACHIEVA SL (FOUR/V-6)

| 3N | L69 | 4-dr. Sed-5P | 15225/16775 | 2917/N/A | N/A |

CUTLASS (V-6)

Model Number	Body/Style Number	Body Type & Seating	Factory Price	Shipping Weight	Production Total
N/A	N/A	4-dr. Sed-5P	N/A	2982	N/A

CUTLASS SUPREME SL (V-6)

| 3W | H47 | 2-dr. Cpe-6P | 18950 | 3283 | N/A |
| 3W | H69 | 4-dr. Sed-6P | 18950 | 3388 | N/A |

EIGHTY-EIGHT (V-6)

| 3H | N69 | 4-dr. Sed-6P | 22495 | 3465 | N/A |

EIGHTY-EIGHT LS (V-6)

| 3H | N69 | 4-dr. Sed-6P | 23795 | 3465 | N/A |

LSS (V-6)

Model Number	Body/Style Number	Body Type & Seating	Factory Price	Shipping Weight	Production Total
3H	Y69	4-dr. Sed-5P	27695	3547	N/A

SILHOUETTE (V-6)

Model Number	Body/Style Number	Body Type & Seating	Factory Price	Shipping Weight	Production Total
3U	M06	3-dr. Minivan-7P	N/A	3721	N/A

REGENCY (V-6)

Model Number	Body/Style Number	Body Type & Seating	Factory Price	Shipping Weight	Production Total
3H	C69	4-dr. Sed-6P	27995	N/A	N/A

BRAVADA (V-6)

Model Number	Body/Style Number	Body Type & Seating	Factory Price	Shipping Weight	Production Total
3T	V06	4-dr. Sport Utility-5P	N/A	4023	N/A

FACTORY PRICE AND WEIGHT NOTE: Beginning with the Achieva SC coupe, prices and weights to left of slash are for four-cylinder engine and to right for V-6.

ENGINE DATA: BASE FOUR (Achieva SC/Achieva SL): Twin cam inline four-cylinder. Cast iron block and aluminum head. Displacement: 146 cu. in. (2.4 liters). Bore & stroke: 3.54 x 3.70 in. Compression ratio: 9.5:1. Net horsepower: 150 @ 5600 rpm. Torque: 155 lb. ft. @ 4400 rpm. Fuel injected (SFI). BASE SIX (Cutlass/Cutlass GLS/Cutlass Supreme SL): Series 3100 60-degree overhead valve V-6. Cast iron block and aluminum heads. Displacement: 191 cu. in. (3.1 liters). Bore & stroke: 3.51 x 3.31 in. Compression ratio: 9.6:1. Net horsepower: (Cutlass/Cutlass GLS) 155 @ 5200; (Cutlass Supreme SL) 160 @ 5200 rpm. Torque: 185 lb. ft. @ 4000 rpm. Fuel injection (SFI). OPTIONAL SIX (Achieva SC/Achieva SL): same aforementioned Series 3100 3.1-liter/191-cid V-6 with SFI. BASE SIX (Eighty-Eight/LSS/Regency): Series II 3800 90-degree overhead valve V-6. Cast iron block and cast iron heads. Displacement: 231 cu. in. (3.8 liters). Bore & stroke: 3.80 x 3.40 in. Compression ratio: 9.4:1. Net horsepower: 205 @ 5200 rpm. Torque: 230 lb. ft. @ 4000 rpm. Fuel injected (SFI). OPTIONAL SIX (LSS) supercharged version of the aforementioned Series II 3.8-liter/231-cid V-6. Compression ratio: 8.5:1. Net horsepower: 240 @ 5200 rpm. Torque: 280 lb. ft. @ 3200 rpm. Fuel injected (SFI). BASE SIX (Silhouette): Series 3400 60-degree overhead valve V-6. Cast iron block and aluminum cylinder heads. Displacement: 205 cu. in. (3.4 liters). Bore & stroke: 3.62 x 3.31 in. Compression ratio: 9.5:1. Net horsepower: 180 @ 5200 rpm. Torque: 205 lb. ft. @ 4000 rpm. Fuel injected (SFI). BASE SIX (Bravada): Vortec overhead valve V-6. Cast iron block and cast iron cylinder heads. Displacement: 262 cu. in. (4.3 liters). Bore & stroke: 4.00 x 3.48 in. Compression ratio: 9.2:1. Net horsepower: 190 @ 4400 rpm. Torque: 250 lb. ft. @ 2800 rpm. Fuel injected (CPI). BASE EIGHT (Aurora) 90-degree dual overhead-cam V-8. Aluminum block and aluminum heads. Displacement: 244 cu. in. (4.0 liters). Bore & stroke: 3.43 x 3.31 in. Compression ratio: 10.3:1. Net horsepower: 250 @ 5600 rpm. Torque: 260 lb. ft. @ 4400 rpm. Fuel injected (SFI).

CHASSIS DATA: Wheelbase: (Aurora) 113.8 in.; (Achieva) 103.4 in.; (Cutlass) 107.0 in.; (Cutlass Supreme) 107.5 in.; (Eighty-Eight) 110.8 in.; (LSS) 110.8 in.; (Silhouette) 112.0 in.; (Regency) 110.8 in.; (Bravada) 107.0 in. Overall Length: (Aurora) 205.4 in.; (Achieva) 187.9 in.; (Cutlass) 192.0 in.; (Cutlass Supreme coupe) 193.9 in.; (Cutlass Supreme sedan) 193.7 in.; (Eighty-Eight) 200.4 in.; (LSS) 200.4 in.; (Silhouette) 187.4 in.; (Regency) 201.6 in.; (Bravada) 180.9 in. Height: (Aurora) 55.4 in.; (Achieva) 53.5 in.; (Cutlass) 56.9 in.; (Cutlass Supreme coupe) 53.3 in.; (Cutlass Supreme sedan) 54.8 in.; (Eighty-Eight) 55.7 in.; (LSS) 55.7 in.; (Silhouette) 67.4 in.; (Regency) 55.7 in.; (Bravada) 63.2 in. Width: (Aurora) 74.4 in.; (Achieva SC) 68.6 in.; (Achieva SL) 68.1 in.; (Cutlass) 69.4 in.; (Cutlass Supreme) 71.0 in.; (Eighty-Eight) 74.1 in.; (LSS) 74.1 in.; (Silhouette) 72.2 in.; (Regency) 74.7 in.; (Bravada) 66.5 in. Front tread: (Aurora) 62.5 in.; (Achieva)

55.8 in.; (Cutlass) 59.0 in.; (Cutlass Supreme) 59.5 in.; (Eighty-Eight) 60.4 in.; (LSS) 60.4 in.; (Silhouette) 61.5 in.; (Regency) N/A; (Bravada) 56.6 in. Rear tread: (Aurora) 62.6 in.; (Achieva) 55.3 in.; (Cutlass) 59.0 in.; (Cutlass Supreme) 58.0 in.; (Eighty-Eight) 60.4 in.; (LSS) 60.4 in.; (Silhouette) 63.3 in.; (Regency) N/A; (Bravada) 55.1 in. Standard tires: (Aurora) P235/60R16; (Achieva) P195/65R15; (Cutlass) P215/60R15; (Cutlass Supreme) P215/60R15; (Eighty-Eight) P205/70R15; (LSS) P225/60R16; (Silhouette) P205/70R15; (Regency) P205/70R15; (Bravada) P235/70R15.

TECHNICAL: Transmission: Four-speed automatic standard on Aurora/Achieva/Cutlass/Cutlass Supreme/Eighty-Eight/LSS/Silhouette/Regency/Bravada. Five-speed manual floor shift available on Achieva SC Series I and Series II/Achieva SL Series I. Standard final drive ratio: (Aurora) 3.48:1 with four-speed automatic trans.; (Achieva) 3.42:1 with four-speed automatic trans.; (Cutlass) 3.05:1 with four-speed automatic trans.; (Cutlass Supreme) 3.43:1 with four-speed automatic trans.; (Eighty-Eight) 2.84:1 with four-speed automatic trans.; (LSS) 3.06:1 with four-speed automatic trans.; (Silhouette) N/A; (Regency) N/A; (Bravada) 3.73:1 with four-speed automatic trans. Steering: (all except Aurora/LSS/Bravada) power assisted rack and pinion; (Aurora/LSS) rack and pinion with magnetic speed-variable assist; (Bravada) integral power steering variable ratio. Front Suspension: (Aurora/Achieva/Cutlass/Cutlass Supreme/Eighty-Eight/LSS/Regency) Independent, MacPherson strut w/ coil springs and anti-roll bar; (Silhouette) dual path upper strut mount, shock absorbers, lower control arms, large diameter anti-roll bar; (Bravada) Independent driving axle w/ upper and lower control arms, torsion bar springs, front stabilizer bar and frame-mounted differential carrier. Rear Suspension: (Aurora) Independent, cast aluminum semi-trailing arm w/ lateral links, coil springs, anti-roll bar and automatic leveling; (Achieva) Trailing twist axle with tubular control arms and open section transverse beam, coil springs and anti-roll bar; (Cutlass) Independent, tri-link strut location; (Cutlass Supreme) Independent, tri-link strut location, transverse leaf spring, anti-roll bar; (Eighty-Eight/LSS) Independent, Chapman strut, coil springs, anti-roll bar; (Silhouette) Twist beam axle, coil springs, canted shock absorbers; (Regency) Independent, strut; (Bravada) Rigid axle design with semi-elliptic leaf springs, stabilizer bar beam, coil springs and anti-roll bar. Brakes: (Achieva/Cutlass/Eighty-Eight/LSS/Silhouette/Regency) anti-lock power front disc, rear drum; (Aurora/Cutlass Supreme/Bravada) anti-lock power four-wheel disc. Body Construction: (all except Bravada) unibody; (Bravada) separate body and frame. Fuel tank: (Aurora) 20.0 gal.; (Achieva) 15.2 gal.; (Cutlass) 15.2 gal.; (Cutlass Supreme) 17.1 gal.; (Eighty-Eight/LSS) 18.0 gal.; (Silhouette) 20.0 gal.; (Regency) N/A; (Bravada) 18.0 gal.

DRIVETRAIN OPTIONS: (Achieva SC/Achieva SL) Series 3100 3.1-liter V-6 ($457). (LSS) supercharged Series II 3.8-liter V-6 ($1022). Transmission: (Achieva SC Series I and Series II/Achieva SL Series I) five-speed manual ($550 credit); Engine block heater ($18).

OPTION PACKAGES: (Aurora) Autobahn package ($395). (Aurora) Gold graphics package ($50). (Achieva SL) sport package ($255). (Achieva SC Series II/Achieva SL Series II) convenience package ($395).

MAJOR CONVENIENCE/APPEARANCE OPTIONS: Remote keyless entry ($125). Chrome-plated wheels ($600-$800). Cruise control ($225). Power sunroof ($695-$745). Heated driver's and passenger's side seats ($295). Astroroof ($595-$995).

Historical Footnotes: Oldsmobile began a campaign, notably on the entry-level Achieva and high-end Bravada, of marking major parts such as the engine, transmission, front fenders, doors, bumpers and hood with separate vehicle identification numbers to thwart theft.

OLDSMOBILE INTRIGUE 1998

Before it had a name, Oldsmobile designers and engineers knew that this car would send the division in a new direction in the midsize market. It wasn't until name research began that it was understood just how far Oldsmobile had gone in repositioning its main midsize entry.

Cutlass was the first name brought to the party. It was a logical candidate for a new high-volume Oldsmobile. It was steeped in company tradition. The name Intrigue, on the other hand, was totally new and, in fact, a late addition in the name research process.

"We needed to understand two things -- what does the name Cutlass stand for and to what extent does the name fit with this new product," said Doug Schumacker, Oldsmobile market re-

search manager. Consumer research results were conclusive and impactful. While the Cutlass name drew positive responses from domestic owners, import-minded customers were less than enamored with it.

The real test came when the Cutlass name was matched with this new midsize entry. "Import owners loved the car, but were dead-set against it being 'branded' as a Cutlass," Schumacker said. "Clearly, this car needed to carry a name that correctly matched the target customer's perception of the vehicle."

The next step was to develop and test name candidates along with the Cutlass name as a benchmark. Similar to the process used to brand the all-new Aurora, a list of name candidates was generated. A well-known branding development company, Lex-

Two views of the 1998 Oldsmobile Intrigue, a midsize four-door sedan. (Oldsmobile photo)

icon, was consulted to create a candidate list. Team members representing a variety of disciplines including marketing, design, advertising, and engineering were also solicited for name ideas.

Armed with a carefully honed list of name candidates, the Oldsmobile research team went out to the car's target customer group in search of an appropriate brand name.

As the research progressed, the name Intrigue clearly emerged as the most appropriate name. Clinic participants felt that not only did the name fit the car well, but the name itself generated positive images about the vehicle.

"We found that the Intrigue name had a synergistic effect with the car," explained Don DeVeaux, Intrigue assistant brand manager. "The name complemented the vehicle in areas that are important to the target market such as 'sporty,' 'luxurious,' and 'rewarding-to-drive,'" DeVeaux said. "It also conjured up an aura of mystery and excitement."

One study participant summed up this feeling best by saying, 'The name alone would get me to look at this vehicle.'

Dramatic departure

Like the Oldsmobile Aurora, the Intrigue represents another dramatic departure from traditional domestic car thinking. Providing a balance of sport and high-level refinement, Intrigue is an expressive and rewarding-to-drive, five-passenger midsize sedan. It is no mistake that customers targeted by Intrigue are those who would have listed upscale midsize imports as their first choice.

Intrigue makes a strong brand character statement in a market segment where it matters most. The sedan combines elements of the award-winning production Aurora and Oldsmobile Antares -- *AutoWeek* magazine's "Concept Car of the (Chicago Auto) Show" in 1995. Sculptured shoulder forms over the wheels and body side contours evoke images of Aurora while crystal clear head and taillamps and interior space efficiencies bring Antares to mind.

Oldsmobile already set new standards in the prestige luxury segment with the Aurora. Intrigue's design includes similar appearance, ride and handling attributes while keeping in mind the needs of its target midsize car customers.

With this sedan, Oldsmobile shifts toward import-oriented consumers. The division's need to make this change is part of its Centennial Plan, which aims to reposition the entire lineup, providing internationally-focused vehicles and unparalleled satisfaction throughout the shopping, buying and ownership experience.

Intrigue Features:

* 3.4-liter DOHC 24-valve V-6 engine
* four-speed automatic transmission
* antilock power four-wheel disc brakes
* daytime running lamps
* driver and passenger airbags
* sport-tuned suspension
* passenger compartment air filtration

Intrigue Dimensions:

Wheelbase: 109.0 inches

Length: 195.9 inches

Width: 73.8 inches

Height: 56.4 inches

Curb Weight: 3,515 pounds

Fuel Capacity: 18 gallons

Tire Size: P225/60R16

Interior view of 1998 Oldsmobile Intrigue

OLDSMOBILE TRUCKS

1904 Oldsmobile Box Body Runabout, OCW

OLDSMOBILE -- Lansing, Mich. -- (1904 - c.1975) -- The first of many light-duty commercial vehicles produced by Oldsmobile was a delivery van version of the company's famous Curved Dash model. It appeared as early as 1904. Between 1905 and 1907, the company produced heavier trucks. The firm became a branch of General Motors and, for a while, stuck chiefly to making passenger cars. However, in 1918, a one-ton truck using an overhead valve four-cylinder Northway engine came on the market for a short stay. It survived until about 1924, after which time the Oldsmobile truck was seen only in export markets. In the 1930s, Oldsmobile engines were used in some GMC truck models. The company's chassis was also used by some "professional car" builders as a platform for ambulance and hearse conversions. Though never the most popular choice of professional carmakers, these conversions were available at least through the mid-1970s from firms such as Superior, and especially Cotner-Bevington. Also of interest was the development of a prototype Oldsmobile sedan delivery in 1950. Only one of these was ever built. From 1968-1970, the American Quality Coach Co. also produced an airport limousine based on the front-wheel-drive Oldsmobile Toronado. It had twin rear axles, eight doors and seating accommodations for 15 people.

1919 Oldsmobile "Economy" Canopy Express, OCW

1919 Oldsmobile "Economy" Canopy Express, OCW

1920 Oldsmobile One-Ton Canopy Express, (J. Vann/CPC)

1919 Oldsmobile One-Ton Rack Body Express, (DFW)

1920 Oldsmobile One-Ton Canopy Express, OCW

231

INTERESTING OLDSMOBILE FACTS

The 1910 Limited had a Warner 100 mph speedometer. The Limited Roadster had a 40-gallon fuel tank.

In 1912 Oldsmobile introduced an automatic gas headlamp lighter.

In 1913 the Model 53 had a 23-gallon gas tank plus a reserve tank of two gallons.

The 1913 Oldsmobiles came with Delco electric ignition and starter at no extra charge.

In 1915 Oldsmobile's cross-town rival, Reo, founded by Ransom E. Olds, after he left Oldsmobile, outsold Oldsmobile two-to-one, 14,693 cars vs. 7,696, respectively.

The 1915 Oldsmobile Model 55 switched to left-hand steering.

In 1915 the four-cylinder Model 42, known as the "baby Olds," was advertised as having valves that were "enclosed and silenced."

The 1917 Oldsmobile Model 37 had a six-volt battery under the front seat.

In 1920 Oldsmobile introduced the Model 46 V-8, followed in 1922 by Model 47, Oldsmobile's second V-8. Oldsmobile now had two V-8s in a relatively small market segment.

In January 1927 four-wheel brakes were introduced on the Model 30 at no extra cost.

The Model F-28 was introduced in 1928 with an all-new six-cylinder engine, which continued until 1933. This was the first all new model since the 1923 Model 30.

In 1929 Oldsmobile introduced the Viking, a two-ton, V-8-powered "companion car."

The Viking went against the trend of smaller companion cars such as the LaSalle, a junior Cadillac.

The Viking had little parts interchangeability with F-series Oldsmobiles and was the only Oldsmobile with the new V-8 engine.

An unforeseen event on October 29, 1929, impacted Viking sales and the Viking was discontinued in 1930. It had a 90 degree, 260 cubic inch V-8 engine with 81 hp.

In 1931 Oldsmobile production was evenly divided between wire and wood wheels. It was also evenly divided between sidemounts and non sidemounts. Sidemounts were finally discontinued at the end of 1938.

In 1932 the fixed external sun visor was eliminated. This was an early step in the streamlining trend of the early 1930s.

1911 Oldsmobile Limited, Oldsmobile photo

Safety glass was standard in all 1932 Oldsmobile windshields and an extra cost option for all other windows.

Hydraulic self-energizing brakes were introduced in all 1934 Oldsmobiles.

In 1935 Oldsmobile introduced an aerodynamic split-V windshield, replacing the flat single piece windshield. This evolved into the split curved windshield in 1948 and the single piece curved windshield in 1950.

The new 1935 Oldsmobile body introduced the all-steel "Turret-Top." The entire roof was stamped from a single steel sheet. It replaced the fabric roof insert and was hailed as a major advancement for durability and safety.

Safety glass was made standard on all windows in the new-bodied 1937 Oldsmobile.

The 1938 Oldsmobile grille extended to the front fenders. This began the gradual evolution of the grille to a horizontal theme from the traditional upright radiator style.

The 1938 Oldsmobile introduced a safety dash. Corners and projections were eliminated through curved surfaces and flush controls.

In 1939 Oldsmobile transferred the three-speed manual shift lever from the floor to the steering column.

All 1939 Oldsmobiles had full trunks after discontinuing the sleek flatback trunk.

The 1939 Oldsmobile 70 and 80 Series could be ordered without runningboards.

The 1939 Oldsmobile 70 and 80 Series introduced the "Sunshine Turret-Top" option, an all-steel sunroof for $37.50. This innovative option, years ahead of its time, was short-lived due to leaks.

Sealed-beam headlights were introduced on all 1940 Oldsmobiles.

The rarest 1940 Oldsmobile was the four-door convertible sedan. It was the first Oldsmobile four-door convertible in almost a decade. Total production for this midyear model was only 50.

Oldsmobile introduced Hydra-Matic transmission to the industry in 1940. By 1941, half of all Oldsmobiles built had this option.

The 1941 Oldsmobile four-door sedan had a sleeper option to convert the rear seat and trunk into a bed. Window screens were optional for mosquito protection.

Turn signals were optional in 1942 for $11.40.

A rear window wiper was a $14.60 option on the 1947 Oldsmobile 98 two-door fastback sedan. It was either factory or dealer installed.

The all-new 1949 Oldsmobile 76 and 88 four-door sedans debuted in fastback and notchback versions. All fastbacks disappeared at the end of 1950.

There were two editions of the all-new 1949 Oldsmobile 88 station wagon. The early 1949s had substantial, but reduced exterior wood. In mid-1949 all exterior wood was replaced with steel, trimmed like wood.

1954 Oldsmobile 98 Starfire convertible, OCW

The 1949-1/2 Oldsmobile 98 introduced the two-door hardtop body-style to the industry, together with Buick's Riviera and Cadillac's Coupe de Ville. The hardtop also debuted the wraparound rear window.

The Oldsmobile ringed-world medallion debuted in 1949. This logo was used through 1957.

The 1949 Oldsmobile Rocket V-8 pioneered the modern short-stroke high-compression, overhead-valve V-8 format that dominated the horsepower race of the 1950s.

In 1950 Oldsmobile introduced the two-door hardtop to both the 88 Series and the entry-level 76 Series.

The 1950 Oldsmobile 88s began the model year with a split curved windshield. It soon made the transition to a single piece curved windshield.

In 1952, Oldsmobile introduced power steering by GM's Saginaw.

The 1953-1/2 Oldsmobile Fiesta convertible introduced a wraparound windshield and body two-tone paint. Although the Fiesta had five more horsepower than the 98s, this did not compensate for the Fiesta's extra 350 pounds.

In 1953 Oldsmobile sold an exclusive 548 Ninety-Eight Fiesta convertibles with a base price of $5,717.

In 1953 Oldsmobile adopted the 12-volt electrical system.

A 1953 two-seat concept car was the first Oldsmobile to carry the Starfire badge. It featured a fiberglass body, wraparound windshield and 200 hp V-8.

The Starfire was named after the Lockheed F-94B Starfire, a Lockheed rocket-firing jet.

In 1953 a devastating fire at GM's Hydra-Matic plant forced Oldsmobile to substitute Buick's Dynaflow twin-turbine transmission in 7,000 Oldsmobiles.

In 1953 Oldsmobile introduced Frigidaire air-conditioning at $550.

Power brakes were introduced as a $32 option in 1953.

The all-new 1954 Oldsmobile body was three inches lower. For the first time, the hood was level with the front fenders.

In 1954 Oldsmobile introduced the first displacement increase for the 1949 Rocket V-8. It went from 303 cubic inches to 324 cubic inches.

Oldsmobile first used the Cutlass name in 1954 on a semi-fastback concept car with fins. The Cutlass name was inspired by the Chance Vought F7U Cutlass, a twin-tail, carrier-based jet fighter.

The 1954 Oldsmobile F-88 concept car had a strong Corvette influence. It was a fiberglass two-seater substituting Oldsmobile Rocket-projectile taillights for the Corvette's spaceship taillights.

In 1955 Oldsmobile introduced tubeless tires in all series.

In 1955-1/2 Oldsmobile introduced the four-door hardtop to the industry. It debuted in all three Oldsmobile series. In a break from tradition, both 88 Series four-door hardtops had 98-style side trim.

In 1955 air conditioning outlets were relocated in the

dash, replacing clear plastic tubes connected to headliner ducts.

Hydra-Matic transmission became standard for the first time on the 1956 Oldsmobile 98s, 16 years after its debut.

In 1957 Oldsmobile re-introduced the station wagon, which had not been available since 1950.

The 1957 Oldsmobile reintroduced a three-piece backlight, the first Oldsmobile three-piece backlight since 1952. It was discontinued promptly in 1958.

The height of the 1957 Oldsmobile was reduced from 60-1/2 inches to 58 inches. An innovative two-piece driveshaft helped realize a lower body with less drive-tunnel intrusion into the passenger compartment. It had an extra U-joint at the cross point of the frame and X-member.

The new 1957 Oldsmobile dash was not symmetrical, a break from the practice since 1953.

In January 1957, the J-2 tri-power option was introduced. It included three two-barrel (3x2v) carburetors plus a special manifold and cylinder head gasket package to boost compression ratio to 10.0:1 as well as dual exhaust.

In 1958 Oldsmobile introduced an air bag suspension system called New-Matic Ride. It was a short-lived option.

The 215 cubic inch aluminum V-8 tooling (for the 1961-1963 Oldsmobile Cutlass/F-85) was later sold to England. It now powers the Range Rover four-wheel-drive station wagon, a more expensive Oldsmobile Bravada-type vehicle.

The 1961 F-85 station wagon introduced a single-piece tailgate hinged at the top.

The Oldsmobile Starfire was introduced in 1961-1/2 as a specially trimmed Super 88 convertible with full-length brushed aluminum side trim plus bucket seats and console.

In April 1962 Oldsmobile introduced the F-85 Jetfire with a turbocharged version of the 215 cubic inch aluminum V-8.

The 1962 Oldsmobile two-door hardtop introduced a new convertible-silhouette style roof with a small rear window and blind C-pillar.

The 1963 Oldsmobile Starfire introduced a stylish concave rear window. This novel roof line was transplanted to the conservative 1964 Oldsmobile F-85 four-door sedan.

The 1964-1/2 Oldsmobile Cutlass 4-4-2 option (code B-09) evolved from the police pursuit package. Initially it had a 330-cid/310-hp V-8 plus heavy-duty shocks and springs.

The 1964-1/2 Vista Cruiser was built on the intermediate F-85 chassis with a five-inch wheelbase stretch plus a raised rear roof with windows. The concept was inspired by the Greyhound Scenicruiser bus, built by General Motors.

In 1965 the 4-4-2 package moved up to the 400 cubic inch V-8 with 345 hp. Subsequently the 4-4-2 designation represented the 400 (or more) cubic inch V-8, four-barrel carburetor and dual exhaust. With this package, 0-60 mph time was 7.5 seconds.

In 1965 the 4-4-2 package cost $190.45 on the F-85, and $156.02 on the Cutlass.

In 1965 Oldsmobile discontinued its full-size 88 station wagon in favor of the Vista Cruiser.

Safety features added for 1966 included front and rear seat belts, back-up lights, outside rearview mirror, windshield washers, padded sun visors and glare-reducing surfaces on wiper arms and instrument panel.

The 4-4-2 became a full fledged series in 1968, the introductory year for the 1968-1972 Cutlass platform.

In 1969 side-impact bars were installed inside doors as a further safety enhancement.

The most potent 1969 Oldsmobile was the 4-4-2 with the 360 hp air-inducted W-30 (option code) package.

The 1970 and 1971 Oldsmobile 4-4-2s had a standard 455 cubic inch V-8, the largest 4-4-2 engine ever offered.

The 1971 Oldsmobile full-size 88s, 98s and Toronado were completely redesigned. They retained the 1971 bodies until the dramatic downsizing of the 88/98 in 1977 and the Toronado in 1979.

The 4-4-2 series reverted back to option status in 1972.

The 1973 Oldsmobile Cutlass was completely redesigned. Pillared sedans replaced two-door and four-door hardtops.

In 1974 Oldsmobile produced only 380 Hurst/Olds models, making it the lowest production edition.

The 1974 Oldsmobile Toronado offered an electric sunroof for $589 that required the power window option.

The 1974 Oldsmobile introduced the production air bag option on the 88/98 and Toronado. It was ordered in limited-volume.

The last "pure" Oldsmobile convertible, a Delta 88 Royale, was built on July 11, 1975.

In 1975 the 4-4-2 option was an appearance-only package. Technically, it was available on six-cylinder models.

The 1975 Hurst/Oldsmobile had a T-top roof called the Hurst hatch. It also had the innovative deletion of the opera window for a retrograde extended B-pillar with poor lane-changing visibility.

The 1975 Cutlass had optional swivel front seats with removable and reversible seat cushions.

The 1977 Oldsmobile Starfire reintroduced four-cylinder engines to Oldsmobile for the first time since 1923.

The 1977 Oldsmobile Cutlass Supreme coupe sales reached 242,874 -- an impressive figure for a single model of a series.

Oldsmobile introduced its first diesel, a 350 cubic inch V-8 in 1978.

The downsized 1977 Oldsmobile full-size 88s actually weighed less than the 1977 midsize Cutlass, anticipating its 1978 downsizing.

The downsized 1978 Oldsmobile Cutlass "aeroback" four-door sedans were fastbacks without a rear hatch. They were one of the largest fastback four-door sedans built.

The 1978 Cutlass four-door aeroback was not popular and had to be extensively and quickly converted back to a notchback for 1980, using the same platform. Sales increased dramatically with the new 1980 notchback, which resembled the first generation 1976-1979 Cadillac Seville.

The downsized 1978 Cutlass had an average weight reduction of 657 pounds.

The 1978 Oldsmobile Cutlass Salon and Calais had an optional five-speed manual transmission.

The Toronado was downsized in 1979 and lost 900 pounds, one of the greatest weight reductions for a downsized car.

In 1979 Oldsmobile introduced its second diesel, a smaller 260 cubic inch V-8 for the Cutlass at $700.

Even after downsizing the Oldsmobile Cutlass Supreme coupe sold an impressive 277,944 cars in 1979.

Completely new sheet metal for the 1981 Oldsmobile Cutlass coupe reduced aerodynamic drag by 15 percent.

The 1981 Oldsmobile Toronado switched to the 4.1-liter, 125-hp Buick V-6 as its base engine.

In 1982 Oldsmobile introduced the Cutlass Ciera as its version of GM's new A-body platform. The A-body was a stretched X-body, used by the Oldsmobile Omega and all the other GM divisions except Cadillac.

The Cutlass Ciera had the longest production run of any single platform Oldsmobile series, continuing from 1982 through 1996, with evolutionary updates.

In 1985 the Oldsmobile 98 (GM C-body) was downsized for the second time since 1977 and converted to front-drive. The 88 followed with front-wheel downsizing in 1986.

The 1990 Oldsmobile Cutlass Supreme roll-bar convertible was introduced in mid-1990, the latest industry introduction of any 1990 car. The 1988 Indy Pace Car prototype did not have the roll-bar.

The 4-4-2 was reborn in 1990 as a $1,680 option package for the Cutlass Calais. It included the Quad 4 engine, four valves per cylinder and two overhead camshafts.

The compact Oldsmobile Achieva was introduced in early calendar 1992. It was an extensive revision of the 1987 Chevrolet Beretta/Corsica platform.

Oldsmobile released 1995 Aurora prototype press photos on December 30, 1992. The prototype was almost identical to the final product.

The 1998 Oldsmobile Intrigue, succeeding the Cutlass Supreme, will have a 3.4-liter V-6 version of the Aurora V-8.

OLDSMOBILE MOTORSPORTS MILESTONES

The Motorsport Aurora V-8 is the heir to Oldsmobile's winning tradition that includes over 100 race wins, 11 Manufacturer's Championships, and 11 Driver's Championships in IMSA road racing competition at the start of the 1996 racing season. Innovative engineering and race-winning technology are hallmarks of Oldsmobile's 99-year history. The following are highlights of this rich heritage:

1897 Olds Motor Vehicle Company incorporated in Lansing, Mich., on August 21, 1897, making Oldsmobile the longest running car company in the United States.

1902 Roy E. Chapin drives a Curved Dash Oldsmobile from Detroit to New York in 7-1/2 days, becoming the sensation of the New York auto show

1903 Ransom E. Olds drives the "Pirate" to a 54 mph speed record at Ormond Beach, Fla.

1905 Two Oldsmobiles stage the first transcontinental race, covering 4,000 miles from New York to Portland, Oregon, in 44 days

1923 Cannonball Baker drives Oldsmobile Model 30A from New York to Los Angeles in 12-1/2 days

1948 High-compression Rocket V-8 introduced

1949 Oldsmobile 88 named Indianapolis 500 pace car; Olds wins six of nine NASCAR Grand National races

1950 Herschel McGriff wins first Pan-American road race in Oldsmobile 88 sedan

1951 Oldsmobile wins 20 of 41 NASCAR Grand National races

1957 Buddy Sampson wins Top Eliminator at NHRA U.S. Nationals with Oldsmobile-powered dragster

1959 Lee Petty wins inaugural Daytona 500

1960 Oldsmobile F-85 introduced with all-aluminum V-8

1962 Oldsmobile introduced first American production turbocharged V-8

1964 Oldsmobile 4-4-2 sport option debuts

The 1903 Oldsmobile Pirate was the first Olds race car. It raced from Ormond to Daytona Beach, Florida, in 1903 and set a land speed record in its class of 54.38 mph. (Oldsmobile photo)

Hershel McGriff (wearing crash helmet) and Ray Elliott drove this "City of Roses" sponsored 1950 Oldsmobile 88 to victory in the 1950 Mexican Road Race, which spanned 2,178 grueling miles between Ciudad Juarez and El Ocotal, Mexico. (Old Cars photo)

1967 Oldsmobile sweeps five classes in Union/Pure Oil Performance Trials at Daytona Beach, Fla.

1968 Toronados finish 1-2-3 in Pike's Peak Hill Climb stock car division; Hurst/Olds introduced

1970 Oldsmobile paces Indy 500; race winner Al Unser receives Oldsmobile 442 convertible

1971 Oldsmobile wins first of 14 NHRA Manufacturers Championship

1978 Oldsmobile scores first IMSA victory in American Challenge event in Talladega, Ala.

1979 Richard Petty wins Daytona 500 with Oldsmobile

1982 Warren Johnson scores first Oldsmobile win in NHRA Pro Stock

1983 15th Anniversary Hurst/Olds produced; Oldsmobile DRCE Rocket V-8 debuts

1984 Oldsmobile named "Official Car Of NHRA"; Olds wins first of 12 consecutive NHRA Manufacturers Championships

1985 Jim Head wins first Oldsmobile Funny Car title at NHRA NorthStar Nationals

1986 Oldsmobile wins first of nine consecutive "Automobile Manufacturer of the Year" awards on *Car Craft* All-Star Drag Racing Team; Warren Johnson breaks 190 mph Pro Stock barrier with Oldsmobile Firenza; Irv Hoerr wins IMSA American Challenge championship

1987 A.J. Foyt drives Quad 4-powered Oldsmobile Aerotech to world closed course speed record (257 mph) and "flying mile" record (267 mph); Pat Austin wins first of four NHRA Top Alcohol Funny Car championships

1988 Paul Gentilozzi scores first Oldsmobile win in SCCA Trans-Am series; Quad 4 engine introduced in Calais, wins first IMSA race; Oldsmobile paces Indy 500 for record eighth time

1989 Bruce Larson wins first Oldsmobile Funny Car championship; Bob Newberry breaks 5-second barrier in Top Alcohol Funny Car with Cutlass Supreme; Oldsmobile Quad 4 wins IMSA Street Stock Touring class drivers and manufacturers championships; Rob Moroso wins NASCAR Grand National championship; Olds wins first of six consecutive Pro Stock Cups

1990 High-performance W41 Quad 4 introduced with Quad 442 Sport Performance Package; Quad 4 sweeps IMSA Street Stock Sport Class drivers and manufacturers championships

1991 Jeff Taylor wins first Oldsmobile Super Stock championship; Quad 4 wins first of three consecutive IMSA International Sedan drivers and manufacturers championship; Quad 4 powers SCCA Oldsmobile Pro Series; Harry Gant wins four straight NASCAR Winston Cup races; Olds sweeps NASCAR Grand National Drivers and Manufacturers Championships

1992 Warren Johnson wins first Oldsmobile NHRA Pro Stock championship; Bob Newberry scores milestone 250th NHRA win for Oldsmobile; Olds wins first of three consecutive SCCA World Challenge drivers championships; Oldsmobile Aerotech breaks 47 speed and endurance records with production 4.0-liter Aurora V-8

1993 Jim Epler breaks 300 mph barrier with Oldsmobile-bodied Funny Car; Olds scores milestone 300th win in NHRA drag racing; Blaine Johnson wins fourth consecutive NHRA Top Alcohol Dragster championship with

Oldsmobile DRCE engine; Olds wins fifth consecutive Funny Car championship; Olds wins IMSA GTS manufacturers championship

1994 Oldsmobile drag racer Kurt Johnson breaks 6-second Pro Stock barrier; Oldsmobile named "Official Car of IMSA"; Brix Racing wins Daytona 24-hour endurance race with Oldsmobile-Spice; Olds wins inaugural IMSA World Sports Car Manufacturers Championship

1995 Motorsport Aurora V-8 introduced, wins six races and eight poles, sweeps GTS-1 Drivers and Manufacturers Championships; Brix Racing Oldsmobile-Spice wins second consecutive IMSA WSC class in Daytona 24-hour race; Olds wins record 12th consecutive NHRA Manufacturer's Cup, tenth consecutive "Automobile Manufacturer of the Year" award, and seventh consecutive Pro Stock Cup; Warren Johnson scores Oldsmobile's milestone 400th NHRA national event victory

1996 Indy Racing League Aurora V-8 announced; Oldsmobile sweeps WSC and GTS-1 classes Rolex 24 at Daytona, scores first overall win by American manufacturer since 1966; Olds wins Sebring 12-hour; Old competes in 24 Hours of Le Mans for first time.

The Riley & Scott Racing Aurora V-8-powered World Sports Car (WSC) class endurance racer competed at the 24 Hours of LeMans in 1996, and qualified seventh on the grid. (Oldsmobile photo)

A motorsports version of the Aurora body design was developed specifically for IMSA GTS-1 competition in 1996. Brix Racing was almost unbeatable since it debuted its twin Auroras at the season-opening 24-hour race at Daytona International Speedway. The Brix Racing GTS-1 Auroras won five of the first six races on the IMSA schedule, including the 24-hour event at Daytona. (Oldsmobile photo)

OLDSMOBILE'S PACE CAR PARADE

This group of 1970 Oldsmobile Cutlass convertible Indianapolis 500 pace car replicas was used in the 500 Festival held in Indianapolis prior to the Memorial Day Classic at the "brickyard." (IMS photo)

Oldsmobile's first Indianapolis 500 pace car was this 1949 88 convertible with special "rocket" trim. It was driven by Wilbur Shaw. (AA)

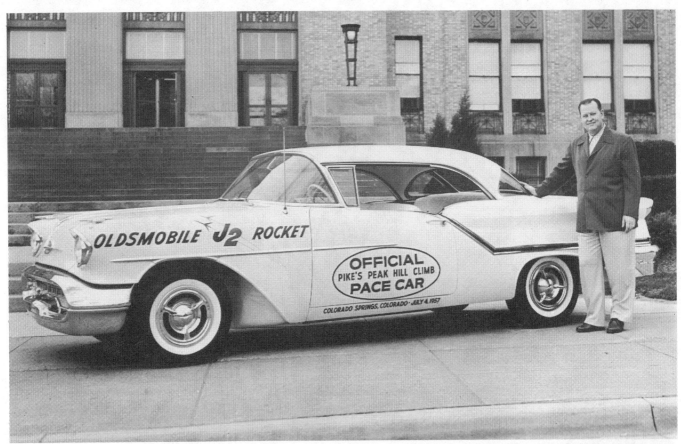

The Indianapolis 500 was not the only recipient of an Oldsmobile pace car. The July 4, 1957, Pikes Peak Hill Climb at Colorado Springs, Colo., was started with this 1957 Golden Rocket 88 Holiday hardtop as the honorary pace car. V.H. Sutherlen, Oldsmobile general sales manager, posed with the car, which was powered by the J-2 Rocket engine linked to a Jetaway Hydra-Matic drive transmission. It was driven up the 12-1/2-mile race course by Pikes Peak Auto Hill Climb Association President and General Manager Lloyd Faddis. (Oldsmobile)

The 1960 Indianapolis 500 was paced by this Olds 98 convertible with Sam Hanks at the wheel. That's speedway owner Tony Hulman behind the wheel in this publicity photo. (IMS)

A 1970 Oldsmobile 4-4-2 convertible paced that year's Indy 500 with Rodger Ward as driver. Chief Steward Harlan Fengler showcased the car in this publicity photo. (IMS)

The 1972 Indianapolis 500 was paced by this Hurst/Olds convertible with Jim Rathmann as driver. Chief Steward Harlan Fengler posed in the car for this publicity photo. (IMS)

Jim Rathmann again was the Indy 500 pace car driver in 1974 when this Hurst/Olds W-30 convertible paced the event. Chief Steward Tom Binford was behind the wheel in this publicity photo. (IMS)

Actor James Garner was the driver of this 1977 Oldsmobile Delta 88 Indianapolis 500 pace car. Chief Steward Tom Binford posed in the car for this publicity photo. (IMS)

A 1985 Oldsmobile Calais 500 convertible paced that year's Indianapolis 500, again with actor James Garner at the wheel. (IMS)

A Quad 4-powered 1988 Oldsmobile Cutlass Supreme convertible paced that year's Indy 500. Pilot Chuck Yeager was the driver. (IMS)

An artist's drawing of the 1997 Oldsmobile Aurora V-8 that was scheduled to pace the 81st running of the Indianapolis 500 as part of Oldsmobile's centennial observance. (The driver of the Aurora pace car had not yet been named as this book went to press.) (Oldsmobile)

Oldsmobile Concept Cars Predicted the Future Subtle *and* Spectacular

by Robert C. Ackerson

Oldsmobiles of the 1950s were best known for their sparkling performance and basically handsome lines, even if at times they sported excessive chrome trim. Having led the rest of General Motors in the use of Hydra-Matic drive in 1940, Oldsmobile, along with Cadillac, had ushered in the era of modern engine design with its 303-cid/135-hp "Rocket" V-8 in 1949.

Somewhat overlooked by automotive historians, perhaps because of these twin technological triumphs, have been the exciting Oldsmobile concept and experimental cars of the postwar years. With a spectacular and popular extravaganza such as the great Motorama events as a showcase, all the General Motors divisions turned out attractive, and at times bizarre, one-off automobiles worthy in retrospect of more than a passing glance.

First displayed at the 1952 Motorama, Oldsmobile's Fiesta convertible was the first and surprisingly hesitant venture by Olds into the world of "Alice in Wonderland." When compared to Oldsmobile's future offerings in the Dream Car sweepstakes, the Fiesta was a fairly attractive but restrained automobile with styling closely patterned after the 1953 production models. This similarity to its assembly line siblings did make it possible for the Fiesta to enter production on a limited basis. A total of 458 Fiestas were sold at the rather hefty price of $5,715. For this amount of cash the Fiesta's owner could justify his purchase to cynical friends by pointing out its wraparound windshield (which had first appeared on the LaSabre in 1951 and was scheduled for production Oldsmobiles, Buicks and Cadillacs in 1954), its power steering/brakes/windows and twin radio antennae and finally its "ultra-ultra" interior with thick carpets and leather-covered cushions. With a 170 bhp version of Oldsmobile's V-8, the Fiesta, while not a sports car, was a suave precursor of the great high performance Oldsmobiles of the late-1960s and early-1970s.

Slightly more exotic was the Fiesta's Motorama runningmate the 200 hp Starfire "XP Rocket", described as "the epitome of daring new automotive design ... an exciting, experimental "Laboratory-on-wheels" that represents all the genius and vision of progressive Oldsmobile engineers." In reality, the Starfire was somewhat less than this bit of literary hyperbole implied. Probably its most innovative feature was its fiberglass body, unusual for a car of its size.

Neither the Fiesta nor the Starfire could hold a candle in terms of styling sensationalism to Oldsmobile's 1954 Motorama offerings, the Cutlass coupe and the F-88 two-seater. As Oldsmobile's General Manager, Jack F. Wolfram noted with a good deal of accuracy and a minimum of bravado, "these Oldsmobile-designed experimental sports cars give our engineers and stylists a free hand in automotive design without limitations." Powered by a 325-cid/250-bhp Oldsmobile V-8 and finished in metallic copper paint, the Cutlass -- like the Starfire, named after a military aircraft used by the United States -- was a striking automobile. Restrained enough to retain its identity as an Oldsmobile yet sufficiently futuristic to turn heads, it was the most radical Oldsmobile dream car yet to appear. A compact two-seater on a snug 110-inch wheelbase, the Cutlass was equipped with a center console containing "competition-type" instruments (including a tachometer) and swivel seats that made entry into and exit from this 51.5-inch high automobile fairly convenient. Some seven years later the Cutlass' rear bumper-fin arrangement would be used on the 1960 Cadillacs with a good deal of success. Two other Cutlass features destined for future popularity were its "Venetian-blind" rear window and (shades of "get your ears on good buddy!") its "radio-telephone."

1953 Starfire: A fiberglass-bodied four-passenger convertible, the Starfire was finished in regal turquoise with white and turquoise leather upholstery. The safety padded instrument panel had five gauges spaced between the speedometer and the radio speaker. Dual back-up lights and exhaust ports are integral with the end bumper guards. Oldsmobile world emblems front and rear and an "88" medallion on the side identified it as an Oldsmobile. The Starfire lent several of its styling ideas to production vehicles. Most notably, the large oval grille (1956 models) and the side trim (1954 models). The wraparound windshield was soon seen on the large series GM cars in 1954 and across-the-board by 1955. The name Starfire came from the F-94 Starfire jet fighter. For many years to come the name Starfire was attached to all Olds convertibles. It then became the name of a luxury series in the 1960s and finally the name Olds called its new small car in 1964. (Oldsmobile photo)

1954 Cutlass: One of two Olds show cars built for the 1954 GM Motorama show, the Cutlass was also named after a fighter plane -- a Navy carrier-based jet. This sports hardtop had a fiberglass body and was finished in highly metallic copper, with copper and white upholstery and interior trim. The concept car's stainless steel wheelhousings were perforated to permit exhaust of engine heat. Overall length of the Cutlass was 188-1/2 inches, road height was 51-1/2 inches and wheelbase was 110 inches. (Oldsmobile photos)

The Cutlass' co-star, the F-88 was a sleek two-seater with a 102-inch wheelbase and a height of only 48 inches. Adorned with metallic gold paint and devoid of superfluous styling clichés, it was an attractive sports car. With 250 hp, a fiberglass body and pigskin upholstery, the F-88 was what the original Corvette should have been.

Oldsmobile's offering for the 1955 Motorama, the "88 Delta, XP-40" was a four-passenger "close-coupled" two-door hardtop with far more conservative styling than its immediate predecessors. Using a chassis and running gear consisting primarily of components from production Oldsmobiles, the Delta was Oldsmobile's way of letting the public know what was in store for them in the late 1950s. Most would agree with Dick Langworth's assessment that "one could not particularly praise the Delta's styling; it predicted the swap-backed horse period into which Olds and others sank during the late 1950s."

But the relatively conservative Delta was followed by what was probably the most spectacular concept car of the entire Motorama era -- the Golden Rocket of 1956. Described by Oldsmobile as "an experimental sports coupe with aerodynamic styling,"

the Golden Rocket was without a doubt the high point of Oldsmobile's fascination with the application of aircraft styling themes to automobiles. Only 49-1/2 inches high, with dorsal fins arising midway on its sweeping rear fenders and endowed with a front end unlike anything seen before, the Golden Rocket was a stunning fantasy with undeniable appeal. Like its ancestors, some of its styling features were destined to appear on future GM production models. In the case of the Golden Rocket it was its split, two-piece rear window design that eventually found a home on the 1963 Corvette Stingray.

Other elements of the Golden Rocket to later have virtually industry-wide use were its 13-inch diameter wheels and first generation flow-through ventilation system. When the fiberglass-bodied, 275-bhp Golden Rocket was exhibited at the Paris Salon in 1957 even the Parisians -- accustomed to a good deal of automotive exotica -- were impressed by its roof panels, which rose to aid passenger entry/exit. In addition, Oldsmobile incorporated seats that rose three inches and swiveled to the outside in a successful effort to reconcile practicality with the Golden Rocket's futuristic design.

246

The engine that powered the Cutlass was a 324-cid/250-hp Rocket V-8 with 9.0:1 compression ratio. (Oldsmobile photo)

Apparently at this time, the realization that the Motorama shows attracted not only a great deal of the public's interest but that of competitors as well led GM to reconsider airing the fruits of its creative genius for all to see, marvel and copy. Thus for the most part the dream and experimental cars that followed the Golden Rocket were essentially production models given custom interiors or color combinations to set them apart. As a result the best Oldsmobile could muster for the auto show circuit in 1957 and 1958 were such items as a Holiday 98 coupe, called the "Mona Lisa," with pearlescent paint and the Carousel, a standard Fiesta station wagon outfitted with rear seats upholstered in vinyl to withstand the abuse of young children. While the kids entertained themselves with a built-in magnetic car game, Mom and Dad enjoyed the luxury of fabric seats up front. Not that all this was bad (the Carousel also featured rear windows and doors operable only by a switch on the instrument panel), but after all those exciting experimental cars with their jazzy airplane derived names, things just weren't the same!

A partial return to those glorious days of yesteryear came in 1959 with the F-88III. Like its earlier versions this trim two-seater was mounted on a 102-inch wheelbase. With a vermilion body and a brushed stainless steel top that rolled back on concealed tracks and stowed beneath the rear deck the F-88III was accurately described by Oldsmobile's Public Relations Department as "a rolling laboratory to test advanced styling and engineering features." Beneath its combination steel and fiberglass body the F-88III fairly shone with interesting technical goodies

including an experimental Hydra-Matic transmission mounted behind the passenger compartment and a special cross-flow aluminum radiator. A bit on the freaky side was the F-88's muffler and exhaust system, which was mounted in front of the engine and had its exhaust outlets mounted forward of the front wheels!

In 1962 with Oldsmobile's F-85 luxury compact receiving a warm reception in the automotive marketplace, the X-215, a two-seater based on the production F-85 convertible was created. Its fiberglass tonneau cover, which incorporated an airfoil-section roll bar, covered the rear seat in a fashion not unlike that Ford used to convert its Thunderbird into a two-seater. Finished in "Firefrost Silver" the X-215 was powered by a turbocharged engine driven through a Hydra-Matic transmission.

The last of the really great concept cars from Oldsmobile came in 1968. Simply called the Toronado Granturismo, it could have easily been put into limited production with a minimum number of changes such as the Fiesta convertible of 1953. Using the running gear of the normal front-wheel drive Toronado but with five inches less overhang and a wheelbase of just 110 inches, it was a taut, agile two-seater, easily the equal of the best European GTs.

Oldsmobile still offered concept cars after the Toronado Granturismo but somehow they lacked the element of design innovation that seemed so much a part of Oldsmobiles such as the F-88, Cutlass and Golden Rocket.

1954 F-88: The second show car for 1954 was this Corvette-size sports car made of fiberglass, which weighed 3,600 pounds. The F-88 was built on a 102-inch chassis with a 167-inch overall length. The F-88 was painted metallic gold with a pigskin interior. It shared the same 324-cid engine as the Cutlass had. (Oldsmobile photos)

The rear bumper unit of the F-88 dropped down to reveal the horizontally-stored spare tire. (Oldsmobile photo)

1955 Delta: The Delta was Oldsmobile's contribution to the GM Motorama for 1955. It was a four-passenger coupe with brushed aluminum roof, wide-set oval recesses housing the headlights, dual fuel tanks in the rear fenders, front seats that swiveled for easy entry and exit and cast aluminum wheels. The Delta was finished in two-tone metallic blue set off by ornamental chrome and the interior was blue aluminum trim and blue leather. Except for the top, the Delta's body was made from fiberglass. The hood width extended from fender crown to fender crown, a chrome cove hid the fender edge. The concept car's wraparound rear bumper blended into the rear fenders. The Delta's overall length was 201 inches, road height was 53 inches and wheelbase was 120 inches. It was powered by a 250-hp Rocket V-8 with a 10.0:1 compression ratio. (Oldsmobile photo)

1956 Golden Rocket: This two-passenger sports coupe with aerodynamic styling was made of fiberglass and was painted metallic gold. Projectile-shaped bumper guards were incorporated at the extreme front and rear of the fenders and the extension of this form was carried for the entire length of the car. As either door was opened, the roof panel automatically rose and the seat also rose three inches and swiveled out for easier entry or exit. Plastic dorsal fins just to the rear of the doors on the fender crown line were lighted in red and served as running lights. The interior was upholstered in blue and gold leather. The car's overall length was 201 inches, road height was 49-1/2 inches and wheelbase was 105 inches. The Golden Rocket was powered by a 275-hp Rocket V-8 with a 9.5:1 compression ratio. (Oldsmobile photo)

1956 Oldsmobile Golden Rocket

1969 Apollo: This space age conception of the 4-4-2 appeared at the 1969 New York Auto Show. It was finished in Fireball red paint with black accent stripes and hood panels. The interior featured four metallic red and black leather "contour couches" and head restraints. (General Motors photo)

1989 Aerotech II: A spin-off of the Olds Aerotech that carried A.J. Foyt to record speeds in 1987, the Aerotech II debuted at the North American Auto Show in Detroit in 1989. The aim of this concept car was to apply the low-drag benefits gleaned from the single-seater Aerotech to a four-passenger sports coupe for highway use. (Oldsmobile photo)

1990 Expression: The family sport sedan debuted at the 1990 Chicago Auto Show. The Expression featured uninterrupted front fascia lines and a unique rear tailgate that doubled as a family entertainment center including Nintendo game center, VCR and built-in vacuum cleaner with outlets throughout the car. It had a metallic orange finish. The Expression was powered by a 230-hp Quad 4 engine. It had a 200.3-inch overall length and 104.9-inch wheelbase. (Oldsmobile photo)

1995 Antares: Named after the brightest star in the southern hemisphere, the Antares debuted at the 1995 Chicago Auto Show. It featured thin, horizontal headlamps and translucent rear taillights for an international focus. Antares featured champagne blue paint and sculptured, six-spoke, 18-inch wheels and high-speed rated tires. (Oldsmobile photo)

TORONADO: OLDSMOBILE'S FRONT-RUNNER IN 1966

It was announced to the press on July 29, 1965, and unveiled in showrooms on September 24, 1965. It was radical. It was risky. And before the ink was dry on all the accolades heaped on it by the automotive press, Oldsmobile's front-wheel drive 1966 Toronado had earned the coveted *Motor Trend* "Car of the Year" award, among other prestigious engineering merits.

The Toronado was the first practical, domestic, full-sized front-wheel drive car since the Cord automobiles of the 1930s. Research on the Toronado dated back to the 1950s. The production "Toro" was assembled in Lansing, Mich., and rode on a wheelbase of 119 inches with an overall length of 211 inches. Both standard and deluxe versions were offered. Thirty-plus years later, with front-wheel drive now the norm in automobiles, the Oldsmobile engineers who created the Toronado can truly be hailed as forward-thinkers in more ways than one.

An artist's rendering of the stylish, front-drive 1966 Toronado. (Oldsmobile photo)

The 1966 Toronado came standard with dual exhaust and chrome exhaust extensions. (Oldsmobile photo)

The Toronado was powered by a 425-cid/385-hp V-8, the only engine available that year for the luxury front-drive Olds. It had a 10.5:1 compression ratio and produced 475 pound-feet of torque. Only premium fuel could be used. (Oldsmobile photo)

An elongated view of the 1966 Oldsmobile Toronado chassis showed the relocation of all powertrain components ahead of the passenger compartment and the advanced torsion bar suspension system. (Oldsmobile photo)

Conspicuous by its absence was the driveshaft tunnel interrupting the floor of the Toronado's passenger compartment, which seated six comfortably. (Oldsmobile photo)

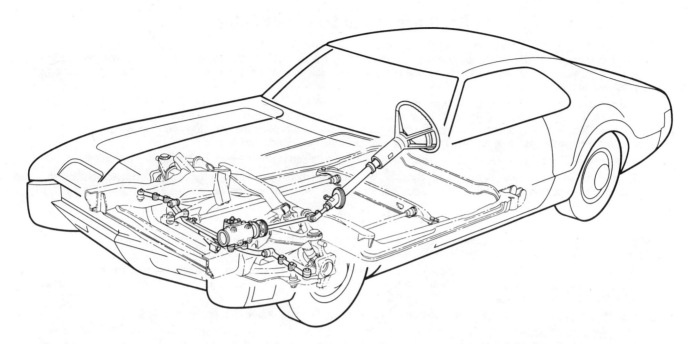

A line drawing of 1966 Toronado that highlights the steering column and steering linkage. The steering column featured a flexible, constant-speed universal joint that isolated vibrations and assured proper steering column angle. Power steering was standard on the Toro and the overall turning ratio was 17.0:1. Lock-to-lock was about 3-1/2 turns compared to nearly five turns for conventional steering. (Oldsmobile photo)

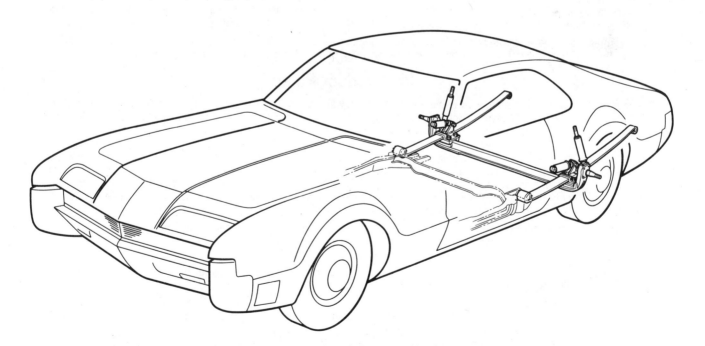

A line drawing of the 1966 Toronado's rear suspension detail. The Toro featured four rear shock absorbers, two on either side, to decrease rear spring "wind-up" and increase braking control. Leaf springs were anchored with rubber bushings and were fastened at the rear to an integral underbody frame. This drawing also shows stamped U-channel axle with fixed spindles bolted on for rear wheels. (Oldsmobile photo)

OLDSMOBILE CENTENNIAL PLAN

A Roadmap to the Division's Future.

On August 21, 1997, Oldsmobile will be the first American automobile maker to celebrate its 100th birthday. By then, a very different car company will be in place, an organization that is far stronger and more dynamic in its response to the competitive challenge. To prepare for the second century of its existence, Oldsmobile has devised and is already executing its Centennial Plan.

The process of sharpening the focus on its future began in 1992 with the arrival of a new Oldsmobile general manager, John Rock. He concluded that Oldsmobile must change in major ways in order to survive. Instead of competing head first with other General Motors brands, Oldsmobile would move to shift its outlook to the popular import models, specifically the most highly regarded Japanese brands: Toyota, Lexus, Nissan, Infiniti, Honda and Acura.

The Centennial Plan, conceived in 1994, rests solidly on two pillars and is summarized by Oldsmobile's mission statement:

The Oldsmobile team will work together to earn and keep its customers by providing internationally-focused vehicles and uncompromised satisfaction throughout the shopping, buying and ownership experience.

Product Pillar

Oldsmobile vehicles executed according to the Centennial Plan are international in scope and import-like in character. A prime example is the Aurora, perhaps the most important and successful new Oldsmobile.

Oldsmobile's product strategy is specifically aimed at younger, better educated and more affluent customers. This group could also be described as import owners or import intenders (those who harbor a preference for import vehicles no matter what they are currently driving).

For specific guideposts help define the Centennial product in more detail -- all future products will be:

Thoughtful By thoughtfully considering customer needs and more carefully executing every detail, future Oldsmobiles will demonstrate a harmony of form and function. Their designs will be sophisticated in their simplicity. Their innovations will be practical and intuitively right for the task. They will evidence an enduring style.

Precise Precision will go far beyond the fit and finish of interlocking body panels. Future Oldsmobiles will be meticulously refined, smooth and effortless to operate. At their core there will be a rigid body structure. Premium materials will be used throughout.

International An international flavor will dominate the entire character of each vehicle. The exterior design will be a balance of function and form. Oldsmobile exterior design themes will be characterized by a clean, uncluttered look. Roomy five-passenger seating will fit neatly within trim exterior dimensions and all-around visibility will be a key feature. Predominantly DOHC powertrains will be balanced with nimble, stable handling, a controlled ride and agile maneuverability.

Rewarding The Rewarding for Oldsmobile ownership will be low life cycle costs, high resale value and the satisfaction of having made a shrewd investment. Each vehicle's design will gratify and inspire its owner throughout is long useful life.

Non-Product Pillar

The other half of the Centennial Plan is the way Oldsmobile will conduct its business affairs in the future. Substantial investment and effort have already gone into the reengineering of the non-product side of the equation to assure that Oldsmobile will soon be regarded as the number one brand in customer care. The Oldsmobile Vision Center in Rochester Hills, Michigan, is, for all intents, a college campus where team members can learn those attitudes and techniques that will change the entire process of selling and servicing the division's products to its constituency. Intensive training focuses on the wants and needs of the customer and stresses the importance of providing a simplified buying experience. Price is vastly de-emphasized by means of a straightforward model strategy and across-the-board simplified pricing. A retailer's consultative approach to selling places the customer in command and the Oldsmobile sales person in the role of information and assistance provider. Respect -- for the customer's time and intelligence -- is at the forefront.

From the showroom floor up to the top levels of Oldsmobiles management, the reengineering process has taken hold to empower every member of the business team with the authority to focus on customer needs.

A major driving force behind the new Oldsmobile is the board of governance, a team of eight wholesale and eight retail members that meet monthly to deal with important issues impacting the business. Many retailers also participate in Board of Governance sub-committees which make important contributions.

Oldsmobile's vision for the future is firmly grounded in the belief that a clear customer focus is the only way to deliver uncompromised satisfaction. Team members are already spreading that attitude by living up to Centennial Plan criteria. While Oldsmobile has survived 100 years, it will soon be a totally new and reconstituted car company. When that message registers -- by demanding consumers' word of mouth rather than by means of television advertising -- there will be genuine cause for celebration.

CONDITIONS

1) EXCELLENT: Restored to current maximum professional standards of quality in every area, or perfect original with components operating and appearing as new. A 95-plus point show car that is not driven.

2) FINE: Well-restored, or a combination of superior restoration and excellent original. Also, an *extremely* well-maintained original showing very minimal wear.

3) VERY GOOD: Completely operable original or "older restoration" showing wear. Also, a good amateur restoration, all presentable and serviceable inside and out. Plus, combinations of well-done restoration and good operable components or a partially restored car with all parts necessary to complete and/or valuable NOS parts.

4) GOOD: A driveable vehicle needing no or only minor work to be functional. Also, a deteriorated restoration or a very poor amateur restoration. All components may need restoration to be "excellent," but the car is mostly useable "as is."

5) RESTORABLE: Needs *complete* restoration of body, chassis and interior. May or may not be running, but isn't weathered, wrecked or stripped to the point of being useful only for parts.

6) PARTS CAR: May or may not be running, but is weathered, wrecked and/or stripped to the point of being useful primarily for parts.

PRICING

OLDSMOBILE

	6	5	4	3	2	1
1901						
Curved dash 1 cyl.						
Rbt	1450	4700	7800	15,600	27,300	39,000
1902						
Curved Dash, 1-cyl.						
Rbt	1450	4550	7600	15,200	26,600	38,000
1903						
Curved Dash, 1-cyl.						
Rbt	1450	4550	7600	15,200	26,600	38,000
1904						
Curved Dash, 1-cyl.						
Rbt	1450	4550	7600	15,200	26,600	38,000
French Front, 1-cyl., 7 hp						
Rbt	1300	4200	7000	14,000	24,500	35,000
Light Tonneau, 1-cyl., 10 hp						
Tonn	1300	4100	6800	13,600	23,800	34,000
1905						
Curved Dash, 1-cyl.						
Rbt	1450	4550	7600	15,200	26,600	38,000
French Front, 1-cyl., 7 hp						
Rbt	1300	4200	7000	14,000	24,500	35,000
Touring Car, 2-cyl.						
Tr	1300	4100	6800	13,600	23,800	34,000
1906						
Straight Dash B, 1-cyl.						
Rbt	1150	3700	6200	12,400	21,700	31,000
Curved Dash B, 1-cyl.						
Rbt	1450	4550	7600	15,200	26,600	38,000
Model L, 2-cyl.						
Tr	1200	3850	6400	12,800	22,400	32,000
Model S, 4-cyl.						
Tr	1300	4200	7000	14,000	24,500	35,000
1907						
Straight Dash F, 2-cyl.						
Rbt	1150	3700	6200	12,400	21,700	31,000
Model H, 4-cyl.						
Fly Rds	1300	4100	6800	13,600	23,800	34,000
Model A, 4-cyl.						
Pal Tr	1400	4450	7400	14,800	25,900	37,000
Limo	1350	4300	7200	14,400	25,200	36,000
1908						
Model X, 4-cyl.						
Tr	1300	4100	6800	13,600	23,800	34,000
Model M-MR, 4-cyl.						
Rds	1300	4200	7000	14,000	24,500	35,000
Tr	1300	4100	6800	13,600	23,800	34,000
Model Z, 6-cyl.						
Tr	1700	5400	9000	18,000	31,500	45,000
1909						
Model D, 4-cyl.						
Tr	1800	5750	9600	19,200	33,600	48,000
Limo	1700	5400	9000	18,000	31,500	45,000
Lan	1650	5300	8800	17,600	30,800	44,000
Model DR, 4-cyl.						
Rds	1750	5650	9400	18,800	32,900	47,000
Cpe	1600	5050	8400	16,800	29,400	42,000
Model X, 4-cyl.						
Rbt	1300	4100	6800	13,600	23,800	34,000

	6	5	4	3	2	1
Model Z, 6-cyl.						
Rbt	2500	7900	13,200	26,400	46,200	66,000
Tr	2550	8150	13,600	27,200	47,600	68,000
1910						
Special, 4-cyl.						
Rbt	1300	4100	6800	13,600	23,800	34,000
Tr	1350	4300	7200	14,400	25,200	36,000
Limo	1450	4550	7600	15,200	26,600	38,000
Limited, 6-cyl.						
Rbt	3400	10,800	18,000	36,000	63,000	90,000
Tr	4000	12,700	21,200	42,400	74,200	106,000
Limo	2350	7450	12,400	24,800	43,400	62,000
1911						
Special, 4-cyl.						
Rbt	1300	4100	6800	13,600	23,800	34,000
Tr	1350	4300	7200	14,400	25,200	36,000
Limo	1300	4200	7000	14,000	24,500	35,000
Autocrat, 4-cyl.						
Rbt	2150	6850	11,400	22,800	39,900	57,000
Tr	2200	6950	11,600	23,200	40,600	58,000
Limo	2200	6950	11,600	23,200	40,600	58,000
Limited, 6-cyl.						
Rbt	3400	10,800	18,000	36,000	63,000	90,000
Tr	4000	12,700	21,200	42,400	74,200	106,000
Limo	2250	7200	12,000	24,000	42,000	60,000
1912						
Autocrat, 4-cyl., 40 hp						
2d Rds	2500	7900	13,200	26,400	46,200	66,000
4d Tr	2500	7900	13,200	26,400	46,200	66,000
4d Limo	2550	8150	13,600	27,200	47,600	68,000
Despatch, 4-cyl., 26 hp						
2d Rds	1300	4200	7000	14,000	24,500	35,000
4d Tr	1400	4450	7400	14,800	25,900	37,000
2d Cpe	1200	3850	6400	12,800	22,400	32,000
Defender, 4-cyl., 35 hp						
2d 2P Tr	1350	4300	7200	14,400	25,200	36,000
4d 4P Tr	1400	4450	7400	14,800	25,900	37,000
2d 2P Rds	1300	4200	7000	14,000	24,500	35,000
2d 3P Cpe	1200	3850	6400	12,800	22,400	32,000
2d 5P Cpe	1150	3700	6200	12,400	21,700	31,000
Limited, 6-cyl.						
2d Rds	3250	10,300	17,200	34,400	60,200	86,000
4d Tr	3750	12,000	20,000	40,000	70,000	100,000
4d Limo	2500	7900	13,200	26,400	46,200	66,000
1913						
Light Six, 6-cyl.						
4d 4P Tr	1250	3950	6600	13,200	23,100	33,000
4d Phae	1300	4100	6800	13,600	23,800	34,000
4d 7P Tr	1200	3850	6400	12,800	22,400	32,000
4d Limo	1250	3950	6600	13,200	23,100	33,000
6-cyl., 60 hp						
4d Tr	2500	7900	13,200	26,400	46,200	66,000
4-cyl., 35 hp						
4d Tr	1600	5050	8400	16,800	29,400	42,000
1914						
Model 54, 6-cyl.						
4d Phae	1550	4900	8200	16,400	28,700	41,000
4d 5P Tr	1500	4800	8000	16,000	28,000	40,000
4d 7P Tr	1550	4900	8200	16,400	28,700	41,000
4d Limo	1300	4200	7000	14,000	24,500	35,000

	6	5	4	3	2	1
Model 42, 4-cyl.						
4d 5P Tr	1200	3850	6400	12,800	22,400	32,000
1915						
Model 42, 4-cyl.						
2d Rds	1150	3600	6000	12,000	21,000	30,000
4d Tr	1150	3700	6200	12,400	21,700	31,000
Model 55, 6-cyl.						
4d Tr	2050	6600	11,000	22,000	38,500	55,000
1916						
Model 43, 4-cyl.						
2d Rds	1100	3500	5800	11,600	20,300	29,000
4d 5P Tr	1150	3600	6000	12,000	21,000	30,000
Model 44, V-8						
2d Rds	1550	4900	8200	16,400	28,700	41,000
4d Tr	1600	5050	8400	16,800	29,400	42,000
4d Sed	850	2650	4400	8800	15,400	22,000
2d Cabr	1500	4800	8000	16,000	28,000	40,000
1917						
Model 37, 6-cyl.						
4d Tr	1000	3250	5400	10,800	18,900	27,000
2d Rds	1000	3100	5200	10,400	18,200	26,000
2d Cabr	950	3000	5000	10,000	17,500	25,000
4d Sed	700	2150	3600	7200	12,600	18,000
Model 45, V-8						
4d 5P Tr	1500	4800	8000	16,000	28,000	40,000
4d 7P Tr	1550	4900	8200	16,400	28,700	41,000
4d Conv Sed	1500	4800	8000	16,000	28,000	40,000
2d Rds	1450	4550	7600	15,200	26,600	38,000
Model 44-B, V-8						
2d Rds	1450	4700	7800	15,600	27,300	39,000
4d Tr	1450	4550	7600	15,200	26,600	38,000
1918						
Model 37, 6-cyl.						
2d Rds	800	2500	4200	8400	14,700	21,000
4d Tr	850	2650	4400	8800	15,400	22,000
2d Cabr	750	2400	4000	8000	14,000	20,000
2d Cpe	550	1800	3000	6000	10,500	15,000
4d Sed	500	1550	2600	5200	9100	13,000
Model 45-A, V-8						
4d 5P Tr	1400	4450	7400	14,800	25,900	37,000
4d 7P Tr	1450	4550	7600	15,200	26,600	38,000
2d Rds	1350	4300	7200	14,400	25,200	36,000
4d Spt Tr	1400	4450	7400	14,800	25,900	37,000
2d Cabr	1300	4200	7000	14,000	24,500	35,000
4d Sed	1050	3350	5600	11,200	19,600	28,000
1919						
Model 37-A, 6-cyl.						
2d Rds	750	2400	4000	8000	14,000	20,000
4d Tr	800	2500	4200	8400	14,700	21,000
4d Sed	500	1550	2600	5200	9100	13,000
2d Cpe	550	1800	3000	6000	10,500	15,000
Model 45-A, V-8						
2d Rds	1250	3950	6600	13,200	23,100	33,000
4d Tr	1300	4100	6800	13,600	23,800	34,000
Model 45-B, V-8						
4d 4P Tr	1300	4100	6800	13,600	23,800	34,000
4d 7P Tr	1300	4200	7000	14,000	24,500	35,000
1920						
Model 37-A, 6-cyl.						
2d Rds	700	2150	3600	7200	12,600	18,000
4d Tr	700	2300	3800	7600	13,300	19,000
Model 37-B, 6-cyl.						
2d Cpe	500	1550	2600	5200	9100	13,000
4d Sed	400	1300	2200	4400	7700	11,000
Model 45-B, V-8						
4d 4P Tr	1050	3350	5600	11,200	19,600	28,000
4d 5P Tr	1100	3500	5800	11,600	20,300	29,000
4d 7P Sed	750	2400	4000	8000	14,000	20,000
1921						
Model 37, 6-cyl.						
2d Rds	650	2050	3400	6800	11,900	17,000
4d Tr	700	2150	3600	7200	12,600	18,000
2d Cpe	450	1450	2400	4800	8400	12,000
4d Sed	400	1200	2000	4000	7000	10,000
Model 43-A, 4-cyl.						
2d Rds	550	1800	3000	6000	10,500	15,000
4d Tr	600	1900	3200	6400	11,200	16,000
2d Cpe	400	1300	2200	4400	7700	11,000
Model 46, V-8						
4d 4P Tr	1000	3100	5200	10,400	18,200	26,000
4d Tr	1000	3250	5400	10,800	18,900	27,000
4d 7P Sed	650	2050	3400	6800	11,900	17,000
Model 47, V-8						
4d Spt Tr	1000	3250	5400	10,800	18,900	27,000
2d 4P Cpe	750	2400	4000	8000	14,000	20,000
4d 5P Sed	1050	3350	5600	11,200	19,600	28,000
1922						
Model 46, V-8						
4d Spt Tr	1000	3250	5400	10,800	18,900	27,000
4d 4P Tr	950	3000	5000	10,000	17,500	25,000
4d 7P Tr	1000	3100	5200	10,400	18,200	26,000
4d 7P Sed	600	1900	3200	6400	11,200	16,000
Model 47, V-8						
2d Rds	950	3000	5000	10,000	17,500	25,000
4d Tr	1000	3250	5400	10,800	18,900	27,000
4d 4P Spt	1050	3350	5600	11,200	19,600	28,000
2d 4P Cpe	700	2150	3600	7200	12,600	18,000
4d 5P Sed	550	1800	3000	6000	10,500	15,000
1923						
Model M30-A, 6-cyl.						
2d Rds	700	2300	3800	7600	13,300	19,000
4d Tr	750	2400	4000	8000	14,000	20,000
2d Cpe	450	1450	2400	4800	8400	12,000
4d Sed	400	1200	2000	4000	7000	10,000
4d Spt Tr	850	2650	4400	8800	15,400	22,000
Model 43-A, 4-cyl.						
2d Rds	750	2400	4000	8000	14,000	20,000
4d Tr	800	2500	4200	8400	14,700	21,000
2d Cpe	450	1450	2400	4800	8400	12,000
4d Sed	400	1200	2000	4000	7000	10,000
4d Brgm	400	1300	2200	4400	7700	11,000
4d Cal Tp Sed	450	1450	2400	4800	8400	12,000
Model 47, V-8						
4d 4P Tr	1000	3100	5200	10,400	18,200	26,000
4d 5P Tr	1000	3250	5400	10,800	18,900	27,000
2d Rds	950	3000	5000	10,000	17,500	25,000

	6	5	4	3	2	1
4d Sed	600	1900	3200	6400	11,200	16,000
2d Cpe	700	2150	3600	7200	12,600	18,000
4d Spt Tr	1050	3350	5600	11,200	19,600	28,000
1924						
Model 30-B, 6-cyl.						
2d Rds	550	1800	3000	6000	10,500	15,000
4d Tr	600	1900	3200	6400	11,200	16,000
2d Spt Rds	600	1900	3200	6400	11,200	16,000
4d Spt Tr	650	2050	3400	6800	11,900	17,000
2d Cpe	450	1080	1800	3600	6300	9000
4d Sed	350	975	1600	3200	5600	8000
2d Sed	350	900	1500	3000	5250	7500
4d DeL Sed	350	975	1600	3200	5600	8000
1925						
Series 30-C, 6-cyl.						
2d Rds	550	1800	3000	6000	10,500	15,000
4d Tr	600	1900	3200	6400	11,200	16,000
2d Spt Rds	600	1900	3200	6400	11,200	16,000
4d Spt Tr	650	2050	3400	6800	11,900	17,000
2d Cpe	350	975	1600	3200	5600	8000
4d Sed	350	900	1500	3000	5250	7500
4d DeL Sed	350	950	1550	3150	5450	7800
2d DeL	350	840	1400	2800	4900	7000
1926						
Model 30-D, 6-cyl.						
2d DeL Rds	700	2150	3600	7200	12,600	18,000
4d Tr	650	2050	3400	6800	11,900	17,000
4d DeL Tr	650	2100	3500	7000	12,300	17,500
2d Cpe	450	1080	1800	3600	6300	9000
2d DeL Cpe	450	1140	1900	3800	6650	9500
2d Sed	350	780	1300	2600	4550	6500
2d DeL Sed	350	840	1400	2800	4900	7000
4d Sed	350	840	1400	2800	4900	7000
4d DeL Sed	350	900	1500	3000	5250	7500
4d Lan Sed	500	1550	2600	5200	9100	13,000
1927						
Series 30-E, 6-cyl.						
2d DeL Rds	550	1700	2800	5600	9800	14,000
4d Tr	500	1550	2600	5200	9100	13,000
4d DeL Tr	550	1700	2800	5600	9800	14,000
2d Cpe	450	1080	1800	3600	6300	9000
2d DeL Cpe	450	1140	1900	3800	6650	9500
2d Spt Cpe	400	1200	2000	4000	7000	10,000
2d Sed	350	900	1500	3000	5250	7500
2d DeL Sed	350	975	1600	3200	5600	8000
4d Sed	350	975	1600	3200	5600	8000
4d DeL Sed	350	1020	1700	3400	5950	8500
4d Lan	400	1300	2200	4400	7700	11,000
1928						
Model F-28, 6-cyl.						
2d Rds	550	1800	3000	6000	10,500	15,000
2d DeL Rds	600	1900	3200	6400	11,200	16,000
4d Tr	600	1900	3200	6400	11,200	16,000
4d DeL Tr	650	2050	3400	6800	11,900	17,000
2d Cpe	400	1200	2000	4000	7000	10,000
2d Spl Cpe	400	1250	2100	4200	7400	10,500
2d Spt Cpe	400	1300	2200	4400	7700	11,000
2d DeL Spt Cpe	450	1400	2300	4600	8100	11,500
2d Sed	350	975	1600	3200	5600	8000
4d Sed	350	1000	1650	3300	5750	8200
4d DeL Sed	350	1020	1700	3400	5950	8500
4d Lan	400	1200	2000	4000	7000	10,000
4d DeL Lan	400	1300	2200	4400	7700	11,000
1929						
Model F-29, 6-cyl.						
2d Rds	750	2400	4000	8000	14,000	20,000
2d Conv	700	2150	3600	7200	12,600	18,000
4d Tr	700	2300	3800	7600	13,300	19,000
2d Cpe	450	1400	2300	4600	8100	11,500
2d Spt Cpe	450	1400	2350	4700	8200	11,700
2d Sed	450	1080	1800	3600	6300	9000
4d Sed	950	1100	1850	3700	6450	9200
4d Lan	450	1140	1900	3800	6650	9500
1929						
Viking, V-8						
2d Conv Cpe	1000	3100	5200	10,400	18,200	26,000
4d Sed	700	2300	3800	7600	13,300	19,000
4d CC Sed	750	2400	4000	8000	14,000	20,000
1930						
Model F-30, 6-cyl.						
2d Conv	800	2500	4200	8400	14,700	21,000
4d Tr	850	2650	4400	8800	15,400	22,000
2d Cpe	400	1300	2200	4400	7700	11,000
2d Spt Cpe	450	1450	2400	4800	8400	12,000
4d Sed	400	1200	2000	4000	7000	10,000
4d Sed	750	2400	4000	8000	14,000	20,000
4d Pat Sed	800	2500	4200	8400	14,700	21,000
1930						
Viking, V-8						
2d Conv Cpe	950	3000	5000	10,000	17,500	25,000
4d Sed	450	1450	2400	4800	8400	12,000
4d CC Sed	500	1550	2600	5200	9100	13,000
1931						
Model F-31, 6-cyl.						
2d Conv	900	2900	4800	9600	16,800	24,000
2d Cpe	450	1500	2500	5000	8800	12,500
2d Spt Cpe	500	1550	2600	5200	9100	13,000
2d Sed	400	1200	2000	4000	7000	10,000
4d Sed	400	1200	2000	4000	7000	10,000
4d Pat Sed	400	1250	2100	4200	7400	10,500
1932						
Model F-32, 6-cyl.						
2d Conv	1000	3250	5400	10,800	18,900	27,000
2d Cpe	500	1550	2600	5200	9100	13,000
2d Spt Cpe	550	1700	2800	5600	9800	14,000
2d Sed	400	1200	2000	4000	7000	10,000
4d Sed	400	1300	2200	4400	7700	11,000
4d Pat Sed	450	1400	2300	4600	8100	11,500
Model L-32, 8-cyl.						
2d Conv	1150	3600	6000	12,000	21,000	30,000
2d Cpe	550	1700	2800	5600	9800	14,000
2d Spt Cpe	550	1800	3000	6000	10,500	15,000
2 dr Sed	400	1300	2200	4400	7700	11,000
4d Sed	450	1400	2300	4600	8100	11,500
4d Pat Sed	450	1450	2400	4800	8400	12,000

1933

Model F-33, 6-cyl.

	6	5	4	3	2	1
2d Conv	900	2900	4800	9600	16,800	24,000
2d Bus Cpe	400	1250	2100	4200	7400	10,500
2d Spt Cpe	450	1450	2400	4800	8400	12,000
2d 5P Cpe	450	1400	2300	4600	8100	11,500
2d Tr Cpe	400	1250	2100	4200	7400	10,500
4d Sed	400	1200	2050	4100	7100	10,200
4d Trk Sed	400	1250	2100	4200	7400	10,500

Model L-33, 8-cyl.

	6	5	4	3	2	1
2d Conv	950	3000	5000	10,000	17,500	25,000
2d Bus Cpe	400	1300	2200	4400	7700	11,000
2d Spt Cpe	450	1450	2400	4800	8400	12,000
2d 5P Cpe	450	1400	2300	4600	8100	11,500
4d Sed	400	1250	2100	4200	7400	10,500
4d Trk Sed	400	1300	2200	4400	7700	11,000

1934

Model F-34, 6-cyl.

	6	5	4	3	2	1
2d Bus Cpe	400	1250	2100	4200	7400	10,500
2d Spt Cpe	400	1300	2200	4400	7700	11,000
2d 5P Cpe	400	1200	2000	4000	7000	10,000
4d SB Sed	450	1140	1900	3800	6650	9500
4d Trk Sed	450	1160	1950	3900	6800	9700

Model L-34, 8-cyl.

	6	5	4	3	2	1
2d Conv	950	3000	5000	10,000	17,500	25,000
2d Bus Cpe	450	1450	2400	4800	8400	12,000
2d Spt Cpe	500	1550	2600	5200	9100	13,000
2d 5P Cpe	450	1500	2500	5000	8800	12,500
2d Tr Cpe	400	1300	2200	4400	7700	11,000
4d Sed	400	1200	2000	4000	7000	10,000
4d Trk Sed	400	1250	2050	4100	7200	10,300

1935

F-35, 6-cyl.

	6	5	4	3	2	1
2d Conv	850	2750	4600	9200	16,100	23,000
2d Clb Cpe	450	1160	1950	3900	6800	9700
2d Bus Cpe	450	1130	1900	3800	6600	9400
2d Spt Cpe	450	1190	2000	3950	6900	9900
2d Tr Cpe	450	1120	1875	3750	6500	9300
4d Sed	350	975	1600	3250	5700	8100
4d Trk Sed	350	1000	1650	3300	5750	8200

L-35, 8-cyl.

	6	5	4	3	2	1
2d Conv	950	3000	5000	10,000	17,500	25,000
2d Clb Cpe	400	1250	2100	4200	7300	10,400
2d Bus Cpe	400	1200	2000	4000	7100	10,100
2d Spt Cpe	400	1300	2200	4400	7700	11,000
2d Sed	350	1040	1750	3500	6100	8700
2d Trk Sed	450	1050	1800	3600	6200	8900
4d Sed	450	1050	1800	3600	6200	8900
4d Trk Sed	450	1090	1800	3650	6400	9100

1936

F-36, 6-cyl.

	6	5	4	3	2	1
2d Conv	950	3000	5000	10,000	17,500	25,000
2d Bus Cpe	400	1250	2100	4200	7400	10,500
2d Spt Cpe	400	1300	2200	4400	7700	11,000
2d Sed	450	1050	1750	3550	6150	8800
2d Trk Sed	450	1080	1800	3600	6300	9000
4d Sed	450	1090	1800	3650	6400	9100
4d Trk Sed	950	1100	1850	3700	6450	9200

L-36, 8-cyl.

	6	5	4	3	2	1
2d Conv	1000	3250	5400	10,800	18,900	27,000
2d Bus Cpe	400	1200	2000	4000	7000	10,000
2d Spt Cpe	400	1250	2100	4200	7400	10,500
2d Sed	950	1100	1850	3700	6450	9200
2d Trk Sed	450	1140	1900	3800	6650	9500
4d Sed	450	1160	1950	3900	6800	9700
4d Trk Sed	450	1190	2000	3950	6900	9900

1937

F-37, 6-cyl.

	6	5	4	3	2	1
2d Conv	1050	3350	5600	11,200	19,600	28,000
2d Bus Cpe	400	1250	2100	4200	7300	10,400
2d Clb Cpe	450	1400	2300	4600	8100	11,500
2d Sed	400	1300	2200	4400	7700	11,000
2d Trk Sed	400	1200	2000	4000	7100	10,100
4d Sed	400	1300	2200	4400	7700	11,000
4d Trk Sed	400	1200	2050	4100	7100	10,200

L-37, 8-cyl.

	6	5	4	3	2	1
2d Conv	1150	3700	6200	12,400	21,700	31,000
2d Bus Cpe	400	1350	2250	4500	7800	11,200
2d Clb Cpe	400	1300	2200	4400	7700	11,000
2d Sed	400	1250	2100	4200	7300	10,400
2d Trk Sed	400	1250	2100	4200	7400	10,500
4d Sed	400	1250	2100	4200	7300	10,400
4d Trk Sed	400	1250	2100	4200	7400	10,600

1938

F-38, 6-cyl.

	6	5	4	3	2	1
2d Conv	1150	3600	6000	12,000	21,000	30,000
2d Bus Cpe	400	1250	2100	4200	7300	10,400
2d Clb Cpe	400	1300	2200	4400	7600	10,900
2d Sed	450	1140	1900	3800	6650	9500
2d Tr Sed	400	1200	2000	4000	7000	10,000
4d Sed	450	1190	2000	3950	6900	9900
4d Tr Sed	400	1200	2000	4000	7000	10,000

L-38, 8-cyl.

	6	5	4	3	2	1
2d Conv	1300	4100	6800	13,600	23,800	34,000
2d Bus Cpe	400	1300	2200	4400	7600	10,900
2d Clb Cpe	450	1350	2300	4600	8000	11,400
2d Sed	400	1200	2000	4000	7000	10,000
2d Tr Sed	400	1250	2100	4200	7400	10,500
4d Sed	400	1250	2050	4100	7200	10,300
4d Tr Sed	400	1250	2100	4200	7400	10,500

1939

F-39 "60" Series, 6-cyl.

	6	5	4	3	2	1
2d Bus Cpe	400	1250	2050	4100	7200	10,300
2d Clb Cpe	400	1250	2100	4200	7300	10,400
2d Sed	400	1200	2050	4100	7100	10,200
4d Sed	400	1250	2100	4200	7300	10,400

G-39 "70" Series, 6-cyl.

	6	5	4	3	2	1
2d Conv	1050	3350	5600	11,200	19,600	28,000
2d Bus Sed	400	1250	2100	4200	7400	10,500
2d Clb Cpe	400	1300	2150	4300	7500	10,700
2d Sed	400	1250	2100	4200	7300	10,400
2d SR Sed	400	1250	2100	4200	7400	10,600
4d Sed	400	1250	2100	4200	7400	10,500
4d SR Sed	400	1250	2100	4200	7400	10,600

L-39, 8-cyl.

	6	5	4	3	2	1
2d Conv	1150	3700	6200	12,400	21,700	31,000
2d Bus Cpe	400	1300	2200	4400	7700	11,000
2d Clb Cpe	450	1350	2300	4600	8000	11,400
2d Sed	400	1300	2150	4300	7500	10,700
2d SR Sed	400	1300	2200	4400	7700	11,000
4d Sed	400	1350	2200	4400	7800	11,100
4d SR Sed	400	1300	2150	4300	7600	10,800

1940

Series 60, 6-cyl.

	6	5	4	3	2	1
2d Conv	1100	3500	5800	11,600	20,300	29,000
2d Bus Cpe	450	1350	2300	4600	8000	11,400
2d Clb Cpe	450	1450	2400	4800	8400	12,000
4d Sta Wag	750	2400	4000	8000	14,000	20,000
2d Sed	400	1300	2150	4300	7500	10,700
2d SR Sed	400	1300	2200	4400	7700	11,000
4d Sed	400	1300	2150	4300	7600	10,800
4d SR Sed	400	1350	2200	4400	7800	11,100

Series 70, 6-cyl.

	6	5	4	3	2	1
2d Conv	1150	3700	6200	12,400	21,700	31,000
2d Bus Cpe	450	1450	2400	4800	8400	12,000
2d Clb Cpe	450	1400	2300	4600	8100	11,500
2d Sed	450	1350	2300	4600	8000	11,400
4d Sed	450	1400	2300	4600	8100	11,600

Series 90, 8-cyl.

	6	5	4	3	2	1
2d Conv Cpe	1750	5650	9400	18,800	32,900	47,000
4d Conv Sed	1800	5750	9600	19,200	33,600	48,000
2d Clb Cpe	600	1900	3200	6400	11,200	16,000
4d Tr Sed	550	1700	2800	5600	9800	14,000

1941

Series 66, 6-cyl.

	6	5	4	3	2	1
2d Conv Cpe	1000	3100	5200	10,400	18,200	26,000
2d Bus Cpe	400	1300	2200	4400	7700	11,000
2d Clb Cpe	450	1400	2300	4600	8100	11,500
2d Sed	400	1250	2100	4200	7300	10,400
4d Sed	400	1250	2100	4200	7400	10,600
4d Twn Sed	400	1300	2150	4300	7500	10,700
4d Sta Wag	1050	3350	5600	11,200	19,600	28,000

Series 68, 8-cyl.

	6	5	4	3	2	1
2d Conv Cpe	1050	3350	5600	11,200	19,600	28,000
2d Bus Cpe	450	1400	2300	4600	8100	11,500
2d Clb Cpe	450	1450	2400	4800	8400	12,000
2d Sed	400	1250	2100	4200	7400	10,600
4d Sed	400	1300	2150	4300	7600	10,800
4d Twn Sed	400	1300	2200	4400	7700	11,000
4d Sta Wag	1050	3350	5600	11,200	19,600	28,000

Series 76, 6-cyl.

	6	5	4	3	2	1
2d Bus Cpe	450	1450	2400	4800	8400	12,000
2d Clb Sed	400	1300	2200	4400	7700	11,000
4d Sed	400	1300	2200	4400	7700	11,000

Series 78, 8-cyl.

	6	5	4	3	2	1
2d Bus Sed	400	1350	2200	4400	7800	11,100
2d Clb Sed	450	1350	2300	4600	8000	11,400
4d Sed	450	1400	2300	4600	8100	11,500

Series 96, 6-cyl.

	6	5	4	3	2	1
2d Conv Cpe	1550	4900	8200	16,400	28,700	41,000
2d Clb Cpe	550	1800	3000	6000	10,500	15,000
4d Sed	500	1550	2600	5200	9100	13,000

Series 98, 8-cyl.

	6	5	4	3	2	1
2d Conv Cpe	1800	5750	9600	19,200	33,600	48,000
4d Conv Sed	1850	5900	9800	19,600	34,300	49,000
2d Clb Cpe	600	1900	3200	6400	11,200	16,000
4d Sed	550	1700	2800	5600	9800	14,000

1942

Special Series 66 & 68

	6	5	4	3	2	1
2d Conv	950	3000	5000	10,000	17,500	25,000
2d Bus Cpe	400	1250	2100	4200	7400	10,500
2d Clb Cpe	400	1300	2200	4400	7700	11,000
2d Clb Sed	400	1250	2100	4200	7400	10,600
2d Sed	400	1250	2050	4100	7200	10,300
4d Sed	400	1250	2100	4200	7400	10,500
4d Twn Sed	400	1300	2150	4300	7500	10,700
4d Sta Wag	1000	3250	5400	10,800	18,900	27,000

NOTE: Add 10 percent for 8-cyl.

Dynamic Series 76-78

	6	5	4	3	2	1
2d Clb Sed	450	1400	2300	4600	8100	11,500
4d Sed	400	1300	2200	4400	7700	11,000

NOTE: Add 10 percent for 8-cyl.

Custom Series 98, 8-cyl.

	6	5	4	3	2	1
2d Conv	1100	3500	5800	11,600	20,300	29,000
2d Clb Sed	500	1600	2700	5400	9500	13,500
4d Sed	500	1600	2650	5300	9200	13,200

1946-1947

Special Series 66, 6-cyl.

	6	5	4	3	2	1
2d Conv	950	3000	5000	10,000	17,500	25,000
2d Clb Cpe	400	1250	2100	4200	7400	10,600
2d Clb Sed	400	1250	2100	4200	7300	10,400
4d Sed	400	1250	2050	4100	7200	10,300
4d Sta Wag	1000	3250	5400	10,800	18,900	27,000

Special Series 68, 8-cyl.

	6	5	4	3	2	1
2d Conv	1000	3100	5200	10,400	18,200	26,000
2d Clb Cpe	450	1400	2300	4600	8100	11,600
2d Clb Sed	450	1350	2300	4600	8000	11,400
4d Sed	400	1350	2250	4500	7900	11,300
4d Sta Wag	1050	3350	5600	11,200	19,600	28,000

Dynamic Cruiser, Series 76, 6-cyl.

	6	5	4	3	2	1
2d Clb Sed	400	1300	2150	4300	7500	10,700
2d DeL Clb Sed (1947 only)	400	1300	2150	4300	7600	10,800
4d Sed	400	1250	2100	4200	7400	10,600
4d DeL Sed (1947 only)	400	1300	2150	4300	7500	10,700

Dynamic Cruiser Series 78, 8-cyl.

	6	5	4	3	2	1
2d Clb Sed	450	1400	2350	4700	8200	11,700
2d DeL Clb Sed (1947 only)	450	1400	2350	4700	8300	11,800
4d Sed	450	1400	2300	4600	8100	11,600
4d DeL Sed (1947 only)	450	1400	2350	4700	8200	11,700

Custom Cruiser Series 98, 8-cyl.

	6	5	4	3	2	1
2d Conv	1000	3250	5400	10,800	18,900	27,000
2d Clb Sed	450	1500	2500	5000	8800	12,500
4d Sed	450	1450	2450	4900	8500	12,200

1948

Dynamic Series 66, 6-cyl., 119" wb

	6	5	4	3	2	1
2d Conv	1000	3100	5200	10,400	18,200	26,000
2d Clb Cpe	400	1250	2100	4200	7400	10,500
2d Clb Sed	400	1200	2050	4100	7100	10,200
4d Sed	400	1250	2050	4100	7200	10,300
4d Sta Wag	1000	3250	5400	10,800	18,900	27,000

Dynamic Series 68, 8-cyl., 119" wb

	6	5	4	3	2	1
2d Conv	1000	3250	5400	10,800	18,900	27,000
2d Clb Cpe	450	1400	2300	4600	8100	11,500
2d Clb Sed	400	1350	2250	4500	7800	11,200

	6	5	4	3	2	1
4d Sed	450	1400	2300	4600	8100	11,600
4d Sta Wag	1050	3350	5600	11,200	19,600	28,000
Dynamic Series 76, 6-cyl., 125" wb						
2d Clb Sed	400	1250	2100	4200	7400	10,500
4d Sed	400	1250	2100	4200	7400	10,600
Dynamic Series 78, 8-cyl., 125" wb						
2d Clb Sed	450	1400	2300	4600	8100	11,500
4d Sed	450	1400	2300	4600	8100	11,600
Futuramic Series 98, 8-cyl., 125" wb						
2d Conv	1050	3350	5600	11,200	19,600	28,000
2d Clb Sed	450	1450	2400	4800	8400	12,000
4d Sed	450	1450	2400	4800	8400	12,000
1949						
Futuramic 76, 6-cyl., 119.5" wb						
2d Conv	1000	3100	5200	10,400	18,200	26,000
4d Clb Cpe	450	1450	2400	4800	8400	12,000
2d Sed	400	1200	2000	4000	7100	10,100
4d Sed	400	1200	2000	4000	7000	10,000
4d Sta Wag	550	1800	3000	6000	10,500	15,000
Futuramic Series 88, V-8, 119.5" wb						
2d Conv	1300	4200	7000	14,000	24,500	35,000
2d Clb Cpe	500	1550	2600	5200	9100	13,000
2d Clb Sed	400	1350	2200	4400	7800	11,100
4d Sed	400	1300	2200	4400	7700	11,000
4d Sta Wag	600	1900	3200	6400	11,200	16,000
Futuramic Series 98, V-8, 125" wb						
2d Conv	1300	4100	6800	13,600	23,800	34,000
2d Holiday	800	2500	4200	8400	14,700	21,000
2d Clb Sed	450	1450	2400	4800	8400	12,000
4d Sed	450	1450	2400	4800	8400	12,000
1950						
Futuramic 76, 6-cyl., 119.5" wb						
2d Conv	1000	3250	5400	10,800	18,900	27,000
2d Holiday	850	2650	4400	8800	15,400	22,000
2d Clb Cpe	500	1550	2600	5200	9100	13,000
2d Sed	400	1200	2050	4100	7100	10,200
2d Clb Sed	400	1250	2050	4100	7200	10,300
4d Sed	400	1200	2000	4000	7100	10,100
4d Sta Wag	750	2400	4000	8000	14,000	20,000
Futuramic 88, V-8, 119.5" wb						
2d Conv	1500	4800	8000	16,000	28,000	40,000
2d DeL Holiday	1000	3250	5400	10,800	18,900	27,000
2d DeL Clb Cpe	600	1900	3200	6400	11,200	16,000
2d DeL	500	1550	2600	5200	9100	13,000
2d DeL Clb Sed	500	1600	2700	5400	9500	13,500
4d DeL Sed	500	1550	2600	5200	9000	12,900
4d DeL Sta Wag	900	2900	4800	9600	16,800	24,000
Futuramic 98, V-8, 122" wb						
2d DeL Conv	1300	4200	7000	14,000	24,500	35,000
2d DeL Holiday HT	850	2750	4600	9200	16,100	23,000
2d Holiday HT	850	2650	4400	8800	15,400	22,000
2d DeL Clb Sed	450	1500	2500	5000	8800	12,500
4d DeL FBk	450	1450	2400	4800	8400	12,000
4d DeL FsBk	450	1450	2400	4800	8500	12,100
4d DeL Sed	450	1400	2300	4600	8100	11,600
4d DeL Twn Sed	500	1550	2600	5200	9100	13,000
NOTE: Deduct 10 percent for 6-cyl.						
1951-1952						
Standard 88, V-8, 119.5" wb						
2d Sed (1951 only)	500	1600	2700	5400	9500	13,500
4d Sed (1951 only)	500	1600	2700	5400	9400	13,400
DeLuxe 88, V-8, 120" wb						
2d Sed	450	1400	2300	4600	8100	11,600
4d Sed	450	1400	2300	4600	8100	11,500
Super 88, V-8, 120" wb						
2d Conv	1000	3100	5200	10,400	18,200	26,000
2d Holiday HT	800	2500	4200	8400	14,700	21,000
2d Clb Cpe	550	1700	2800	5600	9800	14,000
2d Sed	450	1400	2350	4700	8300	11,800
4d Sed	450	1400	2350	4700	8200	11,700
Series 98, V-8, 122" wb						
2d Conv	1050	3350	5600	11,200	19,600	28,000
2d DeL Holiday HT ('51)	850	2750	4600	9200	16,100	23,000
2d Holiday HT	850	2650	4400	8800	15,400	22,000
4d Sed	450	1450	2400	4800	8400	12,000
1953						
Series 88, V-8, 120" wb						
2d Sed	450	1190	2000	3950	6900	9900
4d Sed	400	1200	2000	4000	7000	10,000
Series Super 88, V-8, 120" wb						
2d Conv	1100	3500	5800	11,600	20,300	29,000
2d Holiday HT	850	2750	4600	9200	16,100	23,000
2d Sed	400	1200	2000	4000	7000	10,000
4d Sed	400	1200	2000	4000	7100	10,100
Classic 98, V-8, 124" wb						
2d Conv	1250	3950	6600	13,200	23,100	33,000
2d Holiday HT	950	3000	5000	10,000	17,500	25,000
4d Sed	450	1400	2300	4600	8100	11,500
Fiesta 98, V-8, 124" wb						
2d Conv	2500	7900	13,200	26,400	46,200	66,000
1954						
Series 88, V-8, 122" wb						
2d Holiday HT	850	2650	4400	8800	15,400	22,000
2d Sed	400	1250	2100	4200	7400	10,600
4d Sed	400	1250	2100	4200	7400	10,500
Series Super 88, V-8, 122" wb						
2d Conv	1150	3700	6200	12,400	21,700	31,000
2d Holiday HT	900	2900	4800	9600	16,800	24,000
2d Sed	400	1350	2250	4500	7800	11,200
4d Sed	400	1300	2200	4400	7700	11,000
Classic 98, V-8, 126" wb						
2d Starfire Conv	1450	4550	7600	15,200	26,600	38,000
2d DeL Holiday HT	1050	3350	5600	11,200	19,600	28,000
2d Holiday HT	1000	3250	5400	10,800	18,900	27,000
4d Sed	500	1550	2600	5200	9100	13,000
1955						
Series 88, V-8, 122" wb						
2d DeL Holiday HT	750	2400	4000	8000	14,000	20,000
4d Holiday HT	500	1550	2600	5200	9100	13,000
2d Sed	400	1250	2100	4200	7400	10,600
4d Sed	400	1250	2100	4200	7400	10,500
Series Super 88, V-8, 122" wb						
2d Conv	1150	3600	6000	12,000	21,000	30,000
2d DeL Holiday HT	850	2650	4400	8800	15,400	22,000
4d Holiday HT	550	1700	2800	5600	9800	14,000
2d Sed	400	1350	2200	4400	7800	11,100
4d Sed	400	1300	2200	4400	7700	11,000
Classic 98, V-8, 126" wb						
2d Starfire Conv	1350	4300	7200	14,400	25,200	36,000
2d DeL Holiday HT	950	3000	5000	10,000	17,500	25,000
4d DeL Holiday HT	550	1800	3000	6000	10,500	15,000
4d Sed	500	1550	2600	5200	9100	13,000
1956						
Series 88, V-8, 122" wb						
2d Holiday HT	850	2650	4400	8800	15,400	22,000
4d Holiday HT	550	1800	3000	6000	10,500	15,000
2d Sed	450	1450	2400	4800	8400	12,000
4d Sed	450	1400	2300	4600	8100	11,500
Series Super 88, V-8, 122" wb						
2d Conv	1150	3600	6000	12,000	21,000	30,000
2d Holiday HT	900	2900	4800	9600	16,800	24,000
4d Holiday HT	650	2050	3400	6800	11,900	17,000
2d Sed	500	1550	2600	5200	9100	13,000
4d Sed	450	1500	2500	5000	8800	12,500
Series 98, V-8, 126" wb						
2d Starfire Conv	1400	4450	7400	14,800	25,900	37,000
2d DeL Holiday HT	950	3000	5000	10,000	17,500	25,000
4d DeL Holiday HT	700	2150	3600	7200	12,600	18,000
4d Sed	550	1700	2800	5600	9800	14,000
1957						
Series 88, V-8, 122" wb						
2d Conv	1200	3850	6400	12,800	22,400	32,000
2d Holiday HT	850	2650	4400	8800	15,400	22,000
4d Holiday HT	550	1800	3000	6000	10,500	15,000
2d Sed	450	1400	2300	4600	8100	11,600
4d Sed	450	1400	2300	4600	8100	11,500
4d HT Wag	700	2150	3600	7200	12,600	18,000
4d Sta Wag	500	1550	2600	5200	9100	13,000
Series Super 88, V-8, 122" wb						
2d Conv	1350	4300	7200	14,400	25,200	36,000
2d Holiday HT	900	2900	4800	9600	16,800	24,000
4d Holiday HT	650	2050	3400	6800	11,900	17,000
2d Sed	450	1500	2500	5000	8800	12,600
4d Sed	450	1500	2500	5000	8800	12,500
4d HT Wag	750	2400	4000	8000	14,000	20,000
Series 98, V-8, 126" wb						
2d Starfire Conv	1450	4700	7800	15,600	27,300	39,000
2d Holiday HT	950	3000	5000	10,000	17,500	25,000
4d Holiday HT	700	2300	3800	7600	13,300	19,000
4d Sed	500	1600	2700	5400	9500	13,500
NOTE: Add 10 percent for J-2 option.						
1958						
Series 88, V-8, 122.5" wb						
2d Conv	850	2650	4400	8800	15,400	22,000
2d Holiday HT	800	2500	4200	8400	14,700	21,000
4d Holiday HT	550	1700	2800	5600	9800	14,000
2d Sed	400	1250	2100	4200	7400	10,500
4d Sed	400	1250	2100	4200	7300	10,400
4d HT Wag	550	1800	3000	6000	10,500	15,000
4d Sta Wag	450	1450	2400	4800	8400	12,000
Series Super 88, V-8, 122.5" wb						
2d Conv	1000	3100	5200	10,400	18,200	26,000
2d Holiday HT	900	2900	4800	9600	16,800	24,000
4d Holiday HT	600	1900	3200	6400	11,200	16,000
4d Sed	400	1300	2200	4400	7700	11,000
4d HT Wag	650	2050	3400	6800	11,900	17,000
Series 98, V-8, 126.5" wb						
2d Conv	1150	3600	6000	12,000	21,000	30,000
2d Holiday HT	850	2650	4400	8800	15,400	22,000
4d Holiday HT	700	2150	3600	7200	12,600	18,000
4d Sed	450	1450	2400	4800	8400	12,000
NOTE: Add 10 percent for J-2 option.						
1959						
Series 88, V-8, 123" wb						
2d Conv	850	2750	4600	9200	16,100	23,000
2d Holiday HT	700	2300	3800	7600	13,300	19,000
4d Holiday HT	550	1800	3000	6000	10,500	15,000
4d Sed	400	1200	2000	4000	7000	10,000
4d Sta Wag	400	1250	2100	4200	7400	10,500
Series Super 88, V-8, 123" wb						
2d Conv	950	3000	5000	10,000	17,500	25,000
2d Holiday HT	800	2500	4200	8400	14,700	21,000
4d Holiday HT	650	2050	3400	6800	11,900	17,000
4d Sed	400	1250	2100	4200	7400	10,500
4d Sta Wag	400	1300	2200	4400	7700	11,000
Series 98, V-8, 126.3" wb						
2d Conv	1100	3500	5800	11,600	20,300	29,000
2d Holiday HT	850	2750	4600	9200	16,100	23,000
4d Holiday HT	700	2300	3800	7600	13,300	19,000
4d Sed	400	1300	2200	4400	7700	11,000
NOTE: Add 10 percent for hp option.						
1960						
Series 88, V-8, 123" wb						
2d Conv	850	2750	4600	9200	16,100	23,000
2d Holiday HT	700	2150	3600	7200	12,600	18,000
4d Holiday HT	550	1700	2800	5600	9800	14,000
4d Sed	400	1200	2000	4000	7000	10,000
4d Sta Wag	400	1250	2100	4200	7400	10,500
Series Super 88, V-8, 123" wb						
2d Conv	950	3000	5000	10,000	17,500	25,000
2d Holiday HT	750	2400	4000	8000	14,000	20,000
4d Holiday HT	600	1900	3200	6400	11,200	16,000
4d Sed	400	1250	2100	4200	7400	10,500
4d Sta Wag	400	1300	2200	4400	7700	11,000
Series 98, V-8, 126.3" wb						
2d Conv	1100	3500	5800	11,600	20,300	29,000
2d Holiday HT	850	2650	4400	8800	15,400	22,000
4d Holiday HT	650	2050	3400	6800	11,900	17,000
4d Sed	400	1300	2200	4400	7700	11,000
1961						
F-85, V-8, 112" wb						
4d Sed	350	830	1400	2950	4830	6900
2d Clb Cpe	350	840	1400	2800	4900	7000
4d Sta Wag	350	900	1500	3000	5250	7500
Dynamic 88, V-8, 123" wb						
2d Sed	350	880	1500	2950	5180	7400
4d Sed	350	900	1500	3000	5250	7500
2d Holiday HT	550	1800	3000	6000	10,500	15,000
4d Holiday HT	400	1300	2200	4400	7700	11,000
2d Conv	800	2500	4200	8400	14,700	21,000
4d Sta Wag	450	1140	1900	3800	6650	9500
Super 88, V-8, 123" wb						
4d Sed	350	975	1600	3200	5600	8000

	6	5	4	3	2	1
4d Holiday HT	450	1450	2400	4800	8400	12,000
2d Holiday HT	650	2050	3400	6800	11,900	17,000
2d Conv	850	2750	4600	9200	16,100	23,000
4d Sta Wag	400	1200	2000	4000	7000	10,000
2d Starfire Conv	1150	3600	6000	12,000	21,000	30,000
Series 98, V-8, 126" wb						
4d Twn Sed	400	1250	2100	4200	7400	10,500
4d Spt Sed	400	1300	2150	4300	7500	10,700
4d Holiday HT	500	1550	2600	5200	9100	13,000
2d Holiday HT	700	2150	3600	7200	12,600	18,000
2d Conv	950	3000	5000	10,000	17,500	25,000

NOTE: Deduct 10 percent for std. line values; add 10 percent for Cutlass.

1962

	6	5	4	3	2	1
F-85 Series, V-8, 112" wb						
4d Sed	350	840	1400	2800	4900	7000
2d Cutlass Cpe	350	975	1600	3200	5600	8000
2d Cutlass Conv	400	1200	2000	4000	7000	10,000
4d Sta Wag	350	840	1400	2800	4900	7000
Jetfire Turbo-charged, V-8, 112" wb						
2d HT	450	1450	2400	4800	8400	12,000
Dynamic 88, V-8, 123" wb						
4d Sed	350	900	1500	3000	5250	7500
4d Holiday HT	400	1300	2200	4400	7700	11,000
2d Holiday HT	600	1900	3200	6400	11,200	16,000
2d Conv	800	2500	4200	8400	14,700	21,000
4d Sta Wag	450	1140	1900	3800	6650	9500
Super 88, V-8, 123" wb						
4d Sed	350	975	1600	3200	5600	8000
4d Holiday HT	450	1450	2400	4800	8400	12,000
2d Holiday HT	650	2050	3400	6800	11,900	17,000
4d Sta Wag	400	1200	2000	4000	7000	10,000
Starfire, 345 hp V-8, 123" wb						
2d HT	850	2650	4400	8800	15,400	22,000
2d Conv	1000	3250	5400	10,800	18,900	27,000
Series 98, V-8, 126" wb						
4d Twn Sed	450	1140	1900	3800	6650	9500
4d Spt Sed	450	1160	1950	3900	6800	9700
4d Holiday HT	550	1700	2800	5600	9800	14,000
2d Holiday Spt HT	700	2300	3800	7600	13,300	19,000
2d Conv	900	2900	4800	9600	16,800	24,000

1963

	6	5	4	3	2	1
F-85 Series, V-8, 112" wb						
4d Sed	350	840	1400	2800	4900	7000
2d Cutlass Cpe	350	975	1600	3200	5600	8000
2d Cutlass Conv	400	1300	2200	4400	7700	11,000
4d Sta Wag	350	900	1500	3000	5250	7500
Jetfire Series, V-8, 112" wb						
2d HT	450	1450	2400	4800	8400	12,000
Dynamic 88, V-8, 123" wb						
4d Sed	350	1020	1700	3400	5950	8500
4d Holiday HT	400	1300	2200	4400	7700	11,000
2d Holiday HT	550	1800	3000	6000	10,500	15,000
2d Conv	700	2150	3600	7200	12,600	18,000
4d Sta Wag	450	1080	1800	3600	6300	9000
Super 88, V-8, 123" wb						
4d Sed	450	1080	1800	3600	6300	9000
4d Holiday HT	450	1450	2400	4800	8400	12,000
2d Holiday HT	600	1900	3200	6400	11,200	16,000
4d Sta Wag	450	1140	1900	3800	6650	9500
Starfire, V-8, 123" wb						
2d Cpe	700	2300	3800	7600	13,300	19,000
2d Conv	1000	3250	5400	10,800	18,900	27,000
Series 98, V-8, 126" wb						
4d Sed	450	1080	1800	3600	6300	9000
4d 4W Holiday HT	500	1550	2600	5200	9100	13,000
4d 6W Holiday HT	450	1400	2300	4600	8100	11,500
2d Holiday HT	650	2050	3400	6800	11,900	17,000
2d Cus Spt HT	650	2100	3500	7000	12,300	17,500
2d Conv	1000	3100	5200	10,400	18,200	26,000

1964

	6	5	4	3	2	1
F-85 Series, V-8, 115" wb						
4d Sed	350	900	1500	3000	5250	7500
4d Sta Wag	350	860	1450	2900	5050	7200
Cutlass 3200, V-8						
2d Spt Cpe	350	975	1600	3200	5600	8000
2d HT	450	1140	1900	3800	6650	9500
2d Conv	450	1450	2400	4800	8400	12,000
Cutlass 4-4-2						
2d Sed	350	1040	1700	3450	6000	8600
2d HT	400	1250	2100	4200	7400	10,500
2d Conv	550	1700	2800	5600	9800	14,000
Vista Cruiser, V-8, 120" wb						
4d Sta Wag	350	975	1600	3200	5600	8000
4d Cus Wag	350	1000	1650	3300	5750	8200
Jetstar, V-8, 123" wb						
4d Sed	350	975	1600	3200	5600	8000
4d HT	450	1140	1900	3800	6650	9500
2d HT	400	1300	2200	4400	7700	11,000
2d Conv	700	2300	3800	7600	13,300	19,000
Jetstar I, V-8, 123" wb						
2d HT	600	1900	3200	6400	11,200	16,000
Dynamic 88, V-8, 123" wb						
4d Sed	350	1020	1700	3400	5950	8500
4d HT	400	1200	2000	4000	7000	10,000
2d HT	550	1800	3000	6000	10,500	15,000
2d Conv	800	2500	4200	8400	14,700	21,000
4d Sta Wag	400	1200	2000	4000	7000	10,000
Super 88, V-8, 123" wb						
4d Sed	450	1080	1800	3600	6300	9000
4d HT	400	1300	2200	4400	7700	11,000
Starfire, 123" wb						
2d HT	700	2300	3800	7600	13,300	19,000
2d Conv	900	2900	4800	9600	16,800	24,000
Series 98, V-8, 126" wb						
4d Sed	450	1140	1900	3800	6650	9500
4d 6W HT	450	1450	2400	4800	8400	12,000
4d 4W HT	500	1550	2600	5200	9100	13,000
2d HT	650	2050	3400	6800	11,900	17,000
2d Cus Spt HT	650	2100	3500	7000	12,300	17,500
2d Conv	1000	3100	5200	10,400	18,200	26,000

1965

	6	5	4	3	2	1
F-85 Series, V-8, 115" wb						
4d Sed	200	730	1250	2450	4270	6100
2d Cpe	350	780	1300	2600	4550	6500
4d Sta Wag	200	745	1250	2500	4340	6200
4d DeL Sed	200	750	1275	2500	4400	6300
4d DeL Wag	350	780	1300	2600	4550	6500
Cutlass Series, V-8, 115" wb						
2d Cpe	350	900	1500	3000	5250	7500
2d HT	450	1140	1900	3800	6650	9500
2d Conv	400	1250	2100	4200	7400	10,500
Cutlass 4-4-2						
2d Sed	450	1050	1750	3550	6150	8800
2d HT	400	1300	2200	4400	7700	11,000
2d Conv	550	1700	2800	5600	9800	14,000
Vista Cruiser, V-8, 120" wb						
4d Sta Wag	350	840	1400	2800	4900	7000
Jetstar Series, V-8, 123" wb						
4d Sed	350	820	1400	2700	4760	6800
4d HT	350	1020	1700	3400	5950	8500
2d HT	400	1250	2100	4200	7400	10,500
2d Conv	450	1450	2400	4800	8400	12,000
Dynamic 88, V-8, 123" wb						
4d Sed	350	840	1400	2800	4900	7000
4d HT	450	1140	1900	3800	6650	9500
2d HT	400	1250	2100	4200	7400	10,500
2d Conv	550	1800	3000	6000	10,500	15,000
Delta 88, V-8, 123" wb						
4d Sed	350	900	1500	3000	5250	7500
4d HT	450	1140	1900	3800	6650	9500
2d HT	450	1400	2300	4600	8100	11,500
Jetstar I, V-8, 123" wb						
2d HT	450	1450	2400	4800	8400	12,000
Starfire, 123" wb						
2d HT	550	1700	2800	5600	9800	14,000
2d Conv	650	2050	3400	6800	11,900	17,000
Series 98, V-8, 126" wb						
4d Twn Sed	350	975	1600	3200	5600	8000
4d Lux Sed	350	1000	1650	3300	5750	8200
4d HT	450	1080	1800	3600	6300	9000
2d HT	450	1450	2400	4800	8400	12,000
2d Conv	650	2050	3400	6800	11,900	17,000

1966

	6	5	4	3	2	1
F-85 Series, Standard V-8, 115" wb						
4d Sed	200	730	1250	2450	4270	6100
2d Cpe	350	780	1300	2600	4550	6500
4d Sta Wag	350	780	1300	2600	4550	6500
F-85 Series, Deluxe, V-8, 115" wb						
4d Sed	200	745	1250	2500	4340	6200
4d HT	350	780	1300	2600	4550	6500
2d HT	350	975	1600	3200	5600	8000
4d Sta Wag	350	800	1350	2700	4700	6700
Cutlass, V-8, 115" wb						
4d Sed	200	750	1275	2500	4400	6300
4d HT	350	800	1350	2700	4700	6700
2d Cpe	350	790	1350	2650	4620	6600
2d HT	350	1020	1700	3400	5950	8500
2d Conv	550	1700	2800	5600	9800	14,000
Cutlass 4-4-2						
2d Sed	450	1450	2400	4800	8400	12,000
2d HT	550	1800	3000	6000	10,500	15,000
2d Conv	700	2150	3600	7200	12,600	18,000

NOTE: Add 30 percent for triple two-barrel carbs. Add 90 percent for W-30.

	6	5	4	3	2	1
4d 3S Sta Wag	350	900	1500	3000	5250	7500
4d 2S Sta Wag	350	870	1450	2900	5100	7300
4d 3S Cus Sta Wag	350	950	1550	3100	5400	7700
4d Cus Sta Wag 2S	350	900	1500	3000	5250	7500
Jetstar 88, V-8, 123" wb						
4d Sed	350	780	1300	2600	4550	6500
4d HT	350	840	1400	2800	4900	7000
2d HT	450	1080	1800	3600	6300	9000
Dynamic 88, V-8, 123" wb						
4d Sed	350	800	1350	2700	4700	6700
4d HT	350	900	1500	3000	5250	7500
2d HT	450	1160	1950	3900	6800	9700
2d Conv	400	1300	2200	4400	7700	11,000
Delta 88, V-8, 123" wb						
4d Sed	350	840	1400	2800	4900	7000
4d HT	350	975	1600	3200	5600	8000
2d HT	400	1200	2000	4000	7000	10,000
2d Conv	400	1300	2200	4400	7700	11,000
Starfire, V-8, 123" wb						
2d HT	450	1450	2400	4800	8400	12,000
Ninety-Eight, V-8, 126" wb						
4d Twn Sed	350	860	1450	2900	5050	7200
4d Lux Sed	350	870	1450	2900	5100	7300
4d HT	350	1020	1700	3400	5950	8500
2d HT	400	1300	2200	4400	7700	11,000
2d Conv	500	1550	2600	5200	9100	13,000
Toronado, FWD V-8, 119" wb						
2d Spt HT	400	1300	2200	4400	7700	11,000
2d Cus HT	450	1400	2300	4600	8100	11,500

1967

	6	5	4	3	2	1
F-85 Series, Standard, V-8, 115" wb						
4d Sed	200	730	1250	2450	4270	6100
2d Cpe	350	780	1300	2600	4550	6500
4d 2S Sta Wag	200	730	1250	2450	4270	6100
Cutlass, V-8, 115" wb						
4d Sed	200	750	1275	2500	4400	6300
4d HT	350	780	1300	2600	4550	6500
2d HT	350	1020	1700	3400	5950	8500
2d Conv	600	1900	3200	6400	11,200	16,000
4d 2S Sta Wag	350	780	1300	2600	4550	6500

NOTE: Deduct 20 percent for 6-cyl.

	6	5	4	3	2	1
Cutlass-Supreme, V-8, 115" wb						
4d Sed	350	780	1300	2600	4550	6500
4d HT	350	830	1400	2950	4830	6900
2d Cpe	350	850	1450	2850	4970	7100
2d HT	400	1300	2200	4400	7700	11,000
2d Conv	650	2050	3400	6800	11,900	17,000
Cutlass 4-4-2						
2d Sed	450	1450	2400	4800	8400	12,000
2d HT	550	1800	3000	6000	10,500	15,000
2d Conv	700	2150	3600	7200	12,600	18,000

NOTE: Add 70 percent for W-30.

	6	5	4	3	2	1
Vista Cruiser, V-8, 120" wb						
4d 3S Sta Wag	350	840	1400	2800	4900	7000
4d 2S Cus Sta Wag	350	900	1500	3000	5250	7500
4d 3S Cus Sta Wag	350	950	1550	3100	5400	7700
Delmont 88, 330 V-8, 123" wb						
4d Sed	200	720	1200	2400	4200	6000
4d HT	350	780	1300	2600	4550	6500
2d HT	350	975	1600	3200	5600	8000

	6	5	4	3	2	1
Delmont 88, 425 V-8, 123" wb						
4d Sed	350	780	1300	2600	4550	6500
4d HT	350	840	1400	2800	4900	7000
2d HT	350	1020	1700	3400	5950	8500
2d Conv	500	1550	2600	5200	9100	13,000
Delta 88, V-8, 123" wb						
4d Sed	350	820	1400	2700	4760	6800
4d HT	350	870	1450	2900	5100	7300
2d HT	450	1140	1900	3800	6650	9500
2d Conv	550	1800	3000	6000	10,500	15,000
Delta 88, Custom V-8, 123" wb						
4d HT	350	900	1500	3000	5250	7500
2d HT	450	1170	1975	3900	6850	9800
Ninety-Eight, V-8, 126" wb						
4d Twn Sed	350	900	1500	3000	5250	7500
4d Lux Sed	350	950	1500	3050	5300	7600
4d HT	350	1000	1650	3350	5800	8300
2d HT	400	1200	2000	4000	7000	10,000
2d Conv	600	1900	3200	6400	11,200	16,000
Toronado, V-8, 119" wb						
2d HT	400	1250	2100	4200	7400	10,500
2d Cus HT	400	1300	2200	4400	7700	11,000

NOTE: Add 10 percent for "425" Delmont Series.
Add 30 percent for W-30.

1968

	6	5	4	3	2	1
F-85, V-8, 116" wb, 2 dr 112" wb						
4d Sed	200	745	1250	2500	4340	6200
2d Cpe	350	780	1300	2600	4550	6500
Cutlass, V-8, 116" wb, 2 dr 112" wb						
4d Sed	200	750	1275	2500	4400	6300
4d HT	350	770	1300	2550	4480	6400
2d Cpe S	350	800	1350	2700	4700	6700
2d HT S	350	1020	1700	3400	5950	8500
2d Conv S	600	1900	3200	6400	11,200	16,000
4d Sta Wag	350	780	1300	2600	4550	6500
Cutlass Supreme, V-8, 116" wb, 2 dr 112" wb						
4d Sed	350	780	1300	2600	4550	6500
4d HT	350	830	1400	2950	4830	6900
2d HT	450	1140	1900	3800	6650	9500

NOTE: Deduct 5 percent for 6-cyl.

	6	5	4	3	2	1
4-4-2, V-8, 112" wb						
2d Cpe	450	1450	2400	4800	8400	12,000
2d HT	550	1700	2800	5600	9800	14,000
2d Conv	700	2150	3600	7200	12,600	18,000
Hurst/Olds						
2d HT	650	2050	3400	6800	11,900	17,000
2d Sed	550	1800	3000	6000	10,500	15,000
Vista Cruiser, V-8, 121" wb						
4d 2S Sta Wag	200	745	1250	2500	4340	6200
4d 3S Sta Wag	350	780	1300	2600	4550	6500
Delmont 88, V-8, 123" wb						
4d Sed	350	780	1300	2600	4550	6500
4d HT	350	800	1350	2700	4700	6700
2d HT	350	1020	1700	3400	5950	8500
2d Conv	550	1700	2800	5600	9800	14,000
Delta 88, V-8, 123" wb						
4d Sed	350	800	1350	2700	4700	6700
2d HT	450	1080	1800	3600	6300	9000
4d HT	350	840	1400	2800	4900	7000
Ninety-Eight, V-8, 126" wb						
4d Sed	350	860	1450	2900	5050	7200
4d Lux Sed	350	880	1500	2950	5180	7400
4d HT	350	975	1600	3200	5600	8000
2d HT	400	1200	2000	4000	7000	10,000
2d Conv	550	1800	3000	6000	10,500	15,000
Toronado, V-8, 119" wb						
2d Cus Cpe	450	1140	1900	3800	6650	9500

NOTE: Add 30 percent for W-30.
Add 20 percent for 455 when not standard.
Add 20 percent for W-34 option on Toronado.

1969

	6	5	4	3	2	1
F-85, V-8, 116" wb, 2d 112" wb						
2d Cpe	200	720	1200	2400	4200	6000
Cutlass, V-8, 116" wb, 2d 112" wb						
4d Sed	200	670	1150	2250	3920	5600
4d HT	200	670	1200	2300	4060	5800
4d Sta Wag	200	670	1150	2250	3920	5600
Cutlass - S						
2d Cpe	350	780	1300	2600	4550	6500
2d HT	450	1080	1800	3600	6300	9000
2d Conv	550	1800	3000	6000	10,500	15,000
Cutlass Supreme, V-8, 116" wb, 2d 112" wb						
4d Sed	200	730	1250	2450	4270	6100
4d HT	350	780	1300	2600	4550	6500
2d HT	500	1550	2600	5200	9100	13,000
4-4-2, V-8 112" wb						
2d Cpe	450	1450	2400	4800	8400	12,000
2d HT	550	1700	2800	5600	9800	14,000
2d Conv	700	2150	3600	7200	12,600	18,000
Hurst/Olds						
2d HT	700	2150	3600	7200	12,600	18,000
Vista Cruiser						
4d 2S Sta Wag	200	745	1250	2500	4340	6200
4d 3S Sta Wag	200	750	1275	2500	4400	6300
Delta 88, V-8, 124" wb						
4d Sed	350	840	1400	2800	4900	7000
2d Conv	400	1300	2200	4400	7700	11,000
4d HT	350	900	1500	3000	5250	7500
2d HT	450	1080	1800	3600	6300	9000
Delta 88 Custom, V-8, 124" wb						
4d Sed	350	820	1400	2700	4760	6800
4d HT	350	975	1600	3200	5600	8000
2d HT	450	1140	1900	3800	6650	9500
Delta 88 Royale, V-8, 124" wb						
2d HT	400	1200	2000	4000	7000	10,000
Ninety Eight, V-8, 127" wb						
4d Sed	350	900	1500	3000	5250	7500
4d Lux Sed	350	950	1500	3050	5300	7600
4d Lux HT	350	1040	1700	3450	6000	8600
4d HT	350	1020	1700	3400	5950	8500
2d HT	400	1300	2200	4400	7700	11,000
2d Conv	500	1550	2600	5200	9100	13,000
2d Cus Cpe	350	1040	1750	3500	6100	8700
Toronado, V-8, 119" wb						
2d HT	450	1140	1900	3800	6650	9500

NOTE: Add 30 percent for W-30.
Add 20 percent for W-34 option on Toronado.
Add 20 percent for 455 when not standard.

1970

	6	5	4	3	2	1
F-85, V-8, 116" wb, 2d 112" wb						
2d Cpe	350	780	1300	2600	4550	6500
Cutlass, V-8, 116" wb, 2d 112" wb						
4d Sed	200	720	1200	2400	4200	6000
4d HT	350	780	1300	2600	4550	6500
4d Sta Wag	200	745	1250	2500	4340	6200

NOTE: Deduct 5 percent for 6-cyl.

	6	5	4	3	2	1
Cutlass-S, V-8, 112" wb						
2d Cpe	200	720	1200	2400	4200	6000
2d HT	450	1450	2400	4800	8400	12,000

NOTE: Add 25 percent for W45-W30-W31.

	6	5	4	3	2	1
Cutlass-Supreme, V-8, 112" wb						
4d HT	350	780	1300	2600	4550	6500
2d HT	550	1700	2800	5600	9800	14,000
2d Conv	700	2150	3600	7200	12,600	18,000
4-4-2, V-8, 112" wb						
2d Cpe	550	1800	3000	6000	10,500	15,000
2d HT	700	2300	3800	7600	13,300	19,000
2d Conv	850	2650	4400	8800	15,400	22,000
Rallye 350 112" wb						
2d HT	700	2150	3600	7200	12,600	18,000
Vista Cruiser, V-8, 121" wb						
4d 2S Sta Wag	200	745	1250	2500	4340	6200
4d 3S Sta Wag	200	750	1275	2500	4400	6300
Delta 88, V-8, 124" wb						
4d Sed	200	750	1275	2500	4400	6300
4d HT	350	780	1300	2600	4550	6500
2d HT	350	1020	1700	3400	5950	8500
2d Conv	450	1450	2400	4800	8400	12,000
Delta 88 Custom, V-8, 124" wb						
4d Sed	350	780	1300	2600	4550	6500
4d HT	350	790	1350	2650	4620	6600
2d HT	450	1080	1800	3600	6300	9000
Delta 88 Royale, V-8, 124" wb						
2d HT	450	1140	1900	3800	6650	9500
Ninety Eight, V-8, 127" wb						
4d Sed	350	790	1350	2650	4620	6600
4d Lux Sed	350	820	1400	2700	4760	6800
4d Lux HT	350	850	1450	2850	4970	7100
4d HT	350	840	1400	2800	4900	7000
2d HT	400	1200	2000	4000	7000	10,000
2d Conv	500	1550	2600	5200	9100	13,000
Toronado, V-8, 119" wb						
2d Std Cpe	450	1140	1900	3800	6650	9500
2d Cus Cpe	400	1200	2000	4000	7000	10,000

NOTE: Add 20 percent for SX Cutlass Supreme option.
Add 35 percent for Y-74 Indy Pace Car option.
Add 50 percent for W-30.
Add 20 percent for 455 when not standard.
Add 15 percent for Toronado GT W-34 option.

1971

	6	5	4	3	2	1
F-85, V-8, 116" wb						
4d Sed	200	650	1100	2150	3780	5400
Cutlass, V-8, 116" wb, 2d 112" wb						
4d Sed	200	660	1100	2200	3850	5500
2d HT	400	1250	2100	4200	7400	10,500
4d Sta Wag	200	650	1100	2150	3780	5400
Cutlass -S, V-8, 112" wb						
2d Cpe	350	975	1600	3200	5600	8000
2d HT	400	1300	2200	4400	7700	11,000

NOTE: Deduct 5 percent for 6 cyl.

	6	5	4	3	2	1
Cutlass Supreme, V-8, 116" wb, 2d 112" wb						
4d Sed	350	790	1350	2650	4620	6600
2d HT	500	1550	2600	5200	9100	13,000
2d Conv	700	2150	3600	7200	12,600	18,000

NOTE: Add 15 percent for SX Cutlass Supreme option.

	6	5	4	3	2	1
4-4-2, V-8, 112" wb						
2d HT	700	2150	3600	7200	12,600	18,000
2d Conv	850	2650	4400	8800	15,400	22,000
Vista Cruiser, 121" wb						
4d 2S Sta Wag	200	660	1100	2200	3850	5500
4d 3S Sta Wag	200	670	1150	2250	3920	5600
Delta 88, V-8, 124" wb						
4d Sed	200	660	1100	2200	3850	5500
4d HT	200	720	1200	2400	4200	6000
2d HT	350	975	1600	3200	5600	8000
Delta 88 Custom V-8, 124" wb						
4d Sed	200	670	1150	2250	3920	5600
4d HT	200	745	1250	2500	4340	6200
2d HT	350	1020	1700	3400	5950	8500
Delta 88 Royale, V-8, 124" wb						
2d HT	450	1080	1800	3600	6300	9000
2d Conv	450	1450	2400	4800	8400	12,000
Ninety Eight, V-8, 127" wb						
2d HT	400	1250	2100	4200	7400	10,500
4d HT	350	780	1300	2600	4550	6500
4d Lux HT	350	800	1350	2700	4700	6700
2d Lux HT	400	1200	2000	4000	7000	10,000
Custom Cruiser, V-8, 127" wb						
4d 2S Sta Wag	350	780	1300	2600	4550	6500
4d 3S Sta Wag	350	800	1350	2700	4700	6700
Toronado, 122" wb						
2d HT	400	1200	2000	4000	7000	10,000

NOTES: Add 40 percent for W-30.
Add 20 percent for 455 when not standard.

1972

	6	5	4	3	2	1
F-85, V-8, 116" wb						
4d Sed	200	650	1100	2150	3780	5400
Cutlass, V-8, 116" wb, 2d 112" wb						
4d Sed	200	660	1100	2200	3850	5500
2d HT	400	1300	2200	4400	7700	11,000
4d Sta Wag	200	650	1100	2150	3780	5400
Cutlass -S, V-8, 112" wb						
2d Cpe	350	975	1600	3200	5600	8000
2d HT	500	1550	2600	5200	9100	13,000

NOTE: Deduct 5 percent for 6-cyl.

	6	5	4	3	2	1
Cutlass Supreme, V-8, 116" wb. 2d 112" wb						
4d HT	350	900	1500	3000	5250	7500
2d HT	550	1700	2800	5600	9800	14,000
2d Conv	700	2150	3600	7200	12,600	18,000

NOTE: Add 40 percent for 4-4-2 option.
Add 20 percent for Hurst option.

	6	5	4	3	2	1
Vista Cruiser, 121" wb						
4d 2S Sta Wag	200	660	1100	2200	3850	5500
4d 3S Sta Wag	200	670	1150	2250	3920	5600
Delta 88, V-8, 124" wb						
4d Sed	200	700	1075	2150	3700	5300

	6	5	4	3	2	1
4d HT	200	720	1200	2400	4200	6000
2d HT	400	1200	2000	4000	7000	10,000
Delta 88 Royale, 124" wb						
4d Sed	200	650	1100	2150	3780	5400
4d HT	200	745	1250	2500	4340	6200
2d HT	400	1250	2100	4200	7400	10,500
2d Conv	450	1450	2400	4800	8400	12,000
Custom Cruiser, 127" wb						
4d 2S Sta Wag	200	720	1200	2400	4200	6000
4d 3S Sta Wag	200	745	1250	2500	4340	6200
Ninety-Eight, 127" wb						
4d HT	200	745	1250	2500	4340	6200
2d HT	400	1200	2000	4000	7000	10,000
Ninety-Eight Luxury, 127" wb						
4d HT	350	780	1300	2600	4550	6500
2d HT	400	1250	2100	4200	7400	10,500
Toronado, 122" wb						
2d HT	400	1200	2000	4000	7000	10,000
NOTES: Add 30 percent for W-30.						
Add 20 percent for 455 when not standard.						
1973						
Omega, V-8, 111" wb						
4d Sed	200	650	1100	2150	3780	5400
2d Cpe	200	670	1150	2250	3920	5600
2d HBk	200	700	1200	2350	4130	5900
Cutlass, 112" - 116" wb						
2d Col HT	200	730	1250	2450	4270	6100
4d Col HT	200	685	1150	2300	3990	5700
Cutlass S, 112" wb						
2d Cpe	350	770	1300	2550	4480	6400
Cutlass Supreme, 112" - 116" wb						
2d Col HT	350	780	1300	2600	4550	6500
4d Col HT	200	670	1200	2300	4060	5800
NOTE: Add 10 percent for 4-4-2 option.						
Vista Cruiser, 116" wb						
4d 2S Sta Wag	200	720	1200	2400	4200	6000
4d 3S Sta Wag	200	730	1250	2450	4270	6100
Delta 88, 124" wb						
4d Sed	200	700	1075	2150	3700	5300
4d HT	200	720	1200	2400	4200	6000
2d HT	350	975	1600	3200	5600	8000
Delta 88 Royale, 124" wb						
4d Sed	200	650	1100	2150	3780	5400
4d HT	200	745	1250	2500	4340	6200
2d HT	350	1020	1700	3400	5950	8500
2d Conv	400	1250	2100	4200	7400	10,500
Custom Cruiser, 127" wb						
3S Sta Wag	200	745	1250	2500	4340	6200
2S Sta Wag	200	720	1200	2400	4200	6000
3S Roy Wag	350	770	1300	2550	4480	6400
2S Roy Wag	200	745	1250	2500	4340	6200
Ninety-Eight, 127" wb						
4d HT	200	720	1200	2400	4200	6000
2d HT	350	975	1600	3200	5600	8000
4d Lux HT	350	770	1300	2550	4480	6400
2d Lux HT	350	1020	1700	3400	5950	8500
4d HT Reg	350	780	1300	2600	4550	6500
Toronado, 122" wb						
2d HT Cpe	350	1020	1700	3400	5950	8500
NOTE: Add 20 percent for Hurst/Olds.						
1974						
Omega, 111" wb						
2d Cpe	200	700	1050	2100	3650	5200
2d HBk	200	660	1100	2200	3850	5500
4d Sed	200	675	1000	2000	3500	5000
Cutlass, 112" - 116" wb						
2d Cpe	200	670	1150	2250	3920	5600
4d Sed	200	675	1000	2000	3500	5000
Cutlass S, 112" wb						
2d Cpe	200	670	1150	2250	3920	5600
Cutlass Supreme, 112" - 116" wb						
4d Sed	200	700	1050	2100	3650	5200
2d Cpe	200	670	1200	2300	4060	5800
NOTE: Add 10 percent for 4-4-2 option.						
Vista Cruiser, 116" wb						
4d 6P Sta Wag	150	650	975	1950	3350	4800
4d 8P Sta Wag	200	675	1000	1950	3400	4900
Delta 88, 124" wb						
2d HT	200	720	1200	2400	4200	6000
4d HT	200	650	1100	2150	3780	5400
4d Sed	200	675	1000	2000	3500	5000
Custom Cruiser, 127" wb						
4d 6P Sta Wag	200	700	1075	2150	3700	5300
4d 8P Sta Wag	200	660	1100	2200	3850	5500
Delta 88 Royale, 124" wb						
2d HT	350	780	1300	2600	4550	6500
4d HT	200	670	1150	2250	3920	5600
4d Sed	200	700	1050	2050	3600	5100
2d Conv	400	1200	2000	4000	7000	10,000
NOTE: Add 20 percent for Indy Pace car.						
Ninety-Eight, 127" wb						
4d HT	200	720	1200	2400	4200	6000
2d HT Lux	350	840	1400	2800	4900	7000
4d HT Lux	200	730	1250	2450	4270	6100
2d HT Reg	350	900	1500	3000	5250	7500
4d Reg Sed	200	730	1250	2450	4270	6100
Toronado, 122" wb						
2d Cpe	350	975	1600	3200	5600	8000
1975						
Starfire, 97" wb						
2d Cpe 'S'	150	550	850	1650	2900	4100
2d Cpe	150	550	850	1675	2950	4200
Omega, 111" wb						
2d Cpe	150	550	850	1650	2900	4100
2d HBk	150	600	900	1800	3150	4500
4d Sed	150	550	850	1675	2950	4200
Omega Salon, 111" wb						
2d Cpe	150	575	900	1750	3100	4400
2d HBk	150	600	950	1850	3200	4600
4d Sed	150	600	900	1800	3150	4500
Cutlass, 112" - 116" wb						
2d Cpe	150	650	950	1900	3300	4700
4d Sed	150	550	850	1675	2950	4200
2d Cpe 'S'	150	650	975	1950	3350	4800
Cutlass Supreme, 112" - 116" wb						
2d Cpe	200	675	1000	1950	3400	4900
4d Sed	150	600	900	1800	3150	4500

Cutlass Salon, 112" - 116" wb

	6	5	4	3	2	1
2d Cpe	200	675	1000	2000	3500	5000
4d Sed	150	600	950	1850	3200	4600
NOTE: Add 10 percent for 4-4-2 option.						
Vista Cruiser, 116" wb						
4d Sta Wag	150	575	900	1750	3100	4400
Delta 88, 124" wb						
2d Cpe	150	600	900	1800	3150	4500
4d Twn Sed	150	550	850	1650	2900	4100
4d HT	200	675	1000	2000	3500	5000
Delta 88 Royale, 124" wb						
2d Cpe	150	600	950	1850	3200	4600
4d Twn Sed	150	550	850	1675	2950	4200
4d HT	200	700	1050	2100	3650	5200
2d Conv	450	1140	1900	3800	6650	9500
Ninety-Eight, 127" wb						
2d Lux Cpe	200	670	1200	2300	4060	5800
4d Lux HT	200	660	1100	2200	3850	5500
2d Reg Cpe	200	700	1200	2350	4130	5900
4d Reg HT	200	685	1150	2300	3990	5700
Toronado, 122" wb						
2d Cus Cpe	350	840	1400	2800	4900	7000
2d Brgm Cpe	350	900	1500	3000	5250	7500
Custom Cruiser, 127" wb						
4d Sta Wag	150	600	950	1850	3200	4600
NOTE: Add 20 percent for Hurst/Olds.						
1976						
Starfire, V-6						
2d Spt Cpe	150	575	875	1700	3000	4300
2d Spt Cpe SX	150	575	900	1750	3100	4400
NOTE: Add 5 percent for V-8.						
Omega F-85, V-8						
2d Cpe	150	550	850	1650	2900	4100
Omega, V-8						
4d Sed	150	550	850	1675	2950	4200
2d Cpe	150	575	875	1700	3000	4300
2d HBk	150	575	900	1750	3100	4400
Omega Brougham V-8						
4d Sed	150	575	875	1700	3000	4300
2d Cpe	150	575	900	1750	3100	4400
2d HBk	150	600	900	1800	3150	4500
Cutlass "S", V-8						
4d Sed	150	550	850	1650	2900	4100
2d Cpe	150	650	950	1900	3300	4700
Cutlass Supreme, V-8						
4d Sed	150	550	850	1675	2950	4200
2d Cpe	150	650	975	1950	3350	4800
Cutlass Salon, V-8						
4d Sed	150	575	900	1750	3100	4400
2d Cpe	200	675	1000	1950	3400	4900
Cutlass Supreme Brougham, V-8						
2d Cpe	200	675	1000	2000	3500	5000
Station Wagons, V-8						
4d 2S Cruiser	150	600	900	1800	3150	4500
4d 3S Cruiser	150	600	950	1850	3200	4600
4d 2S Vista Cruiser	150	600	950	1850	3200	4600
4d 3S Vista Cruiser	150	650	950	1900	3300	4700
Delta 88, V-8						
4d Sed	150	575	900	1750	3100	4400
4d HT	150	650	975	1950	3350	4800
2d Sed	150	600	900	1800	3150	4500
Delta 88 Royle, V-8						
4d Sed	150	600	950	1850	3200	4600
4d HT	200	675	1000	2000	3500	5000
2d Sed	150	650	950	1900	3300	4700
Station Wagons, V-8						
4d 2S Cus Cruiser	200	675	1000	2000	3500	5000
4d 3S Cus Cruiser	200	675	1000	2000	3500	5000
Ninety-Eight, V-8						
4d Lux HT	200	700	1050	2100	3650	5200
2d Lux Cpe	200	670	1150	2250	3920	5600
4d HT Reg	200	660	1100	2200	3850	5500
2d Reg Cpe	200	685	1150	2300	3990	5700
Toronado, V-8						
2d Cus Cpe	350	780	1300	2600	4550	6500
2d Brgm Cpe	350	840	1400	2800	4900	7000
NOTE: Deduct 5 percent for V-6.						
1977						
Starfire, V-6						
2d Spt Cpe	150	500	800	1550	2700	3900
2d Spt Cpe SX	150	550	850	1650	2900	4100
NOTE: Add 5 percent for V-8.						
Omega F85, V-8						
2d Cpe	150	475	750	1475	2600	3700
Omega, V-8						
4d Sed	150	575	900	1750	3100	4400
2d Cpe	150	600	900	1800	3150	4500
2d HBk	150	600	950	1850	3200	4600
Omega Brougham, V-8						
4d Sed	150	600	900	1800	3150	4500
2d Cpe	150	600	950	1850	3200	4600
2d HBk	150	650	950	1900	3300	4700
NOTE: Deduct 5 percent for V-6.						
Cutlass - "S", V-8						
4d Sed	150	550	850	1675	2950	4200
2d Sed	150	575	875	1700	3000	4300
Cutlass Supreme, V-8						
4d Sed	150	575	900	1750	3100	4400
2d Sed	150	600	900	1800	3150	4500
Cutlass Salon, V-8						
2d	150	600	900	1800	3150	4500
Cutlass Supreme Brougham, V-8						
4d Sed	150	600	950	1850	3200	4600
2d Sed	150	650	975	1950	3350	4800
Station Wagons, V-8						
4d 3S Cruiser	150	600	900	1800	3150	4500
Delta 88, V-8						
4d Sed	150	600	900	1800	3150	4500
2d Cpe	150	600	950	1850	3200	4600
Delta 88 Royale, V-8						
4d Sed	150	650	950	1900	3300	4700
2d Cpe	150	650	975	1950	3350	4800
Station Wagons, V-8						
4d 2S Cus Cruiser	150	600	950	1850	3200	4600
4d 3S Cus Cruiser	150	650	950	1900	3300	4700
Ninety Eight, V-8						
4d Lux Sed	200	675	1000	1950	3400	4900
2d Lux Cpe	200	675	1000	2000	3500	5000

	6	5	4	3	2	1
4d Regency Sed	200	675	1000	2000	3500	5000
2d Regency Cpe	200	700	1050	2050	3600	5100
Toronado Brougham, V-8						
2d Cpe XS	350	900	1500	3000	5250	7500
2d Cpe	200	720	1200	2400	4200	6000
NOTE: Deduct 5 percent for V-6.						

1978

	6	5	4	3	2	1
Starfire						
2d Cpe	100	360	600	1200	2100	3000
2d Cpe SX	125	380	650	1300	2250	3200
Omega						
4d Sed	125	450	700	1400	2450	3500
2d Cpe	125	450	750	1450	2500	3600
2d HBk	150	475	750	1475	2600	3700
Omega Brougham						
4d Sed	125	450	750	1450	2500	3600
2d Cpe	150	475	750	1475	2600	3700
Cutlass Salon						
4d Sed	125	400	675	1350	2300	3300
2d Cpe	125	400	700	1375	2400	3400
Cutlass Salon Brougham						
4d Sed	125	400	700	1375	2400	3400
2d Cpe	125	450	700	1400	2450	3500
Cutlass Supreme						
2d Cpe	125	450	750	1450	2500	3600
Cutlass Calais						
2d Cpe	150	475	750	1475	2600	3700
Cutlass Supreme Brougham						
2d Cpe	150	475	775	1500	2650	3800
Cutlass Cruiser						
4d 2S Sta Wag	125	450	700	1400	2450	3500
Delta 88						
4d Sed	125	450	750	1450	2500	3600
2d Cpe	150	475	750	1475	2600	3700
Delta 88 Royale						
4d Sed	150	475	750	1475	2600	3700
2d Cpe	150	475	775	1500	2650	3800
Custom Cruiser						
4d Sta Wag	125	450	750	1450	2500	3600
Ninety Eight						
4d Lux Sed	150	500	800	1550	2700	3900
2d Lux Cpe	150	500	800	1600	2800	4000
4d Regency Sed	150	500	800	1600	2800	4000
2d Regency Cpe	150	550	850	1650	2900	4100
Toronado Brougham, V-8						
2d Cpe XS	350	900	1500	3000	5250	7500
2d Cpe	200	720	1200	2400	4200	6000

1979

	6	5	4	3	2	1
Starfire, 4-cyl.						
2d Spt Cpe	125	370	650	1250	2200	3100
2d Spt Cpe SX	125	380	650	1300	2250	3200
Omega, V-8						
4d Sed	125	450	750	1450	2500	3600
2d Cpe	150	475	750	1475	2600	3700
2d HBk	150	475	775	1500	2650	3800
Omega Brougham, V-8						
4d Sed	150	475	750	1475	2600	3700
2d Cpe	150	475	775	1500	2650	3800
Cutlass Salon, V-8						
4d Sed	125	400	700	1375	2400	3400
2d Cpe	125	450	700	1400	2450	3500
Cutlass Salon Brougham, V-8						
4d Sed	125	450	700	1400	2450	3500
2d Cpe	125	450	750	1450	2500	3600
Cutlass Supreme, V-8						
2d Cpe	150	475	750	1475	2600	3700
Cutlass Calais, V-8						
2d Cpe	150	475	775	1500	2650	3800
Cutlass Supreme Brougham, V-8						
2d Cpe	150	500	800	1550	2700	3900
Cutlass Cruiser, V-8						
4d Sta Wag	125	450	750	1450	2500	3600
Cutlass Cruiser Brougham, V-8						
4d Sta Wag	150	475	750	1475	2600	3700
Delta 88, V-8						
4d Sed	150	475	775	1500	2650	3800
2d Cpe	150	500	800	1550	2700	3900
Delta 88 Royale, V-8						
4d Sed	150	500	800	1550	2700	3900
2d Cpe	150	500	800	1600	2800	4000
Custom Cruiser, V-8						
4d 2S Sta Wag	150	500	800	1550	2700	3900
4d 3S Sta Wag	150	500	800	1600	2800	4000
Ninety Eight						
4d Lux Sed	150	550	850	1650	2900	4100
2d Lux Cpe	150	550	850	1675	2950	4200
4d Regency Sed	150	575	875	1700	3000	4300
2d Regency Cpe	150	575	900	1750	3100	4400
Toronado						
2d Cpe	200	675	1000	2000	3500	5000

NOTE: Deduct 5 percent for V-6.
Add 60 percent for Hurst/Olds option.
Deduct 10 percent for diesel.

1980

	6	5	4	3	2	1
Starfire, 4-cyl.						
2d Cpe	150	475	775	1500	2650	3800
2d Cpe SX	150	500	800	1550	2700	3900
Omega, V-6						
4d Sed	150	475	775	1500	2650	3800
2d Cpe	150	500	800	1550	2700	3900
NOTE: Deduct 10 percent for 4-cyl.						
Omega Brougham, V-6						
4d Sed	150	500	800	1550	2700	3900
2d Cpe	150	500	800	1600	2800	4000
NOTE: Deduct 10 percent for 4-cyl.						
Cutlass, V-8						
4d Sed	125	450	750	1450	2500	3600
NOTE: Deduct 12 percent for V-6.						
Cutlass Salon, V-8						
2d Cpe	150	500	800	1550	2700	3900
NOTE: Deduct 12 percent for V-6.						
Cutlass Salon Brougham, V-8						
2d Cpe	150	500	800	1600	2800	4000
NOTE: Deduct 12 percent for V-6.						
Cutlass Supreme, V-8						
2d Cpe	150	550	850	1650	2900	4100
NOTE: Deduct 12 percent for V-6.						
Cutlass LS, V-8						
4d Sed	150	475	750	1475	2600	3700
NOTE: Deduct 12 percent for V-6.						
Cutlass Calais, V-8						
2d Cpe	150	550	850	1675	2950	4200
NOTE: Deduct 12 percent for V-6.						
Cutlass Brougham, V-8						
4d Sed	150	475	775	1500	2650	3800
2d Cpe Supreme	150	550	850	1675	2950	4200
NOTE: Deduct 12 percent for V-6.						
Cutlass Cruiser, V-8						
4d Sta Wag	150	500	800	1550	2700	3900
4d Sta Wag Brgm	150	500	800	1600	2800	4000
NOTE: Deduct 12 percent for V-6.						
Delta 88, V-8						
4d Sed	150	550	850	1650	2900	4100
2d Cpe	150	550	850	1675	2950	4200
NOTE: Deduct 12 percent for V-6.						
Delta 88 Royale, V-8						
4d Sed	150	550	850	1675	2950	4200
2d Cpe	150	575	875	1700	3000	4300
NOTE: Deduct 12 percent for V-6.						
Delta 88 Royale Brougham, V-8						
4d Sed	150	575	900	1750	3100	4400
2d Cpe	150	600	900	1800	3150	4500
NOTE: Deduct 12 percent for V-6.						
Custom Cruiser, V-8						
4d 2S Sta Wag	150	575	875	1700	3000	4300
4d 3S Sta Wag	150	575	900	1750	3100	4400
Ninety Eight, V-8						
4d Lux Sed	150	600	950	1850	3200	4600
4d Regency Sed	200	675	1000	1950	3400	4900
2d Regency Cpe	200	700	1050	2050	3600	5100
Toronado Brougham, V-8						
2d Cpe	350	770	1300	2550	4480	6400

1981

	6	5	4	3	2	1
Omega, V-6						
4d Sed	150	500	800	1550	2700	3900
2d Cpe	150	500	800	1600	2800	4000
NOTE: Deduct 10 percent for 4-cyl.						
Omega Brougham, V-6						
4d Sed	150	500	800	1600	2800	4000
2d Cpe	150	550	850	1650	2900	4100
NOTE: Deduct 10 percent for 4-cyl.						
Cutlass, V-8						
4d Sed	150	475	750	1475	2600	3700
NOTE: Deduct 12 percent for V-6.						
Cutlass Supreme, V-8						
2d Cpe	150	550	850	1675	2950	4200
NOTE: Deduct 12 percent for V-6.						
Cutlass LS, V-8						
4d Sed	150	475	775	1500	2650	3800
NOTE: Deduct 12 percent for V-6.						
Cutlass Calais, V-8						
2d Cpe	150	575	900	1750	3100	4400
NOTE: Deduct 12 percent for V-6.						
Cutlass Supreme Brougham, V-8						
2d Cpe	150	575	875	1700	3000	4300
NOTE: Deduct 12 percent for V-6.						
Cutlass Brougham, V-8						
4d Sed	150	500	800	1550	2700	3900
NOTE: Deduct 12 percent for V-6.						
Cutlass Cruiser, V-8						
4d Sta Wag	150	500	800	1550	2700	3900
4d Brgm Sta Wag	150	500	800	1600	2800	4000
NOTE: Deduct 12 percent for V-6.						
Delta 88, V-8						
4d Sed	150	550	850	1675	2950	4200
2d Cpe	150	575	875	1700	3000	4300
NOTE: Deduct 12 percent for V-6.						
Delta 88 Royale, V-8						
4d Sed	150	575	875	1700	3000	4300
2d Cpe	150	575	900	1750	3100	4400
NOTE: Deduct 12 percent for V-6.						
Delta 88 Royale Brougham, V-8						
4d Sed	150	600	900	1800	3150	4500
2d Cpe	150	600	950	1850	3200	4600
Custom Cruiser, V-8						
4d 2S Sta Wag	150	575	900	1750	3100	4400
4d 3S Sta Wag	150	600	900	1800	3150	4500
Ninety Eight, V-8						
4d Lux Sed	150	650	950	1900	3300	4700
4d Regency Sed	150	650	975	1950	3350	4800
2d Regency Cpe	200	675	1000	1950	3400	4900
NOTE: Deduct 12 percent for V-6.						
Toronado Brougham, V-8						
2d Cpe	350	800	1350	2700	4700	6700
NOTE: Deduct 12 percent for V-6.						

1982

	6	5	4	3	2	1
Firenza, 4-cyl.						
2d Cpe	150	550	850	1675	2950	4200
4d Sed	150	575	875	1700	3000	4300
4d Sta Wag	150	600	900	1800	3150	4500
Cutlass Calais, 4 Cyl.						
NOTE: Deduct 5 percent for lesser models.						
2d Cpe	150	575	900	1750	3100	4400
4d Sed	150	600	900	1800	3150	4500
2d Cpe SL	150	650	975	1950	3350	4800
2d Cpe Int.	200	660	1100	2200	3850	5500
4d Sed Int.	200	670	1150	2250	3920	5600
2d Cpe V-6	200	700	1050	2100	3650	5200
4d Sed V-6	200	700	1075	2150	3700	5300
2d Cpe SL V-6	200	650	1100	2150	3780	5400
4d Sed SL V-6	200	660	1100	2200	3850	5500
Cutlass Ciera, 4 Cyl.						
2d Cpe	200	675	1000	1950	3400	4900
4d Sed	200	675	1000	2000	3500	5000
4d Sta Wag	200	700	1050	2050	3600	5100
2d Cpe Brgm	200	675	1000	2000	3500	5000
4d Sed Brgm SL	75	230	380	760	1330	1900
4d Sta Wag Brgm	200	700	1050	2100	3650	5200
2d Cpe V-6	200	700	1050	2050	3600	5100
4d Sed V-6	200	700	1050	2100	3650	5200
4d Sta Wag V-6	200	700	1075	2150	3700	5300
2d Cpe SL V-6	200	650	1100	2150	3780	5400
4d Sed V-6	200	660	1100	2200	3850	5500
4d Sta Wag V-6	200	670	1150	2250	3920	5600

	6	5	4	3	2	1
2d Cpe Int. V-6	200	670	1200	2300	4060	5800
4d Sed Int. V-6	200	700	1200	2350	4130	5900
Cutlass Supreme						
2d Cpe V-6	200	730	1250	2450	4270	6100
2d Cpe SL V-6	350	780	1300	2600	4550	6500
2d Cpe Int. V-6	350	800	1350	2700	4700	6700
2d Cpe V-8	350	790	1350	2650	4620	6600
2d Cpe Brgm V-8	350	780	1300	2600	4550	6500
Delta 88 Royale						
2d Cpe V-6	200	660	1100	2200	3850	5500
4d Sed V-6	200	670	1150	2250	3920	5600
2d Cpe Brgm V-6	200	700	1200	2350	4130	5900
4d Sed Brgm V-6	200	720	1200	2400	4200	6000
Custom Cruiser V-8						
4d Sta Wag	350	780	1300	2600	4550	6500
Ninety Eight, V-6						
4d Sed Regency	350	780	1300	2600	4550	6500
4d Sed Regency Brgm	350	840	1400	2800	4900	7000
4d Sed Touring Sed	350	840	1400	2800	4900	7000
Toronado V-8						
2d Cpe	350	900	1500	3000	5250	7500
2d Cpe Brgm	350	1020	1700	3400	5950	8500
Custom Cruiser, V-8						
4d Sta Wag	200	675	1000	1950	3400	4900
Ninety Eight Regency, V-8						
4d Sed	200	700	1050	2050	3600	5100
2d Cpe	200	700	1050	2100	3650	5200
4d Brgm Sed	200	700	1050	2100	3650	5200
NOTE: Deduct 12 percent for V-6.						
Toronado Brougham, V-8						
2d Cpe	350	820	1400	2700	4760	6800
NOTE: Deduct 12 percent for V-6.						

1983

	6	5	4	3	2	1
Firenza, 4-cyl.						
4d LX Sed	150	550	850	1650	2900	4100
2d SX Cpe	150	550	850	1675	2950	4200
4d LX Sta Wag	150	575	875	1700	3000	4300
NOTE: Deduct 5 percent for lesser models.						
Omega, V-6						
4d Sed	150	550	850	1650	2900	4100
2d Cpe	150	550	850	1675	2950	4200
NOTE: Deduct 10 percent for 4-cyl.						
Omega Brougham, V-6						
4d Sed	150	550	850	1675	2950	4200
2d Cpe	150	575	875	1700	3000	4300
NOTE: Deduct 10 percent for 4-cyl.						
Cutlass Supreme, V-8						
4d Sed	150	600	950	1850	3200	4600
2d Cpe	150	650	950	1900	3300	4700
NOTE: Deduct 12 percent for V-6.						
Cutlass Supreme Brougham, V-8						
4d Sed	150	650	950	1900	3300	4700
2d Cpe	150	650	975	1950	3350	4800
NOTE: Deduct 12 percent for V-6.						
Cutlass Calais, V-8						
2d Cpe	200	675	1000	1950	3400	4900
NOTE: Deduct 12 percent for V-6.						
Add 15 percent for Hurst/Olds package.						
Cutlass Cruiser, V-8						
4d Sta Wag	150	650	975	1950	3350	4800
NOTE: Deduct 12 percent for V-6.						
Cutlass Ciera, V-6						
4d Sed	150	600	950	1850	3200	4600
2d Cpe	150	650	950	1900	3300	4700
NOTE: Deduct 10 percent for 4-cyl.						
Cutlass Ciera Brougham, V-6						
4d Sed	150	650	950	1900	3300	4700
2d Cpe	150	650	975	1950	3350	4800
NOTE: Deduct 10 percent for 4-cyl.						
Delta 88, V-8						
4d Sed	150	650	975	1950	3350	4800
NOTE: Deduct 12 percent for V-6.						
Delta 88 Royale, V-8						
4d Sed	200	675	1000	1950	3400	4900
2d Cpe	200	675	1000	2000	3500	5000
NOTE: Deduct 12 percent for V-6.						
Delta 88 Royale Brougham, V-8						
4d Sed	200	700	1050	2050	3600	5100
2d Cpe	200	700	1050	2100	3650	5200
NOTE: Deduct 12 percent for V-6.						
Custom Cruiser, V-8						
4d Sta Wag	200	700	1050	2050	3600	5100
Ninety Eight Regency, V-8						
4d Sed	200	700	1075	2150	3700	5300
2d Cpe	200	660	1100	2200	3850	5500
4d Sed Brgm	200	650	1100	2150	3780	5400
NOTE: Deduct 13 percent for V-6.						
Toronado Brougham, V-8						
2d Cus Cpe	350	830	1400	2950	4830	6900
NOTE: Deduct 13 percent for V-6.						

1984

	6	5	4	3	2	1
Firenza, 4-cyl.						
4d LX Sed	150	550	850	1650	2900	4100
2d LX Sed	150	550	850	1650	2900	4100
4d LX Sta Wag Cruiser	150	575	875	1700	3000	4300
NOTE: Deduct 5 percent for lesser models.						
4d Sed Brgm	150	575	875	1700	3000	4300
2d Sed Brgm	150	575	875	1700	3000	4300
NOTE: Deduct 5 percent for 4-cyl.						
Deduct 8 percent for 4cyl.						
Cutlass, V-8						
4d Sed Supreme Brgm	150	650	975	1950	3350	4800
2d Sed Supreme Brgm	150	650	975	1950	3350	4800
2d Sed Calais	200	675	1000	1950	3400	4900
2d Sed Calais Hurst/Olds	200	660	1100	2200	3850	5500
Cutlass Ciera, V-6						
4d Sed	150	600	950	1850	3200	4600
2d Sed	150	600	950	1850	3200	4600
4d Sta Wag Cruiser	150	600	950	1850	3200	4600
4d Sed Brgm	150	650	950	1900	3300	4700
2d Sed Brgm	150	650	950	1900	3300	4700
NOTE: Deduct 8 percent for 4-cyl.						
Cutlass Ciera, V-8						
4d Sed	150	650	975	1950	3350	4800
2d Sed	150	650	975	1950	3350	4800
4d Sta Wag	150	650	975	1950	3350	4800
4d Sed Brgm	200	675	1000	1950	3400	4900
2d Sed Brgm	200	675	1000	1950	3400	4900

Delta 88 Royale, V-8

	6	5	4	3	2	1
4d Sed	200	675	1000	2000	3500	5000
2d Sed	200	675	1000	2000	3500	5000
4d Sed Brgm	200	700	1050	2100	3650	5200
2d Sed Brgm	200	700	1050	2100	3650	5200
4d Cus Sta Wag Cruiser	200	700	1075	2150	3700	5300
4d LS Sed	200	700	1075	2150	3700	5300
NOTE: Deduct 10 percent for V-6 cyl.						
Ninety Eight Regency, V-8						
4d Sed	200	660	1100	2200	3850	5500
2d Sed	200	660	1100	2200	3850	5500
4d Sed Brgm	200	670	1150	2250	3920	5600
Toronado Brgm						
2d V-6 Cpe	350	780	1300	2600	4550	6500
2d V-8 Cpe	350	840	1400	2800	4900	7000

1985

	6	5	4	3	2	1
Firenza, V-6						
4d LX Sed	150	575	875	1700	3000	4300
2d LX Sed	150	575	875	1700	3000	4300
4d LX Sta Wag	150	575	900	1750	3100	4400
NOTE: Deduct 8 percent for 4-cyl.						
Deduct 5 percent for lesser models.						
Cutlass, V-8						
4d Sed	150	650	975	1950	3350	4800
2d Sed	150	650	975	1950	3350	4800
Cutlass Supreme Brougham, V-8						
4d Sed	150	650	975	1950	3350	4800
2d Sed	150	650	975	1950	3350	4800
Cutlass Salon, V-8						
2d Cpe	200	675	1000	1950	3400	4900
2d 442 Cpe	350	820	1400	2700	4760	6800
NOTE: Deduct 8 percent for 4-cyl.						
Deduct 30 percent for diesel.						
Calais, V-6						
2d Sed	200	675	1000	1950	3400	4900
2d Sed Brgm	200	675	1000	1950	3400	4900
NOTE: Deduct 8 percent for 4-cyl.						
Cutlass Ciera, V-6						
4d Sed	150	600	950	1850	3200	4600
2d Sed	150	600	950	1850	3200	4600
4d Sta Wag	150	650	950	1900	3300	4700
Cutlass Ciera Brougham, V-6						
4d Sed	150	650	950	1900	3300	4700
2d Sed	150	650	950	1900	3300	4700
NOTE: Deduct 8 percent for 4-cyl.						
Deduct 30 percent for diesel.						
Delta 88 Royale, V-8						
4d Sed	200	700	1050	2050	3600	5100
2d Sed	200	700	1050	2050	3600	5100
4 dr Sed Brgm	200	700	1075	2150	3700	5300
2d Sed Brgm	200	700	1075	2150	3700	5300
4d Sta Wag	200	650	1100	2150	3780	5400
NOTE: Deduct 10 percent for V-6 where available.						
Deduct 30 percent for diesel.						
Ninety Eight Regency, V-6						
4d Sed	200	670	1150	2250	3920	5600
2d Sed	200	670	1150	2250	3920	5600
4d Sed Brgm	200	685	1150	2300	3990	5700
2d Sed Brgm	200	685	1150	2300	3990	5700
Toronado, V-8						
2d Cpe	350	850	1450	2850	4970	7100
NOTE: Deduct 30 percent for diesel.						

1986

	6	5	4	3	2	1
Firenza, 4-cyl.						
4d Sed	150	600	900	1800	3150	4500
2d Cpe	150	575	900	1750	3100	4400
2d HBk	150	600	900	1800	3150	4500
4d Sed LX	150	600	950	1850	3200	4600
2d Cpe LC	150	600	900	1800	3150	4500
4d Sta Wag	150	600	950	1850	3200	4600
2d HBk GT V-6	150	650	950	1900	3300	4700
Cutlass Supreme V-6						
4d Sed	150	650	950	1900	3300	4700
2d Cpe	150	650	950	1900	3300	4700
4d Sed Brgm	150	650	975	1950	3350	4800
2d Cpe Brgm	150	650	975	1950	3350	4800
Cutlass Salon, V-6						
2d Cpe	200	675	1000	1950	3400	4900
2d Cpe 442-V-8	350	820	1400	2700	4760	6800
NOTE: Add 20 percent for V-8.						
Calais, 4-cyl.						
4d Sed	200	700	1050	2050	3600	5100
2d Cpe	200	700	1050	2050	3600	5100
4d Sed Supreme	200	700	1050	2100	3650	5200
2d Cpe Supreme	200	700	1050	2100	3650	5200
NOTE: Add 10 percent for V-6.						
Cutlass Ciera, V-6						
4d Sed LS	200	700	1050	2100	3650	5200
2d Cpe LS	200	700	1050	2100	3650	5200
2d Cpe S LS	200	700	1075	2150	3700	5300
4d Sta Wag LS	200	650	1100	2150	3780	5400
4d Sed Brgm	200	650	1100	2150	3780	5400
2d Cpe Brgm	200	650	1100	2150	3780	5400
2d Cpe Brgm SL	200	660	1100	2200	3850	5500
Delta 88						
4d Sed	200	650	1100	2150	3780	5400
2d Cpe	200	650	1100	2150	3780	5400
4d Sed Brgm	200	660	1100	2200	3850	5500
2d Cpe Brgm	200	660	1100	2200	3850	5500
Custom Cruiser, V-8						
4d Sta Wag	200	745	1250	2500	4340	6200
Ninety Eight Regency						
4d Sed	200	685	1150	2300	3990	5700
2d Cpe	200	685	1150	2300	3990	5700
4d Sed Brgm	200	670	1200	2300	4060	5800
2d Cpe Brgm	200	670	1200	2300	4060	5800
Toronado						
2d Cpe	350	900	1500	3000	5250	7500

1987

	6	5	4	3	2	1
Firenza, 4-cyl.						
4d Sed	150	600	900	1800	3150	4500
2d Cpe	150	575	900	1750	3100	4400
2d HBk S	150	600	900	1800	3150	4500
4d Sed LX	150	600	950	1850	3200	4600
2d Cpe LC	150	600	900	1800	3150	4500
4d Sta Wag	150	600	950	1850	3200	4600
2d HBk GT	150	600	950	1850	3200	4600

Cutlass Supreme, V-6

	6	5	4	3	2	1
4d Sed	150	650	975	1950	3350	4800
2d Cpe	150	650	950	1900	3300	4700
Cutlass Supreme, V-8						
4d Sed	200	675	1000	2000	3500	5000
2d Cpe	200	675	1000	1950	3400	4900
2d Cpe 442	350	950	1550	3150	5450	7800
Cutlass Supreme Brougham, V-6						
4d Sed	200	675	1000	1950	3400	4900
2d Cpe	150	650	975	1950	3350	4800
Cutlass Supreme Brougham, V-8						
4d Sed	200	700	1050	2050	3600	5100
2d Cpe	200	675	1000	2000	3500	5000
Cutlass Salon						
2d Cpe V-6	200	700	1050	2050	3600	5100
2d Cpe V-8	200	700	1050	2100	3650	5200
Calais, 4-cyl.						
4d Sed	200	700	1050	2100	3650	5200
2d Cpe	200	700	1050	2050	3600	5100
Calais, V-6						
4d Sed	200	700	1075	2150	3700	5300
2d Cpe	200	700	1050	2100	3650	5200
Calais Supreme, 4-cyl.						
4d Sed	200	700	1075	2150	3700	5300
2d Cpe	200	700	1050	2100	3650	5200
Calais Supreme, V-6						
4d Sed	200	650	1100	2150	3780	5400
2d Cpe	200	700	1075	2150	3700	5300
Cutlass Ciera, 4-cyl.						
4d Sed	200	650	1100	2150	3780	5400
2d Cpe	200	700	1075	2150	3700	5300
4d Sta Wag	200	660	1100	2200	3850	5500
Cutlass Ciera, V-6						
4d Sed	200	660	1100	2200	3850	5500
2d Cpe	200	650	1100	2150	3780	5400
4d Sta Wag	200	670	1150	2250	3920	5600
Cutlass Ciera Brougham, 4-cyl.						
4d Sed	200	660	1100	2200	3850	5500
2d Cpe SL	200	650	1100	2150	3780	5400
4d Sta Wag	200	670	1150	2250	3920	5600
Cutlass Ciera Brougham, V-6						
4d Sed	200	670	1150	2250	3920	5600
2d Cpe SL	200	660	1100	2200	3850	5500
4d Sta Wag	200	685	1150	2300	3990	5700
Delta 88 Royale, V-6						
4d Sed	200	650	1100	2150	3780	5400
2d Cpe	200	700	1075	2150	3700	5300
4d Sed Brgm	200	670	1150	2250	3920	5600
2d Cpe Brgm	200	660	1100	2200	3850	5500
Custom Cruiser, V-8						
4d Sta Wag	200	660	1100	2200	3850	5500
Ninety Eight, V-6						
4d Sed	200	670	1150	2250	3920	5600
4d Sed Regency Brgm	200	685	1150	2300	3990	5700
2d Sed Regency Brgm	200	670	1150	2250	3920	5600
Toronado, V-6						
2d Cpe Brgm	350	880	1500	2950	5180	7400

NOTE: Add 10 percent for Trofeo option.

1988

Firenza, 4-cyl.

	6	5	4	3	2	1
2d Cpe	150	550	850	1675	2950	4200
4d Sed	150	575	875	1700	3000	4300
4d Sta Wag	150	600	900	1800	3150	4500
Cutlass Calais, 4-cyl.						
2d Cpe	150	575	900	1750	3100	4400
4d Sed	150	600	900	1800	3150	4500
2d SL Cpe	150	650	975	1950	3350	4800
4d SL Sed	200	675	1000	1950	3400	4900
2d Int'l Cpe	200	660	1100	2200	3850	5500
4d Int'l Sed	200	670	1150	2250	3920	5600
2d Cpe, V-6	200	700	1050	2100	3650	5200
4d Sed, V-6	200	700	1075	2150	3700	5300
2d SL Cpe, V-6	200	650	1100	2150	3780	5400
4d SL Sed, V-6	200	660	1100	2200	3850	5500
Cutlass Ciera, 4-cyl.						
2d Cpe	200	675	1000	1950	3400	4900
4d Sed	200	675	1000	2000	3500	5000
4d Sta Wag	200	700	1050	2050	3600	5100
Cutlass Ciera Brougham, 4-cyl.						
2d Cpe	200	675	1000	2000	3500	5000
4d SL Sed	200	700	1050	2050	3600	5100
4d Sta Wag	200	700	1050	2100	3650	5200
Cutlass Ciera, V-6						
2d Cpe	200	700	1050	2050	3600	5100
4d Sed	200	700	1050	2100	3650	5200
4d Sta Wag	200	700	1075	2150	3700	5300
Cutlass Ciera Brougham, V-6						
2d Cpe SL	200	650	1100	2150	3780	5400
4d Sed	200	660	1100	2200	3850	5500
4d Sta Wag	200	670	1150	2250	3920	5600
2d Int'l Cpe	200	670	1200	2300	4060	5800
4d Int'l Cpe	200	700	1200	2350	4130	5900
Cutlass Supreme, V-6						
2d Cpe	200	730	1250	2450	4270	6100
2d SL Cpe	350	780	1300	2600	4550	6500
2d Int'l Cpe	350	800	1350	2700	4700	6700
Cutlass Supreme, V-8						
2d Cpe	200	750	1275	2500	4400	6300
2d Cpe Brgm	350	780	1300	2600	4550	6500
Delta 88 Royale, V-6						
2d Cpe	200	660	1100	2200	3850	5500
4d Sed	200	670	1150	2250	3920	5600
2d Cpe Brgm	200	700	1200	2350	4130	5900
4d Sed Brgm	200	720	1200	2400	4200	6000
Custom Cruiser, V-8						
4d Sta Wag	350	780	1300	2600	4550	6500
Ninety Eight, V-6						
4d Sed Regency	350	780	1300	2600	4550	6500
4d Sed Regency Brgm	350	840	1400	2800	4900	7000
4d Trg Sed	350	975	1600	3200	5600	8000
Toronado, V-6						
2d Cpe	350	900	1500	3000	5250	7500
2d Cpe Trofeo	350	1020	1700	3400	5950	8500

1989

Cutlass Calais
4-cyl.

	6	5	4	3	2	1
4d Sed	150	600	900	1800	3150	4500
2d Cpe	150	575	900	1750	3100	4400
4d Sed S	150	650	975	1950	3350	4800
2d Cpe S	150	650	950	1900	3300	4700
4d Sed SL	200	700	1075	2150	3700	5300
2d Cpe SL	200	700	1050	2100	3650	5200
4d Sed Int'l Series	350	780	1300	2600	4550	6500
2d Cpe Int'l Series	350	770	1300	2550	4480	6400
V-6						
4d Sed S	200	700	1075	2150	3700	5300
2d Cpe S	200	700	1050	2100	3650	5200
4d Sed SL	200	670	1150	2250	3920	5600
2d Cpe SL	200	660	1100	2200	3850	5500

Cutlass Ciera
4-cyl.

	6	5	4	3	2	1
4d Sed	200	675	1000	1950	3400	4900
2d Cpe	150	650	975	1950	3350	4800
4d Sta Wag	200	720	1200	2400	4200	6000
4d Sed SL	200	685	1150	2300	3990	5700
2d Cpe SL	200	670	1150	2250	3920	5600
4d Sta Wag SL	200	745	1250	2500	4340	6200
V-6						
4d Sed	200	660	1100	2200	3850	5500
2d Cpe	200	650	1100	2150	3780	5400
4d Sta Wag	200	750	1275	2500	4400	6300
4d Sed SL	200	685	1150	2300	3990	5700
2d Cpe SL	200	670	1150	2250	3920	5600
4d Sta Wag SL	350	780	1300	2600	4550	6500
4d Sed Int'l Series	350	790	1350	2650	4620	6600
2d Cpe Int'l Series	350	780	1300	2600	4550	6500

Cutlass Supreme, V-6

	6	5	4	3	2	1
2d Cpe	350	840	1400	2800	4900	7000
2d Cpe SL	350	900	1500	3000	5250	7500
2d Cpe Int'l Series	350	975	1600	3200	5600	8000

Eighty Eight Royale, V-6

	6	5	4	3	2	1
4d Sed	350	840	1400	2800	4900	7000
2d Cpe	350	830	1400	2950	4830	6900
4d Sed Brgm	350	900	1500	3000	5250	7500
2d Cpe Brgm	350	880	1500	2950	5180	7400

Custom Cruiser, V-8

	6	5	4	3	2	1
4d Sta Wag	350	900	1500	3000	5250	7500

Ninety Eight, V-6

	6	5	4	3	2	1
4d Sed Regency	350	900	1500	3000	5250	7500
4d Sed Regency Brgm	350	1020	1700	3400	5950	8500
4d Sed Trg	450	1140	1900	3800	6650	9500

Toronado, V-6

	6	5	4	3	2	1
2d Cpe	350	1020	1700	3400	5950	8500
2d Cpe Trofeo	450	1140	1900	3800	6650	9500

1990

Cutlass Calais
4-cyl.

	6	5	4	3	2	1
2d Cpe	150	650	975	1950	3350	4800
4d Sed	200	675	1000	1950	3400	4900
2d Cpe S	200	675	1000	1950	3400	4900
4d Sed S	200	675	1000	2000	3500	5000
2d Cpe SL Quad	200	660	1100	2200	3850	5500
4d Sed SL Quad	200	670	1150	2250	3920	5600
2d Cpe Int'l Quad	200	670	1150	2250	3920	5600
4d Sed Int'l Quad	200	685	1150	2300	3990	5700
V-6						
2d Cpe SL	200	670	1200	2300	4060	5800
4d Sed SL	200	700	1200	2350	4130	5900

Cutlass Ciera
4-cyl.

	6	5	4	3	2	1
4d Sed	200	675	1000	2000	3500	5000
2d Cpe S	200	700	1050	2050	3600	5100
4d Sed S	200	700	1050	2100	3650	5200
4d Sta Wag S	200	660	1100	2200	3850	5500
V-6						
4d Sed	200	700	1050	2100	3650	5200
2d Cpe S	200	660	1100	2200	3850	5500
4d Sed S	200	670	1150	2250	3920	5600
4d Sta Wag S	200	685	1150	2300	3990	5700
4d Sta Wag SL	200	670	1200	2300	4060	5800
2d Cpe Int'l	200	720	1200	2400	4200	6000
4d Sed Int'l	200	730	1250	2450	4270	6100

Cutlass Supreme
4-cyl.

	6	5	4	3	2	1
2d Cpe Quad	350	780	1300	2600	4550	6500
4d Sed Quad	350	790	1350	2620	4620	6600
2d Cpe Int'l Quad	350	900	1500	3000	5250	7500
4d Sed Int'l Quad	350	950	1550	3100	5400	7700
V-6						
2d Cpe	350	800	1350	2700	4700	6700
4d Sed	350	820	1400	2700	4760	6800
2d Cpe SL	350	830	1400	2950	4830	6900
2d Conv	350	975	1600	3200	5600	8000
4d Sed SL	350	840	1400	2800	4900	7000
2d Cpe Int'l	350	900	1500	3000	5250	7500
4d Sed Int'l	350	950	1500	3050	5300	7600

Eighty Eight Royale, V-6

	6	5	4	3	2	1
4d Sed	350	840	1400	2800	4900	7000
2d Cpe Brgm	350	900	1500	3000	5250	7500
4d Sed Brgm	350	950	1500	3050	5300	7600

Custom Cruiser, V-8

	6	5	4	3	2	1
4d Sta Wag	350	900	1500	3000	5250	7500

Ninety Eight, V-6

	6	5	4	3	2	1
4d Sed Regency	350	975	1600	3200	5600	8000
4d Sed Regency Brgm	350	1020	1700	3400	5950	8500
4d Sed Trg	450	1140	1900	3800	6650	9500

Toronado, V-6

	6	5	4	3	2	1
2d Cpe	350	1020	1700	3400	5950	8500
2d Cpe Trofeo	450	1140	1900	3800	6650	9500

About The Authors

John Chevedden

John Chevedden is an accomplished writer and author of many articles for automotive, aerospace, and business books and magazines. His work on the *Standard Catalog of Oldsmobile* actually began when he was five years old and accompanied his father to the Oldsmobile plant in Lansing, Michigan, to pick up a new Oldsmobile 88.

Upon receiving his MBA, John took a job with General Motors-Hughes Aircraft managing communication satellite projects.

John currently resides in Redondo Beach, California.

Ron Kowalke

Ron Kowalke is a lifelong old car enthusiast. The former news editor for *Olds Cars Weekly News & Marketplace,* he is currently the automotive books editor for Krause Publications. He has authored or co-authored an extensive list of books for the collector vehicle hobby, including the *Standard Catalog of Pontiac, Car Memorabilia Price Guide* and *Trucking in America: Moving the Goods.*

Ron acquired his Oldsmobile "fixation" from his father, Roy, whose daily driver list includes a 1963 F-85, 1984 Cutlass Supreme and 1990 Cutlass Supreme. Ron's first new car purchase was a 1979 Starfire. His "collector car I hope to own $omeday" is the 1950 Olds 98 Club Sedan.

Ron, who lives in Appleton, Wisconsin, is currently working on a sequel to *Antique Auto Wrecks* titled *Old Car Wrecks.*

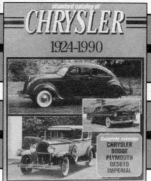

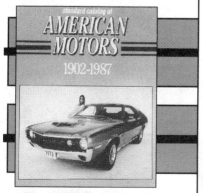

KICK IT INTO HIGH GEAR WITH THESE 5-SPEED BOOKS!

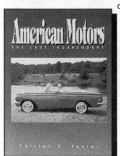

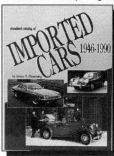
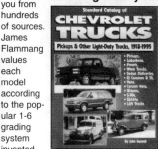
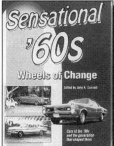

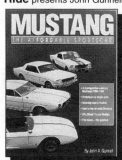

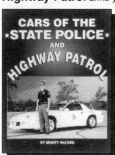
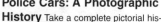

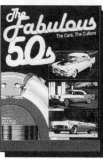

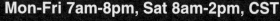

REV UP YOUR ENGINES WITH THESE FAST-MOVING BOOKS!

Standard Catalog of American Cars, 1946-1975, 3rd edition, provides you with answers to your old car questions. This expanded and revised catalog, edited by John Gunnell, gives you technical specifications, information on serial numbers, production totals and much more! 8-1/2x11 SC • 864p • 1,500 photos • **AC03 $27.95**

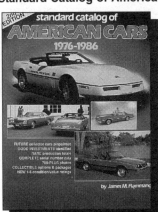

Standard Catalog of American Cars, 1976-1986, 2nd edition James Flammang provides the key factor of production totals to give you a glimpse into the car collecting hobby's future. You'll also find complete technical specifications, serial numbers, and more! 8-1/2x11 SC • 484p • 1,100 photos • **AD02 $19.95**

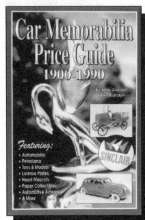

Car Memorabilia Price Guide is packed with memorabilia values in up to six grades of preservation. Rare, clear photos and insights from Ron Kowalke help you identify and price even the most hard-to-find toys, models, hood ornaments, paper collectibles and more. 6x9 SC • 416p • 400 photos • **GAP01 $19.95**

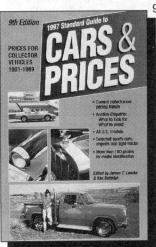

1997 Standard Guide to Cars & Prices, 9th edition Jim Lenzke and Ken Buttolph put you in the driver's seat for the best deals on collector cars from 1901-1989. More than 224,000 current values give you the confidence to deal smart and offer you the marketplace edge. 6x9 SC • 656p • 180 photos • **CG09 $15.95**

The Metropolitan Story and author Patrick R. Foster introduce you to the designers and far-sighted marketers behind this short-lived car. Complete color, trim and production figures. Helpful tips on collecting and restoring the Met, with club listings, parts sources. 8-1/2x11 HC• 208p • 250 b&w photos • 120 color photos • **MET $24.95**

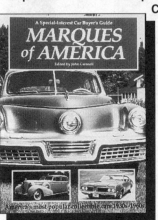

Marques of America - A Special-Interest Car Buyer's Guide details America's most popular collectible cars from the 1930s - 1960s. You'll find a montage of the most remarkable automobiles from the Depression Era through the tumultuous '60s presented by John Gunnell. 8-1/2x11 SC • 264p • 400 b&w photos • 8 color photos • **MA01 $18.95**

Return orders with payment to:

Krause Publications
Book Department ZPB1, Iola, WI 54990-0001